Windows Server® 2008 R2 Remote Desktop Services Resource Kit

Christa Anderson and Kristin L. Griffin
with the Remote Desktop Virtualization Team

PUBLISHED BY
Microsoft Press
A Division of Microsoft Corporation
One Microsoft Way
Redmond, Washington 98052-6399

Library of Congress Control Number: 2010934986

Printed and bound in the United States of America.

Microsoft Press books are available through booksellers and distributors worldwide. For further information about international editions, contact your local Microsoft Corporation office or contact Microsoft Press International directly at fax (425) 936-7329. Visit our Web site at www.microsoft.com/mspress. Send comments to msinput@microsoft.com.

Acquisitions Editor: Martin DelRe
Developmental Editor: Karen Szall
Project Editor: Valerie Woolley and Megan Smith-Creed
Editorial Production: Custom Editorial Productions, Inc.
Technical Reviewer: Alex Juschin; Technical Review services provided by Content Master, a member of CM Group, Ltd.
Cover: Cover Design: Tom Draper Design; Illustration: Todd Daman

Body Part No. X17-21601

I dedicate this book to my family, who has always been supportive, always pushes me to do my very best I can do, and always has a "Go team!" waiting when I really need one.

—CHRISTA

I dedicate this book to Elizabeth Nelson-Lyda and Michael B. Smith for taking me under your wing back in the day, and for always believing in me. You were great mentors and are great friends.

—KRISTIN

Contents at a Glance

Contents

What do you think of this book? We want to hear from you!

Microsoft is interested in hearing your feedback so we can continually improve our books and learning resources for you. To participate in a brief online survey, please visit:

microsoft.com/learning/booksurvey

Chapter 8   Securing Remote Desktop Protocol Connections   401

Chapter 9   Multi-Server Deployments   423

Chapter 10   Making Remote Desktop Services Available from the Internet 507

What do you think of this book? We want to hear from you!

Microsoft is interested in hearing your feedback so we can continually improve our
books and learning resources for you. To participate in a brief online survey, please visit:

microsoft.com/learning/booksurvey

Acknowledgments

This book isn't the work of just two people. We owe many thanks to the combined efforts of a lot of people at Microsoft, our terrific set of editors, and the greater community. (All this said, any errors in this book are the sole responsibility of the authors.)

One of the best things about working at Microsoft is that a lot of very smart (and very helpful) people work there, and we are grateful for the insights of these people. Throughout this book, you'll find Direct from the Source sidebars contributed by members of the product team. We also extend our heartfelt thanks to the members of the product team who sat down with us to explain the finer details of how something worked. From the Remote Desktop Virtualization (RDV) team, we'd like to thank Niraj Agarwala, James Baker, Ara Bernardi, Tad Brockway, Vikash Bucha, Yuvraj Budhraja, Hammad Butt, Rommy Channe, Munindra Das, Silvia Doomra, Samim Erdogan, Rajesh Ganta, Costin Hagiu, Al Henriquez, Travis Howe, Olga Ivanova, Gopikrishna Kannan, Sergey Kuzin, Rob Leitman, Raghu Lingampally, Meher Malakapalli, Benjamin Meister, Ranjana Rathinam, Rajesh Ravindranath, Ray Reskusich, Sriram Sampath, Bhaskar Swarna, and Janani Venkateswaran. Even people from other teams got involved. Many thanks to Kyle Beck, Jeff Heatton, Michael Kleef, Timothy Newton, Mark Russinovich, Tom Shinder, Makarand Patwardhan, Bohdan Velushchak, Paul Volosen, and Jon Wojan for your invaluable assistance. We'd also like to thank Christa's manager, Ashwin Palekar, for his support during this project.

RDS expertise isn't limited to people at Microsoft, either. Remote Desktop Services MVPs as well as MVPs and experts from other disciplines also pitched in to contribute Direct from the Field sidebars and explain the intricacies of related technologies. Many thanks go to Janique Carbone, Brian Ehlert, Ross Harvey, Helge Klein, Russ Kaufmann, Shay Levy, Brian Madden, Patrick Rouse, Greg Shields, Michael Smith, and Mitch Tulloch.

The great team at Microsoft Press had a huge hand in turning this project from an idea into the book you hold in your hands. We'd like to thank Martin Del Re at Microsoft Press for asking us to write the first edition of the book in the first place, Megan Smith-Creed at Custom Editorial Productions, Inc., for great editing and project management on this edition, and Alex Juschin for tech editing the book. The rest of the editorial team at Custom Editorial Productions, Inc., did a terrific job of copyediting and proofing this text. Thank you all!

Finally, we'd like to thank our friends and families for their support during this big project. We couldn't have done it without you. We promise to talk about something else now.

Introduction

Welcome to the *Windows Server 2008 R2 Remote Desktop Services Resource Kit*! This is a detailed technical resource for planning, deploying, and running Microsoft Remote Desktop Services (RDS). Because some features of RDS are brand new, this book is valuable both for those completely new to RDS and those who have used Terminal Services (its former name) in previous versions of Microsoft Windows.

Within this resource kit, you'll find in-depth information about the improvements in RDS introduced in Windows Server 2008 R2. This book combines underlying architectural concepts with practical hands-on instructions that allow you to set up a working RDS ecosystem, understand *why* it's working, and give you some guidance about how to fix it when it's not. You'll also find detailed information and task-based guidance on managing all aspects of RDS, including deploying RD Session Host servers, integrating RDS role services with other key parts of the Windows Server 2008 R2 operating system, and extending the reach of RDS to outside the corporate network. Finally, the companion media includes additional tools and documentation that you can use to manage and troubleshoot RDS role services. Although we mention some third-party tools in the course of this book, this book is fundamentally about running RDS using only the tools found in the operating system. You can do what we've done here using *only* Windows Server 2008 R2. Nor do we get into extensive discussion of any of the third-party tools that many people use with native Remote Desktop Services. For example, many people with high-complexity RDS deployments use management software from Citrix or Quest or other RDS partners, but we don't discuss it here because it's not included with the operating system.

 ON THE COMPANION MEDIA   See the team partner page at *http://www.microsoft.com/windowsserver2008/en/us/rds-partners.aspx* for a list of companies that make products complementing or expanding on Remote Desktop Services in Windows Server 2008 R2.

What's New in Remote Desktop Services in Windows Server 2008 R2?

Remote Desktop Services in Windows Server 2008 R2 took a lot of the improvements added in Windows Server 2008 and added the features people had asked for. Want native support for VDI? It's added to RD Connection Broker. Want fewer logons, security filtering, simplified discovery of available applications and virtual machines (VMs)? It's in the new version of RD Web Access. Want to address problems discovered via Network Access Policies (NAP), not just shut people out of the network? It's in the new edition of RD Gateway. Want improved application compatibility? See RD Session Host for IP address virtualization and dynamic fair share scheduling that proactively prevents one session from taking all the processor cycles. Want to stop installing printer drivers on both sessions and VMs? Easy Print now works for both virtualization options.

For those who went straight to Windows Server 2008 R2 from Windows Server 2003, let's take a look at what the new features add to the former model of a terminal server and a license server.

Simplified Application Delivery and Display

Terminal Services in Windows Server 2003 presented all remote applications from a desktop, completely separating the display of local and remote applications. RemoteApp programs (introduced in Windows Server 2008) launch from a server, but integrate with the local desktop so they look like they're running locally.

Not only do the applications integrate better with the local desktop, they're easier to find and distribute, thus making it easier to support a larger and more complex deployment. One of the issues in enabling remote access is how to get the most complete and up-to-date set of remote resources to your user base. This is especially true when you're providing access to individual applications, not to a full desktop. Using RDS Web Access, you can present links to individual applications or to entire desktops and know that these links will always be up to date. In Windows Server 2008 R2, RD Web Access can present RemoteApp programs from more than one farm as well as VMs. It also, however, supports security filtering so that you can manage an aggregated source for all remote resources but only display to people the ones they should use.

Improved Farm Support

The Session Directory service in Windows Server 2003 offered the beginning of farm support, but was only available for Enterprise SKUs and didn't include any load balancing—it just kept track of where connections had gone. In Windows Server 2008 R2, RD Connection Broker is available on the Standard SKU, supports load balancing, and can broker connections to both sessions and VMs.

Secure Internet Access

One of the key benefits of Remote Desktop Services is its ability to support mobile workers. We had a great (and extremely itinerant) tech editor, RDS MVP Alex Juschin, for this edition of the book. He's got a great description of how he used Remote Desktop Services while completing his part.

> In your book you can mention that I have been reviewing your book all over the world using the RDP protocol to connect to my home in Dublin via 3G or WiFi . I've worked while on a smelly Kebap Bus in Poland, in a freezing hotel in Latvia, while being driven in a high-end coach in Estonia, on the ferry to England, in a pub in Ireland, on a train going down the coast from Belfast, while tasting wine in France, sitting in a nice Brasserie on the island of Jersey, eating Belgian chocolate in Brussels, on a plane to Germany, on a bench with a beautiful view in Zurich, in a café near the Berlin Wall, in a prison in Finland (ok, hotel, but it used to be a prison), and on the highest point of Germany (Zugspitze).

In Windows Server 2003, Terminal Services didn't support secure Internet access except across virtual private networks. In Windows Server 2008 R2, Remote Desktop Services supports connectivity over Secure Sockets Layer (SSL) via RD Gateway. RD Gateway allows you to set up different rules for local and remote access and does not require any client-side setup. Introduced in Windows Server 2008, in R2, RD Gateway now enforces device and resource redirection decisions made at the gateway and supports NAP remediation.

Simpler and Broader Device Redirection

RDS assumes that a lot of people will be working from computers with local resources, and that those people won't want to be cut off from their resources when they're working in their session or VM. It also assumes that the server administrators don't want to spend more time than necessary making these resources available.

Although printer redirection, as it's been known in earlier versions of Terminal Services, still works as it did, Easy Print, introduced in Windows Server 2008, helps simplify printer redirection. Rather than requiring administrators to install printer drivers on the server, Easy Print allows redirected printers to use the drivers already installed on the client computer. In Windows 2008 R2, RD Easy Print works with even more printer types and works from both sessions and VMs.

Part of the rich remote work experience is using local devices. Support for local devices has been expanded through the Plug and Play Device Redirection Framework, introduced in Windows Server 2008.

Simplified License Management

Per-user licensing was introduced in Windows Server 2003 but didn't include any tracking, so you couldn't easily tell if you were in compliance. Windows Server 2008 R2 allows you to track Per-User RDS CAL usage. Additionally, the Licensing Diagnostics feature can help you resolve licensing issues. Windows 2008 R2 RD License servers can now migrate licenses from one server to another without the help of the Microsoft Clearinghouse. This can be done even if a license server is out of commission.

This is only a partial list of new features—Chapter 1, "Introducing Remote Desktop Services," describes the Remote Desktop Services features in Windows Server 2008 R2, and the rest of the book explains how to use them. But these are some of the highlights that show how the role has expanded in management and user experience.

 ON THE COMPANION MEDIA The authors will post data that is relevant to the *Windows Server 2008 R2 Remote Desktop Services Resource Kit* on the book's blog, located at *http://blog.kristinlgriffin.com/*. You can find this link on the companion media.

How This Book Is Structured

Our goal in writing this book is to help you set up a working Remote Desktop Services farm, as well as VDI pooled and personal VMs using all the pieces in the operating system, while understanding the greater context of the circumstances under which Remote Desktop Services is useful, how it works, and how Windows Server 2008 R2 compares to previous versions. This book has twelve chapters.

- Chapter 1, "Introducing Remote Desktop Services," explains where RDS came from and how it has evolved as a platform, what new features are available in this latest iteration, and what you can accomplish with this new version of the product. It also explains how other services support RDS.

- Chapter 2, "Key Architectural Concepts for Remote Desktop Services," dives into RDS internals and relevant Windows Server 2008 R2 internals. It also shows you how to determine the hardware and software you will need to support this product in your environment.

- Chapter 3, "Deploying a Single Remote Desktop Session Host Server," shows you how RD Session Host servers work, and how to install and configure this role service.

- Chapter 4, "Deploying a Single Remote Desktop Virtualization Host Server," explains what VDI is, how Microsoft VDI works, and how to install and configure a RD Virtualization Host and the supporting roles.

- Chapter 5, "Managing User Data in a Remote Desktop Services Deployment," discusses the different types of profiles that work with RDS and how to deploy and troubleshoot user profile solutions and folder redirection.

- Chapter 6, "Customizing the User Experience," discusses how remoting works, promoting good client experience in the remote session, and how to print from RDS sessions.

- Chapter 7, "Molding and Securing the User Environment," explains why you should lock down the RDS environment and how you should do it, and describes how to provide remote assistance to users from within the user session.

- Chapter 8, "Securing Remote Desktop Protocol Connections," discusses RDP encryption, server and client authentication, and how to configure security settings on the RD Session Host server.

- Chapter 9, "Multi-Server Deployments," introduces key concepts for multi-server deployments, shows how to create RD Session Host farms, and explains how to publish applications and display resources through RD Web Access.

- Chapter 10, "Making Remote Desktop Services Available from the Internet," shows you how to install and configure RD Gateway to provide access to RemoteApps, desktop sessions, and pooled and personal VMs to users located outside the corporate network.

- Chapter 11, "Managing Remote Desktop Sessions," shows you how to monitor and terminate processes and users sessions running on an RD Session Host server, how to provide help with remote control, and how to drain RD Session Host servers for maintenance.

- Chapter 12, "Licensing Remote Desktop Services," discusses the new RDS licensing paradigm, including both RDS and VDI licensing. This chapter explains how licenses are tracked and enforced; how RD License server assign RDS CALs; how to install, configure, and maintain RDS License servers; how to diagnose licensing issues with the Licensing Diagnosis tool; and how to migrate licenses from one server to another.

Document Conventions

The following conventions are used in this book to highlight special features or usage.

Reader Aids

The following reader aids are used throughout this book to point out useful details.

READER AID	MEANING
Caution	Warns you that failure to take or avoid a specified action can cause serious problems for users, systems, data integrity, and so on.
Note	Underscores the importance of a specific concept or highlights a special case that might not apply to every situation.
On the Companion Media	Calls attention to a related script, tool, template, job aid, or URL on the companion CD that helps you perform a task described in the text.

Sidebars

The following sidebars are used throughout this book to provide added insight, tips, and advice concerning different Remote Desktop Services features.

NOTE Sidebars are provided by individuals in the industry as examples for informational purposes only and may not represent the views of their employers. No warranties, express, implied, or statutory, are made as to the information provided in sidebars.

SIDEBAR	MEANING
Direct from the Source	Contributed by experts from the product group who provide "from-the-source" insight into how Remote Desktop Services works, best practices, and troubleshooting tips.
Direct from the Field	Contributed by experts external to the product group who have real-world experience working with Remote Desktop Services. Some experts are Microsoft field engineers; others are Microsoft MVPs or other experts.
How It Works	Provides unique glimpses of Remote Desktop Services features and how they work.

Command-Line Examples

The following style conventions are used in documenting command-line examples throughout this book.

STYLE	MEANING
Bold font	Used to indicate user input (characters that you type exactly as shown).
Italic font	Used to indicate variables for which you need to supply a specific value (for example, *file name* can refer to any valid file name).
`Monospace font`	Used for code samples and command-line output.
%VariableName%	Used for environment variables.

Companion Media

In addition to the book itself, you also get a CD that contains some great tools and other resources. System requirements for running the CD are at the back of this book. The CD includes the following resources.

Links

The companion media includes many links to URLs that lead to more information about Remote Desktop Services-related topics, Remote Desktop Services resources, partner web sites, and more. Some of the URLs are referenced throughout the book and some are not

Management Scripts

On the companion media, you will find a collection of scripts illustrating ways to work with Remote Desktop Services using Windows PowerShell and VBScript. We've also included listings in relevant locations in the book so that you can better understand how these scripts support the functionality you're looking for. Although these scripts are intended as samples instead of finished products, they do useful work such as allowing you to easily determine the shadowing permissions on a server or providing application-usage metering not provided in the GUI.

Find Additional Content Online   As new or updated material becomes available that complements your book, it will be posted online. The type of material you might find includes updates to book content, articles, links to companion content, errata, sample chapters, and more. This website is available at *http://go.microsoft.com/fwlink/?LinkId=203980* and is updated periodically.

Support for This Book

Every effort has been made to ensure the accuracy of this book. As corrections or changes are collected, they will be added the O'Reilly Media website. To find Microsoft Press book and media corrections:

1. Go to *http://microsoftpress.oreilly.com*.
2. In the Search box, type the ISBN for the book, and click Search.
3. Select the book from the search results, which will take you to the book's catalog page.
4. On the book's catalog page, under the picture of the book cover, click View/Submit Errata.

If you have questions regarding the book or the companion content that are not answered by visiting the book's catalog page, please send them to Microsoft Press by sending an email message to **mspinput@microsoft.com**.

We Want to Hear from You

We welcome your feedback about this book. Please share your comments and ideas via the following short survey.

http://www.microsoft.com/learning/booksurvey

Your participation will help Microsoft Press create books that better meet your needs and your standards.

> **NOTE** We hope that you will give us detailed feedback via our survey. If you have questions about our publishing program, upcoming titles, or Microsoft Press in general, we encourage you to interact with us via Twitter at *http://twitter.com/MicrosoftPress*. For support issues, use only the email address shown above.

Introducing Remote Desktop Services

You might be reading this book for any of a number of reasons. Perhaps you're an old hand at Microsoft Terminal Server and are interested in seeing what Remote Desktop Services (RDS) in Microsoft Windows Server 2008 R2 can do for you. You might have installed Windows Server 2008 R2 and are now interested in what all these web accesses, gateways, and Remote Desktop Session Host servers do. Maybe you have heard about RDS and are interested in how you might benefit by incorporating it into your environment. For that matter, you might be wondering how RDS compares to other remote access technologies in Windows Server 2008 R2.

Whichever reason you have to be interested in RDS, this book is for you.

This chapter sets the stage for the rest of the book. To understand the evolution of Microsoft Terminal Services (now called Remote Desktop Services), you have to understand where it came from and the ecosystem in which it operates. To understand what you can do with the roles and role services, you have to understand the essential goals of RDS in Windows Server 2008 R2 and the scenarios that it's designed for. And, because RDS isn't an end in itself but a piece of the broader Windows infrastructure, you'll see how RDS roles interact with other technologies, like Windows Server 2008 Hyper-V and IIS.

After reading this chapter, you'll understand the following.

- Why Terminal Services is now known as Remote Desktop Services

- What Windows Server 2008 R2 includes for supporting a RDS environment

- What scenarios the RDS role services are intended to support

- What kinds of new technology enable those new scenarios

- How RDS role services interact with each other

- How RDS role services depend on other Windows Server roles
- What application programming interfaces (APIs) exist for developers to use, and what are some examples of the kinds of features that developers can add to RDS

Where Did RDS Come From?

If you're looking at RDS for the first time with Windows Server 2008 R2, you'd hardly recognize its earliest incarnations. Like Windows Server itself, RDS has changed a *lot* over the years and has become much more comprehensive. It's not important to go through an exhaustive feature list for each edition, but it's useful to see how multi-user Windows has developed since its inception in the mid-1990s.

Citrix MultiWin

The original MultiWin architecture was designed not by Microsoft but by Citrix, who licensed the Microsoft Windows NT 3.51 source code from Microsoft to create multi-user Windows. [MultiWin was originally going to be based on IBM Operating System/2 (OS/2) when Microsoft was part of the OS/2 project, but Windows won.] Citrix created its own product called WinFrame, which was a multi-user version of Windows NT 3.51 and totally separate from the operating system that Microsoft produced.

A First Experience with Multi-User Windows

Christa first experienced multi-user Windows through WinFrame 1.7 in 1997 at an IBM training center in New York's Hudson River Valley. Training lasted multiple days, so there were hotel rooms in the training center. Originally, the training center provided a PC in each guest room, and staff had to deal with the maintenance headaches of that setup. But by that training session in 1997, they'd moved to setting up thin clients (connected to the WinFrame servers) in all guest rooms so that guests could check email and work from their rooms. When attendees checked in, a script automatically created a user account for that person. This is all common now, of course, but at the time, it was heady stuff and a big change from the desktop-centric model of Windows.

Windows NT, Terminal Server Edition

WinFrame was built on Windows NT 3.51. Microsoft licensed MultiWin back from Citrix in 1995 and plugged this multi-user core into the Windows NT 4.0 base operating system to make a new product: Windows Server with multi-user capabilities. The result was Windows NT 4.0 Terminal Server Edition. Citrix no longer provided a stand-alone product but released MetaFrame, which ran on top of Terminal Server Edition (in much the same way that Citrix XenApp runs on Windows Server now) and added some new features and management tools.

Terminal Server Edition was very much a starting point. The operating system was pretty basic, to put it mildly. Almost every installation of Terminal Server Edition ran MetaFrame on top of it, because the base product did little more than provide a multi-user operating system. Even basic functionality such as clipboard mapping was not included. The fact that Terminal Server Edition and the core operating system were different products wasn't great for either Microsoft or its customers. Microsoft had to deal with two sets of operating system service packs, and customers had to purchase a separate product to test server-based computing *and* juggle two different service packs that were not released at the same time. On the plus side, when there was a problem with Service Pack 6 (SP6) for Windows NT 4.0, it was solved by the time SP6 for Terminal Server Edition was released.

Windows 2000 Server

The first real breakthrough in Terminal Services was in Microsoft Windows 2000 Server. For the first time, Terminal Services was a server role in the base server operating system, not a separate product. Why did this matter? There are several reasons. First, the game of juggling incompatible service packs for single-user and multi-user operating systems was over. Second, there was a fundamental change in the way that server-based computing and remote access were perceived. Before Windows 2000, if you wanted to manage a Windows server from the graphical user interface (GUI), you generally sat down in front of it—there was no capability for remote management using Microsoft Remote Desktop Protocol (RDP). The problem was that there is a limit to the number of servers that you can sit in front of during the day, especially when those servers are in different buildings—or even in different cities. Windows 2000 Server introduced Remote Administration as an optional component, allowing server administrators to manage servers even when they *weren't* sitting in front of them. Not only did this make server administration a lot easier, it also came to the aid of Terminal Services, because it gave people a good use case for remote usage and multi-user computing.

Having Terminal Services in Application Server mode available in the core operating system also meant that trying Terminal Server for users required comparatively little effort—setting up a basic pilot could be done with as little effort as installing the role in Application Server mode and letting people use Notepad. In addition, because RDP in Windows 2000 Server added some basic functionality such as client printer redirection and a shared clipboard between local and remote sessions, trying Terminal Server and getting a feel for how users could benefit from shared computing was possible even with only the tools in the core operating system.

Windows Server 2003

The next big step was Microsoft Windows Server 2003, which took some of the decisions made in the Windows 2000 Server timeframe to their next logical conclusions. If Remote Administration is a good thing, why should it be an optional component? Instead, enable it for all Windows server roles and make it an option for the client. And although the basic functionality in Windows 2000 Terminal Server is useful, it doesn't provide a sufficiently rich client experience. Let's enable drive mapping, full color, sound, and other features that were previously possible only with third-party products, so that the remote experience can be a lot more like the local desktop experience.

Another big change to Windows Server 2003 was in management. Windows 2000 terminal servers could be managed only singly. You could configure them remotely, but not collectively. Windows Server 2003 introduced some Group Policy settings for configuring and managing terminal servers, and Terminal Server Manager supported management of remote servers.

Windows Server 2008

Microsoft Windows Server 2008 represented a big breakthrough in Terminal Services functionality. Previous versions of Terminal Services had included only two roles: the terminal server and a license server.

> **NOTE** Although Windows Server 2003 included the Session Directory Server for basic farm support, this role was available only in the Enterprise Edition and was not widely deployed.

If your needs extended beyond remote access to a full desktop on the local area network (LAN), then you needed third-party additions to the role to help you fulfill them. With Windows Server 2008, Terminal Services gained the following advantages.

- Visual integration between locally and remotely running applications
- A web interface for presenting applications on the terminal servers individually
- A secure gateway to enable support for secure access via the Internet
- A session broker to route incoming connections to the most appropriate terminal server
- A printing subsystem that did not require print drivers to be installed on the terminal servers
- Redirection of new types of devices

Windows Server 2008 R2 and RDS

Windows Server 2008 R2 is technically a "minor release" like other R2 releases, but it introduces a lot of changes for RDS. The role service has expanded again to add virtual desktop support (often called VDI, for *Virtual Desktop Infrastructure*). It has also gained some new features, some of the most important being the following.

- Support for connection to Hyper-V based virtual machine (VM) pools of shared VMs and personal VMs assigned to an individual
- Changes to Remote Desktop (RD) Web Access that allow the portal to display resources from multiple RD Session Host servers (formerly known as terminal servers) or farms, and that enable security filtering for RemoteApp programs and VMs

- Improved application compatibility and resource management on RD Session Host Support for Aero Glass remoting and other user experience improvements to RDP 7

- Support for forms-based single sign-on through RD Web Access so that users need authenticate only once in the website to get to all the RemoteApp programs assigned to them

- Improvements to Remote Desktop Gateway to enforce drive redirection policies and enable client remediation when clients do not conform to software rules

- Improved discoverability for license servers for a more reliable connection

DIRECT FROM THE SOURCE

Why VDI?

Michael Kleef, Senior Product Manager
Windows Server Marketing

Microsoft added VDI support to Windows Server 2008 R2 to allow customers further desktop delivery choice in thin client computing. Although Remote Desktop Session Host is a mature product and still provides relevant customer value at the right TCO (total cost of ownership) point, there are times when the level of personalization and isolation that VDI with Windows 7 delivers are important for specific use cases. Applications that require elevated permissions are hard to support on an RD Session Host because one elevated-privilege mistake could affect all users of the server. The isolation of VMs makes it possible to support this type of application using VDI. Another example is native application compatibility; this was largely solved by Microsoft App-V, but it can't solve all application issues in which the application requires a Windows client installation. It's for reasons like this that Microsoft invested in delivering a VDI platform in Windows Server 2008 R2 and extended it further in Service Pack 1 with Dynamic Memory and RemoteFX, to increase VM density and improve the rich user experience.

Most obviously, Terminal Services is now called Remote Desktop Services, and all subroles are renamed to go along with the change. The service was renamed to reflect the much broader scope of the server role, including sessions and the role services needed to get people connected to them, but also hosting of VMs and secure wide area network (WAN) access.

NOTE Because this book is about Windows Server 2008 R2, it uses the current names for the server role and its role services. See Table 1-1 for a list of some of the names you'll come across most often. For a complete mapping of the old and new name for RDS, see *http://technet.microsoft.com/en-us/library/dd560658(WS.10).aspx.*

TABLE 1-1 Mapping TS Names to RDS Names

FORMER NAME	WINDOWS SERVER 2008 R2 NAME
Terminal Services	Remote Desktop Services
Terminal server	Remote Desktop Session Host server
Terminal Services Licensing (TS Licensing)	Remote Desktop Licensing (RD Licensing)
Terminal Services Web Access (TS Web Access)	Remote Desktop Web Access (RD Web Access)
Terminal Services Gateway (TS Gateway)	Remote Desktop Gateway (RD Gateway)
Terminal Services Client Access License (TSCAL)	Remote Desktop Services Client Access License (RDSCAL)
Terminal Services Manager	Remote Desktop Services Manager
Terminal Services Configuration	Remote Desktop Services Configuration

The pattern is pretty obvious; if any names you see don't make sense, look at the list provided at the link.

The Evolving Remote Client Access Experience

Although this book focuses on the server shared-computer experience, not the client, it is important to know that RDS also changed on the client side as the server-side capabilities evolved. Microsoft Windows 2000 Professional did not support incoming remote access connections (nor did Microsoft Windows 9.x), but Microsoft Windows XP, Windows Vista, and Windows 7 all do. Supporting incoming remote connections enabled several new ways to use Windows clients, including

- Remote access to a physical computer from home or another area of the building
- Remote Assistance
- Virtual desktop hosting
- Hosting RemoteApp programs to be displayed in another client operating system (for application compatibility)

Remote access from another computer reflects the reality that many people use more than one computer, and that a home might have more than one computer. Remote Assistance uses the remote control feature of RDS—the ability to permit a second person to see or even take over a remote session—for enabling help desk support, even on desktops. Virtual desktop hosting was one of the chief competitors to session hosting for a long time (and is now part of the service). Features like RemoteApp on Hyper-V allow people to run applications on an older operating system while seeing them on a newer one, even if the application won't run on Windows 7 for some reason.

NOTE Generally speaking, most 32-bit applications can run on a 64-bit platform as long as these applications don't include drivers and don't have a 16-bit installation routine. Web applications designed to run in Microsoft Internet Explorer 6 are one exception to this rule. Internet Explorer 6 is included with Windows Server 2003, but can't be installed on Windows Server 2008 R2. Therefore, if you have Internet Explorer 6–dependent applications and want to display them as RemoteApp programs, you can host them in VMs using RemoteApp for Hyper-V.

RDS shows up in the client versions of Windows even when you don't expect it. It's the technology that enables Fast User Switching and Remote Assistance (to name just two), and a version of the RDP protocol is the basis of Live Mesh.

In short, the story of Remote Desktop Services is the story of how multi-user computing has become less of a niche technology and more of a Microsoft strategy for enabling various scenarios that blur the line between the PC and the data center. Even when they're not called RDS, multi-user computing and the Remote Desktop Protocol have become crucial parts of the core Windows platform.

What Can You Do with RDS?

The preceding section provides a (very fast) look at where RDS came from and how it became part of the core Windows platform for both client and server. You will learn about the technology in depth in later chapters. But what do you *do* with it?

Fundamentally, RDS breaks the hard links between location, client operating system, and capability.

In many ways, this is a natural extension of networking. If you're using a single computer unconnected to any networks, you're limited to the applications and data stored on that computer. If you attach that computer to a network and enable file sharing, you can use data that is not stored on your laptop, and a systems administrator can both back up that data (impossible for someone else to do on an isolated desktop) and secure it. With RDS, you can use not only data stored somewhere else but also applications stored somewhere else. They don't even have to be capable of running on the client computer as long as they'll run on the host. Presentation remoting improves file sharing because the files you use don't have to be accessible to the client computer as long as they're available to the back-end application.

With an isolated PC, you are absolutely tied to what that computer can do. With presentation remoting, the capabilities are more flexible, because what you see isn't necessarily running on the computer where you're working, or even in the same country. This has benefits for security, location, and device independence.

Improved Security for Remote Users

Totally PC-based computing has problems with data security. More and more people work on laptops, and laptops are meant to be taken places. But laptops with data stored on them are a security risk, even if you password-protect the laptop. Unless you take the laptop with you *everywhere*, including lugging it along to dinner instead of leaving it in the hotel room when you're on the road, the data on your laptop is vulnerable to theft. And if someone *really* wants the laptop, it doesn't matter if you take it with you. This doesn't even address the dilemma of leaving the laptop in a taxi or on a train by accident. It happens. BitLocker technology on Windows 7 and Windows Vista protects against theft but does not protect against loss from a misplaced or broken laptop that wasn't backed up.

If the data is on the laptop and you lose the laptop, the data's gone. The obvious solution is not to keep the data on the laptop—store it in the data center instead. But if you're accessing the data center from a remote location via a virtual private network (VPN) and working with large files (in this day of heavy-duty formatting, what file *isn't* large?), it's tempting to keep the file on the local drive while working on it remotely and then copy it back to the network when you're done with it. However, if you work this way, you're back where you started with the data on the local drive.

Information Insecurity

It's not practical to make sensitive information accessible only to people within the four walls of the office, but it's been shown again and again what happens when that information leaves the data center. In November 2009, the Army Corps of Engineers lost a hard drive containing the names and social security numbers of as many as 60,000 current and former Army service members and some civilians. As of this writing, the drive has not yet been recovered. This isn't the first time that sensitive data has been lost to a misplaced laptop or other portable media.

It's not always feasible to store sensitive information only in the data center, accessible solely via secure connection to a Remote Desktop Session Host server behind the perimeter network. Sometimes, the information must be available even when a network connection isn't. But when it is feasible, it's much more secure to keep information where it's least likely to be compromised, stolen, or lost: in the data center.

One solution to the dilemma of how to secure data while keeping it accessible to the people who need it is to keep *everything* in the data center, including the applications required to edit the data. If both the applications and the confidential data are on the network, then it's either impossible to edit the data locally (because no application for doing the editing is installed locally) or not as desirable to do so because there's no reason to download the remote file to the local computer for a more responsive experience. No sensitive data ends up on the client computer; it all stays within the boundaries of the data center.

NOTE Given a sufficiently long distance or sufficiently slow Internet connection, the remote connection will also be slow; and if the network connection isn't totally reliable, it can be frustrating as the session disconnects. As you know all too well, even high-speed networks experience some latency when you're working on one continent and the data center is on another one. But these problems apply to any remote-access scenario and have less chance of accidentally corrupting the original document by attempting to write to it over a slow connection. A disconnected session doesn't lead to data loss—it's just there waiting for its user to reconnect to it.

What if you want people to be able to edit confidential documents when they are in a secure location but not when they're accessing the corporate network from the local coffee shop? Using RDS in Windows Server 2008 R2, you can set up rules that determine which applications a remote user has access to, whether the user has any local drives mapped, and even whether it's possible to cut and paste text between local and remote applications. Security needs can determine the restrictions placed on remote access while still keeping the data easily available when it should be.

Provisioning New Users Rapidly

This is especially useful for temporary workers. If you are providing computer services for someone who will only be around temporarily (for example, a consultant needing a temporary desktop or a temporary worker) then it's good not to need to spend much time on setting up a computer for her, but also good to give her a clean work environment that doesn't require her to work around the detritus left by the previous user of the computer. Through RDS, you can get a new user set up and working almost as quickly as you're able to get her a domain account. In addition, the pooled VM or remote desktop session the person uses will be brand new, with no old settings left from a previous user, which should simplify troubleshooting and training.

Enabling Remote Work

Related to security for mobile workers is remote work. Telecommuting is becoming more common in the workplace. Some help desk suppliers and U.S. government agencies don't even have desks for all their workers, since their workplaces are designed for most people to be working from home most of the time. According to the Status of Telework Report to the Congress (see *http://www.telework.gov/Reports_and_Studies/Annual_Reports /2009teleworkreport.pdf*), over 100,000 people working for the U.S. government teleworked during 2008, with 64 percent of these teleworking at least 1 to 3 days per week. This represents an increase of just under 9 percent since 2007.

Nor is telework a solely North American phenomenon. In 39 percent of western European companies, some people work at home at least part of the time, according to "IT and the Environment," a 2007 paper by the Economist Intelligence Unit.

But working from home has its own set of challenges, not least being the question of how the company can support the desktop environment. Home-based computers can't be easily managed by Group Policy; they can break down with no IT staff immediately available to provide assistance, and people working from home can't always readily talk through a computer-based problem with help desk staff. And how do you update an application when it's time to move from, say, Microsoft Office 2007 to Office 2010? If you've worked remotely for even a brief span of time, you probably have experienced the advantages of mobility and the disadvantages of lack of local support. It's great being able to work from the coffee shop, hotel, or airport lobby; it's not so great acting as your own help desk.

Server-based computing helps enable remote scenarios in several ways. You don't have to worry about home users installing applications that they shouldn't run on the Remote Desktop Session Host servers if you follow basic security procedures (more later on this topic). Since the applications are stored on the RD Session Host servers, they're installed and updated there, not on the clients. And, as discussed in the previous section, "Provisioning New Users Rapidly," using RDS allows the administrator to determine the kind of resource sharing that the local and remote computers should do and which applications are available, depending on the location from which a user is connecting.

Bringing Windows to PC-Unfriendly Environments

Not all the people who need a PC work in an environment that allows them to have one. One example is electronics firms. If you're making circuit boards, you make them within what's called a *clean room*, a room with no dust and which requires a time-consuming process to enter. If you need to use Windows applications in a clean room, you can't use PCs. The fans inside the case kick up dust inside the computer and spread it into the room. In addition, it's not practical to have PCs that might need servicing in any room that takes extensive preparation to enter as a clean room does. Therefore, you need RDS to provide Windows applications to the terminals.

Thin clients are also good for environments where you want access to Windows applications but the circumstances are not PC-friendly, if they've got too much dust or vibration to be good for the PC. Small terminals that can be wall-mounted or carried work better in these circumstances than PCs do. But since these small terminals have very limited memory and CPU power and no disks, you can't run Windows 7 on them. To get access to the latest operating system and applications, you need an RD Session Host server for the terminals to connect to.

PC-less Windows environments include places such as upscale health clubs or city apartment lobbies. Management wants to attract customers by offering the convenience of a personal computer in the lobby or cafe but doesn't want to support computers in these locations. (Bulk can also be an issue when you're trying to squeeze five user work areas into a small counter space.) Windows terminals can connect to an RD Session Host server and present the applications. They're also smaller, cooler, and more reliable than PCs, which can get misconfigured.

It has been said that there's no point to getting thin clients because if you buy PCs, you get more power for the same money. With thin clients, you're not paying for the computing power; you're using very little, comparatively speaking. You're paying for the reduced administration and smaller physical footprint and energy use. This solution is not for everyone, but sometimes thin clients are a better choice than PCs.

Business Continuity and Disaster Recovery

One advantage of RDS is that it enables you to set up user work environments quickly. As long as the servers are available in the data center, they can be made available to users almost as quickly as the user's computer is plugged in and turned on. Using a combination of centralized application installs and Internet access, it's possible to set up a new branch office quickly even if the RD Session Host servers are located offsite. For maximum flexibility and ease of setup, this model assumes that the RD Session Host servers are user-agnostic (that is, all user information, including profiles, is stored elsewhere) and identically configured.

Supporting Green Computing

One of the hot topics (no pun intended) these days is how to make companies and governments greener—how to help them use less energy. IDC, a market-research firm, says that power consumption is now one of systems managers' top five concerns. Companies now spend as much as 10 percent of their technology budgets on energy, says Rakesh Kumar of Gartner, a consultancy. (Only about half of this amount is used to run computers; much of it goes toward cooling them, since for every dollar used to power a server, you spend a dollar to cool it.) Dropping power usage is a win-win situation, really—because companies have to pay for their power, using less energy means that they spend less money on power.

> **NOTE** A December 2007 paper from McKinsey & Company, "Reducing U.S. Greenhouse Gas Emissions: How Much at What Cost?" (*http://www.mckinsey.com/clientservice/ccsi/pdf /US_ghg_final_report.pdf*), shows the marginal costs of reducing carbon dioxide emissions. The cost of reducing the carbon emissions for combined heat and power in commercial buildings is negative. That is, it pays companies to go green.

There's a *lot* of waste in desktop-centric computing. According to IDC, average server utilization levels range from 15 to 30 percent. Average resource utilization rates for PCs have been estimated at less than 5 percent. Because you have to power the processor and memory whether you're using them or not, this represents a lot of waste. Therefore, depending on the needs of the client, there might be quite a bit of room for people accessing their desktops—or at least their applications—from an RD Session Host server. For companies that can reasonably exchange desktop computers for Windows-based terminals, this can represent a huge savings, both in terms of the power drawn by the full desktops and in terms of the air conditioning required to cool the building heated by hundreds of powerful PCs.

Improved Command-Line Support

Windows Server 2008 had a wide array of programmable interfaces that duplicated—and even extended—the capabilities of the GUI. What it didn't have was the best way to get at them. Windows PowerShell supported Windows Management Instrumentation (WMI) but had no remote access capabilities (and finding the right WMI object isn't trivial unless you already know what you're looking for), so you couldn't use Windows PowerShell to manage settings on a server farm. VBScript did support remote access and WMI, but it required knowing how to script. (You also need to learn to use Windows PowerShell to use it, but it's simpler and a lot of basic tasks have cmdlets already prepared.)

Command-line management is simpler in Windows Server 2008 R2 for two reasons. First, the Windows PowerShell team introduced remote access support in Windows PowerShell 2.0. Second, the RDS team created Windows PowerShell objects to map to its WMI structure. It's now possible to easily find the capability that you want according to server role, and the objects are fully supported by standard Windows PowerShell cmdlets. You'll be reviewing throughout this book how to use Windows PowerShell to manage the RDS farms.

> **NOTE** For an example of the kinds of things you can do with Windows PowerShell and RDS, see the RDS team's Script Center site at *http://technet.microsoft.com/en-us /scriptcenter/ee364707.aspx*. Some scripts use VBScript for backward compatibility with previous operating systems.

RDS for Windows Server 2008 R2: New Features

So far, you've seen an overview of some of the ways you might apply server-based computing to meet your company's needs for supporting remote workers or PC-unfriendly environments. Many new features in Windows Server 2008 help you support these scenarios specifically. This book is devoted to letting you know what's new in RDS and how to use it. This section discusses some of the features and how this version of RDS differs from previous versions in ways larger than individual features.

DIRECT FROM THE FIELD

New Features of RDS You Might Not Have Heard Of

Greg Shields, RDS MVP
Partner and Principal Technologist with Concentrated Technology (www.ConcentratedTech.com)

RDS in Windows Server 2008 R2 gets a lot of press, because there's so much in it that's new and exciting. But in among its heavy-hitter updates are a few that you might not know about.

For example, did you know that its *Dynamic Fair Share Scheduling* ensures that each user on the same server gets an equal amount of processor attention? With it, a lightweight user running Microsoft Word can collocate with a heavyweight user performing a software build, or crunching a database query, or any other CPU-intensive activity. Neither session is impacted by the actions of the other.

Remote Desktop IP Virtualization is also new for those finicky applications that require unique IP addresses to function. Without it, all applications running from the same RD Session Host will appear to have the same IP address. With it, an RDS server can virtualize a set of IP addresses so that those applications execute without problems.

Even *Windows Installer* gets improved with Windows Server 2008 R2. In previous operating system versions, Windows Installer wasn't fully Terminal Services–aware. This limitation made the installation of some applications very difficult as concurrent installs would block each other. That awareness is finally present in R2, improving the success rate of installing applications to RDS. Installing MSI packages on an RD Session Host server is the same as installing them on a client computer—they serialize and don't block.

With R2, your options for connecting users to applications become as important as the application delivery itself. This "feature" isn't so much a feature as a completely new way of thinking about *application delivery*. The incorporation of RemoteApp and Desktop Connection in Windows 7 with the RD Web Access in Windows Server 2008 R2 gives you more options for how you connect users to their applications. Depending on your needs, you can deliver RemoteApp programs and VMs via a web page in Internet Explorer, through an .RDP file delivered to the user, or, for those using Windows 7, you can simply populate your users' Start menu.

The Changing Character of RD Session Host Usage

One RDS change in Windows Server 2008 R2 is in the usage assumptions. Windows Server 2003, for example, assumed that administrators will generally run individual servers from the corporate LAN (and probably only one or two of them) since the session brokering piece is available only in the Enterprise edition of the software. Windows Server 2008 assumed that terminal servers would be hosted in farms, that people would run both locally installed applications and RemoteApp programs, and that at least some people would be accessing the RD Session Host servers from the Internet.

RDS in Windows Server 2008 R2 expands on the assumptions in Windows Server 2008 to assume the following, among other things.

- Many users access the corporate LAN from the Internet at least some of the time.
- Users don't always log on from domain-joined computers.

- Users are more likely to use a PC (with some locally installed applications) than a terminal device.
- Users might work from a branch office but still are connected to the domain.
- Some users will run very demanding applications from the data center.
- Applications will be served from a farm of identical servers more often than a single server.
- Some users will be allowed to install applications even in a hosted workspace.
- Some applications should be isolated for best compatibility.

You will learn about some RDS role services here, but a technical walkthrough of these features is less important right now than understanding the business problems that they're designed to solve. The rest of this book will provide design, deployment, and operations guidance.

Supporting VM Users

Sessions are a good way to enable that a lot of people use the same physical hardware. However, sessions don't work for everyone, especially not if desktop replacement is the goal. A session can't permit its users full administrative access to tweak settings through the Control Panel, isn't always friendly to resource-hungry applications (at least, the resource-hungry applications are not always friendly to the other sessions), and doesn't permit users to install applications to use later in exactly the same environment. Nor can you hibernate a session to easily save not just data, but also the work that you were in the middle of completing when you dropped everything and ran to catch the bus. Using a VM, it is literally possible to save your work state.

One new feature in Windows Server 2008 R2 is native support for Virtual Desktop Infrastructure (VDI), which is a short name for "managed virtual machines." Microsoft VDI supports two kinds of VMs. *Personal desktops* are assigned to an individual and can be customized according to whatever rules are in place in the organization. *Pooled desktops* are generally available to anyone with access to the pool. Although it is possible in some cases to make changes to them, there is no guarantee that a user changing a pooled desktop will get the same one the next time they log in—rolling back changes is often normal, to avoid people contaminating the desktop pool with applications and settings they will never reuse.

Each kind of desktop is designed for a different purpose. Personal desktops are for full desktop replacement. Although accessible only via RDP, a personal desktop is controlled by the user it is assigned to, and if a person has a personal desktop, the RD Connection Broker will always attempt to connect them to it first. A personal desktop can replace a physical computer and even has the advantage of making the machine state easy to back up, so moving to a new physical platform doesn't mean losing all settings.

Pooled desktops are more for supporting people who need to run applications that aren't well hosted on an RD Session Host server, even with the new support for fair share processing that prevents a single session from using all the processor power. They can be preinstalled with any applications that the people who need the pool will need.

Pooled desktops can also support an application-compatibly feature released after Windows Server 2008 R2 shipped: RemoteApp on Hyper-V. This feature allows you to run RemoteApp programs from a VM rather than from an RD Session Host server. It's designed to allow computers running Windows 7 that need to run an application that can't run on Windows 7 (for example, a web application based on Internet Explorer 6) from a computer running Windows XP located in the data center. Although each VM can still only support one incoming connection at a time, RemoteApp for Hyper-V makes it possible to support these older applications while retaining the features of Windows 7 on the desktop.

How to Get RemoteApp Technology from a Client

Remoting technology is great for displaying applications that can't run on the client. For example, you can run really demanding applications from a session or a VM to integrate with an older operating system or on hardware that won't support them.

Supporting older applications that won't run on an operating system later than Windows Server 2003 and Windows XP is a bit more problematic. Windows Server 2003 didn't include support for RemoteApp technology, so to run the older applications there would mean publishing only from a full desktop. And up until now, Windows XP didn't support RemoteApp connections (although some companies had solutions that did something functionally similar).

Microsoft has several different technologies that support RemoteApp from client operating systems such as Windows XP. They're all intended for different user scenarios.

XP Mode uses Virtual PC technology to run a Windows XP VM on a computer running Windows 7. People with their own computers would run this to enable themselves to run applications locally that will not run on Windows 7. To get XP Mode, go to *http://www.microsoft.com/windows/virtual-pc/download.aspx*.

MED-V is essentially managed XP Mode (see *http://blogs.technet.com/medv /archive/2009/04/30/windows-xp-mode-in-windows-7-how-it-relates-to-future-ver- sions-of-med-v.aspx*). You'd use this to deploy XP Mode in an organization so that you don't rely on individuals to update their own RemoteApp guest machines.

The catch to XP Mode is that it requires the RemoteApp VM to run locally. Not all computers have the hardware to run two full machines at the same time (required with Type 2 hypervisors like Virtual PC). To make it possible to support RemoteApp from Windows XP, there's RemoteApp for Hyper-V. This model runs the Windows XP guest VMs hosting the RemoteApp programs in a data center and uses RDP to

Continued on the next page

display them on a computer running Windows 7. To get the updates required to use RemoteApp for Hyper-V, go to *http://support.microsoft.com/kb/961742*.

MED-V and XP Mode are outside the scope of this book because they do not use the RDS infrastructure, but RemoteApp for Hyper-V is discussed in more detail in Chapter 3, "Deploying a Single Remote Desktop Session Host Server."

Supporting Telecommuters and Mobile Workers Securely

The way that people work in information fields has changed a great deal over the years. At one time, most information workers (the best way to describe people who need regular access to a shared pool of data to do their jobs) went to where the information was: namely, to the office. When they left the office, they stopped working on anything that depended on that central pool of information. Similarly, when they were in the office, they could easily add to this central pool of information—after all, all this information is created by people—and when they left, they could not continue adding to the central pool of information.

Laptops changed this by giving telecommuters a computer that they could easily take with them, but laptops still didn't have access to the central pool of information that people could access at the office. Widespread Internet access combined with the increasing use of email as a personal information store gave additional access, but email doesn't include *everything* your company knows—just that information included within emails you've sent or received.

The next stage was securely connecting to the corporate network, retrieving the information required, and then downloading it to the laptop. This, of course, required both broad access to high-speed networks for downloading the documents to the local computer and also for the application to be installed locally. It also meant that people needed some way for the laptop to access the data center without creating a security breach or spreading a virus on the corporate network.

Much of the industrialized world today has access to the necessary components: laptops and high-speed networks that are available both at home and in public places such as airports and hotels. The tricky problems that arise include how to regulate which computers are allowed access to the network and how to keep sensitive data off computers vulnerable to theft or loss. There's also the problem of gaining access to the data that mobile workers create while on the road. Data stored on a laptop won't make it back to the corporate network until the road warriors get back from the trip, or at least get some free time to upload all their new data to the central data pool.

RDS long held promise in supporting telecommuters and mobile workers, but the solution included with the operating system didn't have all the tools needed to make this work until Windows Server 2008. Windows Server 2008 Terminal Services changed this, introducing Terminal Services Gateway (TS Gateway). TS Gateway enabled authorized users to access authorized corporate resources securely via RDP tunneled through the Internet. Windows Server 2008 R2 added some enhancements for increased security in the new version of TS Gateway, called Remote Desktop Gateway (RD Gateway).

RD Gateway enables users to access the corporate network—and the centralized data pool—securely via SSL from the hotel or airport or even the beach (if you can keep sand out of your laptop). When combined with RDP file signing and server authentication, RD Gateway provides secure Internet access, giving users some assurance that the RDP file that they launch is a legitimate resource and not a spoofed server set up to capture their logon credentials. RD Gateway can also set policy to protect the data center, controlling which people and computers are allowed to access the data center via this path and letting administrators control what resources they have access to once they get there.

> **NOTE** RD Gateway and SSL aren't the only ways to create a secure connection to the data center from a remote location—VPNs and Direct Access are other access options. But RD Gateway has some advantages, including controlled access to specific resources, which is discussed in detail in Chapter 10, "Making Remote Desktop Services Available from the Internet."

Using Public Computers Without Storing Connection Data

The previous section discussed personal laptops, and that's what most people use to access the data center while on the road. However, it's not reasonable to expect that people will *never* log on except from a computer that they own. For example, you could be connecting to the corporate RD Session Host servers from a computer at your family's home in Tucson, or from a kiosk at an Internet cafe in Darmstadt. In both cases, you need a way to access work resources without leaving any personal data cached on those computers, including an RDP file used to point to the data center.

Remote Desktop Web Access (RD Web Access) has features that enable you to do this. Rather than storing connection settings in an RDP file that you can get in email or save to a desktop, RD Web Access is a secured website that displays icons representing shared desktops and RemoteApp programs. When a user clicks a link, RD Web Access generates the RDP settings for the resource to which the user is attempting to connect. With the advent of forms-based authentication in Windows Server 2008 R2, users can log onto the website once, then use the same credentials to access all RemoteApp programs displayed in the browser.

RD Web Access and RD Gateway are independent role services, but they can be combined to provide secured Internet access without depending on saved RDP files.

Integrating Locally Installed Applications and RemoteApp Programs

RDS in Windows Server 2008 R2 doesn't require a specific client operating system to work; you can connect to a VM or to an RD Session Host server using clients as old as RDP 5.2. (Previous versions of RDP aren't supported because of security improvements in RDP 5.*x*.) However, you'll definitely get the best experience using RDP 7. This version of the client enables some new visual remoting not possible with previous versions. Like Terminal Services in Windows Server 2008, RDS continues to blur the line between client and server.

One feature of RDS depends on a capability in the client operating system and is available only to clients running Windows 7: RemoteApp and Desktop Connections. (For those using Windows Server 2008 R2 as a client, it's also possible to set up this feature from this operating system.) You will learn about this feature in detail in Chapter 9, "Multi-Server Deployments," but in short, it allows users to add icons automatically from applications running in the data center to their Start menu.

> **NOTE** For the best user experience, you should use the latest version of RDP (7, as of this writing) but many features are available even to older versions of the RDP client. See Chapter 6, "Customizing the User Experience," for more details.

Supporting High-Fidelity User Experience over RDP

Early versions of Terminal Services made it very obvious that you were connecting to a remote computer. The color quality was low, you couldn't redirect devices, you couldn't use more than one monitor, the quality of audio redirection wasn't the best, and so forth.

Windows Server 2008 R2 makes it easier to work remotely by supporting the following features.

- True multi-monitor support, including varying layouts and both landscape and portrait orientations.
- Aero remoting for single-monitor sessions on Windows 7.
- Client-side rendering of multimedia and audio Windows Media Player files.
- Improved display of video from Silverlight and Windows Media Foundation.
- Bi-directional audio remoting, including sound recording to a remote session.

Working from Branch Offices

Working remotely isn't a label just for those working from home or while on the road. "Remote" workers might operate in a separate office, but one with resources similar to the corporate office. In this scenario, the network is reliable, the computers are domain-joined . . . but the data center is not in the same physical location as the branch office workers, and onsite IT staffing might be minimal.

Supporting Larger Server Farms

RDS deployments don't consist of just one or two servers anymore, but the tools available in Windows Server 2003 didn't really support farms. (Session Directory Server was available only on the enterprise edition of Windows Server 2003.) Windows Server 2008 R2 RDS is more suited to managing access to multiple servers because it adds additional group policies for server management and the RD Connection Broker enables users to connect to farms instead of single servers.

Other Business Cases for RDS

Administrators benefit from RDS, too.

Regulatory Compliance Requirements

For the IT department, data security and the ability to meet regulatory requirements both remain top priorities. RDS helps secure an application and its data in a central location, reducing the risk of accidental data loss caused by, for example, the loss of a laptop. Key features of RDS, such as RD Gateway and RemoteApp combined with RD Web Access, help ensure that partners, or users, who do not need full access to a company network or computers can be limited to a single application, if needed.

Complex Applications

In an environment with complex applications such as line-of-business (LOB) or customized older software, or in situations in which large and complex applications are frequently updated but are difficult to automate, RDS can help simplify the process by reducing the burden of managing multiple applications across the entire environment. The client machines can access the applications they require from a central source, rather than requiring applications to be installed locally.

Merger Integration or Outsourcing

In the case of a merger, the affected organizations will typically need to use the same LOB applications, although they might be in a variety of configurations and versions. In addition, organizations might also find that they are working with outsourced or partner organizations requiring access to specific LOB applications but not to the full corporate network. Rather than performing a costly deployment of the entire set of LOB applications across the extended infrastructure, these applications can be installed on an RD Session Host server and made available to the employees and business partners who require access, when they need it.

New RDS Technology in Windows Server 2008 R2

New technology in RDS in Windows Server 2008 R2 does a lot to improve the user experience. Part of the goal of this release was to make the remoting unobtrusive so that an application executing remotely should appear to be executing locally. In this section, you will learn about some of the technology in this release that enables this. The rest of this book will go into more detail.

Integration of RemoteApp Programs and Desktops into the Start Menu

Technically, it was possible to integrate RemoteApp icons with the Start menu in Windows Server 2008. To do so, you had to

1. Package the RemoteApp from the RD Session Host server as a Microsoft Windows Installer (MSI) file.

2. Publish this MSI file through Group Policy.

3. Repackage and republish manually as required when the RemoteApp settings changed.

It's not a bad system, and MSI publishing is still the only way that you can support file associations with RemoteApp programs. (It's also the only way you can integrate RemoteApp programs with the Start menu on Windows XP and Windows Vista.) However, it doesn't update automatically, and you can't add more RemoteApp programs to the Start menu without editing Group Policy. Finally, since it requires Group Policy, you can't use this method to publish applications to computers outside the domain.

A new feature called RemoteApp and Desktop Connections avoids these drawbacks. A new application Control Panel item in Windows 7 (and Windows Server 2008 R2) called Remote-App and Desktop Connections can accept a Uniform Resource Locator (URL) for the *publishing feed* created from the farm. This feed aggregates all the RemoteApp programs, VM pools, and personal desktops available. When a user connects to the URL for the feed and presents their credentials, RD Web Access filters the display so that they get links only to resources that they are permitted to use. These links then populate the client's Start menu.

Using RemoteApp and Desktop Connections has the following advantages.

- It allows users to start locally installed applications and RemoteApp programs in the same way: through the Start menu.
- It does not require the computer running Windows 7 to be connected to the domain.
- It updates automatically whenever RemoteApp programs or VMs are added to or removed from the feed, or when permissions change.
- Users have to log on only once to create the connection.
- Finally, this feed is written in XML, an industry standard, and is available to developers to consume in other ways.

Aero Glass Remoting

One of the visual limitations of Windows Server 2008 was that Windows Vista had this great Aero Glass interface . . . but this wasn't available from terminal server sessions. Today, Aero remoting is available when connecting to Windows 7 VMs and Windows Server 2008 R2 sessions from a client running Windows 7—even if the endpoint can't display Aero itself (for example, if connecting to a headless computer).

Aero Glass remoting from Windows 7 is enabled by default; to enable it from Windows Server 2008 R2 requires turning on desktop composition. The details are discussed in Chapter 6.

Aero Glass remoting is available for single-monitor sessions only.

Improved Application Compatibility

One of the interesting questions about applications, especially those that are a little fussy, is whether they will work on an RD Session Host server. Three new technologies in Windows Server 2008 R2 RDS seek to address application compatibility problems.

- Changes to the process of installing MSI packages make the installation process work more as it does on client operating systems. Chapter 3 goes into the details, but the impact is to prevent simultaneous first-time uses of applications based on MSI installs from blocking each other.

- Windows Server 2008 has Windows System Resource Manager (WSRM) for preventing single sessions or processes from using up all the processor time. Windows Server 2008 R2 still supports WSRM, but it also introduces a new feature for preventing this problem in a more proactive manner. Whereas WSRM identifies badly behaving applications and scales back their processor time, Dynamic Fair Share Scheduling (DFSS) works with the scheduler to ensure that a single session never starves other sessions for processor cycles. You'll learn about this in more detail in Chapter 3.

- Finally, IP virtualization makes it possible for a session—or only certain applications running in a session—to have a unique IP address. In previous versions of Terminal Services, all applications on a server would have the same IP address: the server's IP. Although this worked much of the time, it prevented applications or security scenarios that required a discrete IP address. Again, you'll find out more about this feature in Chapter 3.

Support for True Multi-monitor Remoting

Version 6 of the Remote Desktop Connection client introduced monitor spanning, so you could use two or more monitors (up to a resolution of 4096 × 2048) to display a remote session. To get this, you connected to the terminal server using the */span* switch. Span was an improvement over being limited to a single monitor but had some drawbacks.

- The monitors had to be arranged in a row.

- The remote session was still a single-monitor session—just one with a *really* big monitor. Because of this, if you had only two monitors, error messages displayed in the middle of your screen sometimes got bisected or obscured. In addition, maximized applications would take up all the monitor space.

Again, the total supported resolution had to be below 4096 × 2048 (for example, 1600 × 1200 + 1600 × 1200 = 3200 × 1200).

RDS replaces monitor spanning with true multi-monitor support. With multi-monitor support, each monitor on the client machine is redirected individually, so that each monitor (up to 16) is seen as a separate monitor to the remote session. (Group Policy limits it to 10, but it's technically possible up to 16 if you set this value programmatically.) Therefore

- The monitors can be arranged in any configuration that makes sense to the user: a row, a box, an L, and so forth.
- Individual applications will maximize to the size of the monitor they're currently displayed in, not the entire row of monitors.
- Each monitor can have a maximum resolution of up to 4096 × 2048.

True multi-monitor is not supported with Aero Glass remoting. If multi-monitor and Aero Glass remoting are both configured, multi-monitor will take precedence.

Remoting huge and high-resolution displays can take a toll on server performance, so you might want to tweak the maximum supported resolution and maximum supported monitors. For more details, see Chapter 6.

Client-Side Multimedia Rendering

Many modern personal computers, even modest ones, have a lot of power—more than a server does to render all multimedia in a session on the server and then stream it to the client, at any rate.

In Windows Server 2008 R2, the RDS team has improved the media playback experience by efficiently transporting audio/video-based multimedia in a compressed format within the RDP protocol. Rather than being rendered on the server, it's sent to the client to be played back through Windows Media Player. The content will appear to be displaying locally because it is—even though it was originally generated in a remote session. However, it will also be fully integrated with the remote session.

This approach has several advantages.

- It reduces bandwidth usage since data over the wire will be compressed video instead of a succession of bitmaps; the experience is roughly equivalent to running from a file share or video server. Resizing the window won't affect the playback, either.
- It reduces the processing on the server because the server no longer needs to use processor time decoding the video and packaging it on RDP.

To support this, the client must support multimedia redirection and the server must be configured for audio and video playback. This feature is covered in more detail in Chapter 6.

Single Sign-On for Farms

Single sign-on, or having to present a password only once to use resources from your computer, is obviously good for users. Imagine coming to work in the morning and logging on to your computer. Then you click an icon and need to present credentials again. Then you click another icon and need to present credentials again. By 10 A.M., you're probably ready to just go for coffee and forget about working, since productivity clearly isn't happening if you have to log on every time you start an application.

Single sign-on was introduced in Windows Server 2008, but it was improved in Windows Server 2008 R2 with forms-based authentication. Whereas the previous version allowed you to continue to work without re-presenting your credentials when logging into the same server, the current iteration caches your credentials in a secure web form to present any time you attempt to connect to a RemoteApp program.

Extending Easy Print to Client Platforms and Eliminating .NET Dependency

Printer drivers have long been the bane of the terminal services administrator's life. At first, supporting printer drivers was a gamble in which, if the driver didn't crash the terminal server, you'd won. Supporting client-side printers increased the exposure to error-prone drivers by lessening the administrator's control over the drivers installed. When supporting Windows NT drivers on the terminal servers and non–Windows NT drivers on the client (for example, when using Windows 98 as a client to a Windows 2000 Server terminal server), the drivers might not have the same name. This would require the administrator to create driver mapping files that basically say, "When the system refers to *this* driver from within the client session, *that* driver on the terminal server should be used." Otherwise, the print job would not print.

Over time, the drivers got more reliable as the problem became better understood. When both the client and terminal server were based on Windows NT technology, the driver name mismatch problem ceased to be an issue. Then Windows Server 2003 introduced a new Group Policy that permitted only user-mode drivers by default. This removed the chance of installing a poorly written kernel-mode driver that could crash the server, but it still meant that terminal server administrators had to test, maintain, and support a variety of drivers for both corporate printers and mapped client printers (although some companies stopped supporting mapped client printers just to avoid the driver problems).

Another problem with previous iterations of printing was deciding which printers should be mapped to the remote session. If printer mapping was enabled, then all the client printers would map to the terminal server, regardless of whether this was appropriate. Mapping all these printers could also be time-consuming, not to mention increasing the number of drivers that needed to be installed on a terminal server.

Terminal Services in Windows Server 2008 addressed these problems in several ways. First, and simplest, Group Policy allows administrators to map only the client's *default* printer to a terminal session. Second, Easy Print technology avoids the driver problem for clients running Windows Vista and Remote Desktop Connection 6.1. Basically, Easy Print allows users to print from a remote session without having to install any drivers on the terminal session at all. The remote session gets printer settings from the client and even makes calls to the client-side GUI to show the driver configuration panes for the drivers.

Easy Print had two catches, though: It didn't work when connecting to client operating systems (which eliminated most common VDI scenarios) and it required .NET on the client operating system to work. In Windows Server 2008 R2, both those limitations are addressed. Whereas .NET is required to convert the XPS of the data stream to the GDI commands required to print, in Windows Server 2008 R2 and Windows 7, the operating system does this.

To learn more about Easy Print, see Chapter 6.

RDS Roles in Windows Server 2008 R2

Users of Terminal Services in Windows Server 2008 will find most of the roles in Windows Server 2008 R2 RDS familiar. RDS is supported by six role services.

- RD Session Host
- RD Virtualization Host
- RD Connection Broker
- RD Web Access
- RD Gateway
- RD Licensing

RD Session Host

The RD Session Host (known as the terminal server in Windows Server 2008) remains the core piece of the Remote Desktop Services architecture for delivering individual applications and for getting the highest user density for full desktops. A RD Session Host server is different from other types of Windows servers in several ways. Fundamentally, a server with this role installed works a lot more like a workstation than a server.

For example, other server roles are designed to serve one general purpose, such as handling email or database queries. Their priorities are clear: Whatever is at the foreground of that server's purpose gets the lion's share of the processor. A shared server is different. Many people are using it at the same time, so it can't just assume that whichever application is in the foreground is the one that should get all the processing time—which foreground of the 40 or so sessions should it pick? Therefore, all user processes on a Remote Desktop Session Host server have the same priority so that they share the processor more or less evenly among all remote users.

> **NOTE** In Windows Server 2008 R2, a new feature called Dynamic Fair Share Scheduling (DFSS) proactively ensures that the scheduler doesn't allocate too much processor time to any single session. This feature is on by default.

Users connect to an RD Session Host server via the RDP. They make this connection by starting an RDP file that details all the settings for the connection. Users can get to this file from a network share or in email, and it can be automatically generated from a browser or (for clients running Windows 7) the Start menu through RemoteApp and Desktop Connections. When a user starts a remote session, it's protected from other remote sessions running on that computer. Users can't see each other's sessions, and the applications running in those sessions don't share read/write memory. They can have an impact on each other inadvertently (for example, by using demanding applications that take memory away from other users) but there's minimal security risk in having multiple people running sessions on the same RD Session Host server. To say "no security risk" is, of course, not possible, because there are some exceptional cases that could be exploited by an expert with the right tools, but this is generally true.

> **BEST PRACTICE**   RD Session Host servers have a heavy workload supporting all the remote client sessions, so it's generally best to reserve them only for that use.

Chapter 2, "Key Architectural Concepts for Remote Desktop Services," talks about how to size an RD Session Host server; information about how to install and set up the role is included in Chapter 3; and how to set up server farms with the RD Connection Broker is covered in Chapter 9.

RD Virtualization Host

Windows Server 2008 R2 introduces a new kind of supported resource: VMs. (VMs, of course, are not new with Windows Server 2008 R2, but support for them within the RDS infrastructure is.) This role service uses Hyper-V to host VMs. VMs can be pooled (generally available to anyone with access to the VM pool) or personal (assigned to a particular user in AD DS).

Why support VMs as well as sessions? The answer is simple: both are valid means of virtualizing the desktop. For higher density, you want sessions: *Many* more people can run sessions on a single computer than can run VMs, because sessions share a lot of basic infrastructure in the operating system (even though they can't see each other). VMs are a virtual manifestation of a physical machine and thus completely separate from each other. This takes many more resources to support. You can run a dozen sessions on a server with 4 GB of RAM and a modern processor, but this same server would have a hard time supporting more than a couple of VMs running at the same time.

> **NOTE**   True story: At one virtualization event, some people said they had heard about virtualized desktops through VMs first. They'd never heard of sessions and were excited by the possibilities of "lightweight VDI."

The reason why VMs are valuable is related to why they're so resource-intensive: they're a completely isolated environment. A VM is configured with a certain amount of memory and a certain number of processors, reserved for it and not available to other VMs. The operating system is entirely reserved for the use of the VM. That means that whatever happens within the VM does not affect other VMs running on the same physical server. Users can install applications and they will be installed only on that VM. Users can run the most processor-intensive CAD (computer-aided design) software around and they won't drain resources from other VMs. Users can completely misconfigure a VM and cause it to crash, and this will affect only the person currently using it.

In RDS, VMs are often assigned to power users. Those with personal desktops are those who need a complete desktop replacement (albeit one that can be backed up and has all the protection of the data center): those who need to be able to install applications and configure their computers. Personal desktops are also good candidates for applications that require a persistent local data source (that is, they can't store all their data on a network share). Those using pooled desktops are often those who need to run applications that aren't good candidates for virtualization on an RD Session Host for one reason or another—they require a previous version of the browser, are 16-bit (Windows Server 2008 R2 is 64-bit only, and 16-bit applications won't run on that platform), or otherwise just don't fit but will work on a pooled VM.

Chapter 2 covers how to size an RD Virtualization Host server; Chapter 4, "Deploying a Single Remote Desktop Virtualization Host Server," discusses how to set up the role for a single-server installation; Chapter 9 teaches you how to deploy the role in a farm; and Chapter 10 details how to manage larger deployments.

RD Web Access

Remote Desktop Web Access (RD Web Access) integrates with Microsoft Internet Information Services (IIS) to display the icons of authorized RemoteApp programs and VMs in a portal displayed in Internet Explorer and launch the connections. A user authorizes against the portal and can see the icons for all the remote resources allocated to them by the administrator. When he or she clicks an icon, it creates and starts a RemoteApp program in much the same way it would if the RDP file were stored on the user's computer. Using the new forms-based authentication in RDS, after a user authenticates to a portal once, his or her credentials can be used for any resource the user is authorized to access.

When a user starts a RemoteApp program, a session is started on the RD Session Host server that hosts the RemoteApp program, or the VM backing the VM icon. The RD Web Access server does not start the application. As shown in Figure 1-1, it just displays the application icon, creates the RDP file for that application when the user double-clicks that icon (1), and then passes the RDP file to the user to start the application from the RD Session Host (2). RemoteApp programs and desktops started via RD Web Access do not display in the browser but in their own windows (3) and are independent of the browser window. Closing the browser won't disconnect or terminate the connections to the RD Session Host or VM.

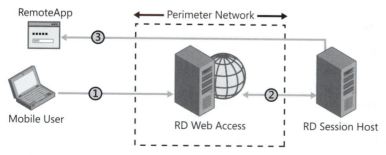

FIGURE 1-1 RD Web Access displays application icons in a browser for the convenience of users.

RD Web Access has many benefits, including the following.

- Users can access RemoteApp programs from a website over the Internet or from an intranet. To start a RemoteApp program, they just double-click the program icon.

- With the new Web SSO feature, after the user authenticates to the website, those credentials are stored and provided for any other connections they initiate—even connections on other servers or other farms.

- RD Web Access can display resources from more than one farm and aggregate them into a single window.

- RD Web Access will display only the resources assigned to a particular person.

- By using RD Web Access, there is much less administrative overhead than that required to maintain and distribute RDP files for connecting to an RD Session Host farm. You can easily deploy programs from a central location and don't have to worry about ensuring that RDP files containing connection information are up to date.

- RD Web Access includes Remote Desktop Web Connection, which enables users to connect remotely to the desktop of any computer where they have Remote Desktop access from the RD Web Access portal.

- RD Web Access works with minimal configuration, but the RD Web Access web page includes a customizable Web Part, which can be incorporated into a customized web page or a Microsoft SharePoint site.

That's how RD Web Access benefits people using a browser . . . but in Windows Server 2008 R2, this role service supports even people connecting without a browser. RemoteApp and Desktop Connections is a new feature in Windows 7 (it's part of the operating system, not the RDP client, so it is not available in previous versions of Windows) that allows RemoteApp and VM icons to be added to a client's Start menu and started from there. The trick is that RD Web Access gets its information about which RemoteApp programs and desktops are available to which users from the publishing service on the RD Connection Broker and makes those resources available through a URL. One URL supports the website you see with a browser, and another supports connections delivered to RemoteApp and Desktop Connections.

Chapter 9 explains how to configure and use RD Web Access and RemoteApp and Desktop Connections.

RD Connection Broker

For the sake of redundancy, it's good practice to have more than one RD Session Host server hosting your remote application set and to load-balance your servers. And it's essentially a given that there will be more than one VM in any deployment using VDI—there might even quite possibly be more than one RD Virtualization Host to run those VMs.

Having multiple endpoints and servers supporting those endpoints allows you to spread out the user load and eliminates the possibility that one server could go down and take out your ability to serve centralized applications. The trouble is that connections are fundamentally made to individual RD Session Host servers, not to groups of them. That is, the final connection is made to the RD Session Host server named RDSH01 (or whatever other name you've given it).

But if your RDP files include the names of individual RD Session Host servers, the connections won't be load-balanced. Nor will they be flexible enough to determine that a user really should be connecting to another RD Session Host server when starting a new application, because he or she already has an application open there. If you've deployed VMs, it's possible to point an RDP file to a particular VM without making any assignments in Active Directory Domain Services—it's essentially the same thing as using RDP to connect to a physical machine identified by name. But assigning VMs by name doesn't allow you to use pooled VMs. Nor can RDP files automatically wake up a VM that's hibernating and prepare it for the connection. If you attempt to make a direct connection to a hibernating VM, the connection will fail.

HOW IT WORKS

An Introduction to Connection Brokering

The RD Connection Broker role service handles the problem of how to connect user requests for sessions or VMs intelligently to the right endpoint, as shown in Figure 1-2. For RemoteApp connections, RD Connection Broker makes this decision according to several criteria, including

- Which farm was the incoming request attempting to connect to?

- Does the person making the connection request already have an existing (active or disconnected) session on that farm?

- If no connection exists, which RD Session Host server has the lowest number of sessions?

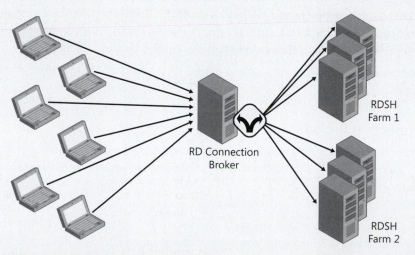

FIGURE 1-2 The RD Connection Broker routes incoming connections to the appropriate RD Session Host server.

For VM connections (see Figure 1-3), the RD Connection Broker makes its decision based on similar criteria.

- Is the VM request for a personal VM?
- If for a pooled VM, does the person requesting already have a disconnected session on a VM?

If no connection exists, the connection is sent to the RD Virtualization Host server that has the lowest number of currently active VMs, and the RD Virtualization Host server prepares a VM for the connection.

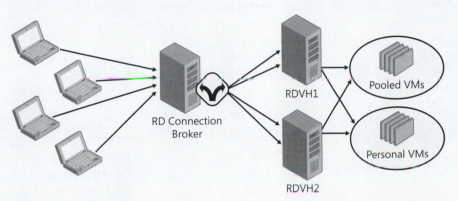

FIGURE 1-3 The RD Connection Broker also brokers connections to VMs on RD Virtualization Host servers.

The RD Connection Broker includes only one form of load balancing—keeping track of how many sessions RD Session Host servers have or how many VMs each RD Virtualization Host is running—but it can be integrated with third-party load balancers that support other criteria such as processor or memory load, time of day, or application.

Chapter 9 explains how to use RD Connection Broker to support RD Session Host farms and pooled and personal VMs.

RD Gateway

In the dark days before Windows Server 2008, if you wanted to connect to a terminal server from the outside world using only the tools in the box, you might have considered opening port 3389 (the port that RDP listens on by default) so that the terminal server could accept incoming connections. Most people didn't do this, however, because of the security hole it opened.

One of the role services of RDS in Windows Server 2008 R2 is Remote Desktop Gateway (RD Gateway). RD Gateway enables authorized remote users to connect to resources on an internal corporate or private network, from any Internet-connected device, whether originally part of the domain or a public computer or kiosk. As shown in Figure 1-4, the network resources can be RD Session Host servers supporting full desktops or RemoteApp programs, VMs, or computers with Remote Desktop enabled. In other words, people accessing the corporate network from the Internet can use RDP to connect to full desktops, individual applications, or even their own desktop computers—it all depends on what the administrator has set up.

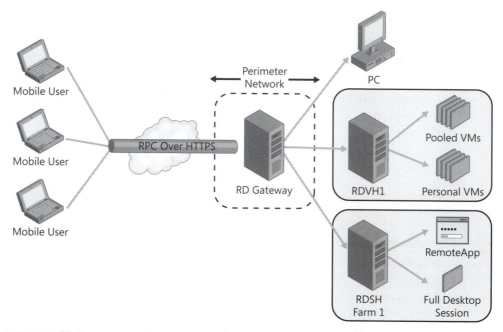

FIGURE 1-4 RD Gateway provides secure access to the corporate network from other networks such as the Internet.

RD Gateway uses RDP over HTTPS to establish a secure encrypted connection between remote users on the Internet and the internal network on which their applications run; this requires only port 443 to be open (which it probably is already for secure Internet connectivity). By doing this, RD Gateway does the following.

- Enables remote users to connect to internal network resources over the Internet by using an encrypted connection, without needing to configure VPN connections.

- Provides a comprehensive security configuration model that enables you to control access to specific internal network resources.

- Provides a point-to-point RDP connection that can be limited, rather than allowing remote users access to all internal network resources.

- Enables most remote users to connect to internal network resources that are hosted behind firewalls in private networks and across Network Address Translators (NATs). With RD Gateway, you do not need to perform additional configuration for the RD Gateway server or clients for this scenario (aside from opening port 443 in the firewall).

The RD Gateway Manager console enables you to configure authorization policies to define conditions that must be met for remote users to connect to internal network resources. For example, you can specify

- Who can connect to RD Gateway (in other words, the users and computers who can connect).
- Which network resources (computers or computer groups) users can connect to.
- Whether device and disk redirection is allowed.
- Whether clients must use smart card authentication or password authentication, or either one.

To enhance security further, you can configure RD Gateway servers and RDC clients to use Network Access Protection (NAP). NAP is a health policy creation, enforcement, and remediation technology included in Windows XP Service Pack 3 (Windows XP SP3), Windows Vista, Windows Server 2008, Windows 7, and Windows Server 2008 R2. Using NAP, system administrators can enforce client computer health requirements, which can include software requirements, security update requirements, required computer configurations, and other settings to connect to RD Gateway.

You can also use RD Gateway server with Microsoft Internet Security and Acceleration (ISA) Server or Forefront Threat Management Gateway (TMG) to enhance security. In this scenario, you can host RD Gateway servers in a private network rather than a perimeter network and host ISA or TMG in the perimeter network. The SSL connection between the RDC client and ISA or TMG Server can be terminated at the Internet-facing server.

The RD Gateway Manager console provides tools to help you monitor RD Gateway connection status, health, and events. With RD Gateway Manager, you can specify events (such as unsuccessful connection attempts to the RD Gateway server) that you want to monitor.

RD Gateway can be used with RDP files stored on clients, with RD Web Access, or with RemoteApp and Desktop Connections. Combined with RD Web Access or RemoteApp and Desktop Connections, you can set up a remote workspace that presents a website with the appropriate application icons and then makes sure that the person connecting or the computer he's connecting from meets the RD Gateway rules.

RD Gateway uses few resources and if sized properly can support hundreds of incoming users, so it can safely be combined with other roles that might be in the perimeter network.

RDS Licensing

The RDS Licensing role service is responsible for keeping track of who has a license to use the RD Session Host servers. Not who's *authorized* to use the RD Session Host server—AD DS user rights or RD Gateway makes that call, depending on what level the administrator is authorizing this connection. RDS Licensing is the license management system that enables RD Session Host servers to obtain and manage RDS client access licenses (RDS CALs) for devices and users that are connecting to an RD Session Host server.

RD Session Host servers can be configured to require either per-user or per-device RDS CALs. You'll learn more about the details of RDS Licensing in Chapter 12, "Licensing Remote Desktop Services," but the basic story is this: Each RD Session Host server determines if the user or the computer connecting to it has a valid license. If it does (and the user has permission to log on), then the RD Session Host server grants the connection. If it does not, then the RD Session Host server attempts to contact a license server to see if a license for that device or user is available. The license server then either allocates a license to the device (per-device RDS CAL) or edits the properties of the user's account in AD DS to show that a license has been used (per-user RDS CAL). If the RD Session Host server cannot connect to an RDS Licensing server, it will issue a temporary license if the RD Session Host server is within its grace period. Access will be granted for up to 120 days.

Servers supporting the RDS Licensing role maintain a database that tracks how RDS CALs have been issued. For per-device RDS CALs, the license is assigned to a computer. For per-user RDS CALs, the license is not actually assigned but its usage is registered in AD DS and can be tracked.

RD Licensing is a low-impact service, requiring very little processor time or memory for regular operations. Memory usage is less than 10 MB. Its hard disk requirements are small, even for a significant number of clients: The license database grows in increments of 5 MB for every 6,000 RDS CALs issued. The license server is active only when an RD Session Host server is requesting an RDS CAL, and its impact on server performance is very low, even in high-load scenarios. Therefore, in smaller deployments, the RDS Licensing role service can be installed on the same computer as the RD Session Host role service. In larger deployments, the RD Licensing role will often be on a separate computer.

Although only accessing the RD Session Host role will trigger the consumption of an RDS CAL, using any part of the RDS infrastructure requires an RDS CAL (or, for VDI-only deployments, a VDI CAL).

How Other Services Support RDS

The RDS role doesn't exist in a vacuum. Several roles help to support the various role services of RDS, and without them, the solution doesn't work. In addition to the core RDS role services and their relationship with each other, it's important to understand their relationship with other Windows Server roles. This section covers these roles and how they support RDS functionality.

What are the roles and how do they fit together? How do they fit with the other non-RDS parts of the Windows infrastructure (Hyper-V, IIS, certificates, and AD DS, among others)?

The Client Connection

Yes, it might be obvious, but it's still worth looking at: The way the client interacts with the role services of RDS defines what the user experience to a particular endpoint will be.

Whether the endpoint is a session on an RD Session Host server, a VM hosted on RD Virtualization Host, or even a physical machine, the fundamental relationship between client and endpoint has three parts: the RDC client, the RDP connection, and the endpoint.

- The RDC client component initiates the connection to the endpoint and receives the data that the server sends to it.

- The server component on the endpoint interacts with the core operating system and takes the information received (for example, sounds being produced, bitmaps being displayed), converts it to RDP commands, and serializes it to be passed to the client.

- The protocol enables the connection between the client and the endpoint; it defines the kind of information that is passed between them via virtual channels.

> **NOTE** Why the distinction between RDP and RDC? RDP is the Remote Desktop Protocol, the protocol that passes user input and application output between client and server. RDC is the Remote Desktop Connection, the client component that initiates and manages the RDP connection.

In short, the client requests the connection, the endpoint formats the calls to the applications and operating system in a way that the client (or server, depending on which way the information flow is going for a particular transaction) can understand, and RDP passes the right information that lets the user communicate with the applications on the server as though they were running locally.

This communication relies on *virtual channels*, bi-directional connection streams provided through RDP. They establish a data pipe between the RDC client and the endpoint to pass specific kinds of information, such as device redirection or sound, between client and server. Virtual channels are a way to extend the functionality of RDP that's been available since Windows 2000 Server, and they are also used by some features of RDS, such as device and sound redirection.

But a lot has changed since Windows 2000 Server, and one of the components that's changed is that the 32 static virtual channels originally made available with RDP 5.1 aren't enough anymore. More kinds of data are now available, and it's clear that there might be more not yet considered. In addition, static virtual channels had a problem: They were created at the beginning of the connection and torn down at the end. If you added a device during the session, it couldn't use virtual channels unless you terminated the connection and then reconnected.

> **IMPORTANT** Terminating a connection ends it completely on the server. A disconnected session still exists on the server and a user can reconnect to it

Therefore, RDS supports *dynamic virtual channels*, virtual channels that the client creates on demand and then shuts down when it's done with them. If you're curious about the interfaces to make dynamic virtual channels work for you (or how they work at all), see the PDF titled "Functionality for RDS Scripters and Developers" on the companion CD.

Hosting VMs

For some time, it has been possible to virtualize Terminal Services roles, but Hyper-V was not a required component of a Terminal Services deployment. In RDS, Hyper-V is required to use the VM hosting feature.

Hyper-V is installed automatically if you choose to install the RD Virtualization Host Role service. Because RD Virtualization Host requires Hyper-V, it is the only RDS role service that cannot be virtualized.

Authenticating Servers with Certificates

Although you don't need a Certificate Authority (CA) server to use RDS, you will definitely need certificates from somewhere.

One of the curious things about RDS is the trust required between client and server. Obviously, the server has to trust the client, since the server is a partial porthole to the corporate network. But the client has to trust the server as well. The client is providing the user name and password for the corporate network, so it's important that the server the client is connecting to is a legitimate endpoint and not a rogue server set up to steal logon credentials.

To ensure that an endpoint's identity can be trusted, you can install a certificate on the server and on the client. To do this, you'll need to get certificates from your own in-house PKI solution, or you'll need to purchase certificates from a public CA.

> **IMPORTANT** All RD Session Host servers in the same farm must use the same certificate for certificate-based authentication.

Certificates are also used to

- Authenticate the identity of an RD Gateway server and allow it to set up a secure channel with the client.
- Sign RDP files
- Provide HTTPS access to the RD Web Access website

Enabling WAN Access and Displaying Remote Resources

Two components of RDS require IIS: RD Web Access and RD Gateway. RD Web Access's need for IIS is pretty apparent: It provides information about the RemoteApp programs and desktops available to a user through two URLs. One URL supports display for RD Web Access and one supports RemoteApp and Desktop Connections.

IIS is also required for RD Gateway. RD Gateway encapsulates RDP traffic over HTTPs, so it requires certain components of IIS.

IIS is installed automatically when you install an RDS role service that requires it.

Updating User and Computer Settings

It's such an obvious choice to use AD DS for a support role that you might not have thought of it, but it's crucial to a functioning centralized computing infrastructure in several ways—not all of which you might have expected. AD DS manages

- The group policies that configure RD Session Host servers and the user sessions running on them.
- Whether or not a user has the right to connect to an RD Session Host server.
- The process of showing that a user has consumed a per-user RDS CAL.

Functionality for RDS Scripters and Developers

It's crucial to understand that RDS is not just a product—although it's definitely that—but it's also a development platform for both independent software vendors (ISVs) and consultants creating custom solutions. Windows Server 2008 added a lot of new APIs for partners, and Windows Server 2008 R2 adds even more. Although a description of how to use all of these APIs is beyond the scope of this book, information available on the companion media highlights some of the platform extensions available to RDS partners through public interfaces.

 ON THE COMPANION MEDIA For a detailed description of the RDS API, please see "Functionality for RS Scripters and Developers" on the companion media. Detailed instructions for using this API are on MSDN.

NOTE Public interfaces (also known as APIs) are interfaces that are, well, publicly available and documented on MSDN so that developers can use them. Private interfaces are not documented. The main difference is supportability. A private interface might change at any time if required by the people who developed it (in this case, Microsoft). An API won't change without notice. Even if you had the option to build solutions based on private interfaces, it would be better to build on the public APIs than on private ones.

Summary

This chapter introduced you to RDS in Windows Server 2008 R2. At this point, you should understand

- How this role has developed since it became part of Windows 10 years ago.

- What RDS is used for.
- The new business cases that Windows Server 2008 R2 RDS now supports.
- The RDS roles that support these new business cases and how they interact.
- How other Windows roles (and the client) support RDS functionality.
- How RDS is a development platform and some of the functionality that scripters and developers can add to it.

In Chapter 2, you'll find out how Windows architecture supports RDS.

Additional Resources

These resources contain additional information and tools related to this chapter.

- To learn more about some fundamental concepts of the operating system that affect RD Session Host and RD Virtualization Host functionality (and sizing), see Chapter 2, "Key Architectural Concepts for Remote Desktop Services."
- To learn how to set up an RD Session Host server, see Chapter 3, "Deploying a Single Remote Desktop Session Host Server."
- To learn how to set up an RD Virtualization Host server to support pooled VMs and personal desktops, see Chapter 4, "Deploying a Single Remote Desktop Virtualization Host Server."
- To learn how to set up user profiles with RDS, see Chapter 5, "Managing User Data in a Remote Desktop Services Deployment."
- To understand how RDP integrates the client and server operating systems for display, printing, and audio and device redirection, see Chapter 6, "Customizing the User Experience."
- To learn how to lock down the user environment with Group Policy, see Chapter 7, "Molding and Securing the User Environment."
- To learn how RDP connections are secured for LAN connections, see Chapter 8, "Securing Remote Desktop Protocol Connections."
- To learn how to use RD Connection Broker to deploy a farm of RD Session Host servers or a pool of RD Virtualization Host VMs, see Chapter 9, "Multi-Server Deployments."
- To learn how to publish resources to RD Web Access and RemoteApp and Desktop Connections, see Chapter 10, "Making Remote Desktop Services Available from the Internet."
- To learn how to use RDS on the Internet, see Chapter 10, "Making Remote Desktop Services Available from the Internet."
- To learn how to manage sessions on an RD Session Host server, see Chapter 11, "Managing Remote Desktop Session Host Sessions."

- To learn how RDS licensing works and how to use an RD License server, see Chapter 12, "Licensing Remote Desktop Services."

- To learn about RDS life-cycle management, see Chapter 13, "Life-Cycle Management for Remote Desktop Services."

- For more details on the APIs available to developers, see the RDS Reference at *http://msdn.microsoft.com/en-us/library/aa383494(VS.85).aspx* or, for longer documents and source code, see the RDS Code Gallery site at *http://code.msdn.microsoft.com/rdsdev.*

- For in-depth developer resources (including code samples and detailed documents), see the RDS team Code Gallery site at *http://code.msdn.microsoft.com/rdsdev.*

CHAPTER 2

Key Architectural Concepts for Remote Desktop Services

Before you start installing Remote Desktop Services (RDS) role services, you must understand the business and technical decisions you'll need to make. This chapter addresses those questions, including both the details of the system architecture that are essential to supporting the two models of application delivery that RDS supports and some of the business decisions that you'll need to make before implementing the technology. Both will help you better plan for the resources required to support what you want to do. The chapter covers such topics as

- Windows Server 2008 R2 internals particularly relevant to sizing RDS roles

- How to size Remote Desktop (RD) Session Host and RD Virtualization servers

- The client requirements for using some new features of RDS

- Characteristics of an application that will run properly on an RD Session Host server

- Technology decisions rooted in business needs, such as the licensing mode or the kinds of client hardware that make the best business sense for your company

NOTE In parts of this chapter, you'll learn about how to do performance scaling on an existing RD Session Host server. When determining how to order the chapters in this book, the decision was made to put planning before installing. For details of the installation process, see Chapter 3, "Deploying a Single Remote Desktop Session Host Server," or Chapter 4, "Deploying a Single Remote Desktop Virtualization Host Server."

Know Your Application Delivery System

Before getting too deeply into the question of the internals of memory architecture or tips for server sizing, you need to know what an RD Session Host server and an RD Virtualization Host server do. Understanding how each application delivery platform works is essential to understanding sizing guidelines.

RDS supports two application delivery platforms: sessions on an RD Session Host and VMs on an RD Virtualization Host.

RD Session Host Servers

A RD Session Host server is a shared workstation for multiple concurrent users. When in use, the server starts applications and loads files into memory. It saves users' files. When users log on to an RD Session Host server, it loads their user profile so that they get the customized work environment that they've come to know and love. This server does everything a workstation does . . . but it does it for many users simultaneously.

In practical terms, this means that an RD Session Host server must

- Try to spread the use of processor time across all sessions so that one session isn't consuming all of it and starving the other sessions.
- Support new users as they log on while still maintaining current users.
- Run many instances of the same applications as efficiently as possible.
- Keep track of how much physical memory is available and use it as efficiently as possible for the greater good of the entire server.
- Isolate the sessions so that the users running applications on the same computer can't see each others' data.

RD Virtualization Host Servers

The RD Virtualization Host application delivery model is a bit different. A RD Virtualization Host server isn't a shared workstation; it's a platform for a collection of individual workstations running in virtual machines (VMs), each with an isolated operating environment. The VMs on an RD Virtualization Host server are completely isolated from each other. They can run different operating systems, use incompatible device drivers, run demanding applications, and even crash without disturbing the other VMs on the same host. As long as the RD Virtualization Host itself is not compromised, the VMs will not be affected by each other.

When you're setting up VMs (more details about this can be found in Chapter 4), you will need to configure how much memory each VM has and the number of processors it's got. Unused memory or processor power won't be shared among the other VMs on the same host server. Therefore, you should have a pretty good idea of what the needs of each VM will be and what hardware you'll require to support them.

Each model for application delivery works a bit differently, but they're fundamentally doing the same thing: letting a large number of people use the same hardware at the same time. Both models require a bit of juggling on the part of the operating system. Your job is to give each type of server enough resources to juggle as efficiently as possible. To do your job, it's helpful to know how the RD Session Host does all these things.

Relevant Windows Server 2008 R2 Internals

This section covers the internal workings of some system components that are most helpful to understanding how an RD Session Host or RD Virtualization Host server allocates system resources to the users it is hosting, including

- What it means to the RD Session Host that Windows Server 2008 R2 comes only in 64-bit
- How VMs work
- How application delivery servers allocate processor cycles to all the users on them
- How application delivery servers perform memory management for sessions and VMs

The following sections will deal mainly with the RD Session Host servers because they're the most different. Although VM hosts are juggling resources among VMs, the VMs themselves are in many ways like single-user operating systems. These sections discuss virtualization and how processor scheduling, memory management, and disk and network access work in that context.

Windows Server 2008 R2 Is 64-Bit Only

One of the most basic things to understand about RDS is that in Windows Server 2008 R2, all server platforms are 64-bit. Windows 7 comes in both 32-bit and 64-bit editions, but server SKUs no longer have this option. Windows Server 2008 was the last 32-bit server platform from Microsoft.

> **NOTE** The Windows Server 2008 edition of this book discussed Physical Address Extensions (PAEs) and Address Windowing Extensions (AWEs). However, neither is supported—or necessary—on a 64-bit operating system, so neither has been included in this edition.

For RD Session Host servers, the move to 64-bit is almost entirely good news. (You'll learn why it's an "almost" in just a moment.) On 32-bit operating systems, the biggest bottleneck for terminal servers has generally been memory, with disk reads and writes coming a close second. A 32-bit operating system can't address more than 4 GB of virtual memory, no matter how much physical memory you install on the server. Windows Server Standard Edition didn't even support the installation of more than 4 GB of physical memory, so it could not take advantage of such workarounds as PAEs and AWEs that let the operating system store and refer to data in more than 4 GB of physical memory even if it couldn't "see" it all at one time. Now, 64-bit Windows can "see" up to 44 exabytes of virtual memory addresses, so it can use all the memory it could ever need without the memory tricks that the 32-bit version of the operating system would have to use.

The reason why 64-bit Windows is almost entirely good news involves the support for older device drivers and older applications. You'll find that 32-bit applications will generally run on a 64-bit operating system without issues. In most cases, an application that can run successfully on a 32-bit terminal server should run on a 64-bit RD Session Host. However, a 64-bit operating system requires 64-bit drivers. Older client printers that you're still attempting to support, for example, might not have 64-bit drivers.

However, even recalcitrant printer drivers don't have to crush your plans to virtualize application delivery. First, if you can use Easy Print (discussed in Chapter 6, "Customizing the User Experience") for your printers, then you won't need printer drivers on the RD Session Host Servers and can just use the drivers installed on the client. Second, if Easy Print isn't an option, you can use RD Virtualization Host to support the users who need the old print devices.

For RD Virtualization Host, having the host run a 64-bit operating system is an unmitigated win—the reason why Hyper-V has always been 64-bit. The guest VMs on the host don't have to run a 64-bit operating system, so they really don't have any application or driver issues as long as the user environment will work in Windows XP SP2 or later. Having 64-bit operating systems just mean that you can install as much memory as you need to support all your VMs.

DIRECT FROM THE FIELD

How Does 64-Bit Windows Perform as an RD Session Host Server?

Jeff Heatton
Operations Engineer, Microsoft

We have recently moved to 64-bit on many of our servers. We see that the same physical server that could support, say, 55 users in 32-bit mode with 4 GB of RAM, can support 150 users with little stress on 64-bit with 8 GB of RAM. The 64-bit solution seems to work extremely well, and I suspect that in our environment, we could scale up further just by adding more RAM. Some servers have seen more than 300 sessions with no performance issues.

We find that with our application the workload is variable by region for the same application, because users have different work patterns in the different regions. The European folks are heavy hitters, whereas the folks in the United States and Asia give the RDS farms an easier time.

How Does an RD Session Host Server Dole Out Processor Cycles?

Nothing happens on a computer without a processor. When a computer serves dozens of users, there's a lot of competition for any available processor cycles. Here, you'll learn about how the RD Session Host server decides who's going to get processor time.

Users run applications, but operating systems don't know anything about applications. The operating system deals with processes and threads that support the application executable. A *process* defines the working environment for an application, including its priority when it comes to being allocated processor time, the image name of the application associated with the process (for example, Winword.exe), the process identifier (process ID, or PID) that the operating system uses to uniquely identify the process, the memory regions allocated to this process by the memory manager, links to parent processes that spawned this new process, and anything else the application would have to know to run and cooperate with other running applications.

Why Processes Need Both Names and PIDs

Why does a process need both an image name (this is the same as the executable name) and a PID? The reason is that image names are not necessarily unique on a server, particularly on an RD Session Host, it's highly likely that more than one instance of the same application will be running, and it is guaranteed that more than one instance of required system processes will be running (see Chapter 3 for more information about the processes common to all sessions).

Since more than one instance could be running in the same session, you can't identify the processes by session. To give Windows and the administrator more control over individual processes, the process manager creates new processes with a PID. You'll often work with PIDs when using the Remote Desktop Manager and query process command-line tools, both discussed in Chapter 11, "Managing Remote Desktop Sessions."

Processes don't do anything themselves. Rather, they define the execution environment and relationships that the executable part of a process, the *thread*, must know about. Threads know details such as the process they're associated with, and their security information, such as their *access token* (the record of the rights the thread has, given the identity of the account who started it) and *impersonation information* (the security credentials being used). They also keep track of their pending input/output (I/O) requests. Like processes, threads have a priority. They inherit their priority range from their process but can adjust their own priority within that range.

One key property of a process or thread is its priority, since that determines how often a thread gets some processor cycles. As you might guess, the higher the priority, the more often a thread gets processor time. Since nothing happens on a computer without processor time to execute instructions, this is critical.

> **NOTE** If you're curious to see how a processor thread priority compares to that of other types of processes, use the Process: Priority Current or Thread: Priority Current performance counters in the Performance Monitor. For example, the Win32 Subsystem process (which has the image name Csrss.exe) has a higher base priority than user applications, so it will get more processor time. This is intentional, as it doesn't matter if an application is responsive if Windows isn't.

One way in which RD Session Host servers differ from other types of servers is in their use of process priority. Other types of servers are generally designed to do one thing really well: They search databases, or manage email, or support websites. Their priorities are clear: The application in the foreground is the one to support. Therefore, the processes and threads belonging to the application in the foreground have a higher priority than those in the background.

> **NOTE** Just because the application in the foreground is the main one supported doesn't mean that the foreground application processes have the *highest* priority. See *Microsoft Windows Internals, Fifth Edition*, by Mark E. Russinovich and David A. Solomon, with Alex Ionescu (Microsoft Press, 2009), for more background on the relative priority of various types of processes.

Unlike other servers, RD Session Host servers don't have one clear priority (in contrast to a server running Microsoft Exchange Server, for example, which focuses on one task: "I *must* get the mail through!"). They have dozens of users to support, all of whom are doing different things and all of whom are expecting a responsive work environment. Because of its conflicting priorities, the only way for a server with the RD Session Host role installed to cope is to prioritize all user application processes and threads equally. Because the processes backing user applications have the same priority, you can approximate the load a server can take by determining how much of the total processor time a user session will require. You'll find out more about *how* to do this with the Performance Monitor later in this chapter in the section called "Using Performance Monitor." But a key point to remember is that the action of installing the RD Session Host role optimizes the operating system for playing this role in your network. An RD Session Host server does not prioritize processes in the same way as a database server or mail server, because the needs of this server are different.

If one session were running a large number of demanding applications, it could potentially affect the performance of other sessions, even though the user applications all have the same priority. Windows Server 2008 addressed this with the Windows System Resource Manager

(WSRM), which would reduce a thread's priority if other user threads in other sessions were being starved for processor cycles. WSRM made sure that processor time was divided evenly among sessions, but it engaged only if a session was being affected. Windows Server 2008 R2 adds a new feature called Dynamic Fair Share Scheduling (DFSS), which changes the way that the scheduler works in the kernel. With DFSS engaged—as it is by default—the scheduler will make sure that the processor time is scheduled evenly among sessions from the beginning. You'll learn more about how DFSS works in Chapter 3.

How Do RD Session Host Servers Use Memory More Efficiently?

RD Session Host servers spread processor time among individual sessions by prioritizing all user application processes in the same way and using DFSS to ensure that no one session uses up all the processor time just because it's running demanding applications. Next, you'll learn how memory works on an RD Session Host server, including

- The differences between user mode and kernel mode
- The relationship between physical storage and virtual memory
- The role of the page file in providing additional physical storage
- How the memory manager optimizes the use of memory
- How memory usage, disk reads/writes, and processor time are related
- How 64-bit only affects virtual memory management on RD Session Host servers

Understanding User-Mode and Kernel-Mode Virtual Address Space

You can't do anything on a computer without a processor, but the threads getting processor time can't do anything without memory to store data in. Operating systems store data that they're currently working with in memory. (Data that they are not currently working with, such as files you've saved and don't currently have open, are stored on the hard disk.) This data can include user data such as files or applications, or system data such as pointers to where data is stored in memory. (Memory is big—*really* big. Even the operating system needs a map to avoid getting lost.)

There are two kinds of memory in your computer. One is physical memory, determined by the amount of RAM installed in the computer. If you have 24 GB of RAM, there are 24 GB of physical memory available to the operating system (minus memory taken by other hardware components). The other is virtual memory, which is determined by the size of the operating system addressing structure. All 32-bit operating systems have a 4-GB virtual memory address space; 64-bit operating systems have a 16-terabyte virtual memory address space—8 terabytes for user-mode processes and 8 terabytes for kernel mode. (If you've heard it said that the 64-bit operating system removes the memory limitation on a terminal server, but you weren't quite sure what that meant, this should put the difference into perspective.) You'll see the 8-terabyte model referred to in the explanation. Virtual memory is supported by two physical storage places: the physical memory of RAM and an area on the hard disk called the *page file* or *swap file*. Therefore, even if a computer running a 64-bit operating system has only 8 GB of RAM installed, it still has an 8-terabyte range of virtual addresses for data storage.

> **NOTE** If you've done the math, you'll notice that 2 to the 64th power is more than 16 terabytes—it's actually 16 exabytes. Windows (and currently available processors) don't currently support 2^{64} bytes, however—they support only up to 2^{44}, or 16 terabytes split evenly between kernel mode and user mode.

This 16 terabytes of virtual memory address space is divided into two regions: kernel space and user space, and the processes that store data in each region are called user-mode or kernel-mode processes. Kernel space, the upper 8 terabytes, is shared by all processes that store data here. User space is specific to each user-mode process. Conceptually, the memory layout looks like that shown in Figure 2-1. All kernel-mode processes know they must share a memory region, but all user-mode processes—not just all sessions, but all processes—think they have their own personal 8 terabytes of user-mode storage. Because this means that virtual memory addresses are duplicated from process to process, one key job of the memory manager is to make sure that user-mode processes don't affect each other when storing memory in their view of user-mode memory.

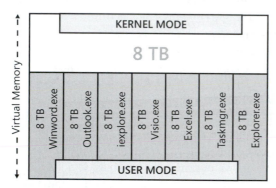

FIGURE 2-1 Kernel-mode memory is common to all processes that store information there; user-mode memory appears specific to each process.

Understanding both user-mode and kernel-mode storage is important to understanding how an RD Session Host server uses memory.

Why Does It Matter Whether Drivers Are User-Mode or Kernel-Mode?

Previous versions of Windows introduced Group Policy to require users to employ user-mode printer drivers. If it's not obvious to you why a policy to require user-mode drivers might be necessary or desirable, read on.

Every component of the Windows operating system is designed to call on memory from a particular section of memory, which is organized into blocks. The amount of memory an operating system can access depends on the addressing scheme it supports. For example, 64-bit operating systems can call on up to 16 terabytes of memory, and this memory is normally divided into two pieces: The upper 8 terabytes is kernel-mode memory and the lower 8 terabytes is user-mode memory. *Kernel-mode* components have access to actual physical memory structures. *User-mode* components have access only to a mapped view of these structures.

Think of the memory structures are a set of interoffice mailboxes. The kernel-mode components have access to the mailboxes themselves—the physical bins that line the wall. User-mode components don't have access to the boxes; instead they indicate that a piece of data should go into the box belonging to, say, Kim Abercrombie or to Michael Pfeiffer. The kernel-mode component creates the mapping that identifies which physical location is associated with Kim Abercrombie and routes the data there, so that even if the boxes are shuffled or Kim gets a new mailbox, the data ends up in the right place. Similarly, if a user-mode component needs data from a location, that component doesn't know the physical location of the data, but calls on it according to its virtual data—"I need the data stored in Kim Abercrombie's mailbox." The kernel-mode component then maps Kim Abercrombie's name to a mailbox location and retrieves the data. The area of memory that a component is designed to use depends on what that component needs to do, how quickly it needs to do it, and how likely it is to have a problem doing it. Almost everything that you *see* happening on a computer occurs in user mode: applications open, windows move, characters appear on the screen as you type, and so forth. Operations running in user mode are protected from each other because they write to virtual locations, not to physical ones. Kernel-mode components ensure that these operations don't write to the same physical locations. For this reason, user mode is also called *protected mode*. If an application running in user mode crashes, it does not affect other applications.

Kernel-mode components are slightly faster than user-mode components because they don't have to translate virtual memory addresses to physical ones; however, they are more vulnerable to error. (That said, "slightly faster" in this context is not a difference that a human can detect.) Kernel mode references the physical memory structures shared among all components on the same computer, so it's possible that two applications could attempt to store information in the same memory space. When this happens, the components crash and it might crash the entire operating system. Printer drivers running in kernel mode on a shared server, therefore, put not just one person's workspace at risk but that of everyone using that same computer. Although printer drivers are more reliable on shared servers than they used to be, it's best to use only user-mode drivers. If you absolutely must use kernel-mode drivers, you must test them before putting them into production.

Technically speaking, the user-mode drivers are only partially user-mode—or at least, they are not able to do all their work from within user mode. They still communicate with a kernel-mode component that puts the data in the physical location where it must go. However, if the user-mode piece fails, this does not affect the kernel-mode area of memory.

The Role of the Memory Manager

How does all this paging take place? Who's in charge of mapping virtual address space to physical memory so that when you try to bring a file into memory, you get the right one? How is it possible that each user-mode process thinks that it has its own 8 terabytes of user-mode memory? All this is handled by a key part of the operating system called the *memory manager*. The memory manager has four main jobs.

- Mapping the virtual address space into physical memory
- Protecting the address space of processes from each other and from the operating system
- Paging data to and from disk
- Managing key system resources such as the paged and non-paged memory pools and system cache

The memory manager works with the I/O manager (responsible for writing to and reading from disk) and the cache manager (some storage for the system cache) to ensure that processes have the data they need as quickly as possible.

In the next sections, you'll learn more about how the memory manager does its job.

Mapping Virtual Memory to Physical Memory

A 64-bit operating system can see 16 terabytes of virtual memory addresses, but the computer in which the operating system is running won't have 16 terabytes of RAM installed. As you can see from Table 2-1, no edition of Windows Server 2008 R2 or Windows 7 supports more than 2 terabytes of installed RAM. (Microsoft doesn't support what it can't test, and systems with more than 2 terabytes of RAM didn't exist.)

TABLE 2-1 Physical Memory Limits by SKU (Editions Supporting RDS Only)

VERSION	RAM SUPPORTED
Windows Server 2008 R2 Datacenter	2 terabytes
Windows Server 2008 R2 Enterprise	2 terabytes
Windows Server 2008 R2 Standard	32 GB
Windows Server 2008 R2 Foundation	8 GB

Not only does the amount of virtual memory exceed the installed RAM, but each user-mode process thinks that it has a dedicated 8 terabytes of storage. Something has to sort out where the data that a process thinks it stored at a particular location is really located. That function is handled by the memory manager.

> **IMPORTANT** The following section applies to user-mode code. Kernel-mode processes don't have the same storage retrieval problem as user-mode processes because there is only one view of kernel-mode memory. It's easy for a kernel-mode process to know which area of physical storage maps to a virtual memory address because there's only one possibility. Kernel-mode processes are (infinitesimally) faster than user-mode processes because they don't rely on the memory manager to map the addresses. It's also the reason that kernel-mode drivers can be so dangerous; they can bypass the memory manager, be wrong about the mapping, and inadvertently overwrite the memory being used by another kernel-mode process.

The way the memory manager keeps track of how virtual addresses correspond to physical locations is much the way you'd do it if someone gave you the same job: It maintains lists mapping each virtual address to a physical location. These lists are called *page tables*. The collection of page tables is organized in the *page table directory*. (A *page* is a contiguous block of memory and the smallest unit of data that the memory manager can work with.) An individual entry on the page table is called a *page table entry (PTE)*. A PTE contains the pointer to an area of physical memory. If you find page directories and PTEs confusing, think of it this way: The page table directory is like a telephone book for each process. Within the telephone book are the pages of listings—the pages are the page tables. Individual addresses on the page tables are the page table entries. With any one of the addresses, you can find a physical location for the information (the *page*).

> **NOTE** The amount of physical memory a process is using at any given time is called its *working set*.

Page tables and page table directories are stored in an area of kernel-mode memory reserved for this memory mapping information. The relationship between virtual memory, PTEs, and physical storage is shown in Figure 2-2.

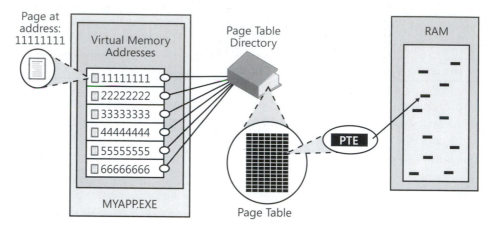

FIGURE 2-2 Virtual addresses get mapped to physical locations with PTEs.

Windows maintains a two-level page table structure of page table directories and page tables. Each process has its own page table directory. Within that page directory are the page tables listing the pages. (A process has to have more than one page table—and hence the page table directory—because the page tables are limited in size.) Within the page tables, the entries are indexed according to where they are on the page. The value of the index tells the memory manager which area of physical storage a virtual memory address points to. A virtual address contains a pointer to the correct page table directory, indexing information that points to the correct page table, and indexing information pointing to the correct PTE, as shown in Figure 2-3.

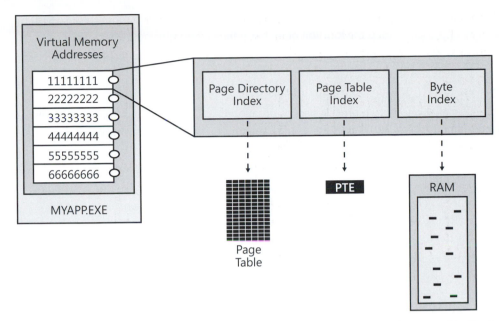

FIGURE 2-3 Virtual memory addresses store indexing information that points to the page table directory, the page table, and the PTE

One of the limitations of Terminal Services on 32-bit Windows is that the telephone book can be only so big because there's a limited amount of space to store the pages. It's as if the size of a community were limited by the size of the telephone book that would fit in each mailbox. No more space available indicates there can be no additional pages in the telephone book. This means that you'll never be able to visit the new family in the neighborhood because they have no entry in the telephone book and you can't find them. In the same way, the size of the space available to store PTE records limits the number of processes that can run even if you have all the RAM in the world available. The number of virtual memory addresses available to user-mode processes appears enormous because each process sees the entire 8-terabyte area. But for this area to be useful, the memory manager must be able to map the virtual address to a physical location, which means creating a page directory, page tables, and PTEs for each process. If the memory manager can't do the mapping, then the process can't start.

Before Windows Server 2008, the area of kernel-mode memory dedicated to PTEs was fixed in size. In Windows Server 2008 and later, kernel-mode memory for these storage structures is allocated dynamically, so that if the memory isn't needed for one structure, it might be available to another. Windows Server 2008 R2 uses more memory than Windows Server 2003, due in part to some changes in the user shell. But if Windows Server 2003 Terminal Server was constrained by the amount of space available for PTEs, it's possible that on the same hardware, the Windows Server 2008 R2 RD Session Host Server could support more users.

Note that 64-bit Windows has another advantage: It's got a lot more room to store System PTEs (the PTEs used to map the location of memory the system is using). The amount of storage in 32-bit Windows is 660 MB; 64-bit Windows has 128 GB.

How Virtual Memory Is Supported

Ideally, the virtual memory a process uses to organize its storage will map to the RAM committed to that process. But RAM is finite, and sometimes it's necessary to store that data elsewhere and then add it to the process working set when required. "Elsewhere" translates to the page file or another area of memory. To start, consider the page file.

The page file is one of those pieces of the memory structure that you've probably heard is very important but perhaps you aren't quite sure what makes it so important. Basically, the page file helps make virtual memory work by adding data storage to the server above and beyond what physical RAM supplies. When RAM gets full, data that isn't being used gets moved to the area of hard disk called the *page file* or *swap file*—that is, the data is paged to disk. When this data written to disk is called on, this produces a *hard page fault*. When a process searches for that data, it goes to where the data was last stored in virtual memory. The memory manager intercepts this request and retrieves the requested data from its location in the page file, paging the data back into physical memory where the process can access it. The page file increases the amount of physical storage for the virtual address space the operating system recognizes and can be used to store the data, but keep in mind that swapping data to and from the hard disk takes some time. When memory is on the hard disk, retrieving it takes longer than if the data is stored in RAM, where it can be called up more quickly. Each page fault takes processor cycles to complete. Each request to read or write to disk has to get in the I/O queue for the hard disk (more about this shortly). And the system slowdowns do add up.

The page file isn't sounding like much of a bargain, is it? You might be wondering why it's important. The sensible thing to do would be to install as much RAM as possible, so that the operating system will have plenty of very fast RAM to store data, instead of swapping data between the RAM and the page file. To a point, you'd be right: More RAM will generally result in a more responsive operating system (and this was especially true on 32-bit operating systems, where memory was likely to be the performance bottleneck).

However, you can't just load up an RD Session Host or RD Virtualization Host server with an equal amount of physical and virtual memory. There are two reasons for this. First, the 64-bit operating system supports 16 terabytes of virtual memory, and the most physical memory you can install on any Windows SKU is 2 terabytes. (For Windows Server Standard, the maximum amount of physical memory supported is 32 GB, and for Windows Foundation Server, the maximum is 8 GB.) Second, all user-mode processes think that they have their very own 8-terabyte area of user-mode virtual memory. Support dozens or hundreds of users on a single server, and they'll often use more virtual memory than you can back with RAM.

BEST PRACTICES Microsoft's best practices for RD Session Host servers suggest that your page file should be two to three times the size of the installed RAM to support all the individual user-mode memory areas for each process. The reasoning is that process creation is expensive—two or three times more so than maintaining the process in memory. Because many people are using the same computer, it's likely that the computer will be creating a lot of processes for all those people. Therefore, every time users start an application, they're engaging in this expensive activity. To keep the RD Session Host server running smoothly, you need more memory than just enough to keep the processes running.

Like other key structures, the page file is larger in 64-bit Windows than 32-bit Windows; 64-bit Windows supports a 256-terabyte page file, and for 32-bit Windows, the maximum size is 16 terabytes.

HOW IT WORKS

Improvements to the Page File System in Windows Server 2008 and Beyond

One change to memory management in Windows Server 2008 (and still relevant in Windows Server 2008 R2) lies in the way the page file works. It's designed to be more efficient than previous versions of Windows in two important ways that allow it to write less often.

First, the fewer write actions the operating system has to take, the better, because every action has a cost. To reduce the number of necessary write options in Windows Server 2003, the memory manager could write only up to 64 KB of data in a single action. Today, that limit has been removed so the memory manager can write data in larger chunks. Most write operations now are approximately 1 MB.

Another improvement to the page file beginning in Windows Server 2008 is that it takes the amount of free physical memory into account before writing to the page file. In previous versions of Windows, the decision to write to the page file was based on the number of *dirty pages* in RAM, or areas where data had been modified. Now, if there's no shortage of RAM, the memory manager will leave the modified data in RAM.

Not all data can be paged to disk. Some important data (important to the functioning of the operating system, not important to a user) must be maintained in RAM at all times. Data that never gets paged is stored in an area of kernel-mode memory called the *non-paged pool*. Kernel-mode processes that store data that can be paged to disk store it in the paged pool. In previous versions of Windows, paged pools and non-paged pools had fixed sizes depending on the amount of RAM installed on the server; beginning with Windows Server 2008, these memory areas had no fixed size but could fluctuate depending on the needs of the operating system (see Figure 2-4).

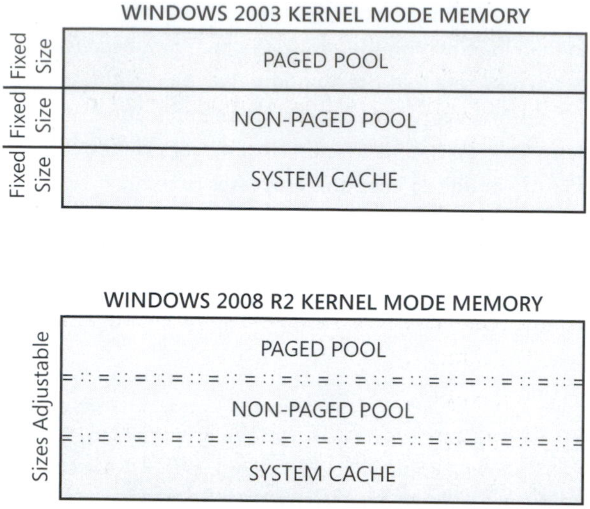

WINDOWS 2003 KERNEL MODE MEMORY

Fixed Size	
Fixed Size	PAGED POOL
Fixed Size	NON-PAGED POOL
	SYSTEM CACHE

WINDOWS 2008 R2 KERNEL MODE MEMORY

Sizes Adjustable	PAGED POOL
	NON-PAGED POOL
	SYSTEM CACHE

FIGURE 2-4 Kernel-mode memory areas supporting important system structures are sized dynamically in Windows Server 2008.

On 64-bit Windows, the maximum size of the non-paged pool is 128 GB, as opposed to 256 MB for 32-bit Windows.

Not all page faults are hard page faults. Sometimes, the data is still stored in RAM, but not in the process working set. For example, it's possible another process might be using the data (see the next section, "Memory Sharing and Copy-on-Write"). Soft page faults cost little in terms of time or system resources, so you don't need to worry about them. Hard page faults, in which the memory manager has to initiate a process to retrieve the data from disk, are much more expensive. When a computer is very low on available RAM and must store a lot of data in the page file, the constant reads and writes are called *thrashing*.

The following points sum up this section.

- A user process expects to find the data it's looking for in its working set.
- If the data is not in the working set, then the memory manager will check to see if it's stored anywhere else in RAM and add it to the process working set (a soft page fault).
- If the data is not in memory, then the memory manager prompts the I/O manager to find the data in the page file on hard disk so it can be added to the process working set (a hard page fault).

Memory Sharing and Copy-on-Write

Earlier you learned that all user-mode processes think they have an 8-terabyte user-mode memory area to themselves. You also discovered that this forces the need for a page file to back the virtual memory addresses, since there's no way that RAM can do it. But the memory load of many modern applications is quite large. On an RD Session Host server support-ing dozens or hundreds of sessions, each running memory-hungry applications that are not designed to be efficient with memory (because applications are still typically designed for a single-user computer), how do you avoid running out of page file as well as RAM?

One way, of course, is to ensure that you've got enough page file. Another way that doesn't require any work on your part is a memory-sharing technique implemented in Windows that allows processes to share memory space—sometimes. This technique is called *copy-on-write* and is related to *shared memory*.

At the basis of copy-on-write is the fact that there's a lot of redundancy in a computer. If two processes need to use the same dynamic-link library (DLL), for example, it is better if they can use the same one—if one can "read over the shoulder" of the other. So long as neither process is modifying the data, this works fine, and it decreases the amount of data that a process must store in memory to support all its threads.

The tricky bit comes when a piece of data that two processes are using needs to be changed by one of them. There are two ways you can avoid having a change by Process B make an impact on Process A. One way is to make a copy of the data for Process B as soon as Process B accesses the shared memory area. This can be wasted effort, though—what if the second process won't change the shared data?

Another way that avoids this wasted effort is the approach that Windows takes: When Process B needs to change the data at the shared location, the memory manager copies the edited data to a new location. The original data is not affected, and the process that must change the data can continue, now using its own copy, as shown in Figure 2-5. Windows works like this; other operating systems might make a copy of the page at the time the sec-ond process must access the same data as the first process.

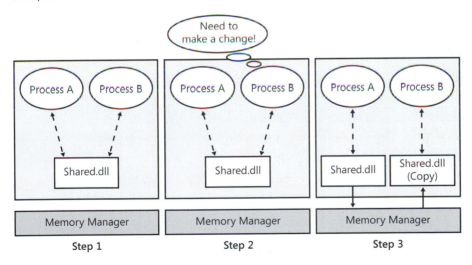

FIGURE 2-5 Copy-on-write allows for more efficient use of physical memory.

The catch to copy-on-write is that applications must be written in a way that allows them to take advantage of it. The Windows operating system can use copy-on-write for itself, but developers must plan for its use in user applications.

How Does Disk Affect Application Delivery?

The last item in our server internals overview is disk performance. Although not everyone considers hard disks when designing an RD Session Host or RD Virtualization Host server, for best results, it's important to keep disk performance and data storage in mind.

Keep Shared Work Environments Generic

Whether you're delivering applications through VMs on an RD Virtualization Host or through sessions on an RD Session Host, it's best to keep the application delivery system homogenous. All the RD Session Host servers in the same farm should have the same applications installed and the same settings configured; all the VMs in the same pool should have the same applications and configuration. Only the following four kinds of data should be on the servers.

- The page file
- The cached user profiles currently in use (while the profiles themselves are stored on a separate file server)
- The operating system
- The applications

You should never store user-specific data like user profiles or user data on a shared application delivery role like an RD Virtualization Host pooled VM or an RD Session Host server. Doing so complicates backups (since data isn't on a central server) and can lead to an inconsistent user experience as users move from VM to VM or connect to a new session. A possible exception to this rule is the personal desktop assigned to a user, because that user will always return to that VM. However, even storing personal data on a desktop has it downfalls because it will complicate restoring files if the only backup is of the VM itself.

> **IMPORTANT** User profiles should not be stored on an RD Session Host server, but rather on a central file share so that there's only one copy of the profile. However, the profile will be cached on the RD Session Host server for the duration of the session it's supporting. See Chapter 5, "Managing User Data in a Remote Desktop Services Deployment," for more details about combining profiles and RDS.

You not only need to think about where you're storing data to facilitate backups and provide a consistent user experience, you need to take disk performance into account. One approach to storing all the data that should be on the RD Session Host or the VMs is to get one big hard disk and keep all the data on it. That way, you can mirror the hard disk and have a backup configuration. For small environments or pilot programs, this might work fine.

For larger deployments, best practice is generally to divide up the three types of data (page file, user profile cache, and the operating system and applications) among three separate hard disks, to avoid waits for disk I/O requests. The problem is that all user activity requires a lot of disk reads and writes. Beginning a user connection, loading a user profile, starting an application, paging some data in memory to disk (or reading data previously paged to disk back into memory)—these are just some of the events that generate disk I/O requests. If these requests begin to stack up, users will see delayed response times. Paging data back into memory from disk, for example, is already relatively slow compared to accessing the same data from physical memory.

Processors and memory are extremely fast. Disks, although fast, are much slower than either RAM or processors. (If you'll recall from the section titled "How Virtual Memory Is Supported" earlier in this chapter, this is why it's good to minimize use of the page file, even though it's critical to your server functioning well.) Ideally, try to have one hard disk spindle for every 20 to 30 users on a given RD Session Host or RD Virtualization Host server. That way, the users' disk requests will be less likely to delay each other.

Understanding the System Cache

As you've seen, writing data to the page file or reading from it is expensive and relatively slow. What if you'll use the data again soon but need to free up some RAM now? What if a user requests one piece of data but is likely to need related pieces close to it in storage? In either case, the memory manager can store some data in an area of kernel-mode memory called the *system cache*.

The file system cache holds data pulled from disk. Without getting too deeply into the minute details of the decision tree (see the "Additional Resources" section at the end of this chapter for some detailed references), when a process requests some data, the request goes first to the area in virtual memory where the process stored the data. If the data is in RAM, then the process can continue with whatever it was doing.

If the data is not in the RAM mapped to the user's virtual address space, the next stop is the system cache, which is a collection of virtual addresses backed by RAM. If the entire request can be satisfied from the system cache (that is, if the process has asked for data A through E, and the cache contains A, B, C, D, and E), then the request never gets as far as the file system. If only part of the data is in the system cache (say, A and B), then the cache manager forwards the request to the memory manager, which then generates a hard page fault and gets the data from the page file or from disk as appropriate.

The larger the system cache, the more efficient the process of retrieving data is. The cache grows as needed (a refinement introduced in Windows Server 2008) but in 64-bit Windows the system cache can be as large as 1 terabyte—much larger than the 1 GB possible on 32-bit Windows.

How Does RAID Affect Disk Performance?

What about RAID? RAID (which stands for "redundant array of independent disks") is one way to increase the uptime of your servers by decreasing the likelihood of a disk failure. The basic idea of RAID is that, rather than using a monolithic disk for all your storage, you combine partitions on multiple disks into a single logical unit. The partition can encompass the entire physical disk or only part of it.

The purpose for combining the multiple disks depends on the scenario. Some forms of RAID are intended for data security by linking two or more disks in a way that maintains a copy of your data. Some increase disk throughput by letting you use two or more I/O paths to support a single logical disk (one spanning multiple physical disks).

> **NOTE** Not all forms of RAID increase server reliability. Some even reduce it by linking two physical disks and making a volume spanning both, so that if one disk fails the entire volume is inaccessible. For the purposes of this book, assume that references are only to the fault-tolerant forms of RAID.

There are two basic kinds of fault-tolerant RAID: disk mirroring (RAID 1) and stripe sets with parity (RAID 5). (RAID 10 is fault-tolerant, but essentially combines 5 and 1.) Mirroring is the obvious winner when it comes to RD Session Host servers, but we'll review both to make it clear why it is a better choice.

DISK MIRRORING

Disk mirroring is the preferred configuration for an RD Session Host server. In this RAID configuration, you have two disks backing a single logical volume. One disk contains the primary partition, and one contains the mirror partition. Each time you write data to the primary partition, it's also written to the mirror partition. When you read data from the primary partition, it can be read simultaneously, on some implementations, from the mirror partition. This means that reads from a RAID 1 configuration could theoretically be twice as fast as reading from a volume encompassing only a single physical disk. Writes do not take twice as long because they can happen asynchronously.

If one disk of a mirror set fails, then a perfect and always up-to-date copy remains on the other disk. If one disk fails, you can restore redundancy easily by breaking the mirror set and replacing the failed disk, then adding the new disk to the mirror set. The disks will re-create the information on the existing disk onto the one you've just added to the mirror set.

RAID 1 reduces the time required to read from disk while not really affecting the write time. It also makes it easy to recover from a disk failure since the data is already fully assembled. About the only disadvantage is that it does not make very efficient use of space because there are two full copies of all data.

STRIPE SETS WITH PARITY

Another contender for a fault-tolerant system is RAID 5, or stripe sets with parity. RAID 5 works differently from RAID 1. Whereas RAID 1 maintains a perfect copy of all the data on a partition on a second disk partition, RAID 5 takes a more space-efficient approach. It writes a slice of data to each disk in the array (a minimum of three disks), but only once across the entire array. Each physical partition then contains both actual data and parity information for data stored on another drive. Therefore, so long as no more than one disk fails, you have either the original data or the parity information required to create the original data.

 CAUTION Be aware that if a second disk fails before you replace one failed disk in a stripe set, you will lose data. This is why some people choose RAID 10, which mirrors striped volumes.

RAID 5 has its advantages. It can use many more disks than RAID 1, and it is more efficient in the way that it stores data because it's not maintaining duplicates of all data—just some of it, plus parity information needed to re-create it in case of disk failure. It can also be more efficient for reads because more than one I/O path can be used. But writing data takes more time with RAID 5 because every time you write data, you must also calculate and write its parity information. Given the large number of reads and writes that an RD Session Host or RD Virtualization Host server will necessarily do, this isn't a good RAID model.

One caution about using RAID on an RD Session Host server: Don't use software RAID. In particular, don't use software RAID 5 (stripe sets with parity), because the calculations required will utilize processor cycles that could be used more profitably elsewhere. Hardware RAID systems have their own processor and will increase disk performance.

How Does Virtualization Affect Resource Usage?

Virtualization was an interesting footnote for Windows Server 2008 Terminal Services (TS). Most TS roles *could* be virtualized for convenience, with the exception at the time of the terminal servers themselves. (You'll learn shortly about the hardware architectural changes that have made virtualizing an RD Session Host server no longer a bad idea, given the right processor architecture.) It wasn't a core scenario, however. In RDS, however, one of the roles depends on virtualization: RD Virtualization Host relies on Hyper-V. Therefore, you'll explore how virtualization works for allocating processor time, memory, disk input/output paths, and networking.

Distinguishing Type 1 and Type 2 Hypervisors

There are two kinds of hypervisors supporting Windows virtualization today: type 1 and type 2, as illustrated in Figure 2-6. If you're not sure of the difference or why it's important, read on.

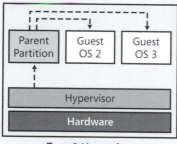

Type 1 Hypervisor   Type 2 Hypervisor

FIGURE 2-6 Contrasting Type 1 and Type 2 hypervisors

A Type 1 hypervisor, in a model also known as *bare metal virtualization*, interacts directly with the computer hardware. In a Type 1 hypervisor such as Microsoft Hyper-V, the hypervisor is the go-between for the system hardware and the *parent*, or *root*, partition, the part of the operating system that manages the VMs. The VMs are also known as the *guests* or the *child partitions*. A Type 1 hypervisor has a parent partition and as many child partitions as it can support and needs.

Type 2 hypervisors (also known as *host-based virtualization*), such as Microsoft Virtual PC, are part of the host operating system. Guest VMs communicate with the host operating system to work with the system hardware.

The main reason to choose each right now depends on where you're planning on running the VM: the data center or the desktop. Since RDS is a data-centric computing model, you'd expect that this model would prefer running the VMs from the data center on a Type 1 hypervisor, and you'd be right. However, if there is a valid reason to use a VM on a desktop computer (for example, to run a demo), as of 2010, it will most likely be on a Type 2 hypervisor. (Type 1 client hypervisors aren't a trivial problem, in part due to the wide variety of client hardware; servers are certified for Hyper-V support.) Because RDS uses Hyper-V, a Type 1 hypervisor, you'll focus on that model in our discussion of virtualization.

You've learned a lot in this chapter about how virtual memory, disk, and processor work in Windows Server 2008 R2. As you'd expect, when VMs are involved, the story gets a bit more complicated. To understand it, you'll walk quickly through the architecture of a Type 1 hypervisor, including

- The role of the parent partition
- How child partitions use memory and processor cycles
- How child partitions access other hardware
- Why you will get better performance using a virtualization-aware guest operating system

If you'd like more details on how hypervisors work, the additional resources at the end of this chapter point you to some sources to learn more about hypervisor architecture.

The Role of the Parent Partition

The parent partition, or root partition, is the liaison for the hypervisor (and occasionally the hardware) and the child partitions. The root partition typically runs a stub operating system such as Windows Server Core to save on memory requirements. Within the root partition are

- The true device drivers for interacting with hardware
- The virtualization service providers (VSPs) used to manage access to synthetic devices from the child partitions (more about this in the section titled "Device Access from Child Partitions" later in this chapter)
- The VM Service that connects the parent partition to the hypervisor
- Worker processes that manage the state of a child partition and perform device emulation (more about this later)

You'll find out more about what all these pieces actually do in the remainder of this section.

How Memory and Processor Allocation Works on Child Partitions

You have been introduced to some of the problems of memory and processor time management across sessions on the same host. As you can imagine, traffic control is complicated when a processor or memory manager must figure out how to coordinate multiple service requests not just from different sessions, but from different VMs—and machines that might not all be running the same operating system.

Processor scheduling and memory management are both handled by the hypervisor itself. This component of the virtualization stack has both a processor scheduler and a memory manager built in. The scheduler manages the access to processor time across all the child partitions and corresponding to the virtual processors in each VM, and the memory manager handles the tracking of where the virtual address for each VM maps to in physical memory.

PROCESSOR TIME

Child partitions don't directly access the processor scheduler; if they did, they'd interfere with each other and it would be impossible to coordinate all the requests. A logical processor (a core in a physical processor is referred to as a *logical processor*) might be used by more than one VM (and likely is), and a VM might be using more than one logical processor. To manage all the processor time requests, the hypervisor represents processors in a child partition as virtual processors (VPs). A child partition can have zero (although you won't get a lot done like that) or more VPs. The number of VPs is not related to the number of logical processors—again, a processor might be accessed by more than one child partition or not accessed at all by some. A virtual processor can be

- Running, when it's actively executing instructions.
- Ready, when it's not executing instructions but is ready to.
- Waiting, when the VP is waiting for instructions that tell it what to do next.
- Suspended, when it's temporarily disabled and won't execute instructions again until taken out of the suspended state.

The hypervisor keeps track of the state of each VP and which logical processor a VP is using. The root partition can access this information.

MEMORY MANAGMENT

Memory management is also more complex on a VM host than on a physical machine. The VMs themselves can't share memory for many reasons, including security isolation, and the memory manager has three areas of memory to manage, not just two (see Figure 2-7). These three areas are

- The system physical address (SPA) space
- The guest physical address (GPA) space
- The guest virtual address (GVA) space

The GPA is the representation of physical memory from the perspective of the guest. Operating systems expect their memory addresses to be numbered beginning at 0 and expect some structures to be in memory at a certain address range, so guests can't really share a view of physical memory without getting confused. The GPA is mapped to the SPA more or less in the same way that the memory manager maps virtual memory addresses to physical memory addresses, as discussed in the section titled "How Do RD Session Host Servers Use Memory More Efficiently?" earlier in this chapter. When a guest operating system accesses memory in the GVA, the request is mapped to the GPA, and from there mapped to the *actual* physical address of the SPA.

All this memory management can use up processor cycles, so VMs—especially those with a lot of memory reads and writes, like RD Session Host servers—will benefit from Second-Level Address Translation (SLAT) technology, as discussed in the section "Can I Run RDS in a VM?" later in this chapter.

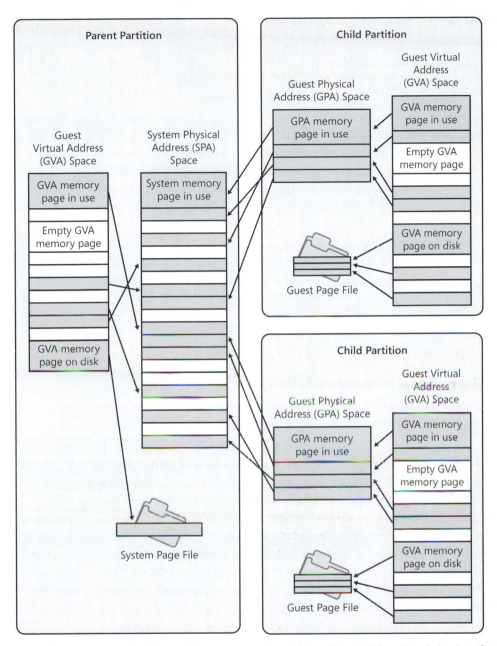

FIGURE 2-7 Memory management with a hypervisor, from "Second Level Address Translation Benefits in Hyper-V R2," by Janique Carbone. Used with permission.

Device Access from Child Partitions

Devices other than processors and RAM are managed separately. Rather than being managed directly by the hypervisor, other types of devices (like network cards and hard disks) use VM worker processes that control the virtual devices (VDs) and give the VMs a way to interact with the devices indirectly. VDs can be *emulated* or *synthetic*.

Emulated devices are accessible to all guest VMs. They're basically a set of I/O ports, memory ranges, and interrupts (all representing device access) that the guest can access and which the hypervisor controls. When a guest tries to use an emulated device (for example, a Legacy Network Card), then the VM worker process is notified. The worker process basically emulates the action requested (for example, a disk read). While the guest VM is distracted, the worker process sends the request to the hypervisor to be executed by the actual disk, then works the results back up the chain to the guest VM.

Emulation is slow but simple, and it works even if the operating system isn't virtualization-aware. It's also available during installation (which is why, after it is installed, you need to install a toolset onto the guest operating system to improve the VM performance and display). But it's not really up to the demands of modern hardware. For better performance, you'll use synthetic devices.

Synthetic devices are supported by VSPs, virtualization service clients (VSCs), and the VMBus. VSPs run in the parent partition. When a child partition attempts to use a synthetic device (for example, to read a file from a virtual disk), the VSC in charge of that particular device sends the request to the VMBus. The VMBus links the child partition and the parent partition. The VMBus then sends the request to the VSP for disk, and this travels via the miniport driver to the hardware. The hypervisor doesn't get involved at all, and this model is much faster.

Enlightenment, or Why Windows 7 Guests *Might* Scale Better

There are reasons to run Windows XP as the guest operating system in a VM, application compatibility (the driver behind the RemoteApp for Hyper-V feature) being one of them (more on this in Chapter 4). However, one of those reasons shouldn't be so you can run more VMs on a single host. Contrary to what you might expect, clients running Windows Vista and Windows 7 might scale better, all else being equal. (This assumes that all VMs are using the same amount of memory. If you're using less memory for the Windows XP VMs, then they will scale better.) The reason for this is that these more recent operating systems were designed to be virtualized and Windows XP was not.

The current operating system kernel contains a technology called *enlightenments*, introduced in Windows Vista and Windows Server 2008 and present in Windows Server 2008 R2 and Windows 7. Basically, enlightenments are code that runs only when the operating system is virtualized. When the code is running, the enlightenments coordinate actions with the hypervisor to make sure that they're interacting with the hardware as efficiently as possible. For example, if updating a cached memory mapping for the child process, without enlightenments, the operating system would instruct the processor to flush the cache for that entry without any caveats, which would slow memory mapping for any other child partition using that cache. Enlightenments allow the guest operating system to let the processor know that it should flush this cache only for the child partition doing the requesting. Other parts of the kernel operate with the same intelligence: When possible, they ask the hypervisor to pass on instructions to carry out *only* for the child partition requesting them, not the entire host and every guest running on it.

Windows 7 and Windows Vista were designed with virtualization in mind. Windows XP, however, was built before Hyper-V. Therefore, you might discover that you can host more Windows 7 VMs than Windows XP VMs per RD Virtualization Host for VMs with the same resource profile. Since Windows 7 guest VMs will also give the best user experience due to their full support for RDP 7 features and Windows XP endpoints can only display RDP 5.2 features, in most cases Windows 7 VMs will be the best choice.

DIRECT FROM THE SOURCE

How Windows 2008 Improves VM Performance

Mark Russinovich
Technical Fellow at Microsoft and co-author of Windows Internals, *5th edition*

One way Windows improves the performance of child VM operating systems is that both Windows Server 2008 and Windows Vista implement enlightenments, which are code sequences that activate only when the operating system is running on a hypervisor that implements the Microsoft hypercall application programming interface (API). By directly requesting services of the hypervisor, the child VM avoids virtualization code overhead that would result if the hypervisor had to guess the intent of the child operating system.

For example, a guest operating system that does not implement enlightenments for spinlocks, which execute low-level multiprocessor synchronization, would simply spin in a tight loop waiting for a spinlock to be released by another virtual processor. The spinning might tie up one of the hardware CPUs until the hypervisor scheduled the second virtual processor. On enlightened operating systems, the spinlock code notifies the hypervisor via a hypercall when it would otherwise spin so that the hypervisor can immediately schedule another virtual processor and reduce wasted CPU usage.

Another way Windows Server 2008 improves VM performance is to accelerate VM access to devices. Performance is enhanced by installing a collection of components, collectively called the *VM integration components*, into the child operating system.

If you run a VM without installing integration components, the child operating system configures hardware device drivers for the emulated devices that hypervisor presents to it. The hypervisor must intervene when a device driver tries to touch a hardware resource to inform the root partition, which performs device I/O using standard Windows device drivers on behalf of the child VM's operating system. Since a single high-level I/O operation, such as a read from a disk, might involve many discrete hardware accesses, it can cause many transitions, called *intercepts*, into the hypervisor and the root partition.

Determining System Requirements for RD Session Host Servers

You've looked at disk, processor, and memory internals in some detail. Armed with your newfound knowledge, answer this: If you have a server running 64-bit Windows Server 2008 R2 Standard Edition with 16 GB of RAM, a three-disk array, two quad-core processors, and a gigabit network, how many concurrent sessions can this RD Session Host server support?

The answer, of course, is that it depends on what the users logged into those sessions are doing. Many times, when you're choosing hardware to support a given situation, you can take a well-established path to choose the hardware. Look at the product documentation for the operating system that you plan to run and the software that you want to buy, and it's easy to tell what the hardware requirements are. Follow those guidelines and you should be all right.

With RD Session Host servers, it's not that easy. Defining hardware requirements for this server role is more difficult than defining them for a server running Exchange Server, for example. A server running Exchange Server has a more predictable load: It sends mail and it receives mail. The mailboxes can be of a predetermined size limit, and the process of sending or receiving an email takes a predictable number of processor cycles. Given all that, if you know how many users are utilizing the server, you can determine what hardware to buy.

RD Session Host servers, in contrast, support individuals who might be doing various kinds of activities with differing types of applications. It's possible to predict the hardware profile required to support 50 users getting email with a fair degree of accuracy. It's much harder to predict the hardware needed to support 50 users on an RD Session Host server who are using a combination of the thousands (to be conservative) of business applications available. To know the load that an RD Session Host server can manage, you must have a very good idea what the individuals using it will be doing.

This might be frustrating to hear, but the most reliable way to determine how many people can use an RD Session Host server simultaneously is to try it: Install the server and the applications, get a representative group of users together, and keep adding users until performance slows to an unacceptable level. Alternatively, you can make some guesses based on a test run or on information derived from one session. Read on for more details about doing a test run or extrapolating usage information from a single representative session.

Baseline RD Session Host Requirements

Saying that you can't know how many people can use an RD Session Host server at the same time given a certain hardware profile isn't to say that there are no guidelines at all. Before getting into some procedures for load testing, let's look at some basic recommendations for RD Session Host hardware.

Memory

Load up on memory. This is always true for an RD Session Host server, because many people will be using applications and loading data into memory at the same time, all in parallel. One person working on eight Microsoft PowerPoint presentations at the same time is bad enough, but 50 individuals doing the same thing can take quite a toll on a server.

Memory was an issue with terminal servers running Windows Server 2003, but it will be more of an issue for RD Session Host servers running Windows Server 2008 R2. The base operating system uses more memory now, for reasons that have nothing to do with RDS. First, the server operating system runs Windows Internet Explorer 8, which uses more memory than Microsoft Internet Explorer 6. Any scenarios that require the Microsoft native browser will be affected by this. Second, the shell in Windows Server 2008 R2 and Windows 7 is more memory-intensive than that in Windows Server 2003 and Windows XP. And with Windows Server 2008, these additional memory consumers will affect an RD Session Host server in particular, because these programs are all about the user experience.

Remember that 64-bit Windows uses more memory than 32-bit; a lot of the standard processes use more memory in the 64-bit version than they do in the 32-bit version. You need about 8 GB of RAM in an RD Session Host Server to bring it to parity with a 32-bit terminal server with 4 GB. However, at 16 GB, the RD Session Host server will start being able to support more users than the 32-bit server can.

Disk

As you saw previously, you must be sure to pay attention to your physical hard disk layout. Everyone thinks about memory when sizing an RD Session server, with processor power another obvious consideration. Not everyone takes disk I/O into consideration, but a server supporting reads and writes for many users needs a wide and unobstructed I/O path. Split data among multiple hard disks (20 to 30 users to a disk spindle, as a guideline) for best performance and use hardware RAID 1 for disk fault tolerance.

Network

Of course, network speed is important to a centralized computing environment. In-house, bandwidth should not be a problem, although you might consider a multihomed server so you can dedicate one network card to Remote Desktop Protocol (RDP) traffic and one to serving file and print requests. Out of the corporate network, you're dependent on networks you might not be able to control. To support remote users, consider a test run to determine the usability via the networks your users have available. What works well on the LAN might be difficult over a digital subscriber line (DSL); what works well via DSL is likely to be difficult over dial-up. Disable any features that use a large amount of bandwidth but aren't required and be sure to set the RDP clients' network hint appropriately for their connection type (see Chapter 6 for more about RDP).

Processor

Processor speed was unlikely to be your biggest bottleneck when running the 32-bit version of Windows Server 2008, but it's more important in 64-bit Windows where memory is no longer constrained. Quad-core processors are common these days; get a motherboard that has additional sockets. The amount of cache is more critical to processor responsiveness than the processor's speed. More cache provides more space to store instructions that are quickly available to the processor to execute. Incremental changes in megahertz (MHz) made a lot more difference when you were moving from 66 MHz to 100 MHz. DFSS, introduced in Windows Server 2008 R2, automatically apportions processor time evenly among sessions.

DIRECT FROM THE FIELD

RDP Network Requirements

Jon Wojan
Senior Premier Field Engineer

Timothy Newton
Support Escalation Engineer Defining Acceptable Performance

How much network bandwidth does a typical remote session require? The answer depends on a variety of factors, including but not limited to the following.

- Pixel dimensions of the RDP session
- Color depth of the RDP session
- Redirected devices in the RDP session and their usage patterns
- Amount of screen redraw done by user workload/multitasking and application repaints in the RDP session
- Compression schemes being used on the RDP channel
- Version of RDP being used

Due to the number of factors involved, any estimate would likely be wrong for more than 90 percent of all scenarios. However, if you want to do some testing on your own, you can use a third-party application that measures network traffic. One option Tim uses is a tool called NetMeter, which shows a little graph of upload and download in real time. Using a tool like this, you can easily see how much is going up and coming down from a given client (or you could run it on the server and see the overall load).

Your goal is to create an efficient and effective user experience. That user experience will be defined subjectively by three main criteria:

- The logon process, including both how long it takes to log on, whether the server seems unresponsive or gives some feedback data, and how many times the user needs to supply credentials. Although the ideal user experience is to avoid logons totally—just sitting down and having applications open is easiest—you can create a reasonable experience if the wait isn't unacceptably long and the process is fairly transparent.

- Application responsiveness is crucial. Users must feel as though applications are responsive from the RD Session Host server or VM. A little lag might be acceptable, but not much, and if the delay is so great that users are typing ahead of the display, the IT department will likely receive complaints.

- Files should load quickly when requested, and print jobs should print. When using the centralized application model, you might get better response times than are possible with desktop-based applications.

NOTE Consider each of these criteria separately when designing a live test. That is, don't try to measure performance data at the same time you're measuring the number of simultaneous logons the server can support. If you mix scenarios, the two tests will interfere with each other. How can you tell how a server will perform on a daily basis if it's stressed out at that moment from too many logons? Sort out the logon bottleneck, and then look to see how the servers will respond to day-to-day usage requirements.

Designing a Live Test

To create a live test, you need to know which applications are going to be run and how the users running them work so you can pick a representative group of users and applications. What is the plan for these RD Session Host servers?

Root the Test in Reality

There's a lot of difference between running a low-impact point-of-sale application and running computer-assisted design (CAD) applications requiring lots of rendering. For a less extreme example, there's even a difference between running Microsoft Office 2003 and Microsoft Office 2007, since the Office 2007 interface is more resource intensive. Test with the applications you expect to be running, not with a random or invented scenario that does not apply to your real-life expectations. If the server isn't doing the work under normal circumstances, then your test results will be meaningless.

> **NOTE** Because of the memory sharing discussed earlier, the first RD Session Host server session might use more memory than that of subsequent consecutive sessions—it depends on the application usage profile. This is why running the live test helps: It shows the effect of multiple instances running.

Generate Typical User Behavior

Similarly, you need to know how your users work. Are they intensive workers who pound at their applications all day (for example, inputting data or writing a long document)? Or will they be up and down, engaging the RD Session Host server on an occasional basis? Just checking the number of open sessions on an RD Session Host server doesn't give you the information you need. Even if there are 100 open sessions, how many are active? How long have the inactive ones been idle?

> **NOTE** You might see references to knowledge workers and task-based workers when researching RD Session Host server sizing. Knowledge workers conform to the profile that was described in Chapter 1, "Introducing Remote Desktop Services"; they need access to the data stored in the data center to do their job. Knowledge workers use many business applications such as Office. Task-based workers generally input or review discrete chunks of data, such as working a cash register displayed as a Windows application. Each profile can involve light, medium, or heavy usage. Someone who's using an RD Session Host server to check their email a few times a day is a knowledge worker, but a light one.

If your final environment will be running a mix of users, try to get that mix represented in your live test. Does your work group include 75 knowledge workers and 25 task-based workers? If so, select three knowledge workers for every task-based worker for your test run.

Ideally, get real workers to participate in this test so that you can receive usage data that accurately depicts typical user actions and needs throughout your workday. For instance, you might know that users typically open files located on a file server from their RD Session Host sessions. You might *not* know that these files are typically 100 MB each. It would be best if this is discovered during your test phase and not during rollout.

Executing the Tests

If your main concern is to determine how many users an RD Session Host server can support during the day, you'll need to build an RD Session Host server using the instructions in Chapter 3. Install the applications you intend to use and make some representative files available to the users involved in the test. These are the steps you'll follow.

1. Start an instance of the Performance Monitor, the Windows Server 2008 R2 performance monitoring tool. Begin monitoring the counters that are not session-specific.

2. Have the users log on.

3. Tune the Performance Monitor to record performance data for the activity in each of the user sessions for session-specific counters.

4. Ask logged-on users to start applications, load files, check email (if that's a part of your test), surf the Web—in short, have them work as they would normally.

5. Let the test continue for a reasonable amount of time—perhaps an hour, or even longer.

6. Review the results and see the strain on the RD Session Host server as recorded by Performance Monitor.

Using Performance Monitor

Most of these steps are fairly self-explanatory, but using performance counters might be new to you. If so, read on for a walkthrough of how the monitoring process works.

COLLECTING THE DATA

To start the tool, click Start, Administrative Tools, and Performance Monitor.

> **NOTE** The process name for this tool hasn't changed from previous versions of Windows Server. You can also start it by selecting Start, Run, Perfmon.exe.

First, build a data collector set. Browse to Data Collector Sets. Right-click User Defined and select New, Data Collector Set, as shown in Figure 2-8.

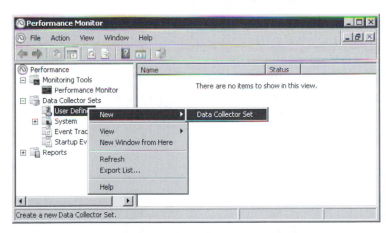

FIGURE 2-8 Start by making a new data collector set.

Name your data collector set using a description of what you are collecting, such as "RDS User Test 1." As shown in Figure 2-9, choose Create Manually (Advanced) and click Next.

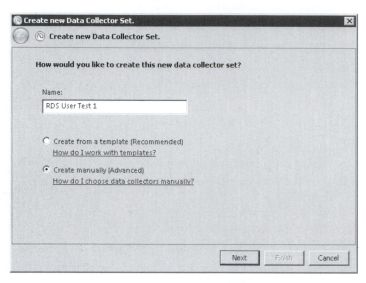

FIGURE 2-9 Create a new data collector set manually.

The goal is to log data, not initiate alerts for error conditions, so choose to create data logs based on performance counters, as shown in Figure 2-10. Click Next.

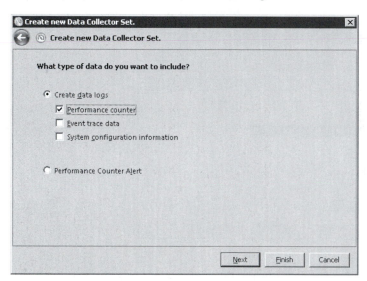

FIGURE 2-10 Create a data log using performance counters.

Next, you need to add performance counters to the collection set. What counters should you include as part of a full test pass? Since you're loading the server with many users, you can take a holistic view of the server rather than just focusing on what's happening within a single session. See Table 2-2 for an example of counters that can tell you about the strain on the server.

> **NOTE**   The counter names still refer to "Terminal Services" for compatibility reasons. When the product was renamed, APIs, registry keys, and performance counters couldn't be renamed, because if they had been, existing customer scripts would have stopped working.

TABLE 2-2 Performance Monitor Counters for a Full Test Pass

COUNTER	DESCRIPTION
Processor: % Processor Time	The percentage of elapsed time that the processor spends to execute a non-idle thread (in other words, the percentage of time the processor is doing anything useful).
Terminal Services Session: Total Bytes	Total number of bytes sent to and from this session via virtual channels. Gives an idea of the traffic coming in and out of the session due to redirected device calls.
Physical Disk: Avg. Disk Queue Length	Average number of I/O requests waiting for the disk. This number should not be more than 2.
Memory: Page Faults/Sec	The rate at which the RD Session Host server is reading from and writing to the page file. Higher numbers indicate that the server might be low on memory for its user load.
Terminal Server Session: WorkingSetPeak	The peak amount of virtual memory backed by RAM for a given session. This shows the demand for physical memory.
Terminal Server Session: % Processor Time	The percentage of processor time a given session uses.

To add a counter, find the appropriate object in the list, as shown in Figure 2-11. Click the icon to expand the list of counters for that object. If you're choosing a session-specific counter, choose the sessions to add it to; to choose all of them, choose <All Instances>.

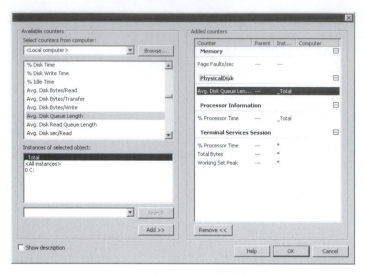

FIGURE 2-11 Choose counters for each object that you want to monitor.

When you're done selecting counters, click OK to display the list of counters that you're monitoring. The default sample selection should be fine. Click Next.

Choose the location where you'd like to save the data (as shown in Figure 2-12) and click Next.

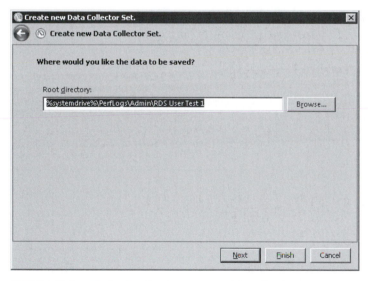

FIGURE 2-12 Specify the location to save your data collection set.

You can either save the data collector set to be initiated manually or edit the properties to set a schedule of when it should start and how long it should last. For the moment, assume that you're going to start it manually, so choose that option from the list shown in Figure 2-13 and click Finish.

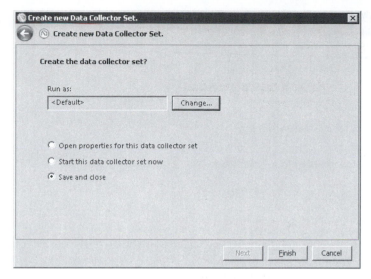

FIGURE 2-13 Save the data collector set to start it later.

When you're ready to begin testing, return to the main screen of Performance Monitor and choose the saved set from the folder of user-defined data collector sets. Right-click to open the context-sensitive menu and choose Start, or click the green Start button, as shown in Figure 2-14.

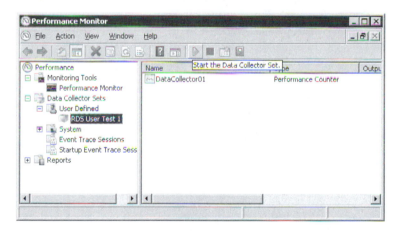

FIGURE 2-14 Start the data collector set.

When you have finished with the test, go back to Performance Monitor, right-click the collector set, and choose Stop, or click the square-shaped Stop button located to the right of the green Start button.

REVIEWING THE DATA

To review the results of your test, go to the Reports area shown in Figure 2-15 to find the report identified with the name that you specified.

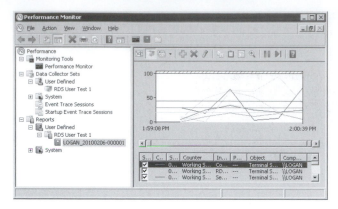

FIGURE 2-15 Find your report.

A report doesn't have to show all the counters that you included in the original data collector set, but by default it does. To remove a counter that you don't need, highlight it in the bottom section on the right pane and click the red X button at the top of the pane (or press the Delete key on your keyboard). Conversely, to add counters you want to show, click the green plus sign at the top of the pane on the right to open the dialog box shown in Figure 2-16. Only the objects for which you selected counters for the specified report will be available.

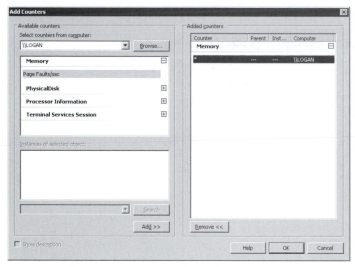

FIGURE 2-16 Choose the counters and specific object instances to display in your report.

Choose the object and the counters that you want to include, and because you are measuring the total user load, make sure that <All Instances> is selected in the Instances Of Selected Object list. <All Instances> is represented by the asterisk (*) symbol in the pane at right. Click OK when you've chosen all the counters.

> **NOTE** The Total option makes a total count for all selected instances; <All instances> tabs each instance individually but monitors all of them.

Finally, click the Change Graph Type drop-down menu to the left of the green plus sign and choose to display the information as a report (or press Ctrl+G twice), as shown in Figure 2-17.

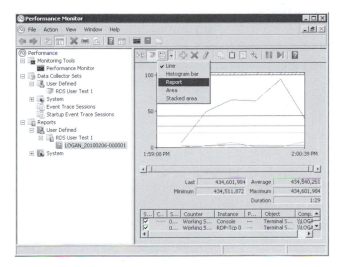

FIGURE 2-17 Change the report view to Report.

You should see data similar to Figure 2-18, displaying the results of your tests.

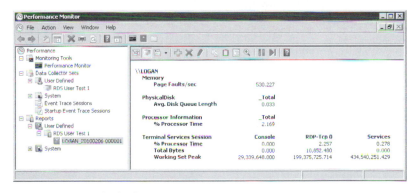

FIGURE 2-18 View the final report.

Using the RD Load Simulation Tool

Performance Monitor will graph or report on set activity periods on your RD Session Host server, but it does not create activity on an RD Session host. And before you go live with a new RD session host environment or add a new application to an existing environment, you should have a good idea that the server can handle the amount of activity that your users will impose upon this machine.

One way to do this is to go through a testing phase, where you have test users log in and use the system while you take readings with Performance Monitor. This is fine if you have those test users and they can spare the time to do this kind of testing.

Another way to understand what your RD Session Host can and can't handle is to simulate user sessions and user activity and monitor the server's performance while it's being taxed. The RD Load Simulation Tool (RDLST) does just that. It simulates user sessions and individual user activity on an RD Session host server, given a set of parameters. You specify how many users you want to simulate, and what you want these users to do (for example, open a document, type some text, create a graphic image, or save the document). The tool will programmatically start remote desktop sessions to the specified RD Session Host from the designated clients and execute specified actions within each session. Based on how the server reacts to the load you put on it, you can get an idea of whether your server hardware is adequate for your needs, exceeds your needs (so you could add more users), or about right. By reviewing the performance data, you can also see which counters are showing strain.

 ON THE COMPANION MEDIA   The RDLST is available at *http://www.microsoft.com/downloads/details.aspx?FamilyID=c3f5f040-ab7b-4ec6-9ed3-1698105510ad&displaylang=en.* This link is also located on the CD.

RDLST includes a controller component, a client agent, and a server agent, as shown in Figure 2-19.

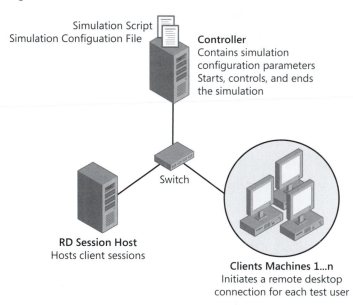

FIGURE 2-19 The RDLST consists of the controller, server agent, and client agent.

The controller is responsible for configuring the test parameters. The test clients and RD Session Host agents connect to the controller. The controller starts the test, monitors its progress, and ends the test.

The clients are used to start remote desktop sessions on the RD Session Host. Then the RD Session Host hosts the remote desktop sessions started from the clients.

The RDLST is not a solution on its own. It requires scripts to perform the actions it is built to run, like starting user sessions, running applications, and performing activities in each user session (such as opening an application and doing some work). Scripts also perform other pre-test and post-test functions, like starting and stopping Performance Monitor on the RD Session Host server and ending user sessions.

The RDLST comes with installation instructions, guidance on how to build scripts to perform tasks specific to your environment, and a reference guide, so there's no need to duplicate that effort. However, you should walk you through an example of how to set up and run a simple test against an RD Session Host server using the following basic steps.

1. Install the agents on the designated test servers and clients.
2. Create test user accounts in Active Directory Domain Services (AD DS).
3. Create the script that will automate the user activities inside the user remote desktop session.
4. Start the server and client agents.
5. Configure Performance Monitor on the RD Session Host.
6. Take a baseline Performance Monitor capture on the RD Session Host.
7. Configure the controller test parameters.
8. Start a Performance Monitor capture on the RD Session Host.
9. Start the simulation from the controller.
10. Run the simulation.
11. Stop the simulation.
12. Stop Performance Monitor data collection on the RD Session Host.
13. Review the Performance Monitor report.

In the next sections, you'll go through these steps in more detail.

Install the Agents on the Designated Test Servers

To begin, set up the controller, the clients, and the server for the test as follows.

- Install the controller tools on a designated server. The controller is responsible for the simulation configuration, and it also starts and ends the test. To install the controller, run the RDLoadSimulationTools MSI file on the controller, and choose the Controller Tools option.

- To set up the clients, run RDLoadSimulationTools MSI on each of the clients that you will use to generate the user sessions, and choose the Client Tools option.

- To set up the server, run RDLoadSimulationTools MSI on the RD Session Host server and choose the Server Tools option. Take care to run the 32- or 64-bit version of the MSI that matches your operating system version.

> **NOTE** This simulation tool example assumes the availability of basic networking services (AD DS, Domain Name System, Dynamic Host Configuration Protocol) and that all test servers and clients can communicate with the other test machines.

Create Test User Accounts in AD DS

For the simulation to start remote desktop sessions, it needs user accounts to log in and start the remote desktop sessions. To be used with the tool, these user accounts need to be set up as follows.

- User account names need to have the same prefix followed by a number suffix (for example, TEST01, TEST02, TEST*nn*).
- All user accounts all need to use the same password.

Create these test user accounts in AD DS and add these accounts to the Remote Desktop Users group on the test RD Session Host. The following PowerShell code (also on the CD as "Create30Users.ps1") will create multiple user accounts automatically, with the same prefix, followed by a number, and place them in a specified organizational unit (OU). In our example, the script creates 30 user accounts, named ASHTEST1, ASHTEST2...ASHTEST30, with the password "P@ssword", placed in the ASH_Users OU.

```
1..30 | ForEach-Object {
New-QADUser `
-ParentContainerASH_Users `
-Name "ASHTEST$_" `
-UserPassword "P@ssword" `
-UserPrincipalName "ASHTEST$_" `
-DisplayName "ASHTEST$_" `
-SamAccountName "ASHTEST$_" `
}
```

> **NOTE** This script uses Quest Software's free Windows PowerShell commands for AD DS, which you can download at *http://www.quest.com/powershell/activeroles-server.aspx* (the link is also provided on the CD).

Create the USER ACTIVITY Script

As noted earlier, the RDLST doesn't run any applications on its own—it's the engine that makes it possible. You'll need to create scripts to execute the applications and simulate user activity. The RDLST guides tell you how to create these scripts, but they also include one example to get you started. For the purpose of demonstrating how to use the tool, you'll use the sample included in the box melded into a single script and included on the CD as Notepad.vbs. This script starts a remote desktop session, logs in a user, opens Notepad, writes some text, and saves the text file. It is started for each of the user sessions invoked by the controller.

> **NOTE** The SendKeys method will be very helpful to you in developing an interactive script. See *http://msdn.microsoft.com/en-us/library/8c6yea83(VS.85).aspx*.

Start the Client and Server Agents

Log on to the clients and servers with an Admin account. Installing the client and server agents adds their icons to the Start menu, so you can start the agents from there or by rebooting the computers. Make sure the firewalls on the client and server machines are turned off or have firewall exceptions for this application in place so that the firewall ignores the agents. For this example, the firewalls are turned off on all participating machines.

The client agents automatically connect to the controller upon execution. When they do, the dialog box for the client agent will say that it is "Connected." The server agent should also connect automatically. If it does not, type the controller server's name into the Controller input box and click Connect.

Configure the Controller Test Parameters

Next, configure the controller with the information that it needs to run the test. Start the Controller software from the Start menu or by starting the executable (in this case, on an x86 operating system) as follows.

```
C:\Program Files (x86)\TSPerfTools\RDLoadSimulationController.exe
```

This starts the Remote Desktop Load Simulation Controller, shown in Figure 2-20. The controller shows the machines that connect successfully in the Status Events section.

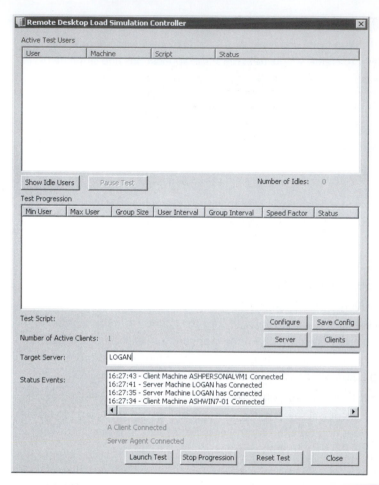

FIGURE 2-20 The Remote Desktop Load Controller shows the test progression and active test users.

In the Target Server input box, type the name of the RD Session Host server. Then click Configure to open the Configuration dialog box shown in Figure 2-21.

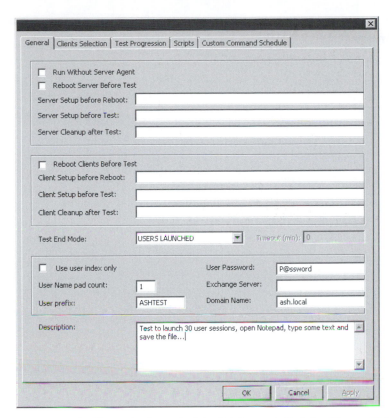

FIGURE 2-21 Configure the General tab to dictate events that should occur on the RD Session Host server before and after the simulation runs.

Manipulate the data on each tab to create the details of how the simulation will work. In the upper section of the General tab, dictate events that should occur on the RD Session Host server before and after the simulation has run its course. For instance, to reboot the server before the test (one way to start the server agent and to end any pre-existing user sessions), select the Reboot Server Before Test check box. The three input boxes in this section are for inputting paths to optional scripts that can be run before or after a simulation to prepare or clean up the RD Session Host server. For instance, at the end of a simulation, you might want to stop the Performance Monitor capture and log off the test users. The second section performs similar tasks for the clients.

ON THE COMPANION MEDIA Note that the first two sections in this simulation example are not used here, but you might need to use them in your testing. A script to log off the test users is located on the CD in the LogOffUsers.cmd file. A script to stop the Performance Monitor capture is on the CD in the StopPerfMon.cmd file.

The Test End Mode drop-down box provides four choices that govern when the controller will conclude that the test is ended.

- **Stay Alive**   The test does not end.
- **Users Finished**   The test ends when all users tell the controller that they are finished using the EndScript function.
- **Users Launched**   The test ends as soon as the controller starts the last user script.
- **Users Launched –Timeout**   The controller will wait for the specified timeout after launching the last user before the test ends.

This example uses the Users Launched option.

First, configure the user accounts. On the User section of the General tab, specify the user names of your test user accounts, the password for these accounts (now you see why they should all have the same password), the name of the server running Exchange Server (if needed), and the domain name. Test user account names in AD DS should match the settings here. User Name Pad Count is the number of digits that will be added to the user name prefix to reference the user names in the simulation. For instance, if the User Prefix is TEST and the User Name Pad Count is 3, then the test will reference the user names TEST001, TEST002, and TEST003.

Next, click the Clients tab and check that the right clients are selected and that each is running the right number of sessions. All clients currently communicating with the controller will be added automatically as test subjects on this tab. Select the Run Test Only On Selected Clients option to modify the participating client list. At the bottom of the page, enter the number of user sessions that you will run from each client. This example specifies that 20 user sessions will be run per client. (Microsoft has tested the tool with up to 50 users per client, but the number that will be able to run ultimately depends on the client hardware.)

Next, design how the load builds from the Test Progression tab. Enter the following numbers according to the simulation needs and then click Add to add the data to the simulation configuration.

- **User range**   Specifies how many users you will activate with this simulation.
- **User Group Size**   Specifies how many users in a group.
- **Interval between users (sec)**   Specifies the number of seconds that the controller waits before starting the next user within the group.
- **Interval Between Groups (sec)**   Specifies how many seconds will pass in between the ending of one group's sessions starting and the beginning of the next user group's sessions starting.
- **Speed Factor**   Specifies how fast the scripts will be run. The scripts will run at the normal speed when the speed factor is set to 1. They will run at double speed when speed factor is 2, and so on.

Figure 2-22 shows the numbers used in this example simulation.

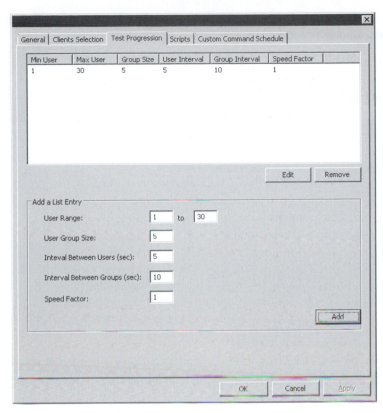

FIGURE 2-22 Add a list entry on the Test Progression tab.

Next, click the Scripts tab to pick the script or scripts that you'll use for the simulation. Click Add Script to open the Add Script dialog box, shown in Figure 2-23.

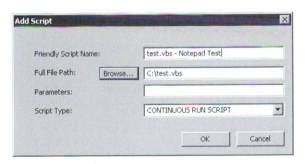

FIGURE 2-23 Enter the full file path to the script to be used in the simulation.

Enter the full path or browse to each script that the RDLST tool will call to start the user sessions on the clients, open remote desktop sessions on the test server, and do some work. Enter a friendly name of each script. The friendly name will be used as the name of the configuration INI file created next. Enter any optional parameters to be passed to the script in the

Parameters input box. This can be left empty if no optional parameters are required. In this example, none are needed. Ignore the Script type pull-down menu because it is disabled in this version of the tool. Click OK. Now highlight the script in the Available Scripts pane and click the Add>> button in the middle panel to add the script to the Selected Scripts list, as shown in Figure 2-24.

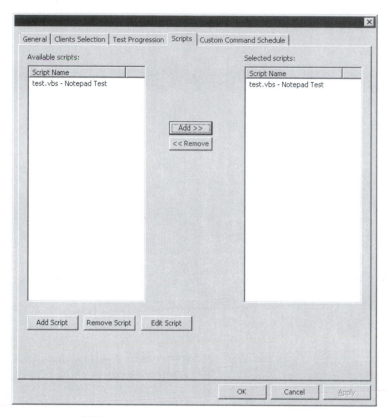

FIGURE 2-24 Add the simulation script to the Scripts tab.

Click the Custom Command Schedule tab. This example does not use any extra added commands, but this tab box allows for custom commands that will be run on servers based on user events. For example, you could configure the test to run a script on the servers when 50 user sessions are started and again when 100 user sessions are started. After you have configured the controller parameters, click OK in the bottom-right corner. Then click the Save Configuration button on the General tab of the controller. This saves the configuration to an INI file that can be used to populate the controller configuration for future tests. Call the configuration file when starting the program to autopopulate the controller configuration with the parameters from the INI file. The example's INI file looks like this.

```
[SCALCONTROLLER]
UserIndexMode=0
ServerAgentMode=1
TClientMode=0
RebootServerMode=0
RebootClientMode=0
UserPadCount=1
UsersPerMachine=20
TestEndMode=2
CommandTimeout=25
TestEndTimeout=0
UserPrefix=ASHTEST
UserPassword=P@ssword
DomainName=ash.local
ExchangeServer=
ServerName=LOGAN
ServerPreRebootCommand=
ServerPreTestCommand=
ServerTestCleanupCommand=
ClientPreRebootCommand=
ClientPreTestCommand=
ClientTestCleanupCommand=
TestDescription=Test to launch 30 user sessions, open Notepad, type some text and
    ;save the file...;
ProgressionListCount=1
Progression1=1-30-5-5-10-1
CommandListCount=0
ScriptListCount=1
ScriptName1=test.vbs - Notepad Test
[AVAILABLESCRIPTS]
ScriptsCount=1
ScriptName1=test.vbs - Notepad Test
[test.vbs - Notepad Test]
filepath=C:\test.vbs
parameters=
type=3
```

If you're running the 32-bit version, the INI file will be saved by default to the c:\Program Files (x86)\TSPerfTools\ folder. The name of the file is the same name as the friendly name of the script input on the Scripts tab. To call it in the future, open a Run box on the Start menu and type:

```
"C:\Program Files (x86)\TSPerfTools\RDLoadSimulationController.exe" SCRIPT-NAME.ini
```

Configure Performance Monitor on the RD Session Host

Configure Performance Monitor on the RD Session Host server to capture data that shows the load that the user sessions place on the server. Refer to the section titled "Using Performance Monitor" earlier in this chapter for how to set up a data collection set. This example uses a data collector set containing the counters listed in Table 2-2.

Take a Baseline Performance Monitor Capture

It's important to know what the performance results look like *before* you start the test so that the true impact of the sessions is clear. To find out, make sure no users are logged onto the RD Session Host server and run the capture by selecting the Data Collector Set made for the simulation and then clicking the green Play button in the top of the right pane. Run the capture for a minute or two. Figure 2-25 show the results of this example's baseline capture report. As expected, very little activity is logged in the resulting report.

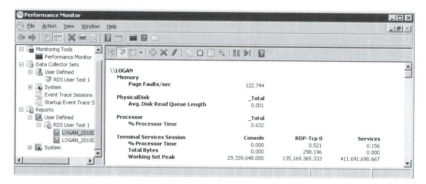

FIGURE 2-25 The RD Session Host server's baseline Performance Monitor results show little activity.

Start the Performance Monitor and Start the Simulation

Performance Monitor needs to run during the session to capture the data. You can either start it manually or from a script; if you'd prefer the latter, use StartPerfMon.cmd on the CD. This script will start Performance Monitor automatically and start a capture given the name of the data collector set. Add this script to the Server Setup Before Test input box on the General tab of the controller configuration.

To start Performance Monitor manually, select the same data collector that was used in the base capture and click Play. Then immediately start the simulation on the controller server by clicking Launch Test.

> **NOTE** You can only start Performance Monitor manually if you are not choosing the Reboot Server Before Test option on the General tab. Otherwise the perfmon log will stop when the server reboots. In the reboot case, you need to set the Perfmonstart.cmd script to run by adding it to the Server Setup Before Test box on the General tab of the controller.

Run The Simulation

After you start the simulation, the first thing you'll see is the user sessions starting on the clients. The active test users will begin appearing in the Active Test Users box on the Controller graphic user interface (GUI). The user sessions will also start appearing in the RD Session Hosts Users tab in Task Manager, as well as in the Simulation agent on the client.

As the simulation progresses, the controller logs status events; you can also view them in real time on the controller's GUI, as shown in Figure 2-26.

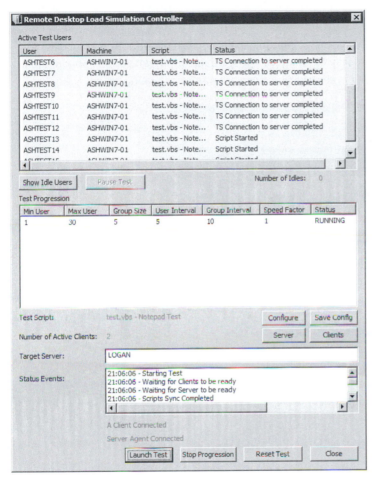

FIGURE 2-26 The Remote Desktop Load Simulation Controller shows user session activity and logs simulation status events.

During the simulation, Task Manager on the RD Session Host will give a quick overview of how the sessions are taxing the server.

Stop the Simulation and Performance Monitor

The simulation is considered over when the Test End Mode specified on the controller's configuration General tab occurs. This example specifies Test End Mode: Users Launched. This means that when all the users have been started, the controller considers the test complete. When the specified Test End Mode is reached, a Test Completed event will be logged on the controller in the Status Events window.

At this time, the user sessions need to be logged off from the RD Session Host either manually using Task Manager or the Remote Desktop Manager or programmatically using a script that is specified in the simulation configuration.

Next, stop the Performance Monitor capture; again, you can either do this manually by clicking Stop or programmatically by using a script specified in the simulation configuration. Figure 2-27 shows the activity in this example simulation from beginning to end.

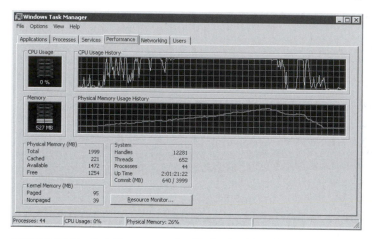

FIGURE 2-27 The Task Manager on the RD Session Host shows the activity throughout the simulation.

Where the peak starts to drop on the Physical Memory usage history is where the simulation ends. The very next plateau shows the user sessions disconnecting. Then the final drop shows the user sessions logging off.

Review the Performance Monitor Report

To get the results of your effort, view the report corresponding to the simulation capture in Performance Monitor on the RD Session Host. The report will be located in the Reports\User Defined folder. Select the report by name, select the option to change the graph type, and select Report. Compare this report to the baseline report taken before the simulation was started. This example's baseline report is shown in Figure 2-28, and the simulation report is shown in Figure 2-29.

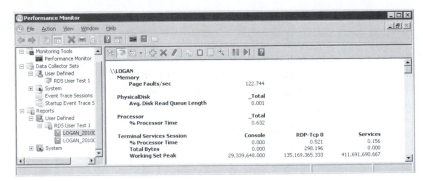

FIGURE 2-28 The report contains data captured when monitoring an RD Session Host baseline configuration.

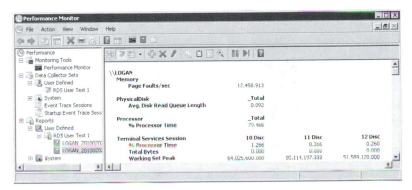

FIGURE 2-29 The report contains data captured when monitoring a RD Load Simulation test running on a RD Session Host server.

In short, using the RDLST will help you determine how many users can work simultaneously on your RD Session Host servers and how well the load corresponds to the hardware you have.

 ON THE COMPANION MEDIA See the book's CD for a link to the RDLST to help you programmatically determine how many people can use an RD Session Host server based on your application set.

An Alternative to Full Testing: Extrapolation

Running a test pass of the RD Session Host server is the best way for you to get a true picture of the session load that your hardware can handle before running a full pilot program. There might be situations, however, in which you will be unable to run through a test pass. If no one is available to help you, and you cannot use the RDLST, you can do a single pass on your own, record the results with the Performance Monitor, and extrapolate the number of users that the server can handle from the results.

You will still need to set up your RD Session Host server and load the applications that you will host. (To learn how to set up an RD Session Host server, see Chapter 3.) Where you can save time is in user testing. Instead of mimicking your user environment with multiple user sessions and with real user help, you can make some estimates by testing with one representative user session and doing some math.

In this test model, most of the counters checked for the full test pass will not help you. You can't really tell much about page file usage with only one user, and with only one session you're not likely to be putting much strain on disk I/O. You can, however, tell what's going on within the session itself.

To find out, create a data collector as discussed earlier in this chapter, including only the Terminal Server Session counters for Working Set Peak and % Processor Time.

> **NOTE** Because your report doesn't have to include every counter you collect data for, you can reuse the one from the earlier walkthrough if you created it as you read.

Run the test as described previously, trying to mimic a user session (that is, open programs your users will open, do some work, print pages, save files, and so on). When you've finished collecting data, select the counters to view, as described previously in this chapter, and choose to show a report of what's happening in that session (as opposed to choosing counter data for <All instances> as in the test pass). View this step in Figure 2-30.

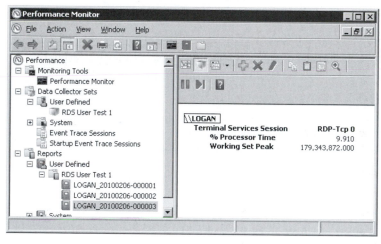

FIGURE 2-30 The report is based on session extrapolation.

Now that you have this report, what does it mean and how can you use it? You can view the data in several ways.

The data shows that the % Processor Time is approximately 10 percent. To determine the maximum users that can be supported with this processor, divide 100 percent by 10 percent; the result is 10 users.

> **NOTE**   You might have multiple processors in your RD Session Host server. Be aware that two processors don't render twice the power of one. Instead, there is a sliding scale.
>
> - Approximately 1.8:1 when going from one to two processors
> - Approximately 1.65:1 when going from two to four processors
>
> Therefore, if you have four processors in your RD Session Host server, you would use the following calculations to compute Max Users.
>
> 100 percent divided by 5 percent = 10 users. Now take into account the other three processors: 10*1.8*1.65 = 30 users at full load.

The processor in this example would be the bottleneck, but that might not always be the case. You must look at the peak working set for the session and weigh that against the amount of RAM in the computer. In this example, the peak working set was about 179 MB. Discounting for the requirements of the operating system, take the remainder and divide it by 250. As you can see, if the RD Session Host has 4 GB of RAM (a very low number for a production RD Session Host server), the RAM should be able to support 16 users running the applications that you ran in your test.

So can this server support 30 users or 16 users? For best results, it pays to be conservative: You should always use the lower number. On a server with this processor, with this amount of RAM, it's safe to guess that you can reasonably support roughly 16 concurrent users.

DIRECT FROM THE SOURCE

Server Sizing Tips

Costin Hagiu
Remote Desktop Services Test Architect, Microsoft

Hammad Butt
Software Development Engineer II (Test), Microsoft

If detailed information about user activity on the RD Session Host or RD Virtualization Host server is not available, then you can make some estimates about how many resources each session will need as follows.

- Allocate a percentage of a processor to a user based on how much CPU you expect users to need for running their tasks. For example, if you expect your users to need approximately 5 percent of the CPU's capacity for their work, expect to have about 20 users per CPU.

- Allocate a working set amount of *x* MB per user. You can approximate the value of *x* by starting the applications that you expect your users to open, working through a normal scenario, and noting the value of Peak Working Set from Task Manager. If this is not possible, make an estimate starting with a minimum of 100 MB per session for a 64-bit operating system.

- Always make sure that the paging file is three times the size of RAM (for example, if the RD Session Host server has 16 GB of RAM, plan on a 48-GB page file).

- Allocate a disk spindle for every 20 users for best performance. User profiles, page files, and system and application files should be on separate physical volumes as far from each other as possible to avoid I/O bottlenecks.

Each of these points will allow you to compute a number of supported users per specific resource. For example, if 5 percent of CPU capacity per user means 20 users per CPU, to compute the number of users that four processors will support, the equation is $20 \times 1.8 \times 1.65 = 60$ users at full load, for a margin of 50 percent of the maximum CPU usage, or 30 users.

You'll likely end up with different results when calculating for different resources. Always use the lowest numbers to avoid overstressing the servers. And of course, keep in mind that this is just an approximate process. There is no guarantee that the system will not run out of resources.

How Many Servers Should You Buy?

Now that you've got a reasonable idea about load, how should you distribute it across servers? Some people question whether it's more cost-efficient to have a single large server that can handle the entire load or to spread the load among more, but less powerful, servers. Is it cheaper to buy one server with 32 GB of RAM or two servers with 16 GB of RAM each?

Be aware that, if initial hardware and software costs are your primary concern, then RDS might not be the ideal platform for you. Using RDS almost certainly *will* increase your upfront costs. Consider the following points.

- You won't save on application licensing. Generally each user needs a license for the applications hosted on the RD Session Host server—sometimes even if a particular person has access to the application but doesn't use it. The exact terms will depend on the application vendor. Check the fine print of the relevant agreement to see how the applications are licensed.

- You probably won't save on desktop hardware. Unless you're starting from scratch—new company, entirely new hardware, and all the rest—you're not likely to get cheaper desktops than those you already have. Client hardware is a sunk cost.

- You will have to buy RD Session Host servers. This is especially true if you propose to virtualize the RD Session Host servers and want to get the benefits of Second-Level Address Translation (SLAT). Older servers won't have this technology.

- You will have to buy RDS client access licenses (RDS CALs) for users to connect to those servers, regardless of how many servers they're connecting to. If you're using any additional management software on those RD Session Host servers, you'll need to purchase those components as well. For example, if you install Citrix XenApp on your RD Session Host servers, you'll also need to purchase both RDS CALs and per-connection licenses from Citrix.

People use RDS for many, many reasons and frequently discover that it's possible to reduce long-term costs and increase productivity. Upfront costs aren't the best way to determine how to build a sustainable platform, however. Reducing capital expenditure isn't generally the goal; reducing operations cost is.

Going back to the original question: Should you have one large server or two (or more) smaller ones? Most often, you'll find more servers—scaling out, not up—to be the more cost-effective and fault-tolerant option. The larger the dual inline memory modules (DIMMs), the more they'll cost. More servers also means more disk I/O paths. In addition, even in a small deployment, with a second or third server, you create some redundancy in your environment by not relying solely on one RD Session Host server.

Other Sizing Questions

Thus far, this discussion has focused on what you need to know to size an RD Session Host server properly when that server is running on a physical computer. Let's take a look at other sizing scenarios.

Sizing RD Virtualization Host Servers

The previous discussion about sizing focused mainly on RD Session Host servers. What about RD Virtualization Host servers—how many VMs can you support per host?

Although the answer to this question still depends on what people are doing on those VMs, sizing VMs is a bit more like sizing physical desktops than like estimating the number of people who can concurrently use an RD Session Host server. With Windows Server 2008 R2, you assign a certain amount of RAM to each VM when creating it, so if you have 10 VMs and x RAM, the absolute maximum of memory that each running VM can have is $x/10$, minus whatever the hypervisor needs to operate. After it's created, you can also tweak the other hardware settings. A decent rule to remember for VMs using RDP for remote display is that you can run 4 VMs per core. Always test, though, because the configuration for those VMs will make or break the sizing.

One consideration you might not think of is the operating system that you're using in the guest VMs. Counterintuitive as it might seem, Windows 7 might scale better than Windows XP even though the Windows XP shell uses less memory. The reason, as discussed earlier in this chapter, is that Windows 7 was designed to take advantage of virtualization and Windows XP was not. Therefore, Windows XP is less efficient when it comes to memory management and processor requests—or any kernel activity, really. Although you might need to run Windows XP for application compatibility reasons in some cases, it might be better to use Windows 7. Again, try it and see.

What About Sizing Other RDS Roles?

Do other RDS role services face the same constraints as a RD Session Host server?

The short answer is "Not really." You will learn about the internal workings of each server role as it's introduced in this book, but here's a quick overview of what other role services are doing.

- An RDS Licensing server provides per-device RDS CALs or updates AD DS to show usage of a per-user RDS CAL on a user account object, depending on whether the RD Session Host server using the license server is in per-user mode or per-server mode. This is not a demanding workload.

- A Remote Desktop Gateway (RD Gateway) server examines incoming connections and permits them or refuses them based on the rules that you set up. If a connection to a resource is permitted, the connection will be proxied through the RD Gateway server. The main constraint on RD Gateway performance is the number of simultaneous incoming connections and the number of network packets in each one compared to the network speed; keep in mind that the server can maintain hundreds of connections.

- A Remote Desktop Connection Broker (RD Connection Broker) examines incoming connection requests and determines which endpoint (RD Session Host server or VM) that they should be routed to based on its brokering logic and the type of endpoint requested. After a connection has been made, the RD Connection Broker is no longer involved, but all incoming connections to all sessions and VMs will go through this server role.

- A Remote Desktop Web Access (RD Web Access) server accepts incoming Hypertext Transfer Protocol (HTTP) connections to generate RDP files on the fly. When delivered, those RDP files provide a direct connection to an RD Session Host server. This server can be sized like any other web server.

In short, with the exception of RD Gateway, other RDS role services generally handle short transactions and then pass the more substantial duties to an RD Session Host or RD Virtualization Host server. The load really isn't very large except during heavy logon times, when they're processing a lot of connections. Ensure that the RD Gateway (and RD Web Access, whichever users are going to first) has sufficient bandwidth to handle the expected load of concurrent incoming connections. Otherwise, the servers should be able to function well if they meet the requirements for Windows Server 2008 R2.

Can I Run RDS in a VM?

Virtualization is one of the hot topics today. Does virtualization mix with RDS?

The answer to the question is, of course, that it depends.

Part of the answer depends on what roles you want to virtualize. Obviously, RD Virtualization Host *requires* you to use Hyper-V to host the VMs. For many other role services (for example, RD Gateway, RD Connection Broker, RD Web Access or RD Licensing), running in a VM will probably work fine, although you might be able to support fewer simultaneous connections in a VM than you can in a physical machine. In fact, for years, Terminal Services administrators have run license servers in virtual computers to make it easier to maintain a backup. (This isn't necessarily supported by Microsoft, depending on the VM platform used, but it is done.)

Virtualizing RD Session Host servers on Hyper-V is supported, but the performance will depend on a few factors. The biggest factor is whether the hardware platform supports SLAT. As was discussed earlier in this chapter, virtualizing complicates memory management. Any operating system has to map virtual memory addresses to physical RAM to retrieve data. Hypervisors have a harder job in that they must keep track of three things.

- Physical memory
- The physical memory each VM guest is using
- The virtual memory each VM guest is using

Remember the page table that the memory manager uses to map virtual memory addresses to RAM? The hypervisor maintains a shadow page table for every guest VM. On a memory-intensive server like an RD Session Host, that's a lot of memory mapping for the hypervisor to keep track of. Every time the guest VM updates the page table, the hypervisor has to update its shadow page table. Although these tables have to be stored in memory, the problem isn't really running out of memory addresses—on a 64-bit operating system like Windows Server 2008 R2, that's not likely to be an issue. It's actually a problem of processor cycles, because the processor has to chew up cycles updating the shadow page tables.

SLAT-enabled processors improve the situation by maintaining the address mappings in hardware, not software. In other words, on a SLAT-enabled server, the hypervisor does not need to maintain the shadow page tables, but this can be done in hardware. The result is that a virtualized RD Session Host server can support more sessions than the number of a virtualized RD Session Host running on non-SLAT hardware. Both memory usage and processor overhead will drop.

How SLAT Reduces Overhead on Virtualized RD Session Hosts

Janique Carbone

Co-author of Microsoft Windows Server 2008 Hyper-V Resource Kit

With respect to memory management, Windows Server 2008 R2 Hyper-V supports a new feature named Second-Level Address Translation (SLAT). SLAT uses AMD-V Rapid Virtualization Indexing (RVI) and Intel VT Extended Page Tables (EPT) technology to reduce the overhead incurred during virtual to physical address mapping performed for VMs. Through RVI or EPT respectively, AMD-V and Intel VT processors maintain address mappings and perform (in hardware) the two levels of address space translations required for each VM, reducing the complexity of the Windows hypervisor and the context switches needed to manage VM page faults. With SLAT, the Windows hypervisor does not need to shadow the guest operating system page mappings. The reduction in processor and memory overhead associated with SLAT improves scalability with respect to the number of VMs that can be concurrently executed on a single Hyper-V server. As an example, the Microsoft RDS team recently blogged about performance tests conducted using an internal simulation tool on a Windows Server 2008 Terminal Services configuration running as a VM on Windows Server 2008 R2 Hyper-V. The results showed that a SLAT-enabled processor platform increased the number of supported sessions by a factor of 1.6 to 2.5 when compared with a non-SLAT processor platform. Overall, Microsoft reports that with SLAT-enabled processors, the Windows hypervisor processor overhead drops from about 10 percent to about 2 percent and reduces memory usage by about 1 MB for each VM.

Although RVI is not required to support workloads running on Windows Server 2008 R2 Hyper-V, if you intend to run memory-intensive workloads like RDS, Microsoft SQL Server, or web services, you should strongly consider using a SLAT-enabled AMD-V or Intel VT platform to take advantage of the performance improvements provided for your virtualized workloads.

If you're running the RD Session Host servers on older Hyper-V hosts that don't support SLAT, then it's still supported if you're using Hyper-V, but your results will depend on how heavily used the RD Session Host servers are. If the load is very light—say only a few users per server—then this might be practical and allow you to avoid dedicating a physical server to an undemanding role. For RD Session Host servers with heavier usage, however, this isn't likely to be a good fit for several reasons.

- **Disk I/O bottlenecks**   You've learned about how best practices for RD Session Host servers recommend that you have one disk spindle—one physical disk, usually—for each 20 to 30 users.

- **Memory constraints**   RD Session Host and RD Virtualization Host servers are memory-hungry. A VM host must have a lot of RAM to support many RD Session Host servers. This VM host could also end up being very expensive. Most servers top out at eight slots for RAM. As of this writing, 8-GB DIMMs cost three to four times as much as 4-GB DIMMs. Financially, you're better off with a second server than one server with twice as much RAM—just using smaller DIMMs.

There is a place for hosting RDS role services (such as a license server) on VMs, however—even if the host does not support SLAT. Connection brokers and license servers don't need a lot of resources to keep running.

Supporting Client Use Profiles

You've heard a lot about servers—and specifically the RDS role—in this chapter. But you also need to consider your users when planning. What kinds of computers do they need? What licensing model should you follow to best support their work patterns?

Client Hardware: PC or Thin Client?

This is another one of those "it depends" situations. The reasons that make thin client devices a requirement for some people just don't apply to all situations, and the same is true for PCs.

> **NOTE**   For those new to RDS, a thin client is a simple computer that is intended to act entirely or almost entirely as a client to a remote endpoint (for example, RD Session Host or VM on an RD Virtualization Host). Clients supporting RDP connections typically run Microsoft Windows CE or an embedded version of Windows. (You'll see some Linux-based thin clients, but the RDP clients on Linux are neither developed by nor supported by Microsoft.)

PCs with local processing power have become so inexpensive that they're a commodity item in many places—look at netbooks for one example. Purchasing thin clients won't generally save you money on hardware. The reasons why you'd choose thin clients are different, as follows.

- When or where PCs won't work well because of space, vibration, and other environmental issues.

- When the cost of maintaining individual, personalized computers is very high because of frequent user turnover.

- When client lockdown is vital. Since thin clients don't generally run applications locally and don't have access to data unless they're connected to the remote endpoint, it's easier to secure them—all security is on the endpoint.

- When a user desktop needs to be extremely replaceable. If a PC stops working and you need to replace it, a full replacement is bulky and, if the PC is customized at all for the user, time-consuming. Replacing a thin client means unplugging one terminal and plugging in the new one.

Thin clients generally work best when it's acceptable for all applications to execute on the remote endpoint (session or VM). It is technically possible to preload a thin client running a full Windows operating system such as Windows XP Embedded with applications, but this would be extremely expensive because of the amount of flash memory and RAM required to store and run those applications locally.

> **NOTE** As of this writing, thin clients running Windows CE Embedded do not support RemoteApp programs, discussed in Chapter 3 and Chapter 9, "Multi-Server Deployments."

Outside of those specialized settings where terminals shine, PCs (whether desktops, netbooks, or laptops) are generally the preferred option for one or more of the following reasons.

- Not all applications might be running remotely. If some applications don't remote well, they might need to be installed on the client.

- The user needs access to the applications when disconnected. Mobile workers often do well with RDS, as discussed in Chapter 1, but travelers also go offline at times, such as when they are on airplanes.

- You plan to use secure access from the Internet via RD Gateway. At this time, RD Gateway does not work with Windows CE, so the lightest-weight thin clients won't work.

- You need local processing power to optimize the remote experience. RDP 7 sends Windows Media Player content from the remote endpoint to the client for processing, which looks terrific. However, this requires being able to process the content locally.

In short, you're most likely to use thin clients to support task-based workers running applications on a LAN, and PCs for users with more complex usage scenarios (offline access, WAN access, and/or a mix of locally executing applications and RemoteApp programs).

What's the Best License Model?

You'll learn about RDS Licensing and how it works in detail in Chapter 12, "Licensing Remote Desktop Services," but RDS CALs are worth a mention when you're planning your RDS deployment.

RD Session Host servers support either per-device or per-user RDS CALs. Per-device RDS CALs are associated with a particular computer (either PC or thin client). Per-user RDS CALs are associated with a particular user. A RD Session Host knows which type of licenses to ask for based on whether you've configured it to be in per-user or per-device mode. RDS does not have concurrent-user licensing.

The answer to "Which license model is better?" can best be answered by "Which will cost the least amount of money while still allowing us to comply with the End User License Agreement (EULA)?" To calculate the answer, just consider whether you have more computers or more users. Organizations doing shift work, where three people might use the same computer, will benefit from the per-device model. Organizations in which the ratio is one user to every computer, or even two computers to every user (for example, if many users have both a desktop computer and a laptop), will benefit from the per-user model.

Each licensing model has a limitation, or at least a consideration. Per-user licensing works only with Windows Server 2003 or later and requires Active Directory/AD DS; you cannot use it in a workgroup or within a domain prior to Windows Server 2003. This is because the license usage is stored as a property to the user's account object. In addition, the license server must be able to update the domain controller to write this property. Although per-device licensing does not have this limitation, the license is associated with a particular device. This can sometimes lead to complications when you retire a PC or are using a thin client that does not store the per-device RDS CALs properly and keeps requesting a new one whenever it connects (not often a problem anymore, but it used to be with some models).

There *is* one other major difference between per-user and per-device licensing in Windows Server 2008 R2: per-device licensing is enforced, whereas per-user licensing is only tracked. This does not mean it is okay to break the EULA. You still need to buy a per-user license for each person accessing one of your RD Session Host servers.

> **NOTE** Only RD Session Host enforces or even tracks licensing, but using any RDS role service (RD Gateway, RD Connection Broker, etc.) requires an RDS CAL. To learn more about how licensing works, see Chapter 12.

What Applications Can I Run on an RD Session Host Server?

OK, you're convinced. You'd like to add RD Session Host servers to your IT infrastructure. One question remains: Can you use these servers to host all your current applications?

This is a great question to which there is no definitive answer. Microsoft does not maintain a list of third-party applications tested with RDS. No current logo program requires ISVs to test applications on RD Session Host severs. Therefore, not all application vendors test their applications on RD Session Host servers. How can you find out what will work well, what will work well with a little help, and what won't work at all?

There are three main ways that you can find out if an application will work on an RD Session Host server (or what you'll need to do to it to make it work well) before actually installing it.

- Ask if the vendor supports the application on an RD Session Host server, and ask about the recommended configuration. If the vendor has not tested the application on a shared server, you might need to get into some details about the application design. Table 2-3 includes some of the details that you should learn about an application before attempting to run it on an RD Session Host server. This is especially applicable to older or proprietary applications; most applications certified to run on Windows 7 should not have any problems running on a Windows Server 2008 R2RD Session Host server. They might be resource-intensive, depending on the application (few application developers design with a shared computer in mind), but they will avoid the design flaws that prevent an application from running properly.

- Check to see if anyone else has successfully run the application on an RD Session Host server. This can be as simple as doing a web search for the name of the application plus "RD Session Host server" ("terminal server" should also work and might generate more hits, because that name has been around longer) or going to the website of an independent software vendor (ISV) who packages applications for automatic deployment on an RD Session Host server. Knowing that it's been done might not tell you how to tweak the application to make it work on an RD Session Host server, but it will at least inform you that it's been done.

- Use the RDS Application Analyzer to examine how the tool operates and whether it's doing anything that will cause problems in a multi-user environment in which a user does not have administrative privileges.

TABLE 2-3 Application Design Questions

CHARACTERISTIC	BACKGROUND	IMPLICATIONS
Will the application setup automatically begin Add/Remove Programs? (Applies to non-MSI programs only.)	An RD Session Host server has a special mode called Install Mode for installing applications properly for multiple users, which the administrator can set from the command line or by using Add/Remove Programs. If the setup routine is started from Windows Explorer or the command line, the server should change modes.	If an application does not install in Install Mode, it will not support personalization for each person using it.
Will the application permit multiple versions to be run on the same RD Session Host server?	Different versions of an application might use identically named but different DLLs.	If more than one version of an application is running on the same RD Session Host server, the applications might have a DLL conflict and not run properly. This issue often can be avoided by creating a server farm to deploy applications or by using App-V.
Does the application separate per-user and per-machine registry data, or does it assume that one user equates to one computer?	Applications might store configuration data in HKEY_LOCAL_MACHINE (the registry hive relating to the computer) or in HKEY_CURRENT_USER (the registry hive relating to the currently logged-in user). RD Session Host servers will have one instance of HKCU for each logged-in user.	Since many people are running applications on the same RD Session Host server, for personalization to be supported, the application must separate per-machine and per-user data.
Does the application separate per-user and per-machine configuration data, or does it assume that one user equates to one computer?	Applications might store configuration data in the system files, but these might not be (and should not be) available to everyone logged on to the shared server. Applications should store personalized data structures by user.	Since many people are running applications on the same RD Session Host server, for personalization to be supported, the application must separate per-machine and per-user data.

Continued on the next page

CHARACTERISTIC	BACKGROUND	IMPLICATIONS
Does the application allow (or disallow) multiple instances of itself to run as appropriate?	Some administrative applications should only be started once to work best. (A disk-management utility that can mount or format disks is one good example.) Business applications on an RD Session Host server should start more than once, but older apps might permit only one instance of themselves.	More than one instance of a management application could end up in inconsistencies in user or machine configuration that might result in serious problems. For business applications, if it will run only one instance, it's useless on an RD Session Host server. It might still run in a VM, however.
Does the application separate computer and user identities?	Some older network applications identify themselves by computer name (or IP) address, but on a shared computer, this doesn't work properly. Applications that have a network presence should be user-specific (like MSN Messenger, for example), not computer-specific (like the old WinChat used to be).	If an application identifies itself by the computer it's running on, then it can't map to a specific user running that application on a shared computer. IP virtualization in Windows Server 2008 R2 does not enable static mappings of user identity to IP addresses.
Does the application assume that the Windows Explorer shell is always present?	Applications should not assume that the Windows Explorer will be available—especially now that RemoteApp programs are used. (In addition, your user configuration for File-Save Locations should not assume that the Desktop is available.)	If an application assumes the Windows Explorer shell is being used, then it might not work properly with RemoteApps.
How does the application communicate with any external hardware resources?	If the application needs to communicate with any external hardware resources, then it should use ports that are supported for redirection.	Hardware requiring ports that are not supported for redirection won't work from within an RD Session Host server session.
Does the application assume that the TEMP directory is persistent?	A user's TEMP directory will be cleaned up when the user logs off a session.	If the application stores data in Temp files, then that data will be deleted with the TEMP directory when the user logs off.

CHARACTERISTIC	BACKGROUND	IMPLICATIONS
Does the application rely on a particular version of Internet Explorer?	You can't install Internet Explorer 6 (for example) on an RD Session Host server, which comes with Windows Internet Explorer 8.	If a web application requires a previous version of Internet Explorer, then you'll need to run it on an operating system that supports it. This might be worked around by using Windows XP in a VM as a host.
The application is available in 16-bit only.	Windows Server 2008 R2 is a 64-bit operating system. It can run both 32-bit and 64-bit applications, but not 16-bit.	A 16-bit application will not run on Windows Server 2008 R2.

If an application won't work on RD Session Host for one of the reasons listed earlier, that doesn't necessarily mean that you must install it on the client, as shown in the following examples.

- If the application requires a previous version of Internet Explorer and won't work with Internet Explorer 8, then you can run the application on a VM running Windows XP. As Chapter 4 will discuss, you can run it either from a desktop or as a RemoteApp program from the client operating system.

- If an application stores data in Temp files, you might be able to keep it working using the *Flattemp* command to keep all temporary data in one folder instead of dividing it during each session.

- If an application assumes that the shell will be Explorer.exe, then you can run it from a full desktop.

- If you need to support multiple versions of an application, then you can deploy the application using a server farm or isolate it with App-V.

- If an application requires administrative privileges to run, you might be able to host it in a VM on RD Virtualization Host.

- You might be able to run 16-bit applications on 32-bit guest VMs running Windows 7 or (if required) Windows XP.

Using the RDS Application Analyzer

Not sure why an application won't work properly? The RDS team developed the RDS Application Analyzer (available from *https://connect.microsoft.com/tsappcompat/Downloads*) to help you answer such questions. In short, the tool will tell you whether an application, running as you would expect to run it on an RD Session Host, will work in that environment, and it can also offer some specific suggestions about why there might be problems. This tool does not need to be run on a Windows Server 2008 R2 RD Session Host; it works fine from a client.

Using the tool is fairly straightforward. To begin, download and install the tool and make sure that the RDS Analyzer Service is running (although the tool does not require a reboot, the service won't start just by being installed). When the service is running, start the tool. You should see a screen like the one shown in Figure 2-31.

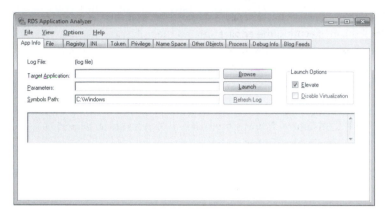

FIGURE 2-31 Start the RDS Application Analyzer by clicking the Launch button.

Don't worry about the Log File section; that's used only if you're loading a log file from memory. To test an application, click Browse to locate the program executable file or type the path to the executable. You don't need to change the symbols path. Before clicking Launch, look at the Launch Options list and choose the right option depending on what you want to test, as follows.

- To run the application with administrative privileges, select Elevate. Users won't generally have these privileges, but selecting this option will allow you to get past any initial privilege issues that might normally shut the application down. For initial testing, don't select this box.

- To run the application as a normal user, clear the Elevate option and leave Disable Virtualization cleared as well.

- To really check an application's compatibility, select Disable Virtualization. This will turn off the registry virtualization enabled in Windows Vista and later to work around application compatibility issues (see the How It Works sidebar here for more details).

Registry Virtualization

Registry virtualization redirects writes from protected areas of the registry to places where the person executing the application has the right to write. For example, if an application attempts to write to HKEY_LOCAL_MACHINE\Software \ASH\, it will redirect automatically to HKEY_USERS\< User SID >_Classes \VirtualStore\Machine\Software\ASH. (Although this write is stored in the user profile, it's stored in the non-roaming section of the profile.)

The goal of this feature is to enable support for applications that write to areas of the registry that the user doesn't have permission to edit or view.

- If an application attempts to open a virtualized key, then the key will be opened with the Max_Allowed rights instead of the security credentials of the person who started the application.

- If an application attempts to write to a virtualized key, then the virtualization intercepts the write and sends it to the virtualized location.

- If an application attempts to read a virtualized key, then the registry will merge the values of the "real" key and the virtualized key. If it doesn't have a virtualized value, then it will report the "real" value. If it has been written to already, then the registry will report the virtualized value.

If you disable registry virtualization in the RDS Application Verifier, then this will tell you if the application that you're testing depends on this feature. If it fails without registry virtualization, you should take this as a warning. Microsoft implemented registry virtualization in Windows Vista to solve application compatibility issues brought about by applications attempting to access protected registry keys, but this feature is intended to be temporary and it might be removed in future versions of Windows—basically, when enough applications no longer need it.

When you've configured the Launch Settings options appropriately, type the path or browse to the executable file to test and click Launch. From here, use the application normally for a while—open and close files, import images, whatever you might do—so you can get a good sense of what file locations and registry keys it's touching. You might see some Debug information updating in the background, but this is only a small part of the results. When you're done, close the application. This will prompt the RDS Application Analyzer to log all the data it collected and display the results, as in Figure 2-32 (showing saved log data and obscuring the name of the application being tested, which is not important to understanding the results).

FIGURE 2-32 The Compatibility Summary contains the results of running the RDS Application Analyzer.

Let's walk through what you're seeing here.

- **File and Registry Access**   The File and Registry tabs show what areas of the operating system the application attempted to access without the right permissions and what the results were. For example, one of the three failed writes that this application made was an attempt to delete a folder under Program Files. The detailed information about this option looked like this.

```
RemoveDirectoryW: Directory (\Device\HarddiskVolume2\PROGRA~1\XXX) only grants
requested 'DELETE' to 'NT SERVICE\TrustedInstaller, NT AUTHORITY\SYSTEM, BUILTIN\
Administrators'
```

As you read this, you can see that only members of the BuiltIn\Administrators group can delete folders in this location, so the action failed.

- **INI Writes**   Few modern applications still reference INI files, but if you run one that does, you'll see it here.

- **Token**   The Token section notes permissions again. If the token required for this application to run is BuiltIn\Administrators, then that application is unlikely to work well on an RD Session Host, where users do not have administrative privileges. An application might use the Administrator rights to do cleanup without assuming that it has them to do the main functions of the application, though.

- **Privilege** This tab tells you more about the level of access that the application demands. If it requires SeDebugPrivilege, then it won't run properly without elevated privileges; it's running as a service. SeAuditPrivileges is not a problem, though—that just allows the process to generate security audit data.

- **Name Space** Name space issues refer to applications attempting to create system objects in a protected namespace. Applications that try to do this will need too many privileges to work without administrative rights.

- **Other Objects** This tab includes issues involving object access that aren't related to the file system or registry entries. Anything listed here is a failed access attempt. The application might still work, but it wasn't able to do something it was attempting to do.

- **Process** This tab lists any issues with process elevation. Again, this will point to an application attempting to elevate its privileges beyond those of a normal user account. Problems here will generally lead to an application failing on an RD Session Host server.

What Version of Remote Desktop Connection Do I Need?

Some features of Windows Server 2008 R2RDS require the latest version of the Remote Desktop Connection (RDC). As of this writing, the latest version is RDC 7, available for Windows XP Service Pack 3, Windows Vista Service Pack 1, and installed on Windows 7.

Tables 2-4, 2-5, and 2-6 are adapted from "How to Detect RDS-Specific Application Compatibility Issues by Using the RDS Application Compatibility Analyzer" on the RDS team blog. They show what the user experience is like for people using RDC 5.2 (the oldest supported version of RDC), 6.1, and 7 to connect to a Windows Server 2008 R2 or Windows 7 endpoint.

> **IMPORTANT** Both the client and server pieces of RDP determine the user experience, and the earlier version will always take precedence if there is a conflict. For example, if you are connecting to Windows XP from an RDC 7 connection, you'll get the remote experience of RDP 5.2, because Windows XP does not have the RDP 7 server component. If connecting to Windows Server 2008 from RDC 7, you'll get the RDC 6 user experience.

TABLE 2-4 The RDC Connectivity Experience

CONNECTING FROM	WINDOWS 7/ WINDOWS SERVER 2008 R2	WINDOWS VISTA SP+	WINDOWS VISTA SP+	WINDOWS XP SP3	WINDOWS XP SP3	WINDOWS XP SP2	WINDOWS XP SP2	DISCUSSED IN
	RDC 7.0	RDC 7.0	RDC 6.1	RDC 7.0	RDC 6.1	RDC 6.1	RDC 5.2	
Access to Remote Desktop sessions	Yes	Yes	Yes	Yes	Yes	Yes	Yes	Chapter 3
Access to RemoteApp programs	Yes	Yes	Yes	Yes	Yes	Yes	No	Chapter 3
Access to personal desktop by using RD Connection Broker	Yes	Yes	Yes	Yes	Yes	Yes	Yes	Chapter 9
Access to virtual desktop pools by using RD Connection Broker	Yes	Yes	Yes	Yes	Yes	Yes	Yes	Chapter 9

CONNECTING FROM	WINDOWS 7/ WINDOWS SERVER 2008 R2	WINDOWS VISTA SP+	WINDOWS VISTA SP+	WINDOWS XP SP3	WINDOWS XP SP3	WINDOWS XP SP2	WINDOWS XP SP2	DISCUSSED IN
Start applications and desktops from RemoteApp and Desktop Connection on client	Yes	No	No	No	No	No	No	Chapter 9
Start RemoteApp programs, virtual desktop, and session-based desktop from RD Web Access	Yes	Yes	Yes	Yes	Yes	Yes	No	Chapter 9
Status & disconnect system tray icon	Yes	Yes	No	No	No	No	No	Chapter 9

TABLE 2-5 The RDC User Experience

CONNECTING FROM	WINDOWS 7/ WINDOWS SERVER 2008 R2	WINDOWS VISTA SP+	WINDOWS VISTA SP+	WINDOWS XP SP3	WINDOWS XP SP3	WINDOWS XP SP2	WINDOWS XP SP2	DISCUSSED IN
	RDC 7.0	RDC 7.0	RDC 6.1	RDC 7.0	RDC 6.1	RDC 6.1	RDC 5.2	
Windows Media Player Redirection	Yes	Yes	No	Yes	No	No	No	Chapter 6
Bidirectional Audio	Yes	Yes	No	Yes	No	No	No	
Multi-monitor Support	True	True	Spanning	True	Spanning	Spanning	No	Chapter 6
Aero Glass Support	Yes	No	No	No	No	No	No	Chapter 6
Enhanced Bitmap Acceleration	Yes	Yes	No	Yes	No	No	No	Chapter 6
Language Bar Docking	Yes	No	No	No	No	No	No	Chapter 6
Easy Print	Yes	Yes	Yes	Yes	Yes	Yes	No	Chapter 6

TABLE 2-6 The RDC Security Feature Experience

CONNECTING FROM	WIN7/R2 RDC 7.0	VISTA SP1 RDC 7.0	VISTA SP1 RDC 6.1	XP SP3 RDC 7.0	XP SP3 RDC 6.1	XP SP2 RDC 6.1	XP SP2 RDC 5.2	DISCUSSED IN
Per-user filtering of RemoteApp programs	Yes	Yes	Yes	Yes	Yes	Yes	na	Chapter 9
Web single sign-on	Yes	Yes	No	Yes	No	No	No	Chapter 9
Web forms-based authentication	Yes	Yes	Yes	Yes	Yes	Yes	No	Chapter 9
RD Gateway-based control of device redirection	Yes	Yes	Yes	Yes	Yes	Yes	No	Chapter 10
RD Gateway system and logon messages	Yes	Yes	No	Yes	No	No	No	Chapter 10
RD Gateway Background Authorization & Authentication	Yes	Yes	No	Yes	No	No	No	Chapter 10
Gateway Idle & Session Timeouts	Yes	Yes	No	Yes	No	No	No	Chapter 10
NAP remediation with RD Gateway	Yes	Yes	No	Yes	No	No	No	Chapter 10

What Role Services Do I Need to Support My Business?

Although Windows Server 2008 R2 has several role services to support the main role of RDS, you don't necessarily need all of them, or you might add them as your needs grow. Some of these might seem obvious, but you might have questions about all of these subjects, so they are worth addressing directly.

- You always need an RDS license server. The RD Session Host server will not continue to accept connections without one, and to be in compliance, you need RDS CALs to use any RDS role.

- You need RD Gateway to support secure access from the Internet via port 443. You do not need RD Gateway to provide secure access within the firewall.

- You need RD Web Access and an Internet Information Services (IIS) server if you intend to display application links in a web browser. RD Web Access will work on both a corporate intranet and on the Internet.

- You don't need RD Connection Broker unless you have more than one server to deliver sessions. It's definitely worth it to have two servers, however. Having an RD Connection Broker allows you to address your servers as a farm rather than as individuals. You will always need RD Connection Broker to support VM delivery.

Summary

After reading this chapter, you should have a good understanding of the internal workings of Windows Server 2008 R2 and how they apply to the RDS roles. You should also have some notion of how to design a test program, how to use the Performance Monitor to estimate the number of users that a server can support, and how to use the Load Simulator. You've covered the client requirements and discussed what server roles you'll need to support different business needs (for example, remote workers).

Best practices for planning a Windows Server 2008 RDS deployment include the following.

- Try to have one disk spindle for each 20 to 30 simultaneous users of the terminal server to avoid I/O bottlenecks.

- Don't install the RD Session Host role service on a VM unless the host supports SLAT. VMs aren't well suited to the disk I/O and memory demands of terminal servers.

- Choose applications wisely. Applications certified for Windows 7 should generally run without problems on an RD Session Host server (aside from any issues relating to resource-intensive applications). A proven track record or official support for execution on an RD Session Host server is ideal.

- Use real-world testing to understand the system and network requirements for the applications and usage profiles you want to support. Estimates based on theory are less useful than experience.

Now that you understand the basic operations of your RD Session Host and RD Virtualization Host servers, the next step is to start setting it up. In Chapter 3, you'll go through the process of setting up your basic RD Session Host environment, and in Chapter 4, you'll do the same for an RD Virtualization Host for a very simple deployment.

Additional Resources

A lot of information is covered in this chapter, and even more background is available. If you'd like more details about Windows internals that are relevant to planning RDS deployments, these resources contain additional information.

- For some tips on capacity planning, see the "Remote Desktop Session Host Capacity Planning in Windows Server 2008 R2" white paper posted at *http://www.microsoft.com/downloads/details.aspx?displaylang=en&FamilyID= ca837962-4128-4680-b1c0-ad0985939063*.

- You've scratched the surface of RDS internals here. For more information about Windows Server internals, see *Microsoft Windows Internals,* 5th ed., by David Solomon and Mark Russinovich, with Alex Ionescu (Microsoft Press, 2009).

- See the CD for a link to the RD Load Simulation and RDS Application Analyzer tools.

- The RDS Team Blog located at *http://blogs.msdn.com/rds*.

- Janique Carbone's article "Second Level Address Translation Benefits in Hyper-V R2" can be found at *http://www.virtualizationadmin.com/articles-tutorials /microsoft-hyper-v-articles/general/second-level-address-translation-benefits-hyper-v-r2.html*.

- To learn what applications others have tested in RD Session Host servers, see *http://www.microsoft.com/rds/compatibility/Default.aspx*.

CHAPTER 3

Deploying a Single Remote Desktop Session Host Server

You don't need a complex deployment to test Remote Desktop (RD) Session Host server capabilities. To begin, it is more important that you understand what the RD Session Host (and the RD Virtualization Host, but that will be covered in Chapter 4, "Deploying a Single Remote Desktop Virtualization Host Server") are doing and how to get them set up properly. Doing this well on a single server will serve you well as you expand and add other roles to your deployment. Therefore, in this chapter, you'll learn about the basics of this role.

- How RD Session Host servers work

- How to install the RD Session Host role service

- Configuring an RD Session Host server for the best user experience

How RD Session Host Servers Work

You probably know *what* an RD Session Host server does: It accepts incoming connections from multiple users and runs unique sessions to support those users as though each person had his or her own computer. What you might not know is *how* it does this. This section discusses the components of the operating system that let these servers do what they do. It covers both the key services directly related to supporting the multi-user remote access architecture and the components that support it for the entire operating system.

Services Supporting RD Session Host

Three services support an RD Session Host server: Remote Desktop Services, Remote Desktop Configuration, and Remote Desktop Services UserMode Port Redirector.

The Remote Desktop Services service enables a computer to accept an interactive logon from another computer. Remote Desktop Configuration enables system configuration that needs to happen in the System Context (meaning that it's highly privileged, even more so than the administrative context). The Remote Desktop Services UserMode Port Redirector enables remote device mapping (used for printers, MP3 players, or client-side drives).

To see the impact of these three services, try stopping them.

If you stop Remote Desktop Services, all remote connections to the computer—including the one you're using (if you stop the service from a remote connection)—will disconnect immediately. That is, any applications open in a remote session will still run on the RD Session Host server, but the remote connection is ended and anyone using that connection will need to log in again to reconnect. If you need to disconnect everyone from the RD Session Host server immediately, stopping this service will make that happen. It will also only disconnect their sessions, not log them off, so their applications will remain open.

If you stop the Remote Desktop Services UserMode Port Redirector, any client-side devices or drives that you have in the remote session will disappear instantly from My Computer in the remote session. Restarting the service will *not* bring the redirected resources back after stopping the service deletes them. If you restart this service, anyone who has client-side devices redirected to their terminal session must disconnect from and reconnect to their session to remap those resources to the remote session. This is because when you stop the service, you're closing down the virtual channels in the Remote Desktop Protocol (RDP) that support device redirection. To bring them back, simply restart the connection.

The Remote Desktop Configuration service is responsible for all Remote Desktop Services and Remote Desktop–related configuration and session maintenance activities that require the SYSTEM context. These include per-session temporary folders, themes, and certificates.

Creating and Supporting a Session

The previous section described the services that support Remote Desktop Services application delivery. The operating system needs to do the following to support the sessions that these services make possible.

- Create the sessions for each person to use.
- Connect the client to the server via a display protocol that allows the two to share data.
- Create a Windows environment for each session.
- Route client input to the correct application on the RD Session Host server and route client output to the appropriate client, including
    - Windows user interface and application screens (from endpoint to client).
    - Mouse clicks and keystrokes (from client to endpoint).
    - Sound (both directions).
    - Redirected devices such as printers and drives.
    - Multimedia display (endpoint to client).
- Package the RDP data for transport over the network protocol [Transmission Control Protocol (TCP/IP), in this case].

Key Processes Loaded at Boot Time

In Windows Server 2008 R2 and Windows 7, key system services run in Session 0, which is not accessible to users. When you boot an RD Session Host server, the operating system loads many new services to support itself. The ones important to its functionality include

- The Session Manager (Smss.exe)
- The Windows Startup Manager (Wininit.exe)
- The Services and Controller Application (Services.exe)
- The Local System Authority (Lsass.exe)
- The Local Session Manager (Lsm.exe)
- The euphoniously named Desktop Window Manager Session Manager (which runs inside an instance of Svchost.exe)
- The Remote Desktop Services service (runs inside an instance of Svchost.exe)

At boot time, the server completes a series of steps to enable RD Session Host functionality.

1. The System process loads the Session Manager.

> **NOTE** The System process is different from other processes (described in Chapter 2, "Key Architectural Concepts for Remote Desktop Services"). It does not host an executable image but exists solely to host operating system threads for the memory manager, cache manager, and other subsystems, as well as device driver threads. See Chapter 2 for more on what these subsystems do.

2. The Session Manager loads another instance of itself.
3. The new Session Manager loads the Windows Startup Manager and then exits.
4. The Windows Startup Manager loads the Services and Controller Application, the Local Security Authority, and the Local Session Manager.
5. The Services and Controller Application loads instances of Svchost.exe for the Desktop Window Manager Session Manager and the Remote Desktop Services service (among others not as relevant here).

To see all this, use Process Monitor. Enable boot logging from the Advanced Boot Options screen as you reboot and restart the RD Session Host server. Restart Process Monitor and then choose Tools, Process Tree to see the boot order. As you can see, the parent instance of the Session Manager keeps running, but after the child instance has completed its tasks, it closes.

You can't find the TermService service (or any other service) in Process Monitor easily to see what it's starting, because many services run within processes called Svchost.exe (to speed logon times, in part) and you can't distinguish them by name. To find out which instance of Svchost.exe a given service is running in and learn more about it using Process Monitor, run Task Manager and click the Services tab. Edit the visible columns to show the Process ID for that service (for this example, TermService) and select Remote Desktop Services from the list. Now you can filter events in Process Monitor to show only that Process ID and easily pick out the correct instance of Svchost.exe in the process tree.

 ON THE COMPANION MEDIA Download Process Monitor from the following link, available on this book's companion media: *http://technet.microsoft.com/en-us /sysinternals/bb896645.aspx.*

Getting the services running in Session 0 sets the stage for the RD Session Host server to begin accepting incoming sessions. The following sections will explain the roles these services play in setting up the user environment for each session.

> **NOTE** To see which processes run in Session 0, run Task Manager. From the Process tab, choose View, Select Columns to open the Select Process Page Columns dialog box. From the list, make sure that the box is selected for Session ID. On the Process tab, you'll now be able to see which processes run in Session 0.

Creating a New Session on the RD Session Host Server

The first stage of creating a session is to connect to the RD Session Host server. In Windows Server 2008 R2, this connection is made through a set of interfaces called the Remote Desktop Protocol Provider. This application programming interface (API) is public, so it can be used not only by RDP but by any protocol to make a connection in a standardized way.

When Windows Server starts, the Remote Desktop Services service starts as well. The service also starts listener objects for RDP or any other protocol that is installed, which in turn listen for client connections. The service and the protocol providers are user-mode objects that communicate by using the APIs discussed in this documentation. The first step for a connection to be made is to start up the listener. When the listener is ready, Remote Desktop Services is ready to begin accepting connections.

The connection process isn't as simple as just turning on the listener. When the listener detects that a client has requested a connection, the listener creates a connection object and passes it to the Remote Desktop Services service to allow this service to configure everything properly. (It also creates a licensing object responsible for making sure the session is licensed.) Setting up the connection takes a number of steps. You'll find out more about the specifics shortly, but broadly, you can identify these steps as follows.

1. Prepare the computer to accept the session and apply the computer settings.
2. Confirm that the user or computer making the connection has a license.
3. Establish a connection, apply the per-user settings, and log the user on.

You might be used to thinking of protocol communication as happening between client and server. Some of the interaction is between the server and clients, but it's mainly the process of the connection object talking to the Remote Desktop Services service to ensure that everything is set up properly for the session.

PREPARING THE COMPUTER TO ACCEPT THE CONNECTION

After the listener detects that a client is attempting to establish a connection, it alerts the Remote Desktop Services service and creates a connection object for the Remote Desktop Services service to configure (shown in Figure 3-1).

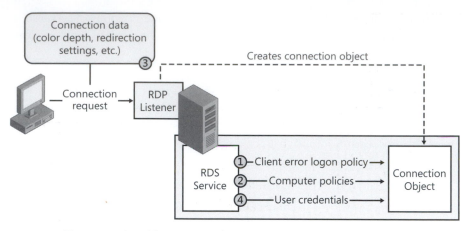

FIGURE 3-1 The connection object prepares the computer to accept a connection.

Here are the steps in this process.

1. The Remote Desktop Services service tells the connection object how it should respond if there are any logon errors.

2. The Remote Desktop Services service tells the connection object about the computer-wide policies that should apply to this session. These policies can contain settings such as the color depth, whether port redirection is enabled, the required encryption level, and the like.

3. Now, the connection gets client connection data from the client. This data includes settings such as whether to hide the title bar, the color depth the client is requesting (which cannot be more than the color depth specified in the connection policies set in Step 2), whether audio redirection should be enabled, and so forth. The client connection policies must fit within the connection policies defined in Step 2: that is, although the client might be more restrictive, it cannot add features that are disabled or restricted in RDS Configuration or Group Policy.

4. Next, the Remote Desktop Services service gives the user credentials to the connection object. (It got them from WinLogon, as described in the section titled "The Role of Services in Creating a New Session" later in this chapter.) Although these credentials are passed in plaintext, they're in plaintext only on the server itself: Even at the lowest level of encryption that RDP supports, data sent from client to server is always encrypted.

CONFIRMING THAT A LICENSE IS AVAILABLE

After the user has been authenticated, the protocol can start working on licensing, as shown in Figure 3-2. It doesn't do this before the user is authenticated so that there's no way for unauthorized users to drain per-device RDS client access licenses (CALs) from the license server and prevent authorized users from getting licenses.

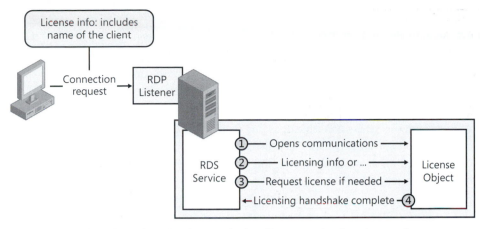

FIGURE 3-2 The Remote Desktop Services service handles connection licensing needs.

Here are the steps in this process.

1. To begin the licensing steps, the Remote Desktop Services service opens communication with the licensing object.

2. The Remote Desktop Services service passes the licensing info from the client to the licensing object, including the name of the client.

3. Next, the protocol requests a license from the client. (If the client can't provide one, the Remote Desktop Services service will request a license.)

4. The Remote Desktop Services service tells the licensing object that the licensing handshake is complete.

LOG THE USER ON AND APPLY PER-USER SETTINGS

When the licensing part of the connection is complete, there are still a few more steps to establish the connection fully, as shown in Figure 3-3.

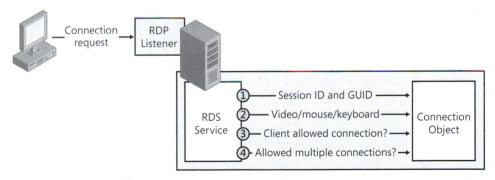

FIGURE 3-3 The remaining steps to establish a connection

Here are the steps in this process.

1. The Remote Desktop Services service tells the connection object the Session ID and its globally unique identifier (GUID) for the new session.

2. Set up the video and mouse/keyboard connections for base connectivity between the client and the session. At this point, the session is initialized. The user is not connected to the session at this point; the session is just prepared for the connection.

3. At this point, the RD Session Host does one final check: Given the user's name and domain (and their security token) and the session ID to which they're attempting to connect, are they allowed to log onto this session? If so, the connection continues; if not, the connection ends.

4. Is the user allowed to have more than one session? If so, what are the session IDs for the sessions that they have available?

At this point, the user logs on and the Group Policy settings corresponding to the user (recall that the computer policies were applied earlier) are applied to the session.

Those are the steps to set up a functioning connection. Let's look a little more at how the services on the RD Session Host support this process.

The Role of Services in Creating a New Session

Windows Server 2008 R2 always runs at least one session for services (Session 0), and additional sessions that users or administrators can interact with. The Session Manager (Smss.exe) for the RD Session Host server is the element of Windows that gets the process started. A new instance of the Session Manager is created. It starts all the processes required to support the session.

When someone attempts to log on to the system, the initial instance of Smss.exe creates another instance (which is of itself—that is, it starts an additional instance of Smss.exe) to configure the new session, just as it did for Session 0. On RD Session Host servers running Windows Server 2008, multiple instances of Smss.exe can run concurrently, enabling faster logons for multiple users (see Figure 3-4). The number of parallel sessions that Session Manager can create at a time depends on the number of virtual processors in the RD Session Host server. For example, a server with four quad-core processors is able to create up to 16 new sessions simultaneously.

> **NOTE** If you're using Network Level Authentication (NLA) for pre-authentication, the logon process works a little differently. NLA and securing RDP connections are covered in Chapter 8, "Securing Remote Desktop Protocol Connections."

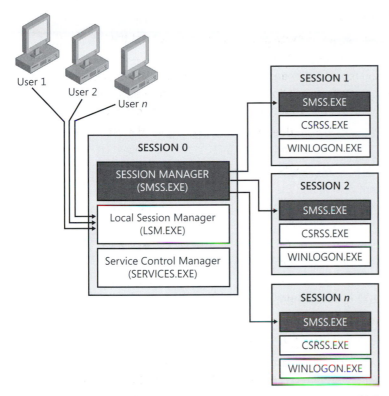

FIGURE 3-4 The Session Manager in Windows Server 2008 R2 can start multiple sessions at once by loading multiple copies of itself.

When the child instance of the Session Manager starts, it starts the Windows subsystem (Csrss.exe and Winlogon.exe) and then exits.

When Smss.exe enables new sessions, it does so with the help of several other services. The Local Session Manager accepts the incoming connections and helps determine whether a computer can connect to the server. The Remote Desktop Services service allows a server to interact with incoming connections. All these services are managed by the Service Control Manager. To recap, see Table 3-1.

TABLE 3-1 Key System Processes for Initiating a Session on an RD Session Host Server

FUNCTION	SUPPORTING COMPONENT	FILE NAME
Create, destroy, enumerate, and manipulate sessions. Prior to Windows Server 2008, it was incorporated into the Terminal Services service. It is now an independent process.	Local Session Manager	Lsm.exe

Continued on the next page

FUNCTION	SUPPORTING COMPONENT	FILE NAME
Check credentials collected by the credential provider and create a token identifying the user.	Local Security Authority	Lsass.exe
Start, stop, restart, and pause Windows services.	Service Control Manager	Services.exe
Create new sessions.	Session Manager	Smss.exe
Enable multiple sessions on a server and provide the run-time interfaces for communication between client session and the operating system. Also known as the Remote Connection Manager.	RDS	Termsrv.dll

Want to learn more about what happens within that new session? Read on . . .

Enabling User Logons to the New Session

Having a session isn't enough. To work, you need a way to log on to it. In addition to starting the Service Control Manager and the Local Session Manager on the terminal server, the Session Manager builds the Windows logon infrastructure in each session, including

- The Client-Server RunTime Subsystem (CSRSS), also known as the Windows subsystem

- The Windows logon process (Winlogon.exe), which starts UserInit and the Logon User Interface Host (Logonui.exe), which in turn starts the credential provider that accepts the user's logon data

> **NOTE** In versions of Windows prior to Windows Vista, Winlogon.exe started the Graphical Identification and Authentication (GINA) dynamic-link library (DLL) specified in the registry. Windows Vista and Windows Server 2008 (as well as Windows Server 2008 R2 and Windows 7) replaced the GINA with a credential provider, identified (if not the default) in HKLM\SOFTWARE\Microsoft\Windows\CurrentVersion\Authentication\Credential Providers. It has a different name, but plays the same basic role for storing credentials. (It doesn't do some other things that a custom GINA could do, however.)

In short, the logon process works by performing the following steps.

1. The Windows subsystem starts the Windows logon process.

2. The Local Session Manager determines whether the incoming connection is allowed at all.

3. The Windows logon process presents the interface to the credential provider so a user can provide credentials such as user name and password, or smart card and personal identification number (PIN).

4. The credential provider passes the credentials to the Local System Authority, which checks them against the security database, which is Active Directory Domain Services (AD DS) for a domain account or the local computer's security account manager for a local account.

Figure 3-5 illustrates how these components work together to allow you to log onto the RD Session Host server.

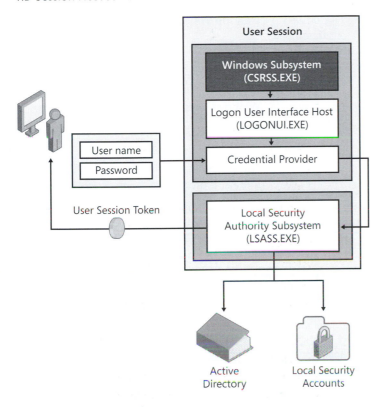

FIGURE 3-5 The Windows logon process

Creating the Base Environment in Each Session

Finally, the Windows user environment needs a shell—a user environment—even if the session will display only RemoteApp programs, not a full desktop. When displaying the full desktop, the usual Windows shell is Explorer (Explorer.exe). If displaying RemoteApp programs only, it's the RDP shell (RDPShell.exe)

When the session begins, the Remote Desktop Services service and Desktop Window Manager running in Session 0 each begin a per-session piece of themselves. The Remote Desktop Services service starts Rdpclip.exe, which supports the shared Clipboard between the session and any locally running applications. The Desktop Window Manager Session Manager starts Dwm.exe, which manages the appearance of windows in the remote session.

Table 3-2 shows the user-mode processes that create the common user environment (minus the applications that you'd also expect to see running). You won't actually see all these from Task Manager.

TABLE 3-2 User-Mode Processes That Support Each Session's Windows Environment

FUNCTION	SUPPORTING COMPONENT	FILE NAME
Create graphical effects used in Aero Glass (for example, Flip and transparent thumbnail views of minimized applications) in video memory, then sends them to the screen when composed.	Desktop Window Manager	Dwm.exe
Display the Windows Shell for desktops.	Windows Explorer	Explorer.exe
Enable clipboard redirection between the session and the client.	Clipboard redirection tool	Rdpclip.exe
Display RemoteApp programs.	The Windows shell for RemoteApp programs	RDPShell.exe
Supply information to management interfaces on the RD Session Host server.	Windows Remote Desktop Services API	Wtsapi.dll

Remote sessions aren't interesting without interaction, however. That's where the last step of passing data between client and server comes in.

Passing Data Between Client and Server

An RD Session Host server doesn't have one session—it has dozens or even hundreds of sessions. An RD Session Host client doesn't necessarily display a single application running from the server farm; it has four or five or perhaps even more . . . and not all of those four or five applications are necessarily running on the same server. How does the data passing between client and server get to the right place? The answer has three parts.

- The session structure
- The use of Session IDs and Process IDs to identify internally *which* instance of an application the system is referring to among the multiple instances running concurrently on the RD Session Host server
- Cooperation between components on the RD Session Host server (that is, common to all sessions) and in the client session (exclusive to one session)

SESSION STRUCTURE

One connection to an RD Session Host server is normally equivalent to one session. In other words, there's never any question on the client as to which session some input should go to, because each session's communication with the RD Session Host server will be handled separately from within the session. Even RemoteApp programs will all run within the same session as long as they're on the same server. The only time you'd have more than one session on the same server is if you deliberately connected to a second desktop and the RD Session Host server was configured to permit more than one session on the same server.

Session isolation has evolved over the years. As you can see from Figure 3-6, the operating system can be session-aware in various areas. At the kernel level, the memory manager (for example) must be session-aware so it can map data to the right set of user-mode addresses (as discussed in Chapter 2). New kernel-mode awareness of sessions was introduced in Windows Server 2008 R2 with Dynamic Fair Share Scheduler (DFSS), which allocates processor time evenly among sessions (DFSS is part of the Process Scheduler component in Figure 3-6).

At the service level, all services run in Session 0 and are session-aware to the extent that they are not mapped to any single user identity. In Windows Server 2008 and later, even system administrators don't interact with Session 0 anymore.

At the session level, there's a separate instance of the Windows subsystem, Windows Logon, Win32k.sys (to prevent one session from being able to manipulate windows in another session), and now in Windows Server 2008 R2, even Internet Protocol (IP) virtualization for WinSock applications (any application written to use the Windows Socket API for communicating with TCP/IP).

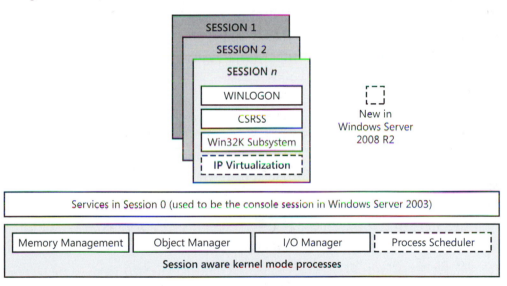

FIGURE 3-6 There is even more session isolation in Windows 2008 R2.

IDENTIFYING PROCESSES

If you're in a single session, how do you get the right data to the right instance of an application and send the feedback to the correct session? One way is that each session has a unique identifier on the RD Session Host server (the Session ID that you can see in the Remote

Desktop Services Manager discussed in Chapter 11, "Managing Remote Desktop Sessions"). Activity within a session is identified to the RD Session Host server by its Session ID, not by the name of the person logged on to the session. Therefore, even if one person has more than one session open on the same server, the server won't confuse the sessions.

The RD Session Host server also avoids confusion through the way the operating system identifies processes. Windows Server 2008 R2 identifies processes running on an RD Session Host server not only by their names but by their Process IDs. (This is true on any Windows operating system, but on an RD Session Host server, it's even more important because of the likelihood that many processes will be duplicated.) A Process ID is also unique on an RD Session Host server. Process IDs are covered in more detail in Chapter 11, as part of the discussion about managing user sessions and processes.

COMMUNICATING BETWEEN SESSION AND RD SESSION HOST SERVER

The following portions of the RD Session Host server are responsible for making sure the right data ends up with the right session after the ownership of Process IDs and Session IDs is sorted out.

- Rdpwsx.dll is the path between RDP and the kernel. It contains
  - Generic Conference Control (GCC) to manage virtual channels, which transport specific types of data between the remote session and the client
  - The Multipoint Communication Service (MCS), which assigns data to virtual channels and sets the priority of each so that GCC can work with all the virtual channels as a single pipe
- The RDP stack has three jobs.
  - Rdpwd.sys transforms display data into RDP commands to be transmitted to the session.
  - Wdtshare.sys encrypts and packages the RDP stream.
  - Tdtcp.sys packages RDP for transport on TCP/IP so that the data can be passed between server and client.

The drivers and libraries supporting data-passing between the RD Session Host server and each client session are listed in Table 3-3.

TABLE 3-3 Key Drivers and Services Sessions for the Entire RD Session Host Server

FUNCTION	SUPPORTING COMPONENT	FILE NAME
Manage the virtual channels, allowing the creation and deletion of session connections and controlling resources provided by MCSMUX.	GCC	Rdpwsx.dll
Accept keyboard input from the sessions.	Keyboard driver for Remote Desktop Services	Kbclass.sys

FUNCTION	SUPPORTING COMPONENT	FILE NAME
Assign data to virtual channels within RDP, set priority levels, and segment data as required. This abstracts the multiple RDP stacks into a single entity.	MCS	Rdpwsx.dll
Accept mouse input from the sessions.	Mouse driver for RDS	Mouclass.sys
Encode display data into RDP commands.	RDP WinStation driver	Rdpwd.sys
Communicate with kernel via I/O Control Interface; contains GCC and MCSMUX.	Interface between display protocol and kernel	Rdpwsx.dll
Package RDP onto TCP/IP.	TCP driver	Tdtcp.sys
Coordinate and manage RDP protocol activity.	RDS device driver	Termdd.sys
Handle user interface (UI) transfer, compression, encryption, and framing.		Wdtshare.sys
Manage device redirection and audio.	RDP device redirection driver	Rdpdr.sys

The client also has some work to do to pass data between the session and the RD Session Host server for processing (see Table 3-4). Win32k.sys is the kernel-mode component of the Windows subsystem that manages mouse and keyboard input and sends it to the right application. Rdpdd.sys is the display driver that packages Windows neatly to be processed by the Remote Desktop Services Device Driver.

TABLE 3-4 Key Services and Drivers Running Within Sessions on the RD Session Host

FUNCTION	SUPPORTING COMPONENT	FILE NAME
Manage the Windows graphical user interface (GUI) environment by taking the mouse and keyboard inputs and sending them to the appropriate application.	Kernel-mode component of the Windows subsystem	Win32k.sys
Capture the Windows user interface and translates it into a form that is readily converted by Rdpwd.sys into the RDP protocol.	RDP display driver	Rdpdd.dll

The communication between each session and client logged into it uses virtual channels. Each kind of data has its own virtual channel so that data transfer can be enabled or disabled selectively. For instance, it's possible to disable clipboard redirection while still allowing other types of data to pass between client and server.

Virtual channels can be static or dynamic. Static virtual channels are created at the beginning of a session and remain until that session is disconnected or terminated. You can't create new static channels during a session. Dynamic virtual channels are created and torn down on demand, such as when a new device is connected to a terminal session. For more information about virtual channels, see Chapter 6.

DIRECT FROM THE SOURCE

Why Do You Need a Separate Instance of Win32k.sys for Each Session?

Sriram Sampath
Senior Development Lead, Remote Desktop Virtualization

The Window management and Graphics Subsystem in Windows primarily reside in a key kernel driver called Win32k.sys. It primarily consists of two subcomponents: the Window Manager (NTUSER) and the Graphics Subsystem (GDI).

In the RD Session Host architecture, there is one instance of this subsystem (Win32k.sys) for each session. The primary motivation behind this is security boundary and strong isolation between sessions. To elaborate, the window station/desktop boundary is considered to be the security isolation boundary for user sessions; it is not possible to send window messages, for example, from one session to another. This creates a very strong isolation environment. Having one instance of Win32k.sys in each session aids us with this.

The Win32k.sys driver is also responsible for loading and managing the display driver associated with each session; this allows different display drivers to be loaded in different sessions. As an example, the NVIDIA driver can be loaded in the physical console session and the RD Session Host server display driver, RDPDD, can be loaded in a different session.

Some other subsystems of the operating system that are session-aware in this manner are

- **Winlogon process**   One for each session
- **Csrss process**   One for each session
- **Object manager**   Some parts of the object, like BaseNamedObjects, are sessionized
- **I/O manager**   One instance for the operating system, but session-aware
- **Plug and Play manager**   One instance for the operating system, but session-aware

Putting It All Together

When you combine the key pieces of a working RD Session Host server environment that both support a session and allow it to communicate with the RD Session Host server, it looks like the overview shown in Figure 3-7.

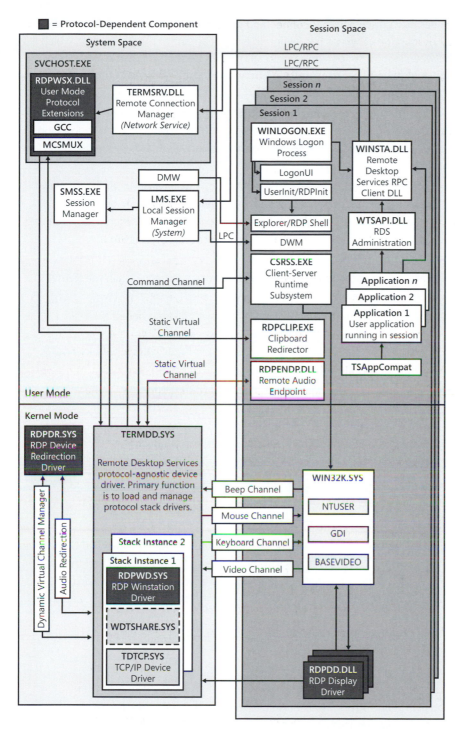

FIGURE 3-7 These are the components of Remote Desktop Services architecture in Windows Server 2008 R2

This model has been discussed in the preceding pages, but there's a lot of data here. First, here is a quick description of what's happening in each quadrant of this illustration, which is broken out between system space (common to all sessions on the RD Session Host server) and session space (unique to each session), and between kernel mode and user mode.

In the upper-left quadrant (System Space, User Mode), the RD Session Host server is starting sessions, accepting incoming connections, and organizing virtual channels. In the upper-right quadrant (Session Space, User Mode), the session runs the following: its Windows logon processes, the Windows subsystem (CSRSS.exe) for presenting all aspects of the user interface, its shell, and its applications.

In the lower-left quadrant (System Space, Kernel Mode), the server is loading and managing the protocol-specific functionality of the session. That is, RDP is only one possible protocol that you can use to interact with a RD Session Host server. ICA, used for connecting to servers with Citrix's XenApp extensions to RD Session Host installed, is another.

In the lower-right quadrant (Session Space, Kernel Mode), the session packages the display data and input data to be processed by the display protocol when working in the Kernel Mode section of System Space.

Installing an RD Session Host Server

Now that you're acquainted with the inner workings of an RD Session Host server, it's time to become familiar with the outer workings of installing and configuring it.

> **NOTE** There is a lot of time spent installing roles during the course of this book, and you might notice some steps are skipped to avoid unnecessary repetition, but it's worth going into detail once so you understand the processes involved.

Installing an RD Session Host Server Using the Administrative Tools Interface

To install the RD Session Host role service, click Start, Administrative Tools, and then Server Manager. Right-click Roles, choose Add Roles to open the Add Roles Wizard, and then click Next to move past the opening page. When you get to the next page of the wizard, you'll see a list of available roles, as shown in Figure 3-8. Select the box next to Remote Desktop Services and click Next.

When you choose to install Remote Desktop Services, the next page of the wizard offers you an overview of the service. Click Next.

> **NOTE** Do not install the RD Session Host role on a server that already has the Active Directory Domain Services role installed. First, it's not good security practice to allow users to connect to a domain controller. Second, should some problem with a user or application require you to bring down the RD Session Host server for maintenance, you'll have a domain controller offline.

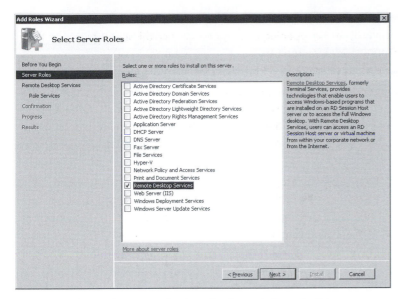

FIGURE 3-8 Choose the Remote Desktop Services role from the list.

Now, you can see why the Add Roles Wizard offered only Remote Desktop Services on the Select Server Roles page; from here (see Figure 3-9), you can choose any of the related role services. For now, stick with adding RD Session Host and click Next.

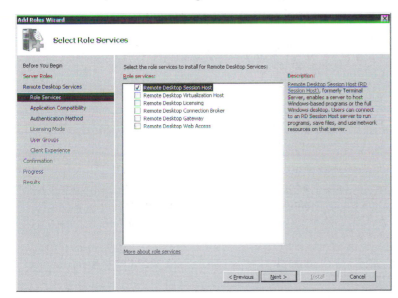

FIGURE 3-9 Choose Remote Desktop Session Host from the list of RDS role services.

Next, you'll see the Application Compatibility page telling you that if you installed applications on the server prior to installing RDS, some of the existing applications might not work in a multiple user environment. (You'll learn more about the reasons for this later in this chapter.) Click Next.

Until now, most questions have been fairly self-explanatory. As shown in Figure 3-10, however, you need to make a decision about whether you want computers logging into the RD Session Host server to support NLA.

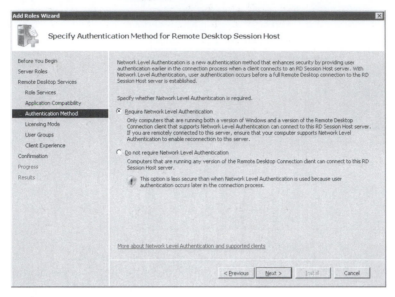

FIGURE 3-10 Choose NLA to protect the server from failed logon attacks or do not require it to support broader access to the RD Session Host server.

NLA requires users to be authenticated before they make a full connection to the RD Session Host server, thus protecting the server from denial-of-service (DoS) attacks using failed logon attempts to use up all the server's processor time.

NLA is supported only for RDC 6.x and later, but more importantly, it employs the Credential Security Provider (CredSSP) to authenticate the user early in the process. You'll find out more about the details in Chapter 8, but for now, you need to know three things.

- Requiring NLA enables you to force users to authenticate themselves before they can create a connection to the RD Session Host server.
- If you require NLA, only clients supporting CredSSP (at least those running Windows 7, Windows Vista SP1 or later, or Windows XP SP3) will be able to connect to the RD Session Host server.
- NLA is not available with Windows Vista RTM or Windows XP SP2; it requires the service pack updates that add support for CredSSP. NLA is not a service of RDP.

> **NOTE** The decision to require NLA isn't final; as with many configuration settings, you can change your mind later by reconfiguring the host.

Next, you can choose the license mode of the RD Session Host server (see Figure 3-11). An RD Session Host server can be in per-user or per-device mode—that is, it can accept either per-user licenses or per-device licenses—but not both at the same time. The incoming connection must present the kind of license that the server is expecting, if the machine or user making the connection already has one. It also means that if the incoming connection *doesn't* present a Remote Desktop Services client access license (RDS CAL) at connection time, and the RD Session Host server has to request one from the license server, then the licenses on the license server must be a type the RD Session Host server is able to accept. This is discussed in more depth in Chapter 12, "Licensing Remote Desktop Services."

> **NOTE** In Windows Server 2003, you had to choose the license mode when installing a terminal server. In Windows Server 2008 and later, you can delay this decision until you are certain what types of licenses will be available. An RD Session Host server in Configure Later mode will not ask incoming connections for a license, but an RD Session Host server can be in this mode only during its grace period (120 days). After that, it will not accept connections without a license server and a licensing mode.

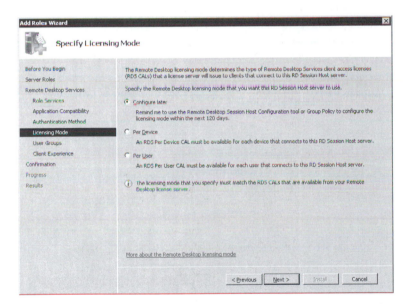

FIGURE 3-11 Choose the appropriate license mode or delay the decision until you have more information.

Why Configure Later?

So, why should people use the Configure Later option? Why not just require people to choose a license mode when they install the server? After all, they can change this mode later using the Remote Desktop Session Host Configuration tool. The reason is simple: That's the way it worked in Windows Server 2003 and it caused some problems.

Before Windows Server 2003, there was only one license mode for terminal servers: per-device. This model was enforced, meaning that a terminal server set up to accept per-device Terminal Services client access licenses (TS CALs) would eventually stop accepting connections from computers unable to present one. This model was also the default mode for terminal servers running Windows Server 2003, but Windows Server 2003 introduced a new license mode for terminal servers: per-user.

The trouble started when people installed the terminal servers without really looking at the license mode option, since this had not mattered before Windows Server 2003. They installed the terminal servers in per-device mode, because that was the default, but often got per-user licenses, because that model fit their needs better. Because the terminal servers weren't set up to use or issue per-user TS CALs, the terminal servers stopped accepting connections. Although the Event Log recorded the problem and (with Service Pack 1 for Windows Server 2003) pop-up windows warned administrators when they logged in, this didn't entirely fix the problem.

Because RD Session Host servers must now be in one mode or the other, part of the solution in Windows Server 2008 and later is a Configure Later option. The RD Session Host licensing mode will eventually need to be configured, but at least the administrator is making a conscious choice when configuring it.

Next, you'll choose who has access to the RD Session Host. Server access is partially determined by user membership in the Remote Desktop Users group (see Figure 3-12). Only members of this group can connect to the RD Session Host server.

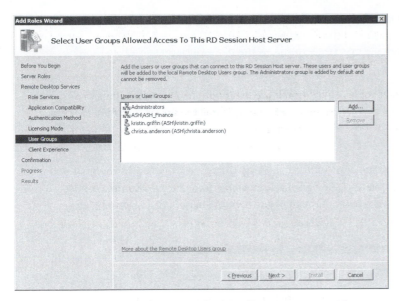

FIGURE 3-12 Add groups to the Remote Desktop Users group to enable user connections.

By default, the local Administrator's group is added already. To add more people to the Remote Desktop Users group, click Add to open the Select Users dialog box. Enter the security group or users to add, click Check Names to validate the name of the accounts, and then click OK. For example, you might add the Domain Users group to the Remote Desktop Users group. (You can do this because Domain Users is a global group and Remote Desktop Users is a local group; global groups can be members of local groups.) Then, you can deny access to groups or users selectively.

Why would you limit who is allowed to use the server? Three reasons, as follows.

- You have a limited number of RDS CALs available, and you don't want to give them to users who don't really need them.

- You have a limited number of application user licenses available for applications on the RD Session Host server, and you don't want to use them unnecessarily.

- You sized the server for a certain number of users, and you want to limit the number allowed to log on to your size limit.

NOTE You can deny even members of the Remote Desktop Users group the right to log on by editing their user account properties in Active Directory Users And Computers, or through Group Policy. They just can't log on if they're not members of the Remote Desktop Users group.

Another option to limit user access is to create a security group called, for example, Company RDS Users. Add only users that need access to the RD Session Host server to this group, and then add the Company RDS Users group to the Remote Desktop Users group.

> **NOTE** If you're not sure of the name of the group or user accounts you want to add, click Advanced, choose the proper domain or computer, and click Find Now to populate the Search Results area. Then you can select the users or groups to add.

After you have added the appropriate users and groups, click Next. On the next page (shown in Figure 3-13), you have a few options available to make the user experience on the RD Session Host include some functionalities users would experience using Windows 7. This screen is new to Windows Server 2008 R2.

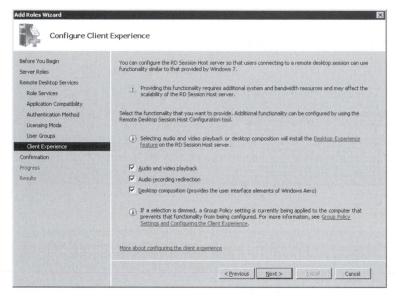

FIGURE 3-13 Options are available to enhance the user experience on the RD Session Host server.

The options available are as follows.

- **Audio And Video playback** Users can listen to audio and view video in their remote desktop session.
- **Audio Recording Redirection** Users can record audio and have this recording redirected to their remote desktop session.
- **Desktop Composition** Enables visual effects including Windows Flip, three-dimensional (3-D) window transition, and glass window frames. This is needed to enable Aero Glass remoting in Remote Desktop sessions.

One thing to consider when enabling these options is the potential impact on the bandwidth provided for the session connections. A user playing back audio and video files will take up more bandwidth than a user editing spreadsheets. How much more depends on how the users work, so if you are enabling these features, it's a good idea to make sure your RD Session Host server load testing includes representative data of these activities. (See Chapter 2 for more information on load testing.)

The last stage is confirming the settings that you specified during the wizard, as shown in Figure 3-14.

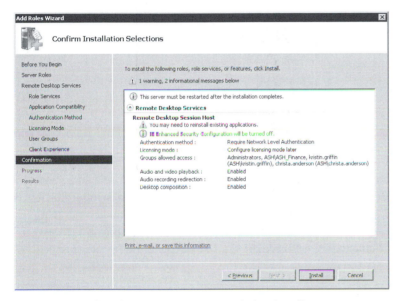

FIGURE 3-14 Confirm the settings in your setup before installing.

To save the configuration at setup, click the Print, E-mail, Or Save This Information link to create and open a simple Hypertext Markup Language (HTML) page that you can then print, email, or save as part of your RD Session Host server configuration documentation. You should seriously consider doing this so you can make a record of the basic installation, particularly if you selected a licensing mode. This information documents the way that the RD Session Host server is set up and will be a guide to the person setting up the second server—or the 20th—who does not want to inspect the server configuration manually to make sure it's consistent across the load-balanced farm.

After you click Install, the server will take some time installing the service. When it's finished, you'll be prompted to restart the server and get a second chance at printing or saving the configuration report. When you click Close, you will be prompted to restart the server.

After rebooting, as you start up again, the RD Session Host server will spend a few minutes processing and making final recommendations, as shown in Figure 3-15.

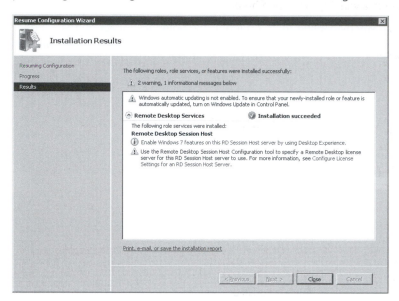

FIGURE 3-15 Complete the installation after rebooting.

You might have already installed Desktop Experience if you chose to enable audio and video playback and/or Desktop Composition features. Desktop Experience is important. As you'll learn in Chapter 6, it's required to enable the Plug and Play framework for automatically detecting client-side plug-and-play devices such as cameras. If you don't install Desktop Experience, you won't be able to redirect these devices seamlessly to the remote connection. You'll also need it for audio and multimedia redirection.

Installing an RD Session Host Server from the Command Line

In Windows Server 2008, you could do a very basic installation from the command line with Servermanager.exe. This executable has been deprecated in Windows Server 2008 R2 and replaced by Windows PowerShell cmdlets.

> **NOTE** To install Windows roles, role services, and features via Windows PowerShell, you must run Windows PowerShell with elevated privileges.

To run server manager cmdlets in Windows PowerShell, first import the Servermanager module like this.

```
Import-Module servermanager
```

To see which commands are available for this module, assign the action of getting the Servermanager module to a variable, as shown here.

```
$sm = Get-Module servermanager
```

Then reference the variable like this.

```
$sm
ModuleType Name                        ExportedCommands
---------- ----                        ----------------
Manifest   servermanager               {Remove-WindowsFeature, Get-WindowsFeat...
```

You can see from the resulting text that there are multiple ExportedCommands available with this module, but they are all not listed here (some are hidden by the ellipsis). To see clearly all the commands offered by this module, type the following command.

```
$sm.exportedcommands
```

```
Name                            Value
----                            -----
Remove-WindowsFeature           Remove-WindowsFeature
Get-WindowsFeature              Get-WindowsFeature
Add-WindowsFeature              Add-WindowsFeature
```

You want to add the RD Session Host server role service, so type **Add-WindowsFeature** to get a long list of all the features you could install on this server. The Remote Desktop Services role services that you can install are shown here.

```
[X] Remote Desktop Services                          Remote-Desktop-Services
    [X] Remote Desktop Session Host                  RDS-RD-Server
    [ ] Remote Desktop Virtualization Host           RDS-Virtualization
    [ ] Remote Desktop Licensing                     RDS-Licensing
    [ ] Remote Desktop Connection Broker             RDS-Connection-Broker
    [ ] Remote Desktop Gateway                       RDS-Gateway
    [ ] Remote Desktop Web Access                    RDS-Web-Access
```

From the resulting list, you now know both the display name (Remote Desktop Session Host) and its corresponding "name" (RDS-RD-Server). Install the Remote Desktop Session Host role by referencing the server role name like this.

```
Add-WindowsFeature RDS-RD-Server
```

A successful install returns the following.

```
WARNING: [Installation] Succeeded: [Remote Desktop Services] Remote Desktop
Session Host. You must restart this server to finish the installation process.

Success Restart Needed Exit Code Feature Result
------- -------------- --------- --------------
True    Yes                      Succes... {Remote Desktop Session Host}
```

Reboot the server to finish the installation process, as instructed. To reboot from Windows PowerShell, type

Shutdown /r

Installing RD Session Host via Windows PowerShell doesn't give you the option of configuring any options. When you install this way, the RD Session Host server will be set up with all the default settings. The Remote Desktop Users group will be empty. In addition, the server will not prompt you for NLA options or the enhanced user experience options (enabling desktop composition, and so on).

> **NOTE** If you have installed and removed this role service in the past, take care to double-check your settings, because some settings (NLA, users added to the Remote Desktop Users group, and so on) will retain the information from the previous install, and if Desktop Experience was installed before, it is likely be installed now unless you specifically removed it.

To remove the role service, type the following command and then reboot the server as specified by the resulting instructions.

```
remove-windowsfeature RDS-RD-Server
WARNING: [Removal] Succeeded: [Remote Desktop Services] Remote Desktop Session
Host. You must restart this server to finish the removal process.

Success Restart Needed Exit Code Feature Result
------- -------------- --------- --------------
True    Yes                      Succes... {Remote Desktop Session Host}
```

Essential RD Session Host Configuration

After installing the service, you have some basic configuration to set up before anyone uses the RD Session Host server. This isn't the only essential configuration you'll be doing—much of this book is concerned with that—but this is what you should do before people start using the server.

Allocating Processor Time

One of the nightmare scenarios for a shared computer is that of the user who is such a heavy user of RAM and processor time that he or she affects even light users. This is sometimes a reason for organizing users based on how much they will stress a server, and sometimes a reason for not putting heavy users onto the shared server at all.

Isolating users on their own computers isn't always ideal (or even possible), and what do you do if people's use patterns change over time? A better answer is to do what you can to even out resource usage automatically.

In Windows Server 2008, to make sure that processor time would be fairly allocated among sessions, you'd configure the Windows System Resource Manager (WSRM). This tool evens out processor time by monitoring processes and lowering their priority if they start affecting the performance of the processes running in other sessions. When a process receives more processor time than others, WSRM lowers its priority for a while so that it waits for threads in other processes to execute. (It's similar to the way in which a process that isn't getting enough time can have its priority temporarily boosted to get its threads through some processor cycles.) WSRM is reactive; for it to get involved, a process must take too many processor cycles.

> **NOTE** A bug in Windows Server 2008 made WSRM very resource-intensive. If you had this problem on Windows Server 2008, see *http://support.microsoft.com/kb/970067* for a solution. This issue was fixed in Windows Server 2008 R2.

The catch with WSRM is that it *is* reactive. Not only that, but it's not enabled by default. In other words, you have to configure it properly, and even if you do, there has to be a problem before WSRM can respond (the delay wouldn't normally be more than a few seconds, but it's worth mentioning). In Windows Server 2008 R2, Windows Server added DFSS, a new feature that operates in the kernel and makes sure that each session is using no more than its fair share of processor time. That is, if a server has five sessions running, then each session should get no more than 20 percent of processor time, but a session does not have to use that much. This feature is enabled by default. You can disable this feature by setting the value of the following registry entry to 0, as follows.

```
HKEY_LOCAL_MACHINE\SOFTWARE\Policies\Microsoft\Windows\SessionManager\DFSS\EnableDFSS
```

If allocating processor time evenly across all sessions works for you, then you're done. If you're interested in weighting sessions—perhaps to let the people facing a tight deadline crunch numbers in their spreadsheets faster—then you can set up weighted sessions using WSRM, as described in the following sections.

CAUTION WSRM has a memory management feature that can limit the size of a process's working set or committed memory. Do not use this feature on an RD Session Host server. First, it is not session-aware; it just limits the memory available to a particular process regardless of where it's running. Second, starving a process of memory will make it run more slowly, which is very frustrating in an interactive application (less so for an application running in the background). If a process is taking up too much memory, then add more memory to the RD Session Host server or (as a last resort) remove the application in question from the farm.

Installing WSRM

To install WSRM, start Server Manager. Right-click Features and click Add Features to start the Add Features Wizard. Scroll down the list to select Windows Server Resource Manager. When you select it, you might be prompted to install an additional component. WSRM requires that you have a database to store historical data, so if the Windows Internal Database isn't already installed (and it could be; it's also used by several other features), you'll be prompted to add that feature. Go ahead and install it if prompted to do so by clicking Add Required Features.

When you click Next, you'll see a confirmation page showing the features that you will install. Click Install to perform the installation.

When the installation is finished, Server Manager will show you that the two features are fully installed. Close the dialog box; you don't need to reboot.

To install WSRM from Windows PowerShell, use the following code to import the module and then start the service.

```
Import-Module servermanager
add-WindowsFeature WSRM
Success Restart Needed Exit Code Feature Result
------- -------------- --------- --------------
True    No             Success   {Windows Internal Database, Windows System...
```

Configuring WSRM for Weighted Remote Sessions

As discussed earlier, it might make sense to give some sessions more processor time than others. DFSS doesn't allow this, but WSRM does. To configure WSRM for this purpose, click Start, Administrative Tools, and Windows System Resource Manager to open the Windows System Resource Manager snap-in shown in Figure 3-16. You'll first be prompted to choose the computer that you want to manage; for now, choose the local server. (You do not need to disable DFSS for this to work.)

CAUTION If you have not already configured Weighted Remote Sessions as the managing policy, then first make sure that no one is logged into the RD Session Host server that you're configuring and then put it into drain mode from RD Session Host Configuration. Changing the managing policy requires a reboot.

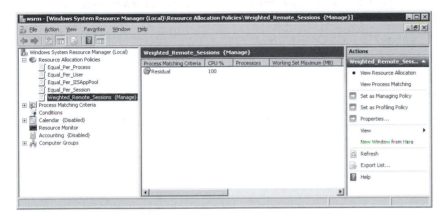

FIGURE 3-16 The WSRM management console

Right-click the Weighted_Remote_Sessions policy and choose Properties from the menu to open the dialog box in Figure 3-17. This dialog box shows all the groups for which you've configured this policy, so it should be empty.

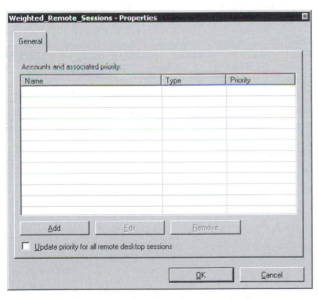

FIGURE 3-17 Add groups to Weighted Remote Sessions.

To add a group, click Add to open the dialog box in Figure 3-18. The Priority options in the drop-down list are Premium, Standard, and Basic. They're in descending order of their priority for getting processor time.

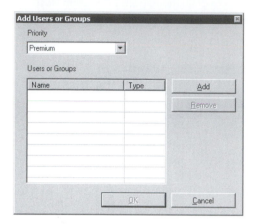

FIGURE 3-18 Add new users or groups to the list.

Click Add to add a new user or group to the list. This will open the dialog box shown in Figure 3-19. This is the standard dialog box for picking users or groups; use it as you normally would for choosing user groups.

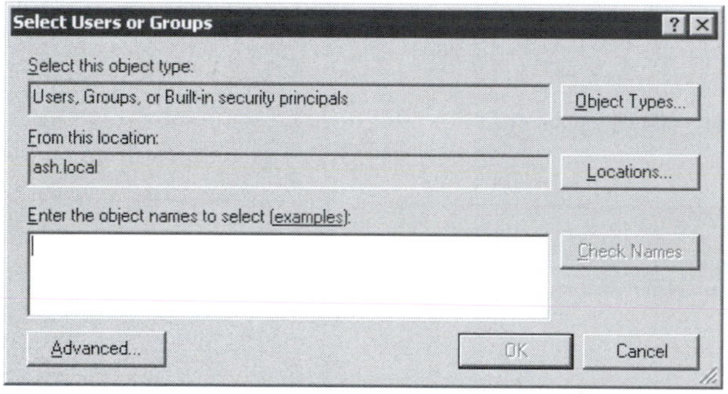

FIGURE 3-19 Set the WSRM properties.

When you've chosen the right users, they'll appear in the Add Users Or Groups dialog box, shown in Figure 3-20. Choose the right priority and click OK. To add more users, click Add.

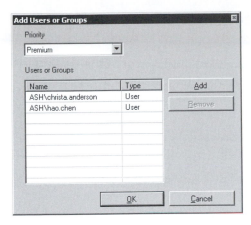

FIGURE 3-20 Set user or group priority.

When you click OK, all the users you've configured so far will be in the Weighted Remote Sessions Properties dialog box, as shown in Figure 3-21. As you can see, the priority of each is listed here. If you need to change a priority, click Edit to return to the Add Users Or Groups dialog box and change the priority as needed. Click OK when you're done.

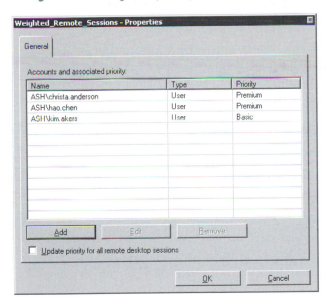

FIGURE 3-21 Configured user accounts are listed.

To finish, click Set As Managing Policy in the right pane to change the default policy to Weighted_Remote_Sessions; doing this makes it possible to give some groups or users more weight. This will require a reboot to start working. (You can also take this step before config-uring the policy, but one way or another, you'll need to reboot the server after changing the default policy in WSRM.)

Enabling Plug and Play Redirection with the Desktop Experience

To enable Plug and Play redirection on the RD Session Host server, install Desktop Experience. This feature requires no configuration and little setup. To install it, simply open the Server Manager and migrate to the list of features. Click the link to add a new feature and then walk through the wizard to select and install Desktop Experience.

You can also enable this feature from Windows PowerShell in Windows Server 2008 R2, using the following code.

```
PS C:\Users\admin> add-WindowsFeature Desktop-Experience
Success Restart Needed Exit Code Feature Result
------- -------------- --------- --------------
True    No             NoChan... {}
```

You will not need to reboot the RD Session Host server after installing or uninstalling Desktop Experience.

Adjusting Server Settings with Remote Desktop Configuration

After you have Desktop Experience set up, the next step to the basic RD Session Host server installation is reviewing the configuration settings in the Remote Desktop Session Host Configuration MMC snap-in shown in Figure 3-22. This tool manages settings on a per-server basis; to manage settings for many RD Session Host servers at a time, use Windows PowerShell or Group Policy as described in Chapter 7, "Molding and Securing the User Environment."

> **NOTE** Not all settings are relevant to a single-server RD Session Host deployment like the one discussed here. For more information about farm and RD Connection Broker settings, see Chapter 9, "Multi-Server Deployments."

Open the Remote Desktop Session Host Configuration tool by clicking Start | Administrative Tools | Remote Desktop Services | Remote Desktop Session Host Configuration. To change a setting (or settings), double-click any single entry in the Edit Settings section to open the Properties dialog box shown in Figure 3-23.

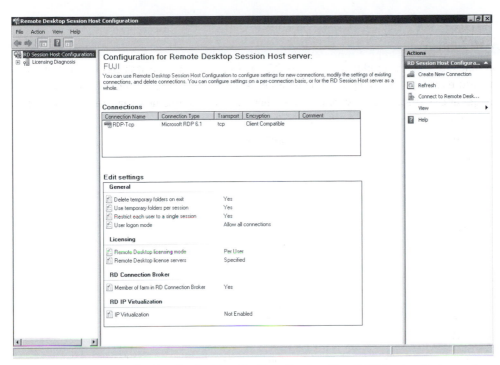

FIGURE 3-22 Use Remote Desktop Session Host Configuration to edit each RD Session Host server's configuration.

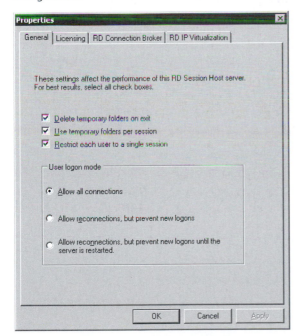

FIGURE 3-23 Clicking any setting in Remote Desktop Session Host Configuration Edit Settings section opens this tabbed Properties dialog box.

You can also configure all these settings through Windows PowerShell, using the new Remote Desktop Services provider, installed along with the RDS role service. To use it, first load the module using the import-module command from within Windows PowerShell, as follows.

```
PS C:\Users\admin> Import-module remotedesktopservices
```

Next, navigate to the RDS provider by issuing either the *Set-Location rds:* or *Cd rds:* cmdlet (they're the same; Cd is just an alias for Set-Location to make it easier for those accustomed to using the command-line interface), as shown here.

```
PS C:\Users\admin> set-location rds:
PS RDS:\>
```

To list the contents of the RDS container, use the *Dir* cmdlet as follows.

```
PS RDS:\> dir
   Directory: RDS:
```

Name	Type	CurrentValue	GP	PermissibleValues	PermissibleOperations
RDSConfiguration	Container		-		Get-Item, Get-ChildItem
RemoteApp	Container		-		Get-Item, Get-ChildItem

The configuration options for an RD Session Host server are in the RDSConfiguration container. Navigate to the RDSConfiguration container like this.

```
PS RDS:\> cd rdsconfiguration
PS RDS:\rdsconfiguration> dir
    Directory: RDS:\rdsconfiguration
```

Name	Type	CurrentValue	GP	PermissibleValues	PermissibleOperations
Connections	Container		-		Get-Item, Get-ChildItem, New-Item
LicensingSettings	Container		-		Get-Item, Get-ChildItem
ConnectionBrokerSettings	Container		-		Get-Item, Get-ChildItem
TempFolderSettings	Container		-		Get-Item, Get-ChildItem
ProfileSettings	Container		-		Get-Item, Get-ChildItem
SessionSettings	Container		-		Get-Item, Get-ChildItem

VirtualIPSettings	Container		-	Get-Item, Get-ChildItem
UserLogonMode	Integer	0	- 0, 1, 2	Get-Item, Set-Item
RDSessionHostServerMode	Integer	1	- 0, 1	Get-Item
TimeZoneRedirection	Integer	0	No 0, 1	Get-Item, Set-Item

Now that you've got the tools to edit the configuration from the GUI or command prompt, the following sections explain the settings found in Remote Desktop Session Host Configuration. You'll come back to some of these settings throughout this book.

General Session Settings

Most often, you won't need to adjust any of the settings on the General tab shown in Figure 3-23.

TEMPORARY FOLDER SETTINGS

The only circumstance under which you're likely to need to change the temporary folder settings is if you are supporting an older application (or a proprietary one) that won't store temporary directories on a per-user basis, but only per computer. Most of the time, there's no reason not to delete per-session temporary files when the user ends the session. Doing this also protects user privacy.

To configure temporary folder settings using Group Policy, go to Computer Configuration | Policies | Administrative Templates | Windows Components | Remote Desktop Services | Remote Desktop Session Host | Temporary Folders. Then proceed as follows.

- To disable deleting a user's per-session temporary folders when they exit, enable Do Not Delete Temp Folder Upon Exit. When this setting isn't configured, the temporary folders will be deleted unless you've specified otherwise using RD Configuration.

- If you enable the Do Not Use Temporary Folders Per Session policy setting a user's temporary files for the user's sessions on a server will be stored in the common Temp folder in the user's profile instead of each session storing temporary files in separate subfolders in this location.

You can also use Windows PowerShell to configure these temporary folder options. Configure the Do Not Delete Temp Folder Upon Exit option like this.

```
PS RDS:\RDSConfiguration\TempFolderSettings> Set-Item DeleteTempFolders X
```

where X is one of these values.

- 1 = Yes (selected in the GUI)
- 0 = No (cleared in the GUI)

Configure the Use Temporary Folders Per Session option like this.

```
PS RDS:\rdsconfiguration\tempfoldersettings> Set-Item UseTempFolders X
```

where X is one of these values.

- 1 = Yes (selected in the GUI)
- 0 = No (cleared in the GUI)

SESSION COUNT

With RemoteApp programs, there is also generally no reason to allow users to maintain more than one session on the same RD Session Host server. All RemoteApp programs started from the same server run in the same session, so they can all use the core processes needed to support the session (for example, Csrss.exe, Winlogon.exe, and Win32k.sys) and save memory. Running in the same session also allows all those applications to use the same instance of the user profile. (Profile issues are discussed in Chapter 5, "Managing User Data in a Remote Desktop Services Deployment," but for now, understand that it's good to have only one copy of your profile open.)

To configure logon restrictions using Group Policy, go to Computer Configuration | Policies | Administrative Templates | Windows Components | Remote Desktop Services | Remote Desktop Session Host | Connections. The setting in question is Restrict Remote Desktop Services Users To A Single Remote Session.

Configure the option to restrict users to a single user session using Windows PowerShell like this.

```
PS RDS:\RDSConfiguration\sessionsettings> Set-Item SingleSession X
```

where X is one of these values.

- 0 = Selected (restrict use to a single session)
- 1 = Cleared (allow multiple sessions)

USER LOGON MODE

The settings for user logon mode depend on whether the RD Session Host server is currently in production or you're planning on taking it down but don't want to abruptly end everyone's sessions. One option applies if you are planning for a reboot (for example, if you cyclically reboot RD Session Host servers to fix old applications with memory leaks), in which case you should choose the option to limit connections until the service restarts. If you're planning on longer maintenance, however, choose to limit connections until you explicitly re-enable them.

To configure the user logon mode using Group Policy, go to Computer Configuration | Policies | Administrative Templates | Windows Components | Remote Desktop Services | Remote Desktop Session Host | Connections. The setting in question is Allow Users To Connect Remotely Using Remote Desktop Services. However, this is one situation in which Group Policy *isn't* the best configuration option. User logon mode is most appropriately set by Group Policy when you're staging a bunch of servers and don't want any of them to go online until you're done. If you're taking an RD Session Host server offline, then it's much easier and faster to adjust this setting using the configuration tools on the server.

Configure the user logon mode from Windows PowerShell like this.

```
PS RDS:\RDSConfiguration\sessionsettings>Set-item USerLogonMode X
```

where *X* equals one of these three values.

- 0 = Allow all connections
- 1 = Allow reconnections, but prevent new logons until the server is restarted
- 2 = Allow reconnections, but prevent new logons at all times

Configuring IP Virtualization

When multiple people are all working from the same server, they're all using the same IP address. For most applications, this is acceptable. Some applications, however, don't work properly unless they have a unique IP address for every connection. Some client/server applications, for example, require this. To allow applications like this to be used on RD Session Host, Windows Server 2008 R2 added IP virtualization to assign a single IP address to each session or to certain applications within a session.

To configure IP virtualization, open RD Session Host Configuration and choose IP Virtualization (or, if you have the server's Properties dialog box already open, turn to the appropriate tab) to show the settings in Figure 3-24.

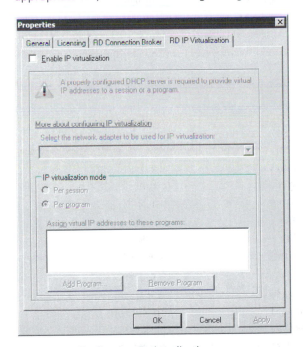

FIGURE 3-24 Configuring IP virtualization

Most of the steps here are pretty intuitive. First, enable IP virtualization. You will need a Dynamic Host Configuration Protocol (DHCP) server available for this, but you won't need to do any configuration on the DHCP server—it's not aware of this feature but just assigns IP addresses as it would normally.

Enable or disable IP Virtualization from Windows PowerShell using this code.

```
PS RDS:\RDSConfiguration\VirtualIPSettings> Set-Item VirtualIPActive X
```

Where *X* is one of these values.

- 0 = Disabled (cleared)
- 1 = Enabled (selected)

Second, choose the network interface adapter to use. You must choose one adapter to use (by default, none will be selected).

To set or modify this setting, IP virtualization must be enabled, and the mode must be set to Per Program (this is the default choice selected when you enable IP Virtualization). Choose the network adapter that will be used for IP Virtualization using Windows PowerShell like this.

```
PS RDS:\RDSConfiguration\VirtualIPSettings> Set-Item NetworkAdapter 00-15-5D-0A-31-68
```

> **NOTE** When using Windows PowerShell, you must specify the Network Adapter by the adapter media access control (MAC) address, not name.

Next, change the virtualization mode if needed. Generally, per-program is the best choice if you can use it. You probably know which applications require unique IP addresses, and a session won't use a virtual IP address if that application is not running. In addition, per-session IP virtualzation won't work on multihomed RD Session Host servers, even if you only pick one NIC. Per-program works on multihomed servers.

Set the Virtual IP mode using Windows PowerShell using this command.

```
PS RDS:\RDSConfiguration\VirtualIPSettings> Set-Item VirtualIPMode X
```

where *X* is one of these values.

- 0 = Per session
- 1 = Per program

If you choose per-program, you'll need to pick the applications that should use a virtual IP address. With this option, all applications configured this way and running in the same session will have the same virtual IP address, while other applications will be using the address of the RD Session Host server's NIC.

Again, you can also configure this setting using Windows PowerShell. The following command adds a program (Notepad.exe) that exists at a specified path (C: Windows\System32\ Notepad.exe) to the list of programs that will be assigned a virtual IP address.

```
PS RDS:\RDSConfiguration\VirtualIPSettings\applications>
    New-Item -Name 'Notepad' -AppPath 'c:\windows\system32\Notepad.exe'
```

Setting the exact path is optional. Add the application name without the exact path to assign a virtual IP address to any program running inside a user session that has the specified application name. The following is an example.

```
PS RDS:\RDSConfiguration\VirtualIPSettings\applications>
    New-Item -Name 'Notepad' -AppName 'Notepad.exe'
```

To remove a program, execute the following command.

```
PS RDS:\RDSConfiguration\VirtualIPSettings\applications> Remove-Item Notepad.exe
```

Two Group Policy settings control this feature. First, you can enable the feature from Computer Configuration | Policies | Administrative Templates | Windows Components | Remote Desktop Services | Remote Desktop Session Host | Application Compatibility. The setting in question is Turn On Remote Desktop IP Virtualization. Second, you can prevent a session from using the RD Session Host server's IP address if no IP address is available for the session by enabling the Do Not Use Remote Desktop Session Host IP Address When Virtual IP Address is Not Available setting.

One point to be aware of with IP virtualization is that using it can double the IP addresses that your organization will need. Everyone's client will have a unique IP address, and everyone's session will have its own IP address (albeit only for the duration of the session). There is no way to configure DHCP to limit the number of addresses in a particular range that should be allocated to sessions. In addition, IP virtualization is enabled on the server, not on a per-user basis, so you can't pick and choose which people should use it. The best way to use it is to limit it to certain applications. Many applications don't need it; use this feature only for applications that do.

RD Session Host Licensing Settings

The next tab of the Properties dialog box allows you to configure the licensing settings, both for the type of license you'll use and the discovery method that the server will use to locate license servers. Getting the correct settings (as shown in Figure 3-25) is crucial for the successful implementation of RDS within your organization.

REMOTE DESKTOP SERVICES LICENSING MODE

An RD Session Host server can be in either per-device mode or per-user mode. The mode that you select depends on the type of licenses you purchase, which depends mainly on the proportion of users to computers. If there are more computers than users (for example, if people using RD Session Host servers can log in from either a work computer or from a home computer), then per-user licensing makes more sense. If there are more users (for example, if the people using the RD Session Host servers are shift workers and three people use the same thin client at different times of day) then per-device licensing makes more sense.

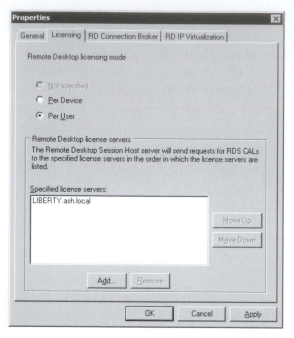

FIGURE 3-25 Remote Desktop Services Licensing settings are critical to RD Session Host availability.

You can change the licensing mode, but whichever mode you pick, you must be sure that the matching license types are installed on the license server that you're using. Otherwise, even if the RD Session Host server can find a license server, it will not be able to allocate licenses to users or computers.

To configure the licensing mode using Group Policy, select Computer Configuration | Policies | Administrative Templates | Windows Components | Remote Desktop Services | Remote Desktop Session Host | Licensing. The setting in question is Set The Remote Desktop Services Licensing Mode. This is an excellent setting to edit using Group Policy, as all RD Session Host servers in a farm are likely to have the same licensing mode. Using this setting avoids accidental errors.

Set the license server mode from Windows PowerShell like this.

```
PS RDS:\RDSConfiguration\LicensingSettings> Set-Item LicensingType X
```

where X is one of these values.

- 2 = Per-device
- 4 = Per-user

View the current licensing mode with the following command.

```
PS RDS:\RDSConfiguration\LicensingSettings> Get-Item LicensingName
```

SPECIFYING A LICENSE SERVER

Previous versions of Terminal Services supported license server discovery, but this method had so many conditions that could cause it not to work properly that RDS removed this feature. You must now specify a license server. Do this in the GUI by clicking Add on the Licensing tab of the Properties dialog box. Then either select a license server from the list of known license servers or add a license server by name or IP address and then click Add. Then click OK.

To add a license server using Windows PowerShell, use the following command and fill in the requested parameters.

```
PS RDS:\RDSConfiguration\LicensingSettings\SpecifiedLicenseServers> New-Item
cmdlet New-Item at command pipeline position 1
Supply values for the following parameters:
Path[0]: Liberty.ash.local
Path[1]:
```

To see the license server added, run this command:

```
PS RDS: \RDSConfiguration
LicensingSettings\SpecifiedLicenseServers> dir
Directory: RDS:\RDSConfiguration\LicensingSettings\SpecifiedLicenseServers
```

Name	Type	CurrentValue	GP	PermissibleValues	PermissibleOperations
Liberty.ash.local	Container		-		Get-Item, Get ChildItem, Remove...

Remove a license server like this.

```
PS RDS:\RDSConfiguration\LicensingSettings\SpecifiedLicenseServers>
   remove-item LIBERTY.ash.local -force
```

> **NOTE** You have to use the *–Force* parameter if the license server you are removing is the last or only license server listed.

To configure RDS Licensing using Group Policy, select Computer Configuration | Policies | Administrative Templates | Windows Components | Remote Desktop Services | Remote Desktop Session Host | Licensing. The setting in question is Use The Specified Remote Desktop Services Licensing Servers. Again, this is a good setting for Group Policy to make sure it's consistent across all servers and that new ones will be configured automatically to match the existing set.

To add one or more servers, type their names in the text box and then click Check Names to validate the names; you should see a confirmation message saying "The servers specified are valid terminal license servers." If you don't receive this confirmation, verify the name. When you specify license servers, their names are added to the RD Session host server's registry in HKLM\SYSTEM\CurrentControlSet\Services\TermService\Parameters\LicenseServers\ SpecifiedLicenseServers.

Specifying a license server isn't always as easy as just typing in a server name, for the following reasons.

- The license servers that you specify must be running Windows Server 2008 or later. It is not possible for a license server running Windows Server 2003 to issue Windows Server 2008 R2 RDS CALs. (A license server running Windows Server 2008 R2 can issue TS CALs for terminal servers running Windows Server 2003, however.)
- You can point to a license server outside the forest. However, if this license server will be issuing per-user RDS CALs, there must be a trust relationship between the two domains. When issuing per-user RDS CALs, the license server needs to be able to contact AD DS on behalf of the person requesting an RDS CAL.

Protocol-Specific Settings

The Connections portion of Remote Desktop Configuration contains information about any protocols supported on the server (double-click RDP-Tcp to see them). In this example, you'll see only Remote Desktop Protocol because that's the native protocol used by Remote Desktop Services and the only one that is installed. Were Citrix XenApp extensions to Remote Desktop Services installed, for example, there'd be another entry here for ICA, the default protocol for user sessions when Xenapp is installed.

Most protocol-specific settings are controlled from the user account properties visible from Active Directory Users and Computers, and the settings that aren't there are included in Group Policy. (If they are set using Active Directory Users and Computers, Group Policy can still override them.) The settings in Remote Desktop Configuration (see Table 3-5) are mainly advisory. In this section, you'll learn what the settings mean and how you might use them.

TABLE 3-5 Protocol Configuration Settings in Remote Desktop Configuration

TAB	SETTINGS CONTAINED	WHEN YOU WOULD EDIT
General	Mainly security settings, including the minimum encryption level set between client and server, whether the server must authenticate itself to the client (RDP security layer vs. SSL), and whether NLA is required. See Chapter 7 for more information about these options.	Hopefully, not often. All modern clients can support Secure Sockets Layer (SSL) connections, which reduces the chance that a rogue terminal server could intercept client authentication data. NLA requires at least RDP 6.1 and CredSSP support on the client.
Environment	Initial program path and settings.	Probably never. Because Windows Server 2008 R2 supports RemoteApp programs, you don't need to specify startup applications.

TAB	SETTINGS CONTAINED	WHEN YOU WOULD EDIT
Sessions	Settings determining behavior when a session has been active, disconnected, or idle for a certain length of time.	Rarely. These settings can be set from Group Policy or Active Directory Users and Computers, and both will override the settings here. Use Group Policy to set consistent connection policies across all terminal servers; Active Directory Users and Computers to set connection policies for individuals.
Logon Settings	Whether to use the client logon information or generic logon credentials.	Rarely. You might use this setting for a special-use RD Session Host server supporting anonymous connections, but generally you'll want to use the user logon credentials.
Remote Control	The rules governing remote control of a user's session.	Rarely. These settings can also be set in Active Directory Users and Computers and Group Policy and by default those settings take precedence. Remote Control settings can also be defined on a per-machine basis through Group Policy.
Client Settings	Maximum color depth and device redirection rules. Most supported devices are enabled by default.	Occasionally, to override client-side settings.
Network Adapter	Chooses the network adapters to support RDP traffic and limits the number of connections that the terminal server will support.	Occasionally, to limit the network adapters being used for RDP connections or to keep connections to the RD Session Host server within the bounds of what it can support.
Security	Users and groups permitted access to the terminal server.	Rarely. As Help will remind you when you switch to this tab, it is best practice to control access via controlling the membership of the Remote Desktop Users group because the results are more predictable.

You can also configure most of these settings using Group Policy. Some of the more useful ones are described in the rest of this chapter; you'll learn more about what these settings are for throughout the book. The Network Adapter and Security tabs do not have related Group Policy settings.

To configure connection security (including enabling server authentication and network-level authentication and client encryption level), select Computer Configuration | Policies | Administrative Templates | Windows Components | Remote Desktop Services | Remote Desktop Session Host | Security. Chapter 7 will discuss the settings in more detail, but the policies in question are as follows.

- Set Client Connection Encryption Level
- Require Use Of Specific Security Layer For Remote (RDP) Connections
- Require User Authentication For Remote Connections By Using Network Level Authentication

To configure device redirection and environment settings, select Computer Configuration | Policies | Administrative Templates | Windows Components | Remote Desktop Services | Remote Desktop Session Host | Device And Resource Redirection. The Printer Redirection and Remote Session Environment subkeys in this same path also include policies to control the user environment, which is discussed in more detail in Chapter 5.

To configure the rules for remote control of a user's session by an administrator, select Computer Configuration | Policies | Administrative Templates | Windows Components | Remote Desktop Services | Remote Desktop Session Host | Connections. The setting in question is Set Rules For Remote Control Of Remote Desktop Services User Sessions. You'll find out more about the use of remote control in Chapter 11.

Checking Configuration with the Best Practices Analyzer

Although many configuration choices are left to you to determine what's best for your environment, some configurations must be done in a certain way for a feature to function. For example, users cannot connect to the RD Session Host server if they are not in the Remote Desktop Users Group. Other best practices aren't necessarily a problem, but the server will function better and be less exposed to risk if it conforms to them—for example, to support pre-connection user authentication (which prevents DoS attacks from unauthorized users initiating sessions that they can't start), you need to enable NLA.

Best Practices Analyzer (BPA) is a server management tool in Windows Server 2008 R2. BPA can help you conform to recommended best practices by scanning installed roles on a server and reporting any violations. (Some violations will require immediate action and some are advisory, but all are intended to highlight any potential problems with the server configuration.) You can run the BPA for the local computer or remotely, and because it's built on Windows PowerShell, it also works from the command line so that you can run reports on an entire farm programmatically.

In this example, we'll show you how to run the BPA for Remote Desktop Services. The product group can update BPA as part of recommended updates, so you might have additional options by the time you read this book.

The BPA works by identifying certain best practices for a role and then programmatically checking the configuration to make sure that the settings support the best practices. [All configuration is stored in Windows Management Instrumentation (WMI).] If a setting does not support a recommended best practice, then the report gives feedback about the issue and a recommended fix.

To start using the BPA, open the Server Manager and scroll down to the Remote Desktop Services role, as shown in Figure 3-26. You'll see a link that says Scan This Role (circled here).

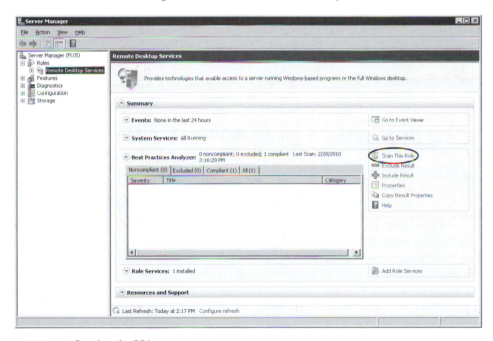

FIGURE 3-26 Starting the BPA

Click the link to display the page shown in Figure 3-27. You'll see a progress bar as the scan continues. When it's done, you'll see a report. In this case, it's showing that the Remote Desktop Users Group is not populated.

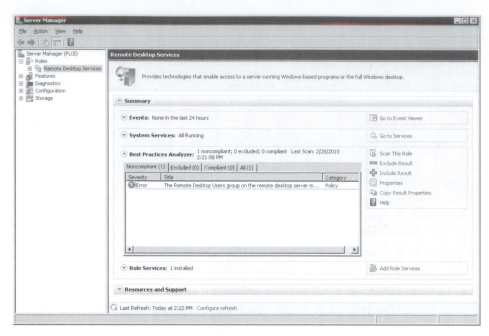

FIGURE 3-27 The BPA Report on RD Session Host

Again, additional rules will be added to the BPA as you add Windows updates, so you might see other rules to check. Other roles have rules, too, so the results of the scan will depend on what roles are installed.

Installing Applications on an RD Session Host Server

Installing an application on an RD Session Host server is different from installing the same application on Windows 7. When you install an application on Windows 7 (or Windows Server 2008 R2 when not configured as an RD Session Host server), you're generally prompted to choose whether you want to install that application for all users of the computer or just for the user who is currently logged on. The installation performed for all users differs from the installation performed for a specific user. The differences between these choices (there are some exceptions among application vendors, but this is what Microsoft recommends for v2 profiles) are explained in Table 3-6.

TABLE 3-6 Recommended Installation Options for Windows Server 2008 R2 and Windows 7

OPTION	COMMON SETTINGS	CURRENT USER
Shortcuts	Installed in Public profile	Installed in current user's profile
Listing in Programs And Features in Control Panel	For all users	For the current user only

OPTION	COMMON SETTINGS	CURRENT USER
COM registration	HKLM\Software\Classes	HKCU\Software\Classes
Run with executive privileges	Yes	Optional
Storage location for icons and transform files	%WinDir%\Installer\ {ProductCode}	%UserProfile%\AppData\ Microsoft\Installer\ {ProductCode GUID}

There are few surprises here: the per-user installation stores all relevant data in the user's profile. An all-users installation stores the relevant data on a per-computer basis (or in the Public folder so that the RD Session Host server is ready to add more users to the application).

Which Applications Will Work?

This subject was briefly mentioned in Chapter 2, in the discussion of how to use the RDS Application Analyzer, but you'll learn about it in more detail here.

Most newer applications will run on an RD Session Host server, but you can't assume that every application will perform successfully. As you know if you've used Terminal Services in the past, not all applications work on a shared server (and that is especially true for older applications). Sometimes the problem is that the application is too resource-intensive to share, or it might require too many graphical updates to update the client-side display properly (rendering applications come to mind). But sometimes the problem is more subtle than that.

Broadly speaking, most application compatibility problems come from one of these sources.

- Microsoft Internet Explorer 6 dependency
- Installation
- Concurrent resource usage
- Permissions issues
- Privacy issues
- Performance issues
- Device redirection issues

Let's look at each of these in more detail.

Internet Explorer 6 Dependency

Some older web-based applications were written with a dependency on Internet Explorer 6. These applications won't run on Windows Server 2008 R2 because it uses Windows Internet Explorer 8. Internet Explorer cannot be virtualized with App-V, so if you need to run these applications remotely, you'll need to either set up a terminal server running Windows Server 2003 or run the application from a virtual machine (VM) running Windows XP (as described in Chapter 4).

Application Installation

Many application installations are designed for a single-user computer. This means that such an application was created with certain assumptions—for example, that it's acceptable to store personal settings in HKLM (which would mean that the application doesn't customize properly; machine-wide means all settings apply to all users), or to store settings in INI files in the Windows directory (which causes all users to have the same application settings).

One application-compatibility setting that is available to developers to avoid these kinds of problems is the */TSAWARE* option, which is in a program's header file. For example, applications designed to be multi-user-aware should not use INI files to store settings. The */TSAWARE* switch provides a workaround for applications that were not necessarily designed for a multi-user environment so that if an application does use INI files, the RD Session Host server will accommodate this during installation by creating virtual Windows directories for each user in which to store the INI files. Without this option, applications using INI files will have a single configuration file, and everyone using the application will have the same settings.

Unfortunately, there's no way for an administrator to check to see if the */TSAWARE* option has been set in an application. If you have a homegrown application that depends on INI files, however, you can check with the developer to see if it is TS-aware so that INI files will be stored on a per-user basis.

Another potential installation issue introduced with Windows Server 2008 R2 is that of 16-bit installers, specifically the stub component some applications use to check the machine type before the 32-bit installation engine runs. 32-bit applications can run on a 64-bit platform; the 64-bit Windows Installer can handle them. 16-bit applications cannot. That said, Microsoft realized that this could be an issue and addressed it for certain installers. If an application uses any of the following installers (listed in HKLM\Software\Microsoft\Windows NT\CurrentVersion\NtVdm64)

- Microsoft Setup for Windows 1.2
- Microsoft Setup for Windows 2.6
- Microsoft Setup for Windows 3.0
- Microsoft Setup for Windows 3.01
- InstallShield 5.*x*

then, when you start the installation, Windows will remove the 16-bit installer that starts the 32-bit installation engine and replace it with a 32-bit version. This list can't be extended. If your application uses another installation engine, you will need to convert it to use a 32-bit installer to make it work on Windows Server 2008 R2.

Concurrent Resource Usage

Many instances of the same application run concurrently on an RD Session Host server. If the applications want to use the same physical port, write to the same files, or write to the same portions of the registry, they won't work on an RD Session Host server. If two applications attempt to write to the same file at the same time, this can lead to data corruption; if they write to the same file at different times (perhaps to the same INI file, as discussed in the previous section), then this can lead to unexpected behavior.

Privacy Issues

Although the architecture of an RD Session Host server session is designed to keep session memory areas separate, applications also must honor this in the way they share files. If those files store any private data (for example, the web pages that a user has viewed), then the applications can't use the same files.

Performance Issues

By definition, applications running on an RD Session Host server must share hardware resources, including disk input/output (I/O), processor time, and physical memory. If an application needs a lot of any of those, then it's probably not a good fit for an RD Session Host server. (Even the DFSS mechanism only divides processor time more evenly—it doesn't make more of it.) Similarly, some applications don't remote well over high-latency networks. As you'll see in Chapter 6, RDP 7 has continued the trend of more efficient usage of resources to better display high-quality multimedia in Windows Media Player, but some Flash and Silverlight applications might not display well over a wide area network (WAN).

Device Redirection

As discussed in Chapter 5, Windows Server 2008 R2 RD Session Host servers can redirect new kinds of resources. They can't, however, redirect *everything*—or at least, they can't support all features (for example, ActiveSync) if they do. Devices that need but don't get this redirection will not work in a remote session.

What can you do about these limitations of applications and device redirection? First, you can do some checking ahead of time so that you will know which applications will work and which will not. One option is to search some websites to find out what applications have been packaged to work on a shared server, because if someone else has been able to make the application work, then at least you know that it can be done. (The software provider visionapp, for example, maintains a list of this kind at *http://visionapp.com/1701.0.html?&ftu= 7074772b28*.) Another option is to analyze the applications themselves, using the Application Analyzer tool available on the companion CD and described in Chapter 2.

Storing Application-Specific Data

Installing applications on a shared server is somewhat different from both the per-user or all-users installation option performed on a single-user operating system. The situation is different; in this case, you want all users who access the RD Session Host server to be able to use the application, but you also want them to be able to maintain their settings in their profiles so those settings will follow them between servers. Therefore, when you install applications on an RD Session Host server, the operating system combines the two approaches. Application binaries are stored to be accessible to anyone connected to the server, but the operating system stores some settings in a particular part of HKLM called the *shadow key*. The location of this key will vary with the operating system and application type, as follows.

- 64-bit versions of Windows Server 2008 R2 store shadow key information for 32-bit applications in HKLM\Software\Wow6432Node\Microsoft\Windows NT\CurrentVersion\Terminal Server\Install\Software.

- 64-bit versions of Windows Server 2008 R2 store shadow key information for 64-bit applications in HKLM\Software\Microsoft\Windows NT\CurrentVersion\Terminal Server\Install\Software.

> **NOTE** Like APIs, registry key names didn't change when Terminal Services became Remote Desktop Services in Windows Server 2008 R2. That would have broken applications that relied on the Terminal Server name.

The shadow key stores configuration settings for all the applications installed on the RD Session Host server, divided by publisher. When a user logs on, the contents of this key are copied to her profile, so long as the contents of the key are newer than the contents in the profile. The operating system determines the relative age of the configuration data in the user profile and in the shadow key by comparing timestamp values of two registry keys, both of which have recorded last write-time in seconds since 1970. The key in the user profile is LastUserIniSyncTime, stored in HKCU\Software\Microsoft\Windows NT\CurrentVersion\Terminal Server; the date of the shadow key is stored in LatestRegistryKey in HKLM\SOFTWARE\Microsoft\Windows NT\CurrentVersion\Terminal Server\Install\IniFileTimes.

> **NOTE** The iniFileTimes key is hidden, so don't expect to see it in the registry if you look for it.

If the profile is newer, the settings aren't copied; if the configuration in the shadow key is newer, the user profile is updated with the data in the shadow key. You don't want to update the central data source, so the user profile will *never* update the shadow key.

32-Bit Applications in a 64-Bit World

Windows Server 2008 R2 is only 64-bit, but it's not practical to assume that 64-bit versions of all applications will be available. To work around this problem, 64-bit Windows implements the WOW64 emulator. This user-mode emulator loads a 32-bit version of NTDLL.dll, used by applications to make system calls. When a 32-bit application calls on NTDLL.dll to interact with the operating system in some way (for example, to read from or write to disk), WOW64 intercepts the call (this is not an expensive operation because it, like the application it's working with, runs in user mode) and sends the request to the 64-bit operating system. In other words, the 32-bit application and the 64-bit operating system don't have to know about each other.

To enable 32-bit applications to take advantage of some of the additional memory space 64-bit applications get, application creators can compile the applications with the IMAGE_FILE_LARGE_ADDRESS_AWARE flag set in the image header. Using this flag doesn't give the 32-bit applications the full 8 terabytes of user-mode virtual memory addresses that 64-bit applications can use, but it does double their virtual memory space to 4 GB.

In addition to needing some way to communicate with the operating system, it's important to separate registry data for 32-bit and 64-bit applications so that they don't load the wrong DLLs or overwrite each other's configuration data. Therefore, 64-bit applications on a 64-bit server use the keys and values stored in HKLM\Software, and the 32-bit applications use the keys and values stored in HKLM\Software\Wow6432Node. Under each key, the structure is approximately the same.

It would be impossible to support 32-bit applications on a 64-bit operating system if all 32-bit applications had to be rewritten to support this compatibility key. Instead, to make this work, 64-bit versions of Windows use *registry redirection* to intercept calls to the registry. If a 32-bit application (or component, for that matter) tries to read from or write to the registry, then the operating system's WOW64 subsystem intercepts the request and redirects it to the appropriate path of the registry. If 64-bit applications attempt to access the registry, the WOW64 subsystem ignores the call.

Sometimes both 32-bit and 64-bit applications need the same data, but they must read it from their own section of the registry. For data that both versions need, the operating system employs *registry reflection*. Registry reflection updates both the 32-bit section and the 64-bit section. This is done mainly for operations such as file association (HKLM\Software\Classes) to ensure that the same application always opens a file with a particular extension. Registry reflection ensures that the contents

Continued on the next page

of the Classes key are maintained in parallel for both the 32-bit and 64-bit sections of the registry.

For our purposes here, the implications of this are that 64-bit versions of Windows maintain two areas for shadow keys: one for 32-bit applications and one for 64-bit applications.

Avoiding Overwriting User Profile Data

You might have noticed that the decision to overwrite or not overwrite the user profile is done solely by the relative age of the data in the profile and the shadow key. If you install and deploy more servers to the farm, the new servers will have a newer date than the older servers. This can lead to problems, because the newer RD Session Host servers overwrite the user-updated data in the user profile because it's (apparently) newer. As an example of how this could affect the user, let's say that you had an RD Session Host server with Microsoft Office 2010 installed on it. You allow users to customize their application experience, so they change which toolbars are visible. When you deploy a new RD Session Host server in the farm, the default settings on the new server will have a newer timestamp than the user profile timestamp. When the user logs onto the new server, the changes the user had made and grown to rely on would be overwritten with the default options on the new server. You can get around this problem in one of several ways.

- Create new servers from images of old servers.
- Ensure that the shadow key timestamps on the new servers are older than the user profile.
- Remove the keys from the shadow key.
- Prevent updates to existing profile data.

Edit the Shadow Key Timestamps

Because the decision to write or not is based on whether the information in the user profile is older than the data in the shadow key, one approach is to ensure that the shadow key is always older than any data in the user profile. You can set the clocks back on new servers before installing applications. The number of seconds since 1970 is determined by the clock on the operating system, not the system clock on the motherboard, so it's not hard to fool. You just need to ensure that you're consistent about the date to which you set the RD Session Host servers.

 ON THE COMPANION MEDIA An after-the-fact approach could be to change the timestamps on the registry keys. One way to do this is with a freeware tool like the Registry Time Stamp Tool from Immidio, linked from the companion media.

Removing Sections from Shadow Keys

Another way to prevent the keys from being updated in the user profile is to delete them from the shadow key. If you do so, of course they won't be added to the user profile, and you'll need to apply them with logon scripts.

The advantage to this approach is that it ensures that the keys won't overwrite the user profile. The disadvantage is that it takes some work to set this up, and more to maintain it. You need to delete the contents of the shadow key on all RD Session Host servers, and you must ensure that all users get the keys added to their session. In addition, if you add more applications, you must update the logon scripts.

Selectively Disabling Registry Writes

Rather than removing the contents of the shadow key, you can control registry propagation selectively. To do this, go to HKLM\Software\Microsoft\Windows NT\CurrentVersion\Terminal Server\Compatibility\RegistryEntries*PathName*, where *PathName* is the path to the key that you don't want updated (located in HKCU\Software). For example, if you examine the contents of this path, you'll see that Microsoft\Windows\CurrentVersion\Explorer\Shell Folders is already there.

> **NOTE** For 32-bit applications on a 64-bit operating system, edit the path to HKLM\
> Software\Wow6432Node\Microsoft\Windows NT\CurrentVersion\Terminal Server\
> Compatibility\RegistryEntries*PathName*.

The tricky part here lies in the value assigned to this key to control propagation. By default, Microsoft\Windows\CurrentVersion\Explorer\Shell Folders has a value of 108 hexadecimal. This value is actually the result of compatibility bits. A value of 8 hex means that the path points to a 32-bit application. The 100 hex comes from the configuration of registry mapping. If this bit is set (which means it has a value of 100), then new entries from the system master registry image will be added to the user profile when the application is started, but no existing data in the profile will be deleted or changed. If this bit is not set (has a value of 0, or isn't present), the operating system deletes and overwrites the user's registry data if it is older than the system master registry data.

Therefore, to prevent Win32 application registry settings from being updated in the user profile, provide the path to the key in HKEY_USERS where that application data is stored and give it a value here of 108 in hex.

Populating the Shadow Key

How does this data get into the shadow key in the first place? The answer depends on the type of application installation. Applications that install from Microsoft Windows Installer files (MSIs) work differently from applications that install from .exe files, and the changes can have real implications for the way the shadow key captures registry settings.

Two Models for Application Installation on Windows Server 2008 R2

Ara Bernardi
Senior Software Development Engineer

Not all applications install in exactly the same way. The following information describes how MSIs differ from applications that do not install from MSIs.

The Pre-MSI Model

In the pre-MSI model, applications are typically installed by running a custom Setup.exe file or a common installation tool such as InstallShield. Such setups do not visibly distinguish per-user configuration from per-machine configuration, so there is no easy way for servers to capture the per-user related changes and propagate such changes to each user's hive. Therefore, installations are done in Install Mode, which records any registry key operation in that session, no matter what process makes the changes. For example, if the administrator decides to change his or her home page while installing an application in Install Mode, that change will also be recorded. Therefore, it is important not to take any actions while an installation is ongoing that do not pertain directly to the installation. When the installation finishes, the session should be put back into Execute Mode.

The related commands are *Change user /install* and *Change user /execute*. The "recording" of registry key changes is saved in the registry under HKLM\SOFTWARE\Microsoft\Windows NT\CurrentVersion\Terminal Server\Install\Software.

While in Install Mode, changes to the Start menu are also tracked, and then those changes are moved to the public menu so that shortcuts are visible to all users.

When a user logs on, Userinit.exe checks to see if the user's hive under HKCU\Software has or is missing keys from the equivalent path above. If anything is added, or changed, it compares the two paths and takes appropriate action by adding keys/values from the HKLM path.

The MSI Model

Applications with MSI-based setup install differently. Since the advent of MSI, a centralized service is now responsible for installation, so there is no need to track registry key changes made by any or all programs in a session. Instead, we need to track only the registry key changes made by the MSI infrastructure. Additionally, MSI has options to make per-user installation appear as a global installation for all users (although this is mostly limited to user interface elements such as the Start menu or Desktop shortcuts). Since applications continue to install registry keys (in

HKCU) during installation, we need to record such changes and propagate them to every user. We must track these changes, but the scope is limited to changes made by the MSI infrastructure. Therefore, there is no need to put the session into Install Mode. Instead, we have a private contract with the MSI service to capture the HKCU-related changes.

MSI detects that it is running on an RD Session Host server and makes all per-user changes in the system context instead of a user's context, which means that instead of changes to installer's HKCU, changes go into System's HKCU (which is HKU\.DEFAULT\Software). Before MSI makes any per-user changes, it makes a reference copy of HKU\.DEFAULT\Software, after which MSI runs and makes all the required changes while installing the application package.

When MSI has finished the installation, it signals the end of this transaction, which runs a side-by-side comparison of the before and after states of the HKU\.DEFAULT\Software trees. When the comparison is complete, MSI saves the delta in HKLM\SOFTWARE\Microsoft\Windows NT\CurrentVersion\Terminal Server\ Install\Software. When a user logs on, the same model as before is used to copy registry keys into the user's hive.

One final note: MSI permits a model of installation called *custom actions*, which is a type of installation that MSI doesn't support natively, but which is implemented by a custom DLL that has been loaded by a vendor. This custom action can do whatever it wants, including rebooting the machine. Therefore, on RD Session Host servers, MSI is hard-coded to refuse a per-user installation by a regular (non-administrator) user.

When you run an MSI file to install an application, this action sends a message to the TSAppCompat component to prepare for installation. This component then creates a snapshot of HKCU\.Default\Software and saves it.

NOTE One issue with installing applications in previous versions of Terminal Services is that the MSI installations don't install the same way on client and server versions of the operating system. On the client, install operations (performed when a user runs a MSI-installed application for the first time) were queued, but an install on a server (for example, to set up Office for first-time use) would block any other installations. This meant that only one person could apply his or her per-user settings at a time. This was changed in Windows Server 2008 R2, so that on both server and client, the MSI installer will queue installation requests and process them in order.

Now, the TSAppCompat component checks the contents of HKCU\.Default\Software to compare the before and after versions, including all insertions, deletions, and changes. Having done so, it creates a delta of all the changes. This delta is what now populates the shadow key.

Only the contents of HKCU\.Default\Software are monitored. If the MSI starts another DLL (an infrequently used option), then the effects of that DLL will be ignored.

The Change user command that comes with RDS and used when you run an installation routine such as Setup.exe is another matter. When you put the RD Session Host server session into Install Mode with the command *Change user /install*, a different component named Advapi32 monitors all registry changes—*all* changes, not just the changes that have anything to do with installing the application. So long as the server is in Install mode, then the changes are recorded and copied to the user profile when they log on. For example, if you change the home page for Internet Explorer, you'll be recording this data and changing it for everybody.

Summary

This chapter has discussed the essentials of setting up a Remote Desktop Session Host server infrastructure. By now, you should be familiar with how RD Session Host servers create sessions, validate user logons, and issue licenses to authorized users or computers.

Best practices for RD Session Host server configuration include the following.

- When configuring more than one server, use Group Policy, not the RD Session Host Configuration tool. When adjusting settings on a per-server basis, it's too easy to introduce inconsistencies among servers, and inconsistencies now can lead to a lot of troubleshooting later.
- DFSS evenly distributes processor time across user sessions; you need to use WSRM only if giving some users greater priority than others.
- Do not use the memory management features of WSRM on an RD Session Host server.
- Install the Desktop Experience feature to enable Plug and Play redirection.
- Use the BPA to check RD Session Host settings.

Additional Resources

The following resources contain additional information and tools related to this chapter.

- To learn more about setting up Group Policy objects for managing user settings, see Chapter 6, "Customizing the User Experience."
- To learn more about how to manage RD Session Host servers as a group, see Chapter 9, "Multi-Server Deployments."
- For more details about related Windows Server 2008 R2 architecture, see Chapter 2, "Key Architectural Concepts for Remote Desktop Services."

Deploying a Single Remote Desktop Virtualization Host Server

Prior to Windows Server 2008 R2, Virtual Desktop Infrastructure (VDI) was not part of Microsoft's presentation remoting package [even though Microsoft technology in the form of Remote Desktop Protocol (RDP) and the Windows operating system was used to enable another company's VDI solution]. In this chapter, you will learn about this new role, how it works, and how to set it up for a single-server deployment. (Deploying multiple RD Virtualization Host servers works the same way as deploying one. Although SCVMM is out of scope for this book, it will help you manage VMs across multiple hosts. See *http://www.microsoft.com/systemcenter/en/us/virtual-machine-manager.aspx* for more information on SCVMM.)

What Is VDI?

But first, what *is* VDI?

At its most basic, Virtual Desktop Infrastructure (VDI) is a deployment design that puts the user desktop on a virtual machine (VM) in the datacenter, rather than on the physical computer at someone's desk. Some degree of connection and image management is usually implied in VDI.

Speaking generally, VDI can range in complexity, as follows.

■ Example 1: One VM assigned to each person with a virtual desktop, with that person connecting to that desktop via the Remote Desktop Connection (RDC) client, specifying the desktop's name or Internet Protocol (IP) address

- Example 2: A personal desktop assigned to a user, but the user doesn't have to know what the VM's name is—just that he or she wants to connect to the machine
- Example 3: A pool of desktops available to a set of users on a temporary basis

A few things vary with the different kinds of complexity.

- The discovery process
- The user control over the VM
- The ease of delivery

First, there's the process of discovering and connecting to the right VM. In the first example, it's obvious: You go to the desktop that you have specified by name in the RDP file and hope that the VM is turned on. In the second and third examples, there must be some intelligence somewhere to get you to the right endpoint and make sure the VM is ready to accept connections.

The degree of administrative control also varies with the type of VDI. In the first two examples, one user will always use the same VM. As the IT manager, you can allow that user whatever degree of control over this virtual desktop that you see fit. In the pooled case, users can't alter the shared pool of desktops. If they did, they'd either lose whatever changes they made (if you'd configured the VM to discard changes and roll back to its saved state at logoff) or they'd be messing up the VM for the next user (if you hadn't).

Finally, the VDI delivery models differ in how easy it is to personalize the VM and the applications installed on it. Again, the first two models make it easy. Even if you don't allow users to install their own applications, the VMs can still have a specific set of applications designed for a specific user's needs. The pooled model makes it difficult to support much personalization because all VMs in the pool must have the right applications for all people who use them, and personal installs don't work in this model.

> **NOTE** App-V can offer some degree of personalization. For more information on App-V, see *http://www.microsoft.com/systemcenter/appv/default.mspx*.

If the VMs in a pool are assumed to be homogeneous, personal changes will lead to user confusion.

In the end, though, it's all VDI: putting a client operating system on a VM to be accessed remotely. The steps required for the user to find the VM, the degree of customization the user can make, and level of user control over this VM are the variables.

One more thing about Microsoft VDI: It's not just about a single role service. Although the Remote Desktop Virtualization Host (RD Virtualization Host) role service is essential to enabling this VDI model, it's complemented by two other role services. As shown in Figure 4-1, RD Web Access displays the VM icons for users to discover, and RD Connection Broker gets a user to the right endpoint based on the kind of connection requested and the load balancing rules in place. Even the RD Session Host gets involved in a small way: This role service supports the redirector, an essential piece required for sending connection requests to RD Connection Broker.

Active Directory Domain Services (AD DS) also plays a key part in supporting VDI. AD DS stores the user account objects that the RDS roles can use to see what the user should see when they log into RD Web Access (since not all users might have access to all pools). The user account objects also store the mappings for personal desktops to users, as applicable.

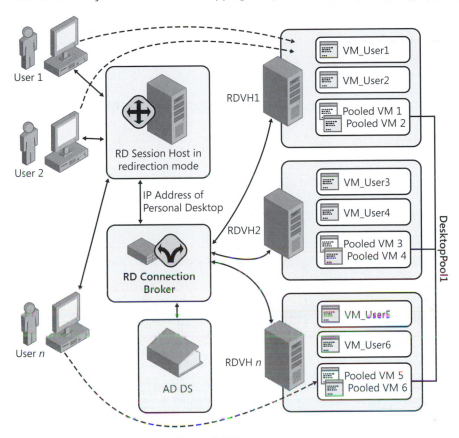

FIGURE 4-1 Role services support Microsoft VDI.

> **NOTE** The information in the rest of this chapter explains exactly how a user ends up connected to their requested VM. For now, the key take-away is that all of the role services in Figure 4-1 play a part in the process.

What *isn't* VDI? VDI isn't just about virtualizing existing desktops, or using a tool such as System Center Virtual Machine Manager (SCVMM) to image a desktop computer and move it into the data center. It's true that there is a small amount of benefit in running a desktop from a VM. It's easy to back up and therefore to restore, so a crashed desktop computer doesn't block a user from working. Fundamentally, though, there's a lot more benefit in viewing VDI as part of a strategy for reducing management costs than in just putting desktops in the data center. Done well, VDI can reduce some operating costs; but done poorly, it becomes a somewhat more expensive way of having physical desktops with a good local backup.

How Microsoft VDI Works

The first sort of VDI—the one that has each user with an RDP file connecting to a single VM by name—isn't really part of Microsoft's version of VDI. This is mostly because it's both very simple to set up and very hard to manage on any kind of scale. All you have to do to get this model working is install Hyper-V and then set up some VMs for people to use, but there are no tools to manage the VMs, the connections, or ensure that the VMs are ready to accept connections when people want to use them.

Microsoft VDI is designed for connecting to pooled and personal VMs. Pooled VMs are available to anyone who is a member of the Remote Desktop Users group on each VM, and personal desktops are assigned to users in AD DS and available only to the person to whom they're assigned. To support this display of and connection to personal and pooled VMs, the RDS components include the following.

- A publishing infrastructure to assign VMs or the use of a pool to people (optional)
- A connection broker to route the connection request to the most appropriate VM
- A redirector (an RD Session Host in redirection mode) to send the connection to the connection broker
- The VM Host agent on the RD Virtualization Host to prepare the VMs for connections
- A Hyper-V hypervisor on the RD Virtualization Host
- A client component that displays the user's set of VMs (and RemoteApp programs)
- AD DS to store the information about which users have personal desktops assigned to them and a place to look up the user SID so that RD Web Access can determine which VM pools a user should see

> **NOTE** The publishing infrastructure is optional, but it makes connection management easier. Publishing RemoteApp programs and VMs is discussed in more detail in Chapter 9, but the basic story is that the publishing infrastructure handles the chores of updating RDP files and getting them to users as you add more resources or delete existing ones. Without the publishing service, you'd have to keep sending users updated RDP files.

The terminology can get a little tricky. For example, when you're talking about connecting to a client operating system running in a VM, which one is the client? When discussing VDI, use the following terms to explain what's happening.

- The computer that is running the RDC client and that someone sits in front of is called the *client*. This is consistent with terminology when connecting to a session.

- The VM that this person is connecting to is the *endpoint*, or the *guest* (a guest of the RD Virtualization Host it's running on). A session on an RD Session Host can also be an endpoint.

- Preparing a VM to be used (for example, bringing it out of hibernation) is called *orchestration*.

- Moving a VM to a new RD Virtualization Host is called *placement*. Placement is not part of the basic RDS VDI solution but might be supported via a filter plug-in.

The rest of this chapter covers the mechanics of how you install and configure the RDS roles required to support VDI. For now, the focus is on the mechanics of how people discover personal desktops and pooled VMs, and how the connections they make get to the appropriate endpoints.

The Central Role of the RD Connection Broker

Without the RD Connection Broker, there is no VDI. As shown in Figure 4-2, the RD Connection Broker is central to the operation of this feature—the "brain." It keeps track of client connections to personal and pooled VMs, determines the kind of connection a user is requesting, and finds the right endpoint for the request.

From the perspective of the RD Connection Broker, it does not matter how a client makes a connection request. Someone can request a connection by clicking an icon in RD Web Access, starting an RDP file from the desktop or a network share, by manually using Remote Desktop Connection (RDC), or by connecting to RemoteApp and Desktop Connections on the client running Windows 7 and clicking an icon on the Start menu. In all these cases, the request is brokered by RD Connection Broker. RD Connection Broker works with RDP clients back to RDP 5.2 (which was available for Windows XP SP2 and Windows Server 2003), so the vast majority of Microsoft RDP clients are supported.

It also does not matter to the RD Connection Broker on which RD Virtualization Host the VM resides. RD Connection Broker is capable of keeping track of multiple RD Virtualization Hosts, as well as all their personal and pooled VMs, even if those pools span multiple servers.

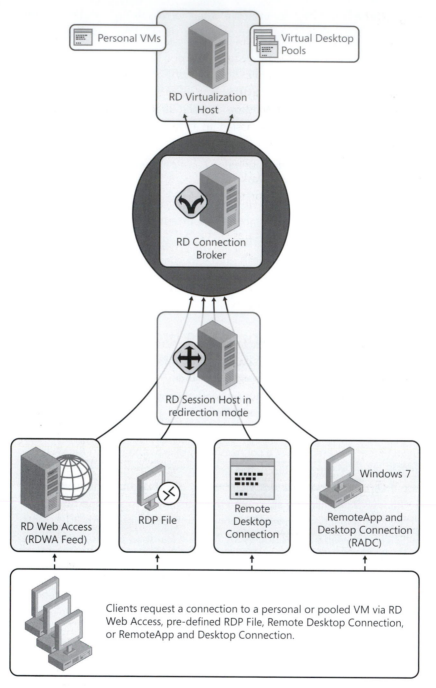

FIGURE 4-2 RD Connection Broker is in charge of connecting users to personal and pooled VMs.

Discovering a VM

The first step of using a VM is discovering that a VM exists. To allow users to discover VMs, the administrator assigns a personal desktop or creates a VM pool from the RemoteApp and Desktop Connections Manager on the RD Connection Broker. When an administrator assigns a personal VM, this assignment is recorded in the user account properties in AD DS. (Active Directory in both Windows Server 2008 and Windows Server2008 R2 support this user account property.) Both personal and pooled VMs are added to the publishing feed that populates both Remote Desktop Web Access and RemoteApp and Desktop Connections on clients running Windows 7. This publishing feed is customized for each user's security credentials, so that one user does not see another's personal desktop. RemoteApp program display is also filtered according to which users have permission to use which applications. That said, all VM pools are visible to all consumers of the feed.

When a user—let's call her Kim Akers—navigates to the RD Web Access page, she's prompted for her credentials. Those credentials go to the publishing service on RD Connection Broker, which then looks them up in AD DS to determine what resources—RemoteApp programs and VMs—have been assigned to those credentials. The browser will then display a filtered look of the RemoteApp programs and VMs to which Kim has access. Again, Kim will see all the pools.

If Kim were connecting to the feed through RemoteApp and Desktop Connections on the client running Windows 7, the process would be pretty similar. The main difference is that Kim would see the VM (as well as RemoteApp icons to which she has access) in a folder on her Start menu. Conceptually, her connection process looks like Figure 4-3.

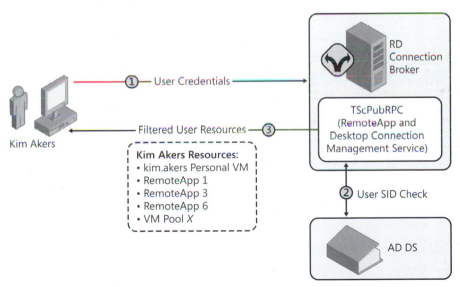

FIGURE 4-3 How VM discovery works

> **NOTE** It's also possible to save an RDP file that points to a personal VM or pool and email that file to someone or put it on a network share. If you do that, the connection process will be the same, but users can skip the discovery step (the process of finding out what VMs are available to you). Distributing RDP files manually saves a few steps in publishing but complicates the process of updating available resources, especially in large environments.

Brokering a Connection

Kim initiates the brokering phase by clicking the personal desktop or pooled VM icon. At this point, she's requested a type of resource, like access to a VM pool, and the brokering must get her to the most appropriate location based on the server load and what she's asked for.

The RD Connection Broker is built to be flexible both in terms of determining what kind of resource Kim wants to connect to (a VM or a session) and the rules governing which connection is most appropriate. It does this by using a couple of different kinds of plug-ins: *resource plug-ins*, which are used for a specific kind of resource, and *filter plug-ins*, which are used in combination with a particular resource plug-in to tweak the rules governing which resource is chosen and what happens to prepare it for a connection. The brokering service communicates with the resource plug-ins to engage them as appropriate for the type of connection. It also gets the VM IP address back from the VM resource plug-in to inform the client of its final endpoint. See Figure 4-4 for a diagram of the relationship between the component parts.

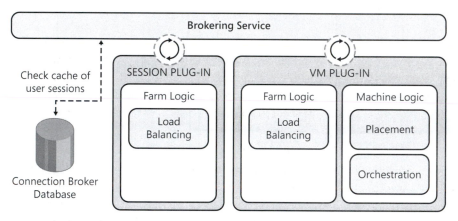

FIGURE 4-4 The Brokering service on the RD Connection Broker engages with the appropriate resource plug-in.

RD Connection Broker comes with two resource plug-ins: a session plug-in used for connecting to RD Session Host servers and a VM plug-in used to connect to personal and pooled VMs. Each of these resource plug-ins comes with built-in internal logic that the RD Connection Broker uses to determine where a connection should go and how it's made ready to accept connections. By default, the VM plug-in will distribute VM requests evenly among all RD Virtualization Host servers available. Because our basic scenario includes only a single server, all connections will go there, but if more were available, then it would use a round-robin technique to distribute the VM requests. Resource plug-ins are stored on the RD Connection Broker in HKLM/System/CurrentControlSet/Services/Tssdis/Parameters/Resource.

Figure 4-5 shows the settings for the VM resource plug-in. (This RD Connection Broker has only the VM Resource plug-in because there are currently no RD Session Host farms configured on it.) The value for IsEnabled must be 1 for the plug-in to function, and the system must be able to identify the plug-in by name, class ID (the unique identifier for a COM object), and provider.

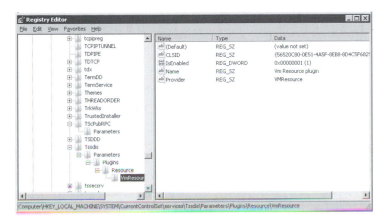

FIGURE 4-5 Built-in VM resource plug-in

Although RDS comes with only two plug-ins (again, the RD Session Host plug-in doesn't show here because this RD Connection Broker is not connected to an RD Session Host farm), independent software vendors (ISVs) can implement resource plug-ins for other kinds of endpoints as well, such as blade PCs or physical desktops. The brokering logic used to connect to and prepare those resources would depend on how the ISV had implemented the resource plug-in and the rules that were included. These rules could be built into the resource plug-ins or implemented as filter plug-ins to the main resource plug-in, as the ISV saw fit.

To change the default behavior of the resource plug-in, you'd add a new filter plug-in and associate it with that resource plug-in. For example, you might want to change the way that load balancing works. Rather than sending VM requests to each RD Virtualization Host in turn, an ISV might create a product to send them to the host server with the lowest processor stress, or the lowest number of currently running VMs. In that case, the ISV doesn't have to change the underlying logic to connect to a VM—just the rules by which it happens. Filter plug-ins can control behavior for load balancing (picking the right endpoint), orchestration (readying a VM for a connection), or placement (putting a VM on a host). Filter plug-ins are stored on the RD Connection Broker in HKLM/System/CurrentControlSet/Services/Tssdis/Parameters/Filter.

Each filter plug-in is associated with a single resource plug-in, and more than one filter plug-in can be active at one time. To determine which filter plug-in's rules will prevail in case of a conflict, you can set priority when implementing the filter plug-in. Filter priority is set in HKLM/System/CurrentControlSet/Services/Tssdis/Parameters/Filter/*n*, where *n* is a whole number greater than 0.

Orchestrating a VM

Discovery and brokering get a user 95 percent of the way to a working VM, but not 100 percent. The final stage is *orchestration*, which means to make the VM ready for connections. Orchestration is an important step. Without it, the VM would have to be constantly on, waiting for a connection. Orchestration makes it possible to put a VM to sleep and wake it up on demand, saving hardware resources on the host.

> **NOTE** Although the Microsoft VDI model also supports placement, RDS alone doesn't implement placement; add-ons might. If you're using RDS only, then the VMs you run will need to be on the hosts where they will be running.

As shown in Figure 4-6, during orchestration, the VM Host Agent finds a VM on the RD Virtualization Host that doesn't already have a connection and wakes it. You can watch this from Hyper-V Manager. A sleeping VM will wake up and be ready to accept incoming connections. The key part of this is the VM Host agent—without that, the hypervisor has no way to know that it needs to wake up the VM. The WTS application programming interface (API) shown here is for managing the VM sessions. In Chapter 11, "Managing Remote Desktop Sessions," you will learn more about how you can use tools built on this API to interact with sessions and VMs.

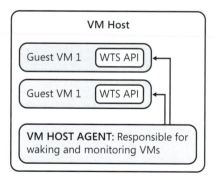

FIGURE 4-6 The VM Host Agent wakes up and monitors the VMs on the RD Virtualization Host.

Connecting to a VM Pool

When Kim gets the icon representing the VM pool or personal desktop, she can click it to initiate the connection process. Let's start with the pooled VM case (shown in Figure 4-7) and assume that she is making a new connection and does not have any disconnected sessions available. Kim would proceed with the following steps.

1. Kim clicks the icon representing the VM pool. Doing so opens the RDP file associated with that icon, which then populates the fields of MSTSC.DLL with the information in the RDP file. MSTSC.DLL sends this connection request to the redirector. (The redirector is an RD Session Host server that has been configured not to accept incoming connections, but only forward requests to the RD Connection Broker.)

2. The redirector sends the request to the RD Connection Broker. Although broken out as separate machines in Figure 4-7, to better illustrate the connection process, the RD Connection Broker can be on the same server as the redirector, and this is in fact recommended.

3. The RD Connection Broker inspects the information that MTSC.DLL sent and learns that Kim is attempting to connect to a VM and the VM is a pooled VM. The RD Connection Broker activates the VM resource plug-in. Knowing that Kim requested a VM pool, the RD Connection Broker checks its connection database to see whether Kim already has a disconnected session on a VM in the pool. It knows this because the VM Host Agent on each RD Virtualization Host updates the RD Connection Broker when a VM's state changes.

4. Having a found a VM Host, the VM plug-in sends a request to the VM Host agent on the RD Virtualization Host server and asks that the VM be prepared for Kim's connection.

5. The VM Host agent orchestrates the VM (and restores it to a ready state if it is hibernating) and, when it's ready, gets its IP address.

6. The VM Host agent passes the IP address to the RD Connection Broker.

7. The RD Connection Broker sends the IP address to the redirector.

8. The redirector sends the IP address to the client from which Kim made the original request.

9. Kim is seamlessly disconnected from the RDP connection to the redirector and reconnected to the VM using the IP address that the redirector sent to her computer.

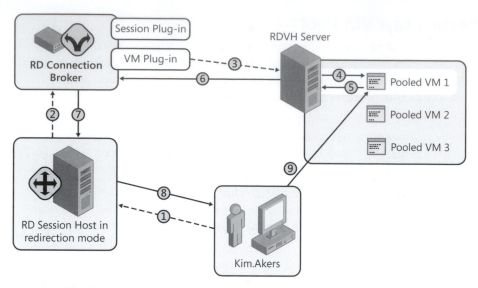

FIGURE 4-7 Kim Akers connects to a VM pool.

How did the RD Connection Broker determine that Kim wanted to connect to a pooled VM? The answer lies in the RDP file she was using. The following line entry contained in the RDP file connects a user to a pooled VM because of the *1* after *vmresource* and the Pool ID. The Pool ID is the way that the RDP file and RD Connection Broker identify the pool, as opposed to the friendly name that people use.

```
loadbalanceinfo:s:tsv://vmresource.1.VM-POOL-ID-GOES-HERE
```

If the code included a 2 instead of a 1 and no Pool ID, that would have indicated a personal VM. However, because the default load balancing sends a user to a personal VM if he or she has one, this line isn't really required for connecting to personal VMs.

Connecting to a Disconnected Session

If Kim had already had a session, this process would have changed slightly at Step 3. If Kim already has a session on a VM, there's no need to do load balancing—you want her to return to the VM where she has that session so she can continue working. Therefore, in that case, the VM Plug-in will contact the VM Host agent on the RD Virtualization Host server where the VM is placed and ask it to ready the VM to accept connections. When it's ready, the IP address will be returned to Kim's computer, as described in the previous section.

Rolling Back a VM

Rolling back a VM means reverting a VM's state to a prior point in time. This is done by taking a "snapshot" of the VM and then using it to return to the state the VM was in when the snapshot was taken. Think of a snapshot as a static picture of a VM. When a VM is rolled back, any changes made to the VM beyond the point when the snapshot was taken are reversed.

CAUTION It's best to snapshot a VM when it's turned off, so that the VM doesn't preserve any temporary data that you don't want to be part of the pooled VM. Do ensure that the VMs are gracefully powered down; if you just turn the VM off in Hyper-V instead of gracefully shutting down, then the VM will not start normally and will show the boot menu to choose normal or safe mode.

Those who've used Terminal Services in the past to access sessions might wonder why rollback is an issue. When you're done with a session, you just log off and, except for changes written to your profile, any changes that you made while the session was active are gone. This is because an RD Session Host server is, in best practice, properly locked down to avoid user changes to the system itself.

VMs in a pool are different, however. Each user who logs on to a particular VM will see the same VM that the previous user had, not a unique session on a server. So the changes made by one user (new application installs, and so on) will still be there when one user finishes and logs off and the next user connects to that VM. Therefore, the user experience over time could vary considerably from VM to VM because changes made (by each user) to the VMs in the pool would be retained. Troubleshooting would become more complicated, because a VM's configuration would no longer be predictable. Enabling rollback on all the VMs in a pool ensures that any changes made to these VMs while a user was logged in will be discarded, thus maintaining a consistent environment for all users each time they connect to a VM in the pool.

 CAUTION Because any changes made while a user is logged on to the VM will be discarded, it is very important to update VMs while they are not in use and to then take another snapshot after this maintenance. Otherwise, those updates will also be discarded.

Connecting to a Personal Desktop

Had Kim been attempting to connect to a personal desktop, the process would have changed slightly at Step 3 in Figure 4-7. If Kim clicks on the icon to log in to her personal desktop, the VM plug-in on the RD Connection Broker should make sure she connects to that VM. RD Connection Broker can determine that she's asking for a personal desktop by adding the following line in the RDP file (either created by RD Web Access or stored in a saved RDP file).

```
loadbalanceinfo:s:tsv://vmresource.2
```

VMResource shows that she's asking for a VM, and 2 indicates that a personal VM is requested. (A 1 signifies a pool.)

When Kim clicks the icon to connect to her personal desktop, she's prompted for her credentials. When she provides her credentials to log on, she's passing them to the RD Connection Broker. RD Connection Broker checks those credentials against Active Directory and finds the name of her personal VM, stored in her user account properties. After the personal VM is located, the VM plug-in on the RD Connection Broker will contact the VM Host where her personal desktop is located and prompt the VM Host Agent there to orchestrate the VM and return the VM's IP address. The redirector returns the IP address to Kim, and the RDP client on her computer will silently disconnect from the redirector and reconnect to the personal VM.

Installing Supporting Roles for VDI

RD Virtualization Host is a new role service to RDS and is essential to Microsoft VDI, but, as discussed already, it doesn't act alone. Without RD Web Access, there's no easy way to discover the VM pool or personal desktop. Without the RD Connection Broker, there's no way for a connection to get to the right VM and have the RD Virtualization Host wake it up. Without the supporting roles, RD Virtualization Host is essentially a hypervisor with some extra—and unused—capabilities.

> **NOTE**   This implementation assumes that machines are domain joined and AD DS is available for user SID checks and RemoteApp and VM filtering.

Figure 4-8 shows a bird's-eye view of what must happen to each role service and to the VMs to support Microsoft VDI. It is also available in the files Microsoft-VDI-Setup-Steps.vsd and Microsoft-VDI-Setup-Steps.xps on the companion media.

To support Microsoft VDI, you'll need to do the following.

- Install the RD Virtualization Host.
- Install and configure the RD Connection Broker (including the redirector on the same computer).
- Install and configure RD Web Access to allow users to discover the VMs.
- Configure the VMs to work with VDI.
- Create pools and assign personal desktops as required.

The next sections explain how to accomplish each of these steps.

- Install RDVH Role Service
- Rename Personal VMs to match the VM computer name!
- Snapshot each pooled VM
- Rename each snapshot: RDV_Rollback

RDVH1

For every pooled or personal VM:

- Enable Remote Desktop and add users to Remote Desktop Users group
- HKLM/System/CurrentControlSet/Control/TerminalServer/AllowRemoteRPC = 1
- For RemoteApp for HyperV: HKLM/System/CurrentControlSet/Control/TerminalServer/fDenyTSConnections = 0
- Make Firewall Exception for Remote Service Management
- Set RDP Protocol Permissions

RD Session Host in Redirection Mode

- Install RDSH role service

Note: The RD Session Host will be put into redirection mode by the RD Connection Broker when you run the Virtual Desktops Wizard.

RD Connection Broker

- Install RD Connection Broker Service
- Add RD Web Access server to the TS Web Access Computers group (or add it to the RemoteApp and Desktop Connection Properties in the Remote Desktop Connection Manager)
- Run Virtual Desktops Wizard, specify:
  - The RDVH server
  - The RDSH server as the Redirector
  - The RD Web Access server
- Run the Create Virtual Desktop Pool Wizard

RD Web Access

- Install RDWA Role service
- Add appropriate users to the TS Web Access Administrators group so they can manage the website (local administrators already have this right)
- Add the RD Connection Broker server as a "source"

Client PC

- Run RemoteApp and Desktop Connections from Control Panel– add the feed referencing the RDWA server: *https://RDWA-Server-Name/RDWeb/Feed/webfeed.aspx*

FIGURE 4-8 Configuring role services to support Microsoft VDI

Installing the RD Virtualization Host

Installing the RD Virtualization Host role service is simple. This feature depends on Hyper-V, so RD Virtualization Host is the only RDS role service that cannot be virtualized itself.

Assuming that no RDS roles are installed on the server, you will begin to install RD Virtualization Host by opening Administrative Tools/Server Manager and choosing Roles from the menu in the left pane. Click the Add Roles link. You'll see the Before You Begin page; click Next when you are sure that you have met the recommendations to have a strong administrator password, have configured required Static IPs, and have installed the latest updates.

From the Select Server Roles page, choose Remote Desktop Services from the list. You should see the Hyper-V role service already installed as shown in Figure 4-9 (if you don't, you'll be prompted to install it when you select the role service).

> **NOTE** If you have installed RDS on this server already, begin the process from the Add Role Services link in the Role Status section of the Roles page in Server Manager. This will skip the first couple of steps and take you directly to the Select Role Services page.

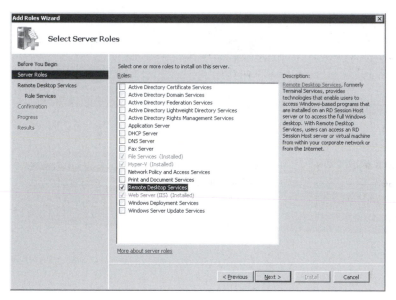

FIGURE 4-9 Hyper-V is a requirement for the RD Virtualization role service.

Click Next to open the Introduction To Remote Desktop Services page and then click Next again to open the Select Role Services page.

On the Select Role Services page, select the check box next to the Remote Desktop Virtualization Host role service and click Next, as shown in Figure 4-10.

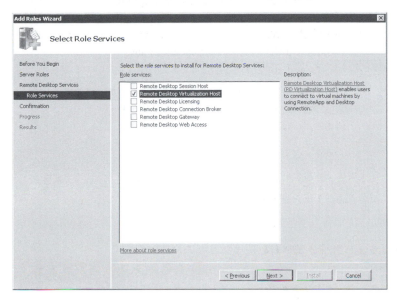

FIGURE 4-10 Select the Remote Desktop Virtualization Host role service.

Confirm your installation selections on the next page and click Install. When the installation is complete, the Installation Results screen should indicate that the installation succeeded. Click Close.

Back in the Server Manager, browse to the Roles selection and highlight Remote Desktop Services, and you will see the Remote Desktop Virtualization Host Agent running in the System Services section, as shown in Figure 4-11. This agent is responsible for orchestrating VMs, so it's essential to this role service's function.

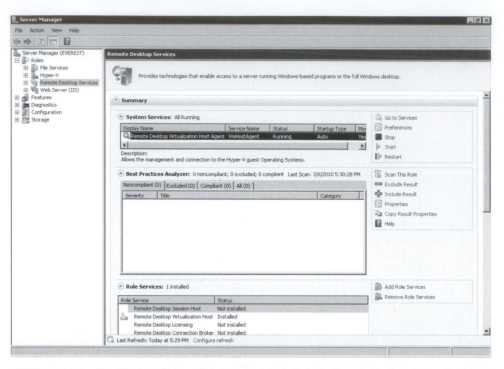

FIGURE 4-11 After the RD Virtualization Role Service is installed, the Remote Desktop Virtualization Host Agent service appears in the Server Manager.

At this point, the RD Virtualization Host is ready to support virtual desktop pools and personal desktops. Before setting those up, let's continue by installing the broker.

Installing RD Virtualization Host Role Service via Windows PowerShell

To install RD Virtualization Host role service via Windows PowerShell, import the Servermanager module as follows.

```
Import-Module servermanager
```

Then run the Add-WindowsFeature command and reference the RD Virtualization Host role service as follows.

```
Add-WindowsFeature RDS-Virtualization
```

The RD Virtualization Host role requires the Hyper-V role, and it will be installed during this installation procedure if it is not already present. If your machine does not meet the requirements for Hyper-V, the installation of RD Virtualization Host role service will fail and show you this message.

```
Add-WindowsFeature : Hyper-V cannot be installed. The processor on this computer is
not compatible with Hyper-V. To install this role, the processor must have a supported
version of hardware-assisted virtualization, and that feature must be turned on in the
BIOS...
Success Restart Needed Exit Code Feature Result
------- -------------- --------- --------------
False   No                       Failed    {}
```

Installing RD Connection Broker

Installing the RD Connection Broker role service is simple. The RD Connection Broker can be run on a VM if you've decided to virtualize your environment.

Assuming that no RDS roles are installed on the server, you will begin to install RD Connection Broker by opening Administrative Tools/Server Manager and choosing Roles from the menu in the left pane. Click the Add Roles link. You'll see the Before You Begin page; click Next when you are sure you have met the recommendations to have a strong password, have configured required Static IPs, and have installed the latest updates. From the Select Server Roles page, choose Remote Desktop Services from the list.

> **NOTE** If you have installed RDS on this server already, begin the process from the Add Role Services Link in the Role Status section of the Roles page in Server Manager. This will skip the first couple of steps and bring you directly to the Select Role Services page.

Click Next to open the Introduction To Remote Desktop Services page and then click Next again to open the Select Role Services page.

On the Select Role Services page, select the check box next to Remote Desktop Connection Broker and click Next, as shown in Figure 4-12.

The RD Connection Broker requires an RD Session Host server configured in redirection mode (for the sake of convenience, we'll call that server the redirector because that's its job) to pass it incoming RDP connections. As discussed earlier, the RDP requests don't go directly to the RD Connection Broker but to the redirector. For simplicity, set up the redirector on the same computer as the RD Connection Broker. To do this, also choose RD Session Host from the list shown in Figure 4-12.

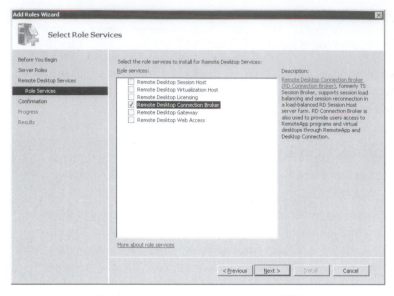

FIGURE 4-12 The RD Connection Broker is a role service of RDS.

Confirm your installation selections on the next page and click Install. When the installation is finished, the Installation Results screen should indicate that the installation succeeded. Click Close. The RD Connection Broker is now installed and ready to be configured for pooled and personal VMs.

To install RD Connection Broker via Windows PowerShell, first import the Servermanager module as follows.

```
Import-Module servermanager
```

Then run the Add-WindowsFeature command and reference the RD Web Access role service as follows.

```
Add-WindowsFeature RDS-Connection-Broker
```

The results of a successful installation will look like this.

```
Success Restart Needed Exit Code Feature Result
------- -------------- --------- --------------

True    No             Success   {Remote Desktop Connection Broker}
```

To remove the RD Connection Broker role service via Windows PowerShell, use this command.

```
Remove-WindowsFeature RDS-Connection-Broker
```

Configuring RD Web Access

RD Web Access is instrumental to discovering VMs, but its scope goes beyond that to include RemoteApp programs, VMs, full desktop sessions, and even physical desktops. For more information on how to install and configure this role service for different scenarios, see Chapter 9. For this circumstance, we will assume that you have installed the role service and want to configure it to serve VMs only.

To publish pooled and personal VMs via RD Web Access, the role service needs to be configured with a source for which the website will display personal and pooled VMs. For this scenario, you need to configure RD Web Access to pull information from RD Connection Broker, so the first thing that you need to do is add the RD Web Access server to the TS Web Access Computers group on the RD Connection Broker server. After you have done this, it's time to configure RD Web Access from the website itself. Access it by doing either of the following.

- Select the Remote Desktop Web Access Configuration tool listed in the Remote Desktop Services folder in Administration Tools.

- Open Windows Internet Explorer and type the following URL.

  ```
  https://servername/RDWeb
  ```

  where *servername* is the name of your RD Web Access server. You can also substitute *localhost* for the server name if you are accessing the website from the server itself.

A fresh install of the RD Web Access website will configure the site as a secured site using a Hypertext Transfer Protocol Secure (HTTPS), and it will have a Secure Sockets Layer (SSL) certificate assigned to it automatically. The certificate will be a self-signed certificate, with the server FQDN representing the certificate common name. For example, if you were to install RD Web Access on a server called Colfax.ash.local, the self-signed certificate assigned to the certificate is made for Colfax.ash.local and signed by Colfax.ash.local. However, accessing the site by either of these methods will produce an error page that says the following.

```
The security certificate presented by this website was not issued by a trusted
   certificate authority.
The security certificate presented by this website was issued for a different website's
   address.
Security certificate problems may indicate an attempt to fool you or intercept any data
   you send to the server.
```

This is expected behavior; the certificate assigned does not have a common name that is referenced in the URL opened by the RD Web Access Configuration tool (it uses localhost instead of the server FQDN), nor is the certificate trusted by default. Click the Continue To This Website link and you will get a logon screen.

> **NOTE** Chapter 10, "Making Remote Desktop Services Available from the Internet," explains how to avoid this error.

Members of the local administrators group are allowed to configure RD Web Access by default, so log on with an administrator account, as shown in Figure 4-13.

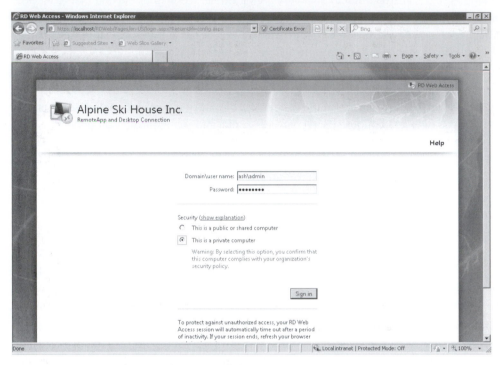

FIGURE 4-13 Log on to the RD Web Access website.

Enter your user name in the form of *domain/user name*, enter your password, and click Sign in.

> **NOTE**   In the security section of this page, you have the option of selecting whether you are accessing this website from a public or private computer. If you choose the option This Is A Public Or Shared Computer, then the timeout for the website login is shorter than if you choose the option This Is A Private Computer.

Next, you will be taken to the Configuration tab of the website, as shown in Figure 4-14.

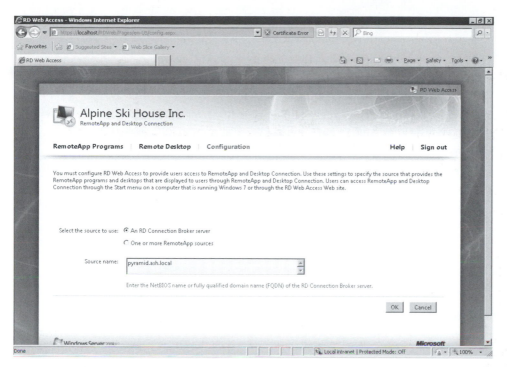

FIGURE 4-14 Add a source for RemoteApp programs and desktops to RD Web Access.

When you access personal and pooled VMs, you must specify an RD Connection Broker server as the source because this is the server that is aware of those personal VM assignments and VM pools. Select the An RD Connection Broker Server option and enter the fully qualified domain name (FQDN) of the RD Connection Broker server. Click OK.

> **NOTE** If you did not add the RD Web Access server to the TS Web Access Computers group on the RD Connection Broker server, you will see the following error.
>
> RD Web Access was not able to access the RD Connection Broker server specified. Ensure that the computer account of the RD Web Access server is a member of the TS Web Access Computers security group on the RD Connection Broker server.

Configuring the RD Connection Broker Server

After you have the role services installed that this VDI solution requires, it's time to do some basic configuring of the RD Connection Broker server. This role service depends on the availability of other RDS role services to do its job, so you need to tell the server about these other role services. The Configure Virtual Desktops Wizard walks you through this configuration. It will prompt you for the following information.

- The name of the RDSH redirector from which it will be receiving incoming requests, and to whom it will be sending fulfilled request information.

- If you need to provide redirection for clients using RDC 6.1 or earlier, then you will provide the alternative server name, which basically is the same redirector server, but uses a different issued Domain Name System (DNS) host record.

- If you will require connections to go through RD Gateway, then you will provide this RD gateway information (you'll find out more about this in Chapter 11).

- If you will sign the RDP files created for pooled and private desktop connections, you will provide the digital certificate used to sign these files (discussed in more detail in Chapter 8, "Securing Remote Desktop Protocol Connections").

Start the wizard by clicking the Configure Virtual Desktops link in the Actions pane of the Remote Desktop Connection Manager. As shown in Figure 4-15, this will open the wizard's Before You Begin page.

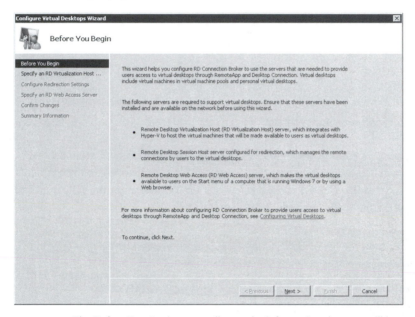

FIGURE 4-15 The Before You Begin page tells you the information that you will be providing in the following pages.

Click Next to select the RD Virtualization server(s) that will support your VM pools and personal desktops, as shown in Figure 4-16. You can use one or more RD Virtualization Host servers to support the pool.

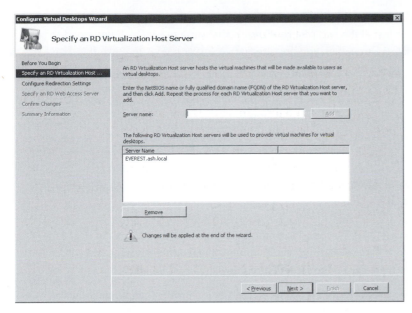

FIGURE 4-16 Provide the names of the RD Virtualization servers that will provide personal and pooled VMs.

After choosing the RD virtualization host server, click Next to configure the redirection settings, as shown in Figure 4-17.

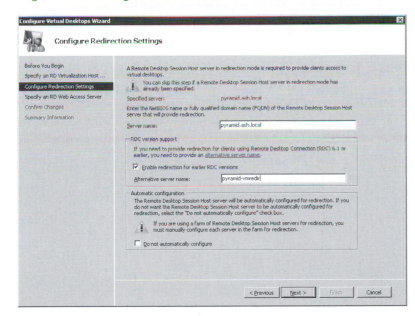

FIGURE 4-17 Provide the name (and the alternative name, if you want) of the RD Session Host redirector.

Add the name of the redirector (this can be the same machine as the RD Connection Broker if you chose to install the two role services on the same machine). If you need to support clients using RDC 6.1 or earlier, add an "alternative server name" to make this work. You create an alternative name by adding another Host record (an A or AAAA record) to DNS with an unique name that points to the IP address of the RD Session Host server that is in redirection mode. For example, Figure 4-17 shows that the alternative name for the redirector server is pyramid-vmredir, so the DNS entry added to DNS would be pyramid-vmredir.ash.local and would map to the same IP address as the DNS entry that is already created for this server: namely, pyramid.ash.local.

Configuring RD Session Host Server Role Service for Redirection Manually

You don't *have* to let the wizard automatically configure the RD Session Host server appropriately for its redirection duties. If you don't, however, you will need to do this manually on the server. Here's how.

1. Add the RD Session Host server name to the Session Broker Computers group on the RD Connection Broker server.

2. On the RD Session Host server, open the RD Session Host Configuration tool, and in the middle pane, double-click Member Of Farm In RD Connection Broker.

3. On the RD Connection Broker tab, click Change Settings.

4. In the Remote Desktop Virtualization section, select the Virtual Machine Redirection option.

5. At the bottom of the RD Connection Broker Settings screen, enter the name of the RD Connection Broker server and click OK.

You will see a warning dialog box that tells you the changes that will be made to the RD Session Host if you put it in redirection mode. In short, those changes mean that people will not be able to use the RD Session Host to run RemoteApp programs or full desktops. Click Yes and then click OK on the Properties dialog box that appears.

When you're finished, click Next to indicate the RD Web Access server that will enable discovery, as shown in Figure 4-18.

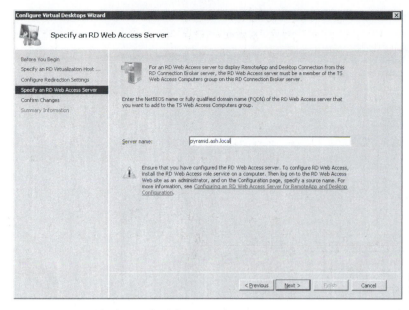

FIGURE 4-18 Provide the name of the RD Web Access server.

Specify the RD Web Access server that will provide access to pooled and personal VMs to users. In this example, the RD Web Access server and the RD Connection Broker are the same server, but they do not have to be. When you've chosen the server, click Next to review the changes, as in Figure 4-19.

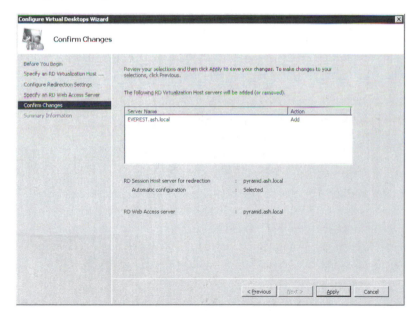

FIGURE 4-19 Review and confirm your selections and then apply them.

When you're sure that you have set up the RD Connection Broker server correctly, click Apply to finish and view a summary of the settings (shown in Figure 4-20).

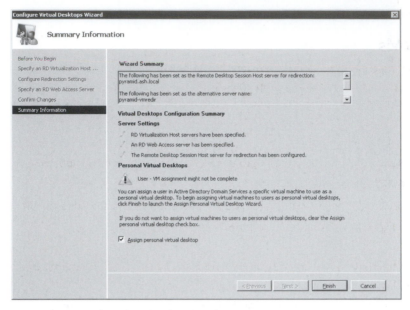

FIGURE 4-20 Complete the wizard to view the summary.

Notice that no personal VMs are yet assigned—hence the yellow warning symbol. This isn't necessary to configure a VM pool, though.

These settings can be adjusted at any time. To access the configuration pages, in Remote Desktop Connection Manager, select RD Virtualization Host and then right-click and choose Properties to view or edit the settings on the Redirection Settings tab. These settings should be familiar to you because you configured them using the wizard previously.

> **NOTE** Because we haven't yet discussed the roles of the RD Gateway or digital signature, we won't discuss those tabs of the Properties dialog box until Chapter 10 and Chapter 8, respectively.

If you use a text editor to open a pooled or personal VM RDP file RD Web Access created (for example, one that was provided in RemoteApp and Desktop Connections on clients running Windows 7), you'll notice something a bit odd: the primary full address setting value will be that of the alternate server name, and the alternate full address setting will have the primary server name as its value, like this:

```
alternate full address:s:pyramid.ash.local
full address:s: pyramid-vmredir
```

This is more of a curiosity than anything else; don't edit the RDP file to reverse the settings and do not change the settings in the Remote Desktop Connection Manager to reflect the settings in the RDP file.

Setting Up VMs

VDI is built for delivering client operating systems, and the in-box solution supports Windows XP SP3, Windows Vista SP1, and Windows 7. To prepare a VM to be used as a pooled or personal VM, you need to make a few adjustments to the operating system. On each VM, you must do the following.

1. Enable Remote Desktop.

2. Add the people who will be using the VM to the Remote Desktop Users group.

3. Enable RemoteRPC on the VM.

4. Give the RD Virtualization Host server the required permissions to orchestrate the VM.

5. Create firewall exceptions for Remote Desktop Protocol and Remote Service Management.

6. Reboot to restart the Terminal Services service and use the new permissions (required for Windows XP VMs only).

We will go through each of these steps in detail, but if this looks like a lot of work to do on every VM, you'll be glad to know that you don't have to: Microsoft has provided a script to do this prep work. Download the script from *http://gallery.technet.microsoft.com/ScriptCenter /en-us/68462b23-0890-4dbd-95b6-8de5763e4f68*. The script works on VMs running Windows 7, Windows Vista, and Windows XP operating systems.

When you run the script, you might see two more command-line boxes appear and then disappear. This is expected; the script calls Netsh.exe to make firewall exceptions, and you are seeing Netsh running in a command prompt.

Both personal and pooled VMs must be in a domain. All members of a pool must be in the same domain, but there are no specific requirements for the AD DS schema. All personal desktops must be in a native-mode domain; you can use the additional functionality in the User Account Properties tab to assign a personal VM if you use Windows Server 2008 R2. (Windows Server 2008 doesn't have the graphical user interface for this, so you will need at least one domain controller running Windows Server 2008 R2 or a computer running Windows 7 with the Remote Server Administration Tools installed to make the assignment.)

Enable Remote Desktop and Add Users to the Remote Desktop Users Group

Remote Desktop is not enabled by default on client operating systems. To permit incoming RDP connections to a client, you must enable them. To do so, go to the Control Panel and open System. Click the Remote Settings link on the left side of the dialog box to open the tabbed dialog box shown in Figure 4-21.

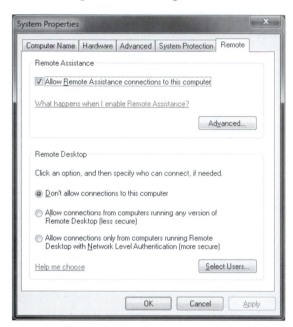

FIGURE 4-21 Enable Remote Desktop.

To enable connections, choose one of the two options. If the computers that you'll be using to connect to this VM are running Windows Vista or later, you can choose the option requiring Network Level Authentication (NLA), which requires that a user provide credentials before establishing a session with the endpoint. If they'll be running other operating systems (for example, earlier versions of Microsoft Windows CE), allow connections from any version of Remote Desktop.

> **NOTE** Chapter 8 discusses how NLA works.

Before any users can log on to a computer running Windows via RDP—server or client—their user account must be added to the Remote Desktop Users group on the client. (Administrators are built into this group, which is why this step is not required for remote administration.) To select users to be added to this group, click Select Users (or Select Remote Users in Windows XP), as shown in Figure 4-21, to open the dialog box shown in Figure 4-22 (the domain and user name are deleted in the dialog box shown here).

FIGURE 4-22 Add users to the Remote Desktop Users group.

If you click Add, you'll open the Select Users dialog box. Browse to the desired user group (or individuals, as required) and add them.

Enable RemoteRPC

Remote Procedure calls (RPCs) allow other processes to connect with the operating system. They're required to allow the VM Host Agent to wake up the VM. To allow RPC connectivity, set the value of AllowRemoteRPC to 1 in the location HKLM/System/CurrentControlSet/Control/Terminal Server, as shown in Figure 4-23.

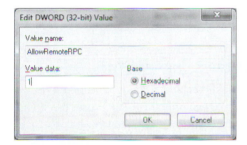

FIGURE 4-23 Enable RemoteRPC.

Create Firewall Exceptions for RDP and Remote Service Management

By default, traffic for Remote Desktop and Remote Service Management (which uses named pipes and RPCs) are not allowed to pass through the firewall. To enable this traffic, go to the Control Panel and open the Windows Firewall configuration tool shown in Figure 4-24.

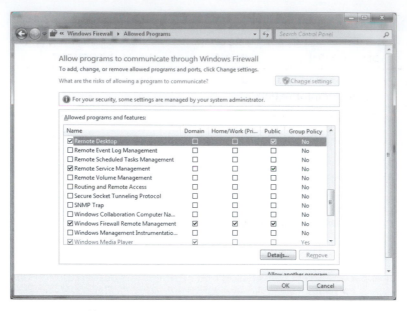

FIGURE 4-24 Enable Remote Desktop through the firewall.

Select the check boxes for both services to enable this traffic through the machine firewall and then click OK.

For Windows XP, you will not see these options in Firewall. Run these commands at a command prompt to accomplish these configuration changes.

```
netsh firewall set service type=REMOTEDESKTOP mode=ENABLE profile=ALL
netsh firewall set service remoteadmin enable subnet
```

Configure RD Virtualization Host RDP Permissions

During this step, you're giving the RD Virtualization Host machine account appropriate RDP permissions on the VM. As you might have noticed while exploring RDP-TCP Properties on an RD Session Host server, the Security tab has an Advanced button. Click it to view the Advanced Security Settings, and you can click Edit to display the Permissions Entry dialog box with the permission settings shown in Table 4.1.

TABLE 4-1 Available and Required Permissions for the RD Virtualization Host Server to Manage VMs

SETTING	DESCRIPTION	PROGRAMATIC VALUE	REQUIRED BY RDVH FOR VM MANAGEMENT
Query Information	Query sessions and servers for information	0	Yes
Set Information	Configure connection properties	1	Yes (used to set query, logoff, and disconnect permissions)
Remote Control	View or actively control another user's session	4	No
Logon	Log on to a session on the server	5	No
Logoff	Log off a user from a session	2	Yes
Message	Send a message to another user's sessions	7	No
Connect	Connect to another session	8	No
Disconnect	Disconnect a session	9	Yes
Reset	Reset (terminate) a session	6	No
Virtual Channels	Use virtual channels	3	No

We've included the programmatic values in this table to make it easier to follow what the next commands (and the script that you saw a link to earlier) are doing. Essentially, it's allowing the RD Virtualization Host server to query the VM status via RDP, log off the connection, and disconnect a session.

To allow the RD Virtualization Host to manage the VM, you'll need to edit these settings on each VM. Because the client operating system does not have the RD Session Host UI, you'll need to execute the following commands at a command prompt.

```
wmic /node:localhost RDPERMISSIONS where TerminalName="RDP-Tcp" CALL AddAccount
    "contoso/rdvh-srv$",1
wmic /node:localhost RDACCOUNT where "(TerminalName='RDP-Tcp' or TerminalName='Console')
    and AccountName='contoso//rdvh-srv$'" CALL ModifyPermissions 0,1
wmic /node:localhost RDACCOUNT where "(TerminalName='RDP-Tcp' or TerminalName='Console')
    and AccountName='contoso//rdvh-srv$'" CALL ModifyPermissions 2,1
wmic /node:localhost RDACCOUNT where "(TerminalName='RDP-Tcp' or TerminalName='Console')
    and AccountName='contoso//rdvh-srv$'" CALL ModifyPermissions 9,1
Net stop termservice
Net start termservice
```

ON THE COMPANION MEDIA   This code is contained in batch files on the companion media called RDP-Permissions.bat (for Windows Vista and Windows 7) and RDP-Permissions-XP.bat (for Windows XP). To use these files, edit the variables DOMAINAME and RDVH-SERVERNAME to reflect your domain name and RD Virtualization Host server name.

Giving RD Virtualization Host Access to VMs Running Windows XP

Rajesh Ravindranath
Software Development Engineer II, Remote Desktop Virtualization team

The process of setting up a VM is the same whether or not the VM is running Windows XP SP3 or Windows 7. However, Windows XP does not make the RDPERMISSIONS and RDACCOUNT aliases available to WMIC, the Windows Management Instrumentation (WMI) command-line tool, so you need to call the WMI interfaces slightly differently from the way you do with Windows 7. To give the RD Virtualization Host server the right permissions on a Windows XP VM, run the following commands at a command prompt.

```
WMIC.exe /node:localhost /namespace://root/cimv2 PATH
    Win32_TSPermissionsSetting where TerminalName="RDP-Tcp" CALL
    AddAccount "contoso/rdvh-srv$",1
WMIC.exe /node:localhost /namespace://root/cimv2 PATH Win32_TSAccount
    where "(TerminalName='RDP-Tcp' or TerminalName='Console') and
AccountName='contoso//rdvh-srv$'" CALL ModifyPermissions 0,1
WMIC.exe /node:localhost /namespace://root/cimv2 PATH Win32_TSAccount
    where "(TerminalName='RDP-Tcp' or TerminalName='Console') and
    AccountName='contoso//rdvh-srv$'" CALL ModifyPermissions 2,1
WMIC.exe /node:localhost /namespace://root/cimv2 PATH Win32_TSAccount
    where "(TerminalName='RDP-Tcp' or TerminalName='Console') and
    AccountName='contoso//rdvh-srv$'" CALL ModifyPermissions 9,1
```

Enabling Rollback (Pooled VMs Only)

To keep pooled VMs in a pristine state, you'll need to enable rollback on them to discard any changes made while a user was logged on. Essentially, you'll create a snapshot for each VM and rename it RDV_Rollback. When the VM Host Agent puts the machine into a saved state, it will restore the snapshot.

To enable rollback on a VM, perform the following steps.

1. Log on to the RD Virtualization Host server using an Administrator account.

2. In Administrative Tools, open Hyper-V Manager.

3. Under Virtual Machines, right-click a running VM and then click Snapshot. Wait while the system creates the snapshot.

4. When the snapshot is complete, rename it to RDV_Rollback.

Rollback occurs when the user logs off the VM. The VM is saved and then immediately reverted and returned to its state at the time of rollback. Make sure that the VM is in the state you want it to be in when you're rolling back before making the snapshot.

Creating Pools

There's really no relationship between a VM pool and the server on which it's located; the pool boundaries are not driven by the hosts' capacity. A VM pool can be on a single server, or it can be spread across multiple servers. An RD Virtualization Host server can have one pool's VMs on it or more than one. Because a pool does not have to be located on a single server, you can add capacity just by adding new servers and adding the VMs from those servers to the pool.

To create a VM pool, go to Administrative Tools/Remote Desktop Services/Remote Desktop Connection Manager on the RD Connection Broker. From the left pane, right-click RD Virtualization Host Servers and choose Create A Virtual Desktop Pool to start the wizard, as shown in Figure 4-25.

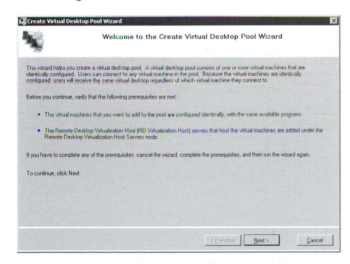

FIGURE 4-25 Review settings for the pool before beginning.

The advice that the wizard gives here is important. First, the VMs in a pool should all be identical, or else the user's experience will change depending on which VM he or she connects to. This pertains to operating systems too: Windows 7 VMs should be in one farm, and any Windows XP VMs should be in another. In addition, make sure that the RD Connection Broker already is aware of about the RD Virtualization Host where you've set up the VMs to populate the pool. When you're sure of both of these items, click Next to select VMs to add to the pool.

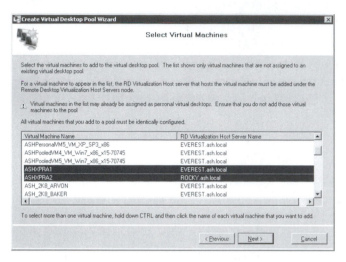

FIGURE 4-26 Choose VMs to populate the pool.

Choose the VMs by highlighting them (to select more than one, hold down the Ctrl key and click each VM that you want to add), as shown in Figure 4-26. Notice that it is much simpler to choose the right VMs if you are very explicit about the VM configuration (defining the operating system, whether it's 32-bit or 64-bit, and so forth). All VMs on the RD Virtualization Host will be displayed here, whether they are running client or server operating systems. The VMs selected in this example will back a pool of Windows XP SP3 VMs.

NOTE   Microsoft VDI is for supporting client operating systems, but, especially in small deployments where one piece of hardware supports many roles, it's possible that an RD Virtualization Host server could have VMs running a server operating system.

When you've selected all the VMs, click Next to continue to the Set Pool Properties page shown in Figure 4-27.

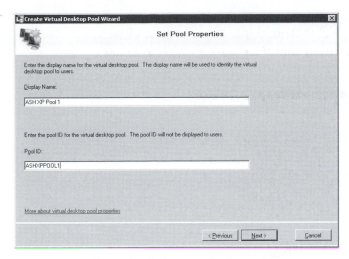

FIGURE 4-27 Configure the display name for the pool.

Type a display name for the pool (notice that, to make it easier to determine the pool's contents, we named it according to the operating system of the VMs in it). Then enter a Pool ID for the pool. The Pool ID is used by the RDP file to identify the pool. When you are done, click Next to review the settings, as shown in Figure 4-28.

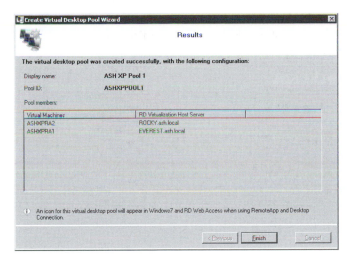

FIGURE 4-28 Review the farm settings for the VM pool.

In this example, the VMs are actually located on two different RD Virtualization Host servers, so both are listed here. Click Finish to close the wizard.

Assigning Personal Desktops

Personal desktops are dedicated to one person. Technically, users could connect and use a VM without RDS, just like a desktop, provided they knew the name of the VM and the user was added to the Remote Desktop Users group on that VM (as part of setting up the VM). Assigning a user a personal desktop in the RD Connection Broker means that the user does not need to know the name of the VM, create an RDP file, or configure an RDC connection to access the VM. All of this is done automatically for the user and is provided as a link in RD Web Access or as a link on the user's Start menu on computers running Windows 7.

After you have prepared a VM to be used as a personal VM (see the section entitled "Setting Up VMs" earlier in this chapter for details on how to do this), you are ready to assign it.

To assign a VM, open the Remote Desktop Connection Manager on the RD Connection Broker, expand RD Virtualization Host Servers, right-click Personal Virtual Desktops, and choose Assign Personal Desktops to users, as shown in Figure 4-29. Alternatively, in the Actions pane, click Assign Personal Desktops to assign to each user.

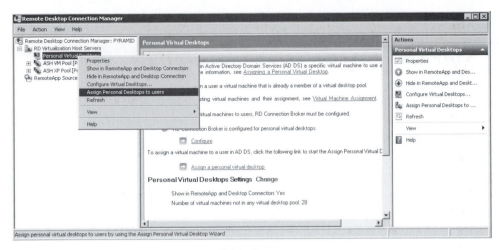

FIGURE 4-29 Assign personal desktops to individual users.

Clicking the link will start the Assign Personal Virtual Desktop Wizard shown in Figure 4-30.

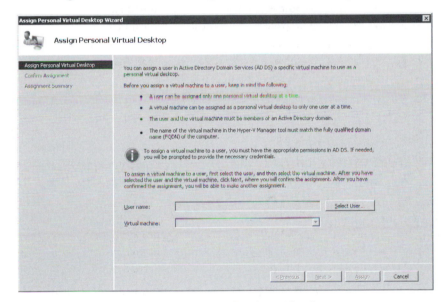

FIGURE 4-30 Open the Assign Personal Virtual Desktop Wizard.

The first page of the wizard offers general guidelines about personal desktops: They can be assigned to only one user at a time, each person can only have one desktop at a time, both user and VM must be domain members, and the name of the VM must match the name in the Hyper-V Manager. (For more specifics about the domain requirements for personal desktops, see the following sidebar.)

AD DS Schema Requirements for Personal Virtual Desktops

Janani Venkateswaran
Program Manager II, Remote Desktop Virtualization

Microsoft's VDI solution offers two deployment scenarios: virtual desktop pools and personal virtual desktops. Virtual desktop pools do not depend on a specific AD DS schema level; however, personal virtual desktops do need a Windows Server 2008 or Windows Server 2008 R2 schema.

Following are the AD DS requirements for personal virtual desktops.

- To deploy personal virtual desktops, your schema for the AD DS forest must be at least Windows Server 2008. To use the added functionality provided by the Personal Virtual Desktop tab in the User Account Properties dialog box in Active Directory Users And Computers, you must run Active Directory Users And Computers from a computer running Windows Server 2008 R2 or from a computer running Windows 7 that has Remote Server Administration Tools (RSAT) installed.

- You must use a domain functional level of at least Windows 2000 Server native mode. The functional levels Windows 2000 Server mixed mode and Windows Server 2003 interim mode are not supported.

Next to the User Name input box, click Select User . . . and choose a user from AD DS to whom you want to assign the VM. When you've done so, the Virtual Machine drop-down menu will become active. From the drop-down menu, select the VM to be assigned to this user. All available VMs on all RD Virtualization Host servers that are added to RD Connection Broker will be listed in the Virtual Machine drop-down menu. When you've chosen the VM, click Next. Confirm the assignment as shown in Figure 4-31 and then click Assign.

Finally, on the Assignment Summary page, either click Finish or select the check box to assign more VMs. Selecting the check box will enable the Continue button, allowing you to assign more VMs to users. Then, when you click Continue, the wizard will restart, and you will go through the same procedures for each VM that you want to assign.

When you are finished assigning VMs to users, clear the Assign Another VM To Another User check box. The Continue button will change to a Finish button. Click Finish, and you are done.

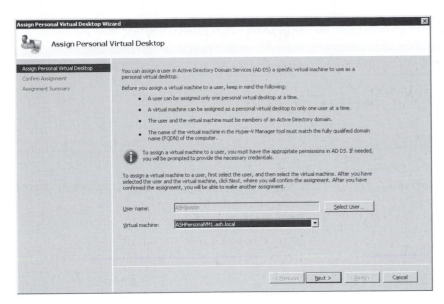

FIGURE 4-31 Confirm the VM assignment.

Creating an RDP file for a User to Connect to a Personal or Pooled VM

If you'd like to experiment with personal VMs without needing to use discovery, here's how. Creating an RDP file to give to users to connect to their personal VMs is a matter of adding a few extra settings to a saved RDP file.

Start by opening Remote Desktop Connection (Mstsc.exe). In the Computer Name input box, add the name of the Remote Desktop Session Host server that is put in redirection mode. Enter the user name of the user that will be receiving and using this RDP file. Doing this adds the following lines to the RDP file (the user name in this example is Kristin, and the RD Session Host server in redirection mode is Humpback.ash.local).

```
username:s:kristin
full address:s:humpback.ash.local
```

Save the file and then open it in a text editor (like Notepad.exe). Now add the following line (and, of course, save the file once more).

```
use redirection server name:i:1
```

If any consumers of this RDP file will be using RDC 6.1 client or earlier, then you also need to add the alternative name of the RD Session Host server in redirection mode that is specified on the Redirection Settings tab of the RD Connection Broker Virtual Desktop Properties dialog box. The example line of code here specifies the server name humpback-vmredir.

```
alternate full address:s:humpback-vmredir
```

Creating an RDP file used to connect to the VM pool is the same process as creating an RDP file to connect to a personal VM, with one difference. You must specify the VM Pool ID, so that the redirector knows that the user needs to connect to the VM pool, instead of a personal VM. To do so, add the following line to the RDC file.

```
loadbalanceinfo:s:tsv://vmresource.1.VM-POOL-ID-GOES-HERE
```

The VM Pool ID is located on the General tab of the VM Pool Properties dialog box in the RD Connection Broker. The 1 in the previous line signifies that a pooled VM is requested. A 2 indicates a personal VM, but if a personal VM exists for a user, then the RD Connection Broker will send them there automatically, even without the 2 specified; that's how load balancing works for VMs. It's similar to the way that the broker will always reconnect a user to a disconnected session instead of starting a VM.

Configuring Personal and Pooled VM Properties

For both pooled and personal VMs, you can control the following RDP settings for all personal VMs and on a per pool basis.

- Display name and pool ID (pools only)
- Whether to show the personal or pooled VM in RD Web Access
- Automatically saving VMs after a given time period
- Device and resource redirection
- Display settings
- Custom RDP settings (like audio settings)

To configure RDP settings for all personal VMs, in Remote Desktop Connection Manager, expand RD Virtualization Host Servers, right-click the Personal Virtual Desktops, and choose Properties. Doing so will bring up the Personal Virtual Desktops Properties tabbed dialog box, as shown in Figure 4-32.

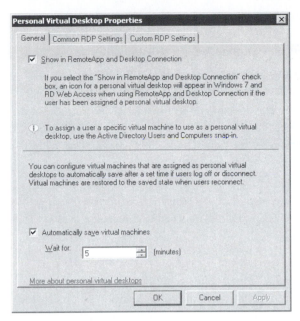

FIGURE 4-32 Configure personal VM RDP settings via the Personal Virtual Desktops Properties tabbed dialog box.

On the General tab, enable users to see their personal virtual desktop (should they be assigned one) in RD Web Access and in their Start menu by selecting the check box next to the option Show In RemoteApp And Desktop Connection.

> **NOTE** You can also toggle showing and hiding personal VMs in RADC and RD Web Access by right-clicking Personal Virtual Desktops and then choosing the setting from the shortcut menu.

To save power on your RD Virtualization host servers, set your personal VMs to go into a saved state when a certain amount of time has passed after a user logs off or is disconnected. Machines are saved in the state they are in at that time, and they are restored to this state when needed again. To set this option, select the Automatically Save Virtual Machines check box and then choose a time in minutes (with a minimum of 5) to wait before the VM is put into a saved state.

Next, select the Common RDP Settings tab. Here you can control device and resource redirection by selecting the check boxes next to the resources you want the user to have access to in the remote session. By default, all redirection is allowed. You can also control the following display settings.

- **Allow Font Smoothing**   Font smoothing is allowed by default. To disable it, clear the check box next to Allow Font Smoothing.

- **Multiple Monitor Use**   By default, the session will use all client monitors when connecting to the personal VM remote session. To use only one monitor, clear the check box next to Use All Client Monitors When Connecting To A Remote Desktop.
- **Color Depth**   By default, this is set to high quality (32 bit). Change the session color depth by opening the corresponding drop-down menu and choosing 15, 16, or 24 bit.

To specify custom RDP settings (settings that are configurable in an RDP file but not set on the preceding two tabs), click the Custom RDP Settings tab. Here you can input RDP settings including audio redirection settings, custom desktop height and width, and whether Windows key combinations are applied to the local or remote computer.

> **NOTE**   For details on RDP settings you can customize, see *http://technet.microsoft.com /en-us/library/ff393699(WS.10).aspx*. The link is also available on the companion media. For a full list of RDP settings, see Appendix A.

Custom settings you input cannot overwrite settings already configured in Remote Desktop Configuration Manager. If a setting is invalid or tries to overwrite a setting that is already configured, you will get an error and you will need to remove the custom setting.

To configure RDP Settings on a per-VM-pool basis, right-click the VM pool you want to configure and choose Properties. The pool's Properties dialog box will appear. These settings are identical to the settings available to personal VMs, except that on the General tab you can also edit the pool display name (the name that appears in RD Web Access and RADC) as well as the Pool ID (the ID that RD Connection Broker uses to identify the pool). Change these settings by editing the text in the corresponding text boxes. When you are done editing RDP settings for pools or personal VMs, click OK to save the changes.

Personal and pooled VM RDP settings are also configurable via PowerShell. To get to these settings, import the RDS Module.

```
Import-Module RemoteDesktopServices
```

Navigate to the personal or pooled VMs section.

```
cd connectionbroker\virtualdesktops\pools\
```

Then navigate further to PersonalVirtualDesktops or to a named pool and edit settings using the set-item command.

Using RemoteApp for Hyper-V for Application Compatibility

Thus far in this chapter, you've learned about VMs in the context of desktop replacement. They also have an additional use: application compatibility. Using VMs, you can upgrade the client operating system on the desktop to Windows 7 while continuing to run applications that require Windows XP. One obvious example of this would be a web application requiring Microsoft Internet Explorer 6. That version of Internet Explorer doesn't come with Windows 7, and you can't virtualize it using App-V. Windows Server 2003 Terminal Services doesn't support RemoteApp programs, either. Without this feature, you'd have one option: set up a Windows Server 2003 terminal server and run the application from there on a full desktop.

RemoteApp for Hyper-V makes this unnecessary. This feature enables a client running Windows XP SP3 (or Windows Vista, or Windows 7) to serve RemoteApp programs to a computer running Windows 7 (or technically, to any computer running the RDC 7 client). The endpoint can still support only a single connection—that's how an RDP connection to a client operating system works—but this feature can enable you to use Windows 7 on the desktop while exporting older applications to the newer platform.

One connection doesn't mean one RemoteApp. If a VM is providing more than one RemoteApp program, then a user can run as many as required; all will run on the same VM, in the same session.

> **NOTE** This feature also allows Windows 7 and Windows Vista to serve RemoteApp programs. However, most applications that run on either of those platforms will run on Windows Server 2008 or Windows Server 2008 R2. Rather than using RemoteApp for Hyper-V, it might be more cost-effective to run RemoteApp programs that don't require Windows XP from a terminal server/RD Session Host. This is because a client operating system can support only a single active remote connection.

When you run a RemoteApp from a guest operating system, it will retain the look and feel of the operating system that it's running on. That is, if the endpoint is running Windows XP, the RemoteApp will have the Windows XP title bar and controls.

If you've heard of a feature called XP Mode, you might have noticed that this sounds extremely similar. For those who haven't, when running a computer in XP Mode, you use Microsoft Virtual PC to run a guest VM of Windows XP on the local computer and run applications from there. This works well in many cases. RemoteApp for Hyper-V differs from XP Mode in being appropriate in the following cases.

- **When the client can't run Virtual XP or can't support two operating systems running at the same time**   Netbook computers are one good example of this situation. They can run Windows 7, but you're not likely to be happy running Windows 7, Virtual PC, and Windows XP at the same time on a low-power computer.

- **When the user needs the application only occasionally, or only for a few minutes at a time**   If someone's using an application for 5 minutes an hour, it's either a waste of computing resources to keep the Windows XP VM running or a waste of time to keep starting it whenever you need the application.

Configuring RemoteApp on Hyper-V

To use RemoteApp on Hyper-V, you must configure both the client and the endpoint, as follows.

- The VM must be running Windows XP SP3 (Professional Edition), Windows Vista SP1 (Enterprise or Ultimate Edition), or Windows 7 (Enterprise or Ultimate Edition).

- The VM must have the update to enable RemoteApp delivery (Windows XP and Windows Vista only) and you must edit the registry to allow the RemoteApp program to start.

- The client must have the RDC 7 client installed and an RDP file configured to connect to a RemoteApp.

- Set Group Policy to disconnect sessions on the endpoint after a certain amount of time.

Let's start with the endpoint.

Configuring the VM

To configure the VM, first install the update that enables this feature. Again, this is not required for Windows 7, but it is required for Windows Vista SP1 and Windows XP SP3. The update is available only for 32-bit operating systems.

To install the hotfix for Windows XP, navigate to *http://www.microsoft.com/downloads /details.aspx?FamilyID=2f376f53-83cf-4e5b-9515-2cb70662a81b&displaylang=en* and choose to download the hotfix.

When it's downloaded and you run it on Windows XP, you'll be prompted to install KB961742-v3.exe. Click Run to unpack the installation and begin. The steps are simple.

1. Review the opening page and note that you might need to restart the computer after installing the hotfix.

2. Agree to the license terms.

3. Let Setup check the current configuration.

4. When prompted, click Finish to end the installation and prompt the reboot.

> **IMPORTANT** The hotfix for Windows Vista is located at *http://www.microsoft.com /downloads/details.aspx?displaylang=en&FamilyID=097b7478-3150-4d0d-a85a-6451f32c459c*. When you have installed the update, install the application that you want to publish as you would normally.

When the application is installed, you'll need to permit people to initiate a connection to the VM by starting that application. To use the Microsoft terminology, you're adding it to the allow list. To do so, you'll be editing the Registry.

On the VM, enable RemoteApp for Hyper V by changing the following value from 0 to 1.

```
HKLM/Software/Microsoft/Windows NT/CurrentVersion/Terminal Server/TsAppAllowList/
    fDisabledAllowList = 1
```

ON THE COMPANION MEDIA The registry import file to change this key is located on the companion media as a file called DisabledAllowList.reg. The code of this file is

```
Windows Registry Editor Version 5.00
[HKEY_LOCAL_MACHINE/SOFTWARE/Microsoft/Windows NT/CurrentVersion/
    Terminal Server/TSAppAllowList]
"fDisabledAllowList"=dword:00000001
```

Readying the Client

The client must have RDP 7 installed. RDP 7 is preinstalled on Windows 7; you can download it to install on 32-bit Windows XP or Windows Vista as well (see the section entitled "Additional Resources" later in this chapter for the location of the download).

Editing the RDP File

When the hotfix is installed and the VM rebooted, you're ready to configure an RDP file to access a RemoteApp program. Open an RDC on the client PC and configure the RDC as if you were going to access the full desktop of the VM. Save this file, naming it something like the name of the application that it will ultimately open (such as Remote Notepad).

Right-click the RDC file and open it with a text editor like Notepad. Edit the following two lines to match the following.

```
remoteapplicationmode:i:1
alternate shell:s:rdpinit.exe
```

Then add the following lines (edit them to suit your needs).

```
RemoteApplicationName:s:FRIENDLY NAME FOR APP GOES HERE (example: Remote Notepad)
RemoteApplicationProgram:s:PATH TO APP GOES HERE (example: %windir%/system32/notepad.exe)
DisableRemoteAppCapsCheck:i:1
Prompt for Credentials on Client:i:1
```

Those settings will work if you have just one machine. But most likely you will have multiple computers providing these RemoteApp programs, configured as a VM pool. If so, then the RDP file needs adjusting to connect to the pool. The computer name that you enter will need to be the name of the RD Session Host server redirector, and you need to add this line to the RDP file.

```
loadbalanceinfo:s:tsv://vmresource.1.POOL-ID-GOES-HERE
```

After you've configured the RDP file appropriately, then anyone attempting to use the RemoteApp VM pool will be routed to the most appropriate endpoint for their session, just as they would for a full desktop. If a user attempts to start a second RemoteApp program that is provided by VMs in the pool, then the RD Connection Broker will route their connection request to the VM where they're already running a RemoteApp. This is because the first step of brokering is to see if the person attempting to connect already has a session running.

Configuring a Time Limit for Disconnected Sessions on the Endpoint

When a user starts a RemoteApp program on a VM running RemoteApp for HyperV, when the user closes the application, their session on that VM remains active, and stays active, even if the VM is put into a saved state. When the VM is restored, the last user who had started the RemoteApp will still be logged on to that machine. In addition, because clients can have only one session going at a time, this computer is now effectively only usable by that user. That is, *no* other users will be able to start a RemoteApp on this machine.

Fortunately, you can set a time limit for disconnected sessions on the endpoint via a Group Policy object (GPO). Here's how.

1. Create an organizational unit (OU) for your endpoint(s) in Group Policy Manager, add the endpoint computers to this OU, and then create a GPO and enable this setting.

   ```
   Computer Configuration | Policies | Administrative Templates | Windows Components
   | Remote Desktop Services | Remote Desktop Session Host | Session Time Limits |
   set the time for disconnected sessions
   ```

2. When you have enabled the setting, choose a time period after which a disconnected session will be ended.

3. Apply the GPO to the Endpoint OU that you just created and reboot the endpoints (because computer policies are applied at startup).

Can You Use RemoteApp for Hyper-V *Without* RDS?

It is technically possible to use the RemoteApp feature on any client, whether it's a VM on Hyper-V (or any hypervisor, really) without RD Virtualization Host, a blade, or a physical desktop. We do recommend using this feature as part of RDS, however. Combining this feature with a connection broker is likely to lead to the most efficient use of resources with the simplest management.

As a reminder, each VM can sustain only a single connection at a time, even though it's publishing RemoteApp programs like an RD Session Host server. Without a broker in the mix, connecting to one or two people can effectively monopolize the farm if they connect to a different VM each time.

If you dedicated a RemoteApp for each person's exclusive use and saved the VM's name in the RDP file for each RemoteApp, you could pull this off. However, this isn't a very efficient way of allocating resources. The VMs won't be available for anyone else's use, and if you're not using RD Virtualization Host and the RD Connection Broker, you'll need to make sure that they're turned on and ready for their owners to use. It's more effective to arrange the VMs for RemoteApp on Hyper-V in a dedicated pool. Just modify the pooled RDP file as described in this section to support publishing RemoteApp programs from a VM.

Troubleshooting: Why Did a Pooled VM Connection Fail?

A user clicked an icon to connect to a pooled VM, and the connection didn't work. Why not? Here are two things that can go wrong during the connection, aside from the standard "you didn't configure this properly" errors reported at *http://technet.microsoft.com/en-us/library/ee891400(WS.10).aspx*.

Waking the VM . . .

This is about the elusive "Waking the VM..." message and eventual timeout. There are a few reasons for this, all of which have to do with not having the client configured correctly. You will receive this error for the following reasons.

- The VM has not been prepared properly. You will experience this situation when any of the preparation was not done, including the exceptions in the firewall, the registry entry adjustments, or the WMIC commands.

- The VM was prepared properly, but the Rollback snapshot was taken before the preparation was finished, and as a result, the VM can 't accept connections.

Unable to Verify Settings . . .

Another scenario that produces obscure errors in the Event Log is one in which the RD Connection Broker has issues connecting the client to the requested VM. The user tries to initiate a connection to a pooled or personal VM, but he or she receives an error message saying that the connection could not be established because the Connection Broker was unable to verify the settings in the RDP file. On the Connection Broker, the following two errors are logged in the TerminalServices-SessionBroker-Client event log.

```
Event ID 1296:
Remote Desktop Connection Broker Client failed while getting redirection
    packet from Connection Broker.
User : ASH/kristin
HRESULT = 0x80070490
```

followed by

```
Event ID: 1306:
Remote Desktop Connection Broker Client failed to redirect the user
    ASH/kristin.
HRESULT = 0x80070490
```

Remedy this situation by re-running the Configure Virtual Desktops Wizard on the RD Connection Broker server. You do not need to change any of the settings (unless they are wrong, of course). Just re-run the wizard with the same settings as you had before, and the RD Connection Broker will resume working properly.

Summary

Adding VM support to RDS increases the number of scenarios that RDS can support. Although sessions still allow you to get more people per server, VMs have their own advantages. Personal desktops enable complete desktop replacement, moving the personal computers into the data center and providing more central management. Pooled VMs allow a set of people to share a more isolated environment than a session can provide. RemoteApp for Hyper-V allows you to serve applications from a client running Windows XP to a Windows 7 desktop, even if the client running Windows 7 can't run a local hypervisor.

After reading this chapter, you should know the following.

- When to use VMs instead of sessions
- When to use personal and pooled VMs
- How to set up VM pools and personal desktops
- How discovery, brokering, and orchestration work
- How to use RemoteApp for Hyper-V to publish applications from a Windows XP VM

Additional Resources

The following resources contain additional information and tools related to this chapter.

- The hotfixes to enable RemoteApp display on Windows XP SP3 are online at *http://www.microsoft.com/downloads/details.aspx?FamilyID=2f376f53-83cf-4e5b-9515-2cb70662a81b&displaylang=en.*
- The hotfix to enable RemoteApp display on Windows Vista SP1 is available from *http://www.microsoft.com/downloads/details.aspx?displaylang=en&FamilyID=26a2de17-8355-4e8d-8f33-9211e48651fb.*
- Error messages relating to RD Connection Broker are documented at *http://technet.microsoft.com/en-us/library/ee891400(WS.10).aspx.*
- For information on customizing the RDP settings used in Personal and Pooled VMs, see Chapter 6, "Customizing the User Experience."
- For instructions on installing RD Web Access, and for configuring RD Web Access to provide access to RD Session Host desktops and RemoteApps, see Chapter 9, "Multi-Server Deployments."
- For information on using RD Gateway to access pooled and personal VMs, as well as other RDS resources from outside your corporate network, see Chapter 10, "Making Remote Desktop Services Available from the Internet."

CHAPTER 5

Managing User Data in a Remote Desktop Services Deployment

Thus far in this book, you have learned how to set up a single Remote Desktop (RD) Session Host server or a simple Microsoft Virtual Desktop Infrastructure (VDI) deployment. Those deployments aren't yet production-ready, though: No applications are available, the connections aren't secured, you haven't yet defined the devices and experience to redirect, and the profiles and Folder Redirection aren't yet set up.

Properly configured profiles and Folder Redirection go a long way toward a good user experience for users working via remote connection to the data center. Because profiles weren't originally designed for remote work environments, this can sometimes be tricky. Remote Desktop Services (RDS) independent software vendor (ISV) partners have developed some products to help make a highly flexible system for complex environments. This chapter, however, shows you how best to configure profiles and Folder Redirection using the tools that come with Windows.

The basic elements of a user workspace are the configuration settings in the user's profile and the default locations to save data. After reading this chapter, you will understand the following.

- How roaming, local, and mandatory profiles work
- Why virtualization can complicate implementing profile strategies
- Best practices for storing and managing profiles
- How to use Folder Redirection to unify user default locations between local and remote applications

- The benefits and drawbacks of using mandatory profiles to maintain a consistent look and feel
- How to secure the desktop to prevent users from saving files to it and why this is important
- How to support profiles across servers running both Windows Server 2008 R2 and Windows Server 2003, or Windows 7 and Windows XP virtual machines (VMs)

How Profiles Work

A *profile* is a collection of settings and documents that define a user's work environment, sometimes referred to as a user's "personality." A user's profile includes both configuration data and personal data such as documents and pictures. Personal data in the profile can be stored on the desktop or in one of the folders associated with the user account (for example, My Documents). The profile also includes user specific settings, such as the following.

- Changes that you make to application layouts, such as adding buttons, changing the layout, and adding a default signature
- Changes to system settings that are unique to the user experience, such as changing your desktop background, screen saver, and keyboard layout

Machine-wide settings such as firewall settings are *not* stored in the user profile.

Documents and supporting files that are part of your profile are stored in a unique user profile folder (and subfolders). Local and roaming profile settings are stored as a single file (called NTUSER.DAT), not as a collection of individual settings. NTUSER.DAT is stored in the root of each user's profile folder. Mandatory profile settings are stored in NTUSER.MAN; this file can be shared among multiple users because it is read-only.

> **NOTE** Super-mandatory profiles label the folder where they're stored with the .man suffix, like this: *//servername/sharename*/mandatoryprofile.man/. Super-mandatory user profiles are similar to normal mandatory profiles except that users with super-mandatory profiles cannot log on when the server that stores the mandatory profile is unavailable. Users with normal mandatory profiles can log on with the locally cached copy of the mandatory profile. Use super-mandatory profiles only when you want to have absolute control of the user profile—so much so that you can't take the chance that a cached copy might be out of date.

While a user is logged in, the NTUSER.DAT file is loaded temporarily into HKEY_CURRENT_USER (HKCU) in the registry of the computer that user is logged on to; the documents are stored in the subfolders within the profile folder, as shown in Figure 5-1. You will find out in detail about the parts of a profile—both the registry and the data folders—later in this chapter. But first let's examine the different types of profiles.

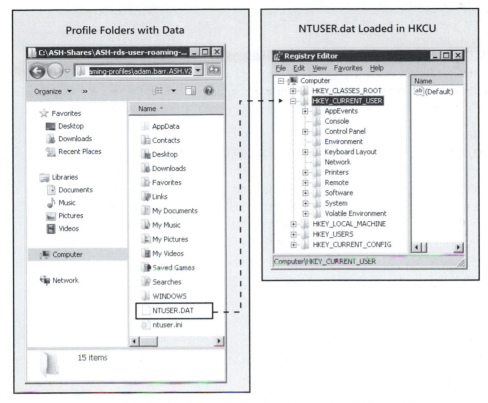

FIGURE 5-1 The user profile contains personal settings and data such as folders and the user-specific registry settings.

Types of Profiles

As alluded to in the previous section, there are three types of profiles: local, roaming, and mandatory. Local profiles are stored on and used from a single computer and store data in NTUSER.DAT. Roaming profiles are stored on and used from a network share, so they're available to any computer that can access that particular network share. They also store data in NTUSER.DAT. Mandatory profiles are often centrally located like roaming profiles, but whereas local profiles and roaming profiles are read-write, mandatory profiles are read-only. They store their settings in NTUSER.MAN.

Local profiles are usually fast to load because they are stored on the computer the user is using. When a user logs on, the local profile will load from its local location on the hard drive and populate HKCU. When the user logs off, the contents of HKCU (including any changes that the user made) will be written back to the local hard disk and overwrite the previous version of the file.

Roaming profiles afford the most flexibility in a remoting environment because they're stored in a central location accessible to all VMs and RD Session Host servers. They're also read-write, so users can adjust their settings. When a user logs onto a session or VM (or a computer, for that matter), the roaming profile will load from its network location and populate HKCU in the registry. When the user logs off, the contents of HKCU (including any changes that the user made) will be written back to the network location and overwrite the previous version of the file.

Mandatory profiles are loaded to HKCU when a user logs on, just like a roaming profile, but they aren't written back to their storage location at logoff—all changes to the profile are just discarded.

How Profiles Are Created

A user does not start with a user profile. The profile is created the first time that a user logs onto a machine. Mandatory profiles are the exception to this, and even the mandatory profile, which is used by multiple people, has to initially come from somewhere. To fully understand profiles, you need to know how profiles are initially created. This will come in handy later in this chapter, when you learn how to create a mandatory profile and also how to customize a default profile.

All profiles are created from a "default profile." Each RD Session Host—actually, every computer—has a local default user profile (located at C:\Users\Default in Windows Vista and later) for this purpose. Depending on which type of profile will be used and how you have implemented the profile strategy, the process of making user profiles varies slightly.

If your users will use local profiles (for instance, if you have only one RD Session Host), new user profiles will be created by making a copy of the local default profile located on the computer that the user logs on to. This copy will go into a new folder labeled by the login name of the user.

If your users will use roaming profiles, when a new user logs on to a server for the first time, a new profile is created for him by making a copy of a default user profile. Domain joined computers will first look for a network default user profile (stored in the netlogon share on a domain controller and replicated to other domain controllers). If it does not find one in the network share, then it will use the local default profile located on the computer to which the user logged on.

User Profile and the Registry

The registry is organized into sections called *keys,* which align with a particular configuration option. For example, computer-wide settings are stored in HKEY_LOCAL_MACHINE (HKLM), whereas user-specific settings are stored in HKEY_CURRENT_USER (HKCU). As with all versions of Microsoft Windows NT since it was first released, Windows Server 2008 R2 and Windows 7 maintain user-specific settings in HKCU for each user logged on to the computer.

You can see how HKCU works and reflects changes to the user environment by following the process outlined in the following How It Works sidebar, "Observe How Changes to the Environment Are Reflected in the Registry."

HOW IT WORKS

Observe How Changes to the Environment Are Reflected in the Registry

One easy way to watch how HKCU changes as you customize your environment is to make a change and watch the contents of the registry, as follows.

1. Run Regedit.exe and confirm that you want to run it when prompted.

2. Navigate to HKCU\Control Panel\Colors\ and look at the value of the Window key. If you're using the default Windows 7 color scheme, the value of this entry should be 255 255 255. (Full saturation of red, blue, and green values show up as white on a monitor. Values of 0 for all three show up as black. If you ever studied color theory, this is a demonstration that black is the absence of color.)

3. Right-click the Desktop and choose Personalize from the context menu to open the Personalization window.

4. Click Window Color And Appearance. In the Appearance Settings dialog box, click Advanced to open the aptly named Advanced Appearance dialog box. From here, select Window from the Item drop-down list. Change Color 1 to light gray and click OK.

5. Click OK in the Appearance Settings dialog box. The screen will adjust for a moment, and then the background color of windows will turn light gray.

6. If you examine the value of HKCU\Control Panel\Colors\Window, you'll see that it's now 192 192 192.

In Windows Server 2008 R2 and Windows 7, HKCU contains the subkeys described in Table 5-1. Even if you're logging on to a Windows Server 2008 R2 RD Session Host server from an earlier operating system such as Windows XP, the profile in the RD Session Host session corresponds to the server platform. These are still the registry keys that apply to the session, not the client computer operating system. There might be additional subkeys in this section; it depends on which applications you have installed. For example, if you install Microsoft Outlook, you'll see an Identities key.

TABLE 5-1 Subkeys of HKCU in Windows 7 and Windows Server 2008 R2

SUBKEY	DESCRIPTION	MAPS TO
AppEvents	Sounds played on system events.	Control Panel\Sounds
Console	Command window settings such as window size, colors, and buffer size.	Command Prompt\Properties
Control Panel	User desktop appearance settings, mouse and keyboard settings, power policy, and accessibility.	Control Panel
Environment	Environment variable definitions.	Control Panel\System\Advanced
EUDC	Customized characters that users install for viewing and printing documents when standard fonts don't support them. Applies to East Asian font sets.	Control Panel\Fonts
Keyboard Layout	Edits the keyboard layout. Useful if your operating system is displaying in one language but you want to use the keyboard layout of another one (for example, displaying in English but arranging the keyboard as though you were in Germany).	Control Panel\Regional and Language Options
Network	Network drive mappings and settings.	Control Panel\Networks
Printers	Printer connection settings.	Control Panel\Printers
Remote (Remote Access in Windows 7)	Contains settings to be applied to remote sessions (for example, ClearType or wallpaper) for each session. The subkey corresponds to the Session ID.	
Session Information	Information about the current session, such as how many applications are open.	Not stored—populated during the session
Software	Personal settings for all software installed for that user.	Individual applications
System	Contains the current control set for that user (drivers and services to run at startup).	Not stored—populated on startup
Volatile Environment	Environment variables for the current logon session.	Not stored—populated for each session

Data is stored in HKCU only for the duration of the session, while data stored in HKLM persists until the reboot. Most pieces of the registry are saved in files called *hives* and are loaded as necessary. When a hive file is opened, it's reloaded into the registry. Therefore, HKCU is stored as a hive in a file called NTUSER.DAT that is loaded at user logon. Each user logged on to an RD Session Host server sees his or her own version of HKCU.

How does this data get loaded? When you log on to a computer, the User Profile Service loads the hive file from the location specified in your user account properties and populates HKCU for that session. When you log off the computer, the hive file is written back to its storage location as NTUSER.DAT. If you happen to be logged on to more than one computer at a time, two copies of your profile will be open, populating the contents of HKCU on each computer.

> **NOTE** Profiles can be cached on the server to speed up logons if you set the corresponding Group Policy. However, even if you enable caching, when a user logs off the RD Session Host server, the corresponding branch of HKCU is cleared. You'll find out more about caching user profiles in the section entitled "Caching Roaming Profiles" later in this chapter.

In addition to loading HKCU with the contents of your profile, logging on to an RD Session Host server updates two parts of HKLM, the computer-wide section of the registry. HKLM\Software\Microsoft\Windows NT\CurrentVersion\Profile List (Figure 5-2) contains a list of all profiles cached on the computer. It also lists the profiles used by the System account, Network Service account, and the Local Service account. As you can see, machine accounts have profiles just like user accounts do.

The users are identified by security identifiers (SIDs), but you can distinguish them by browsing the keys. The values show the path to both the local cache (the ProfileImagePath key value shown in Figure 5-2) and to the roaming profile folder share (the CentralProfile key value shown in Figure 5-2), so it's not hard to map user names to profiles.

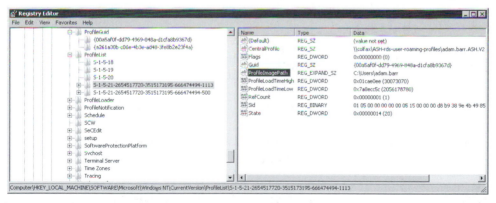

FIGURE 5-2 Loading a profile into a remote desktop session updates the Profile List key for the entire RD Session Host server.

When you log off an RD Session Host server, the two keys with your SID are locked. They don't actually go away, but if you attempt to open the key associated with a user who is currently logged off, you'll get an error message telling you that the system cannot find the file specified. Log on again, and the key with the same SID will be repopulated.

Although loading a profile adds two keys to the registry that never go away, most of the time it doesn't matter. As discussed in the section entitled "The Consequences of Deleting a Profile Folder from Windows Explorer" later in this chapter, it *does* matter should you choose to delete a profile. Deleting the file doesn't delete the registry keys associated with it. Therefore, always use the correct tools to delete profiles; otherwise those users won't be able to load their profiles properly when they log on again.

How Profile Changes Are (Not) Merged

The operating system loads the contents of NTUSER.DAT into HKCU at logon and saves back to NTUSER.DAT at logoff, in the same way that you might open a Microsoft Word document when you log on, type in it for a while, and then save the document when you log off. This has some important implications for a remote environment.

As an example, imagine this scenario: You are logged on to two different computers and you open a new Word document in each session. In Session 1, you type "Every Good Boy Does Fine." In Session 2, you type "All Cows Eat Grass." You save the file in Session 1 as Myfile. docx. Next you save the file in Session 2 as Myfile.docx in the same location, confirming that you want to overwrite the old file when prompted.

The next time you open Myfile.docx, the file will say only "All Cows Eat Grass." The phrase "Every Good Boy Does Fine" has been overwritten. In short, the files are not merged; they're written back to the save location, and the version last written to that location is the only one you'll see.

So it is with profiles, which are just another type of file. If you log on to two sessions, each of which is using the same roaming profile, you will have two copies of your profile open. If you make changes to the open profile, you'll see them at the time, but they won't be saved into NTUSER.DAT until you log off. (Unlike the Word .docx file, the file system won't ask if you want to overwrite the profile file.) As in the previous example, if you have a profile open in Session 1 and in Session 2, log off Session 1 and then log off Session 2, only the changes made to the Session 2 copy of the profile will appear when you log on again and reload that profile. The only difference from the document scenario is that the operating system won't ask you if you want to overwrite the previous version.

 CAUTION One implication of the way profiles work is that you shouldn't use the same profile for local sessions and remote sessions. If you do, then by definition, every time you log on to your computer and then log on to an RD Session Host server, you will be opening two copies of your profile. You will almost certainly lose profile data this way.

You might be wondering whether opening two RemoteApp programs from a single RD Session Host server opens one or two copies of your profile. The answer depends on the version of Windows Server hosting the session, and how you're starting the applications. On a terminal server running Windows Server 2003, you could create a Remote Desktop Protocol (RDP) session that would open a single application instead of displaying the entire desktop. (As noted in Chapter 1, "Introducing Remote Desktop Services," not many people did this because the experience wasn't very user-friendly, but it was possible.) If you presented individual applications this way, then each time a user opened an application on the same server, he would open a separate session and therefore a separate copy of the profile.

Windows Server 2008 improved on this design in two ways. First, it introduced RemoteApp programs. All RemoteApp programs started from the same server by the same user account run in the same session, so they open only a single copy of your profile. Second, when deciding where to route incoming connections to an RD Session Host server farm, the RD Connection Broker will check to see if a user already has an open session on an RD Session Host server in the farm. If it does, then the user will be routed to the same session to start the application. So, what is the result? You have preference to the server where you already have an open connection, *and*, so long as you're connecting to only a single server, only one copy of the profile will be open because all RemoteApp programs will run in the same session.

Profile Contents External to the Registry

Not all parts of a profile are stored in HKCU. The same folder that contains the NTUSER.DAT file also contains other folders that contain user data as well as application-specific data. In Windows Vista and Windows Server 2008, the profile includes the folders listed in Table 5-2. (More folders might be available, depending on which applications you have installed.)

TABLE 5-2 Folders Associated with a Windows 7 or Windows Server 2008 R2 Profile

FOLDER	DESCRIPTION
AppData	Default root location for user application data and binaries.
Contacts	Used to store contact information and is also the address book for Windows Mail, the successor to Microsoft Outlook Express (Windows Mail is not included in Windows 7 or Windows Server 2008 R2).
Desktop	All items stored on the desktop, including files and shortcuts.
Documents	Default root location for all user-created files (spreadsheets, text documents, and so on).
Downloads	Default location for all files downloaded using Windows Internet Explorer.
Favorites	Bookmarked Uniform Resource Locators (URLs) in Internet Explorer.
Links	File and folder shortcuts; these show up under the Favorites menu on the left side of an Explorer window.
Music	Default root location for all music files.

Continued on the next page

FOLDER	DESCRIPTION
Pictures	Default root location for all image files.
Saved Games	Default location for saved games.
Searches	Default location for saved searches performed from the Search Programs And Files input box on the Start menu.
Videos	Default root location for all video files

Beginning in Windows Vista and Windows Server 2008, the profile structure changed from Windows XP and Windows Server 2003. (Windows 7 and Windows 2008 R2 retain this new profile structure.) The new structure uses more folders to organize the data.

Notice that Windows XP and Windows 2003 were not mentioned in Table 5-2. This is because profiles have evolved over time and the structure of profiles has changed. Windows XP and Windows Server 2003 profiles are called version 1 (V1) profiles; profiles using the structure of Windows Vista and Windows Server 2008 and later are called version 2 (V2) profiles. A V2 user profile folder is distinguished from its predecessors by an added .V2 extension.

Version 2 profiles generally use more folders than those of Windows XP, but V1 top-level folders such as NetHood and PrintHood were moved inside the AppData folder beginning in Windows Vista. Table 5-3 (adapted from the Microsoft document "Managing Roaming User Data Deployment Guide" located at *http://technet.microsoft.com/en-us/library/cc766489(WS.10).aspx*) shows the differences in the default root profile folder structure between V1 and V2 profiles.

TABLE 5-3 Profile Folder Structures of V1 and V2 Profiles

V2 PROFILE FOLDERS (WINDOWS VISTA AND LATER)	V1 PROFILE FOLDERS (WINDOWS XP AND WINDOWS SERVER 2003)
Now AppData\Roaming	Application Data
Contacts	Not Applicable
Desktop	Desktop
Downloads	Not Applicable
Favorites	Favorites
Links	Not Applicable
Documents	My Documents
Music	In My Documents
Pictures	In My Documents
Videos	Not Applicable
Saved Games	Not Applicable

V2 PROFILE FOLDERS (WINDOWS VISTA AND LATER)	V1 PROFILE FOLDERS (WINDOWS XP AND WINDOWS SERVER 2003)
Searches	Not Applicable
Tracing	Not Applicable
Now in AppData folder	My Recent Documents
Now in AppData folder	NetHood
Now in AppData folder	PrintHood
Now in AppData folder	Send To
Now in AppData folder	Start Menu
Now in AppData folder	Templates
Now in AppData folder	Local Settings
Now in AppData folder	Cookies

As you might have noticed in Table 5-3, the Local Settings folder from V1 profiles does not exist in V2 profiles, and many V1 profile folders are now consolidated under the AppData folder in V2 profiles. Why does this reorganization of data matter?

One big accomplishment of the V2 profile reorganization is that machine-specific data is now separated from user-specific data. V1 profiles kept machine-specific and user-specific data scattered through the profile. V2 profiles sort this data and do a better job of separating user-specific data from data that is either too large to roam with the user or is specific to a particular machine and therefore should not roam.

In V2 profiles, the AppData folder now has three subfolders that separate this kind of data.

- **AppData\Roaming**   Data that is user-specific and should roam with the user profile
- **AppData\Local**   Data that is either machine-specific or too large to roam with a user's profile folder, for example, an Outlook .OST file
- **AppData\LocalLow**   Data for "low-integrity" apps (such as browser-based apps) to store data

Table 5-4 (which was adapted from the Microsoft "Managing Roaming User Data Deployment Guide") shows where certain V1 profile data is stored in the V2 profile structure.

TABLE 5-4 Data Storage Reorganization from V1 to V2 Profiles

V2 PROFILE DATA LOCATIONS	V1 PROFILE DATA LOCATIONS
...\AppData\Local	Local Settings\Application Data
...\AppData\Local\Microsoft\Windows\History	Local Settings\History
...\AppData\Local\Temp	Local Settings\Temp
...\AppData\Local\Microsoft\Windows \Temporary Internet Files	Local Settings\Temporary Internet Files

Continued on the next page

V2 PROFILE DATA LOCATIONS	V1 PROFILE DATA LOCATIONS
...\AppData\Roaming\Microsoft\Windows\Cookies	Cookies
...\AppData\Roaming\Microsoft\Windows\Network Shortcuts	NetHood
...\AppData\Roaming\Microsoft\Windows\Printer Shortcuts	PrintHood
...\AppData\Roaming\Microsoft\Windows\Recent	Recent
...\AppData\Roaming\Microsoft\Windows\Send To	Send To
...\AppData\Roaming\Microsoft\Windows\Start Menu	Start menu
...\AppData\Roaming\Microsoft\Windows\Templates	Templates

NOTE The "Managing Roaming User Data Deployment Guide" is available at *http://technet.microsoft.com/en-us/library/cc766489%28WS.10%29.aspx.*

Because V1 profiles and V2 profiles are so different, you can't use the same profiles for Windows Server 2008 R2 RD Session Host servers that you did for terminal servers running Windows Server 2003or Windows XP VMs. The structures of the profiles don't match.

You'll learn later in this chapter how to allow Windows Server 2003 and Windows Server 2008 profiles to coexist. (See the section entitled "Sharing Folders Between Windows Server 2003 and Windows Server 2008 Roaming Profiles" later in this chapter.) This is important both for supporting mixed deployments of terminal servers running Windows Server 2003 and Windows Server 2008 R2 RD Session Hosts, and for supporting Windows 7 VM pools and Windows XP VM pools. (The changes to the profile structure between the operating systems are one reason why you should not combine Windows 7 and Windows XP VMs in the same pool.)

Introduction to Folder Redirection

Although these data folders are stored by default in the user's profile folder, they don't have to be. In fact, in most cases, it's best if some of them aren't. Here's why.

First, keeping user data within the profile folder increases the profile size. Assuming that you're storing profiles on a central share instead of on individual RD Session Host servers (and, for reasons you'll see shortly, this is a good assumption), this can slow logons. A large profile increases the time that it takes for users to log on and log off (because the data in the profile must be cached on the RD Session Host server). In Windows Server 2008 R2, if the profile cache on a server exceeds the quota allocated to the profile cache, it will delete the most recently used profiles, but there's still no reason to fill the cache with user data.

Second, if you're using mandatory profiles and you don't redirect folders outside the profile folder, users will not be able to save files to the standard personal folders such as Documents. The files will look like they're saving, but they won't be retained. This will cause users a great deal of grief and bring you many unsolvable calls to the Help desk.

> **NOTE** The Recycle Bin is a hidden file in the root of the profile folder. You can't redirect it, and even if you're using mandatory profiles, you will still be able to send files to the Recycle Bin.

The third reason applies to VMs, whether pooled or personal. In the case of a personal desktop, saving files locally preserves them, but it complicates file restore because the files are stored in the VM. To restore the files saved on the local VM, you'd need to restore the VM from backup. Saving the files separately makes it easier to restore them, and the easiest way to do that is to enable Folder Redirection. In the case of *pooled* VMs, Folder Redirection is essential. As with mandatory profiles, saving files to local folders on a pooled VM can lead to lost data. As discussed in Chapter 4, "Deploying a Single Remote Desktop Virtualization Host Server," the most common configuration for pooled VMs is to roll back changes at user logout so the VM remains pristine. That rollback means that any documents saved to the VM would be lost. (Some ISV solutions actually delete the VM on each use and re-create it, which has the same effect.)

For these reasons, it's good practice to use Folder Redirection with RDS, whether connecting to VMs or sessions. You'll learn how to do this in the section entitled "Centralizing Personal Data with Folder Redirection" later in this chapter. For now, just know that redirecting profile folders means just that: storing profile subfolders and the data within them, outside the main root profile folder.

How Virtualization Complicates Storing User Configuration and Files

This topic will be discussed a lot in this chapter, but to begin, you need to be very clear about why virtualization complicates user profiles and the way users store data. Fundamentally, it's because profiles were originally designed for logging into one place at a time, and when using RDS, you might be logged into more than one remote session.

RDS supports five remoting work scenarios.

- RemoteApp programs running from an RD Session Host server and displayed alongside locally running applications
- RemoteApp programs running from a VM (most often a Windows XP VM)
- A full desktop session on an RD Session Host server
- A pooled VM, which might be running any version of a Windows client operating system
- A personal VM, which might be running any version of a Windows client operating system

Figure 5-3 shows the intricate matrix of user profiles and redirected folders for users who access multiple desktop and RDS environments.

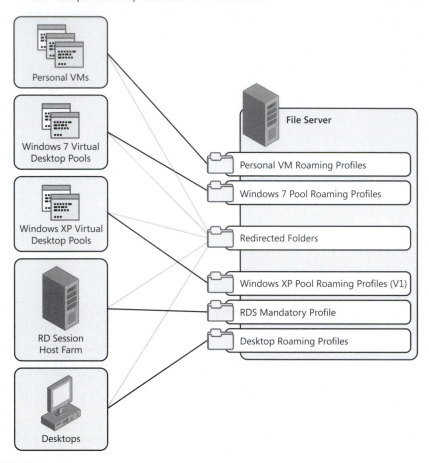

FIGURE 5-3 Providing a consistent environment for RDS environments becomes more complicated with virtualization.

So what does it mean to have all these virtualization environments available?

Using more than one or two types of virtualization can lead to profile proliferation. It's relatively simple if you use one type of virtualization. For example, if you normally work from a desktop running Windows 7 and use RemoteApp for Hyper-V to run a couple of Windows XP applications as RemoteApp programs, then you will have two profiles—one for the RemoteApp session and one for local use. Add a session to that and you could potentially have three profiles to manage. Similarly, the more server farms that a person will need to access to run RemoteApp programs, the more likely that she will have multiple copies of her profile open at once. This is a good argument against farm proliferation.

Operating systems that use V1 profiles can technically use the same V1 profile (and the same goes for operating systems that use V2 profiles). Whether this is a good idea depends on whether the settings in the profiles are appropriate to both local and remote sessions. Also, keep in mind that if you have a copy of your profile open in two sessions, then you might lose changes if you edit both copies.

Storing Profiles

By default, when you log on to a computer running Windows 7 for the first time (unless you've set up roaming profiles), you'll create a new profile in its local profile directory (%SystemRoot%\Users). This profile directory will have your name as a logon alias; it will contain your folders and NTUSER.DAT (which is a hidden file, so you won't see it unless you've enabled viewing hidden files). If left alone, thereafter you'll store everything in that location. Documents will default to Documents, images will default to Pictures, and where music is stored by default is left as an exercise for the reader. All will be well . . . so long as that's the only computer you use. If it's *not* the only computer you use, however, life gets somewhat more complicated.

Thus far, you have learned how to set up only a single RD Session Host server. However, to provide redundancy and better scale, you'll need to have multiple RD Session Host servers organized into a farm. When a user logs on to an RD Session Host server farm, the connection is passed from an RD Session Host server to the RD Connection Broker. If the user trying to connect has no current sessions, the RD Connection Broker picks the RD Session Host server with the lowest number of active sessions and sends the user there, as shown in Figure 5-4. Each time a user connects, the RD Connection Broker decides anew which server the user should connect to, based on the number of connections that each server is actively supporting and whether the user already has a session open somewhere. The user connects to the server with the fewest active connections or the one where the user already has an open session. It is likely (and highly recommended) that users will log off when not using their RD Session Host server session, so if you use local profiles for RD Session Host server sessions, then over time, a user will have a local profile on all the servers in the farm.

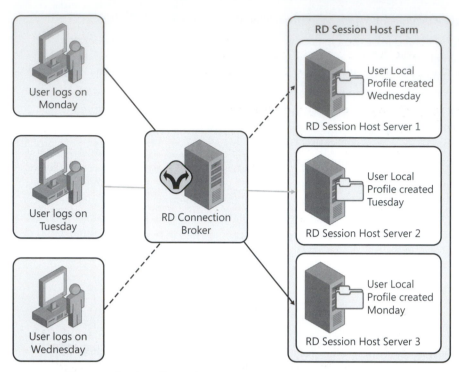

FIGURE 5-4 If you use local profiles with RD Session Host or pooled VMs, a user could eventually have local profiles on every server in the farm or every VM.

This might not sound so bad. The user's logons will occur quickly because the profile isn't loaded from the network but rather from the local computer. But when the user makes a change here and there, over time, her desktop will look completely different depending on which RD Session Host server (or pooled VM) she logs on to. (If user data is part of the profile—if you haven't redirected profile folders—the user will be even more confused because the data that she saved in one local My Documents folder won't be in another one.) If she makes a *bad* change, that change could well lead to a Help desk call that can be tricky to figure out until you determine to which RD Session Host server she is connected. This is especially true because the problem might vanish if the user logs off and then logs back on and the RD Connection Broker sends her to a different RD Session Host server.

To avoid this scenario, all the RD Session Host servers should use the same copy of the profile, which means that you need to use roaming (or mandatory) profiles stored on a network share. When a user logs on, the User Profile Service looks at the user account properties to see where the profile reserved for RD Session Host server sessions is kept and loads it from there.

When a user logs off, the profile is either deleted from the RD Session Host server or retained in the local cache, depending on the Group Policy settings applied to the RD Session Host servers. For faster logons, cache the profile. Just ensure that there's enough space on the hard disk holding the cache to support everyone who might need to cache their profile there.

Providing a Consistent Environment

The ways in which you can provide applications to users has grown, and keeping the user experience consistent across these different environments has become even more complicated. Now you must design and implement a profile strategy that takes into account the following.

- Users can use more than one endpoint type at the same time.
- Microsoft VDI can include both V1 (in Windows XP) and V2 profiles (in Windows Vista and later).
- One user can have multiple profiles.

Expect Multiple Profiles

As you offer more ways to present applications to users, delivering user configuration data in the profile gets more complicated. For example, instead of having users logging onto a single desktop and doing all of their work on that local machine, you can now offer full desktops in a session, RemoteApp programs, personal VMs, pooled VMs, and even RemoteApp programs *from* VMs. Each of these application delivery solutions has a unique environment, and therefore, when using the RDS, we recommend implementing different user profiles for each of these unique environments. The problem with this is that users expect to have the same experience wherever they log on. This is not really possible when users have multiple unique environments.

The Last Write Wins

The benefits of having multiple profiles far outweighs the profits of not having them. Implementing a unique profile for each environment helps to overcome the "Last Write Wins" problem. This is exactly what it sounds like: If a user logs on to multiple places (multiple RDS farms, for example) and those farms have all been set up so that the user utilizes a single roaming profile, then that single roaming profile gets overwritten each time the user logs off each farm. Each time the profile used in a session is copied back to the roaming profile share, it overwrites what was previously there.

The user profile is made of both folder data and registry data. You might not experience much data getting overwritten in the folder areas because you can open only certain files in certain environments (as shown in Figure 5-5). However, the user profile stored in HKCU is all contained in one file: NTUSER.DAT. As Figure 5-5 shows, if the user has a profile open in two different sessions, the second logoff will overwrite any changes saved to the profile at the first logoff.

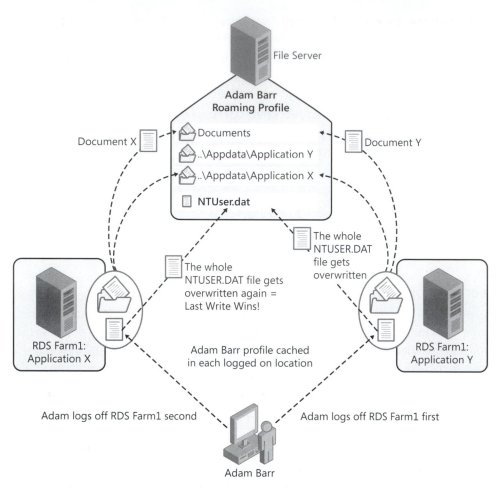

FIGURE 5-5 The Last Write Wins.

For this reason, we recommend creating multiple farms only when necessary.

> **NOTE** There are third-party products that will allow you to use the same profile in multiple environments and will still avoid the Last Write Wins problem. Please see the RDS Partner page at *http://www.microsoft.com/windowsserver2008/en/us/rds-partners.aspx* for more details on these products on partner offerings.

Design Guidelines for User Profiles

Each of the following affects how you save user-specific configuration settings and data for use with RDS.

- Local profiles generally aren't suited to deployments of more than one RD Session Host server because the user experience will be different on every RD Session Host server.

- Large roaming profiles can increase logon and logoff times. The User Profile Service must copy the files to the endpoint and then copy them back to the profile when storing files on a personal VM can complicate backups and restoring data.

- Rollback reverts all changes to a pooled VM to the state when you took the snapshot.

- Profile settings are stored as a flat file written back to the profile storage location at logoff.

The following sections explain how these facts affect your design.

Balance Flexibility and Lockdown

Local profiles aren't a good fit for RDS deployments larger than a single server. Storing local profiles on RD Session Host servers in a multi-server environment will cause the following problems.

- It leads to an inconsistent user experience and can create problems that are hard to troubleshoot because they're linked to logging onto a specific RD Session Host server.

- It fills up an RD Session Host server hard disk with duplicate copies of a profile (that is, the profile will be stored on each RD Session Host server that a user logs on to).

- It requires that you back up the RD Session Host server because it now holds user data.

You have two remaining choices: roaming profiles and mandatory profiles. Neither choice is always appropriate. The option that you pick depends on the amount of control you want and have authority to implement.

Roaming profiles can be freely edited by their owners within the limits defined by Group Policy (discussed in Chapter 6, "Customizing the User Experience"). That is, if you've defined the wallpaper for a user group via Group Policy, that will be the wallpaper every time anyone in that user group logs on. If you haven't specified the wallpaper using Group Policy, anyone is welcome to change the wallpaper when connecting to the RD Session Host server. Like local profiles, roaming profiles store user configuration data in NTUSER.DAT.

Mandatory profiles differ from roaming profiles in that their owners can edit them, but any changes that they make will not be saved to the profile. This can speed up logoff times because nothing is written back to the network share where you've stored the mandatory profiles. More insidiously, mandatory profiles don't save any data to folders stored within the profile folder. You *must* use Folder Redirection if using mandatory profiles, if you want users to be able to save data to their personal folders. In fact, that's worth highlighting in a cautionary note.

 CAUTION If you use mandatory profiles or pooled VMs with rollback enabled, you *must* configure Folder Redirection to allow users to save files to their personal folders that are part of their profiles.

The core choice between mandatory and roaming profiles is the tradeoff of flexibility versus control. Mandatory profiles eliminate the chance of a user making a bad change that can't be fixed by logging off and logging back on again. Mandatory profiles also speed logoff times because they don't need to be written back to the share.

However, mandatory profiles don't allow users the degree of personalization that many people have come to expect from Windows. In addition, mandatory profiles don't allow other applications to save data to the profile either. This means that some security applications that require giving users a private key [such as the encrypted file system (EFS)] don't work with mandatory profiles. The choice will depend on your corporate culture, your need to use applications that require private keys, and the ability of the IT department to control the desktop.

 ON THE COMPANION MEDIA One solution to the choice between roaming profiles and mandatory profiles is not to choose. Use mandatory profiles and combine them with a mechanism that allows users to save selected settings and have them applied at logon. Windows Server 2008 does not include this functionality, but several RDS ISVs or consulting partners do. You can find an example of this functionality—a tool named Flex Profiles—from the following link on the companion media: *http://www.immidio.com/flexprofiles*.

Use Folder Redirection

Whether you're using roaming profiles or mandatory profiles, it's best practice to use Folder Redirection with sessions or pooled or personal VMs.

If you're using roaming profiles, Folder Redirection will ensure that the profile stays small. A large profile will slow both logon and logoff times. The fastest approach is to use local profiles, but for reasons already discussed, you don't want to combine local profiles with RD Session Host servers.

If you're using mandatory profiles, then use Folder Redirection selectively. Any folders stored in the profile folder will become read-only. For some folders, this is very bad news because people won't be able to save their documents or pictures in their personal folders. But for some folders, this is exactly what you want. For example, if you don't want people to remove icons from the Start menu permanently, leave the Start Menu folder in the profile folder. See the section entitled "Centralizing Personal Data with Folder Redirection" later in this chapter for how to implement Folder Redirection.

Compartmentalize When Necessary

It is generally best practice to maintain different profiles for different environments because different types of virtualization can have different user configuration requirements. Don't go crazy creating different profiles for every possible occasion, but make sure your profile plan supports the various ways people use RDS. Compartmentalizing can also help avoid accidental overwrites.

- You might need V1 profiles to access terminal servers running versions of Windows earlier than Windows Server 2008, and V2 profiles to access RD Session Host servers.

- Implement roaming profiles for use with VM pools to keep the user experience consistent and avoid losing profile changes to rollback.

- Personal VMs can use a local profile for faster logons.

- To avoid the Last Write Wins problem, avoid users opening the same profile on multiple machines at the same time.

Prevent Users from Losing Files on the Desktop

There are a couple of cases where it's really important to prevent users from saving files to the desktop.

Users can lose, or misplace, data when using RemoteApp programs if you're not careful about Folder Redirection. Here's why: The Desktop folder contains everything that you can see on the desktop—files and shortcut icons. Many users are used to saving documents to the desktop. This is acceptable if you're actually seeing the full desktop, but if you're using RemoteApp programs, users don't *see* their desktop in the RD Session Host server session. Users could save data to the desktop and then not know where that data actually is because they can't see it. (They could open a document if they moved to the Desktop path when opening a file, but just double-clicking a document on the session desktop is not possible in this scenario.) To prevent users from saving files to the desktop, you can make the desktop read-only and trigger an error message if the user tries to save files to the desktop. To do this, you'll need to do the following.

- Redirect the Desktop folder to an external share.

- Set the permissions on this external share to read-only.

NOTE For instructions on how to create a read-only desktop, read the section entitled "Creating a Safe Read-Only Desktop" later in this chapter.

If you keep the Desktop folder in the profile folder and use mandatory profiles, then people can save files to the desktop . . . as long as they are logged on. When the user logs off, however, no changes are saved, including saved files on the desktop. The same thing will happen to users of VM pools with rollback enabled; anything saved by the user to the VM during each session will be discarded once the VM snapshot is invoked.

In both cases, redirect the desktop to a folder so users can save data there without it being discarded at logoff.

NOTE For instructions on implementing Folder Redirection, see the section "Centralizing Personal Data with Folder Redirection" later in this chapter.

Upload Profile Registry Settings in the Background

NTUSER.DAT is updated only when a user logs off. A user who does not log off isn't saving changes. This can lead to data loss. A new policy in Windows Server 2008 R2 enables this file to be uploaded while the user is logged on, as follows.

Computer Configuration |Administrative Templates | System | User Profiles | Background upload of a roaming user profile's registry file while user is logged on

Configure the setting to upload NTUSER.DAT on a set schedule (at a certain time of day) or at a set interval, designated in hours.

> **NOTE** This setting does not upload any other profile data, just the contents of HKCU.

Speed Up Logons

People are sensitive to the amount of time it takes to log on to a session. If it takes too long, you'll have problems with people leaving their sessions open rather than logging off. This is a security risk, has the potential to lock files that more than one person might need to edit, and keeps processes open on the RD Session Host server. You can disconnect and terminate sessions forcibly using Group Policy, but this has other drawbacks.

To encourage people to log off, make the logon process as painless as possible. You've already learned about using Folder Redirection to minimize the size of a profile. To speed things up, you can also employ Group Policies to do the following.

- Cache roaming profiles.
- Limit the amount of time an RD Session Host server or VM will try to load the user profile before using a temporary profile.
- Set an upper limit on the size of a user profile.
- Process group policies asynchronously.

New to Windows Server 2008: Speeding Up Logoffs

Speeding up logons is important, but when it's Friday afternoon and you want to get out of the office, logoffs are just as important. There are two ways in which Windows Server 2008 and later help logoffs take less time.

You can limit the size of a profile using Group Policy (and help this limit by redirecting the folders out of the policy). This policy, Limit Profile Size, is set per user and is located in User Configuration | Policies | Administrative Templates | System | User Profiles.

Prior to Windows Server 2008, there was a nasty catch when it came to profile quotas: Windows was serious about enforcing this limit. If you made your roaming profile larger than Group Policy allowed, Windows would prevent you from logging off until you made the profile smaller. In Windows Vista and later, you can log off, but if the profile is larger than the size permitted by Group Policy, the profile changes won't get written back to the roaming profile storage area.

Before Windows Server 2008, another issue that could delay logoffs (or prevent you from unloading your roaming profile altogether) was applications or drivers that left handles to the registry open (in other words, they started to use it but never broke the connection). Microsoft had a separate tool called the User Profile Hive Cleanup Service (in an application called UPHClean) that checked for these open handles and closed them so users could log off. In Windows Server 2008 and later, UPHClean functionality is handled by the User Profile Service.

Caching Roaming Profiles

To reduce the time that it takes to log on to an RD Session Host server, the server will cache the roaming profiles. Ordinarily, RD Session Host servers attempt to retrieve the roaming profile from its central location. In cases when the network connection to the profile server is too slow or not working, however, being able to log on with a locally cached copy of your profile can at least speed things up. Caching stores a copy of the profile on the RD Session Host server. This profile cache isn't used if the original roaming profile is available, but it can speed up logons in the case of slow or absent network connections.

Caching profiles is not without its drawbacks. It consumes hard disk space on the RD Session Host server. It can also prevent new users from logging on if the space allocated to cached profiles gets filled up. If you do cache profiles, make sure that you've got sufficient space for your user base and use Group Policy to delete profiles that aren't being used.

 CAUTION   Don't delete user profiles from the RD Session Host server using Windows Explorer or the delete command-line tools, because this does not clean up the registry entries associated with the profile and can affect the user's ability to log on again. Configure the RD Session Host servers with Group Policy to delete any profiles unused for a given period.

Process Group Policy Asynchronously

Caching user profiles also means that you can use asynchronous processing of Group Policy, a policy processing model introduced in Windows Server 2008. You can apply Group Policy synchronously or asynchronously. If you apply it synchronously (the default model for a server), logon doesn't complete until the Group Policy settings that apply to that user are applied. If you apply Group Policy asynchronously (the default action for a desktop), the user can log on while Group Policy is being applied. Asynchronous processing can lead to changes in the user environment after users have logged on but will speed up logon times if Group Policy processing is slowing things down. For a review of the connection process, see Chapter 3, "Deploying a Single Remote Desktop Session Host Server."

Allow asynchronous Group Policy processing by enabling the following Group Policy setting.

Computer Configuration | Policies | Administrative Templates | System | Group Policy | Allow Asynchronous User Group Policy Processing When Logging On Through Remote Desktop Services

This policy works only when logging on to an RDS session host. It's not needed when logging on to desktop pools, because a desktop operating system already processes Group Policy asynchronously by default.

Deploying Roaming Profiles with Remote Desktop Services

This section discusses managing roaming profiles in an RDS environment, including the following.

- Creating roaming profiles
- Converting an existing local profile to a roaming profile
- Creating a default network profile
- Using Group Policy to set up the roaming profile storage area automatically
- Implementing a Group Policy infrastructure that supports these policies, including security filtering and loopback policy
- Managing roaming profiles cached on the RD Session Host servers

Creating a New Roaming Profile

To implement roaming profiles, you will need to

1. Create a network share in which to store the roaming profiles.
2. Configure the user accounts (through Active Directory Users And Computers or Group Policy) to use roaming profiles.
3. Have each user log on and create the roaming profile.

First, create a shared network location to store the roaming profiles. On the file server, create a new folder and set the appropriate NTFS and share permissions, using the guidelines in Table 5-5.

TABLE 5-5 Recommended Share and NTFS Permissions for an RDS Roaming Profiles Storage Folder

USER ACCOUNT	PERMISSION TYPE	NTFS PERMISSIONS
Authenticated Users group	Share	Full Control
Creator Owner	NTFS	Full Control, subfolders and files only
Local System	NTFS	Full Control on this folder, subfolders, files
User/Group whose profiles will be stored in the folder	NTFS	List Folder Content/Read, Create Folders/Append Data, all on this folder only

How Profile Folders Are Named

Sergey Kuzin
Software Development Engineer II

The way that a user's profile folder is named depends on the circumstances in which it's created. The user My Name (with user name Myname) with an account in Domain1 will store his profile in one of two places: \RDS-Roaming-Profiles\Myname or \RDS-Roaming-Profiles\Myname.Domain1.

The best case is to add the domain name to the profile path; this disambiguates the path when there are two (or more) users with the same name living in different domains. For example, in a large corporate network, you might have Domain1\Myname (that's me) and Domain2\Myname (some other user). When Domain1\Myname logs on to a legacy terminal server the profile created for him will be ...\Myname. If Domain2\Myname later wants to store his profile on the same server, he will have a problem. That's why you add *.domain* to the profile path, so that users with the same name but from different domains would have different profiles. So ideally, you always want to add *.domain* to the profile path.

But then, what do you do with profiles that were created before you made this change and don't have *.domain* in the name? Leave them as is. But in this case, how do you know which user this particular profile belongs to? You use permissions to determine that. When the User Profile Service creates a new profile, it gives full control to the user whom this profile is created for. So, if Domain1\Myname has explicit full control permission to the ...\Myname folder, then this profile belongs to me and not to Domain2\Myname. That's why you have this logic when creating profile names.

Here is the logic you use to create the profile path.

Continued on the next page

1. Attempt to locate the ...*username.domain* path. If it exists and the user has explicit permissions to it, then use it.

2. If the user does not have explicit Full Control access to ...*username.domain* or this folder does not exist, then try to access ...*username*.

3. If ...*username* exists and the user has explicit permissions to it, then use it.

4. If the user does not have explicit Full Control access to ...*username* or the folder does not exist, then use ...*username.domain*.

As you can see, by default you always create the folder with ...*username.domain*. Only when the ...*username* folder exists and the user has explicit Full Control access to it do you use it. Again, it's always best to include the domain name in the profile path so that two people with the same user name with accounts in different domains can store their profiles in the same central share.

When you've set up the profile location, configure the user account to use roaming profiles. This process varies slightly for profiles used with RD Session Host servers and for profiles used with pooled and personal VMs. You will see these differences as you step through this process. It's easiest if you configure this via Group Policy, but you will also see how to do it on a per-user basis.

Remote Desktop Session Host

To configure a user account to use roaming profiles, perform the following steps.

1. Open Active Directory Users And Computers, right-click a user's account, and choose Properties.

2. For Remote Desktop Session Host situations, navigate to the Remote Desktop Services Profile tab and type the Profile Path location using the format ***servername**share name*\%username%.*DomainName***, as shown in Figure 5-6.

The variable %username% inserts the user account name into the profile path, so you don't have to customize the path for each person when adding new accounts manually or through a script. You don't need to add the .V2 extension to this path, either; it will be added automatically because the profile will be a 2008 version profile. The next time the user logs on to the RD Session Host server, he will use the roaming RDS profile.

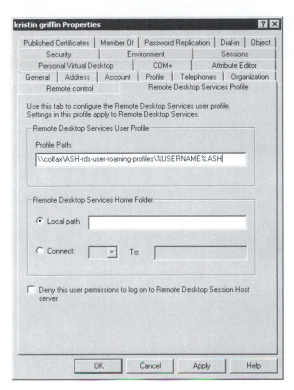

FIGURE 5-6 Enter the Remote Desktop Services profile path.

Virtual Machines

Pooled and personal VMs do not use Remote Desktop Services profiles. A pooled or personal VM is really a virtualized client desktop and acts accordingly—that is, it uses regular profiles. For these VM scenarios, enter the profile share's UNC path on the Profiles tab of the user account Properties dialog box, shown in Figure 5-7.

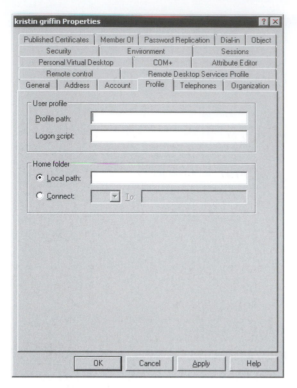

FIGURE 5-7 Specify the profile used for pooled and personal VMs on the Profile tab, not the Remote Desktop Services Profile tab.

When the user is configured to use roaming profiles, it's time to create the profile. This happens when the user first logs on to the RD Session host server (or the pooled/personal VM). When the user first logs on, the following happens.

1. The User Profile Service creates a profile folder for the user in the specified path.

2. The User Profile Service copies the default profile on the RD Session Host server or VM to give the user a profile.

3. When the user logs off, the User Profile Service copies the profile to its storage location in the specified network share. The user will be the owner of the folder and therefore will be the only one to have access to the folder and its contents.

Although a user profile folder is for the user, if Administrators also have permissions they can delete a corrupted profile or perform other maintenance easily. To permit this, give the Domain Admins group Full Control NTFS rights to the parent folder, and pre-create roaming profile folders for each user in the roaming profiles share. Make sure that the user has full control of his profile folder, subfolders, and files and that the user is also the owner of the folder. The simplest way to do this is to use Group Policy; if you keep your RD Session Host servers or pooled VMs in their own organizational unit (OU), you can also create a computer Group Policy object (GPO) with Loopback Processing enabled and give administrators access to profile contents by enabling the following GPO setting.

Computer Configuration | Policies | Administrative Templates | System | User Profiles | Add The Administrators Security Group To The Roaming User Profile Share

For more information on Loopback Processing and using Group Policy to create and manage RDS roaming profiles, see the section entitled "Using Group Policy to Manage Roaming Profiles" later in this chapter.

DIRECT FROM THE FIELD

Managing Roaming Profiles Without Admin Access to the File Server

Bohdan Velushchak
Operations Engineer, MSIT

To use roaming profiles, you need a file server to store them on. In a smaller deployment, you can have administrative rights to the file server as well as the terminal servers, but enterprise deployments often segregate ownership. If you aren't an administrator of the file server, you can't manage the folders directly—you'll need to ask the file server administrator. Even the Group Policy setting Add The Administrators Security Group To Roaming User Profiles will not help if the RDS administrator is not a member of the Administrators group on the file server. You could lobby to become a member of the Administrators group on the file server, but this is counter to Least Privilege Access principles.

You can resolve this situation with a logoff script. Use Icacls.exe to include RDS administrators to the user profile's permissions during logoff from user's security context. This works because the user has full access permissions to her profile, so she can add necessary permissions for RDS Administrators. For example, the Logoff script might look like this.

```
Icacls.exe //<profile root>/%username%.%userdomain%.v2 /grant
    <RDS Admins group>:
F /T /Q
```

Add this script to each user through Group Policy: User Configuration | Windows Settings | Scripts | Logoff Script. Now you can manage that profile folder.

There are two reasons to do this at logoff, not logon. First, if the user is logging on for the first time, the profile folder might not yet exist, so the settings wouldn't apply until the second time. If the user never logged in again, you couldn't delete her profile without the help of the file server administrators. Second, if the profile is large, it takes some time for Icacls.exe to go through the whole tree. Users do not like long logon times, so why make them wait to start working? Let the script process permissions when they're done working and are less concerned about time.

Converting an Existing Local Profile to a Roaming Profile

Sometimes you will want to convert existing local profiles to roaming profiles. This can apply if you are converting a traditional desktop deployment to an all-RDS deployment, and you are willing to risk that the local profile settings are appropriate for the remote work environment.

> **NOTE**   It's often unwise to convert a local profile that a user has been using on a personal desktop to a Remote Desktop Services roaming profile. The user might have administrative access to her personal computer and could have installed numerous applications and made many customizations that don't apply to the shared (and more locked-down) world of RD Session Host servers.

Converting local profiles to roaming profiles is really simple. Configure all user accounts to use roaming policies as described earlier, and specify that cached copies of the profile should be deleted. When users log on to the server where their local policy resides and then log off, their local profile will be copied to the network share that you specified. The cache on the server will be deleted and only the roaming profile in the network share will remain.

You might have done this conversion in Windows Server 2008 using the Copy To button in the User Profile Properties dialog box. This is no longer possible on a server running Windows 2008 R2 or a client running Windows 7—the button has been disabled.

DIRECT FROM THE SOURCE

Why the Copy To Button Is Disabled

Kyle Beck
Program Manager, Microsoft

The Copy To button is now disabled, because even though this button was used to overwrite a profile with another profile, it was unsupported to use it to edit the default profile. It was unsupported because the source profile was just copied wholesale into the default profile—the Copy To button performed a complete copy of everything in the source profile over the default profile. This could lead to errors in the registry because references to the source user would persist on any new user created from the new default profile. Because it was an unsupported method, its behavior was updated; the default profile is now the only one that is copyable using this button.

The removal of this functionality doesn't prevent you from converting local profiles to roaming profiles or even overwriting one user's profile with another's. Removing the functionality prevents you from overwriting the default user profile with another user profile. People often overwrote the default user profile with a customized one from another user to deploy customized profiles to new users. As described in the Direct from the Source sidebar entitled "Why the Copy To Button Is Disabled," doing this was unsupported (although popular) as far back as Windows XP, because although this "worked" for many people, it actually was not a clean process. It could lead to problems if that profile had been used at all, and it would also "tattoo" the profile with inappropriate settings and naming, such as the following.

- A list of that user's frequently run programs.
- The user's documents folders will be incorrectly called Administrator's Documents.
- The user might have access to Administrative Tools (this is incorrect for regular users).
- Windows 7 libraries will be broken.

 ON THE COMPANION MEDIA There are other implications to overwriting the default user profile with a user profile by way of the Copy To button. See this article (also on the companion media) for more information: *http://blogs.technet.com /deploymentguys/archive/2009/10/29/configuring-default-user-settings-full-update- for-windows-7-and-windows-server-2008-r2.aspx*. This article also discusses some options for customizing the default profile in Windows 7.

Customizing a Default Profile

Customizing the default profile is one way to ensure that all new RDS users start with the same settings. The only supported method for customizing the default profile is to use the Sysprep.exe tool (built into Windows 7 and Windows Server 2008 R2) to overwrite the default profile with the profile that you are logged onto when you run Sysprep.exe. Here are the steps.

1. Log on as an administrator and customize the profile as needed. This is the profile that will be copied over the default user profile.

2. Create an Unattend.xml file and add a line of code to it to tell it to copy the profile of the user logged on over the default profile when the system reboots. The line you add is

   ```
   <CopyProfile>true</CopyProfile>
   ```

   The following is example code for a 64-bit version Unattend.xml file with the extra line of code added.

   ```
   <?xml version="1.0" encoding="utf-8"?>
   <unattend xmlns="urn:schemas-microsoft-com:unattend">
   <settings pass="specialize">
   <component name="Microsoft-Windows-Shell-Setup" processorArchitecture="amd64"
   publicKeyToken="31bf3856ad364e35" language="neutral" versionScope="nonSxS"
       xmlns:wcm="http://schemas.microsoft.com/WMIConfig/2002/State"
       xmlns:xsi="http://www.w3.org/2001/XMLSchema-instance">
   <CopyProfile>true</CopyProfile>
   </component>
   </settings>
   <cpi:offlineImage cpi:source="catalog:e:/clg files/64-bit/install_windows 7
       ultimate.clg" xmlns:cpi="urn:schemas-microsoft-com:cpi" />
   </unattend>
   ```

3. Save this Unattend.xml file to C:\Windows\System32\Sysprep.

4. After you have the Unattend.xml file in place, open a command prompt and type the following command.

```
sysprep.exe /oobe /reboot /generalize /unattend:unattend.xml
```

> **NOTE** The article at *http://support.microsoft.com/kb/973289* explains how to do this, but at the time of this writing, the syntax is incorrect. Use the one provided here.

After you run this command, the server will reboot. When it comes back up, the default profile will be overwritten with the one that was logged in when you ran Sysprep. *Now* you can highlight the default profile and use the Copy To button to copy the profile to a network share to be used for roaming profiles.

> **CAUTION** Don't run Sysprep on a production machine. The Sysprep command resets the computer SID as well as eliminating system-specific data like the computer name and the domain affiliation. It can also remove unique hardware drivers and can reset the Windows activation key. If you are using VMs, then one workaround is to take a snapshot of the VM before running Sysprep. After you are done running Sysprep, rebooting, and copying the default profile to another location, apply the snapshot and the VM will be rolled back to its prior state.

Creating a Default Network Profile

You have already learned (in the section titled "How Profiles Are Created" earlier in this chapter) when a network default user profile would be used to create new user profiles. Using a default network profile to create new roaming profiles might benefit your roaming profiles implementation because it ensures that when new profiles are created, they all stem from the same source.

Reasons Not to Create a Network Default Profile

Creating a network default profile can work well to deploy customized profiles in low-complexity environment. But it's not always the best solution.

First, there is no way to distinguish when a network default profile should be used to create a new roaming user profile. As discussed earlier in this chapter, in complex remoting scenarios, it's possible for people to have more than one remoting profile, and if you point them to the same starting point, they will start with the same profile in all scenarios. For example, a new profile created when the user logs on to a Windows 7 pooled VM would stem from the same network default user profile that is used to create a new user roaming user profile for use in an RD session host server

Assuming that you can use a network default profile for all your scenarios, on Windows 2008 (and Windows 7) you can copy a local default profile to the NETLOGON share on a domain controller, following these steps.

1. Log on to the server with an admin account.

2. From the Run box, browse to the domain controller: \\DOMAIN CONTROLLER\ NETLOGON

3. Create a folder in the NETLOGON share and name it Default User.v2.

4. From Server Manager, click Change System Properties, navigate to the Advanced tab, and then click the Settings button in the User Profiles section.

5. Select the Default Profile from the list of profiles stored on the server and click Copy To.

6. Browse to or type the network path \\DOMAIN CONTROLLER\NETLOGON Default User.v2.

BEST PRACTICE   Ensure that the profile doesn't contain any unnecessary data. A large default network profile will slow down the initial profile creation process because new profiles have to pull this large amount of data across the network.

Using Group Policy to Manage Roaming Profiles

You've seen how to dictate who uses roaming profiles by settings this up on a per user basis in Active Directory Users And Computers. If you have more than a few users, it's easiest to create a GPO that dictates the RDS roaming profile location for everyone who logs on to a farm. This section explains how to do this and how to set up the Group Policy infrastructure that you'll need.

The single most important part of successfully using roaming profiles with RD Session Host servers is to set up the RD Session Host server environment OU and create the GPOs correctly. Group Policy has many different uses, but it all comes down to making changes to many computers or many users all at once.

There are two broad categories of Group Policy: computer settings and user settings. Computer settings are applied at boot time, or on an RD Session Host server (see Chapter 2, "Key Architectural Concepts for Remote Desktop Services," for more details), when a session starts (to apply the settings to the session). User settings are applied when the user logs on to the session. Because settings are applied to users at logon, they don't have to be saved as part of a user's account properties. Because they're applied second, settings applied to a user will control when there's a conflict.

Because of the order in which user and computer Group Policy is applied, when managing RD Session Host server settings, you'll almost always use an additional GPO to enforce *loopback policy processing*. In short, loopback policy reapplies the user-specific settings that are placed on the OU where Loopback Processing is enabled after the normal user GPOs are applied. The result is that settings placed on the RD Session Host server OU will always take precedence in case of a conflict. If you have blocked GPO inheritance on the RDS OU, then only the user policies that you place on the OU will be implemented for your users. You'll find out more about loopback policies in the section entitled "The Ins and Outs and Ins of Loopback Policy Processing" later in this chapter.

There's some overlap between the computer- and user-specific settings in Group Policy, but you'll generally find that you'll need both to configure the users' working environment. When setting up an RD Session Host server environment, where it's important not just that you are logging on but that you're using an RD Session Host server, you'll *definitely* need both.

 ON THE COMPANION MEDIA The following explanations assume that you have permission to manage Group Policy for your RD Session Host servers. If this is not the case, you'll need to provide the instructions to the administrator controlling Group Policy for your organization and let him or her fit them into corporate management policy. This is one way to organize your RD Session Host server GPOs, but it is not the only possible model. GPO architecture is unique to the particular situation. For example, for some organizations, blocking inheritance might not be an option for business policy reasons. For more information on Group Policy modeling, see "Design Considerations for Organizational Unit Structure and Use of Group Policy Objects," located at *http://technet2.microsoft.com/windowsserver/en /library/2f8f18cf-a685-48db-a7be-c6401a8fb6341033.mspx?mfr=true*. (This article was written for Windows Server 2003, but it still applies.) You can also find the link on this book's companion media.

Controlling Group Policy Processing for an RDS Environment

When you have multiple users working on one computer, you need to control the environment as much as possible. The easiest way to do this is to perform the following steps.

1. Put RD Session Host server farms and all VMs pools into their own OUs.

2. Block inheritance of all GPOs that are not specifically enforced. (You might not have this option, depending on company policy.)

3. Place computer and user GPOs on these OUs to specify the settings to be implemented for each pool and farm.

Here's how to do all this.

ORGANIZE FARMS AND POOLS INTO OUS

First, create an OU for each RD Session Host farm or VM pool. (Because all members of a farm or pool are homogenous, they should all be in the same OU.) Open Active Directory Users And Computers, right-click the domain, and choose New, Organizational Unit. Name it after the farm (for example, RDSH Farm1) and then drag all computer objects in the farm or pool into the OU (see Figure 5-8).

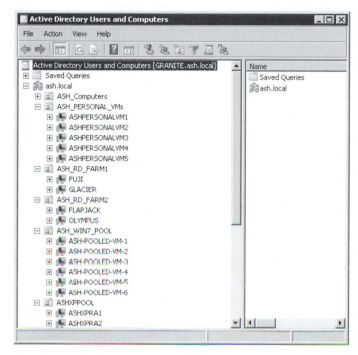

FIGURE 5-8 Create OUs for your RD Session Host server farms and VM pools.

BLOCK GPO INHERITANCE

Next, if possible in your organization, block GPO inheritance for this OU. This ensures that only computer settings set by GPOs linked to this OU will apply to the computers in this OU. It also ensures that with Loopback Processing enabled, only user settings set by GPOs linked to this OU will be applied to users logging on to the computers in this OU; other GPOs set at the domain or site level will not be applied.

To block inheritance for a farm or pool OU, open the Group Policy Management console (GPMC; do this by clicking Start, Programs, Administrative Tools, and Group Policy Management), right-click the RD Session Host server's OU, and choose Block Inheritance. If possible, also do this for your pooled VM OUs. Personal VMs can be controlled like this, but more likely they will act as regular desktops in your environment and will treated as such in the case of Group Policy processing.

IMPORTANT Company policy might prevent you from blocking inheritance. You can still know exactly what policies are going to be applied to the users and computers in your OUs; it will just take more effort because you will have to know about all Group Policies applied at higher levels.

CREATE GPOS FOR USER AND COMPUTER SETTINGS

There are multiple ways to set up policies, but it is usually easiest if you separate computer- and user-specific settings into different policies. Although one policy might contain both user- and computer-specific settings, it's simplest to isolate the two types of settings unless your environment is very small or your user base is very homogenous. This allows you to create a consistent model of RD Session Host server management while still allowing you the flexibility to apply different policies to different groups of users and computers (that is, using a GPO on multiple OUs if the functionality is needed in multiple places). Create two different types of GPOs: a computer GPO and user GPOs, as shown in Figure 5-9.

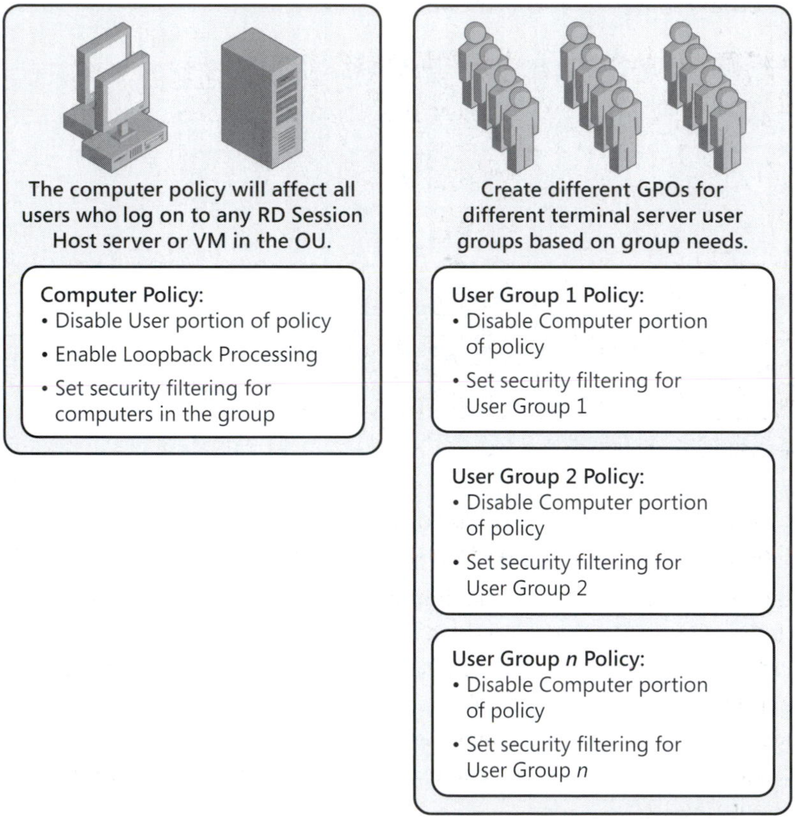

The computer policy will affect all users who log on to any RD Session Host server or VM in the OU.
Computer Policy:
• Disable User portion of policy
• Enable Loopback Processing
• Set security filtering for computers in the group
Create different GPOs for different terminal server user groups based on group needs.
User Group 1 Policy:
• Disable Computer portion of policy
• Set security filtering for User Group 1
User Group 2 Policy:
• Disable Computer portion of policy
• Set security filtering for User Group 2
User Group n Policy:
• Disable Computer portion of policy
• Set security filtering for User Group n

FIGURE 5-9 Create separate user and computer GPOs for the RDS environment.

To create the GPOs, open the GPMC (by clicking Start, Programs, and Administrative Tools). Right-click the Group Policy Objects folder in the left pane, found under your domain folder, and choose New to open the dialog box shown in Figure 5-10.

Name the computer policy something descriptive, such as RDS Computer GPO, and then click OK.

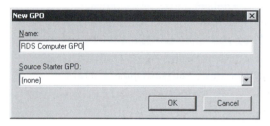

FIGURE 5-10 Create an RD Session Host server computer policy.

Next, create another policy that will hold user-specific settings, naming it something like RDS User GPO. Click OK, and you will be back in the GPMC, with a list of available policy objects that includes the ones you just created, as shown in Figure 5-11.

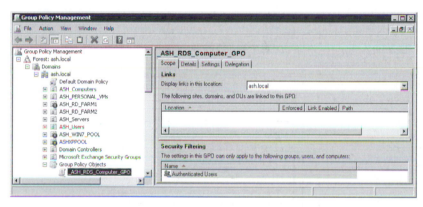

FIGURE 5-11 Create computer- and user-specific GPOs.

Next, ensure that each GPO is specific to one type of settings—computer or user. This is optional, but this will give you more control over your RDS environment.

Click the Details tab in the upper portion of the right pane. Here, there's a GPO Status drop-down list with four options: All Settings Disabled, Computer Configuration Settings Disabled, Enabled, and User Configuration Settings Disabled. For your computer-specific GPOs, make sure that no user-specific settings will be applied by setting the Status to User Configuration Settings Disabled. Follow the same process to create a new user-specific GPO. For the User GPO, navigate to the drop-down menu on the Details tab and set the GPO Status to Computer Configuration Settings Disabled.

Updating Group Policy

Active Directory Domain Services (AD DS) does not immediately send user Group Policy changes down to the computers to which they apply. The Group Policy engine on the computer actually pulls the GPO changes from AD DS at specific intervals, called the *refresh interval*. By default, the refresh interval is 90 minutes (plus a random time ranging from 0 to 30 minutes). To immediately see the effects of changes that you make to GPOs, you can force this refresh. Open a command prompt on your RD Session Host server and type **gpupdate /force**. Most computer policies can be updated just by doing this; a few (like Folder Redirection) will require a reboot.

The Ins and Outs and Ins of Loopback Policy Processing

Outside an RD Session Host server environment, you often apply Group Policy based on the persona of the user logging on. If you don't want Adam Barr to open Control Panel, for example, you probably feel much the same way about this whether Adam Barr is logged on to his desktop computer or his laptop. Similarly, if you don't care whether he is running Control Panel, then you continue not to care whether he's logged on to his desktop or his laptop. It's his space—let him mess it up. (The Help desk might feel differently about this, but that's another matter.)

As discussed in "Using Group Policy to Manage Roaming Profiles" earlier in this chapter, the computer policy will always be applied first, then the user policy. If a user policy and a computer policy conflict, the user policy will "win," because it's applied last. Any Group Policy stored locally on the computer is applied first. Next, policies placed at these levels are applied in order (local, Site, Domain, OU), as shown in Figure 5-12.

In case of conflicts, the policy applied last wins. For example, computer policies set on a computer OU will override conflicting policies set at the domain level. And user policies will overwrite computer policies in conflicting situations (some settings can be set for a computer and also for a user) because they are applied after computer policies.

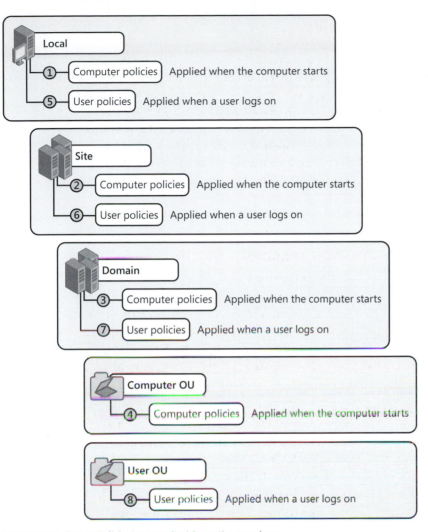

FIGURE 5-12 Group Policies get applied from the top down.

On a personal computer, it's perfectly acceptable to have the identity of the person logging on define the final settings for Group Policy. But RD Session Host server farms and pooled VMs are location-specific or context-specific situations in which *where* you are matters even more than *who* you are. For example, you might decide that it's acceptable for users to use clipboard redirection when connecting to personal VMs, but for security reasons, you don't want them using clipboard redirection when connecting to an RDS server farm hosting sensitive data. You need policies applied based on which computer you are logged on to. In this case, you will apply loopback policy processing to tell the Group Policy engine to apply the user GPOs that are applied to a computer OU (for example, to an RDS farm OU) after applying the user GPOs that are normally applied during logon. With loopback policy processing enabled, GPO processing will now work as shown in Figure 5-13.

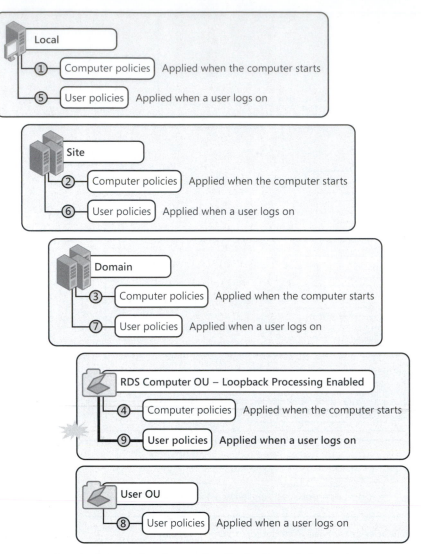

FIGURE 5-13 Loopback Processing changes the effective Group Policy results.

When the RD Session Host server starts, computer GPOs are applied. When the user logs on to the RD Session Host server, the User GPOs are applied to the session. Then, because loopback policy processing is enabled, User GPOs that are applied to the RD Session Host server OU are applied last. In addition, if you have blocked inheritance, it's possible that the *only* GPOs that will be applied are computer and user GPOs that are placed specifically on the OU.

To enable Loopback Processing, right-click the Computer GPO applied to the RD Session Host server OU and choose Edit. The Group Policy Management Editor opens the GPO. Go to Computer Configuration, Policies, Administrative Templates, System, and Group Policy and find the User Group Policy Loopback Policy Processing Mode node in the pane on the right. Double-click it and you will see the dialog box shown in Figure 5-14.

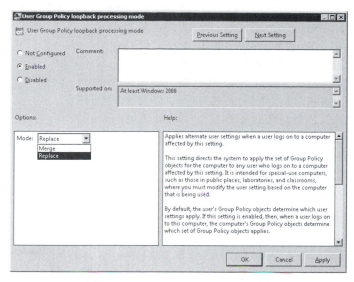

FIGURE 5-14 Enable loopback policy processing from the User Group Policy Loopback Processing Mode Properties dialog box.

HOW IT WORKS

Applying Loopback Policy

Loopback policy can apply to users in one of two ways: Merge Mode and Replace Mode.

- In Merge Mode, loopback policy processing will apply the user GPOs placed on the RD Session Host server OU along with the other normal user GPOs applied from the OU where the user account resides. If there is a conflict, then the user GPOs applied to the RD Session Host server OU will prevail.

- In Replace Mode, the Group Policy engine ignores all other user GPOs from the User OU and applies only the user GPOs applied to the RD Session Host server OU.

Merge Mode and Replace Mode affect only GPOs placed on the OU where the user account resides. User GPOs placed at higher levels (for example, at the domain level) will still be applied unless you have specifically blocked inheritance on the OU where the computers reside.

Whether you choose Merge Mode or Replace Mode depends on your goals and how you've set up the rest of your environment. If users are using the same GPOs to

Continued on the next page

log on to the RD Session Host servers and to their local desktops, their user settings might not mesh well with a shared environment. If that's the case, then you'd pick Replace Mode. If you want the user experience to be as similar as possible for both local and remote logons, then Merge Mode might be more appropriate because it will preserve user-specific policies. The main thing you'll need to watch out for is that GPO settings from the GPOs applied to the user do not cause problems for your user when she is logged on to an RD Session Host server (or pooled VM). Using Merge Mode is more work because it requires a lot of considering of individual policies and their effect on a remote workspace.

Fine-Tuning GPOs with Security Filtering

A GPO works because by default, anyone in the Authenticated Users group can use it, and Authenticated Users means "anyone who is logged on to the domain." (Computers also log on to the domain, so they're also members of Authenticated Users.)

If you have groups of users with specific needs controlled by Group Policy, you can create a User Policy for each user group and then use Security Filtering to apply each User GPO to a specific user group. For example, this technique could come in handy if you give access to multiple applications in one farm but only have licensing enough for a subset of users. You could block certain users from running that application, thus meeting software licensing compliance requirements. To narrow the scope of to whom (or to what) these policies will apply, double-click the GPO in the Group Policy Objects folder and navigate to the Scope tab in the right pane. In the Security Filtering section on this tab, modify Security Filtering to include the specific users group for which you want settings in the GPO to apply, as shown in Figure 5-15.

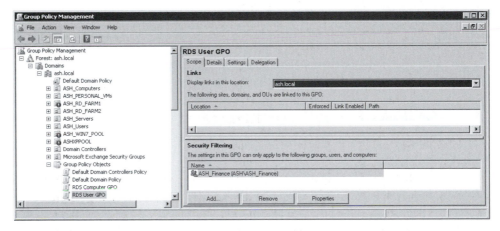

FIGURE 5-15 Add users to the GPO Security Filtering section of the ASH TS Users Policy.

Using Group Policy to Define the Roaming Profile Share

After you have a Group Policy infrastructure set up, you can create a policy to create roaming profile folders in the proper folder share location automatically.

The Group Policy setting to set the path for RDS roaming profiles is a computer setting. Right-click your Computer Policy GPO and choose Edit. Expand the GPO to Computer Configuration | Policies | Administrative Templates | Windows Components | Remote Desktop Services | Remote Desktop Session Host | Profiles. In the pane at right, double-click Set Path For Remote Desktop Services Roaming User Profile, shown in Figure 5-16.

> **NOTE** It might seem counterintuitive to set the RDS roaming profile path for computers, not for users. But the RD Session Host servers must know where to find the roaming profile so the User Profile Service can load it when a user logs on.

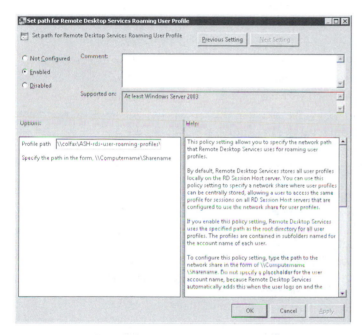

FIGURE 5-16 Set the path for Remote Desktop Services Roaming User Profile storage.

Select the Enabled option and type the RDS roaming profile share location in the Profile Path text box. If you use Group Policy to set the RDS roaming profile path, then the profile folders that are created take the form of *username.domainname*.V2; you do not need to add the %username% variable, the domain name, or the .V2 extension. This is in contrast to defining the path to the Remote Desktop Services profile folder by editing the user account properties through scripting or through Active Directory Users And Computers, where you must specify the *username* and *domainname* variables to create the folder properly.

If the profile folders are created automatically when the user logs on, then the user gets sole access to the profile and is also set as the owner of the profile folder. To permit administrators to access the profile, enable the following GPO setting: Computer Configuration | Policies | Administrative Templates | System | User Profiles | Add The Administrators Security Group To Roaming User Profiles. With this GPO setting enabled, the following permissions are placed on newly created user folders.

- **User**   Full Control, owner of folder
- **SYSTEM**   Full Control
- **Administrators**   Full Control (This is the local administrators group of the server where the profiles are stored, which also contains the Domain Admins group.)

You can also pre-create user profile folders and set permissions as required. For more information about profile folder permissions, see the section entitled "Converting an Existing Local Profile to a Roaming Profile" earlier in this chapter.

With this GPO setting configured, users accessing the RD Session Host servers in this OU now have a roaming profile created and stored in the designated share.

Configuring Roaming Profile Paths for VMs

Pooled and personal VMs will run client operating systems. Setting an RDS roaming profile path on these machines simply won't work. They are client machines, and for the most part, they should be treated as such. To configure the roaming profile path for client machines, use this GPO setting: Computer Configuration | Policies | Administrative Templates | System | User Profiles | Set Roaming Profile Path For All Users Logging On To This Computer.

Enter the share name where your profiles are stored and add the %username% variable to the end of the path so that each user gets a unique profile folder, as follows.

```
\\servername\sharename\%username%
```

Speeding Up Logons

One of the biggest challenges that IT professionals face in an RDS environment is to provide a user experience that feels as much like a local computer as possible. Users want to log on quickly, work steadily, get their job done, and get out. If they find that they have to wait longer to log on than they like, the Help desk will hear about it, or people will look for ways to circumvent the data center.

Roaming profiles are usually the best choice for RDS. Centralizing the profile on a network share makes it possible to always have the same experience no matter what RD Session Host server or VM a user is logged into—even new ones that were just added. Centralizing also simplifies backups. However, if you don't take steps to avoid it, profiles grow over time. By default, a profile contains not only configuration data but also user documents. Assuming that a user saves files to the folders there for that purpose, the profile will grow. Big profiles slow down logons and logoffs due to the massive amounts of data that must be copied to the remote location.

There are several things you can do to speed logons.

- Take advantage of the new behavior of Group Policy caching among servers in a farm to reduce the time needed for the first login.
- Enable Folder Redirection.
- Manage policy caching.
- Limit profile size.

Let's start with the one that requires no configuration.

Roam Group Policy Cache Between RD Session Host Farm Servers

Group Policy is cached on a computer to speed up logon times. The first time someone logs on to an RD Session Host server, her Group Policy settings won't be cached there. A new feature of Windows Server 2008 R2 copies the Group Policy cache to all servers in a farm. That way, once a user has logged on to one member of the farm, her GP cache will be available on all servers in the same farm.

Enable Folder Redirection

When a user logs on to an RD Session Host server, his roaming profile has to be copied to that RD Session Host server. When the user logs out, the changed profile must be copied back to the roaming profile storage location. Note that you are writing the entire profile back, not just the changes to the profile. Imagine if one of your users saved 30 GB of data in his Documents folder. He would log on to the RD Session Host server and then go get a cup of coffee (or even go to lunch) while waiting for the profile to copy itself to the server. Now imagine if all your users had that much data stored in their Documents folder. If they all come in at 9 A.M. and try to log on to the RD Session Host server, logons could quickly consume all your network bandwidth. Soon the water cooler or break room would be very popular, and no one would get any work done.

Profile caching also suffers if you experience profile bloat. *Profile caching* saves a copy of the user profile on the RD Session Host server so that, if the network is slow to retrieve the saved profile from its file share, the user can still log on using the cached copy. (When you log on to an RD Session Host server, a copy of your profile is saved there as a matter of course. If you enable profile caching, the profile isn't deleted when you log off.) However, if the profiles in the cache are too large, the space allocated for them will fill up, and people won't be allowed to log on because there's no room to store their profiles. There are Group Policies to remove older data in the cache if room runs out, but it's better if you can avoid this problem entirely.

The simplest step that you can take to avoid profile bloat is to enable Folder Redirection. Folder Redirection has two advantages: it keeps user data out of the profile to keep the profile smaller, and it allows differential synching (so that if only part of a file is changed, that part will be saved to the central location, rather than copying the entire file). You'll learn how to set up Folder Redirection in the section "Centralizing Personal Data with Folder Redirection" later in this chapter.

Limit Profile Size

One way to reduce the impact of caching profiles on the RD Session Host servers is to limit the size of the profiles. Although too many profiles can still fill up the hard disk, smaller cached profiles have less impact. To limit profile size, open your RDS User GPO and browse to User Configuration | Policies | Administrative Templates | System | User Profiles. Locate the policy Limit Profile Size and enable it.

If you're redirecting folders, the size of the profile shouldn't be a major concern. NTUSER.DAT is a fairly small file. The exact size depends on the profile, but it's not much; check the size of some representative NTUSER.DAT files to gauge the space needed to allocate space for profiles.

Manage the Profile Cache on RD Session Host Servers

Another way to keep the size of the cache on the RD Session Host servers from getting too large is to delete old copies of the user roaming profiles. You can also limit the profile cache size if you're concerned about running out of room on the servers.

PROGRAMMATICALLY MANAGING THE CACHE

You can use two computer Group Policy settings to delete unused cached profiles on RD Session Host servers in the RD Session Host Farm OU automatically. Both policies are located in Computer Configuration | Policies | Administrative Templates | System | User Profiles.

- **Delete Cached Copies Of Roaming Profiles**   Enabling this setting deletes a user's cached profile when the user logs off. This setting ensures that the loaded profile is always the most recent. However, the cached profile provides a fallback configuration to load if the actual profile isn't available for some reason. If you delete cached profiles, then if the actual profile can't be loaded, the user will get a temporary profile and any changes he makes to it will be discarded when the user logs off.

- **Delete Unused Profiles**   Windows Server 2008 R2 has a new Group Policy setting that limits the size of the overall roaming profile cache (located in the %SystemDrive%\ Users directory). If the size of the profile cache exceeds the configured size, RDS deletes the least recently used copies of roaming profiles until the overall cache goes below the quota. The policy setting is found in Computer Configuration | Administrative Templates | Windows Components | Remote Desktop Services | Remote Desktop Session Host | Profiles | Limit The Size Of The Entire Roaming User Profile Cache.

> **NOTE** Although you can apply the Delete Cached Copies Of Roaming Profiles GPO setting to pooled and personal VMs, it doesn't accomplish anything useful. Pooled VMs get rolled back (if set up to do so) when a user logs off, so the user profile cache is cleared as part of the rollback function. And personal VMs are, well, personal. They will have one profile cached on the machine. You will have enough room for one user profile cache in this instance. Deleting the profile cache on a personal desktop will just increase logon time and has no advantages.

Another way to make sure that your servers do not run out of disk space due to an overgrown profile cache is to put a cap on the cache size. If the size of the entire cache exceeds the limit set by this policy, the server will delete the oldest profile in the cache until the overall size drops below the threshold you set. The GPO setting is located at Computer Configuration | Administrative Templates | Windows Components | Remote Desktop Services | RD Session Host | Profiles | Limit The Size Of The Entire Roaming User Profile Cache.

Enable this setting and enter the following numbers.

- A monitoring Interval (in minutes): The interval at which the profile cache size is checked.
- Maximum cache size (in GB): This is the threshold. If the cache grows beyond this number, the oldest profiles start getting deleted.

DELETING CACHED PROFILES MANUALLY

Deleting cached profiles manually sounds too simple to bother explaining, but it's more subtle than it might appear. Cached profiles are kept in the %SystemDrive%\Users directory. However, the obvious approach doesn't work. If you do the obvious—look at the profiles, check the dates, note that some profiles haven't been used in a while, and delete them—you will prevent the owners of those deleted profiles from being able to log on to the RD Session Host server and load their roaming profiles, at least without some help from you. See the section entitled "The Consequences of Deleting a Profile Folder from Windows Explorer" later in this chapter for more information. For now, let's see how you can avoid extra work.

The problem is that cleaning up old profiles isn't just a matter of deleting some old directories. The registry maintains a list of profiles in HKLM\Software\Microsoft\Windows NT\CurrentVersion\ProfileList. Sort through that key (see Figure 5-17), and you'll see entries for everyone who currently has a profile cached on the server. Although the keys themselves are identified by the SIDs of the user accounts, you can see the names of the profile paths by examining the contents of the keys.

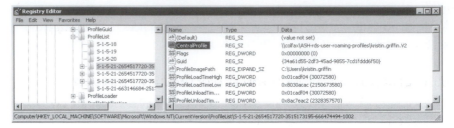

FIGURE 5-17 When you cache a profile on a server, it automatically creates a corresponding registry entry.

> **NOTE** Examining this key can also help you troubleshoot profile problems. If a user seems to be getting his standard profile to log on to the RD Session Host server, check the contents of CentralProfile (see Figure 5-17). If this entry is blank, that person is using a local profile.

If you just delete the profile from Windows Explorer, the entries in the registry remain, which confuses the server, as explained in the next section.

The cleanest way to delete unused profiles is to let Group Policy delete the old and unused profiles. You can also delete cached roaming user profiles from the User Profiles section of System Properties on the RD Session Host server. Log on to the RD Session Host server as an administrator. Go to Start, Control Panel, System, and click Change Settings. The System Properties dialog box will appear. Select the Advanced tab. In the User Profiles section, click Settings… to open the User Profiles dialog box, shown in Figure 5-18.

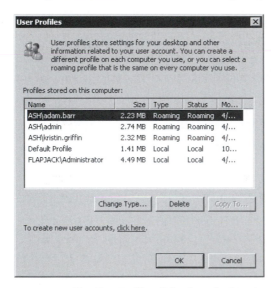

FIGURE 5-18 The User Profiles dialog box displays the profiles stored on the computer.

Highlight the roaming profile that you want to delete and then click Delete. When you see a dialog box confirming that you want to delete the profile, click Yes and the roaming profile cache is deleted. Click OK.

THE CONSEQUENCES OF DELETING A PROFILE FOLDER FROM WINDOWS EXPLORER

Just in case you decide to try deleting a profile folder from Windows Explorer, here's what will happen. If you delete an unused profile folder from Windows Explorer, the next time that user with that folder logs on, he will be unable to load his roaming profile. A temporary roaming profile will be created for him, profile changes that he makes will be discarded at logoff, and Event ID 1511 is logged in the Windows Application event log stating that Windows cannot find the local profile and is logging him on with a temporary profile.

Deleting that directory caused a problem because you didn't clean up the cached profile completely. For each cached profile stored in %SystemDrive%\Users\%UserName%, the User Profile Service creates a registry entry for this profile at HKLM\Software\Microsoft\Windows NT\CurrentVersion\ProfileList, shown in Figure 5-19. This registry key is named according to the user SID.

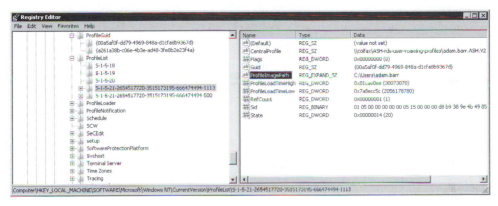

FIGURE 5-19 The RDS roaming profile cache registry entry for user Adam Barr

The ProfileImagePath key in this folder indicates the cache location, which by default is %SystemDrive%\Users\%UserName%. (The network location where the roaming profile is stored is in the CentralProfile key.)

If you delete the user's locally cached profile folder and that user starts a session on that RD Session Host server, he will get a temporary profile. The registry entry corresponding to the user's cached profile is renamed. The SID part stays the same, but it is given an extension of .bak, as shown in Figure 5-20.

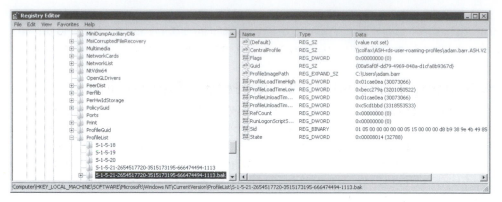

FIGURE 5-20 The old registry key for the profile that was deleted incorrectly now has a .bak extension.

In addition, a new key is created in its place. The newly created registry entry is named after the user SID just as before. However, the ProfileImagePath key inside the new folder now points to %SystemDrive%\Users\TEMP, as shown in Figure 5-21.

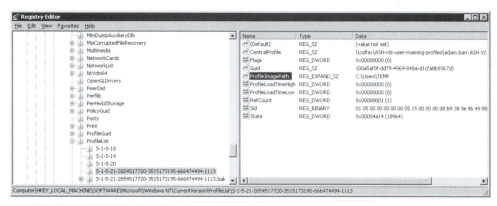

FIGURE 5-21 A new registry entry is created, but the ProfileImagePath key points to %SystemDrive%\Users\TEMP.

Therefore, the entry that used to work now has a .bak extension and is not usable, and the profile actually being used is a temporary profile. When the user logs off, his temporary profile is not copied back to the central profile storage location on the fileserver.

Deleting the profile from the System Properties dialog box User Profiles section no longer works either. Most likely, the profile will not even be listed in the dialog box. If it is, it most likely means that the user has not logged off completely. If you do manage to select it and click Delete, you get an error message: "Profile not deleted completely. Error – The system cannot find the file specified."

To rectify this, you must manually delete the abandoned registry entry that has the .bak extension. You might also need to reboot the server. Only then can the user log on to the RD Session Host server and have his roaming profile correctly cached once again on the server.

Centralizing Personal Data with Folder Redirection

The single biggest thing that you can do to affect profile size, simplify backups, and speed logons and logoffs is to redirect user-specific storage out of the user profile. By default, user data folders such as Documents are in the profile, but they don't have to be. Instead you can create a pointer to a network share where the data actually lives. Users will still store files in their personal folders, but the user data won't be roamed, so it will not affect the time required to load the profiles at logon.

Folder redirection is fundamentally very simple. If you go to HKCU\Software\Microsoft\Windows\CurrentVersion\Explorer\User Shell Folders, you'll see every folder in your profile and the current location of that folder. If Folder Redirection is not turned on, then all entries will look like this: %USERPROFILE%\Music. The goal is to get rid of the %USERPROFILE% variable and replace it with a new location.

You can't redirect all folders, but you can redirect the ones with the biggest impact on profile size. These folders are

- **AppData(Roaming)** Contains a user's application settings that are not computer-specific and therefore can roam with the user
- **Desktop** Contains any items a user places on his desktop
- **Start Menu** Contains a user's Start menu
- **Documents** Contains documents saved to the default location
- **Favorites** Contains a user's Internet Explorer favorites
- **Music** Contains a user's music files saved to the default location
- **Pictures** Contains a user's pictures saved to the default location
- **Video** Contains a user's video files saved to the default location
- **Contacts** Contains a user's contacts saved to the default location
- **Downloads** Contains a user's downloads saved to the default location
- **Links** Contains a user's Favorite links from Internet Explorer
- **Searches** Contains a user's saved searches
- **Saved Games** Contains a user's saved games

Before you redirect these folders, you need a place to redirect them to. Create a shared folder on the server where you want to store the redirected folders and set permissions on this folder according to the user profile folder permissions that were described in Table 5-5.

To redirect the folders to this share, open the GPMC, create or select an existing user GPO, right-click it, and choose Edit. Go to User Configuration | Policies | Windows Settings | Folder Redirection, as shown in Figure 5-22.

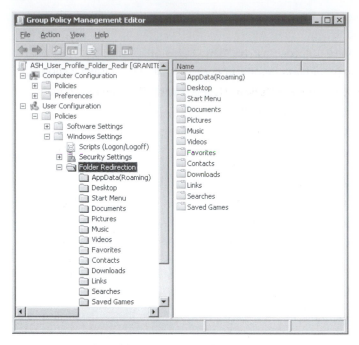

FIGURE 5-22 Set the Folder Redirection policy.

Right-click the AppData(Roaming) folder and choose Properties to open the dialog box shown in Figure 5-23.

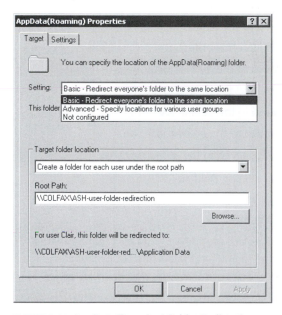

FIGURE 5-23 AppData(Roaming) Folder Redirection properties dialog box

To specify the location of the AppData(Roaming) folder, choose between two options in the Setting drop-down menu.

- **Basic   Redirect Everyone's Folder To The Same Location** This means just what it says; all AppData(Roaming) folder data for every user will go to the same location.
- **Advanced   Specify Locations For Various User Groups** To store user data in different locations based on user group membership, choose this option.

The menu contents will vary depending on the type of folder redirection you choose. If you choose Basic, then you get a Target folder location drop-down menu with three choices.

- **Create A Folder For Each User Under The Root Path** Choose this option to put each user's profile data into a folder under the root path named according to the user name. In the Root Path text box, specify the location of your designated Folder Redirection share. In most cases, this is the best option.
- **Redirect To The Following Location** Choose this option to redirect all user data to the same location. You'd do this if you wanted all users to use the same Desktop or Start Menu folder. Choose this option only if you want everyone to write to the same user-specific folders.
- **Redirect To The Local Profile Location** Don't choose this option. Your profiles roam, and you want your profile folders redirected to the network share.

Click the Settings tab, as shown in Figure 5-24.

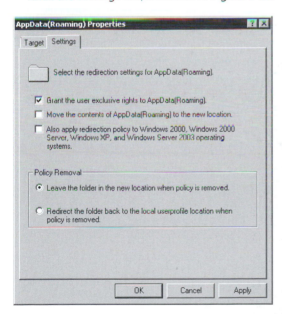

FIGURE 5-24 Grant The User Exclusive Rights To AppData(Roaming) is enabled by default. Clear this check box to let administrators manage the redirected folder.

By default, Grant The User Exclusive Rights To AppData(Roaming) is enabled. If you leave it this way, then the user will own this folder, and only she will be able to access this data. To enable managing this folder, clear this box so that the rights from the parent folder will be inherited. For example, if you give Domain Admins full control of the parent folder, then this group will have access to the redirected user folders as well.

If your users already have these folders before you set up Folder Redirection, then you must set up the existing folders in one of two ways (otherwise, Folder Redirection will fail).

- The user needs to be the owner of the folder and can be granted exclusive rights to the folder.
- If the user does not need to be the owner of the folder, clear this box.

All the folders listed in this GPO section have the same choices to pick from, except for the Pictures, Music, and Video folders. These folders have an extra setting that you can choose for the location of the folder: Follow The Documents Folder. This means that these folders will be stored in the user's Documents folder, wherever that folder is redirected.

To move the contents of the existing folder to the new folder outside the profile, select the Move The Contents Of "The Name Of The Folder Being Redirected" check box to the new location.

 ON THE COMPANION MEDIA When redirecting a folder using Group Policy, one of the options is Move The Contents. Unless you select this option, a duplicate link will be left behind, even when that folder is completely empty, meaning that users will see two Documents folders, two Music folders, and so forth. For tips on how to avoid the "duplicate link" problem, see *http://blogs.technet.com/deploymentguys /archive/2008/05/01/dealing-with-duplicate-user-profile-links-in-windows-vista.aspx*. You can also find the link on this book's companion media.

Sharing Personal Folders Between Local and Remote Environments

Because the RemoteApp programs are designed to blur the line between the remote computer and the local computer, it might make sense for you to help this along by using the same folder to store user-specific documents. This eliminates the problem of having to remember whether you were saving a file from a local or a remote application to know where the file would be stored.

Sharing Folders Between Windows Server 2003 and Windows Server 2008 R2 Roaming Profiles

The easiest profile environment to manage is homogenous: All users work only in RD Session Host servers, and all servers of sessions are running Windows Server 2008 R2. However, there are good reasons why you might need to support both V1 and V2 profile structure at the same time.

- Some users work both on the RD Session Host server and on VMs running Windows XP (perhaps because they're using RemoteApp on Hyper-V).
- You're migrating to Windows Server 2008 R2 RDS from Windows Server 2003 Terminal Services, and some of the older servers are still in use as you convert.

V1 profiles and V2 profiles are not compatible. Therefore, if you have some active 2003 RD Session Host servers, you will need to keep two sets of profiles for your users—one to log on to the 2003 servers and one to log on to the 2008 servers. And you might need even more profiles if users are also using pooled and personal VMs, and/or RemoteApp programs on Hyper-V. However, Folder Redirection can be used to bridge the gap.

Not all 13 folders that can be redirected in Windows Server 2008 R2 can be redirected in Windows Server 2003, but some can. You can share the data in these folders between the 2003 profiles and the 2008 profiles. On the Settings tab of each folder in the Folder Redirection container is an option called Also Apply Redirection Policy To Windows 2000, Windows 2000 Server, Windows XP And Windows Server 2003 Operating Systems. For some folders, this option is available, but on others (the ones that will not redirect for downlevel operating systems), it appears dimmed and is unavailable. Table 5-6 shows which of the folders can be redirected for Windows 2000, Windows XP, and Windows Server 2003.

TABLE 5-6 Profile Folder Redirection Capabilities for Various Versions of Windows

FOLDER	CAN THE FOLDER BE REDIRECTED FOR EARLIER OPERATING SYSTEMS?	DETAILS
AppData(Roaming)	Yes	If you enable the setting Also Apply Redirection Policy To Windows 2000, Windows 2000 Server, Windows XP, And Windows Server 2003 Operating Systems, the following folders within AppData(Roaming) are not redirected: Start Menu, Network Shortcuts, Printer Shortcuts, Templates, Cookies, and Sent To. These folders are redirected if you do not enable this setting.
Desktop	Yes	

Continued on the next page

FOLDER	CAN THE FOLDER BE REDIRECTED FOR EARLIER OPERATING SYSTEMS?	DETAILS
Start Menu	Yes	In Windows Server 2003, the contents of the Start Menu folder are not copied to the redirected location. It is assumed that the Start Menu folder has been pre-created. Therefore, if you do not pre-create the Start Menu folder and place it in the redirected location, the default Start Menu folder located in the user's Windows Server 2003 roaming profile location is used instead.
Documents	Yes	
Pictures	Depends	If the check box for Documents is selected, this folder will follow the Documents folder for earlier operating system profiles. If Documents is not redirected, however, then this folder cannot be redirected.
Music	Depends	If the check box for Documents is selected, this folder will follow the Documents folder for earlier operating system profiles. If Documents is not redirected, then this folder cannot be redirected.
Video	Depends	If the check box for Documents is selected, this folder will follow the Documents folder for earlier operating system profiles. If Documents is not redirected, then this folder cannot be redirected.
Favorites	No	NA
Contacts	No	NA
Downloads	No	NA
Links	No	NA
Searches	No	NA
Saved Games	No	NA

ON THE COMPANION MEDIA   For more information on Windows Server 2003 and Windows XP Profiles and Folder Redirection, see *http://technet2.microsoft.com /windowsserver/en/library/06f7eebc-2ebb-47c5-8361-1958b58078cc1033.mspx?mfr=true*. You can also find the link on this book's companion media.

NOTE   Some custom applications might not respond well to having the AppData folder redirected. But not redirecting AppData could lead to profile bloat, especially if your applications write a lot of data to this location. For situations like this, consider using App-V to deploy the problem application. For technical resources on sequencing with App-V, see *http://www.microsoft.com/systemcenter/appv/dynamic.mspx*.

Setting Standards with Mandatory Profiles

One issue with roaming profiles is that users can change them. On the one hand, that's the point. On the other hand, changes can cause problems. If users can change their profiles, they can delete icons, accidentally resize their toolbar so that it disappears, add wallpaper that slows their logon time, and so on.

One way to avoid this is to set policies controlling what users can and cannot do, and Chapter 7, "Molding and Securing the User Environment," explains how to do this. Another way to prevent users from making permanent changes to their profile is to make the user profile read-only. A user can change settings, but those settings will not be saved when the user logs off the RD Session Host server.

Profiles that don't change are called *mandatory profiles*. Mandatory profiles on a central store are copied to the RD Session Host server at logon, but they are not copied back at logoff. Any profile changes that occur are discarded at the end of the user session. Many companies will not implement mandatory profiles because users find them too constricting, but combined with Folder Redirection, they might give your users enough flexibility. Some third-party profile solutions also require the use of mandatory profiles—it depends on how the products are implemented.

Although it's possible to give every user a unique mandatory profile, it's not ideal. One of the best things about mandatory profiles is that because the profile will never be changed, all users can use a single mandatory profile, creating much less maintenance work for administrators. If a change needs to happen to the profile, there is only one place to make the change, instead of many if every user had his or her own individual profile.

Mandatory profiles are great in many respects, but you need to be careful when implementing them to make sure each user who logs on will not be susceptible to registry changes from other users. See the Direct from the Field sidebar that follows for more details.

Mandatory Profiles: Insecure By Default?

Helge Klein
IT Architect, sepago

Mandatory profiles are generally considered fast and secure because they usually are small in size and cannot be modified by the user. Although that is true—mandatory profiles stay pristine indefinitely—there is more to security than read-only access.

Mandatory profiles are a variant of roaming profiles: A master copy on a file server is copied to the RDS session host during logon. The resulting local copy is secured with file system ACLs that grant full access to the user, but to no one else (except administrators and SYSTEM). All is safe and secure—except in the case of mandatory profiles.

A user profile consists not only of file system data, but also of a registry hive (stored in the file NTUSER.MAN) that is mounted to HKU\<SID> and accessible from within a session via the well-known name HKCU. In contrast to the file system, registry permissions are not changed during logon because that is not necessary—at least with roaming profiles where the master copy of each hive already has the correct permissions.

Not so with mandatory profiles. The creation of a mandatory profile involves changing registry permissions on the master copy to full access for "Everyone." And because many users are logged on simultaneously to an RDS session host, each server's registry consists of many users' hives that are readable and writeable by everyone, not just the owner of the individual user profile.

So on an RD Session Host server where mandatory profiles are used, a user can simply open Regedit (if not blocked from doing so), navigate to HKU\<Some other user's SID>, and read/write at will.

Consequences

Users being able to read/write somebody else's HKCU hive poses a potentially grave security problem. At least two types of attacks can be envisioned: eavesdropping and damaging. Here are some simple examples.

Many applications store a list of most recently used (MRU) files in HKCU (for example, Word: HKCU\Software\Microsoft\Office\12.0\Word\File MRU). By reading such lists, attackers can gain information about which documents another user is editing.

Applications and the operating system itself need and expect write access to HKCU. Because a user always has write access to HKCU, programs do not handle the absence of such permissions well. By changing permissions on another user's hive (for example, removing write access), an attacker could effectively break another user's session, making it impossible to start and use even the most trivial programs—most applications that store their settings in HKCU would be affected.

How to Fix

The following workarounds can help fix this security vulnerability.

1. Make sure that remote registry editing is limited to administrators.

2. Block access to the registry via software restriction policies. This includes, but is not limited to, Regedit.exe, Cmd.exe, Reg.exe, scripts and batch files, and other custom (downloaded) tools. In essence, in order to avoid this problem exclusive white-listing is required.

3. Re-ACL (change the security permissions on) each registry hive after it is loaded and replace "Everyone" with the current user.

Converting Existing Roaming Profiles to Mandatory Profiles

Setting up mandatory profiles is very similar to setting up roaming profiles using Group Policy. To convert a roaming profile to a mandatory profile, you first need to have roaming profiles working, either by setting the RDS Roaming Profile path in the user's account properties in Active Directory Users and Computers, or by using Group Policy. For information on how to set up roaming profiles, see the section entitled "Using Group Policy to Manage Roaming Profiles," earlier in this chapter.

Assuming you have roaming profiles implemented, when a user logs on, her profile is stored in a subdirectory of the designated roaming profile share. To make the user's profile mandatory, in the user's profile folder, locate NTUSER.DAT and change its extension to .man (see Figure 5-25). Then change the NTFS permissions for the user from Full Control to Read & Execute (so she can't change the extension back). The next time the user logs on, she will be using a mandatory profile.

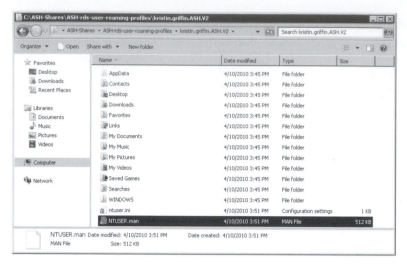

FIGURE 5-25 To convert a roaming profile to a mandatory profile, change its extension.

No changes that the user makes to the profile will be saved. But combining mandatory profiles with Folder Redirection will give users some control over their session and allow them to change their Favorites, Documents, Desktop, and other settings without compromising the configuration data loaded in HKCU.

Creating a Single Mandatory Profile

If you have many users, you probably won't want to convert each roaming profile to a mandatory one—that would negate one of the main reasons to implement mandatory profiles: less configuration and maintenance. To give everyone the same experience, you can create one mandatory profile for everyone to use. Here are the steps to do so.

1. Create a network share to store the mandatory profile (for example: //Colfax/ASH-Mandatory-Profile). Make sure to configure the permissions on this folder correctly. Table 5-7 and Table 5-8 outline the necessary share and NTFS permissions that need to be set on this folder.

TABLE 5-7 Share Permissions for a Mandatory Profile Storage Folder

USER ACCOUNT	SHARE PERMISSIONS
Administrators	Full Control
Authenticated Users	Read

TABLE 5-8 NTFS Permissions for User Accounts for a Mandatory Profile Storage Folder

USER ACCOUNT	NTFS PERMISSIONS
SYSTEM	Full Control, this folder, subfolders, files
Administrators	Full Control, this folder, subfolders, files, Owner
Authenticated Users	Read & Execute, this folder, subfolders, files

2. Create a folder within the folder created in Step 1, name it something appropriate to indicate it is a mandatory profile, and append the .V2 extension (for example: ASH.RDS.MAN.V2).

3. Because using the Copy To button now works only for the Default user profile, this is the profile you will copy to the share you created in Step 1. On the RD Session Host server, from Server Manager, click Change System Properties and select the Advanced tab. In the User Profiles section, click Settings. Highlight the Default User, and click Copy To. In the Copy To dialog box, type or browse to the shared folder location that you created in Step 1. Click Permitted To Use, add Everyone, and click OK.

> **NOTE** If you choose to create a customized mandatory profile, use Sysprep to over-write the Default User profile on the machine that you will copy from. For more on customizing the default user profile and using the Copy To button, and how to use Sysprep to customize the Default User Profile, see the sections earlier in this chapter entitled "Converting an Existing Local Profile to a Roaming Profile" and "Customizing a Default Profile."

4. Rename NTUSER.DAT in the resulting profile (in the file share created in Step 1) to NTUSER.MAN. You will need to change the folder options to show hidden files and folders to see this file.

5. Create appropriate GPOs by doing the following.

   - Edit the Computer GPO setting as follows: Computer Configuration | Policies | Administrative Templates | Windows Components | Remote Desktop Services | Remote Desktop Session Host | Profiles | Set Path For Remote Desktop Services Roaming User Profile to point to the share created in Step 2, for example: //colfax/ ash-rds-mandatory-profile/ASH.RDS.MAN). Do not include the .V2 extension.

   - Enable the Computer GPO policy setting as follows: Administrative Templates | Windows Components | Remote Desktop Services | Remote Desktop Session Host | Profiles | Use Mandatory Profiles On The RD Session Host Server

   - Enable the Computer GPO settings as follows: Computer Configuration | Policies | Administrative Templates | System | User Profiles | Add The Administrators Security Group To Roaming User Profiles

6. Apply the GPOs to the RD Session Host Server OU (in Group Policy Manager on a domain controller).

7. Reboot the RD Session Host servers and test by logging in as a regular user.

Creating a Safe Read-Only Desktop

One curious side effect to not being able to save anything to a mandatory profile is that any folders remaining in the profile (that is, not redirected) will not save changes either. For example, if you do not redirect the Desktop folder and if users save files to the desktop, those files will be discarded when they log off. There won't be any error, and the file will be on the desktop during the session, but the files won't be there when the users log on again. To put it mildly, this could be confusing. However, if you're using Remote App programs, you don't really want people saving files to the desktop because not being able to see the desktop will make those files hard to find.

To keep the desktop read-only but make sure people *know* it is read-only, redirect the desktop to a read-only folder as described in the section entitled "Centralizing Personal Data with Folder Redirection" earlier in this chapter. This will both prevent users from saving files to the desktop (which you want) and alert them to the fact that they can't save files to the desktop (which you also want). If they try, they will get an error. They still can't save anything to the desktop, but at least they will *know* that they can't.

Decrease Logon Times with Local Mandatory Profiles

The main reason to house a mandatory profile on a network share is to make it easier to update when you have a farm environment. But it's also worth noting that logon times can be decreased significantly by keeping a mandatory profile local to the server because the profile doesn't get pulled down from the network share when the user logs on.

Maintaining local mandatory profiles is more work, because any changes to the mandatory profiles will need to be made to the mandatory profile on each server. But the increase in logon speed might make this worthwhile to you, especially if you have only a few RD Session Host servers in a farm or you don't often need to change the profile. Again, testing this fully in your environment will tell you if it makes sense for your setup.

To use local mandatory profiles, perform the following steps.

1. Create a folder on each machine called something like "Mandatory_Profile.V2" and set the appropriate NTFS profile folder permissions as specified in Table 5-8.

2. Copy a default profile to the new Mandatory Profile folder, giving Everyone permission to use it when you perform the copy.

3. Convert this local profile to a mandatory profile by changing the extension of NTUSER.DAT to make it NTUSER.MAN.

4. Enable the GPO setting as follows: Computer Configuration | Policies | Administrative Templates | Windows Components | Remote Desktop Services | Remote Desktop Session Host | Profiles | Use Mandatory Profiles On The RD Session Host Server.

5. Enable the Computer GPO setting as follows: Computer Configuration | Policies | Administrative Templates | Windows Components | Remote Desktop Services | Remote Desktop Session Host | Profiles | Set Path For Remote Desktop Services Roaming User Profile. Point to the local mandatory profile location, such as C:\Mandatory_Profile. Do not include the .V2 extension.

6. Do this on each machine in the farm or pool.

Profile and Folder Redirection Troubleshooting Tips

Many people find the combination of RD Session Host servers and profiles daunting. And it's true—things don't always work the way you expect them to. Table 5-9 describes some common errors, possible solutions, and the sections in the chapter where you'll learn how to fix each problem.

TABLE 5-9 Profiles and Folder Redirection Troubleshooting Tips

PROBLEM	SOLUTION	ADDITIONAL INFORMATION IN THIS CHAPTER
Policies appear to be set correctly, but aren't being applied.	Force a policy update by using Gpupdate or by rebooting.	See the sidebar entitled "Updating Group Policy."
Folders are not being redirected to the proper location or roaming profiles are not being loaded.	Check event logs to make sure that share is available on the network and has appropriate permissions.	See the sections entitled "The Consequences of Deleting a Profile Folder from Windows Explorer" and "Centralizing Personal Data with Folder Redirection."
Group Policy settings aren't being applied to the right computers, groups, or users.	Check the security filters and make sure that you've included the correct groups.	See the section entitled "Fine-Tuning GPOs with Security Filtering."
Folders from profiles from earlier operating systems aren't redirecting properly, but Windows 7 and Windows Server 2008 R2 profile folders are redirecting.	Make sure you've enabled earlier Folder Redirection for that GPO.	See the section entitled "Sharing Folders Between Windows Server 2003 and Windows Server 2008 Roaming Profiles."

Continued on the next page

PROBLEM	SOLUTION	ADDITIONAL INFORMATION IN THIS CHAPTER
Users cannot load their roaming profiles when they log on, and they see a message that they will be logged on with a temporary profile.	You might have deleted the cached profile manually using Windows Explorer. Delete the old registry keys and use tools such as the profile management utility or Delprof to delete profiles.	See the section entitled "Deleting Cached Profiles Manually."
Testing Mandatory Profiles returns the error "Access is denied."	Make sure you set the Everyone group to be permitted to use the profile when you use the Copy To button to create the mandatory profile. If necessary, delete the profile that is not working and redo it.	

Summary

Although roaming profiles (read-write or read-only) are often the best model for storing user profiles in an RDS environment, the complications involved in making them work *well* can be daunting. This chapter has explained how profiles work, including how the User Profile Service loads and saves configuration data. You've learned about best practices, including how to keep profiles manageable in size to speed user logons and how Folder Redirection and profile caching also contribute to faster logons. You've seen how to set up Group Policy to enable automatic profile creation and how to use security filtering and loopback policy processing to ensure that the policies are applied correctly with RDS. Finally, you've learned how to set up and use mandatory profiles with RDS and how to prevent users from losing files when using mandatory profiles.

- There are three types of profiles: local, roaming, and mandatory (including super-mandatory).

- Combining roaming profiles with Folder Redirection is generally the best way to store user data in remote environments. Folder Redirection is very important for keeping logon times short and profile sizes small.

- Mandatory profiles work best when you don't want to save any changes to the profile and have prevented users from writing files to profile folders.

- Profiles don't merge—they overwrite. For best results, open only one copy of the user profile at a time. For this reason, you should generally not use the same roaming profile for both local logons and RD Session Host server logons.

- Implementing Group Policy correctly from the beginning is key to making roaming profiles work.
- Folder Redirection is very important to making profiles work properly, as follows.
  - Folder Redirection keeps profiles small.
  - Folder Redirection reduces the data that must be written back to a file stored in a profile folder.
  - Using Folder Redirection, you can share folders between two profiles for better integration of local and remote user experiences.
  - If using mandatory profiles, you must use Folder Redirection to allow users to save files to any of their normal document storage locations (for example, Documents and Favorites).

Additional Resources

The following resources will extend your knowledge of topics addressed in this chapter. All links are available to you on this book's companion media.

- For more information on user profile management (with or without RDS), read the following.
  - "Managing Roaming User Data Deployment Guide," available online at *http://technet.microsoft.com/en-us/library/cc766489%28WS.10%29.aspx* and for download from *http://go.microsoft.com/fwlink/?LinkId=73760*.
  - "Using User Profiles in Windows Server 2003," located at *http://technet2.microsoft.com/windowsserver/en/library/23ee2a30-5883-4ffa-b4cf-4cfff3ff8cb71033.mspx?mfr=true*.
- For more information about how to configure device redirection, see Chapter 6, "Customizing the User Experience."
- To learn how to lock down the server, see Chapter 7, "Molding and Securing the User Environment."
- For more information about publishing RemoteApp programs, see Chapter 9, "Multi-Server Deployments."
- For more information about enabling RD Session Host server farms with RD Connection Broker and multi-server management, see Chapter 9.

Customizing the User Experience

I f you're reading this book sequentially, by this point you have the basic virtual machine (VM) or session delivery system enabled, and you've configured profiles and folder redirection for your environment. At this stage, you're ready to move on to what most users would consider the critical part of remoting: the user experience. After reading this chapter, you'll know more about the following points.

- How the core features of Remote Desktop Protocol (RDP) 7.0 work

- How the remote experience will vary depending on the version of RDP a user employs to get to Windows 7 or Windows Server 2008 R2

- How RDP 7.0 and RemoteFX differ in their approaches to remoting

- How to configure the remote experience so that client-side devices work in remote sessions

- How to configure printing with and without RD Easy Print

How Remoting Works

Remote Desktop Services (RDS) is all about the RDP. Without RDP, RDS just isn't very exciting. In this section, you'll examine how RDP works. You'll start with the basics of how static virtual channels, dynamic virtual channels, and protocol data units cooperate to send data, and then move on to a deeper look at how the individual features use virtual channels and Protocol Data Units (PDUs).

New Features in RDP 7.0

Each version of RDP adds new features to improve the user experience. RDP 7.0 introduces a number of changes to the remoting protocol that are designed to make the remote session feel more like working on the local computer.

- Multimedia remoting
- True multi-monitor support
- Audio recording from the local session to the remote session
- Desktop composition (Aero Glass) remoting from a session
- Language bar redirection

All these features require having Windows 7 or Windows Server 2008 R2 on the endpoint, and they are not available for /admin connections to a server running Window Server 2008 R2.

Multimedia Remoting

Using Remote Desktop Connection (RDC) 7 with Windows 7 and Windows Server 2008 R2, audio and video content, played back by using Windows Media Player, is redirected from the RD Session Host server to the client in its original format and rendered by using the client's resources. Other multimedia content, such as Silverlight and Windows Presentation Foundation (WPF), are rendered as bitmaps on the server. The bitmaps are then compressed and sent over to the client.

Multiple Monitor Support

Remote Desktop Connection (RDC) 7, with Windows 7 or Windows Server 2008 R2, enables support for up to 16 monitors. This feature supports connecting to a remote session with any monitor configuration that is supported on the client. Programs function just as they do when they are running on the client. All monitors connected to the client will show the remote session; you can't choose to exclude a monitor to show only local programs.

Audio Recording Redirection

RDC 7, with Windows 7 and Windows Server 2008 R2, redirects audio recording devices, such as microphones, from the client to the remote desktop session. This can be useful for organizations that use voice chat or Windows Speech Recognition.

Desktop Composition

RDC 7, with Windows 7 and Windows Server 2008 R2, supports Aero Glass remoting and display of other advanced graphics features within an RD Session Host session. Desktop composition works only with a single monitor.

Language Bar Redirection

Using RDC 7 with Windows 7 and Windows Server 2008 R2, you can use the language bar on the client to control the language settings within your RemoteApp programs.

What Defines the Remote Client Experience?

Distinguishing RDP 7.0, RDC 7, and the actual user experience can be confusing. There are three pieces that facilitate remoting (shown in Figure 6-1).

- **The RDC application on the client**   This application comes native to an operating system, but can be upgraded. You don't have to upgrade the operating system.

- **The RDP listener on the endpoint**   The Winstation driver on the endpoint listens for incoming RDP connections and sends data to the client computer. The listener is built into the operating system, so to upgrade it, you have to upgrade the operating system.

- **The RDP**   The protocol that the RDC and the listener use to pass data between the local and remote computer.

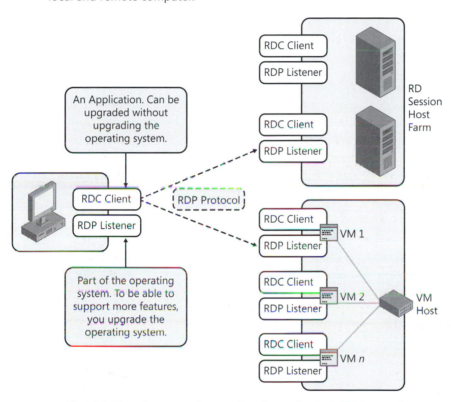

FIGURE 6-1 The RDP Client, listener, and protocol work together to facilitate remoting.

The three of these combined define the client experience. The protocol itself passes data, the RDC sends data from the client and handles it when received, and the Winstation driver on the remote computer sends data from the server and receives it.

The listener and the RDC client support versions of the RDP protocol. Table 6-1 describes the remoting experience attainable given different combinations of RDC and the RDP listener. (Although the user interface in the RD Session Host Configuration tool says RDP 6.1, the experience is RDP 7.0.) There is no user interface to display the version of the RDP listener on client operating systems, but this is the version built in to the operating system. (To see the version on client SKUs, go to HKLM\SYSTEM\ControlSet001\Control\Terminal Server\Wds\Rdpwd.)

> **NOTE** It's a bit confusing that the RDP listener name in RD Session Host Configuration says "6.1" when the protocol experience is 7. It does this because, as you can see in HKLM\SYSTEM\ControlSet001\Control\Terminal Server\Wds\Rdpwd, the name of the Winstation driver (the session driver, and stored in WdName) is "Microsoft RDP 6.1." It could just have easily been "Fred." Regardless of the name of the driver, the experience you will get when connecting to a Windows Server 2008 R2 or Windows 7 endpoint with RDC 7 is that of RDP 7.0.

RDC 7.0 will appear in the Windows XP and Windows Vista RDC About dialog box as version 6.1.7600. "7600" is the RTM version number of the Windows 7 build. It will also say that RDP 7.0 is supported.

TABLE 6-1 RDP Protocol and Listener Support Matrix

	WINDOWS XP SP3	WINDOWS VISTA SP1, SP2	WINDOWS SERVER 2003 SP1,SP2	WINDOWS 7	WINDOWS SERVER 2008 SP1, SP2	WINDOWS SERVER 2008 R2
RDC can support up to	RDP 7.0	RDP 7.0	RDP 6	RDP 7.0	RDP 6.1	RDP 7.0
RDP Listener Supports	RDP 5.1	RDP 6.1	RDP 5.2	RDP 7.0	RDP 6.1	RDP 7.0

> **NOTE** Table 6-3 in the section entitled "How the RDC Version Affects the User Experience—or Doesn't" later in this chapter further defines this matrix.

When connecting from a client to an endpoint, the remoting experience will be the lowest common denominator of what the RDC can support and what the RDP listener on the endpoint can support. For example, if you connect from a machine running Windows XP to another machine running Windows XP, even if you have installed RDC 7, the experience will be that of RDP 5.1, because the RDP listener on Windows XP supports only up to RDP 5.1. Another example: If you connect from a machine running Windows 7 to a machine running

Windows Server 2008 R2, RDP 7.0 is supported by both the client and the listener, so that is the experience you will get.

The RDP protocol connecting the RDC and the endpoint is split into *virtual channels*. Virtual channels are dedicated paths that carry particular kinds of data. For example, different channels support print jobs, clipboard sharing, drive redirection, and so forth. In Windows Server 2008 R2, virtual channels operate in both user mode and kernel mode (see Chapter 2, "Key Architectural Concepts for Remote Desktop Services," for a description of user mode and kernel mode). Remote audio and the clipboard redirector both have virtual channels in user mode, whereas plug and play devices communicate via kernel-mode virtual channels.

To pass data between client and server, both ends of the channel must exist and be enabled. That's why it's possible to turn off drive redirection on an RD Session Host server without having to override this setting on the client—the server just isn't listening on that channel. It's also why it's not possible to use a given virtual channel unless it is supported by both client *and* server. You can't, for example, use the RDP 7.0 client to enable Plug and Play (PnP) Device Redirection on a terminal server running Windows Server 2003. The client supports that channel, but the server does not.

HOW IT WORKS

Why Don't I Get Language Bar Redirection When Connecting to Windows XP from Windows 7?

When the product group blogged about RDP 7.0 on the RDS Team Blog, some people wanted to know if the new protocol would enable new features on earlier versions of Windows. For example, would someone using RDP 7.0 on the client get language bar support when connecting to Windows XP? Would they get *any* new functionality?

The short answer is "Not really." This is because of the way that virtual channels work. Almost all features available with RDS rely on virtual channels. (One exception to this rule is the integration of RemoteApp and Desktop Connections in the Start menu of Windows 7. That feature actually depends on the client operating system itself.) If the virtual channel isn't on both ends of the connection, then the feature doesn't work.

Because remoting functionality requires support on both ends of the connection, the new features of RDP 7.0 are available *only* if you're connecting to an endpoint that supports them. Windows XP listener supports RDP 5.1, and Windows Vista SP1 supports RDP 6.1, so the user experience will fall back to whatever that version can handle.

Until Windows Server 2008, all virtual channels were created at the beginning of the session and severed when the session was ended by the client or the server—these are *static channels*. Windows Server 2008 introduced a new kind of virtual channel called a *dynamic virtual channel* (DVC) that an application can create after the session has begun, and which it can sever before the session ends. DVCs make it possible to add new redirected devices to a session after it's started. If you relied on static channels entirely, then it would not be possible to plug in a camera (for example) to the client and have it show up in an active remote session. Instead, you'd have to plug the camera into the universal serial bus (USB) port before beginning the session.

 ON THE COMPANION MEDIA   Although it's possible to connect to an RD Session Host server using RDP 5.2 or later, applications using DVCs require RDP 6.1 or later; the IWTSVirtualChannelManager interface that manages the connections has a minimum requirement of RDP 6.1. You can get RDP 6.1 in Windows XP SP3 and Windows Vista SP1, or download RDC 7 for both these operating systems from *http://support.microsoft.com/kb/969084*.

Separating data into virtual channels is how this architecture allows you to selectively disable client-side redirection. It's possible to enable printing but disable drive redirection, or to enable clipboard redirection but disable PnP devices. The following section explores in detail how virtual channels work.

The Foundation of RDP: Virtual Channels and PDUs

With a very few exceptions, the communication between the endpoint and the client—and therefore the remoting experience—is enabled through virtual channels and Protocol Data Units (PDUs). RDP describes the general guidelines for how data gets from point A to point B, but the actual data is passed along the virtual channels, and the negotiation of how the data is sent is done through PDUs.

Static Virtual Channels

RDP has been passing data through static virtual channels from its inception. Static virtual channels are created at the beginning of a session and remain in place until the session is disconnected. RDP can have a maximum of 31 static virtual channels, which is one reason why DVCs are useful. They're the basis for all remoting; even the features that use DVCs (see the section entitled "Dynamic Virtual Channels" later in this chapter) depend on static virtual channels, because DVCs run in a static virtual channel.

RDP goes through eight steps to set up static virtual channels for a connection.

1. The client initiates the connection and the endpoint responds. Notice that the client always initiates.

2. The server and client exchange some basic information about the connection, including the following.

- Whether they can both support multiple monitors
- The client display height and width
- The color depth requested
- The type of keyboard
- The client operating system build number and RDP version
- What kind of security the client will use
- How the client will provide credentials (for example, whether it's using CredUI)
- The number of virtual channels requested

NOTE   For more details on the security negotiations, see Chapter 8, "Securing Remote Desktop Protocol Connections."

3. The client and server hook up the virtual channels.

4. If the client is using standard RDP security, the client and server set up session keys for the connection (again, you'll cover this in more detail in Chapter 8). After this point, all subsequent RDP traffic will be encrypted using the session keys, according to the level of security set on the client and enforced by the server.

5. The client sends the user name and password to the server.

6. The server and client negotiate whether the client has or needs a license, and then the server arranges to allocate the client a license if the client doesn't already have one.

NOTE   For details on licensing, see Chapter 12, "Licensing Remote Desktop Services."

7. The server tells the client what capabilities it supports, and the client acknowledges this information. The server capabilities sent during this step includes features such as the following.

- RemoteApp support
- Desktop composition support
- The level of compression supported

8. Finally, the client and server finalize the connection details. After the client has received this, it can start sending keyboard and mouse input to the session, and the server can begin sending graphical updates to the client.

The following features of RDP use static virtual channels.

- Clipboard redirection
- DVCs
- RemoteApp programs
- Audio output
- Smart card redirection
- File system redirection
- Serial port redirection
- Legacy printer redirection (not RD Easy Print)
- Session shadowing

An RDP connection might not have all these static virtual channels in place. During the capability negotiations between client and server, policies applied to the endpoint (and client) will be taken into consideration. Therefore, even if the operating system could technically support, say, file system redirection, if file system redirection is turned off due to Group Policy or turned off on the RDC, then the feature won't be supported and the static virtual channel won't be created.

Dynamic Virtual Channels

Dynamic virtual channels (DVCs), introduced with Windows Server 2008, are virtual channels that connect the client to an application running on the server (for example, Windows Media Player). Because they're linked to applications, they can be created after a session begins and destroyed before it ends. DVCs allow you to add remote support for a device (such as a camera) during a session without having to plug the camera into the client's USB port before beginning the session.

DVCs leverage the static virtual channel architecture. At the beginning of the connection, when the static virtual channels are created, a DVC Server Manager negotiates capabilities with the DVC Client Manager (including the version of DVC supported) and initializes the DVC path. Then, when an application wants to open one or more DVCs, the path is already prepared. The DVC Manager on the server keeps all the DVCs straight (and avoids confusing data between applications) by assigning each DVC an identifier. All traffic for a particular DVC is marked with its channel's identifier. Either the client or the server can initiate a DVC request, and any data sent between client and endpoint using DVCs is not acknowledged by the recipient.

There are two versions of the DVCs. Version 1 allows an application to communicate with the other end of the connection. Version 2 adds the ability to prioritize the data within the DVCs in case some data is more time-sensitive than other data. For example, multimedia remoting is very time-sensitive, or else the user will detect a lag. Printing using RD Easy Print is less so.

The following features of RDP use DVCs.

- RD Easy Print
- PnP Remoting
- Multimedia Remoting
- Audio Recording from client to session
- Composited Remoting (required to enable effects like Aero Glass remoting)

Protocol Data Units

PDUs are not specific to RDP by any means, but their role within RDP is often to help negotiate the respective capabilities of client and endpoint to help RDP transport data as required. (PDUs can also transport data if required.) Throughout this section, when describing how the client and endpoint are negotiating how they can communicate, this negotiation uses PDUs.

Basic Graphics Remoting

The most obvious thing that RDP does is update the client display with the graphical updates in the session. Without that, there isn't much to the experience. In this section, you'll learn about the basic graphics remoting that RDP does and how it draws the desktop to look better.

Basic graphics remoting does what it sounds like: It gets the graphical data from the server to the client. As basic graphics remoting uses static virtual channels, it does not require a very advanced RDP client to support it (Windows Server 2008 R2 and Windows 7 both support connections from RDP 5.2, even though you might not get a full complement of features). It is also the basis for more advanced graphics capabilities like composited remoting and multimedia redirection.

Basic graphics remoting has to be able to do the following things.

- Distinguish between multiple endpoints when sending graphical updates to the client
- Make the session as responsive as possible
- Stop sending graphics updates to the client when the session is disconnected or the remote window is hidden

Basic graphic remoting is enabled when the client and the server establish a connection, as described in the connection sequence in the section entitled "Static Virtual Channels" earlier in this chapter. After the connection is there, the two ends can work out how to handle the other aspects of graphics remoting, such as multimedia remoting or desktop composition.

Distinguishing Between Sessions

When the connection is established, the server keeps track of which session a process is running in and associates that process with the session ID for each session. Because the operating system has to know which process generated keyboard or mouse input, it will associate the process with the session. (Although a client operating system endpoint can support only a single interactive session at a time, Fast User Switching means that it might have more than one session logged on at once.)

Minimizing Data Sent

One way to send graphical updates is commonly known as "screen scraping"—sending bitmap images of the display on the endpoint to the client for display. This method is simple, makes it possible to support a wide array of client devices, and allows for high-fidelity rendering of all graphical updates, but over lower-bandwidth connections, it's inefficient and leads to a very choppy display. Therefore, RDP does primitive remoting whenever possible, not bitmap remoting. In primitive remoting, the endpoint sends the instructions for how and where to draw, say, a rectangle to the client, rather than sending the picture of the rectangle and its precise position. RDP will send bitmaps when it needs to—when remoting Silverlight applications, for example—but when it does, the display speed is reduced because it has to send more data.

Another way that RDP can minimize the data sent is by using a codec on the endpoint to communicate with a codec on the client. When this option is available (see the section entitled "Advanced Graphics Remoting" later in this chapter), then the codecs can send the data to the client for rendering; this might not reduce the amount of bandwidth required because the data still has to get to the client computer somehow, but to the user, it will appear to be updated more quickly and will generally look better.

Finally, RDP can use a cache for graphical data sent to the client. With the exception of bitmaps, caches are stored in memory, not on disk, and are wiped clean when the session is disconnected. Client and server negotiate their caching capabilities when the connection is being established, but the cache might contain the following.

- Bitmap images
- Colors used in drawing the screen updates
- Glyphs (characters) that the client types, both singly and in groups
- Fill areas (for example, those needed to paint the desktop color)
- Graphics device interface (GDI) primitives, cached by both client and server

Each piece of the cache has an ID. When the endpoint is going to send a graphical update that might be cached, the server will tell the client what it plans to send, and the client can look to see if it's already got it. If it does, then it will use the bitmap, or glyph, in the cache. If it does not, the server can send the update. If the server wants to use the GDI primitives cache, it will tell the client exactly where to look in its own cache for that instruction.

Why Microsoft RemoteFX?

Tad Brockway
Principal Product Unit Manager, Remote Desktop Virtualization

I have been passionate about desktop centralization for many years, even before I joined the Microsoft Remote Desktop Virtualization team in 1998. Prior to joining Microsoft, I was a UNIX developer. (We didn't call the scenario "desktop centralization" at that time. We called it "X Windows.")

The promise of Virtual Desktop Infrastructure (VDI) is that user desktops can be centralized in such a way as to move complexity and state from the desktop into the datacenter. To execute on this promise, we needed to allow people to use a broad range of endpoint devices without compromising on the user experience. To this end, we are developing a remoting approach that complements traditional graphics remoting capabilities and works for endpoint devices ranging from PCs to the most lightweight of thin clients.

Up to now, graphics remoting protocols like RDP have approached remoting in a client-centric way. *Client-centric remoting* intercepts graphics on the host device and then efficiently forwards the intercepted graphics "primitives" (for example, "Draw Rectangle" or "Draw Line") to the client device. The client endpoint renders the primitives using a client-side counterpart for each graphics intercept point on the host. Client-centric remoting originated when there was limited bandwidth from the datacenter to the user desktop and when the vast majority of applications were developed on top of the same Windows graphics API: GDI.

Client-centric remoting relies heavily on the rendering capabilities of the client software and hardware. The chief benefit to client-centric remoting is that it's a very bandwidth-efficient way of remoting graphics types that can be intercepted high in the software stack and sent as primitives. But when the client and host don't both support a particular graphics type, either the application fails to run properly or the two sides negotiate down to a least common denominator graphics construct: a bitmap. Bitmaps require more bandwidth than primitives because they have to detail how to remote *everything*. For example, the primitive representation of "Draw Line" would simply include the *X* and *Y* coordinates for the line start and the line finish. The bitmap representation of the line would have to describe at least the *X* and *Y* coordinates for every single point on the line.

If you have a powerful client device with a rich software stack and your host has all the right graphics intercept points, a client-centric graphics remoting can give you a great user experience over a relatively low-bandwidth connection. But if you have a less complex client device, are missing some important graphics intercept points on the host, or both, client-centric remoting will result in gaps in the experience, such as choppy video or missing graphics.

Today, bandwidth is less expensive and more widely available, and Windows users want a wide array of graphics types (for example, Silverlight, Adobe Flash, DirectX, Aero Glass, Windows Media, and so on). These changing conditions call for the addition of a new model that can support all graphics types, including 3-D, by sending highly compressed bitmaps to the endpoint device in an adaptive manner. We call this *host-centric remoting*.

You can ensure a consistent user experience for a wide array of devices if you follow the VDI model and move a large portion of the client software and hardware into the datacenter. With host-centric remoting, all the graphics can be intercepted on the host at a very low layer in the software stack. All graphics are rendered on the host into a single frame buffer (a temporary holding station for graphical updates) that represents the user's display. Changes to the frame buffer are sent to the client at a frame rate that dynamically adapts to network conditions and the client's ability to consume the changes. The changes are sent to the client endpoint as highly compressed bitmaps by using an encoding scheme optimized for Windows desktop content. The basic graphics requirement for the client endpoint is that it supports the ability to decode and display the highly compressed bitmaps that it receives from the host. At a minimum, the client needs the decoder counterpart to the encoder that was used on the host, as well as a basic graphics display capability.

Host-centric remoting requires more bandwidth than client-centric remoting. However, it delivers a consistent experience for every aspect of the modern Windows desktop regardless of the capability of the client-side device.

If you're wondering which remoting model to choose, you don't have to. If you have a client device with a rich software stack and advanced processing capabilities, client-centric remoting makes sense. But to deliver completely on the promise of VDI for less powerful client devices, you also need host-centric remoting. We are adding RemoteFX as a new capability or "payload" to the RDP platform, while continuing to support and enhance our existing client-centric model. Whichever remoting model you use, the fundamentals of RDP are unchanged. RDP includes the same authentication, encryption, device redirection, and transport capabilities, independent of the remoting model being used.

Compressing RDP Data

RDP supports two kinds of bulk compression (compression done on all virtual channels, as opposed to compressing individual channels). Both compress only when sent from server to client, not from client to server. Standard bulk compression compresses all the data going through RDP channels using a lossless technique known as *Huffman compression*. (Lossless compression doesn't lose any data during the compression/decompression process.)

> **NOTE** Huffman compression encodes data based on the frequency of symbols in the data stream. If a symbol appears more often, its representative code is shorter than a character that appears only once. For more information on Huffman compression, see *http://www.huffmancoding.com/my-family/my-uncle/huffman-algorithm*.

Windows Server 2008 added a new codec, called NSCodec, for improving graphics compression over the wide area network (WAN) for 32-bit and 24-bit graphics (used only with RDC 5.1). This lossy compression algorithm is controlled by the following Group Policy object (GPO).

Computer Configuration | Administrative Templates | Windows Components | Remote Desktop Services | RD Session Host | Remote Session Environment | Set Compression Algorithm For RDP Data

This compression mode is off by default because it is more memory-intensive on the endpoint (which can reduce the number of sessions that an RD Session Host server can support). However, it allows RDP to perform better over slower networks. To the user, the images still look fine—your eye puts the images together in the same way it does for a newspaper image. The more data that is lost in the compression process—which generally correlates to a higher degree of compression—the grainier the connection will look.

NSCodec works by degrading the graphics slightly (almost imperceptibly to the user), using the following techniques.

- Splitting and combining color planes, which basically means sending all the color information at once instead of treating two types of colors as different "layers" in the image and sending them separately.
- Color space conversion (required for chroma subsampling)
- Chroma subsampling and super-sampling, which reduces the variation in colors between adjoining pixels (which the human eye is less sensitive to) while maintaining the intensity. Reducing the color fidelity significantly reduces the amount of data that needs to be sent.
- Color loss reduction

When the client and endpoint are negotiating their mutual capabilities (see the section entitled "Static Virtual Channels" earlier in this chapter), they determine whether the client supports both lossy compression (and how much color loss the client will tolerate) and chroma subsampling. Both require at least RDP 6.1 on the client.

Tuning RDP Performance for LANs and WANs

Remote work lives and dies by the responsiveness of the session. It doesn't matter how many features are available—if the session feels slow, then people won't use RDP. Therefore, it's important to make RDP feel as responsive as possible when only limited bandwidth is available.

First, limit the unnecessary data traveling between client and server when bandwidth is at a premium. Don't map drives unless required, use RD Easy Print if possible, and consider the tradeoff between looks and performance when it comes to color depth, because more color depth means more data. You can configure the maximum color depth via Group Policy at Computer Configuration | Administrative Templates | Windows Components | Remote Desktop Services | RD Session Host | Remote Session Environment | Limit Maximum Color Depth. Just enable the policy for your RD Session Host organizational unit (OU), and when clients connect, they will use the maximum color depth specified in Group Policy (15 bit to 32 bit) up to the maximum that the endpoint supports.

Second, choose your bulk compression algorithms carefully. RDP uses a version of the Microsoft Point-to-Point Compression (MPPC) protocol described in RFC 2118. MPPC maintains a buffer for data to be sent between server and client. There are two main versions in Windows Server 2008 R2 and Windows 7 (and Windows Server 2008 and Windows Vista SP1). The default compression algorithm uses an 8-KB buffer to store data for each PDU. Another compression algorithm uses a 64-KB buffer for each PDU and also implements Huffman encoding. Huffman encoding is, in short, a way to find out how often a given piece of data recurs and package the data as efficiently as possible based on that frequency. The algorithm with the 64-KB buffer is more appropriate for slower connections, but it uses more memory. To change the compression algorithm, enable the Group Policy at Computer Configuration | Administrative Templates | Windows Components | Remote Desktop Services | RD Session Host | Remote Session Environment | Set Compression Algorithm For RDP Data. Because client and endpoint will both use the same compression algorithm, when the client connects, it will tell the endpoint what it can support.

Third, choose your features wisely. Like Windows Server 2008, Windows Server 2008 R2 enables ClearType remoting, which makes ClearType fonts look the same in a remote session as they do on the local terminal server. Unfortunately, performance is affected adversely when ClearType remoting is used. Ordinary text remoting displays fonts as characters—*glyphs*, to use the technical term. ClearType remoting displays fonts as bitmaps, as pictures of fonts. This reduces the likelihood that the client will be able to pull the right character from its cache where it stores recently received data. If it can't, then it will need the endpoint to send the character again. ClearType remoting is off by default and isn't recommended for wide area network (WAN) connections.

As you can see, the choices you could make depend on the amount of bandwidth available and are computer-wide. If you need to support both local and remote users, one option would be to define a parallel farm for use via RD Gateway only. (For more about RD Gateway, see Chapter 10, "Making Remote Desktop Services Available from the Internet.") If you did this, then you could use the compression algorithm optimized for low-bandwidth scenarios and limit the color depth, then provide greater color depth and a memory-optimized compression algorithm on the endpoints for local use.

Sending Updates Only When the Session Is Active

There's no point in sending frequent graphical updates when the user isn't interacting with the session. When the session doesn't need updates—when the user has minimized the window or disconnected from the session—the session on the endpoint remains active, but the client doesn't get updates.

When the client sends a request to disconnect, the server will first refuse the request and then reply with an error to prompt that disconnecting will end the connection, but the session will remain active. If the user on the client confirms the request, the connection will be disconnected and the endpoint will stop sending graphical updates.

Advanced Graphics Remoting

Basic RDP displays the desktop and applications on the endpoint in a window on the client. Composited remoting, introduced with Windows Server 2008 R2 and Windows 7, improves the remote display by drawing all windows separately from each other to achieve a 3-D effect, which is required for Aero Glass remoting, window previews, and other advanced graphics remoting features. To make this work, RDP must be able to send the contents of each application layer separately and then send them to the Desktop Window Manager on the client to reassemble them appropriately.

Advanced graphics remoting is available only when the client has a single monitor. If the client uses more than one monitor in a remote session, this feature is disabled even if it is enabled on the endpoint.

To enable advanced graphics remoting, open Server Manager on the host. In the Client Experience section, make sure that you've selected the box for Desktop Composition. Windows 7 Enterprise and Ultimate don't require additional configuration to support this feature.

The RDP 7.0 FAQ

When the product group posted the RDS Team Blog entry announcing RDP 7.0 for Windows XP SP3 and Windows Vista SP1, we got a lot of questions. For easy reference, we've organized and answered them here.

What Operating Systems Is RDC 7 Available For?

All versions of Windows 7 and Windows Server 2008 R2 come with RDC 7. You can install RDP 7.0 on 32-bit Windows XP SP3 and 32-bit Windows Vista SP1 and SP2. (The RDC upgrade is not available for 64-bit versions of Windows XP and Vista because the code base for 64-bit XP is different and there wasn't enough user demand to justify the huge increase in test cost.) For thin clients, RDP 7.0 is available for Windows Embedded Standard 2009 and Windows Embedded POSReady 2009.

> **NOTE** Windows 7 Premium allows outbound RDP connections. It does not permit incoming RDP connections.

A separate installation of RDP 7.0 is not supported on earlier server operating systems as a client, and if you hack the install to install RDP7 on a server SKU (there are instructions floating around the web for this, but none are supported or endorsed by Microsoft), then this will not enable the new features of RDP7 on the endpoint.

As of this writing, there is no RDP 7.0 for Apple Macintosh operating systems, just a basic connectivity. Microsoft does not make or support an RDP client for Linux.

Which Endpoints Will Give Me All the Features of RDP 7.0?

To get all the features of RDP 7.0, you'll need to connect to Windows 7 Enterprise or Ultimate edition, or Windows Server 2008 R2 with the RD Session Host role service installed. Administrative connections to RD Session Host servers or connections to other Windows 7 SKUs will get a limited set of features. Windows 7 Premium cannot be an RDP endpoint.

Does RDP 7.0 Support Tablet Input?

No.

If Using Windows Server 2008 R2 as a Client and Connecting to Windows 7, Will You Get All Features of RDP 7.0?

Yes, as long as you're connecting to Windows 7 Enterprise or Ultimate edition. When you connect to Windows 7 Professional, some features, such as multimedia redirection, bidirectional audio, and true multi-monitor support, will not be available.

Can I Use RDP 7.0 to Make Windows 7 Support Multiple Sessions?

No. Client SKUs support only a single active session at a time. This is by design; multiple sessions aren't covered by the End User License Agreement (EULA).

Can I Split the Remote Display to Show Both Local and Remote Desktops?

If a monitor is connected to the client, it will be used to display the remote session. Using the tools provided, it is not possible to specify that a particular monitor should be used for displaying the remote session and another should be used for displaying the local desktop. It's also not possible to hook up an external display tool (like a projector) and show the local window on the projected image and the remote session on the client's monitor (or the reverse).

Moving the Client Experience to the Remote Session

It's been said of RDS that it "makes it like being there, only better." Let's see what you can do to let users bring their personal work habits to the remote session without causing trouble for you or the other users sharing that RD Session Host server or pooled and personal VMs.

The following sections discuss both per-user and per-computer settings that define the client experience. Not all user-experience configurations can be managed at the user level in Group Policy. Where applicable, the discussions include the settings in RD Configuration Tool and Active Directory Users And Computers, for those not using Group Policy to configure all settings.

Which Client Devices Can You Add to the Remote Session?

Most supported client devices require little setup to use in a remote session, as long as you meet the system requirements. For PnP redirection, make sure that you've installed the Desktop Experience feature on each RD Session Host server or Windows 7 computer. For RD Easy Print, make sure that you've installed RDP 6.1 or later on each client. RDP 7.0 is best as it does not require the Microsoft .NET Framework on the client, whereas RDP 6.1 does.

You can configure device and resource redirection in one of four ways.

- Using Group Policy (highest priority)
- Using Active Directory Users And Computers on a per-user basis (printer redirection only; second priority)
- Using the Remote Desktop Session Host Configuration on a per-server basis (third priority)
- Using the RDC on a per-connection basis (fourth priority)

The priorities mean that although configuration at these levels will be merged for the connection, if device redirection is not allowed at any of these levels, the redirection will be disabled for the user or machine(s) the setting affects. For example, if drive redirection is left unconfigured in Group Policy but enabled in RDC, it will be enabled for the connection. But if you enable drive redirection in RDC, yet it is disabled at the server level (in Remote Desktop Session Host Configuration), drive redirection to that server will be disabled. A lower-priority setting might be able to disable a setting enabled at a higher priority, but it can never enable something disabled at a higher priority.

Not all policies are configurable through all tools. Group Policy exposes all policies (except for the drives and devices plugged in later settings); other tools expose a subset. Because of the different ways you can control device and resource redirection, the options can be confusing. Table 6-2 summarizes the types of devices and resources that can be redirected; whether they can be controlled by Active Directory Users And Computers, RDC, Remote Desktop Session Host Configuration, or Group Policy; and what that controlled state is set to by default.

TABLE 6-2 Default Drive and Resource Redirection Settings for Active Directory Users And Computers, RDC, Remote Desktop Session Host Configuration Tool, and Group Policy Settings

	ACTIVE DIRECTORY USERS AND COMPUTERS USER ENVIRONMENT TAB	RDC 7	REMOTE DESKTOP SESSION HOST CONFIGURATION	GROUP POLICY
Audio and video playback	Not configurable from here	Enabled	Disabled	Not configured; disabled by default for server endpoints; enabled by default for client endpoints
Limit audio playback quality	Not configurable from here	Not configurable from here	Not configurable from here	Not configured; default setting is Dynamic
Audio recording	Not configurable from here	Disabled	Enabled	Not configured; by default enabled when the endpoint is Win7 but disabled when the endpoint is Windows Server 2008 R2

	ACTIVE DIRECTORY USERS AND COMPUTERS USER ENVIRONMENT TAB	RDC 7	REMOTE DESKTOP SESSION HOST CONFIGURATION	GROUP POLICY
Printer redirection	Enabled	Enabled	Named Windows printer; enabled	Not configured; enabled by default
LPT redirection	Not configurable from here	Not configurable from here	Enabled*	Not configured; enabled by default
Clipboard redirection	Not configurable from here	Enabled	Enabled	Not configured; enabled by default
Smart card redirection	Not configurable from here	Enabled	Not configurable from here	Not configured; enabled by default
Serial ports/ COM port redirection	Not configurable from here	Not Enabled	Enabled	Not configured; enabled by default
Drive redirection	Has no effect**	Not enabled	Enabled	Not configured; enabled by default
Drives connected to later	Not configurable from here	Not enabled	Not configurable from here	Not configurable from here
PnP device redirection	Not configurable from here	Not enabled	Enabled	Not configured; enabled by default
Devices plugged in later	Not configurable from here	Not enabled	Not configurable from here	Not configurable from here
Default to main client printer	Enabled	Not configurable from here	Not configured	Not configured; enabled by default

*In Remote Desktop Session Host Configuration, LPT port redirection will be disabled and not able to be edited (the check box will be shaded and unavailable to check) if this Group Policy setting, Use Remote Desktop Services Easy Print Printer Driver First, is enabled. The setting is located at Computer Configuration | Policies | Administrative Templates | Windows Components | Remote Desktop Services | RD Session Host | Printer Redirection.

**Although there is a setting on the Environment tab in the user account Properties dialog box available from Active Directory Users And Computers, this setting has no effect. It was originally designed to be used by the Citrix MetaFrame add-on to Windows 2000 Remote Desktop Services (before RDP supported drive redirection), and it isn't used by RDP.

By default, most device redirection is not specified at the Group Policy level (the policies are available but not configured). To control device redirection via Group Policy, the GPOs that you would modify (and apply to the OU where the endpoint resides) are located at Computer Configuration | Policies | Administrative Templates | Windows Components | Remote Desktop Services | Remote Desktop Session Host | Device and Resource Redirection. They are

- **Allow Audio And Video Playback Redirection**   Audio and video playback redirection is disabled by default when connecting to a Windows 2008 R2 RD Session Host server but enabled for Windows 7, Windows Vista, or Windows XP. If this setting is unconfigured, audio and video playback redirection can be controlled using the Remote Desktop Session Host Configuration on a per-server basis.

- **Allow Audio Recording Redirection**   Audio recording redirection is not allowed by default when connecting to a Windows 2008 R2 RD Session Host server, but it is allowed by default when connecting to a Windows 7 endpoint. To change this default behavior, toggle this GPO (to Enabled for RD Session Host Servers, or Disabled for Windows 7 endpoints).

- **Limit Audio Playback Quality**   You can limit the quality of audio playback by enabling this setting. Limiting audio playback quality can help save bandwidth over slow WAN links. You can set the audio playback to High (no compression), Medium (some compression, latency determined by the codec used), or Dynamic, which determines the best choice of playback quality given the bandwidth available to the connection.

- **Do Not Allow Clipboard Redirection**   Enable this policy to disable clipboard redirection to an endpoint. Clipboard redirection can also be controlled on a user basis in Group Policy with this GPO: User Configuration | Policies | Administrative Templates | Windows Components | Remote Desktop Services | Remote Desktop Session Host | Device and Resource Redirection | Do Not Allow Clipboard Redirection.

- **Do Not Allow COM Port Redirection**   Enable this policy to disable COM Port redirection. By default, COM Port redirection is allowed for RDS sessions. If your users don't need it, stop COM Port redirection by enabling this setting. If you disable this setting, then COM Port redirection is always allowed. If this setting is left unconfigured, COM port redirection is not specified by Group Policy but can be specified using RD Configuration Tool on a per-server basis.

- **Do Not Allow Drive Redirection**   Enable this policy to disable drive redirection to an endpoint.

- **Do Not Allow LPT Port Redirection**   This setting does affect LPT printers. However, it will have no effect if you're using RD Easy Print because that's not redirected—it's just sent to the client for processing. This setting can also be configured from either Active Directory Users And Computers or the Client Settings tab for RDP in Remote Desktop Session Host Configuration. Enable this policy to disable LPT Port redirection to an endpoint.

- **Do Not Allow Supported Plug And Play Device Redirection**   By default, this is not controlled by Group Policy, and users can choose to enable Plug And Play Redirection in the RDC client. Enable this policy to disable Plug And Play Redirection. It can also be controlled on a per-server basis using RD Session Host Configuration.

- **Do Not Allow Smart Card Device Redirection**   By default, smart card redirection is enabled for RDP 6.1 and later. Enable this policy to disable drive redirection to an endpoint.

- **Allow Time Zone Redirection**   Time zone redirection is not allowed by default, and it is configurable only by GPO. See the section entitled "Redirecting Time Zones" later in this chapter for more information. Time zone redirection also does not work for pooled and personal VMs running client operating systems.

> **NOTE**   Although these policies are listed in the Remote Desktop Services section of Group Policy, they apply to pooled and personal VMs as well (except for time zone redirection).

You can also disable redirection of specific types of supported plug and play devices with GPOs located at Computer Configuration | Administrative Templates | System | Device Installation | Device Installation Restrictions, but you need to know the Device IDs or Device globally unique identifiers (GUIDs) of the devices for which you wanted to disable redirection. For example, to block redirection of a camera, enable the GPO called Prevent Installation Of Devices Using Drivers That Match These Device Setup Classes and input the Device Class of the specific device for which you want to block redirection.

To find out what a device's GUID is, open Computer Management, select Device Manager, right-click a device, select Properties, select the Details tab, and in the Properties drop-down box, choose Device Class GUID. Right-click the value and choose Copy.

You can also alert the user that the device redirection has been blocked by policy restrictions by sending a pop-up message to the remote session. Enable either of these two GPOS and add a text message.

- Display A Custom Message When Installation Is Prevented By A Policy Setting
- Display A Custom Message Title When Device Installation Is Prevented By A Policy Setting

By default, device redirection is allowed on a per RD Session Host server (except for audio and video playback). To disable specific device redirections, open the Remote Desktop Session Host Configuration on the server, double-click RDP-Tcp, select the Client Settings tab, and select the check box next to any of the following devices that you do *not* want to redirect.

- Drive
- Windows Printer
- LPT Port
- COM Port
- Clipboard
- Audio And Video Playback (disabled in RD Configuration by default)

- Audio Recording
- Support Plug And Play Devices
- Default To Main Client Printer

Note that Default To Main Client Printer is more of an option than a redirection, but it is located in this panel. This toggles whether or not to make the client default printer the default printer in the remote session.

Assuming that you've not disabled device redirection by GPO or at the server level, any remaining device redirection setup occurs on the client. (If you have disabled device redirection at the GPO or server level, then there's nothing to be done on the client—nothing that you do on the client will override Group Policy or choices made at the server level.) Run the Remote Desktop Connection (RDC) client. To configure device redirection, click the Options button in the RDC dialog box and select the Local Resources tab. The Printers and the Clipboard options are on this tab, but to choose to redirect other devices, you'll need to click More to open the dialog box shown in Figure 6-2.

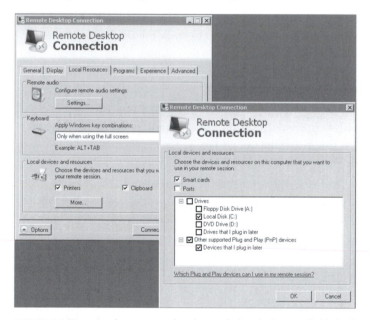

FIGURE 6-2 You can choose to make plug and play devices available in the remote session.

If you use smart cards for user authentication in your environment, then smart cards must be redirected so users can use them to authenticate their remote sessions. As shown in Figure 6-2, smart cards are redirected by default.

Serial port devices are not remoted by default; not many devices use serial connections these days. Likewise, drives are not remoted by default. Expand the Drives option to select particular drives that you want to make accessible in the remote session. (One option is Drives That I Plug In Later, so you can opt to add USB drives to the remote session using DVCs.)

Plug and play devices are not remoted by default, so you'll need to enable their redirection to use them in the session. In Figure 6-2, there is a camera plugged into the client. If you select the check box next to Other Supported Plug And Play (PnP) Devices, when you connect to the remote session, the RD Session Host server will install the redirector driver and then display the drive in My Computer as though it were locally attached, as shown in Figure 6-3.

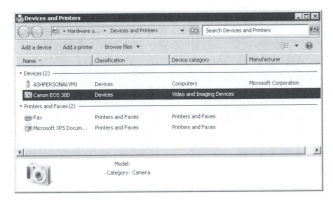

FIGURE 6-3 Redirected devices appear in the remote instance of My Computer, just as they do in the local instance.

> **IMPORTANT** If you don't see the PnP device automatically in the remote session—if instead the endpoint prompts you to install drivers—then you probably haven't previously installed the Desktop Experience, which is required to use the PnP Device Redirection Framework.

Redirected devices, such as the camera in the example, will disappear when unplugged and then will reappear when you plug them in again. When the session ends, all redirected devices disappear from the endpoint.

Pros and Cons of Redirecting Resources

Providing remote access to resources has both benefits and drawbacks. The more remote devices that you enable, the richer the client experience becomes, as it is more like the desktop client experience. But more redirected devices can lead to unintended consequences.

Obviously, redirecting drives opens a security hole. When a local drive is redirected to the remote session, storing data to the local drives is easy. This is true from a desktop computer on the corporate network, of course, but a desktop or corporate-sponsored laptop is trusted. A personal laptop or a public computer in a hotel or coffee shop is not. Not only that, but even a trusted laptop can be lost or stolen. A laptop with corporate data on it is much more valuable than the cost of replacing the hardware. If you enable drive redirection, you're also vulnerable to data from the client making its way to the endpoint. Drive redirection is full duplex; data can travel in both directions. It is not possible to restrict data to one direction.

Therefore, it's necessary to make sure that you restrict remote user access to key drives from remote sessions.

Perhaps less obviously, redirecting devices to a remote session might affect the experience for the person who's benefiting from the redirection. Those remote devices must pass data back and forth between client and endpoint. The more data you pass, the more competition there is for bandwidth between client and server. RDP compresses data well (see the How It Works sidebar entitled "Tuning RDP Performance for LANs and WANs" earlier in this chapter), and it is quite responsive for LAN connections, but it can still be affected by large file transfers, like any other network—it's just that large file transfers don't affect the user's typing when working locally.

Redirecting print devices can also ease management at the expense of performance. Because printing to redirected printers is much easier with RD Easy Print, it might be tempting to always print to redirected printers. This can be a good policy, but keep in mind the physical location of the printers. Every time the print job has to travel across the network, that's one hop across a relatively slow connection. (A LAN might be quite fast, but it's still slower than passing data between components on the same computer.) So if a client has a locally installed printer, that's one hop. If the client has a network connection to a TCP/IP printer, that's two hops (one to get to the client and one to get to the printer). If the client is connecting to a print server with connections to other printers, that's three hops: one to get to the client, one to get to the print server, and one to get to the printer.

Attaching the printers to the RD Session Host server works sometimes, but it doesn't always work well. One disadvantage is that this puts you right back to installing all the printer drivers on the RD Session Host server, with the management overhead that entails. For another reason, clients might be nowhere near the RD Session Host server—perhaps not even in the same country. But it's worth keeping the "hop" count in mind when designing the printer arrangement, balancing it against the management requirements.

The bottom line is that the decisions you make about device redirection will be based on the circumstances in which you're deploying RDS and the scenarios that you'll need to enable.

Device and File System Redirection

In addition to core graphics remoting, RDP supports sharing a number of resources between the client and the session on the endpoint. These resources can include items like the clipboard, printers, the file system, and even some plug and play devices like cameras. Unlike graphics and keyboard/mouse remoting, you can have a remote session without supporting any of these features; the user will just find the experience more like using the local computer if you do this.

Changing Bandwidth Allocation for RDP Connections

Makarand Patwardhan
Software Development Engineer

When running applications in a remote connection, multiple applications send data from server to client. These applications compete for available bandwidth, and over a slow connection, you might find that the session responsiveness suffers. This problem manifests itself most severely when printing a large document over a low bandwidth connection. The printer data competes for available bandwidth with the video rendering, thus deteriorating the graphics rendering significantly.

Beginning in Windows Server 2008 and Windows Vista, we fixed this problem by allocating a fixed percentage of bandwidth to video updates to the client. The rest goes to virtual channel traffic for redirected devices. By default, this allocation is 70 percent for video and 30 percent for virtual channel data. When bandwidth usage is constrained, video data is guaranteed to get 70 percent of the available bandwidth, so the session will remain responsive.

Although this scheme solves the problem effectively, there could be some scenarios in which you might want to tweak it a bit. You can adjust these settings by editing the registry. Please note that these edits are *not* supported, and you will need to reboot the RD Session Host server to see the changes take effect.

View or add the following list of registry values that affect the bandwidth allocation behavior. These are all DWORD values under HKLM/SYSTEM/CurrentControlSet/Services/TermDD.

- **FlowControlDisable**   When set to 1, this value will disable the new flow control algorithm, making it first-in–first-out (FIFO) for all packet requests. This provides results similar to Windows Server 2003. (Default for this value is 0.)

- **FlowControlDisplayBandwidth/FlowControlChannelBandwidth**   These two values together determine the bandwidth distribution between display and virtual channels (VCs). You can set these values in the range of 0–255. For example, setting FlowControlDisplayBandwidth = 100 and FlowControlChannelBandwidth = 100 will make the bandwidth distribution equal between video and VCs. The default settings are 70 for FlowControlDisplayBandwidth and 30 for FlowControlChannelBandwidth, thus making the default distribution equal to 70–30.

- **FlowControlChargePostCompression**   This value, if set to 1, bases the bandwidth allocation on post-compression bandwidth usage. The default for this value is 0, meaning the bandwidth distribution is applied on precompressed data.

Clipboard Redirection

The system clipboard allows users to transfer data between applications that are running on the same computer. First, a user copies data from one application, which places that data on the clipboard. Next, the user pastes it in another application. Because the clipboard stores the data, it's possible to paste multiple times. Because the clipboard will store data in multiple formats, it's possible to share information between applications that support different formats—for example, you can paste data from Microsoft Word to Notepad, even though Notepad does not support the .docx format. Any application that uses the clipboard can share data between the local and remote session.

Clipboard redirection allows you to share the following between local and remote applications.

- Generic data
- Palette data to preserve the color of the data on the clipboard
- Metafile data for storing an image in an application-agnostic format
- The list of files to be transferred
- File Stream data for transmitting pieces of an image (instead of the whole file) or separating the copy action for multiple files

To set up redirection, the client and server go through the following steps to initialize the connection shown in Figure 6-4.

1. The server tells the client the capabilities that it supports.
2. The server tells the client that it is ready and waiting.
3. When it hears that the server is ready, the client transmits its capabilities to the server.
4. The client notifies the server of a location on the client file system that can be used to deposit files being copied to the client. To use this location, the server must be able to access it directly. At this point, the client and the server capability negotiation is complete.
5. The server and client synchronize the Clipboard Formats that each supports, by mimicking a copy operation on the client by forcing it to send a Format List PDU.
6. The server confirms the list of supported formats.

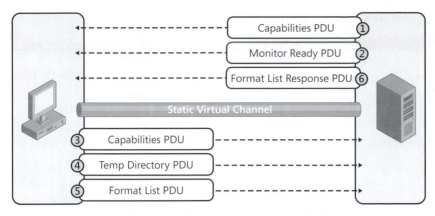

FIGURE 6-4 Here is the clipboard redirection connection initialization sequence.

Two sequences comprise the data transfer between the clipboards on each end of the virtual channel: the copy sequence and the paste sequence. These sequences together copy data on the server clipboard to the clipboard of a client.

The copy sequence synchronizes the list of available formats across the client and the server clipboards. The endpoint is notified when the user updates the contents of the clipboard so it doesn't have to keep polling the keyboard to get updates. When the clipboard is updated on the server, it sends a Format List PDU to the client containing an updated list of formats that are available on the endpoint. The client updates its clipboard format list and sends a Format List Response PDU back to the server.

The paste sequence transfers data from the server to the client clipboard. It gets invoked when an application on the endpoint requests data from its clipboard. When an application on the server requests data from the clipboard, the endpoint sends a Format Data Request PDU. The Format Request PDU contains a format ID of the type of data requested. The client responds by Format Data Response PDU containing the data requested from its local clipboard.

> **NOTE** If the data requested is a file, a File Contents Request PDU and File Contents Response PDU are used to implement the transfer of files.

Figure 6-5 depicts a clipboard copy/paste function over an RDP connection. In the following scenario, there is data on the client clipboard that is requested from within the RDP session hosted on the server. Here are the steps.

1. Data from a client application gets copied to the clipboard.
2. The clipboard notifies the virtual channel on the client.
3. The VC on the client sends an updated Format List to the server.
4. The server's VC receives the Format List and updates the clipboard on the server.

5. The server's VC acknowledges that the update happened successfully.

6. The application on the server requests data.

7. The server's VC requests the data from the client.

8. The client's VC gets the data or file from the client's clipboard.

9. The client's VC sends the requested data or file back to the endpoint.

10. The VC on the server sends the data or file to the clipboard.

11. The clipboard sends the data to the application.

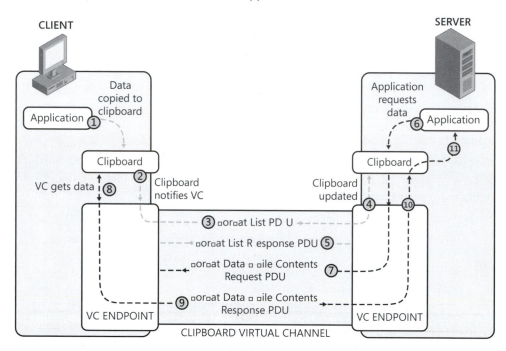

FIGURE 6-5 Clipboard redirection in action.

File System Redirection

File system redirection refers to the redirection and access of client-side file storage hardware from a remote desktop session. This is accomplished by the File System Virtual Channel Extension. It runs over a static virtual channel called RDPDR. The File System Virtual Channel Extension provides access to client-side non-volatile resources (including hard drives, floppy drives, and flash drives) from within an RDP session by redirecting input/output (I/O) requests and responses between the file system drivers on the client and the file system drivers on the server.

NOTE Device redirection is called an extension to basic RDP because it enhances the core RDP capabilities of graphics remoting and enabling mouse and keyboard input. The extension is also used as a base by other RDP extensions for printers, ports, and smart cards.

First, the protocol has to be initiated. The initiation sequence consists of an "announce and reply" exchange, a capabilities exchange, and a device list exchange between the client and the server, as follows.

1. The server and client exchange version information, and the client sends a Client ID to the server.

2. The client sends its computer name to the server.

3. Then the server and client exchange their capabilities—the list of features that will be sent over the virtual channel. The capabilities list in these exchanges can include both file system capabilities and capabilities for other extensions that piggyback on the File System Virtual Channel extension (such as the Port Virtual Channel Extension and the Print Virtual Channel Extension). If the capability is not included in this exchange, then the feature will not be supported over the channel and the subsequent device will not be redirected.

4. The server confirms that it got the client ID.

5. The client sends a Client Device List Announcement Request to the server containing information on all the devices that will be redirected, including file system devices, printers, serial ports, parallel ports, and smart cards. The server sends a Server Devices Announce Response message to the client indicating the success or failure of each device initiation.

After a successful initiation sequence, local file system devices can be used in the remote session as if they were local. The file system VC extension takes care of forwarding various I/O requests and responses between the client and server (reads, writes and queries, control requests, and so on) to the redirected devices.

Even though file system redirection uses static virtual channels, devices (for instance, flash drives) can be attached to the client and to the existing remote session while the session is active. When a new device is added to the client, the client notifies the endpoint and the endpoint confirms the changes. When a device is removed from the client, the client notifies the server that the drive is no longer available. Figure 6-6 illustrates how these communications facilitate drive (and other resource) redirection.

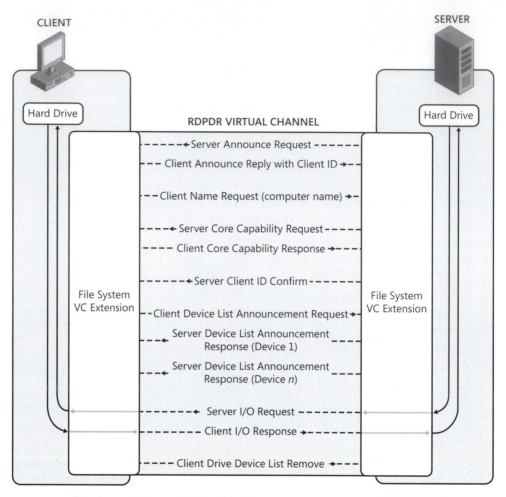

FIGURE 6-6 File system redirection sequences are shown here.

Devices Connected to Client-Side Ports

The Serial and Parallel Port Virtual Channel Extension stipulates the communication used to enable serial and parallel port redirection between a client and a server. Port redirection allows applications on a server to use the physical ports on the client.

The Serial and Parallel Port Virtual Channel Extension piggybacks on the File System Virtual Channel Extension (discussed in the previous section, "File System Redirection.") Therefore, the File System Virtual Channel Extension must be initialized before serial or parallel ports can be redirected. After the File System Virtual Channel Extension is initialized, the ports on the client get enumerated and a matching pseudo-device gets created on the server. The endpoint pseudo-device that corresponds to the client port gets created like this.

1. The port redirection extension enumerates the local serial and parallel ports that need to be redirected, and the File System Virtual Channel Extension sends the information (containing unique IDs for each device) to the server.

2. When the server receives this request, it creates a pseudo-port device that emulates the client device. The pseudo-device's ID matches the port ID on the client.

3. When the server creates the pseudo-port, it sends a Server Create Request to the client to open an instance of the port device.

Now that the pseudo-port is created on the server, the session can start using the port.

The pseudo-port acts as a sort of intermediary between the application and the client when the port is used, sharing information that it receives from one with the other. Whenever an application on the server opens the pseudo-device, the server sends a message to the client containing application request parameters, and the client processes the data. Whenever an application on the server requests a read, write, or control operation on the pseudo-device, the port sends a corresponding message to the client for processing. The client in return processes the requests and sends a corresponding message back to the port containing the results of the request. The port forwards the results to the application that made the initial request. For these transactions, the server must maintain an association between the I/O requests from the applications and the responses from the client. It does so by tagging them with a matching ID called a FileID.

When an application attempts to close the port instance to the pseudo-device, the end-point sends the request to the client. The client processes the request and responds with a confirmation (or an error).

Printers

For older printing models (RD Easy Print runs in its own DVC, so it does not use this extension), the RDS Print Virtual channel extension allows redirection of client-side printers in a remote session running on a server. The RDS Print VC Extension is a subprotocol within the RDP File System VC Extension and will only operate when the File System VC extension is working.

As part of the File System VC Extension setup, the client prepares and sends a Client Device List to the server (see the section entitled "File System Redirection" earlier in this chapter for more information) containing information on all the devices that will be redirected. The Print VC Channel Extension helps to create this list by preparing the printer device data (enumerating the printer queues, determining what printers will be redirected, and so on) that goes into the Client Device List. When the server receives the list, it creates a pseudo-printer queue that represents the client-side printer.

> **NOTE** For more details on configuring RD Easy Print and standard printer redirection, see the section entitled "Printing with RDP" later in this chapter.

Plug and Play Devices

The Device Redirection Framework introduced in Windows Server 2008 and installed when you install the Desktop Experience uses DVCs to enable Plug and Play (PnP) Device Redirection. This framework makes it possible to redirect certain types of devices from a client to a remote session. (Right now, it works only for specific types of devices, but the framework is designed to support potentially any kind of plug and play device.) Both local and remote applications can use the redirected devices, and the devices are visible only to the session in which they are started. Here's the really good part—this process works without installing drivers for those devices on the endpoint. The device redirection framework uses the client-side drivers to enable the devices.

As far as possible, you won't want to install drivers on a server or VM. Device drivers are not always reliable. If a driver crashes, it can affect the person using it (a user-mode driver) or crash the endpoint (a kernel-mode driver). Unfortunately, device drivers enable the operating system to communicate with hardware, so you don't have a choice about using them. Microsoft doesn't make all Windows drivers, so its control over this problem is limited.

RD Session Host Server in Windows Server 2008 R2, as well as Windows 7, is designed to minimize the dependency on device drivers. As you'll see in the section entitled "When You Cannot Use RD Easy Print" later in this chapter, it's not always possible to avoid using device drivers to enable client-side devices, and you will learn how to support them when you can't avoid using them. But PnP Device Redirection and RD Easy Print help reduce the problems associated with using drivers. They don't eliminate drivers entirely—you still need device drivers on the client—but they do keep the drivers off the server, as long as the client-side drivers support the framework.

 ON THE COMPANION MEDIA   The guidelines for creating a conforming driver information file (INF) are located in "Device Driver INF Changes for Plug and Play Device Redirection on Terminal Server," located at *http://www.microsoft.com/whdc /driver/install/ts_redirect.mspx.*

The PnP Device Redirection Framework uses the components shown in Figure 6-7.

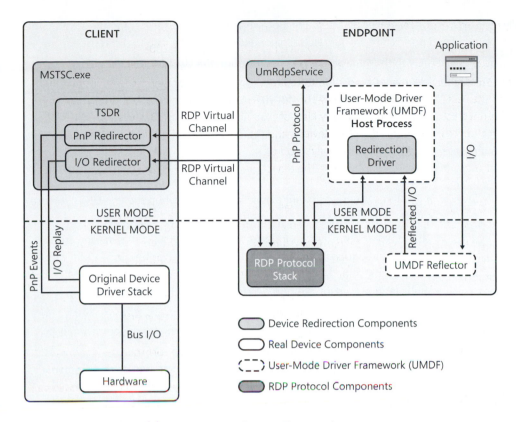

FIGURE 6-7 Architecture of the PnP Device Redirection Framework.

On the client side is the RDC (Mstsc.exe), with a PnP redirector and an I/O redirector. [You can see these two components on the client in the form of the Remote Desktop Device Redirector (RDDR) in the System Devices section of the Device Manager.] RDDR manages two aspects of communicating with client-side mobile devices.

- Inventory of which devices are present, their capabilities, and the data on them, handled by the PnP manager and passed to the PnP redirector

- Reads from and writes to those devices (I/O replay), handled by the input/output (I/O) manager and passed to the I/O redirector

The PnP manager and I/O redirector both communicate with the driver stacks for the devices they're managing, which then communicate with the hardware. The RDDR sends this communication to the session on the server via two virtual channels: one each for PnP-related traffic and I/O-related traffic.

On the server, the two virtual channels backed by RDDR both communicate with the Rdpdr.sys device driver in the RDP stack, which handles device redirection for RDP sessions. The PnP protocol passes the device management and I/O data between the RDP stack in kernel mode and the Remote Desktop Services User Mode Port Redirector service (the

UMRDP service), which makes device redirection work. By sending the data to the session, the PnP protocol and port redirection service allow the devices to show up in the session.

Communication with those devices is handled through the User-Mode Driver Framework (UMDF). The UMDF is part of the standard Windows operating system—it's not specific to RD Session Host servers—and was originally developed to support devices such as cameras and portable music players. The UMDF has three components.

- Driver manager (user mode) in the form of the UmRDP Service
- Reflector (kernel mode)
- Host process (user mode)

The *driver manager* is a system-wide Windows service started when the first UMDF device is installed. It manages the host process and responds to messages from the reflector.

The *reflector* is the proxy for the kernel-mode stack for the drivers. It lives in the kernel, but it is not a driver—its role is to send messages to the correct driver running in user mode. Every time an application makes an I/O request involving an application using the UMDF, the request goes through standard security vetting and is then passed to the reflector.

The *host process* is a child process of the driver manager (so that if it crashes, it won't bring down the driver manager). The host process accepts messages from the driver manager (to load drivers) and from the reflector (to accept requests to those drivers).

The three components work together like this: An application makes an I/O request that requires a user-mode driver. (Which one isn't important for the general case described here.) The request goes to the reflector. The reflector passes this request to the UMDF framework within the host process. The framework either sends the job to the appropriate driver or sends it back to the reflector if no driver is available. Next, the reflector sends the request back to the driver manager to tell the host process to load an additional driver.

The UMDF host can manage any compatible user-mode driver. In this case, RDS has implemented a redirector driver whose job is to communicate with Rdpdr.sys in the RDP protocol stack. Therefore, the redirector driver's job is to accept the messages passed to it by the reflector, which receives those requests from the application running in the remote session that's trying to access the redirected device.

For example, the pieces can communicate something like this.

1. An application running in the remote session makes a request to copy a picture from a client-side media device.

2. The I/O request (to copy a file from the plug and play device) goes to the kernel-mode UMDF reflector.

3. The UMDF reflector passes the request to the UMDF host process, which determines that the request came from the remote desktop session and uses the UMDF driver manager to route it to the user-mode redirection driver.

4. The redirection driver sends the request to Rdpdr.sys, in the protocol stack.

5. Rdpdr.sys sends the request to the Terminal Server Device Redirector (TSDR) on the client via the VCs.

6. TSDR communicates with the I/O manager to satisfy the request.

Today, only devices supporting the Media Transfer Protocol (MTP) and Picture Transfer Protocol (PTP) can be redirected using the PnP Device Redirection Framework (and not all devices supporting those protocols are supported with RD Session Host Servers or pooled and personal VMs). However, the framework is designed to be extensible, so other types of devices can be redirected as well.

Redirecting Time Zones

If all users are accessing RD Session Host servers from within the same building, they are all working within the same time zone. If the workforce is mobile or spread over a wide geographic area, trying to work from a non-local time zone can get disorienting for the users. This isn't uncommon; many large companies have several locations within a country, and quite a few—even small companies—must support people outside their own country and maybe even outside their own continent. If the data center is in New York but one part of the development team is working from California and accessing remote applications to keep project logs, using the New York time zone in remote sessions can be very confusing.

Starting with Windows Server 2003, Terminal Services has been able to redirect the client's time zone to the remote session. In Windows Server 2008 R2, the RD Session Host server does the math, subtracting or adding time according to the relative time zones, and then presents the adjusted time in the client session. The time *zone* is sent to the RD Session Host server, not the actual time. If the users manually adjust their time on their computers but don't change the time zone, then the difference will not show up in the remote session. In Windows Server 2008 and Windows Server 2008 R2, this setting is available as a user policy as well as a computer policy, so you can selectively redirect time zone information.

The Group Policy setting controlling time zone redirection is Allow Time Zone Redirection. If you want to configure it for users or groups of users, it's located at User Configuration | Policies | Administrative Templates | Windows Components | Remote Desktop Services | Remote Desktop Session Host | Device And Resource Redirection.

> **NOTE** Although time zone redirection has been supported since Windows Server 2003, the user policy controlling was introduced in Windows Server 2008. In Windows Server 2003, you could enable or disable this setting only on a computer-wide basis.

Configure this setting on a computer-wide basis by enabling the same policy in Computer Configuration | Administrative Templates | Windows Components | Remote Desktop Services | Remote Desktop Session Host | Device And Resource Redirection. By default, time zone redirection is turned off (the policy is not configured). To turn it on, enable the policy. All RDC clients capable of returning the client computer's time zone (RDP 5.1 and later) will do so. To disable it, either don't configure the policy or disable it.

> **NOTE** The time zone redirection GPOs work only on RD Session Host servers, not when connecting to pooled or personal VMs.

Playing Audio

RDP 7.0 supports two kinds of audio redirection from endpoint to client: one using host-based rendering and one using client-based rendering. In the first, the audio is rendered on the server and sent to the client. In the second (introduced in RDP 7.0), the audio is sent from the endpoint to the client for rendering. The first version has great backward compatibility as this feature was introduced in Windows Server 2003. The second, available only with RDP 7.0 and when connecting to Windows 7 or Windows Server 2008 R2, has the advantage of perfectly synching audio and video playback because they're rendered on the client.

In addition to remoting audio from endpoint to client, RDS can remote audio from client to endpoint, enabling users to record themselves at their computers while working in a remote location.

Basic Audio Remoting

Basic audio remoting has existed in Terminal Services since Windows Server 2003 and Windows XP. This feature allows audio to be generated in a session and sent to the client for playback. This feature relies on a static virtual channel set up at the beginning of the session and removed at the end.

Audio playback has three aspects: initialization (to negotiate the client and server capabilities and set up the communication to something they can both handle), transferring the data to the client for rendering, and sending updates to reflect the volume and pitch (so that when users raise the volume in the session for a song they like, the song plays louder on the client). This communication takes place using static virtual channels and (for Windows XP and Windows Server 2003 clients and endpoints only) User Datagram Protocol (UDP).

During the initialization phase, the client and server figure out their relative capacities that will govern how they communicate for the remainder of the connection. These capacities include the version, the supported audio formats, and whether the client can accept UDP traffic (and, if it can, whether the communication will use UDP or a static virtual channel). Figure 6-8 depicts this process.

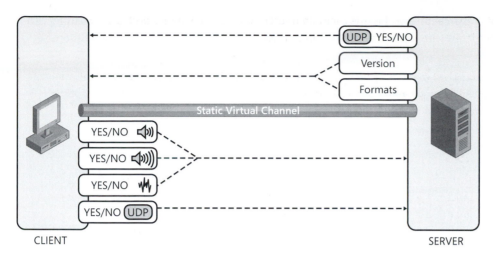

FIGURE 6-8 Audio redirection negotiation

The steps of the process are as follows.

1. The server sends a packet to the client via static virtual channel, describing its version information and the audio formats that it supports.

2. The client responds with a packet to the server, also via static virtual channel, using flags to indicate the following.

    *   The client can consume audio data. (If this flag isn't set, then the endpoint won't send audio data to the client.)

    *   The client can change the volume on the audio if it's changed in the session.

    *   The client can adjust the pitch if it's changed in the session.

3. The server and client sort out whether to use UDP to send the audio traffic to the server.

    If the client is running Windows XP SP 1 or later, then the client can accept the audio data sent to it via UDP. The fact that it can doesn't mean it *will*—the server might override the client and send the information via static virtual channel. The decision process works like this.

    *   If the server is running Windows XP SP1 or earlier, it will always use UDP communications if the client supports them.

    *   If the endpoint is running Windows XP SP2 or SP3, then if the client version is greater than 5 (meaning that the client is running Windows XP SP2 or later) the server will send audio data to the client via UDP.

    *   If the server is running Windows Vista or Windows Server 2008, or Windows 7 or Windows Server 2008 R2, then the server will always use static virtual channels to send the audio data to the client, even if the client can use UDP.

After the client and server have established how they can communicate, clients using UDP will work out with the server which port they're using and get the UDP communications set up.

> **NOTE** Although audio traffic sent via UDP isn't covered by RDP encryption, part of the UDP configuration is setting up encryption between the client and server.

If the communication is happening on static virtual channels and both server and client are running Windows 7 or Windows Server 2008 R2, then they will work out how much control the session can have over the audio. There are three flags that the client can send to tell the server how it wants to adjust the audio quality.

- For the lowest-quality audio, the server dynamically adjusts the audio format to best match network bandwidth (the size of the pipe) and latency (the speed of the pipe).
- For medium quality, the server picks a format that the client supports that is also the best compromise between quality and available bandwidth.
- For high quality, the server chooses the audio format the client supports that also will deliver the best audio, regardless of the bandwidth requirements.

That just set up the communications between client and server, but the actual data transfer is much simpler. In a nutshell, when communication happens along a static virtual channel, the server first tells the client what audio to expect next (with a short segment of the actual content), then sends the audio. After each transmission, the client sends an acknowledgment.

To adjust the volume of the audio being sent to the client, the server will send a packet telling the client what the volume should be (in absolute terms, not relative to what it might have been previously).

Multimedia Redirection

Multimedia redirection, introduced with Windows 7 and Windows Server 2008 R2, is a bit different from standard audio redirection. In this feature, any content that can be played with Windows Media Player can be sent to the client to be rendered using the client's copy of Windows Media Player, as long as the following conditions apply.

- The server is running Windows 7 Ultimate or Enterprise edition or is an RD Session host server.
- The user is not connecting with an /admin connection.
- The client is connecting via RDC 7.
- The client has Windows Media Player installed.

At a high level, in multimedia remoting, multimedia content is sent from client to server via a single DVC. Within the DVC are subchannels for sending the audio and video updates (see Figure 6-9).

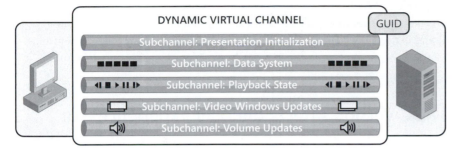

FIGURE 6-9 Multimedia remoting over DVC uses subchannels

There are several aspects to making this work.

- Negotiate the client and server capabilities and setting up the virtual channel, identified with a GUID so that the server always knows which channel to send data to and which client is sending it messages.

- Initialize the presentation of the data when Windows Media Player starts in the remote session and ending the remoting when the multimedia ends.

- The data is streamed to the client for playback.

- As the multimedia plays, the server sends messages to the client to let it know the playback state (for example, paused, rewound, or fast-forwarded).

- The server notifies the client if the video window on the endpoint changes in size or moves.

- The server notifies the client if the volume set in the session changes so the client can adjust accordingly.

To enable advanced graphics remoting, open Server Manager on the host. In the Client Experience section, make sure that you've checked the box for Audio and Video Playback. Windows 7 Enterprise and Ultimate edition endpoints don't require additional configuration to support this feature.

Recording Audio from Client to Server

Another new feature of RDP 7.0 (requiring both a Windows 7 or RD Session Host endpoint and the RDC 7 client) is often called *bidirectional audio*. Because RDP has supported audio remoting since Windows Server 2003 and Windows XP, the real new feature here is that you can send sound from the client to the server—once again, really blurring the line between the desktop and the data center. This feature enables new functionality, like making voice recordings in a remote session.

To enable advanced graphics remoting, open Server Manager on the RD Session Host server. In the Client Experience section, make sure that you've checked the box for Audio recording redirection. Windows 7 Enterprise and Ultimate edition don't require additional configuration to support this feature.

To record from within a session, you'll need to enable this feature on the client. Open the RDC client and expand the options. Select the Local Resources tab and click the Settings button in the Remote Audio section. In the Remote Audio Recording section, make sure that Record From This Computer is selected.

How the RDC Version Affects the User Experience—or Doesn't

Some people expect that upgrading to the RDC 7 client will give them all the features of RDC 7 immediately. And it will—as long as the server you're connecting to is capable of supporting all the features of RDP 7.0. If it's not, the connection will support to the set of features that both client and server can handle. The endpoints that can support the full set of RDP 7.0 features are Windows 7 Enterprise and Ultimate editions and Windows Server 2008 R2 with the RD Session Host role service installed. Everything else will get some variant depending on its technical capability or the features available to that edition. See Table 6-3 for some examples of how the user experience will vary depending on the version of client and server, and the maximum supported client for each operating system.

> **NOTE** For the sake of readability, this table will not attempt to show the myriad subcases (for example, the user experience when connecting to an RD Session Host server via an /admin connection). The most important thing to remember is that the full set of RDP 7.0 features is available *only* when connecting a Windows Server 2008 R2 RD Session Host server or a Windows 7 Enterprise or Ultimate edition computer, and using the RDC 7 client.

TABLE 6-3 Determining the User Experience

CLIENT OPERATING SYSTEM	MAX SUPPORTED RDC	SERVER	RDP EXPERIENCE
Windows 7 or Windows Server 2008 R2	RDC 7	Windows Server 2008 R2 RD Session Host Server or Windows 7 Ultimate and Enterprise edition	RDP 7.0
Windows Vista SP1, SP2	RDC 7	Windows Server 2008 R2 RD Session Host Server or Windows 7 Ultimate and Enterprise edition	RDP 7.0

CLIENT OPERATING SYSTEM	MAX SUPPORTED RDC	SERVER	RDP EXPERIENCE
Windows XP SP3	RDC 7	Windows Server 2008 R2 RD Session Host Server or Windows 7 Ultimate and Enterprise edition	RDP 7.0
Windows Vista RTM	RDC 6.1	Windows Server 2008 R2 RD Session Host Server or Windows 7 Ultimate and Enterprise edition	RDP 6.1
Windows XP SP2	RDC 6.1	Windows Server 2008 R2 RD Session Host Server or Windows 7 Ultimate and Enterprise edition	RDP 6.1
Windows XP SP1	RDC 5.2	Windows Server 2008 R2 RD Session Host Server or Windows 7 Ultimate and Enterprise edition	RDP 5.2
Windows 7 or Windows Server 2008 R2	RDC 7	Windows Vista (all versions)	RDP 6
Windows 7 or Windows Server 2008 R2	RDC 7	Windows XP SP3	RDP 5.2

As you can see from Table 6-3, the RDP experience is never greater than the lowest RDP version supported on the client and server (remember that an RDC client connects to an RDP listener version on the server). Installing RDC 7 on the endpoint does not update the listener; it just updates the client component. There is no way to upgrade the listener without upgrading the server's operating system. Therefore, whichever has the lowest version (client RDC or server listener) is the version that will determine the user experience.

For the specifics of the user experience when connecting to an RD Session Host server or Windows 7 Enterprise or Ultimate edition, see the following sections.

Connectivity Experience

Table 6-4 describes how users can connect to the RemoteApp programs and VMs assigned to them. For basic connectivity, the version of the server isn't critical: as long as users have permission to make the connection (and the server isn't running Windows 7 Premium, which does not allow incoming RDP connections), this will work.

TABLE 6-4 Client RDC Version Determines the Connectivity Experience

CONNECTING FROM	DESCRIPTION	RDC 7	RDC 6.1	RDC 5.2
Access to Remote Desktop sessions	Users can connect to a full desktop session.	Yes	Yes	Yes
Access to RemoteApp programs	Users can run RemoteApp programs alongside locally installed applications.	Yes	Yes	No
Access to personal desktop by using RD Connection Broker	Users can broker connections to VMs assigned in Active Directory Domain Services (AD DS).	Yes	Yes	Yes
Access to virtual desktop pools by using RD Connection Broker	Users can broker connections to VM pools.	Yes	Yes	Yes
Start applications and desktops from RemoteApp and Desktop Connection on client	Users can start VMs or RemoteApp programs assigned to them from their Start menu.	Yes (Windows 7 only)	No	No
Start RemoteApp programs, virtual desktop, and session-based desktop from RD Web Access	Users can start VMs or RemoteApp programs assigned to them from RD Web Access.	Yes	Yes	No
Status and disconnect system tray icon	Users can disconnect connections to RemoteApp programs and VMs via a system tray icon. Available only when starting RDP connections associated with a RemoteApp and Desktop Connection feed.	Yes (Windows 7 only)	No	No

User Experience

Table 6-5 describes the features available to users when they are connected. This time, version matters: Assume here that the server is an RD Session Host server or Windows 7 Ultimate or Enterprise edition. Windows 7 Professional (for example) will not have the full complement of features.

In Table 6-5, the "true" and "spanning" descriptions for multi-monitor support detail the way the feature manifests. In true multi-monitor support, the video driver on the endpoint can distinguish between all the monitors connected to the display and treats them independently. In the spanning multi-monitor support available with RDP 6.0 and 6.1, the endpoint's display driver treats all client-connected monitors as a single device. There's one catch to true multi-monitor support: It does not work with Aero Glass. If you have more than one monitor, Aero Glass will be disabled.

TABLE 6-5 User Experience to RD Session Host or Windows 7

CONNECTING FROM	DESCRIPTION	RDC 7	RDC 6.1	RDC 6.1	RDC 5.2
Windows Media Player Redirection	Enables content hosted in Windows Media Player controls to be redirected to the client for decoding on users' computers. This both improves the quality of the video and ensures that video and audio are always in sync.	Yes	No	No	No
Bidirectional Audio	Redirects audio recording devices such as microphones on the client to the remote session. Useful with voice recognition and applications that record audio.	Yes	No	No	No
Multimonitor Support	Windows Vista and Windows Server 2008 endpoints, only support monitor spanning. RD Session Host and Windows 7 include true multi-monitor support for up to 16 monitors and work for both Remote Desktop and RemoteApp programs.	True	Spanning	Spanning	No
Aero Glass Support	Windows Server 2008 did not support Aero Glass remoting for sessions. This is now supported in Windows Server 2008 R2 RDS in sessions with a single monitor.	Yes	No	No	No

CONNECTING FROM	DESCRIPTION	RDC 7	RDC 6.1	RDC 6.1	RDC 5.2
Enhanced Bitmap Acceleration	Improves the remote display of graphics-intensive applications like Microsoft PowerPoint, Flash, and Silverlight.	Yes	No	No	No
Language Bar Docking	Allows users to use their docked language bar with their RemoteApp applications just as they do with the local ones, instead of relying on the floating language bar.	Yes (Windows 7 to RD Session Host server only)	No	No	No
Easy Print	Allows users to print to their local printers from RemoteApp programs and VMs without needing to install print drivers on the host. Both RD Session Host servers and clients running Windows 7 support RD Easy Print.	Yes	Yes	Yes	No

Printing with RDP

Some years ago, people used to talk a lot about "the paperless office." They seem to have mostly given up on the idea now, and with good reason: Even as you print less information, there is a lot more information created that does have to be printed. Printing isn't going away.

In addition, with display remoting, printing has some new challenges. There are two ways to print from a remote desktop session.

- Print to a printer installed directly on the server (a session on an RD Session Host server, or a VM)
- Print to a printer that has been redirected to the remote desktop session from the client

Both of these methods have advantages and disadvantages, which you will find out more about in the next sections. Because RDS now supports both sessions and VMs, the information includes printing capabilities for pooled and personal VM scenarios, as well as printing from RD Session Host server sessions.

Printing to a Directly Connected Printer

The simplest way to provide printing capabilities from an server is to install the printer directly onto it. Every user logging onto the server will (given the proper permissions) have access to the printer, no matter where he or she is remoting from. The printer can be a network printer (perhaps shared from a print server), a directly connected printer (via USB or parallel port connection), or an IP-based printer located on the LAN.

Printing to directly connected printers on a high level works like this.

1. An application creates a print job and sends it to the print spooler.

2. The spooler does any conversion necessary and sends the resulting spool file to the printer driver (or to the spooler on another machine, for example, a print server, which will pass it to its printer driver).

3. The printer driver sends the file to either a GDI print device or an XML Print Specification (XPS) print device.

HOW IT WORKS

Basic GDI and XPS Printing

A GDI printer accepts enhanced metafile (EMF)–formatted files, and an XPS print device accepts XPS formatted files, so depending on what type of initial file an application creates (XPS or EMF), it might need to be converted to the format that is accepted by the print device.

> **NOTE** For more information on the GDI and XPS print paths, refer to MSDN at *http://msdn.microsoft.com/en-us/library/ms742418.aspx*.

Figure 6-10 maps the different scenarios for printing to a GDI print device from different types of applications.

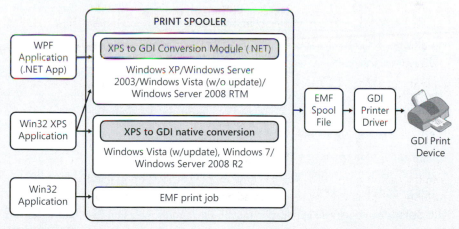

FIGURE 6-10 Files printed to a GDI print device might need conversion depending on the file type initially created.

A .NET application will create a print job and send it to the print spooler, where it goes through the .NET XPS to GDI conversion module (when native conversion is not available). The print spooler processes the resulting EMF file and sends the print job to the print driver, which sends the job to the print device.

If an application creates an XPS file, it must go through conversion to be printed on a GDI print device. In Windows Vista (with the platform update), Windows 7, and Windows 2008 R2, conversion is now native, so .NET no longer needs to be installed to do this (Windows XP Vista without the Platform update, Windows Server 2003, and Windows Server 2008 RTM still need to use the NET conversion module). The spooler sends the resulting EMF file to the printer driver, and the driver sends the print job to the GDI print device.

If an application creates an EMF file, it needs no conversion. The print spooler passes the EMF file to the printer driver and the printer driver sends the print job to the GDI print device.

Figure 6-11 maps out different scenarios for printing to a XPS print device from various types of applications.

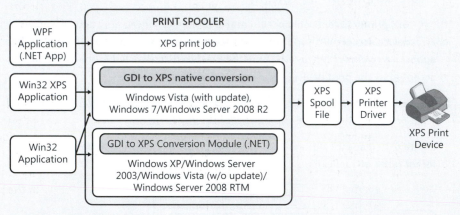

FIGURE 6-11 Files printed to an XPS print device might need conversion depending on the file type initially created.

A .NET application creates an XPS file. No conversion is necessary to print to an XPS print device. The print spooler sends the print job to the printer driver, and the printer driver sends the job to the print device.

If an application creates an XPS file, it needs no conversion. The print spooler passes the XPS file to the printer driver, and the printer driver sends the print job to the XPS print device.

A GDI file created by an application must go through conversion to be printed on an XPS print device. In Windows Vista (with the needed platform update), Windows 7, and Windows 2008 R2, conversion is now native, so .NET no longer needs to be installed to do this. (Windows XP, Vista without the platform update, and Windows Server 2003 and Windows Server 2008 RTM still use .NET conversion module here.) After the file is converted, the spooler sends the resulting print job to the printer driver and the driver sends the job to the XPS print device.

XPS supports true what-you-see-is-what-you-get (WYSIWYG), greater color depth, and faster printing than GDI. When you print to XPS, you create an Extensible Markup Language (XML) file that, like an EMF file, explains exactly what the desired output should look like, but most of the time, an XPS spool file is smaller than an EMF one.

Installing the printer drivers on the endpoints works well in scenarios where the print devices, print servers, and endpoints are all located on the same LAN, preferably where workers can reach this printer easily on foot. It's easier to implement for RD Session Host servers than VMs—there's less installing because VMs are single-user—but it's technically possible on both.

BEST PRACTICES If you install printers on your endpoints, you will want to isolate the printer drivers from the print spooler (a technology new to Windows 7 and Windows Server 2008 R2) to prevent badly behaved printer drivers from crashing the spooler. Refer to the section entitled "Printer Driver Isolation" later in this chapter for more details.

Attaching a printer directly to the server is not such a good idea in highly distributed scenarios, especially if there's a WAN involved. Printing speeds can be dramatically affected by high-latency networks. Not only that, but you could have users walking a long way for a printed document—possibly to Germany from New York, if the printers are all clustered around the RD Session Host servers in the Frankfurt data center. Finally, installing printers on each pooled or personal VM is a hassle to manage. When it's not practical to attach the printers to the endpoints, the benefits of print redirection really stand out.

Printing via Redirected Printers

Print redirection allows users to utilize the printers that are installed on their client from within a remote desktop session. It does not matter if the print device is local to the client, IP-based, mapped from a print server, or a Portable Document Format (PDF) or XPS printer. All these types of printers can be redirected to the remote desktop session.

For users to print from a remote session, two things must happen.

- The printer must show up in the remote session.
- The print job must get to the printer on the client.

Windows Server 2008 R2 supports two printing models: a model for use with RDC 6.1 and later that uses the drivers installed on the client and a model for previous versions of the RDP client (also used with Windows Server 2003) that uses drivers on the printer. The following sections explain how printer redirection works for RDP 6.0 clients and earlier, and how the RD Easy Print model works; both might be applicable to Windows Server 2008 R2.

The Legacy Printing Model for Remote Desktop Services

The legacy printing model requires a matching printer driver installed on both the client and the endpoint for it to work—and part of matching means, "The names must match." For instance, if the client has access to an HP LaserJet 6L printer, for printer redirection to work for this printer, the endpoint would need to have a matching driver installed, and the driver name must match from client to server *exactly*.

> **NOTE** On the server side, you do not need a matching printer installed—just the printer driver. On a Windows Server 2008 R2 RD Session host server, you add print drivers by adding and then deleting a printer (leaving the driver behind) or by highlighting a printer that is already installed, clicking the Print Server Properties link, navigating to the Drivers tab, and clicking Add.

ENUMERATING PRINTERS IN THE REMOTE SESSION

Chapter 3, "Deploying a Single Remote Desktop Session Host Server," explained how session creation works. One component of session creation is enumerating (that is, finding and creating a list of) any printers on the client so they can be redirected to the server. Several components are involved in the redirection.

- Winlogon.exe, the Windows Logon process in the client session
- Winsta.dll, used for configuring the session
- Termsrv.dll, the remote connection manager
- Rdpwsx.dll, a user-mode component on the server that handles the connection sequence for remote connections using RDP
- Rdpdr.sys, the kernel-mode RDP device redirection driver
- Spoolsv.exe, the print spooler on the server
- Usbmon.dll, which handles all the dynamic printer ports (dynamic because they are created and destroyed with the remote session) on the RD session host server
- Mstscax.dll, the RD session host server client, which enumerates the printers on the client and their names, drivers, and settings
- System Event Notification Service (SENS), which monitors system events such as RDS session connects and disconnects and logon/logoff events and delivers them to the applications needing them

To redirect client-side printers to the remote desktop session automatically, these components cooperate in the following ways.

1. The client, Mstsc.exe, connects to a server and goes through the connection and logon sequence. Winlogon.exe remains loaded in the user session, as does Winsta.dll, used for configuring the terminal session.

2. Via Winsta.dll and the remote connection manager, Rdpwsx.dll is notified of the new connection and notifies Rdpdr.sys.

3. Rdpdr.sys sends a packet requesting that the printers for the new session be enumerated.

4. The client collects the following information from the client and sends it to the session, where it is passed by Rdpwsx.dll to Rdpdr.sys.

   - Printer configuration data available, including name, driver name, paper orientation, default status, and so forth—everything standard for a Windows printer, but nothing contained outside the Windows printer configuration dialog boxes

   - Print queues and their port names

   - Manually created print queues created during previous logons (listed in subkeys under HCKU/Software/Microsoft/RD session host server Client/Default/Add Ins/ RDPDR on the client)

5. Rdpdr.sys creates a corresponding print port for each queue the client sends up, naming them TS*XXX*, where *XXX* is a number, counting from 001. You can see this on the RD Session Host server by clicking a printer, clicking the Printer Server Properties link, and selecting the Ports tab, shown in Figure 6-12.

FIGURE 6-12 Rdpdr.sys creates a corresponding print port for each queue that the client sends.

> **NOTE** Group Policy controls whether all printers are redirected, or just the client default printer. If it's the latter, only the client default printer is created in the remote session.

6. Rdpdr.sys also tells the PnP application programming interfaces (APIs) that new printers are available. These APIs notify the spooler (Spoolsv.exe) of the new printers for that connection. The spooler has Usbmon.dll enumerate the available ports, as copied from the client and renamed on the session. The spooler updates the client's registry to make the printers available to them.

> **NOTE** In Windows Server 2003, the spooler service was not session-aware and updated HKCU for everyone logged on to the RD session host server, so that users ended up with printers in their profiles that belonged to other users. They couldn't use them, but they were recorded in the registry. The CPU cycles the spooler service used in order to write to all the copies of HKCU strained the RD Session Host server. This has been changed in Windows Server 2008 so that a user's printers are written only to the user's copy of HKCU.

7. Winlogon.exe notifies SENS that the session is created. SENS waits for disconnect or logoff events so that it can tell Rdpdr.sys when to tear down the mapped ports.

8. SENS does the following.

- Ensures that the printer has a corresponding driver available on the endpoint
- Sets the client's default printer to be the default printer in the session
- Adds the new printer queue to its list of devices
- Sets the default security for the printer so that the logged-on user has read/write/ print permissions to the printer queue and the administrator has full control

The printers should now appear in the remote session as TS001 to TS00*n*. If the printers are not appearing, check the following.

- The client and the server must have a matching driver installed for each printer that will be redirected. If there is no driver match, you will see event ID 1111 logged in the System Event Log on the endpoint.

- Client printers are allowed to be redirected. This policy can be set in RD Session Host Configuration (in the RDP settings), in Active Directory Users And Computers, and in Group Policy. You'll find out more about how to do this in the section entitled "Controlling Printer Redirection" later in this chapter. Printer redirection abilities are also controlled by the Printers check box located on the Remote Desktop Connection client's Local Resources tab.

- Rdpdr.sys must be functioning properly. If no devices are being redirected and policy permits redirection, open Device Manager and inspect the contents of System Devices to find the RD Session Host server Device Redirector and see if it's working properly.

- The Remote Desktop Services UserMode Port Redirector service on the server must be running. If it's not, then start it and disconnect and reconnect all sessions. Because printer queues are built at the beginning of the connection, simply restarting this service won't restore printer queues.

- The Print Spooler service on the server must be running.

PRINTING FROM A REMOTE SESSION

Now that the printers are listed in the remote session, let's see how a print job gets to a redirected printer when RD Easy Print is not used. Printing involves a large number of moving parts, but this high-level view will show you how it works for remote desktop sessions.

1. The application on the server starts the print job. The RDC notifies the RDP graphics subsystem of the printers installed on the client.

2. Then the application creates the print job—either an EMF or XPS file—that contains all the instructions needed to render that picture while maintaining the picture's original size, resolution, and layout.

3. The GDI or XPS Print API passes the file to the spooler. This file can be saved to disk if many print jobs are queued for a particular printer.

4. Assuming that the print job is going to a redirected port (identified as TS*XXX*), the spooler sends the print job to the dynamic port monitor (Usbmon.dll).

5. The dynamic port monitor transfers the spool file to Rdpdr.sys, which sends the data to the appropriate RDS client, where it's sent to the appropriate printer.

To sum up, most of the processing is done on the server, the drivers must be present on the server (so that the GDI or XPS Print API can format the data stream appropriately for the selected printer), and there's a lot of data conversion (for example, EMF files actually get converted to RAW format when its sent to a PostScript printer). Every time you convert data from one format to another, there's a risk of data loss.

The RD Easy Print Architecture

Before RD Easy Print, printing from remote sessions was not an easy task. IT administrators had to deal with the following.

- **Kernel-mode drivers**   In the old days of kernel-mode drivers, a buggy driver could— and sometimes did—crash the terminal server. For this reason, the use of kernel-mode drivers has been blocked by default since Windows Server 2003.

- **Driver name mapping**   When the client and server were not running on the same kernel (for example, clients running Microsoft Windows 98 and the server running Microsoft Windows 2000 Server), the drivers often didn't have the same name. You had to map them in an INF file manually to make printing to a redirected printer work at all. (You will learn how to do this later in this chapter, in case you cannot use RD Easy Print and need to use the older printing method. Tweaking name mappings have some other advantages, too.)

- **Driver testing and distribution**   You had to test drivers before installing them on the terminal server, and after they were tested, distribute them to all the other terminal servers.

- **Bandwidth usage**   Printing could take up a lot of bandwidth, which could slow the session when the user printed documents.

In short, supporting printing with terminal servers has historically been a lot of work. Unfortunately, because the paperless office has yet to materialize (and probably won't, at least in the near future), it's necessary to continue supporting the process.

It's said that the definition of insanity is to keep doing the same thing and expecting different results. Because drivers on the server are hard to support, Windows Server 2008 decided to leave the printing insanity behind by eliminating printer drivers on the terminal server as much as possible. Instead, beginning with Windows Server 2008 and now with Windows Server 2008 R2 and Windows 7, printing over RDP uses a new architecture based on the XPS print format to allow jobs printed to a redirected printer to use the client-side printer drivers instead of requiring printer drivers on the server.

RD Easy Print is supported by clients running RDP 6.1 or later. The older format described previously is still supported for older versions of RDP, but RD Easy Print is the preferred method because of its lower management and bandwidth overhead. As explained previously, Windows 7, Windows 2008 R2, and Windows Vista and Windows 2008 with a platform upgrade all support XPS natively. Windows 2003 and Windows XP require .NET Framework to do the conversion to XPS.

Like older printing methods, RD Easy Print must render data into a WYSIWYG format and pass that data from the endpoint to the client where the printer is located. Where Easy Print differs is in the rendering and spooling process. Basically, Easy Print takes a print job request and does only enough processing on the server to get the print job to the client, as illustrated in Figure 6-13.

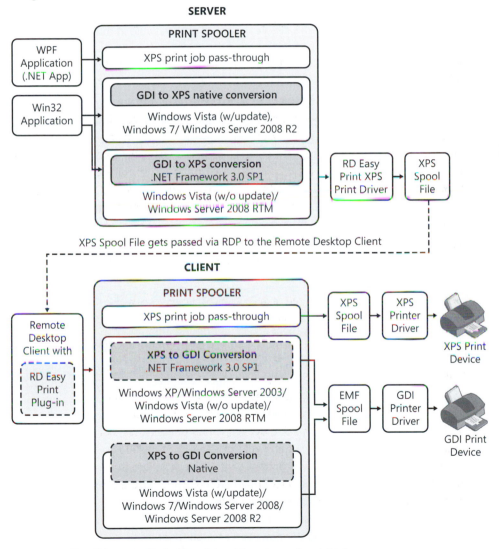

FIGURE 6-13 Easy Print uses client-side printer drivers to create print jobs.

The printing process works like this.

1. The user starts a print job from an application running in the remote session.

2. The print job is converted to an XPS file, natively (this step is skipped if the file is already in XPS format).

3. The XPS file is sent to the RD Easy Print plug-in in the RDC client.

4. XPS files destined for an XPS printer are passed to the XPS print driver. XPS files destined for a GDI printer are converted to EMF spool files and then passed to the GDI printer driver.

5. The print job goes to the printer.

The most important concept to remember in this process is that you don't have to install printer drivers on the server. RD Easy Print uses a proxy driver on the server to pass print jobs to the client for printing. Because of this, all client printers are available in the remote desktop session. By using RD Easy Print, you no longer have to match drivers on the endpoint with drivers on the client, and there is no risk of server crashes due to crashing kernel-mode print drivers or spooler crashes stemming from a problem driver.

Like other device redirection, RD Easy Print uses virtual channels to let you configure the printing properties application directly on the client. When a user clicks a printer's preferences from a session, the RD Easy Print driver on the endpoint intercepts this call and sends the request to the RD Easy Print plug-in on the RDC client. The client calls the client-side printer driver, which brings up the printing preferences dialog box on the client. Therefore, the preferences that you get when you print from a client are the same preferences that you get when printing from an RDS session.

Printing from Remote Desktop Services

One of the most important parts of moving the client experience to the remote session lies in printing.

> **NOTE** Although the following discussions are about printing, they apply to faxing as well. Faxing works just fine with RD Easy Print—simply set up the fax on the client. When the client chooses to send a fax, the client-side dialog box opens to prompt the user for the contact information. Scanning is not supported in native Windows Server 2008 R2, but it is enabled by several third-party products.

Requirements for Easy Print

To take advantage of RD Easy Print, the clients need to be running RDC 6.1 or later, and the endpoints need to be running Windows Server 2008, Windows Server 2008 R2, or Windows 7. RDC 7 comes with Windows 7 and is available for Windows Vista SP1 and Windows XP SP3. RDC 7 is the preferred client, and Windows Server 2008 R2 or Windows 7 the preferred endpoint. In the previous version of Terminal Services, the .NET Framework was also required to convert XPS to GDI for output on GDI printers and to convert XPS to GDI for output with XPS printers. One of the biggest improvements to RD Easy Print in Windows 7 and Windows Server 2008 R2 is that the .NET Framework is no longer needed to do this conversion—it's built into the operating system. In addition, with the right service pack and platform update installed, Windows Server 2008 and Windows Vista no longer require the .NET Framework either when acting as clients.

> **NOTE** The platform update for Windows Vista and Windows Server 2008 is downloadable from the Microsoft website at *http://support.microsoft.com/kb/971644*. Windows Server 2008 requires Windows Server 2008 Service Pack 2 in order to install the update, and Windows Vista requires Windows Vista Service Pack 2.

Windows XP still requires the .NET Framework 3.0 SP1 or later be installed. Table 6-6 provides a list of situations in which the .NET Framework is no longer required to use RD Easy Print.

TABLE 6-6 Scenarios in Which the .NET Framework Is No Longer Needed to Use RD Easy Print

CLIENT	SERVER
Windows Vista SP2 with RDC 7 and KB971644 installed (*http://support.microsoft.com/kb/971644*)	Windows Server 2008 R2
Windows Vista SP2 with RDC 7 and KB971644 installed	Windows 7
Windows 7	Windows Server 2008 R2
Windows 7	Windows 7
Windows Server 2008 with SP2 and KB971644 installed	Windows 7
Windows Server 2008 R2	Windows 7
Windows Server 2008 with SP2 and KB971644 installed	Windows Server 2008 R2

RD Easy Print is not meant for all situations. So it's not available, for example, from a Windows 7 client remoting to a Windows XP server. RD Easy Print is also not available in any session when you make an administrative connection (mstsc /admin). Table 6-7 and Table 6-8 show situations in which RD Easy Print will and will not work. This is helpful when you're trying to determine what's wrong, only to realize that the server that you attempted to use RD Easy Print on was a domain controller to which you had an administrative connection.

> **NOTE** Some of these scenarios work or don't work depending on whether or not RD Session Host Server role service is installed on the server. These are noted by entries in the last column.

TABLE 6-7 Scenarios When RD Easy Print Will Work

CLIENT	SERVER	IF
Windows Server 2008 R2	Windows Server 2008 R2	RDSH is installed
Windows Server 2008	Windows Server 2008 R2	RDSH is installed
Windows 7 Professional	Windows Server 2008 R2	RDSH is installed
Windows 7 Ultimate/Enterprise	Windows Server 2008 R2	RDSH is installed
Windows 7 Ultimate/Enterprise	Windows Server 2008 R2	RDSH is not installed
Windows XP SP3 and .NET Framework 3SP1 and higher	Windows Server 2008 R2	RDSH is installed
Windows Server 2008 R2	Windows Server 2008	Terminal Services is installed
Windows 7 Ultimate/Enterprise	Windows Server 2008	Terminal Services is installed
Windows XP SP3 and .NET Framework 3SP1and higher	Windows Server 2008	Terminal Services is installed
Windows Server 2008 R2	Windows 7 Ultimate/Enterprise	
Windows Server 2008	Windows 7 Ultimate/Enterprise	
Windows 7 Ultimate/Enterprise/ Professional	Windows 7 Ultimate/Enterprise/ Professional	
Windows XP SP3 and .NET Framework 3SP1 and higher	Windows 7 Ultimate/Enterprise	
Windows Server 2008	Windows Server 2008	Terminal Services is installed

TABLE 6-8 Scenarios in Which RD Easy Print Will NOT Work

CLIENT	SERVER	IF
Windows Server 2008 R2	Windows Server 2008 R2	RDSH is not installed
Windows Server 2008	Windows Server 2008 R2	RDSH is not installed
Windows 7 Professional	Windows Server 2008 R2	RDSH is not installed
Windows XP SP3 and .NET Framework 3 SP1and higher	Windows Server 2008 R2	RDSH is not installed
Windows Server 2008 R2	Windows Server 2008	Terminal Services is not installed
Windows 7 Ultimate/Enterprise	Windows Server 2008	Terminal Services is not installed

CLIENT	SERVER	IF
Windows XP with SP3 and .NET Framework 3 SP1and higher	Windows Server 2008	Terminal Services is not installed
Windows Server 2008 R2	Windows 7 Professional	
Windows Server 2008	Windows 7 Professional	
Windows XP with SP3 and .NET Framework 3 SP1and higher	Windows 7 Professional	
Windows Server 2008 R2	Windows XP SP3 and .NET Framework 3 SP1 and higher	
Windows Server 2008	Windows XP SP3 and .NET Framework 3 SP1 and higher	
Windows 7 Ultimate/Enterprise/ Professional	Windows XP SP3 and .NET Framework 3 SP1 and higher	
Windows XP SP3 and .NET Framework 3 SP1and higher	Windows XP SP3 and .NET Framework 3 SP1 and higher	
Windows Server 2008	Windows Server 2008	Terminal Services is not installed

NOTE In some instances (noted in Table 6-8), you can get RD Easy Print to work with Windows 7 Professional, but it is not supported officially.

Printing with RD Easy Print

Making RD Easy Print work requires no setup on the client or the server so long as your clients meet the requirements. Observe RD Easy Print at work in the following examples. Here's the domain breakdown.

- The domain is a Windows Server 2008 R2 domain named Ash.local.
- The Windows Server 2008 R2 RD Session Host servers are named FUJI and GLACIER. They are configured as a farm called Farm1.ash.local.
- ASHPersonalVM1 is a client PC running Windows 7.
- ASHPersonalVM5 is a client PC running Windows XP SP3.

ASHPersonalVM1 meets RD Easy Print Requirements natively—it comes with RDC 7 and also has XPS conversion capabilities built into the operating system (no need to add the .NET Framework). ASHPersonalVM5 is running RDP 6.1, which is required for RD Easy Print. The client running Windows XP still requires .NET Framework 3.0SP1 or later—you must download and install it separately.

Let's review the scenario: A user logs on to ASHPersonalVM1. Some printers are available, as shown in Figure 6-14.

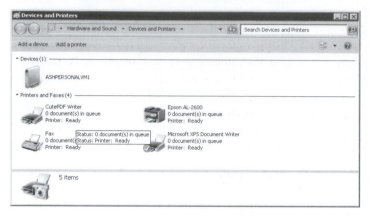

FIGURE 6-14 Printers are available on the client PC.

The user creates a session on Farm1.ash.local. Opening the Printers console in the session, you can see that all four printers have been redirected and are available in the remote desktop session. The redirected printers are designated by the name of the printer plus the redirected session ID number (which is redirected 3 in this example), as shown in Figure 6-15.

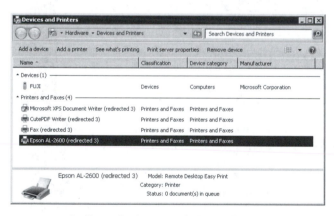

FIGURE 6-15 Redirected printers are designated by the session ID number.

> **NOTE** In the older printing model, redirected printers were named according to this format: Client Printer Name (from Client Computer Name) in session number *X*. In Windows Server 2008 and Windows Server 2008 R2, redirected printer names now follow this format: Client Printer Name (redirected session ID). This makes it easier to read the names and distinguish them from other printers when many printers are available.

Highlighting the printer reveals the driver used for the printer in the lower section of the window (as the Model). As the highlighted printer in Figure 6-15 shows, the printer is using the Remote Desktop Easy Print Driver.

The user opens Notepad, creates a text file, and then chooses File, Print. The Print dialog box appears, and the user selects the default redirected printer and then clicks the Preferences button in the upper-right area of the printer dialog box. The printer Properties dialog box appears. If the RDP session is open in full-screen mode, the printer Properties dialog box appears to be part of the session. But if the RDS session is viewed in a smaller window, as shown in Figure 6-16, the user can actually drag the printer Properties dialog box out of the window. That is because this dialog box is running not in the remote desktop session but from the local computer, because it's using the local driver.

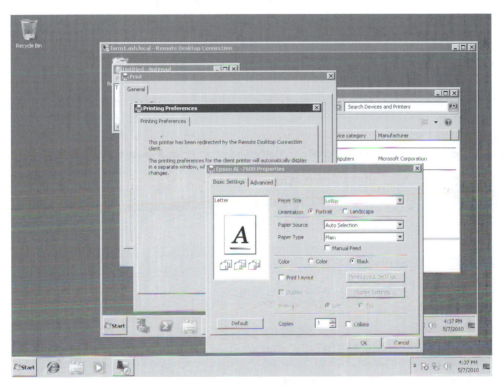

FIGURE 6-16 The Printing Preferences dialog box is superimposed over the session window.

Although you can't see it directly, printing to a redirected printer using RD Easy Print brings up another dialog box located right behind the printer Properties dialog box. It opens when you select Print Preferences, stating that the printer has been redirected by the RDC client and the printing preferences will display in a separate window.

When You Cannot Use RD Easy Print

RD Easy Print works a lot of the time, but it does not work all the time. With so many print-ers out today, you are bound to run into a few that just do not respond well to RD Easy Print (either they won't print or they print badly). In these cases, you will need to rely on the older printing method—installing drivers on the endpoint.

The RD Easy Print driver is installed by default on Windows XP SP3 and later, and using the RD Easy Print driver for printer redirection is also enabled by default. To make the server look for printer drivers instead of using the RD Easy Print driver, you must change the sequence in which the RD Easy Print driver will be used. The endpoint will try to use the RD Easy Print driver for printer redirection first and resort to other printer drivers only if the RD Easy Print driver is not available. Set one of the following GPOs to reverse this (make the endpoint use printer drivers first, and then RD Easy Print).

- On a computer basis: Computer Configuration | Policies | Administrative Templates | Windows Components | Remote Desktop Services | Remote Desktop Session Host | Printer Redirection | Use Remote Desktop Easy Print Printer Driver First

- On a user basis: User Configuration | Policies | Administrative Templates | Windows Components | Remote Desktop Services | Remote Desktop Session Host | Printer Redi-rection | Use Remote Desktop Easy Print Printer Driver First

If this policy is enabled or not configured, the server reflects its default behavior: RD Easy Print driver first, other drivers second. To make the server look for other printer drivers before it attempts to use RD Easy Print, set the policy to Disabled. This does not disable RD Easy Print, but the server will attempt to use the RD Easy Print driver only if a matching printer driver is not available.

HOW IT WORKS

Removing the RD Easy Print Driver

The RD Easy Print driver is installed by default. You can delete it, but it will rein-stall again when you reboot. It's also available for manual reinstallation as part of the Windows Server 2008 R2 driver set. If you do remove the RD Easy Print driver from the endpoint and your endpoint is running Windows 7 or has the RD Session Host role service installed, then no redirection will happen at all if the preceding GPO is enabled or not configured. The endpoint will attempt to use the RD Easy Print driver that is missing and will not look for other printer drivers to use; printer redirection simply fails. There is no supported method for removing the RD Easy Print driver permanently.

Distributing Drivers to Endpoints

If you have problems using RD Easy Print with certain printer models, you'll need to revert to the older printing model, which means installing printer drivers on the server. The challenge here is how to get the drivers onto the endpoints (and distribute them to other endpoints after they are tested).

If a printer driver is included with the operating system, the server will install the driver automatically if it's needed and the person attempting to use it has the right permissions. But what if the printer driver is not included in the operating system?

You can use Group Policy and the Print Management Console (PMC) to distribute the drivers without touching every server. You install the printers (so that the drivers are installed) but then you *delete the printers*. This second step is critical, because it keeps users from being confused by printers that they can see but don't have permission to print to or that do not actually connect to an actual print device.

In Windows Server 2008 R2 and Windows 7, you can use Group Policy to deploy the printers to each server. When you apply and then remove the GPO, the printers get removed, but the drivers remain. Here are the steps to perform.

1. First, add the printers by opening the PMC, right-click the printer server, and choose Add Printer to open the Network Printer Driver Wizard. The printers do not have to work because they are only temporary to facilitate distributing the printer drivers.

2. After your printers are installed, use the PMC to create the GPO for deploying printers. (PMC is installed as part of the Print Server role.) In the PMC, navigate to the Printers section, right-click each printer that you want to deploy, and choose Deploy With Group Policy, as shown in Figure 6-17.

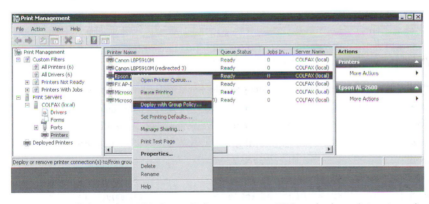

FIGURE 6-17 Click Deploy With Group Policy to create a GPO to deploy printers to endpoints.

3. Browse and select the GPO that you want to use to contain the printers that you will distribute, or, if you want to use a new GPO, click the Create New Group Policy Object icon, as shown in Figure 6-18.

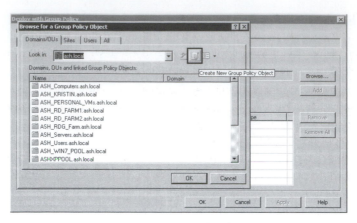

FIGURE 6-18 Create a new GPO to use to distribute printers.

4. Name the new GPO something descriptive, like "Deploy_Printers_To_Endpoints," and click OK. Select the check box next to the computers that this GPO applies to (per machine). Then click Add to add the printer to the list. Then click OK. Do this for every printer that you want to deploy.

> **NOTE** If you look at this GPO in the Group Policy Management console (GPMC), you will see the path for which the setting is located: Computer Configuration | Policies | Windows Settings | Printer Connections. But if you try to create a policy manually (not using the PMC), you won't be able to get to the Printer Connections GPO. It will not show up in the GPMC.

5. When the GPO is complete, apply it to each OU where your servers reside. Next, forcibly update the policies on the endpoints by running *gpupdate /force* or rebooting. The printers will now be installed.

6. Finally, after you've ensured that the printers are deployed correctly to the servers, remove the printers by deleting the GPO and forcing the update. The printer is removed from the server, but the drivers are still available. (You can see this by opening the Print Server Properties tab on the Devices And Printers console (you must have a printer installed and selected for this button to be available).

Mapping Printer Driver Names on Client and Endpoint

In the past (for instance, with clients running Windows 98 remoting to a server running Windows Server 2003), there were some cases where printer drivers made for the client operating system and the corresponding printer driver made for the server were not named the same way. For example, the printer driver for a printer HP LaserJet *X* made for the client could be named Hewlett Packard LaserJet *X* for the server—that is, the names do not match exactly. This was most often a problem when the drivers were written for entirely different operating systems. Without going into detail, Windows 7 and Windows Server 2008 R2 are fundamentally very similar. Windows 98 and Windows Server 2003 were not—their architectures were entirely different. Because Windows 98 and Windows Server 2003 were so different, printer manufacturers did not always make sure the drivers had the same name.

Name mismatches were (and occasionally still are) a problem when remoting using printer drivers because if the names don't match exactly, the mapping does not occur. The workaround for this was to create an INF file on the endpoint that tells the endpoint that Driver *X* equaled Driver *Y* (in this example, HP LaserJet *X* = Hewlett Packard LaserJet *X*). The server would read this file and make the printer driver match, and then it could redirect the printer. This driver name mismatch might not happen with newer operating systems, but the workaround has another use. Should you decide to implement the older printing model, you can use this technique to minimize the number of printer drivers that you have to install on your endpoint; you can create one-to-many mapping (one driver on the server to many printer drivers on the client). The server will use the *one* driver that you tell it to use whenever it encounters a need for any of the drivers that you map to that single driver. For instance

- Brother MFC-230C = Brother MFC-235C
- Brother MFC-230C = Brother MFC-239C
- Brother MFC-230C = Brother MFC-240C

NOTE Some printers might not work with specified drivers. Also, you might lose some functionality when using one driver in place of another. For instance, one driver might allow you to print in Booklet style, and another might not. You will need to test printer driver mapping fully to see what printer drivers will map to certain printers, and also what functionality you might lose by doing so.

To find the server driver name and the client driver name that you want to map, the driver name is specified in the printer properties of an installed printer. Right-click an installed printer and go to the Advanced tab of the Printer Properties dialog box. The printer driver name can also be found in the Print Server Properties dialog box. Do this by opening the Print Server Properties dialog box, selecting the Drivers tab, highlighting the driver, and clicking Properties.

Here is how to implement the mapping.

1. Create an INF file that contains the mappings (name it PRINTDRIVERMAP.inf). Store the file in C:\Windows\System32\ on the endpoint. The file should look like this (but containing your unique mappings).

```
[Printers]
;"Client Printer Driver Name" = "Server Printer Drive Name"
"Client Printer Driver X" = "Server Printer Driver W"
"Client Printer Driver X" = "Server Printer Driver X"
"Client Printer Driver y" = "Server Printer Driver Y"
"Client Printer Driver Z" = "Server Printer Driver Z"
```

The file needs to have the section title [Printers] because it gets referenced next in the registry keys that need to be put in place on the endpoint to invoke the mapping process.

2. Navigate to the Rdpwd folder and choose New, String Key. Name the keys PrinterMappingINFName and PrinterMappingINFSection, respectively. Creating the following registry keys will tell the endpoint to look for printer driver mappings in the Printers section of the PRINTDRIVERMAPS.inf file.

- HKLM\System/Currentcontrolset\Control\Terminal server\Wds\Rdpwd\PrinterMappingINFName

- HKLM\System\Currentcontrolset\Control\Terminal server\Wds\Rdpwd\PrinterMappingINFSection

3. Then set the registry key values by doing the following.

- Double-click the PrinterMappingINFName key and type **PRINTDRIVERMAP.inf**.

- Double-click the PrinterMappingINFSection key and type **Printers**.

ON THE COMPANION MEDIA A script to automate this work is located on the companion media in the Printer-Driver_Mapping-Setup.PS1 file. It creates the INF file PRINTDRIVERMAP.inf in the C:\Windows\System32 directory on each server in the specified OU (and overwrites the file if it is already there). If also creates the needed registry keys for each computer in an OU (and overwrites the values if the keys are already there).

Controlling Printer Redirection

Printer redirection can be enabled or disabled at three tiered levels: per-connection, per-machine, or per-group of computers, as shown in Figure 6-19. In this image, the broadest bar controls in case of any conflicts in policy.

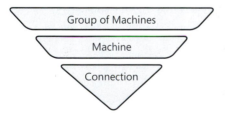

FIGURE 6-19 Printer redirection is controlled on tiered levels.

If printer redirection is disabled at any of these levels, printer redirection will be disabled for the user or machines that the setting affects—and therefore, everything below that level.

Controlling Printer Redirection per Connection

Printer redirection is enabled by default in the RDC client. To disable it, click Options, select the Local Resources tab, and clear the Printers check box in the Local Devices And Resources section. Then either save the RDP file or click Connect. This setting, at the lowest section of the pyramid (Figure 6-19), affects only the connection made or subsequent connections made from the resulting saved RDP file.

Controlling Printer Redirection per Server

Printer redirection is controlled on a machine basis in the RD Session Host Configuration tool on an RD Session Host server (no individual machine control exists on VM pools or personal VMs). It is allowed by default. To turn it off, open RD Session Host Configuration, double-click RDP-Tcp, select the Client Settings tab, select the check box next to Windows Printers in the Redirection section, and then click OK. Even if you allow printer redirection in the RDC, if it is disabled on the RD Session Host server, then it is disabled for all sessions hosted by the server.

Controlling Printer Redirection for Multiple Endpoints

Use Group Policy to control printer driver redirection for multiple computers. Set the following GPO, and then place the GPO on the OU that holds the computers that you want to affect.

Computer Configuration | Policies | Administrative Templates | Windows Components | Remote Desktop Services | Remote Desktop Session Host | Printer Redirection | Do Not Allow Printer Redirection

If you enable this policy, users will not be able to redirect print jobs to their local computer printers. If you do not configure or disable this policy, printer redirection is allowed.

Because this setting is not configured by default, printer redirection at this level is allowed but can still be affected at the other levels (by computer or by session). If this policy is enabled, it will take precedence over settings at the other levels.

Managing Print Settings with Group Policy

There are a few other Group Policy settings that you can use to configure print redirection further. The following Group Policy for printer settings is configured in the following location.

Computer Configuration | Policies | Administrative Templates | Windows Components | Remote Desktop Services | Remote Desktop Session Host | Printer Redirection

The Group Policies are

- **Use RD Easy Print Printer Driver First**   You encountered this setting earlier in this chapter. If this policy is enabled or not configured, the endpoint tries to use the Easy Print driver to redirect client printers first. Only if the Easy Print driver isn't available will it look for a printer driver on the endpoint that matches the printer driver on the client. This does not disable Easy Print, but the endpoint will use Easy Print only if a printer driver is not available.

- **Specify RD Session Host Server Fallback Printer Driver Behavior**   Fallback printer driver behavior tells the endpoint that if it cannot find a printer driver match to a printer driver on a computer, then it should attempt to use an alternate printer driver. Fallback printer drivers are HP DeskJet 500, HP DeskJet 500C, HP LaserJet 4/4M PS, and HP Color LaserJet 5/5M PS. This setting is disabled by default.

- **Redirect Only The Default Client Printer**   Clients might have many printers installed on their client PCs; by default, all will be redirected to the session. To decrease resource usage on the endpoint, you can enable this policy such that only the default printer on the client PC will be redirected to the session.

- **Do Not Set A Default Client Printer To Be The Default Printer In A Session**   By default, the client's default printer is the default printer for the remote session. If you enable this setting, there is no default printer for the remote session.

> **NOTE**   The Use Remote Desktop Easy Print Driver First and the Redirect Only The Default Client Printer settings can also be used in a User GPO at User Configuration | Policies | Administrative Templates | Windows Components | Remote Desktop Services | Remote Desktop Session Host | Printer Redirection.

Printer Driver Isolation

New to Windows 7 and Windows Server 2008 R2, the Printer Driver Isolation feature enables printer drivers to be separated from the print spooler process (Spoolsv.exe) and either run in a separate process that is shared by other printer drivers (shared isolation mode) or isolated into their own process (isolated mode). If the isolated printer driver has issues, it crashes only its own process (or the shared process) and does not take down the print spooler on the server or endpoint. This is good news if you have to install drivers on your endpoint (either in conjunction with RD Easy Print or instead of using RD Easy Print).

> **NOTE**   The RD Easy Print driver is installed by default on Windows 7 and Windows Server 2008 R2 (set to Shared Isolation Mode by default). You can see this by right-clicking the driver in the Print Management Console and selecting Set Driver Isolation. In the resulting list, the selected isolation setting will have a check mark next to it.

Like other printing settings, Printer Driver Isolation is controlled in a tiered fashion, by Group Policy, by the printer driver INI file, and by the Print Management Console. Here are the options.

- If you want, you have the option of controlling overall Printer Driver Isolation on a computer by setting the following GPO.

  Computer Configuration | Administrative Templates | Printers | Execute Print Drivers in Isolated Processes

- If this policy is disabled, then driver isolation is disabled for all drivers on the affected computers. If this policy is enabled or not configured, then it is allowed.

- If Printer Driver Isolation is allowed (or not configured) by Group Policy, next the printer driver INI file is checked to see if the printer driver supports isolation. If the Printer Driver Isolation key DriverIsolation is missing or is set to 0, the driver does not support Printer Driver Isolation. If the DriverIsolation key is set to 2, the driver does support isolation.

- If the driver supports Printer Driver Isolation, it is loaded by default into a separate process called Printisolationhost.exe (instead of being loaded into Spoolsv.exe) along with other printer drivers that are configured for shared isolation. If a driver does not support isolation, the driver will be loaded into Spoolsv.exe.

NOTE All native drivers for Windows 7 and Windows Server 2008 R2 support Printer Driver Isolation, and by default, they will run in shared mode unless otherwise dictated.

This default functionality can be overridden by Group Policy and on each individual printer driver using the Print Management Console.

Printer drivers that are compatible by default run in shared mode. But you can override this on a per-driver basis in the Print Management Console. To do this, right-click each driver and choose Shared, Isolated, or None.

NOTE If GPO dictates that printer isolation is disabled, isolation mode settings from the Print Management Console are ignored.

You can also force printer drivers that are not compatible with Printer Driver Isolation to run in shared mode or to adhere to the settings in the Print Management Console by enabling the following GPO.

Computer Configuration | Administrative Templates | Printers | Override Print Driver Execution Compatibility Setting Reported By Print Driver

The options for this GPO are

- **Enabled** The printer driver will run in shared mode or as specified in the Print Management Console.

- **Disabled Or Not Configured** The Printer Driver Isolation is determined by the key setting in the printer driver INI file.

> **NOTE** For more on Printer Driver Isolation, see *http://msdn.microsoft.com/en-us/library/ff560836%28VS.85%29.aspx*.

Troubleshooting Printing Issues

This section explains how to solve some common problems that people face when dealing with redirected printers.

If printer driver redirection is not working at all between a client and endpoint, make sure printer redirection is allowed (as outlined in the section entitled "Controlling Printer Redirection" earlier in this chapter).

- The Remote Desktop Client configuration allows printer redirection.

- The RD Session Host server allows printer redirection (in the RD Configuration Tool).

- Group Policy allows for redirection on the endpoint OU.

Also, the print spooler (started by default) needs to be running on both client and endpoint. Check Services.msc to make sure it is still running.

Interpreting Event ID 1111

Event ID 1111 logged in the endpoint's system event log indicates a printer driver mismatch. This can occur in two different scenarios.

- If you are trying to redirect printers to an RD Session Host server or a Windows 7 endpoint using the RD Easy Print driver and the driver is missing from the endpoint

- If you are using regular printer drivers to redirect printers and the driver is missing or the driver name does not match

Double-check that either RD Easy Print driver is installed on both the client and the endpoint or that you have matching printer drivers on the client and the endpoint.

Margin or Character Errors Occur When Using RD Easy Print

There are a few updates that correct margin errors on Windows Vista, Windows Server 2008, and Windows XP SP3. If you are experiencing margin errors when printing using the RD Easy Print driver, consult the following Knowledge Base (KB) articles to see if these hotfixes pertain to your implementation. (The links for these articles are also available on the companion media.)

- *http://support.microsoft.com/kb/959442*   The edges of a document are truncated when you try to print the document by using Terminal Services Easy Print from a client that is running Windows XP SP3, Windows Vista SP1, or Windows Server 2008.

- *http://support.microsoft.com/kb/946411*   When you print an XPS file on a computer running Windows XP SP2 or SP3, the characters in the XPS file print incorrectly.

> **NOTE**   Other formatting problems and corresponding KB articles that pertain to these issues are mentioned in the RDS Team Blog at *http://blogs.msdn.com/rds /archive/2009/09/28/using-remote-desktop-easy-print-in-windows-7-and-windows-server-2008-r2.aspx*.

Easy Print Is Not Printing (Windows Server 2008 Only)

This fix pertains to Window Server 2008 (not Windows Server 2008 R2). If your users are connecting via TS Gateway and your print jobs leave the server and then just disappear, check this KB article to see if this fix applies to you: KB968605—"TS Easy Print Not Printing." You'll find this article at *http://support.microsoft.com/kb/968605*.

Using Generic Text Driver

As of this writing, there is a known issue pertaining to using RD Easy Print with printers that are set to use Generic Text Only mode. Unfortunately, there is no known solution at the moment. See the following Microsoft forum thread for more details: *http://social.technet. microsoft.com/Forums/en/windowsserver2008r2rds/thread/cd8792cb-e826-4f35-bdaf-c5b-29ca58ca8*. If you experience this problem, try using a printer driver instead of the Easy Print driver. Do this by installing a matching driver on the client and the server and disable the option to use the Easy Print driver first.

Summary

From the user's point of view, the remoting experience is the most important aspect of RDS. If the screen doesn't look good, the audio doesn't sound good, or the print jobs don't print, the user has a bad experience.

After reading this chapter, you should have learned the following.

- The relationship between the RDC client, the RDP protocol, and the RDP listener, and how the three elements define the user experience

- The RDP features introduced with Windows 7 and Windows Server 2008 R2

- How all features of RDP related to the remote experience work

- How to enable and configure features of RDP

- How to print via RDP, with and without Easy Print

Now that you know how RDP provides the "like being there, only better" experience for users, you will learn in the next chapters how you, the administrator, can lock down the user desktop (Chapter 7, "Molding and Securing the User Environment") and protect the network connection (Chapter 8).

Additional Resources

This chapter examines in depth how RDP works. For more information, the following MSDN sites provide the original documents detailing how the protocol works.

- Basic RDP Remoting: *http://msdn.microsoft.com/en-us/library /cc240445(v=PROT.10).aspx*

- Graphics Acceleration: *http://msdn.microsoft.com/en-us/library /cc241537(v=PROT.10).aspx*

- Graphics Compression: *http://msdn.microsoft.com/en-us/library /ff635378(v=PROT.10).aspx*

- Desktop Composition: *http://msdn.microsoft.com/en-us/library /cc216513(v=PROT.10).aspx* and *http://msdn.microsoft.com/en-us/library /dd358323(v=PROT.10).aspx*

- Dynamic Virtual Channels: *http://msdn.microsoft.com/en-us/library /cc241215(v=PROT.10).aspx*

- Basic Audio Remoting: *http://msdn.microsoft.com/en-us/library /cc240933(v=PROT.10).aspx*

- Clipboard Redirection: *http://msdn.microsoft.com/en-us/library /cc241066(v=PROT.10).aspx*

- Easy Print: *http://msdn.microsoft.com/en-us/library/cc242947(v=PROT.10).aspx*

- Printer Redirection: *http://msdn.microsoft.com/en-us/library/cc242116(v=PROT.10).aspx*

- Audio Input Redirection: *http://msdn.microsoft.com/en-us/library /dd342521(v=PROT.10).aspx*

- Multimedia Remoting: *http://msdn.microsoft.com/en-us/library /dd342975(v=PROT.10).aspx*

- Serial and Parallel Port Redirection: *http://msdn.microsoft.com/en-us/library /cc242856(v=PROT.10).aspx*

- File System Redirection: *http://msdn.microsoft.com/en-us/library /cc241305(v=PROT.10).aspx*

- Plug and Play Redirection: *http://msdn.microsoft.com/en-us/library /cc242231(v=PROT.10).aspx*

The following resources contain additional information and tools related to this chapter.

- Want more information about RDP performance? See the white paper linked at
  http://blogs.msdn.com/rds/archive/2010/02/05/announcing-the-remote-desktop-protocol-performance-improvements-in-windows-server-2008-r2-and-windows-7-white-paper.aspx.

- Download RDC 7 for Windows Vista SP1+ and Windows XP SP3 at
  http://blogs.msdn.com/rds/archive/2009/10/28/announcing-the-availability-of-remote-desktop-connection-7-0-for-windows-xp-sp3-windows-vista-sp1-and-windows-vista-sp2.aspx.

- You can download the Remote Desktop client for Macintosh at
  http://www.microsoft.com/mac/products/remote-desktop/default.mspx.

- New Windows 7 printing architecture can be downloaded at
  http://download.microsoft.com/download/5/E/6/5E66B27B-988B-4F50-AF3A-C2FF1E62180F/CON-T572_WH08.pptx.

- Microsoft Most Valuable Professional Emeritus Vera Noest has put together a great list of hotfixes and updates pertaining to printing, which can be found at
  http://ts.veranoest.net/ts_printing.asp.

Molding and Securing the User Environment

If you're reading this book in order, at this point, your users can use their virtual machines (VMs) or sessions. The servers are set up, the profiles and folder redirection are all configured, and user devices are redirected. The only catch is that now the user work environments are wide open.

Giving users non-secured work environments might be all right. As you'll learn in this chapter, the rules for security will likely vary with the kind of work environment that you're supporting. RD Session Host servers need to be locked down because the server hosting the sessions is persistent and the machine is shared, so one person's error can have lasting impact on a lot of people. Pooled VMs using rollback—so the VM rolls back to a saved state each time a user logs off—need less security because you don't want users running malware but don't need to worry about permanent changes to the VMs. Also, personal desktops should be governed by the same rules that you've applied to physical desktops.

This chapter will show you how to enable and yet still control your users' devices and desires, meaning that you'll understand how to map the client-side experience to the remote environment . . . but you'll do so in a way that doesn't negatively affect the servers or the end users. The following topics will be discussed.

- Locking down the servers (and why you should do so)
- Optimizing the user experience
- Configuring remote control of a session
- Securing access to the RD Session Host server

The primary focus of this chapter is RD Session Host server environments. This is because pooled VMs revert when a user logs off, and personal VMs should be handled the same way that you handle physical user desktops in your company. This doesn't mean that you won't tweak pooled or personal VMs. For instance, it's possible that you will not want a user installing or running rogue software from a pooled machine, even if it will revert to its original state after logoff. Therefore, if a setting or procedure is specific, either only to RD Session Host servers or only to pooled or personal VMs, we will say so. Otherwise, assume that the tactic, setting, or procedure applies to both kinds of implementations.

Locking Down the Server

Sometimes, it's not obvious that you *need* to lock down the server. RemoteApp programs (introduced in Chapter 4, "Deploying a Single Remote Desktop Virtualization Host Server," and explored more deeply in Chapter 9, "Multi-Server Deployments"), introduced in Windows Server 2008, visually integrate applications running on the server with applications running on the local computer. This makes it easier to avoid losing applications and can simplify training because you don't have to teach inexperienced users how to find the applications that they need or how to move between a local and a remote desktop. No one ever sees a separate desktop; they just see the application that they need to run. When users close the last RD RemoteApp they have open, the session on the RD Session Host server ends.

If no one sees a desktop, why would you need to lock down the server? The answer has to do with how RemoteApp programs work. A RemoteApp in a session is still in a session, with the same access to the Windows environment that an application on a full desktop has. A savvy user can find out pretty easily that Ctrl+Alt+End opens Task Manager on the remote session, and that when you have Task Manager open, you can get to the Run box. When you get to Run, you can run nearly any application or command on the RD Session Host server that isn't locked down.

We're *Star Wars* enthusiasts. As Yoda might say, "Ctrl+Alt+End leads to the Task Manager. The Task Manager leads to Run. Run leads to suffering."

Displaying only a single application is no replacement for locking down the server. This section discusses the Group Policy settings that you use to accomplish this.

As the discussion here goes through the process of locking down the server, keep your personal situation in mind. This is not a complete list of what you *must* do. This is a description of what you *can* do. First, some of these settings will overlap—the same goal can be accomplished using different settings, so it will be up to you to choose what settings or methods of lockdown work for your circumstances. Second, for practical reasons, you might not be able to use every setting discussed in the next pages. Shutting down Windows Internet Explorer will close one back door, but if the main reason that you run an RD Session Host server is to provide access to a browser-based application, then blocking access to Internet Explorer isn't a viable option. Test all policies before deploying them to make sure that the combinations that you've chosen haven't disabled any functionality you need.

Restricting Device and Resource Redirection

As was discussed in Chapter 6, "Customizing the User Experience," device redirection is a big part of making a remote application feel like a local application. Device redirection allows users to open local files in remote sessions or save files to their local computers, copy data back and forth, play and record audio, and so forth.

Integration between local and remote computers sounds great . . . until you really need to enforce security on corporate data. For example, by default, client drives and the clipboard are visible in a remote connection, but both open a security hole from the data center to a remote computer. Drive redirection allows users to copy or even save sensitive data from the corporate network to a possibly unsecured computer.

The rule of thumb for device and resource redirection is that more is not necessarily better. Disable redirection that you don't need. As you can see from the descriptions in Chapter 6, disabling unnecessary devices both cuts down on bandwidth resources that might be used for other functions and can reduce server and sensitive data exposure.

> **NOTE** For details on how device redirection works when applied at the user, machine, or Group Policy level, see Chapter 6.

Restricting Device and Resource Redirection Using Group Policy

You can configure device and resource redirection by setting the corresponding device or resource Group Policy settings to the appropriate state. Note that these are computer policies, not user policies. You configure device redirection based not on who someone is, but what machine she is working on.

The following computer policies are located at Computer Configuration | Policies | Administrative Templates | Windows Components | Remote Desktop Services | Remote Desktop Session Host | Device And Resource Redirection.

- **Allow Audio Redirection** You might want to disable audio redirection if you're not running any applications that require it because it takes up more bandwidth.

- **Do Not Allow Clipboard Redirection** What if you'd generally like to enable clipboard redirection but have one or two sensitive applications? Because RemoteApp programs running on the same server for the same user are all running within a single session and in the same user context, it's not possible to disable clipboard redirection on a per-application basis. To be that specific, you'll need to isolate the applications requiring the higher level of security on separate servers and disable clipboard redirection on those servers.

- **Do Not Allow COM Port Redirection** To disable COM port redirection, enable this policy. Not many resources use COM ports these days.

- **Do Not Allow Drive Redirection** Redirecting user drives to the session enhances the feel of the session but opens a security hole. RDS drive redirection works two-ways: Any data that users can access from the terminal session can be copied from it, and they can copy data to any drive to which they have access. To turn off drive redirection for users or computers, enable this policy.

- **Do Not Allow LPT Port Redirection**   LPT ports are used to access older printers. If you don't have a need to redirect these devices, enable this policy.
- **Do Not Allow Supported Plug And Play Device Redirection**   Enable this policy to disable redirection for Plug and Play devices such as cameras.
- **Do Not Allow Smart Card Device Redirection**   Enable this policy to disable smart card redirection.

Drive redirection is an obvious security hole (it allows users to transfer files from their remote session to their local hard drive and vice versa), but printing can also create a security problem. To disable all printer redirection, enable this policy, found in the computer's Group Policy settings: Computer Configuration | Policies | Administrative Templates | Windows Components | Remote Desktop Services | Remote Desktop Session Host Server | Printer Redirection | Do Not Allow Client Printer Redirection. By default, it is not configured; if it is not configured, printer redirection can be controlled via Active Directory Users And Computers, Remote Desktop Connection (RDC), or the RD Configuration Tool.

You can also disable redirection of specific *types* of supported plug and play devices. For example, you might not want to block all plug and play device redirection, but you don't want to allow floppy disk or CD-ROM drive redirection specifically. The Group Policy object (GPO) to do this is located at: Computer Configuration | Administrative Templates | System | Device Installation| Device Installation Restrictions | Prevent Installation Of Devices That Match Any of these Device IDs.

> **NOTE**   The redirection-oriented group policies mentioned in this section are covered in more detail in Chapter 6.

Restricting Printer Redirection Using Active Directory Users And Computers

Only printer redirection can be controlled via Active Directory Users And Computers. To do so, open Active Directory Users And Computers, double-click a user account, click the Environment tab, and select or clear the check box next to Connect Client Printers At Logon. This setting is enabled by default.

The client-side printer is the default printer in the remote session. To disable this setting, clear the Default To Main Client Printer check box.

> **NOTE**   There is also a Connect Client Drives At Logon option; it is checked by default. However, this setting has no effect. It was originally designed to be used by the Citrix MetaFrame add-on to Microsoft Windows 2000 Remote Desktop Services before the Remote Desktop Protocol (RDP) supported drive redirection, and it isn't used by RDP.

Restricting Device and Resource Redirection Using the RD Session Host Configuration Tool

You can also disable device and resource redirection from Remote Desktop Session Host Configuration, but remember that this means configuring each server separately. You cannot configure device and resource redirection for pooled or personal VMs using RD Session Host Configuration.

To disable drive and resource redirection from Remote Desktop Session Host Configuration, open the RDP client Properties dialog box by double-clicking RDP-Tcp and then navigating to the Client Settings tab shown in Figure 7-1. Select the check boxes corresponding to the type of redirection that you want to disable. Click Apply and then click OK.

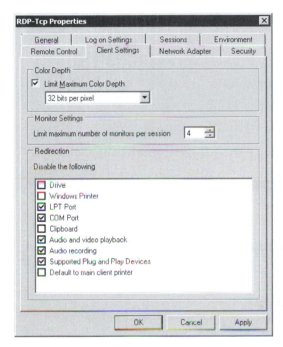

FIGURE 7-1 Restrict redirection by selecting the check boxes on the Client Settings tab of the RDP-Tcp Properties dialog box.

Preventing Users from Reconfiguring the Server

You really don't need users to reconfigure a single RD Session Host server without your knowledge, let alone an RD Session Host server farm that you are trying to keep consistent. At the very least, this nullifies your change management policies; at worst, it could render the server unusable. For pooled VMs, even though the VM will be reverted to its previous state when the user is done with it, for security reasons (and to lower support costs), it might be advantageous to restrict access to parts of the system that the user has no reasonable cause to access. Set the following Group Policy settings to help limit server (and pooled VM) changes to the ones that you know about and authorize.

Restricting Access to the Control Panel

User Configuration | Policies | Administrative Templates | Control Panel

- **Prohibit Access To Control Panel**   Users should have no need to access the Control Panel. Enabling this setting removes Control Panel from the Start menu and Windows Explorer, so users won't have access to Control Panel, nor will they be able to run any of the Control Panel items.

> **NOTE**   When you enable this setting, you prevent administrators from installing any Windows Installer (MSI) package onto the RD Session Host server, even if Deny is explicitly set for the Administrator account. Therefore, to install applications, you'll need to disable this policy. While installing, disable remote logons.

Restricting Printer Driver Installation

Computer Configuration | Policies | Windows Settings | Security Settings | Local Policies | Security Options

- **Devices: Prevent Users From Installing Printer Drivers**   Enabling this setting prevents users from adding printer drivers to an RD Session Host server as part of adding a network printer. This policy does not affect administrators and does not pertain to adding a local printer.

Preventing Access to the Registry

At first, thinking that users might run Regedit.exe leads to worst-case scenarios. The truth is, on an RD Session Host server, domain users are restricted to writing to their own keys. That said, you don't want users wandering through the registry. To prevent access to tools that enable direct read and write capabilities to the registry, use the following two policies.

User Configuration | Policies | Administrative Templates | System

- **Prevent Access To Registry Editing Tools**   By default, access to the registry (on a limited basis) is allowed. Enable this setting to prevent access to the registry.
- **Disable Regedit From Running Silently**   Enable this setting to prevent users from running regedit with the /s switch. For instance, a user could run *regedit /s Filename.reg* from a command prompt and import a file into the registry even though Prevent Access To Registry Editing Tools is enabled.

Preventing Access to Windows Automatic Updates

To prevent Windows updates from being applied automatically to production RD Session Host servers, disable Windows Automatic Updates. This lockdown isn't about users as much as it is about making sure that changes aren't made unintentionally and without full testing. These policies are

User Configuration | Policies | Administrative Templates | System

- **Windows Automatic Updates**   Enabling this setting prevents Windows from automatically searching for, downloading, and installing updates. If this setting is not configured or disabled, Windows will download updates to the server automatically.

User Configuration | Policies | Administrative Templates | Windows Components| Windows Update

- **Remove Access To All Windows Update Features**   Enabling this setting blocks access to the Windows Update website and removes the Windows Update link from the Start menu and from the Tools menu in Internet Explorer. Notifications about updates will cease and automatic updating is disabled.

Closing Back Doors on RD Session Host Servers

Much of locking down the RD Session Host server involves closing back doors (places where users could run executables) on the server. This minimizes unintended consequences caused by users running the command prompt, browsing the network, or browsing the computer.

Restricting Access to the Start Menu and Networking Items

The Start menu enables access to programs and tools in full desktop sessions. Figure 7-2 outlines the Start menu program areas, which are important to understanding how the policies being discussed here work and interact.

The taskbar is also a back door to the operating system, offering easy access to the Address, Links, and Desktop toolbars. Unless you restrict access to the Start menu and taskbar, you've left many holes open on the server. For example, leaving the Run box exposed could lead to a user executing rogue software on the server.

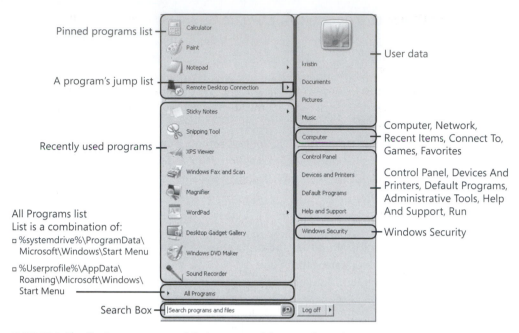

FIGURE 7-2 The Start menu areas and their sources of data are shown here.

To lock down the Start menu and taskbar, use these Group Policy settings, which are accessed in the following location.

User Configuration | Policies | Administrative Templates | Start Menu And Taskbar

- **Prevent Changes To Taskbar And Start Menu Settings** Being able to make changes to the taskbar and the Start menu gives users the opportunity to access programs such as Internet Explorer, email programs, network shares, and Internet websites via the Address bar, Links, and so on. Enabling this setting blocks access to the Properties dialog box that users see when they right-click the taskbar. It also removes the Taskbar and Start menu items from the Taskbar And Settings Menu Properties dialog box. It does not stop users from turning on taskbar toolbars.

- **Show QuickLaunch On Taskbar** By default, the QuickLaunch toolbar is shown on the taskbar when a user logs on. This can be helpful if you want to place application links for your users on this bar—for instance, by preconfiguring the default user profile. Just be aware that users can delete icons from the QuickLaunch toolbar, which might generate Help desk calls. Users can also turn this toolbar on and off. Hide the Quick-Launch toolbar and prevent users from turning it on by disabling this setting.

- **Remove Access To The Context Menus For The Taskbar** Enabling this setting prevents users from turning taskbar toolbars on and off.

- **Remove Programs On Settings Menu** Enabling this setting removes access to the Control Panel, Printers, and Network Connections folders from the Start menu.

- **Remove Common Program Groups From Start Menu**   Enabling this setting displays only items pulled from the user's profile in the Start menu. Items from the Public User profile will not be merged and available on the user's Start menu in the All Programs list or on the desktop.

- **Remove The Pinned Programs List From The Start Menu**   Enabling this setting removes the pinned programs list from the Start menu and prevents users from pinning programs to the Start menu. By default, Internet Explorer and an email client can be pinned to this menu; this setting removes their links by clearing the corresponding boxes on the Simple Start menu customization control panel.

- **Remove the All Programs List From The Start Menu**   All Programs is normally made of a combination of the public users' programs and an individual user's programs portion of the profile. Enabling this setting removes the All Programs menu from the Start menu. This includes links to Accessories, the Startup folder, and other program links that you might not want to be accessible.

- **Remove Network Connections From Start Menu**   Enabling this setting denies users access to the Manage Network Connection link in the Network And Sharing Center.

- **Remove Network Icon From Start Menu**   Enabling this setting removes the Network icon from the Start menu; however, it still appears and is accessible in the Control Panel and Windows Explorer.

- **Remove Favorites Menu From Start Menu**   Although the Favorites menu is not shown by default, enabling this setting prohibits users from displaying the Favorites menu via the Properties of the Start menu, thus prohibiting easy access to Uniform Resource Locators (URLs) from the Start menu.

- **Remove Run Menu From Start Menu**   Enabling this setting removes the Run option from the Start menu, Task Manager, and Windows Explorer. In addition, users will not be able to enter a local file path or a Universal Naming Convention (UNC) path into the Internet Explorer address bar. The key combination Windows Logo+R no longer brings up the Run box if this setting is enabled.

- **Remove Drag And Drop Context Menus On The Start Menu**   Enabling this setting prevents users from dragging links to the Start menu. However, it does not prevent access to the Start Menu Properties dialog box.

- **Do Not Search Internet**   Enabling this setting prevents the Windows Search box from searching Internet history or Favorites. This can decrease user access to URLs that could point to executables or other potentially harmful script files.

- **Do Not Search Programs and Control Panel Items**   Enabling this setting keeps users using the Search box on the Start menu to search for programs or Control Panel items on the RD Session Host server. This will prevent searching the RD Session Host server for programs that users might not need to run or which might be harmful.

Removing Icons from the Desktop

Placing icons on the desktop is a very easy and direct way to access some information if you're displaying full desktops instead of RemoteApp programs. However, you might not want users looking at the System properties of My Computer or mapping a drive so easily. You can remove icons from the desktop with these settings, accessible from the following location.

User Configuration | Policies | Administrative Templates | Desktop

- **Hide And Disable All Items On The Desktop**   Enabling this setting hides and disables all items on the desktop, including the Recycle Bin and My Computer. Users will not be able to access My Computer from the desktop and gain access to unauthorized data and programs by mapping a network drive. (These programs are still available from other locations, such as the Desktop toolbar on the taskbar, however.)
- **Remove Computer Icon From The Desktop**   This policy removes the Computer icon from the desktop as well as within Windows Explorer, and from the Desktop toolbar on the taskbar, preventing users from right-clicking My Computer and mapping a drive.

Restricting Access to CD-ROM and Floppy Drives

CD-ROM and floppy drives (if your servers even *have* floppy drives) on the server should not be a large security risk. If you have any level of physical security on the servers hosting the VMs and sessions, users won't be able to insert their own CDs and floppy disks into a server that is located behind a locked door. In the interest of securing the server, however, you can enable these policies that limit access to these external drives except from local connections while still keeping the drives available for local use. They are available in the following location.

Computer Configuration | Policies | Windows Settings | Security Settings | Local Policies | Security Options

- Devices: Restrict CD-ROM Access To Locally Logged-On User Only
- Devices: Restrict Floppy Access To Local Logged-On User Only

Preventing Access to the Command Prompt

The command prompt isn't a back door to the server as much as a front door. If you can get to the command prompt, you can run any executable to which you have access and permission to run. To disable the command prompt, configure the policy in the following location.

User Configuration | Policies | Administrative Templates | System

- **Prevent Access To The Command Prompt**   Enable this setting to prevent users from using the command prompt.

Removing Access to Task Manager

The Task Manager is only one step removed from the command prompt, as it provides access to the Run button. Therefore, it's good to remove this source of temptation in sessions. For VMs, you might want to leave it open so people can have more control over hanging applications or other Task Manager tools—it depends on whether you view access to Run as acceptable. This policy is available in the following location.

User Configuration | Policies | Administrative Templates | System | Ctrl+Alt+Del Options

- **Remove Task Manager**   Enable this setting to prevent users from executing new tasks (starting programs) or changing the priority of processes via the Task Manager.

Restricting Access to Internet Explorer and the Internet

One way to block Internet access is to block the only browser installed by default—Internet Explorer. To block access to Internet Explorer completely, create a Software Restriction Policy or AppLocker rule (more about this in the section entitled "Preventing Users from Running Unwanted Applications" later in this chapter) that denies Internet Explorer from running.

You can also inhibit access to Internet Explorer by hiding its icon and removing access to Windows Updates. These options are accessible from the locations given here.

User Configuration | Policies | Administrative Templates | Start Menu And Taskbar

- **Remove Links And Access To Windows Update**   Although the Windows Update website is available only to administrators, users can use Windows Update from the Control Panel (if you have not blocked access to it) to open Internet Explorer. If you are not blocking Internet Explorer access, enable this setting.

User Configuration | Policies | Administrative Templates | Desktop

- **Hide Internet Explorer Icon On Desktop**   This policy does not prevent users from starting Internet Explorer another way, but it removes the Internet Explorer icon from the desktop and from the QuickLaunch toolbar on the taskbar.

Sometimes blocking Internet Explorer is not practical. To *limit* access via Internet Explorer, you can configure a proxy setting on the browser to point to an internal web page telling users that Internet access has been blocked, and disable the ability to change the proxy settings. This will allow access to intranet sites while keeping users off the Internet. To do so, configure the following policies, found in these locations.

User Configuration | Policies | Windows Settings | Internet Explorer Maintenance | Connection

- **Proxy Settings**   Set the proxy settings to a false internal address or to an internal website that tells users that Internet access is forbidden from Remote Desktop Services (RDS). Select the Do Not Use Proxy Server For Local (Intranet) Addresses check box.

User Configuration | Policies | Administrative Templates | Windows Components | Internet Explorer

- **Disable Changing Proxy Settings**   Enable this setting so users can't disable or change the proxy setting that you defined.

If users need to access Internet Explorer to reach the Internet, you can at least stop them from changing browser settings by enabling the following settings controlling the display of the tabbed Tools dialog box, available in this location.

User Configuration | Policies | Administrative Templates | Windows Components | Internet Explorer | Internet Control Panel

- **Disable The Advanced Page**   Enabling this setting blocks access to the Advanced page defining the security settings for Internet Explorer. (The Advanced page has other functions, but the security settings are most important to the safety of your RD Session Host servers.)

- **Disable The Connections Page**   Enabling this setting blocks access to the Connections page, where users can configure VPN and proxy settings.

- **Disable The Content Page**   Enabling this setting blocks access to the Content page, where ratings and certificates are managed.

- **Disable The General Page**   Enabling this setting blocks access to the General page, where the home page settings, display settings, and browsing history are managed.

- **Disable The Privacy Page**   Enabling this setting blocks access to the Privacy page, which defines settings for blocking pop-up windows and the security settings for pages.

- **Disable The Programs Page**   Enabling this setting blocks access to the Programs page, where email clients, default browser notifications, and browser add-ons are managed.

- **Disable The Security Page**   Enabling this setting blocks access to the Security page, where zone trust levels (and zone memberships) are set. This is another important page to lock down.

Restricting Access to System Drives

The goal is to keep users out of drives on the server. Users aren't storing data on a session or pooled VM, so they don't need to be able to do anything other than run the applications allotted to them. By default, ordinary users can't do much to the system drives—if they try to delete important files or published applications, they are prompted for administrative credentials. If they run management tools such as Remote Desktop Services Configuration on the RD Session Host server, they can view options but can't edit them. However, there's no reason for users to be poking around the system drive, so you need to know how to keep them from doing this. The following options are found in this location.

User Configuration | Policies | Administrative Templates | Windows Components | Windows Explorer

- **Remove Map Network Drive And Disconnect Network Drive**   Enabling this setting removes the ability to map a network drive by right-clicking My Computer or from the Tools menu in Windows Explorer and Network Sharing Center.

- **Remove Windows Explorer's Default Context Menu**   Enabling this setting removes the window that users get when they right-click an item in Windows Explorer; for instance, enabling this policy would disable right-clicking My Computer located on the desktop, which provides users with a menu with the option to map a network drive or manage the computer.

- **Hide These Specified Drives In My Computer**   This setting does just what it says: It hides the drive letters that you specify. It does not block access to the drives via other methods such as Run. Limit this setting to specific drive letters if you have mapped drives that users must have readily available. To really prevent access, use it in combination with the Prevent Access To Drives From My Computer policy.

- **Prevent Access To Drives From My Computer**   Enable this setting for drives A through D to prevent access to those drives, which are most likely the system drives, the floppy drive (if present—it's not likely), and the CD-ROM drive. Users will see the drives but cannot open or search them. Limit this setting to specific drive letters if you have mapped drives that users need to access. This setting is useful to prevent users adding local drives to libraries.

Controlling Libraries

Libraries, introduced with Windows 7 and Windows Server 2008 R2, don't fundamentally change the need to lock down the RD Session Host server or pooled VMs, but they do give you another reason to do it. Libraries are designed to encourage users to add more storage locations, and you really don't want users to add locations on the local hard disk. As discussed in Chapter 5, "Managing User Data in a Remote Desktop Services Deployment," storing files on the hard disk complicates backups (for RD Session Host servers) and can lead to destroyed data (for pooled VMs set to rollback at user logoff). Let's talk about how to configure libraries to prevent users from saving files locally.

First, you'll need a little background, because libraries are new. Libraries don't contain anything themselves—they are collections of associated folder locations. These collections are stored in Extensible Markup Language (XML) files (one for each library) with names like Music.library-ms. All libraries are stored in C:\Users*UserName*\AppData\Roaming\Microsoft\Windows\Libraries, meaning that they can be part of the roaming user profile if you have one. (Even if you're using a local profile, the library data will still be stored in the same place.) If you're using roaming user profiles, users do not have to re-create their libraries every time they log on to a new RD Session Host server or pooled VM. There are four default libraries: Documents, Videos, Pictures, and Music.

The library description files include information like the Security ID of the owner, the folder type (different types of files use different types to display different kinds of data differently), and the default save location for the library. Although you can read this file in Notepad, it's not very informative, and it's not recommended that you edit it manually because it would be easy to mess up.

> **NOTE** C++ developers can edit this file programmatically using the IShell Library Interface documented on MSDN at *http://msdn.microsoft.com/en-us/library /dd391719(v=VS.85).aspx*. There is no Windows PowerShell or Windows Management Instrumentation (WMI) interface to manipulate libraries, unfortunately.

The main issue with libraries is that by default, the Documents library (for example) contains two folders: My Documents and Public Documents. If you have set up folder redirection, My Documents will be the path to the redirected folder, which is what you want. My Documents is the default save location, which is also what you want.

However, the library also surfaces the Public Documents folder on the C drive (in Users\ Public\Documents), which is *not* what you want. It's possible that there could be some reason why you'd want to store documents there that all the users could see, but that's not a great plan most of the time, for reasons explained in the first paragraph. You also don't want people adding more locations on the C drive and scattering files randomly on the RD Session Host hard disk or on a pooled VM that will be overwritten when users are finished with it— annoyed users will be calling the Help desk looking for their missing files. To prevent users from storing files in Public Documents or anywhere else on the C drive, you should use NTFS permissions and the Hidden attribute to lock down the C:\Users\Public folder.

Preventing Users from Running Unwanted Applications

Your goal is to prevent users from running any applications to which you have not granted access. As Chapter 9 discusses, publishing applications via the RemoteApp Manager adds them to the *allow list* of applications that can be started locally. The allow list controls which RemoteApp can be used to begin a session. However, after a user makes a connection to the RD Session Host server, the allow list has no further effect. This section talks about the default ways to restrict program access.

The Simplest Way to Lock Down an RD Session Host Server

Brian Madden
Remote Desktop Services MVP

What's the simplest thing you can do to lock down an RD Session Host server? Remove the Execute permissions from everywhere they don't need to be. Do users really need to be able to execute programs from their home drives, temporary Internet files, or the Outlook attachment cache folder? Of course not! By preventing them from doing so using this method, you remove about 99.99 percent of all possible ways to execute "rogue" software on your RD Session Host server.

Whether you remove these permissions via Group Policy (with a Software Restriction Policies disallowed path rule or by using AppLocker) or via good old-fashioned editing of NTFS permissions depends largely on your environment and what else you might be doing. But the bottom line is that there are only a few folders from which users actually must be able to run programs (such as the Windows and Program Files folders, for example). For everything else on a server (and the network), remove those permissions.

User Configuration | Policies | Administrative Templates | System

- **Don't Run Specified Windows Applications**   This is the block list approach—starting with everything and then defining applications that are not allowed to run. Blacklists aren't the most effective way to manage applications because executable names change (or new executables are created) and block lists don't take changes into account.

  This policy does not stop users from copying the executable file from another computer, renaming it, and running the same application under another name. A better way to block application execution is to implement Software Restriction Policies.

- **Run Only Specified Applications**   This is a whitelist approach—starting from nothing and then adding programs that are allowed to run. This approach is more secure than the block list approach because it does restrict even new executables, but it can be difficult to implement because of unexpected application dependencies.

  Enabling this setting and adding executables to the corresponding list prevents all programs except the ones on the list from running. However, it does not stop users from copying an executable file from another computer, renaming it to match an application known to be exempt, and running it that way.

Computer Configuration | Policies | Administrative Templates | Windows Components | Remote Desktop Services | Remote Desktop Session Host | Connections

- **Allow Remote Start Of Unlisted Programs**   When disabled, this policy prevents users from starting any application via RDP other than the ones specified in the allow list. Again, be aware that this does not affect locally run programs. If you log on to the RD Session Host server and are presented with a desktop, then you can still run other programs that are not on the Remote-Apps list.

Because the Group Policy settings don't check for anything except the file name, a better approach to blocking application execution is to implement Software Restriction Policies.

Using Software Restriction Policies

Software Restriction Policies (SRPs) block unauthorized applications, scripts, macros, or any other executables from running on an RD Session Host server or a VM.

> **NOTE**   AppLocker, which is discussed next, supersedes SRP for Window 7 and Windows Server 2008 R2. Although SRPs will work with Windows 7 and Windows Server 2008 R2, you will most likely use AppLocker instead because it's a lot simpler. For all other operating systems, you will continue to use SRP to restrict application access.

SRPs are implemented through Group Policy and checked every time a piece of software is run. An SRP can be set as a user policy or a computer policy (or both), which means that administrators have the flexibility to allow or deny software for groups of users or for everyone who logs on to the session or VM.

Depending on how you set up the policy, one of two things happens. Either the software is expressly denied (or not allowed) by the policy and it does not run, or the software is specifically allowed (or not denied) by the policy and it executes. The reason that software can be seen as either expressly allowed or not denied and vice versa is because there are three ways to set up the policy.

A Software Restriction Policy is made up of two parts: a security level and additional rules. The security level is an overall rule that reflects the method that you will use to restrict software access. Three security levels are available at the following location.

Computer Configuration | Policies | Windows Settings | Security Options | Software Restriction Policies | Security Levels

> **NOTE**   These GPO settings will be available after you create a policy.

- **Unrestricted** This is the least secure method. It allows all programs to be executed except those that you specifically deny. This is commonly called "blacklisting."

- **Basic User** This method is considered an intermediate level of security. Unless there is an exception found for this rule, software will run as a normal user (without administrative privileges).

- **Disallowed** This is the strictest, but also the most secure, method. It does not allow any programs to run except those that you specifically allow. If you choose to use this method, take care to test the policy fully before activating it on production computers, so you find all software dependencies. This approach is commonly called "whitelisting."

When you have chosen your security level, make exceptions to this overall rule for specific applications or for types of applications or code. You can do this by creating additional rules with a different default rule applied. There are four types of additional rules that you can create to make exceptions to the security level, at the following location.

Computer Configuration | Policies | Windows Settings | Security Settings | Software Restriction Policies | Additional Rules

These GPO settings will be available after you create a policy.

- **Hash Rule** A *hash* is a digital fingerprint of a piece of software. Using the piece of software as an input to an algorithm, the algorithm then creates a representation (a hash) of the piece of software based on its contents instead of other ways, such as its location or its name. If you change anything about the software, its hash is no longer valid and it will not execute.

- **Certificate Rule** A certificate rule uses code-signing digital certificates to identify software. You can issue code-signing certificates to your software and use them to identify the software on the RD Session Host server by checking the digital signature in the certificate.

NOTE The Basic User security level is not supported for certificate rules.

- **Path Rule** This rule identifies a specific path of an application and only the application in that path can be allowed or denied. A specific piece of code (such as Winword. exe) can be expressed in the path, or the path can point to a folder. If the latter, all code in the folder is allowed or denied. For example, if you host Microsoft Office 2010 applications on your RD Session Host server, you can point to the Microsoft Office installation directory. All code in that directory will be allowed or denied depending on the policy security level and additional rule settings. Environmental variables, UNC paths, registry paths, question marks, and asterisk wildcards can be used in path rules.

- **Network Zone Rule** This rule applies only to MSI files, so it is probably not very useful in locking down an RD Session Host server except when installing software. The network zone rule allows or denies software installation (for MSI files only) based on which Internet zone it was downloaded from.

These rules are applied from the most specific to the most general. Certificate rules are extremely specific about the software they represent, followed by hash rules, then path rules, and finally, Internet zone rules are the least specific. Any software not covered by one of these additional rules is controlled by the default security level (default rule).

For example, let's create an SRP that will affect domain users in the following ways when they log on to your RD Session Host server(s).

- Domain users can run Office 2007 applications.
- Domain users cannot run Internet Explorer.
- Domain users cannot run Cmd.exe or Control.exe (Control Panel).
- Domain users cannot run any software on the RD Session Host server that is not installed on the RD Session Host server. For instance, if a user copies Cmd.exe from her local computer to the roaming profile desktop and then tries to start this application from the RD Session Host server, you want the action to fail.

This example assumes you have your RD Session Host servers placed in their own organizational unit (OU), and if you have multiple RD Session Host servers in the same farm, that they are configured identically. See Chapter 9 for more about RD Session Host farms.

Because you want to affect the domain users group when they log on to the RD Session Host server, create a Software Restriction Policy in the user section of a GPO, located here.

User Configuration | Policies | Windows Settings | Security Settings | Software Restriction Policies

> **NOTE** The Software Restriction Policy setting for Computers is located at Computer Configuration | Policies | Windows Settings | Security Settings | Software Restriction Policies.

Open the Group Policy Management console (GPMC) and create a new GPO; in this example, it is named RD Software Restriction Policy. Then navigate to the Software Restriction Policies folder, right-click the folder, and choose New Software Restriction Policies.

To keep software that is not installed from running, you need to disallow all software from running and then make exceptions to this rule for software located in specific places on the server.

Click the Security Levels folder, and in the right pane, right-click Disallowed and choose Set As Default. Now you need to create the exceptions to this default rule. So you don't lock yourself out, and so you can run applications installed on the RD Session Host server, Microsoft creates two exceptions to the Disallowed security level and places them in the Additional Rules folder when you create a new SRP. They are

- %HKEY_LOCAL_MACHINE\SOFTWARE\Microsoft\WindowsNT\Current Version\ SystemRoot%

  The security level for this additional rule is set to Unrestricted; it allows access to items in the server system root folder (C:\Windows). Users need access to some items in the Windows folder to log on, so keep this setting.

- %HKEY_LOCAL_MACHINE\SOFTWARE\Microsoft\Windows\Current Version\ProgramFilesDir%

  The security level for this additional rule is set to Unrestricted and allows access to the items in the Program Files Directory. Internet Explorer happens to be installed to this directory, so delete this rule, because one of the goals is to block access to Internet Explorer.

Users currently have unrestricted access to Cmd.exe and Control.exe because of the additional rule that allows unrestricted access to the Windows folder; Windows contains the System32 folder, which is where these applications reside. Therefore, you need to make additional rules to deny access for these specific applications. Right-click the Additional Rules folder and choose New Path Rule. Enter the path to Cmd.exe in the Path text box (C:\Windows\System32\Cmd.exe), change the security level to Disallowed, type a description of the rule, and click OK. Then do the same thing for Control.exe.

To allow Office software to run, create another path rule, type the path to Office (typically C:\Program Files\Microsoft Office), and change the security level to Unrestricted. Type a description of the rule and click OK. To apply this GPO to the Domain Users group, change the security filtering on the GPO by removing the Authenticated Users group and adding the Domain Users group. Apply the GPO to the OU where the RD Session Host server(s) reside, and then you are done.

Now, if you don't already have loopback policy processing enabled, create a computer GPO, apply loopback processing, and then apply the GPO to the RD Session Host server OU. This applies the user's SRP to the users specified in the user's SRP security filtering.

If you set SRPs using a computer GPO, you will likely want to forgo applying this policy to the local administrator account. To do this, click the Software Restriction Policies folder, double-click the Enforcement setting, and choose to Apply Software Restriction Policies To The Following Users: All Users Except Local Administrators. Click OK.

Using AppLocker

Although older operating systems will continue to rely on SRP to control software access, AppLocker, which is new to Windows Server 2008 R2 and Windows 7 (Ultimate and Enterprise editions), supersedes SRP for these new operating systems and provides an enhanced software restriction feature set. In fact, while AppLocker has some similarities to Software Restriction Policies, it is actually a completely new feature built using different technology.

> **NOTE** Windows 7 Professional can be used only to create AppLocker rules—the rules cannot be enforced in this version.

AppLocker has quite a few advantages over SRPs.

- AppLocker rules can be applied to specific users or user groups (whereas SRP rules apply to all users).

- Unlike hashes, AppLocker rules can survive version upgrades and location path changes because they can be based on digital signatures.

- AppLocker policies can be run in audit-only mode, so you can determine the effect of a rule before you deploy it.

- AppLocker rules are wizard-driven, so they're easy to set up. Because you can import and export them, it's also easy to move rules from a test to a production environment.

- AppLocker organizes file formats into four *collections* [executables, installers, scripts and dynamic-link libraries (DLLs)] to provide simple ways to build multiple rules that together can provide more detailed restrictions.

- AppLocker has Windows PowerShell support via AppLocker cmdlets.

You can still use SRPs with Windows 7 and Windows Server 2008 R2, but if AppLocker rules and SRPs exist in the same GPO, AppLocker rules policies will supersede any SRP policies for Windows 7 and Windows Server 2008 R2. Older operating systems will use only the Software Restriction Policies.

> **NOTE** You don't have to upgrade your infrastructure to support AppLocker. A computer running Windows Server 2008 R2 or Windows 7 is needed to create the rules, but they can be housed on a Windows Server 2003 or 2008 domain controller.

AppLocker is similar to SRP in that you create whitelists (rules that specifically allow access to files) and block lists (rules that specifically deny access to files) to control access to files and folders on computers. You create rules as needed, for four predefined file categories (collections): executables, scripts, installers, and DLLs.

> **NOTE** DLL rules are turned off by default, because DLL rules can affect machine performance. Take caution when creating and enforcing DLL rules and test thoroughly before deployment.

AppLocker Underlying Philosophy: Admit Nothing, Deny Everything

AppLocker's basic approach is one of extreme control: Do exactly what the rules dictate, and deny all other access for executables in that collection. It does this indiscriminately for both whitelists and block lists. In other words, if no rules are set for a specific collection, then all access is allowed. The minute that you create a rule for a collection, only what is allowed in that rule is applied, and all other access is denied.

This approach is important to understand because it can have some unexpected consequences. For example, if you allow domain administrators access to all executables, that is great for them. But by creating only this rule, you inherently deny everyone else access to any executables on the machine. This means that users can't even access the computer remotely because Winlogon.exe, Explorer.exe, and other executables needed to establish and access a session (full desktop or RemoteApp—it doesn't matter which) are denied.

To help you avoid this pitfall, when you first create a rule, AppLocker will prompt you to let it create a set of "default" rules to make sure that you don't lock people out of the machine. Of course, you can hone these rules to suit your needs.

AppLocker Rule Conditions

Again, the four collections are executables, installers, scripts, and DLLs. AppLocker rules for these four collections are based on the following three conditions.

- **Publisher**   The rule is based on the file's digital signature and the extended attributes of that signature. A digital signature contains the following specific information (attributes) about the file.

  - **Publisher**   Example: O=MICROSOFT CORPORATION, L=REDMOND, S=WASHINGTON, C=US

  - **Product Name**   Example: WINDOWS® INTERNET EXPLORER

  - **File Name**   Example: IEXPLORE.EXE

  - **File Version**   Example: 8.0.7600.16385

  When you create an AppLocker rule based on a file's publisher, you browse and select the signed file, and the publisher attributes retrieved from the file's digital signature. By default, all four of these attributes are used to determine access eligibility, but you can choose how detailed the rule is applied by moving the slider in the graphical user interface (GUI) to include or exclude certain attributes, as shown in Figure 7-3.

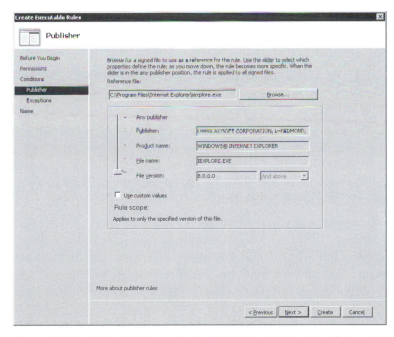

FIGURE 7-3 AppLocker Publisher rules are based on a combination of the extended attributes of the file's digital signature.

NOTE You can customize publisher rules by selecting the Use custom values check box shown in Figure 7-3 and editing the attribute values as needed.

- **Path** The rule will affect a specific file or all files in a specific folder. Both of these options are set by specifying (by typing or browsing to) the path of the file or folder.
- **File Hash** File Hash rules are based on a digital fingerprint of a file. Using the file (an executable, script, installer, or DLL) as an input, an algorithm generates a representation (a hash) of the file. If you change anything about the file, its hash is no longer valid, and allow rules will no longer work.

AppLocker Rules Affect Specific Computers and Users

Overall, AppLocker rules are applied to computers or to OUs containing computers. However, each rule configuration allows you to choose what users or user groups the rule will affect. For example, you can make a rule allowing administrators to run all executables on your RD Session Host servers, and another rule allowing users to run only executables in the Windows folder (so they can log on) and also in the Office folder (so they can run their Office applications). You place these rules on the OU where the RD Session Host servers reside, and the rules apply to all computers in the OU.

AppLocker Exceptions

To facilitate even more detailed control over file access, you can also make exceptions to each rule. For example, you could allow access to all executables in the Programs folder for User Group A, except for certain applications within the Programs folder that you wish to deny to User Group A.

AppLocker Deny Rules

Similar to making allow rules, you can also create deny rules. Deny rules specifically deny access to a file or group of files. However, you can't just create a deny rule and expect everything else to be allowed, because the mere action of creating a rule for a collection means that everything that is not allowed is intrinsically denied for the collection. By doing this, you would basically deny what you put in the rule and then deny everything else as well.

So what is the purpose of deny rules if AppLocker is designed to deny everything except what is specifically allowed? Deny rules, like rule exceptions, help you create a more precise matrix of what is allowed and what is denied. Exceptions will apply to the user(s) contained only in the rule where the exception is made. Deny rules allow you to specify exceptions to rules based on user or user group because you can create a separate deny rule and apply it to a subset of users.

AppLocker Audit Mode

AppLocker is powerful. To help you determine the real effects of the rules that you make, AppLocker provides an "audit only" mode, in which you can log the effects of rules so that you can determine the overall results of rules before you put them into production. When AppLocker rule collections are set to Audit Only mode, actions that the rules would have affected (allowed or denied) will be logged in the Event Viewer of the machine where the action was committed. For example, if a user executes CMD.exe on an RD Session Host server where an AppLocker rule that was enforced would have denied the action, the following event would be logged in the RD Session Host server Event Log at Event Viewer/Application and Services logs/Microsoft/Windows/AppLocker/EXE and DLL/.

```
Event Id 8003: %SYSTEM32%\CMD.EXE was allowed to run but would have been prevented from
running if the AppLocker policy were enforced.
```

Implementing AppLocker

The following example shows how to implement AppLocker policies for an RD Session Host farm. This example shows how you can create, audit, and enforce AppLocker policies that will do the following.

- Give administrators full access to the machine
- Enable access for the ASH_Users group to the Microsoft Office folder on the RD Session Host server farm members, except for Microsoft Excel
- Provide the ASH_Users group the ability to start a remote desktop session by granting access to files in the Windows folder, except CMD.exe, Powershell.exe, Regedit.exe, Wscript.exe, and Cscript.exe
- Block all users except administrators from running any scripts or installers on the machine

First, for AppLocker rules to affect machines, those machines must be running the Application Identity Service. The service is not started by default, and the service setting is set to Manual. You might want to change the default service setting from manual to automatic, so that whenever you start the servers in the farm, AppLocker will work without you needing to turn the service on manually.

 ON THE COMPANION MEDIA A script that starts the AppIDSvc service and also sets the service startup parameter to Automatic for all computers in a specified OU is located on the companion media as Start-AppIDSvc.ps1.

Also, be aware that users who have administrator rights on machines and VMs that are controlled by AppLocker policies can render the policies useless by simply disabling the AppIDSvc service. Make sure that users do not have this ability in any RDS session or pooled/personal VM scenario.

AppLocker rules can be created from different sources.

- Directly in the local policy of the machine on which the policies will apply
- On another machine running Windows 7 or Windows Server 2008 R2 with the same software installed as the production environment, and also the Remote Server Administration Tools (RSAT) installed

Either way you create your rules, you should first implement them in a test environment and then audit them in a production environment before enforcing them. This two-step process will cut down on unforeseen consequences negatively affecting user access in an RDS environment.

In this example, you will see how to create policies directly on a farm member (the RD Session Host server's name is FUJI) that is currently not accepting connections. Then you will see how to export the rules to an XML file and import them into a GPO that will be applied to an RD Session Host farm in Audit mode. When it's clear that the AppLocker policies accomplish the intended goals but do not affect the users negatively, it's safe to change the GPO to Enforce mode.

First, create and export the AppLocker policies by completing these steps.

1. On RD Session Host server FUJI, open the Local Security Policy, browse to the Application Control Policies folder, and expand the AppLocker folder.

2. Right-click Executable Rules and choose Create Default Rules. Three executable rules will appear in the right pane, as shown in Figure 7-4. By creating the default rules, you have already given the BUILTIN/Administrators group full access to all files on the machine, because this is one of the default rules.

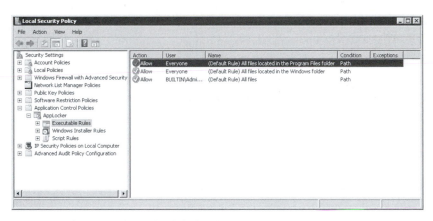

FIGURE 7-4 The Executable Rules default rule is set.

3. Adjust the first rule to allow a specific user group ASH_Users (instead of Everyone) to access the Office executables, except for Excel, as follows.

   a. Double-click the first rule highlighted in Figure 7-4. On the General tab, select the user group that you want to affect (in our example, ASH_Users). Keep the Allow option selected.

b. On the Path tab, click Browse Folders and browse to the folder where the Office executables are located: %PROGRAMFILES%\Microsoft Office*.

c. On the Exceptions tab, add a publisher exception by clicking Add, browsing to the Excel executable, and then clicking OK.

d. Click OK again to apply the changes to the default rule.

4. Double-click the second default rule shown in Figure 7-4 [named (Default rule) All files located in the Windows folder] and adjust it to allow ASH_Users to access all executables in the Windows folder. Then make an exception to the rule and deny access to CMD.exe, Powershell.exe, Regedit.exe, Wscript.exe, and Cscript.exe, as follows.

a. Double-click the highlighted rule. On the General tab, replace the Everyone group by clicking Select and choosing the appropriate user group to whom you want this rule to apply (ASH_Users). Leave the Allow option selected.

b. Leave the %WINDIR% path on the Path tab as is.

c. On the Exceptions tab, add five exceptions, one for each executable to which you want to deny this group access. Leave the Publisher exception type selected. Click Add, browse to cmd.exe, and click OK. Do the same for the other four executables. When the exceptions list is complete, as shown in Figure 7-5, click OK to apply the changes to the rule.

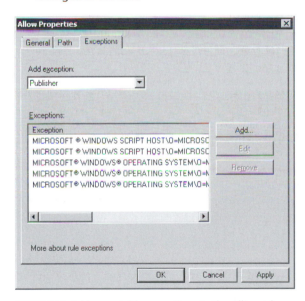

FIGURE 7-5 Add executable exceptions to the Allow rule.

5. The easiest way to block all users except administrators from running any scripts on the machine is to invoke the creating of "default script rules" and then delete the ones that you do not want to use.

a. Select and right-click the Script rules node in the Local Security policy, and then choose Create Default Rules. Three default rules will be created, as shown in Figure 7-6.

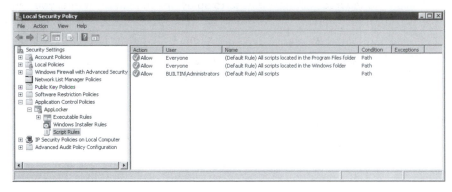

FIGURE 7-6 Create Script Rules default rules.

b. Select the first two rules and then right-click and choose Delete.

You are left with one rule that allows the BUILTIN/Administrators group to run all scripts on the machine, but no one else will be allowed to do so because of the inherent Deny rule that is enforced.

> **NOTE** Deleting the other two default rules prevents the Everyone group from running scripts located in the Program Files folder and the Windows folder, but if your applications need this ability, then you should adjust the rules or add new rules to suit your needs.

6. To block all users except administrators from running any installers on the machine, follow the steps laid out in Step 5, but do so using the Windows Installer Rules node.

7. Now you will export the rules that you have created to an XML file and import them into a GPO. Right-click the AppLocker node and choose Export Policy. Choose a path to save the file, enter a file name (our file name is ASH_Farm1_AppLocker_Rules), and click Save.

8. When you export rules from the local security policy, they are not deleted. Delete them for now because they have not yet been tested in a non-production environment. Right-click the AppLocker node and choose Clear Policy. This reverts AppLocker to its original unconfigured state. If you need to adjust the rules in the future, you can do so by re-importing the policy XML file that you created and adjusting and re-exporting the policy; but for now, there is no reason to leave them in place.

After you have created the rules XML file, create a new GPO (using Group Policy Manager) and then import the XML file into the AppLocker node in the GPO, as shown in Figure 7-7.

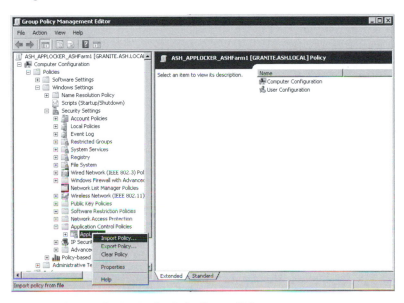

FIGURE 7-7 Import the AppLocker Policy into a GPO.

Auditing AppLocker Rules

Next, because you are in the testing phase of this implementation, you need to set the AppLocker rules to be audited only, not enforced. Right-click the AppLocker node and choose Properties. On the Enforcement tab, make sure the Configured check box is selected for each of the three rule collections, and then choose Audit Only from each of the three drop-down lists, as shown in Figure 7-8. Click OK to save the settings.

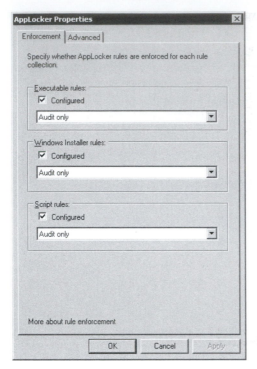

FIGURE 7-8 Set the AppLocker rules to Audit Only mode.

Next, you apply the new GPO to the OU that contains the servers that you want to affect. In this example, you apply the rule to the ASH_RD_Farm1 OU, containing two RD Session Host servers (FUJI and GLACIER). Now, when users log on to the farm, AppLocker logs the actions the user takes that are allowed and the actions that would be denied had the AppLocker rules been enforced. These logs are in the Event Viewer\Applications and Services Logs\Microsoft\Windows\AppLocker folder on the RD Session Host server where the user session is running. In our example, Excel was blocked from starting. As you can see in Figure 7-9, the event log shows that had the AppLocker rule been enforced, the user would have been denied access.

After you have tested and adjusted the AppLocker rules fully to suit your needs, change the enforcement of the rules shown in Figure 7-8 from Audit Only to Enforce Rules and click OK to save the change. Your rules will now be enforced. Any changes that you need to make in the future can be done so directly in the GPO (if you know the text you need to enter), or you can import the rules again to a machine that is not currently hosting or accepting connections, make changes to the rules there, export the new rule set, and re-import them into a GPO.

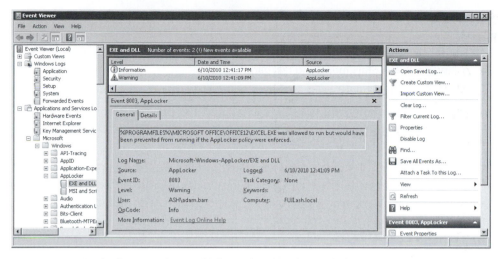

FIGURE 7-9 AppLocker logs warnings and information regarding audited AppLocker rules in the Event Viewer of the server where the user session runs

Creating a Read-Only Start Menu

Lockdown is important, but it's not the only reason to tweak the user experience. You can also customize the experience to simplify it so that people don't have to see menu items that they will never use and which will only confuse them.

The ultimate goal for an RDS environment, be it pooled/personal VMs or a session on an RD Session Host server, is to help people work. If you make it easy for people to get to their applications by removing the clutter they don't need, you're working toward that goal.

You could customize the default user profile so that when users log onto a session or VM, their profile will contain customized settings for the Start menu. This might be fine if you have one small pool of VMs or one RD Session Host server, but managing this kind of setup for many servers would be a daunting task for little benefit. In addition, you would still need to lock things down so the user could not change these settings later. Therefore, a better approach is to customize the Start menu (on a per-user or user-group basis) by redirecting the Start menu to a read-only Start Menu folder. Then, you set a few GPOs to hide other Start menu areas (to cut down on unnecessary items) and remove unneeded items from the other Start menu areas). Here's how to do it.

1. Create a network share or use an already-existing network share (for example, you might use the same share that you use to store the user's redirected folders).

2. In the network share, create a folder called Start Menu and place shortcuts to the items that you want in the folder. Adjust the folder NTFS permissions so that users have read-only rights.

3. Create a GPO that redirects the Start menu for all users who log on to the machines in the OU to this one location and place the GPO on the appropriate OU.

4. Set the following GPOs (some of which were mentioned earlier in the section about locking down the Start menu and taskbar).

   User Configuration | Policies | Administrative Templates | Start Menu and Task Bar

   - **Remove Common Groups From Start Menu**   This does not place items from the All Users group in the user's Start menu located at C:\ProgramData\Microsoft\Windows\Start Menu\Programs.

   - **Remove Pinned Programs List From The Start Menu**   Enabling this setting removes the items stored in the QuickLaunch folder of the user profile. For example, you could use a roaming user profile with QuickLaunch items stored at \\FILE-SERVER\ASH-user-folder-redirection\kristin.griffin\AppData\Roaming\Microsoft\Internet Explorer\Quick Launch\User Pinned\Start Menu.

   - **Remove The Network Icon From The Start Menu**   This removes the network icon from the right side of the Start menu.

5. Remove the Control Panel icon from the Start menu by enabling the following GPO.

   User Configuration | Policies | Administrative Templates |Control Panel | Prohibit Access To The Control Panel

6. Provide administrative tools on the right side of the Start menu, while eliminating this for regular users (who should not have a need for these tools). On each RD Session Host server remove NTFS permissions for the Everyone group and the Users group from the following folder: C:\ProgramData\Microsoft\Windows\Start Menu\Programs\Administrative Tools.

The result of these few steps is a consistent Start menu for users even if they are using roaming profiles and folder redirection. The same items will be available in the All Programs menu each time the user logs on, and to add or change this menu, you only have to maintain the one redirected Start Menu folder.

What's also nice about this arrangement is that different users can see different icons, effectively giving them a different Start menu depending on who they are. To do this, just change the NTFS permissions on each icon in the Start Menu redirected folder. Users who do not have NTFS permissions to the icon will not see the icon in their Start menu.

You can also redirect different user groups to different Start menus (that is, different Start Menu redirected folders) and achieve the same effect. This requires that you create and maintain multiple GPOs that redirect the Start menu to different folders, on a user-group basis. Just remember to set the appropriate NTFS permissions on the redirected folder and also to remove the Authenticated Users group from the GPO security filtering and add the specific users and user groups that you want to use the GPO.

Keeping the RD Session Host Server Available

You have seen how to secure the sessions and VMs and how to simplify the user's view of the desktop. Some Group Policy settings allow you to improve the user experience through limiting access or shortening logon times.

Allowing or Denying Access to the RD Session Host Server

Although users cannot log on to the RD Session Host server unless they are members of the local Remote Desktop Users group on that RD Session Host server, you can control the ability of users to log on via Group Policy. Use the following setting.

- Computer Configuration | Policies | Administrative Templates | Windows Components | Remote Desktop Services | Remote Desktop Session Host | Connections | Allow Users To Connect Remotely Using Remote Desktop Services

  This setting controls whether users can access the RD Session Host server remotely. An RD Session Host server will not accept any user logons until the Remote Desktop Users group is populated. This policy gives you more detailed control over who has access to the RD Session Host servers so that you can prevent unauthorized users from consuming licenses that you had intended for people who need them.

> **NOTE** It's also possible to prevent logons to the RD Session Host server via Active Directory Users And Computers; one option in the user account Properties dialog box defines whether users are allowed to log on to the RD Session Host server (they are, by default). Although it might appear that Group Policy or Active Directory Users And Computers settings are good ways to prevent people from logging on during server maintenance, they're really not, because the policy might not apply in time and you might not have Active Directory Domain Services (AD DS) control anyway. To lock out users during maintenance, run the following command on the RD Session Host that you need to work on.

```
change logon /disable
```

Limiting the Number of RD Session Host Server Connections

For application licensing reasons or performance reasons, you might want to limit the number of simultaneous connections to the server. Do this with the following GPO setting.

- Computer Configuration | Policies | Administrative Templates | Windows Components | Remote Desktop Services | Remote Desktop Session Host | Connections | Limit Number Of Connections

  Enable the Limit Number Of Connections setting to limit the total number of simultaneous connections that can be active on an RD Session Host server. If you have 100 users, and each user is limited to one session, you know that you can limit the number of connections to approximately 100 and not interfere with user access. This also ensures that you won't allow more connections than are needed.

Setting Session Time Limits

The GPOs to set time limits on active, idle, and disconnected sessions are located at:

Computer Configuration | Policies |Administrative Templates | Windows Components | Remote Desktop Services | Remote Desktop Session Host | Session Time Limits

Setting session time limits can be a delicate balancing act. For example, the longer that disconnected sessions are available before being terminated, the more time users have to re-connect. Reconnecting to an existing session is faster than creating a new session, and recon-necting to an existing session keeps the user locked into a particular RD Session Host server.

However, disconnected sessions still require some memory. Not much memory is needed because when a session is disconnected, the data stored in physical memory is high on the list to be paged to disk, but it does require some. If the RD Session Host server is memory-con-strained, disconnected sessions could affect performance. To set a time limit on disconnected sessions, enable and configure the following policy.

Set The Time Limit For Disconnected Sessions

You can also set session limits defining how long sessions might be active or idle before they're disconnected. However, you can't set session time limits for individual RemoteApp programs. All RemoteApp programs using the same session will follow the same rules.

Taking Remote Control of User Sessions

You've probably experienced the following situation: You have a problem with your computer or with an application. Something just isn't right—for example, you can't format the spread-sheet the way you want, even though you're sure you're doing it properly. Someone stops by your desk and asks what's going on. When you explain that the spreadsheet isn't working properly, your co-worker asks you to show him what's not working while he watches. You do it again, and it works perfectly this time.

You can make this happen on an RD Session Host server even without someone standing behind you. One way in which remote sessions on an RD Session Host server can be useful is that it is simple to troubleshoot problems by shadowing a user's session. Sessions running on an RD Session Host server are easy to monitor using the Remote Control tool in Remote Desktop Services Manager or the command-line shadow tool.

> **NOTE** As discussed in Chapter 11, "Managing Remote Desktop Sessions," although VMs are not visible in the Remote Desktop Services Manager, you can shadow them from the command prompt if you know the session ID for the VM. Chapter 11 discusses how to do this in the explanation of how to use shadow for runtime management.

In brief, Remote Control works by intercepting the output of the RDP graphics driver. When a session is shadowed, rather than sending the output to only one session, the RDP graphics driver sends the screen updates and mouse and keyboard inputs to two sessions: the session being shadowed and the session doing the shadowing. This is why you can't shadow a session unless you're in an RDP session yourself.

Chapter 11 discusses how to use Remote Control, but for now, let's focus on the permissions options and how to set them.

NOTE By default, only members of the Administrators or Domain Administrators group are allowed to shadow sessions on the RD Session Host server, so you don't need to worry about users spying on each other. The Shadow command and Remote Control option in RD Session Manager don't work for users unless you specifically give them permissions to use them by assigning them the Remote Control permission on the RDP listener. This setting gives a user the ability to shadow any session controlled by those listener properties, so use it with discretion.

There are two levels of interaction with a Remote Control session. First, you can use it to view the user setting. This setting allows both the user and the administrator to see the session at the same time, but only permits the user to interact with it. The other option is to allow the administrator to interact with the user's session.

There are three options for Remote Control.

- You can disable it entirely. This setting will prevent administrators from using Remote Control on user sessions. This is the most secure option, but it's also the least helpful.

- You can enable it but require the user's permission for an administrator to connect to the session.

- You can enable it and not require any notification.

The option that you pick will obviously depend on the circumstances. Disabling shadowing might be necessary when privacy rules in your organization don't permit it. Requiring notification allows you to use this capability but still reassure the users that no one can see their desktop without their knowledge or permission. Also, not requiring notification allows the administrator to audit user activity, which is a requirement in some organizations.

You can define the way Remote Control works on a per-server basis through RD Session Host Configuration, for specific users in AD DS user account properties, or by using Group Policy.

To configure Remote Control settings for individual RD Session Host servers, go to Start, Administrative Tools, Remote Desktop Services and open RD Session Host Configuration. In the Connections section at the top of the middle pane, double-click RDP-Tcp to open the RDP-Tcp Properties dialog box, and then go to the Remote Control tab shown in Figure 7-10.

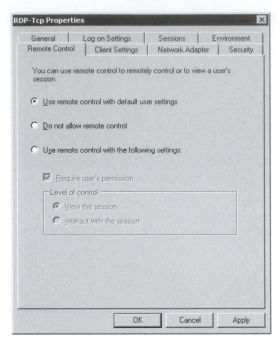

FIGURE 7-10 Configure computer properties for Remote Control.

As you can see, the default settings allow the per-user settings to override. To configure Remote Control settings on a per-user basis, open Active Directory Users And Computers and open a user's account Properties dialog box, as shown in Figure 7-11.

To set remote settings using Group Policy, configure Set Rules For Remote Control Of RD Session Host Server User Sessions. You can set the policy on a per-computer or per-user basis. For computers, the policy is located in Computer Configuration | Policies | Admin Templates | Windows Components | Remote Desktop Services | Remote Desktop Session Host | Connections. For users, it's in User Configuration | Policies | Windows Components | Remote Desktop Services | Remote Desktop Session Host | Connections. Enable the policy and then edit the settings to pick the appropriate option, as shown in Figure 7-12.

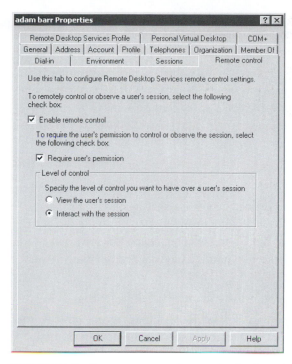

FIGURE 7-11 Configure user account properties for Remote Control.

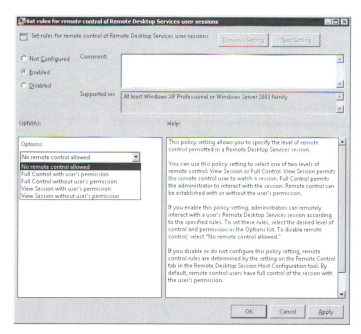

FIGURE 7-12 You can edit the Remote Control Group Policy for users or for all RD Session Host servers.

If you don't configure the policy or any remote control settings, then the settings in Active Directory Users And Computers will take effect by default, and Remote Control sessions will be allowed with the user's permission, with administrators allowed to interact with the session.

Unless there's a really good reason to configure Remote Control settings differently for discrete sets of people, you should configure them for all RD Session Host servers in the same way. Having different policies for different people could easily confuse administrators and render the Remote Control option less useful.

Summary

Hosting shared desktops and applications in the datacenter is a delicate balance between providing a rich user experience (as discussed in Chapter 6) and locking down the server to avoid one user from affecting others, as discussed in this chapter. (Some lockdown can also apply to any desktop, whether it is in the datacenter or it is a physical desktop that you want to control.)

Here are some of the best practices covered in this chapter.

- Use Group Policy to configure user settings if possible. All settings are in Group Policy, and some are represented in either Active Directory Users And Computers or the Remote Desktop Services Configuration Tool.
- Lock down the RD Session Host server by removing the ability to browse the operating system and permitting only authorized executables to run.
- Avoid confusing people who work in sessions and pooled VMs by hiding local files in libraries and preventing people from writing to those local locations.
- On Windows 7 VMs and Windows Server 2008 R2 RD Session Host servers, use AppLocker to prevent unauthorized applications from running.
- Creating a read-only Start menu can help simplify the experience for people who need a full desktop but shouldn't be confused by too many options.
- Limit usage of the RD Session Host servers and limit session counts to keep control of licensing for applications licensed on a per-connection basis and to optimize performance on the RD Session Host servers.
- Configure Remote Control settings to enable session auditing as well as enable the Help Desk to assist users remotely.

Additional Resources

The following resources are related to topics covered in this chapter. You can also find the links on this book's companion media.

- For more information about Software Restriction Policies, see *http://go.microsoft.com /fwlink/?LinkID=92567*.

- An introduction to AppLocker is located at *http://technet.microsoft.com/en-us/library /dd560656(WS.10).aspx*.

- For some ideas of how to manage AppLocker via Windows PowerShell, see *http://blogs.msdn.com/b/powershell/archive/2009/06/02/getting-started-with-applocker-management-using-powershell.aspx*.

- To download RDP 7 for Windows Vista SP1 and later, go to *http://www.microsoft.com/downloads/details.aspx?familyid=AC7E58F3-2FD4-4FEC-ABFD-8002D34476F4&displaylang=en* for 32-bit systems, and *http://www.microsoft.com/downloads/details.aspx?familyid=11E7A081-22A8-4DA7-A6C5-CDC1AC51A1A4&displaylang=en* for 64-bit systems.

- To download RDP 7 for Windows XP SP3, go to *http://www.microsoft.com/downloads /details.aspx?FamilyId=72158b4e-b527-45e4-af24-d02938a95683&displaylang=en*.

- To download RDP 6.1 for Windows XP SP2, go to *http://www.microsoft.com/downloads /details.aspx?FamilyId=6E1EC93D-BDBD-4983-92F7-479E088570AD&displaylang=en*.

- For an introduction to libraries in Windows 7, see *http://msdn.microsoft.com/en-us /magazine/dd861346.aspx*.

Securing Remote Desktop Protocol Connections

Chapter 7, "Molding and Securing the User Environment," discussed some approaches to locking down the server or VM to protect them from malice or error. Isn't that enough?

Locking down the server is important, but it assumes that you've *already* made a secure connection to the server. That assumption doesn't consider the possibility of the connection—or the communication between the client and server—being compromised in some way. For example

- An existing connection could be intercepted and the data flow compromised.

- The user could connect to a malicious server and type his or her logon credentials for the owner of the server to capture.

- A client not authorized to connect to the Remote Desktop (RD) Session Host server could make repeated attempts to connect, tying up resources on the RD Session Host server as it tries to authorize the connection, thus preventing authorized users from connecting.

The catch to mitigating all these connection vulnerabilities is that the logon experience is a critical part of a successful RD Session Host server deployment. If the connection experience is bad, then the users accessing the RD Session Host server will be unhappy with the service. Therefore, you must keep the data stream secure but also make it as fast as possible. This chapter explains the key Windows components that tackle this problem, including the following.

- Remote Desktop Protocol (RDP) encryption
- Server authentication

- Network Level Authentication (NLA)
- Single sign-on (SSO)

Figure 8-1 shows the features that will be discussed and the technologies supporting each feature.

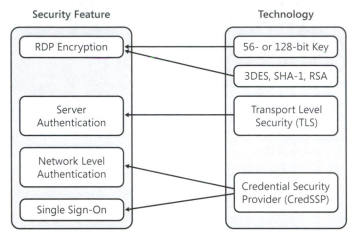

FIGURE 8-1 Key RDS communication security features and supporting technologies are presented here.

Core Security Technologies

Communication security in RDS depends on three core pieces.

- Encryption of the data stream
- Transport Layer Security (TLS) for establishing a secure connection between client and server, in which the server has proved its identity.
- The Credential Security Service Provider (CredSSP) for enabling SSO and NLA to prove that a user has the right to log on before the server creates a session.

Transport Layer Security

TLS is the Internet Engineering Task Force (IETF) standard based on Secure Sockets Layer (SSL) v3, published by Netscape. Some of the enhancements that TLS has include new message alerts, the ability to chain certificates to an intermediary certificate authority (CA) certificate instead of the root CA certificate, and slightly different encryption algorithms from SSL. Although TLS is based on SSL, the two are incompatible. However, TLS can implement a mechanism by which it can fall back to SSL v3 if necessary.

To establish communication between client and server using TLS, the client and server go through the process described in the following steps. (This isn't specific to RDP connections; RDP just has the option of using TLS.) This process is similar to the negotiations described in Chapter 7, in which client and server negotiate their mutual capabilities. There are two requirements for this to work properly.

- The client must trust the server SSL certificate that is used to verify the server's identity.
- The connection between server and client must use High or FIPS encryption. Low encryption only encrypts the traffic from client to server, not server to client, so it's not a secure way to send security capabilities or shared secrets.

If these two requirements are met, the client and server establish communication as follows.

1. The client sends a hello message along with a random fixed-length value. The server responds with a random fixed-length value. During this exchange, the client tells the server the compression methods, ciphers, and hashes that it supports. It also sends its protocol version and a session ID to the server. (The session ID identifies the communication channel; this is not the Session ID on an RD Session Host server.)

2. The server picks the highest compression method that they both support and the cipher and hash function from the client's list, and tells the client which one it has chosen. If there's a minimum set on the server and the client can't meet this minimum, the connection will fail.

3. The server sends its digital certificate to the client. This certificate contains the server's name, the trusted CA that signed the certificate, and the server's public key.

4. The client verifies that the certificate is valid and trusted (the certificate used to sign the server certificate is located in the client's Trusted Root Certification Authorities store). Then it creates a pre-master secret, encrypts it with server public key, and sends it to server.

5. The server receives and decrypts the pre-master secret with its private key. This server is the only one that can do this because it is the only server with the matching private key.

6. Now that both server and client have the pre-master secret and both random numbers exchanged at the beginning of the process, they use these values to generate the 48-byte master secret (also known as the *shared secret*). After the master secret is generated, they delete the pre-master secret.

7. Both client and server then hash the 48-byte master secret and use it to generate the MAC secret (the session key used for hashing) and the WRITE key (the session key used for encryption). The keys are used to encrypt and decrypt the communication for this session. After the session is over, the keys are discarded.

See Figure 8-2 for an overview of how TLS allows the client and server to set up a secure communication link.

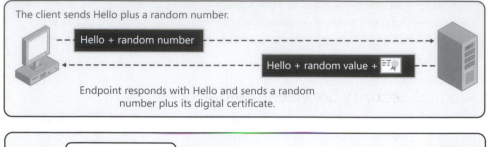

The client sends Hello plus a random number.

Hello + random number

Hello + random value +

Endpoint responds with Hello and sends a random number plus its digital certificate.

Pre-Master Secret

#$%^&

The client creates a pre-master secret, encrypts it using the public key from the endpoint's certificate, and sends it to the endpoint.

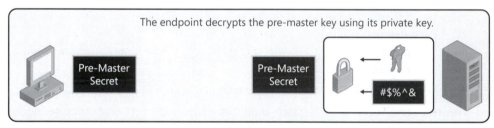

The endpoint decrypts the pre-master key using its private key.

Pre-Master Secret

Pre-Master Secret

#$%^&

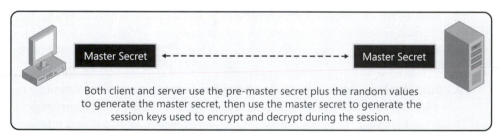

Master Secret

Master Secret

Both client and server use the pre-master secret plus the random values to generate the master secret, then use the master secret to generate the session keys used to encrypt and decrypt during the session.

FIGURE 8-2 Secure communication with TLS

If any step of this sequence doesn't work, the connection has not been fully secured. What happens then depends on the settings on the Advanced tab of the Remote Desktop Connection (RDC) client. In the case of authentication failure, a user can choose to do any one of the following.

- Connect anyway, without notifying the client that there was a problem authenticating the server
- Warn the client but still allow the connection (the default)
- Deny the connection outright if it can't be verified

The exception is if the server requires a certain level of security (for example, High encryption). If the server has requirements and the client can't meet them, the connection will fail. By default, the client and server will negotiate and use the most secure connection settings that they both support.

Credential Security Service Provider

Credential caching, introduced in Windows Vista and Windows Server 2008, enables two features: one that helps the user and one that helps protect the server. To help the user, credential caching allows users to store credentials for a particular connection so they don't need to provide them every time they connect to that server. To help the server, credential caching enables a feature to provide credentials to the server before it establishes a session, thereby avoiding the overhead of a session if the user is not authorized.

The piece that makes credential caching work is the Credential Security Service Provider (CredSSP). CredSSP is available on Windows 7, Windows Vista, Windows Server 2008, and Windows XP SP3. It's not linked to the version of RDC being used because CredSSP is part of the operating system.

CredSSP delegates user credentials to a trusted server via a channel secured using TLS. After it has those credentials, the trusted server can impersonate the user and log on to itself without waiting for a user to present credentials.

CredSSP enables two features: front authentication and SSO.

- For NLA, CredSSP provides the framework that allows a user to be authenticated to an RD Session Host server before fully establishing the connection.
- For SSO, CredSSP stores user credentials and passes them to the RD Session Host server to automate logon.

> **NOTE** Because Microsoft Internet Information Services (IIS) doesn't use CredSSP, you can't use CredSSP to pass credentials to RD Web Access. Users will need to authenticate against RD Web Access to store their credentials in the site (see Chapter 9, "Multi-Server Deployments"). After users are authenticated, they will not need to authenticate again to start RemoteApp programs.

- For reconnecting to a session within a farm, CredSSP speeds the process of passing the connection to the correct server by allowing the RD Session Host server to see who is logging on without having to create an entire session (using NLA in a slightly different scenario).

How CredSSP Authenticates the Server and Client

Credssp enables mutual authentication of server and client, as shown in the following illustration.

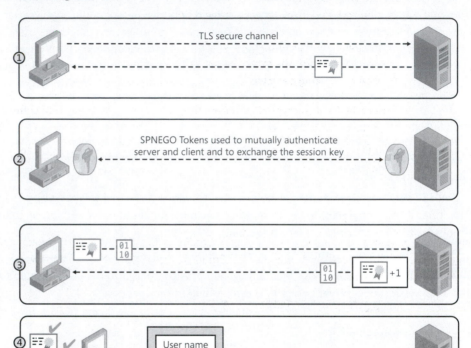

This authentication process is described in the following steps.

1. The client initiates a secure channel with the server using TLS, and the server passes back its certificate with its name, CA, and public key. Only the server is identified; the client remains anonymous at this point.

   NOTE Although the client uses TLS to establish the secure connection, this isn't full server authentication. The client and server don't need to have a mutually trusted CA root.

2. When the session has been established and a session key is created, CredSSP uses the Simple and Protected GSS-API Negotiation (SPNEGO) protocol to authenticate the server and client mutually, so that they know they can trust each other.

Basically, this mechanism lets the client and server agree on an authentication mechanism that they both support, such as Kerberos or NTLM.

3. After the mutual authentication finishes, CredSSP on the client encrypts the server's certificate with the session key created during Step 2 and sends it to the server. The server receives the encrypted certificate, decrypts it using its private key, and then adds 1 to the most significant bit of the certificate number. It then encrypts the result and sends it back to the client.

   NOTE The purpose of performing a function on the certificate is to ensure that no one can intercept the exchange between client and server and spoof the server without being detected.

4. The client reviews the encrypted certificate that it gets from the server and compares it to the certificate it has.

5. Assuming the results match, CredSSP on the client sends the user credentials to the server.

Managing the CredSSP Store

Users can save, edit, and delete credentials in the CredSSP store. To save the credentials to use with SSO initially, select the Remember My Credentials check box in the Windows Security dialog box shown in Figure 8-3.

FIGURE 8-3 You can store credentials in CredSSP.

After they're saved and you have made an initial connection, you can edit them (for example, if you change your password, as CredSSP will not automatically update password changes) by clicking the Edit link in Figure 8-4.

FIGURE 8-4 You can edit or delete stored credentials.

If you choose to edit the saved credentials, you'll see a dialog box like the one used to log on. Your domain and user name will be displayed and your password credentials will be left blank. If you choose to save credentials using another user name, you can also click Use Another Account to start over completely. Use this option to update a stored password after you've changed it.

If you click the Delete link, you'll remove that stored credential from the CredSSP store. A dialog box will prompt you to confirm the action and then clear that saved user name and account information from the cache. Use this option to delete credentials you accidentally saved or which are no longer needed.

Enabling CredSSP (Windows XP SP3 Only)

CredSSP is enabled by default in Windows Vista and Windows 7. Although CredSSP is available in Windows XP SP3 (it's included in the service pack), it's disabled by default. To enable it, you'll need to modify two registry keys as described here.

- In HKLM/SYSTEM/CurrentControlSet/Control/Lsa, and in Security Packages, data type REG_MULTI_SZ, append Tspkg to the list of security providers already present.

- In HKLM/SYSTEM/CurrentControlSet/Control/SecurityProviders, make sure that Credssp.dll is present. You can't use Group Policy to configure SSO in Windows XP SP3.

You must reboot the client for the changes to take effect.

> **NOTE** You can enable CredSSP on an XP SP3 client programmatically with the script at this location: *http://gallery.technet.microsoft.com/ScriptCenter/en-us/41a472e1-9660-4813-be4f-4b81a5345d75*.

Using RDP Encryption

Because there's a lot of open network between the user running the application on an RD Session Host server and the server running the application, it's important to encrypt the traffic going between them so that it can't be intercepted. By default, RDP traffic will be encrypted as strongly as the client can support it—128-bit, if you're using RDP 5.2 or later. Both the RD Session Host server and the client are configured to let the client and the server negotiate the highest level of encryption that both can support.

Understanding Encryption Settings

RDP clients support three levels of encryption: Low, High, and FIPS-compliant.

Low security uses only a 56-bit key to encrypt traffic and will not support server authentication [see the section entitled "Authenticating Server Identity (Server Authentication)" later in this chapter]. It also encrypts only traffic going from client to server, not that going from server to client. This security model is workable only if data is flowing in just one direction, and therefore it is not suitable for any features enabling bidirectional data flow, such as client drive mapping. (Even in this case, the video stream sent to the client could be intercepted.) As you can see, Low security is the level of last resort. The main reason you'll use it is if you are deploying a wide area network (WAN) acceleration device, which will need to see the traffic sent from server to client to compress it in the best manner. The WAN acceleration device can use its own method of encryption since the Microsoft encryption from server to client is disabled.

High security uses a 128-bit key to encrypt data going between client and server; it encrypts traffic going in both directions. You can use High security to support TLS-based server authentication. High security supports server authentication.

FIPS-compliant security uses FIPS-compliant algorithms for encrypting the data flow between the client and the server. Federal Information Processing Standard (FIPS) describes the standards for key generation and key management. There's no such thing as FIPS encryption, but many encryption mechanisms are FIPS-compliant. Only algorithms submitted to the National Institute of Standards and Technology (NIST) can be considered FIPS-compliant. FIPS-compliant security supports server authentication for RDP connections.

When you require FIPS compliance through the RD Configuration tool, you're defining the security algorithms that the server can use. For example, it defines the way that TLS works. As of this writing, it will use Triple Data Encryption Standard (3DES) for encrypting the TLS traffic, RSA for the public key exchange, and the Secure Hashing Algorithm (SHA-1) for the TLS hashing.

Even if you don't choose to use server authentication, when FIPS compliance is required via Group Policy, RDP encryption will use the 3DES algorithm. The server uses FIPS algorithms for more than just establishing secure communications between RDP client and server. Again, the FIPS-compliant algorithms might change with time as more algorithms are tested and determined to be compliant. On Windows Server 2008 R2, the Encrypted File System (EFS) behavior won't change regardless of this setting; the default algorithm is the FIPS-compliant 256-bit Advanced Encryption Standard (AES) algorithm. On previous versions of Windows, requiring FIPS compliance would make EFS fall back to 3DES.

You can configure the RD Session Host server to use FIPS-compliant algorithms either from Group Policy or from RD Session Host Configuration. If you set Group Policy to require FIPS compliance, this will override the Remote Desktop Services–specific Group Policy that sets the RDP Encryption level to High.

> **NOTE** Because NIST certification takes some time, it is possible that the FIPS-compliant algorithm might not be the strongest one available. More recent algorithms might not have been certified yet.

Choosing Encryption Settings

The policy that you use to set RDP encryption levels depends on the level of security that you're setting. By default, the client and server will negotiate the most complex algorithm that they both support. You can change the encryption to Low or, far more likely, require all connections to use a High or FIPS-compliant encryption algorithm. If you do so, clients that do not support these algorithms will not be able to connect to the server. The main reason you'd use Low encryption today is if you're also deploying a WAN accelerator that needs to be able to read the traffic going to the client and has its own encryption mechanism.

Authenticating Server Identity (Server Authentication)

One danger of communicating with a remote computer that requires you to supply your credentials is that the server might not be what you think it is. If it's a rogue server impersonating a real one, you could inadvertently type your credentials into the wrong server, thereby giving attackers everything that they need to connect to your domain or server.

RDP includes encryption, but the protocol does not have any means to authenticate the server. That's where TLS and CredSSP come in. Domain users and individual servers can be authenticated with Kerberos on the local area network (LAN). Server farms by default can't because the farm has no identity in Active Directory Domain Services (AD DS) for the Kerberos ticket to look up. (See the following section, "Establishing a Kerberos Farm Identity," to see how you can give a farm a Kerberos identity and how to set up farms to use Kerberos.) For LAN scenarios, you can use Kerberos to authenticate to the farm. To authenticate to a farm or servers over the Internet, you'll use TLS rather than Kerberos.

> **NOTE** For more information on TLS, see the section entitled "Transport Layer Security" earlier in this chapter.

Establishing a Kerberos Farm Identity

Prior to Windows Server 2008 R2, Kerberos authentication did not recognize farms—just individual servers. Therefore, to authenticate a server's identity, you had to use certificates. Beginning in Windows Server 2008 R2, you could add server farms to AD DS and authenticate the farm. This allows you to save the time and expense required to install certificates on all servers, and it also makes it much easier to deploy new servers in the farm quickly, because you won't need to install certificates on them. You still need to know how to use certificates, since Kerberos authentication still does not work over the Internet, but this feature can save you from needing to install certificates on all farm members if using a full RDS deployment on the LAN.

When the farm has a Kerberos identity, the farm's account credentials are stored on the RD Connection Broker server. The broker then provides each server in the farm with the farm's account credentials. RD Session Host servers use the farm's account credentials as supplemental to the individual server credentials.

There is no user interface to add servers to a farm, but there are scripts for doing so. To see how to establish a Kerberos farm identity programmatically, see *http://blogs.msdn.com/b /rds/archive/2009/05/20/creating-kerberos-identity-for-rd-session-host-farms-part-i-using-the-remote-desktop-services-provider-for-windows-powershell.aspx.*

Creating Test Certificates for a Server Farm

If you're setting up a pilot before going into production, you might want to do this before investing in certificates or setting up a private CA for "real" certificates. You can use self-signed certificates for this, but, as this section notes, the process might work differently from the way you expect! The fundamental issue is that self-signed certificates are typically created for a server, not a farm.

> **NOTE** The following instructions are not intended for a production deployment; they are for testing only. For production, we strongly recommend that you use certificates issued by a trusted CA or create a Kerberos identity for the server farm.

Computer Certificates versus Farm Certificates

When connecting to a farm, you use the farm name (such as Farm1.ash.local). When the certificate for an RD Session host farm member is being checked, you get a dialog box showing that RDC is securing the remote connection. If you generated a self-signed certificate on a server in the farm using the RD Configuration Tool, this certificate will be for the server and is stored in the Remote Desktop/Certificates folder in the Certificates Microsoft Management Console (MMC) snap-in. SSL and computer certificates are stored in the Personal/Certificates folder in the Certificates MMC snap-in.

Server Authentication checks the name that you enter in Remote Desktop Client with the name issued in the certificate that is specified in RD Configuration Tool on the RD Session Host server that it connects to. However, this certificate was generated for a server, not a farm. Therefore, when you try to connect to the farm, you will get the error shown in Figure 8-5.

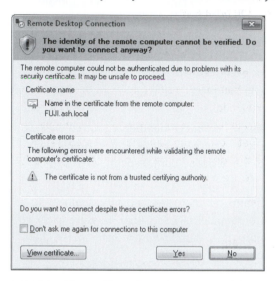

FIGURE 8-5 The certificate is not from a trusted CA, according to this dialog box.

This error is a bit misleading. The certificate will not be seen as trusted because the self-signed certificate is not located in the client's trusted root store. Even if the self-signed certificate were located in the client's trusted root store, however, the name on the certificate is wrong, and you would still get this error.

> **NOTE** You could disregard the error and still connect. If the certificate was generated from a CA (not self-signed), the inability to validate it would be severe enough to prevent the user from connecting to the server.

To use a self-signed certificate to test farm access, you need the name specified on the certificate to be the name of the farm, and you need to install that certificate in the trusted root store on all clients so that the client trusts the certificate.

The trouble is, there's no way to use any RDS tool to generate a self-signed certificate that meets those needs.

If you thought you'd be clever and use RD Gateway to generate a self-signed certificate (see Chapter 10, "Making Remote Desktop Services Available from the Internet," to learn how), you might at first think that you are successful. It will generate a self-signed certificate, and the name will be whatever you specify, but you can't export the private key. The result is that you will be able to import that certificate into the certificate store on the RD Session

Host server, but it won't be usable in RD Session Host Configuration because it's missing the private key. If the RD Gateway and one RD Session Host server in the farm were on the same machine (which is a bad idea, for reasons that are covered in Chapter 10), this would work for that server, but you couldn't use the farm certificate for any other servers in the farm, because when you imported the certificate, it would lack the private key.

Using SelfSSL.exe

RDS doesn't have any tools to help you create a self-signed farm certificate. However, the IIS6 Resource Kit *does* have a tool that will do this. You can download the II6 Resource Kit from *http://support.microsoft.com/kb/840671*. You're looking for the tool called SelfSSL.exe. Here's how to generate a self-signed farm certificate to test server authentication in a pilot deployment. Again, for production, you should get a certificate signed by a trusted CA. (You will get an error if you run SelfSSL on a machine that does not have IIS installed; however, the certificate will still be created and is usable.) There are three steps.

- Generate the certificate using the farm name.
- Export the certificate.
- Import the certificate on each server in the farm.

GENERATING THE CERTIFICATE

1. Open an elevated command prompt by right-clicking the command prompt icon in the Start menu and choosing Run As Administrator. Then navigate to the location of the SelfSSL.exe executable file with the following command.

   ```
   cd C:/Program Files/IIS Resources/SelfSSL
   ```

2. Type the command to create the certificate, filling in the name of your farm for *CN* (for example, farm.ash.local).

   ```
   selfssl.exe /N:CN=<farmname> /K:2048 /V:365 /T
   ```

3. When prompted to replace the SSL settings for site 1 (Y/N)? choose Y. You should get the following success message.

   ```
   The self-signed certificate was successfully assigned to site 1.
   ```

EXPORTING THE CERTIFICATE

1. Open an MMC, add the Certificates (computer) snap-in, and navigate to the Personal store. Here, you should see your certificate. Right-click the certificate and choose Export (shown in Figure 8-6).

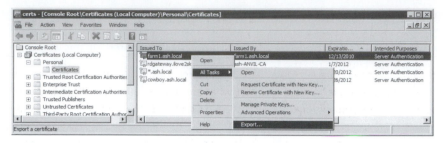

FIGURE 8-6 Use the Certificates MMC to export the certificate.

2. Click Next and then choose the option to export the private key and click Next again.

3. Choose the PFX format and click Next.

4. Add a password for the file and click Next.

5. Add a path and file name to export to, click Next, and then click Finish.

To use this certificate to test, it will need to be imported to the Personal Store on all RD Session Host servers in the farm, as well as to the Trusted Root Certification Authorities Store on the clients you use to test.

> **NOTE** The certificate will contain the private key, and normally you would not add this type of certificate to clients, which is another reason that this is for testing purposes only. If you would rather add a certificate to clients that does not have the private key, re-export the certificate without the private key and import that certificate to the clients.

IMPORT THE CERTIFICATE

1. Open an MMC, add the Certificates (computer) snap-in, and navigate to the Personal store. Right-click and choose Import...

2. Browse to where you stored your PKF file representing the certificate with the private key, choose the PKF format in the drop-down box (so you will be able to see your file), and then add your file.

3. Enter the password for the file and click Next.

4. Choose Place All Certificates In The Following Store. If Personal is not already chosen, select it, click Next, and then click Finish.

5. Repeat steps 1-4 for each test client but add the certificate to the Trusted Root Certification Authorities Store.

Authenticating Client Identity with Network Level Authentication (NLA)

Authenticating the server protects the client from connecting to a malicious RD Session Host server masquerading as a legitimate one, but what about protecting the RD Session Host server from malicious connections? As discussed in Chapter 3, "Deploying a Single Remote Desktop Session Host Server," the process of starting a connection—even just presenting a logon screen—requires the server to create many of the processes required to support a session (for example, Csrss.exe and Winlogon.exe). Session creation is expensive, so creating even this much of a session—only to be told that the user trying to access the RD Session Host server doesn't have the required credentials—is both a security vulnerability and a performance hit.

One way to reduce both the security hit and the performance hit is to enable connections only from computers that support NLA. NLA uses CredSSP to present user credentials to the server before the server has to create a session.

You might have noticed that when you connect to an RD Session Host server with the RDC 6.*x* or later client, you don't connect to the RD Session Host server logon screen to provide your credentials. Instead, a local dialog box pops up to take your credentials on the client (see Figure 8-7). This dialog box is the front end of CredSSP.

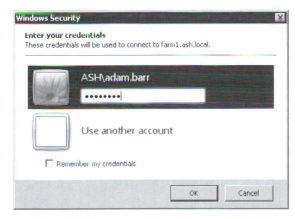

FIGURE 8-7 The Windows Security dialog box is the user interface for CredSSP.

When you type your credentials into this dialog box, even if you don't choose to save them, they go to the CredSSP, which then passes the credentials to the RD Session Host server via a secure channel. Only if the RD Session Host server accepts the credentials will it begin building a session for this user.

> **NOTE** You might also see NLA referred to as *front-side authentication*. It's the same thing, but with a different name.

On clients that support CredSSP and RDP 6.*x* and later, the clients will always use NLA if it's available. You can also configure the RD Session Host server to permit connections only from computers that support NLA, using Group Policy or on a per-server basis using RD Session Host Configuration. Because CredSSP, the technology that supports NLA, is part of the operating system rather than part of RDP, the client operating system must support CredSSP for NLA to work. Therefore, although there is an RDC 6.0 client available for Windows XP SP2, this doesn't enable Windows XP SP2 to use NLA. Clients running Windows XP SP3, Windows Vista, and Windows 7 all support CredSSP. Also, RDC will tell you if it supports NLA in the About screen. To see this, click the Computer icon in the upper-left corner of the RDC and choose About. The About screen will say if it supports NLA, as shown in Figure 8-8.

FIGURE 8-8 The RDC About screen will say if it supports NLA.

> **NOTE** You can also restrict Windows Vista and Windows 7 to accept connection requests only from clients that support NLA. To do so, go to Control Panel | System | Remote Settings. From the Remote tab of the System Properties dialog box, select the option restricting incoming connections to those that can support NLA.

Speeding Logons with Single Sign-on

Time spent typing credentials into a dialog box is wasted time, in the eyes of the user who is less concerned about system security than in getting work done. After all, security is not the user's job. It's acceptable to present credentials once to an RD Session Host server, but when you access multiple servers, it's much more irksome.

SSO enables domain-joined clients to store their credentials and present them automatically each time they connect to a new RD Session Host server. After you provide your user name and password once, you won't have to do so again as long as you're connecting via the same credentials. SSO saves credentials according to the resource you're connecting to, so connections to individual RD Session Host servers will still prompt you for credentials in a way that connecting to a farm via its farm name will not.

Configuring the Security Settings on the RD Session Host Server

The section entitled "Core Security Technologies" earlier in this chapter explained the details of using various connection security mechanisms. This section explains how to configure those settings using the RD Session Host Configuration and Group Policy.

 ON THE COMPANION MEDIA This resource kit also contains a script for configuring the security settings programmatically using Windows PowerShell. See the companion media for the script called Set-RDP-Security.ps1.

Configuring Connection Security Using RD Session Host Configuration

All per-server connection security settings are configured from the General tab of the protocol listener Properties dialog box. To get here, go to Administrative Tools | Remote Desktop Services | Remote Desktop Session Host Configuration and then double-click RDP-Tcp in the Connections section of the middle pane. The General tab is shown in Figure 8-9.

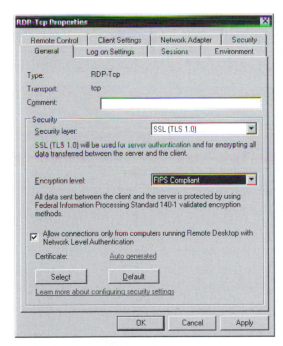

FIGURE 8-9 Edit connection security from the General tab of the RDP-Tcp listener Properties dialog box.

Configuring Encryption

All per-server connection security settings are configured from the General tab of the protocol listener Properties dialog box. To get here, go to Administrative Tools | Remote Desktop Services | Remote Desktop Session Host Configuration and then double-click RDP-Tcp in the Connections section of the middle pane. Set the encryption level. You must choose either High or FIPS-compliant encryption if you want to support server authentication. High encryption uses the strongest key strength of the server; FIPS-compliant encryption uses an encryption algorithm that has been tested by NIST.

> **NOTE** FIPS-compliant algorithms are not necessarily stronger than High security on all platforms; it depends on what's installed and what's been tested. The point of FIPS compliance is to serve as a policy measure for networks that must conform to these guidelines.

Configuring Server Authentication

Set the server authentication settings from the Security Layer section. The default is Negotiate, meaning that client and server will both use TLS for server authentication if it's supported. There's no real reason to mandate using RDP Security Layer, which does not support server authentication, but you can edit this setting to force server authentication using TLS. If the server can't be authenticated, then the client behavior can be set from the client RDP file settings configured on the Advanced tab of the RDC.

- Do Not Connect If Authentication Fails
- Warn Me If Authentication Fails
- Always Connect, Even If Authentication Fails

You can choose the certificate that the server should use to authenticate itself by clicking the Select button near the bottom of the screen. If you click Select, you can get more details about the certificate, including what it's used for, the name of the CA backing it, and when the certificate expires.

Configuring Network Level Authentication

To require the use of NLA for connecting to the RD Session Host server, select the appropriate check box on the General tab. Doing so will prevent any clients that do not support NLA (namely, any client running RDC prior to version 6.*x* and any operating system not supporting CredSSP) from connecting to the server. Only clients running Windows 7, Windows Vista, and Windows XP SP3 support CredSSP. NLA is not required by default.

If users are still prompted for their credentials, look at the Log On Settings tab of the RDP protocol. For credential caching to work, Always Prompt For Password should not be checked. By default, it isn't.

To require NLA connections to VMs running client SKUs, open the System item in the Control Panel and go to the Remote tab. In the Remote Desktop section, ensure that the option Allow Connections Only From Computers Running Remote Desktop With NLA (more secure) is selected.

Configuring Connection Security Using Group Policy

RD Session Host Configuration edits security settings for only a single server. To edit settings on multiple servers, you'll need to use Group Policy. Group Policy also includes security options not available through the RD Configuration graphical user interface (GUI).

Configuring Encryption Levels

To set the minimum encryption level, go to Computer Configuration | Policies | Administrative Templates | Windows Components | Remote Desktop Services | Remote Desktop Session Host | Security and then enable the Set Client Connection Encryption Level policy, choosing Low Level, High Level, or Client Compatible from the drop-down list.

- To require FIPS using Group Policy, go to Computer Configuration | Policies | Windows Settings | Security Settings, Local Policies | Security Options. Find The System Cryptography: Use FIPS Compliant Algorithms For Encryption, Hashing And Signing setting and enable it.

 CAUTION Enabling this policy causes the RD Session Host servers to use FIPS-compliant algorithms for *everything*, not just for RDP connections. Therefore, be aware that requiring FIPS can cause problems with some websites and applications that require inter-server communication.

Configuring Server Authentication

To configure server authentication policies, go to Computer Configuration | Policies | Administrative Templates | Windows Components | Remote Desktop Services | Remote Desktop Session Host | Security.

To require server authentication, enable the Require Use Of Specific Security Layer For Remote (RDP) Connections Group Policy object (GPO) and choose SSL (TLS 1.0) from the list of security layers. (RDP, you might recall, does not support authentication; choosing this option encrypts the traffic but does not authenticate the server.) If you leave the setting at Negotiate (the default), the clients will attempt to use TLS if they support it.

Group Policy allows you to control the template used for server authentication to make sure that the RD Session Host server presents the right one.

To do this, enable the Server Authentication Certificate Template GPO and provide the name of the template to use. If you do, then the server will choose only from among certificates using that template with a name matching the server name. If there's more than one certificate to choose among, the server will choose the certificate with the latest expiration date. If you've already specified a certificate to use for server authentication, the RD Session Host server will ignore this setting. To configure NLA via Group Policy, go to Computer Configuration | Policies | Administrative Templates | Windows Components | Remote Desktop Services | Remote Desktop Session Host | Security.

To require NLA, enable the Require User Authentication For Remote Connections By Using Network Level Authentication policy. Disabling or not configuring this policy means that NLA is not required.

Summary

Securing the server is important when the client is connected, but securing the connection protects the communication between server and client. In this chapter, you've learned how to protect the connection from interception, spoofed servers, and denial of service (DoS) attacks using connection security.

Some best practices for RDS connection security include the following.

- Use High or FIPS encryption if at all possible. Low encryption does not allow server authentication, so it should be used only when WAN accelerators require it.

- If using RDS only on the LAN, create a Kerberos farm identity rather than relying on certificates. Doing this will make it easier to enlarge the farm while still allowing server authentication.

- Use self-signed certificates only for testing, not in a production environment. Self-signed certificates, as the name indicates, are self-signed—they are not signed and validated by a trusted third party. Clients must have the same self-signed certificate placed in their Trusted Root Certification Authorities Store in order to trust the certificate.

- Require NLA both to prevent DoS attacks on the servers and speed farm connections, because NLA prevents the need to create a full session on the redirecting RD Session Host server.

Additional Resources

These resources contain additional information related to this chapter.

- If you need a refresher on Windows PowerShell support for Remote Desktop Services, see Chapter 1, "Introducing Remote Desktop Services."

- For more details on how client-server negotiations work, see Chapter 6, "Customizing the User Experience."

- For more information about CredSSP, see *http://www.wipo.int/pctdb/en/wo.jsp?IA=WO 2007033087&DISPLAY=DES* or *http://download.microsoft.com/download/9/5 /E/95EF66AF-9026-4BB0-A41D-A4F81802D92C/%5BMS-CSSP%5D.pdf*.

- For the details of how TLS is implemented in Windows Server 2008 R2, see *http://msdn.microsoft.com/en-us/library/dd207968(v=PROT.10).aspx*.

- For more about how the connection sequences work, see "Remote Desktop Protocol: Basic Connectivity and Graphics Remoting Specification," available for download from *http://msdn.microsoft.com/en-us/library/cc240445.aspx*.

- For a description of the Credential Security Support Provider (CredSSP) in Windows XP SP3, see *http://support.microsoft.com/kb/951608/*.

- Although a comparison of NTLM and Kerberos is outside the scope of this book, you can find the specifications for NTLM and Microsoft's implementation of Kerberos online at *http://msdn.microsoft.com/en-us/library/cc236622(v=PROT.10).aspx* (NTLM) and *http://msdn.microsoft.com/en-us/library/cc233855(v=PROT.10).aspx* (Kerberos).

Multi-Server Deployments

Previous chapters in this book have covered how to set up individual servers for very simple deployments of full desktops on one server (in Chapter 3, "Deploying a Single Remote Desktop Session Host Server") and a Remote Desktop (RD) Virtualization Host server for providing virtual machines (VMs; in Chapter 4, "Deploying a Single Remote Desktop Virtualization Host Server"). However, you haven't spent all this time learning about profile management with Remote Desktop Services (RDS) and how to configure client experience and security settings via Group Policy just to set up a single server. You'll need multiple servers for scale and redundancy.

In this chapter, you'll learn how to deliver VMs and RemoteApp programs from more than one server, including the following topics.

- Creating an RD Session Host farm
- Publishing applications from RemoteApp Manager
- Assigning applications to users
- Displaying resources from multiple farms and RD Virtualization host servers through RD Web Access
- Enabling users to discover RemoteApp programs, RD Session Host full desktop sessions, and VMs through the RD Web Access website and RemoteApp And Desktop Connections

Key Concepts for Multi-Server Deployments

When talking about multi-server deployments, it's helpful to make sure that everyone agrees on terminology.

RD Session Host Farms

An RD Session Host farm is a group of RD Session Host servers that are all delivering the same application set and are associated under the same farm name. For best results, all servers in a farm are assumed to have the same software: the same version of the operating system, the same updates, and the same versions of applications. This is important because connections to a farm are load-balanced across the entire farm. If the servers are different, users' experience will vary depending on which server they connect to, and this will confuse users and lead to Help desk calls. It's acceptable if the hardware in the farm varies a bit, as long as you take this into account when weighing the servers. A server that has only 75 percent of the capacity of other servers should have only 75 percent of the weight in load-balancing.

If you need to deliver more than one application set, you can do this with more than one farm. In Windows Server 2008 R2, RD Web Access, as well as RemoteApp and Desktop Connections (a new feature in Windows 7 and Windows Server 2008 R2), can be supplied with resources from more than one farm, or even individual RD Session Host servers.

RemoteApp Internals

RemoteApp programs are applications that run on the endpoint and display on the client but are displayed alongside the client-side applications. All RemoteApp programs running on the same computer run in the same session, although the desktop is not visible. This reduces the overhead on the servers and minimizes the number of copies of the profile that are open. (See Chapter 5, "Managing User Data in a Remote Desktop Services Deployment," for an explanation of why this is important.)

RemoteApp programs work a little differently from applications displayed from a full remote desktop because they must integrate with the locally installed applications. In essence, the server sends the entire desktop to the client, but you can't see the desktop. The client-side components create their own application windows to mirror those in the remote session and display them on the client.

Chapter 3 explains the processes and startup mechanism for a remote session. With RemoteApp programs, the process is a little different; the client and server must be even more closely aligned. When a client starts its first RemoteApp, the process works as illustrated in Figure 9-1.

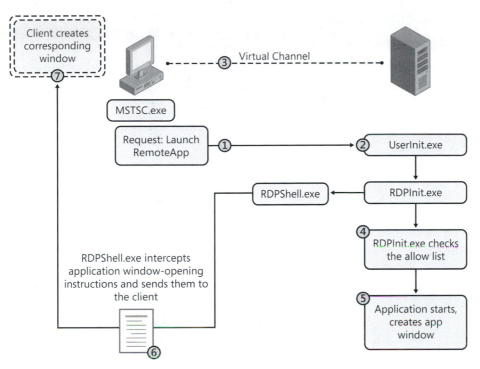

FIGURE 9-1 RemoteApp programs use a special shell to display application windows.

The following steps (numbered accordingly in Figure 9-1) explain this process.

1. The client connects to the server and starts a RemoteApp session (but does not yet start the application).

2. The session is created. Userinit.exe is started, and it in turn starts Rdpinit.exe. Rdpinit.exe manages Rdpshell.exe, the RemoteApp shell (in lieu of Windows Explorer).

3. The server-side and client-side components connect via a virtual channel used especially for RemoteApp communication.

4. Rdpinit.exe checks the allow list for the application. If the application is in the allow list, the RD Session Host server starts the application.

5. The application starts and creates an application window.

6. Rdpshell.exe intercepts the application window-opening instruction and sends it to the client.

7. The client creates a corresponding window to match the one on the RD Session Host server.

   From here, the user interacts with the remote session as usual.

As you can see, communication between the remote session and client is key to making this work. Let's explore RemoteApp components in more detail.

Server-Side Components

On the server, several components must cooperate to ensure the following.

- Only applications currently in the allow list can be started as RemoteApp programs.
- The client-side proxy window must open and close in sync with the invisible application window in the remote session.

The following components make this possible.

- Rdpinit.exe
- Rdpshell.exe
- Rdpdd.dll
- The application window

Figure 9-2 depicts how the RemoteApp components work together to create the user experience. For more information about the broader RD Session Host session architecture, see Chapter 3.

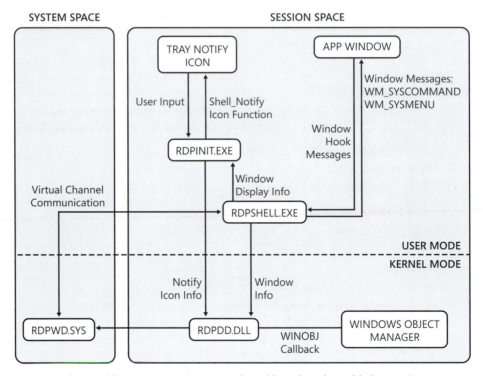

FIGURE 9-2 Server-side components in user mode and kernel mode enable RemoteApp programs.

Rdpinit.exe is the RemoteApp equivalent of Userinit.exe, which starts logon scripts and starts the user shell. Rdpinit.exe starts the Rdpshell.exe and updates the client-side taskbar via Rdpdd.dll. Rdpinit.exe also handles the logoff logic: When no more RemoteApp program application windows are open and no processes are running in the user session that haven't yet exited, Rdpinit.exe disconnects or logs off the session in accordance with the rules set in Group Policy. (You can't configure this setting on the RD Session Host server.)

The Group Policy object (GPO) setting that controls when a RemoteApp is logged off is Computer Configuration | Policies | Administrative Templates | Windows Components | Remote Desktop Services | Remote Desktop Session Host | Session Time Limits | Set Time Limit For Logoff Of RemoteApp Sessions. To set a time limit that RemoteApps will stay disconnected before they are logged off, enable this setting and then choose a time limit from the drop-down menu.

Rdpshell.exe is the shell, the RemoteApp equivalent of Explorer.exe. It keeps track of changes to application windows (for example, opening and closing) and sends them to the client-side components so that the application window visible to the client behaves exactly like the application window in the invisible shell. Rdpshell.exe also keeps track of any Connect/Disconnect/Reconnect events to the remote session, so the application window on the client side disappears or reappears as appropriate.

Rdpdd.dll is the kernel-mode Remote Display Protocol (RDP) display driver in the session. This component receives the Windowing and System Tray Icon notifications from Rdpinit.exe and Rdpshell.exe and updates the display accordingly. It also sends all display updates on the terminal server to the client.

Client-Side Components

On the client side, other components cooperate to make the RemoteApp visible on the desktop and update the application window in the remote session (see Figure 9-3). These components of the RDC client specific to RemoteApp programs include

- The RemoteApp plug-in
- The Windowing plug-in
- The input and drawing orders handlers
- The RemoteApp proxy window
- The Notify icon

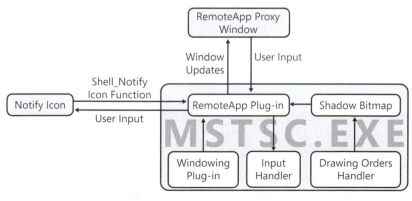

FIGURE 9-3 Client-side components help enable RemoteApp programs.

These components have the following jobs.

- The Windowing plug-in collects the window positioning information from the remote session and passes it to the RemoteApp plug-in.

- The drawing orders handler collects the window appearance information and feeds it to the shadow bitmap.

- The shadow bitmap sends bitmaps to the RemoteApp plug-in to draw the application window.

- The RemoteApp plug-in receives all the drawing and positioning information and collects all the input for that window to send back to the RD Session Host server. It also collects user feedback on the window state and position and sends it to the remote session to update the application window there.

The RemoteApp proxy window is the window for the RemoteApp; the Windowing plug-in positions it correctly, and the shadow bitmap draws it. The Notify icon displays the Remote-App program's icon in the taskbar.

RemoteApp Programs and Multiple Monitors

When a client has more than one monitor attached, RemoteApp programs might work a little differently, depending on whether they're displayed using monitor spanning (introduced in Windows Server 2008) or true multi-monitor support (introduced in Windows Server 2008 R2).

> **NOTE** Generating video display takes some processor power and memory on the RD Session Host server; the larger the display, the more power it takes. If every person using the RD Session host server uses lots of monitors, this could affect scale on the RD Session Host.

One of the new features of Windows Server 2008 was *monitor spanning*, wherein a session on a terminal server expanded to fit all the monitors connected to the client. When the client connects to the server using monitor spanning (for any monitor configuration), it tells the RDP display driver (Rdpdd.sys) the size of the monitor attached to it, adding the monitor resolutions together (see Figure 9-4). Rdpdd.sys accepts this and treats the multiple monitors as one big monitor. It isn't aware that multiple monitors are connected; it simply uses the size of the total display area, up to 4096 × 2048 pixels, to arrange windows. (If you exceed the total display area on your monitors, the display will only be up to 4096 × 2048.)

To enable monitor spanning, connect to the remote server by using the */span* option with Mstsc.exe: Type **mstsc.exe /span** in the Run box of the Start Menu or add the entry **span monitors:i:1** to the RDP connection file. In the absence of this entry, monitor spanning is disabled for desktop connections.

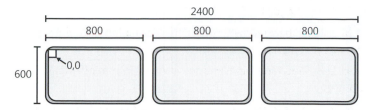

FIGURE 9-4 Individual monitors add up to a single large monitor sized 2400 × 600.

Because spanned monitors are seen by the RDP display driver as a single entity, there are some restrictions on configuration. First, all the monitors must be set to the same resolution, because to the server, they're all the same monitor. If you don't set all the monitors to the same resolution, then even if monitor spanning is enabled, the desktop will be confined to your primary monitor. Second, the monitors must be set up in a horizontal configuration, as in Figure 9-4; the spanning is intended to go from left to right. Third, the leftmost monitor must be the primary monitor so that both client and server start counting in the upper left as 0,0 when deciding how to arrange pixels on the screen.

One limitation of monitor spanning is that it really isn't a multi-monitor solution so much as a way to support a large display. The desktop extends across the entire space (meaning that you might want to use an odd number of monitors to avoid message boxes—which typically pop up in the middle of the screen—being split between two monitors). In addition, maximized applications maximize across the entire space, which can make them inconveniently wide. RemoteApp programs makes monitor spanning more multi-monitor-like by exploiting what it knows about the monitor window size to maximize applications to the monitor in which you've got them, and at the same time making it possible to move them around. For example, start Microsoft PowerPoint as a RemoteApp while two monitors are connected to your client. Both monitors are set to 1280 × 800. The newly started RemoteApp will appear maximized on Monitor 1. To move it, click the Restore Down button and drag the window to Monitor 2. When you maximize it again, the RemoteApp will appear in the confines of the second monitor instead of being spread across every monitor connected to the client. If you position a RemoteApp across two monitors, it will maximize the one in which more of its window is displayed, as shown in Figure 9-5.

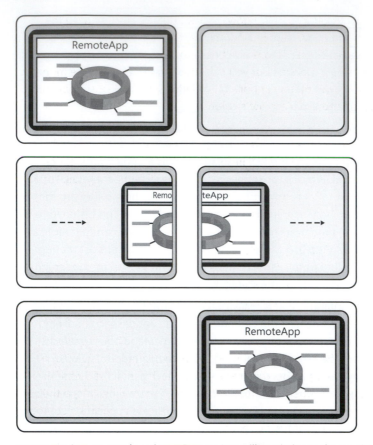

FIGURE 9-5 In a spanned session, a RemoteApp will maximize to the monitor on which more of its window is displayed.

How do RemoteApp programs know where to draw the application window? When running RemoteApp programs, as you modify the application window on the client (maximize it, minimize it, and so forth), these changes are sent to the application window on the RD Session Host server. Although the server doesn't know that there are multiple monitors, the client does. When you maximize a RemoteApp in a client-side monitor, it maximizes to the monitor on which you have it displayed. It then reports its new size to the remote application window. The result is that the application window is sized for a single monitor, not the entire spanned area.

If you are monitor spanning, before connecting to the RemoteApp, you have to configure the monitors on the client to the same resolution. If you don't, you will see some odd behavior. RemoteApp programs displayed on one monitor might "leak" into the display on another one. (For example, a File, Open menu might be partially displayed on Monitor 1 when the application's primary display is on Monitor 2.)

True multi-monitor support, introduced in Windows Server 2008 R2, doesn't have the limitations of spanning. The monitors are handled independently, so the arrangement doesn't matter to the display and the monitor resolutions don't have to match. RemoteApp programs display as though they're on a single monitor, but you can stretch them to fill all the monitors if you wish. Windows 7 has multiple monitor support, but Windows 7 does not support Aero when you are using multiple monitors in a remote session.

> **NOTE** Enable true multi-monitor support by using the running Mstsc.exe file with the */multimon* switch or by adding the Multimon:i:1 line of code to an RDP file. Your monitors must also be pre-setup in whatever configuration you want to use in the RDP session.

Creating and Deploying a Farm

Deploying a single RD Session Host server has some drawbacks. The company can outgrow the hardware capabilities of a single server, and losing that server means no one can work. Creating a server farm of identical RD Session Host servers provides a scalable and redundant application hosting platform.

A RD Session Host *server farm* consists of two or more RD Session Host servers with the same software configuration (for example, security settings and device redirection policies) and application sets, all represented under a single farm name so that they appear to the client as a single server. Server farms are load-balanced so that the workload is distributed evenly among all farm members. Because the servers are configured the same way, it does not matter to users which server they get directed to. All servers should provide the same user experience.

Even when RD Session Host servers are clustered into a farm, the final connection is always between a client and a single RD Session Host server. When you're connecting to individual servers, connecting is simple: The RDP file or RDC client points to a specific server, and assuming that the user is authorized to connect, the connection is made. There's no ambiguity about where the connection should go. A multi-server deployment adds a layer of complexity because the user session must be directed to a particular server—without the user needing to specify *which* server.

Without load-balancing, RD Session Host server load will not necessarily distribute evenly according to the number of connections coming in. The load-balancing has to be smart enough to take into account the possibility of disconnected sessions already running on RD Session Host servers, the load that each server is capable of handling as far as usage per session goes, and other factors. Therefore, you need two mechanisms to determine to which server a connection request should ultimately be sent:

- A way to take the initial connection requests and send them to a brokering mechanism designed to take into account variables specific to the farm environment
- A brokering mechanism that determines which farm server is best suited to accommodate the session ultimately and then sends the connection to the chosen server

The initial connection is handled by a load balancer or redirector. The brokering is handled by a RDS role service called RD Connection Broker. Read on to learn more about each of these mechanisms.

Distributing Initial Farm Connections

Clients don't talk to the RD Connection Broker role service directly; they connect to a farm, which sends this connection to the RD Connection Broker to let it find the right endpoint. When a user connects to a farm, the connection is intercepted by an RD Session Host server farm member and is redirected to the RD Connection Broker. If there are a lot of incoming connections, you can distribute them via software load-balancing among RD Session Host servers in the farm. Alternatively, you can dedicate an RD Session Host server to only redirect farm requests, not to support user connections as well.

There are three in-box ways to distribute the incoming connections via software to avoid overloading a single farm member with redirection requests: round robin DNS (RR DNS), Network Load Balancing (NLB), and a dedicated redirector.

> **NOTE** Because hardware load balancers are not included with RDS, this chapter will not cover them, but they are an option. Remember that a hardware load balancer is a single point of failure unless you buy redundant hardware.

RR DNS creates multiple host records for the same host name. Each time a request for that host name is made, the Domain Name System (DNS) server returns the host records in consecutive order. It's easy to set this up. The catch to this method is that, if a host goes offline, DNS continues routing people to that server as long as the host record remains in its database.

NLB distributes incoming connections evenly across each load-balanced server on the principle that if the incoming requests are evenly distributed, the traffic should be, too. NLB is best for load-balancing servers when the connections are very short, like web servers, or in this case, the initial connection in a farm that is participating in RD Connection Broker load-balancing. NLB is more complicated to set up than RR DNS, but it's capable of detecting when a server is no longer available and will not attempt to send connections to it.

A dedicated redirector is an RD Session Host server whose sole role is to redirect initial connection requests to RD Connection Broker. To avoid asking working RD Session Host farm servers to handle incoming connections, you can dedicate a server to do this work. The only catch to using a dedicated redirector is that it represents a single point of failure.

Choosing Between RR DNS or NLB for Initial Routing

Both RR DNS and NLB come with Windows Server 2008 R2. Which should you use?

RR DNS is very easy to set up, but it has two limitations: One is that client-side DNS caching can result in clients resolving DNS requests with cached records instead of receiving a reply from the DNS server. This means that RR DNS is bypassed completely. Second, RR DNS does not know when a server goes offline, so it will continue to reply to requests with the host record of the unavailable server, resulting in 30-second delays for clients who receive this reply.

For these reasons, you might choose to use NLB, which distributes incoming connections evenly across the load-balanced servers. Although NLB is not ideal for load-balancing among RD Session Host servers, it's fine for creating the initial connections, because they don't last long. NLB does not rely on DNS the way that RR DNS does, so it does not have a problem with cached DNS entries. NLB also detects when a server in the cluster goes offline and will stop sending requests to the downed server.

You will learn how to implement the initial load-balancing options in the section entitled "Deploying RD Session Host Farms" later in this chapter.

Connection Brokering in a Farm Scenario

That's the load-balancing part. The brokering part comes in when it matters where the incoming connection goes. For web services, for example, if you're connecting to a server, it really doesn't matter which one you connect to, because your connection retains no state and won't last very long. For RD Session Host server sessions, though, it matters a great deal. For instance, it's far better for you to maintain all connections belonging to the same user on a single server—and in a single session—for the following reasons.

- Only one copy of your profile will be open (see Chapter 4 for more details).
- The overhead on the RD Session Host servers will be reduced because session creation is expensive and there's a minimum set of processes needed to support an RDS session (see Chapter 3 for more details).

With NLB, you can define affinity for a particular server so that all incoming requests from an Internet Protocol (IP) address or class of IP addresses will go to a particular server, but this isn't quite what's wanted either. Many connections coming from behind a firewall, for example, could all appear to be from one address—the firewall's IP address. The result would be one server having to deal with all those connections. You really need a brokering option that can answer two questions about incoming connections and route connections accordingly.

- Does the user attempting to make this connection already have a session open on an RD Session Host server in the farm?

- If not, which server has the lowest number of sessions?

RD Connection Broker makes those decisions about how to distribute incoming connections to a farm.

You learned about RD Connection Broker with Virtual Desktop Infrastructure (VDI) in Chapter 4. In terms of pooled and personal VMs, RD Connection Broker communicates with VDI servers and with Active Directory Domain Services (AD DS) to collect data about pooled and personal VMs that are available for connection. RD Connection Broker determines the kind of connection a user is requesting, finds the right endpoint for the request, and keeps track of client connections to personal and pooled VMs. For RDS farm scenarios, RD Connection Broker provides

- Session-based load-balancing, which evenly distributes RDS sessions to servers in the farm according to the server capabilities and the number of connections it's hosting

- Session reconnection, reconnecting users to their disconnected sessions

- Session draining, slowly draining sessions from an RD Session Host server that must go offline (for example, due to maintenance needs) by not allowing new connections to the server

- Access to multiple RemoteApp sources via RD Web Access

RD Connection Broker can run on any version of Windows Server 2008 R2 that supports RDS. The servers connected to it can run Windows Server 2003 or later. That said, servers running Windows Server 2003 can take advantage of the session reconnection feature, but cannot be part of a load-balanced farm. Clients need a minimum of RDC 5.2 to use RD Connection Broker Load Balancing.

As described in Chapter 4, the RD Connection Broker is made flexible through a model of plug-ins to the base brokering mechanism. Different types of resources have their own resource plug-ins that contain the logic required to find the most appropriate target for that type of connection and to prepare for connection. For example, the Session Plug-in load-balances based on the number of sessions on each RD Session Host server. Independent software vendors (ISVs) can change the logic for finding and preparing the endpoints by implementing filter plug-ins to the resource plug-ins, or they can make RD Connection Broker support entirely new types of resources by adding their own resource plug-ins.

RDS Farm Connection Brokering in Action

Each RDC request for a farm goes through these steps to reach its final destination server (see Figure 9-6).

1. The client requests a connection to an RD Session Host server farm. A load balancer finds a redirector to handle the initial connection and to redirect the connection to the RD Connection Broker.

2. The user authenticates to that RD Session Host server. If the client supports NLA (see Chapter 7, "Molding and Securing the User Environment"), this reduces the overhead on the RD Session Host server by authenticating the user without creating a session.

3. The RD Session Host server that received the incoming connection (henceforth called the redirector) passes the contents of the RDP file to the RD Connection Broker.

4. RD Connection Broker examines the RDP data to find the desired type of connection. If it's for a session, it activates the RD Session Host resource plug-in. This plug-in first determines whether there's already a session in the farm for this user. It does this by checking its database, which stores the information shown in Table 9-1. If so, the plug-in can tell which server it's on and what the Session ID is.

> **NOTE** It can also tell whether the session is displaying a full desktop or RemoteApp programs. This is important because the two sessions have different shells.

If the user does not already have an active session, the RD Connection Broker finds the server that contains the fewest active sessions. RD Connection Broker sends the result of its efforts (which includes the IP address of the RD Session Host server that the client should connect to) to the redirector.

5. The redirector sends the IP address to the client.

6. The client silently disconnects from the RD Session Host that redirected the connection and reconnects to the RD Session Host server using that IP address.

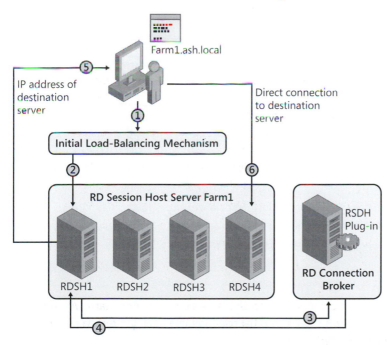

FIGURE 9-6 Connection requests get directed to RD Session Host servers using RD Connection Broker.

TABLE 9-1 Routing Information Stored by RD Connection Broker

RD CONNECTION BROKER DB FIELD	DESCRIPTION
Source-server-ID	Name of the server that the session resides on.
Session-ID	Session ID for the session.
Username	User name of the user logged on to the session.
Domain	Domain to which the user belongs.
TS-Protocol	Protocol used to connect the session. This will be RDP.
Session-creation-date-and-time	Time and date the session was created.
Disconnection-date-and-time	Time and date that the session was disconnected (if applicable).
Application-type	Session type (displaying desktop or RemoteApp programs).
Resolution-width	The resolution width of the RDP session (for example, 1024).
Resolution-height	The resolution height of the RDP session (for example, 768).
Color-depth	The color depth in the session.

HOW IT WORKS

RD Connection Broker Routing Methods

RD Connection Broker can support two kinds of load-balancing redirection: IP address redirection and routing token redirection. RR DNS and NLB use IP address redirection; hardware load balancers such as Cisco's Content Switching Module might use routing token redirection.

IP address redirection, used when clients can connect directly to servers in the farm, is the default for RD Connection Broker. It works like this.

1. The client connects to the initial load balancer and is routed to an RD Session Host server, where the client is authenticated. If the client supports NLA, the client doesn't have to create a full session to be authenticated, speeding up the process.

2. The RD Session Host server redirects the connection request to the RD Connection Broker.

3. The RD Connection Broker finds the most suitable endpoint for the connection request and gets its IP address.

4. RD Connection Broker returns the answer to the RD Session Host server, which passes the encrypted load-balance packet to the client. The packet contains the IP address of the chosen RD Session Host server.

5. The client connects directly to the RD Session Host server IP address specified in the load-balance packet.

When the load-balancing configuration requires that all initial traffic go through the load balancer, clients can't connect using IP addresses. In that case, the load balancer must support RD Connection Broker routing tokens. Clients get routed to the appropriate RD Session Host server like this.

1. The client connects to the initial load balancer and is routed to an RD Session Host server, where the client is authenticated.

2. The RD Session Host server queries the RD Connection Broker for the RD Session Host server to which this client should be redirected.

3. RD Connection Broker returns the answer to the RD Session Host server.

4. The RD Session Host server tells the client to connect again to the load balancer, but this time, it gives the client a routing token to give to the load balancer.

5. The routing token contains the IP address of the chosen RD Session Host server.

6. The client connects directly to the RD Session Host server IP address specified in the routing token.

You might be wondering how RD Connection Broker keeps track of the RD Session Host servers. What happens if one goes offline, and how will the RD Connection Broker know if it does? For that matter, what will it do if a server goes offline?

To keep track of RD Session Host server status, the RD Connection Broker keeps track of whether the connections that it redirects to the RD Session Host servers in the farm actually go through. If a redirection attempt succeeds, that's great—the RD Session Host server is available. If a redirection attempt fails, then there *might* be a problem with the RD Session Host server or the network—but it's not definite, because there was only one attempt. Therefore, 60 seconds after the initial redirection request, the RD Connection Broker starts pinging the RD Session Host server that didn't respond. If the RD Session Host server does not respond to a set number of pings (a default of 3, at a default interval of 10 seconds apart) then the RD Connection Broker removes that RD Session Host server from its database.

This back-and-forth means that, about two to three minutes from the time the RD Connection Broker attempts to send a connection to an unavailable RD Session Host server, the RD Connection Broker will stop looking for the server. Removing an RD Session Host server from the farm by deleting it from the TS Session Directory Computers group will not delete it from the RD Connection Broker's database.

If you take a server offline, you can speed up the process of purging the database by shortening the intervals at which it looks for the RD Session Host server. These are controlled by three registry keys located under HKLM/SYSTEM/CurrentControlSet/Services/Tssdis /Parameters in the RD Connection Broker's registry. Conveniently, all these values are in decimal, so they're easy to interpret. The three that you need to concern yourself with are the following.

- TimeBetweenPings (default value of 78 hexidecimal, or 120 seconds)
- NumberFailedPingsBeforePurge (default value is 3)
- TimeServerSilentBeforePing (default value is 60; the value is in seconds)

To decrease or increase the interval between when RD Connection Broker attempts to connect and when it purges the RD Session Host server from the database, edit these settings. Just be aware that a connection problem or the server being offline isn't the only reason why an RD Session Host server might not respond.

 ON THE COMPANION MEDIA You can use the SBDatabaseDump.vbs script found on the companion media to dump the contents of the RD Connection Broker database. Just edit as needed for your deployment.

How NLA Speeds RD Connection Broker Routing

Munindra Das
Software Development Engineer II

Before Windows Server 2008, when a terminal server in a farm received a connection request, it created a temporary session to authenticate the user and load user policies. If no local disconnected session was present, it queried the TS Session Directory to see if there was a disconnected session for the user on another computer in the farm. If a disconnected session was found, a redirection request was sent to the client to connect to the other server instead. The temporary session was then discarded.

The temporary session creation resulted in significant delay in completing the connection because a full logon occurs in the session. Also, the user experience was unpleasant because the user saw two welcome screens, first for the temporary session and then again for the redirected session. The new technique addresses these drawbacks when a connection is made using the new RDC client with CredSSP.

Windows Server 2008 introduced a new technique to improve the redirection scenario. Clients that support NLA can pass their credentials to the terminal server (now the RD Session Host server). The RD Session Host server (acting as a redirector) hosting the temporary connection can use those credentials to authenticate that the user is allowed to log on to the farm and can pass those credentials to the RD Connection Broker to help it look for an existing connection associated with those credentials. If RD Connection Broker finds a disconnected session on another computer in the farm, it immediately sends a redirect packet to the client, and the client subsequently connects to the redirected server. Hence, no temporary session is created before the connection is redirected. This change improves security because the client must be authenticated even before it makes the connection, and it also improves performance because the first RD Session Host server doesn't have to create a temporary session.

It's also worth mentioning that users will get an error if they try to access individual farm members from a client computer by connecting to an individual server name. However, a client can still access individual farm servers by IP address (the client will get warnings about the IP address not being the name of the server, but eventually, the user would be allowed to connect). To stop this, enforce Server Authentication on the clients by using the following GPO.

Computer Configuration | Policies | Administrative Templates | Windows Components | Remote Desktop Services | Remote Desktop Connection Client | Configure Server Authentication For Client

Enable the policy and choose Do Not Connect If Authentication Fails from the drop-down menu. Then click Ok to save the changes and apply the GPO to the organizational unit (OU) where client computers reside.

> **NOTE** Administrators can access RD Session Host servers by server name even if they are part of a farm.

Deploying RD Session Host Farms

Technically, you could create a farm using only RR DNS or NLB, but this farm wouldn't use a kind of load-balancing suitable for longer connections and can't inform RD Web Access of its resources. To create a load-balanced RD Session Host server farm that can deliver a list of resources to RD Web Access, you must do the following.

- Install the RD Connection Broker role service.
- Allow RD Session Host servers to join RD Connection Broker.
- Set up initial load-balancing among the RD Session Host servers so they can route temporary sessions to RD Connection Broker.
- Configure the RD Session Host servers join a farm.

Chapter 4 explains how to install the RD Connection Broker role service, which you need to do because you must have a connection broker to deliver pooled and personal VMs. To perform the additional setup, read on.

Permit RD Session Host Servers to Join RD Connection Broker

Installing the RD Connection Broker creates a new local security group named Session Broker Computers. You must add RD Session Host servers to this group to permit them to work with the RD Connection Broker. To do so, open Server Manager, expand Configuration/Local Users And Groups/Groups, and then double-click the Session Broker Computers security group in the right pane. On the Members tab, click Add, type the RD Session Host server computer accounts, and click OK twice.

The same RD Connection Broker can support multiple farms, so all RD Session Host servers will go into the same security group.

> **NOTE** If the RD Connection Broker server is also a domain controller, you can't use Server Manager to add RD Session Host servers to the Session Directory Computers group; use Active Directory Users And Computers to do this instead.

Set Up Initial Load-Balancing

Set up RR DNS or NLB to distribute incoming initial connections evenly across the farm.

RR DNS

Setting up RR DNS is very easy: Just add a DNS host entry for the farm name that points to each server in the farm. For example, one of our farms consists of two servers, whose DNS entries map to the following IP addresses.

```
Fuji.ash.local = 10.10.10.110
Glacier.ash.local = 10.10.10.112
```

To implement RR DNS, add two more host entries pointing to the corresponding IP addresses as follows.

```
Farm1.ash.local = 10.10.10.110
Farm1.ash.local = 10.10.10.112
```

> **NOTE** If you use RR DNS, you should also lower the Time To Live (TTL) of the DNS entries so the DNS cache on the clients gets updated frequently. This will cut down on clients bypassing RR DNS completely or possibly trying to access a dead server. To change the TTL on DNS entries in DNS Manager click View, Advanced. Then right click the DNS entry, select Properties, lower the TTL value, and click OK.

NLB

To avoid problems with stale DNS entries, you might decide to implement NLB. To configure an NLB cluster, you need to complete the following steps.

1. If you have a network adapter dedicated to NLB, you need to configure it.
2. Install the NLB Manager on a host node or other management machine.
3. Configure the NLB cluster.
4. Add a DNS entry mapping the farm name to the cluster IP address.

Before Windows Server 2008, it was advised to use two network adapters on each cluster member: one for NLB traffic and one for other traffic. If you used only one network adapter per host in Unicast mode, one host could not communicate with another—each server would see itself as both the initiating and destination computer. Beginning with Windows Server 2008, however, NLB was re-engineered so that implementing NLB in Unicast mode on one network adapter now allows for host-to-host communication. So now you have a choice: You can use one network adapter for all communication, or you can limit NLB traffic to its own network adapter. In our implementation example, you will use two network adapters: one reserved for NLB traffic and one for other traffic (like remote administration).

> **IMPORTANT** Using two network adapters turns off per-session IP virtualization on RD Session Host servers, so if you need to use per-session IP Virtualization, then use one network adapter for NLB. Per-program IP virtualization is not affected by two network adapters.

CONFIGURE THE NLB NETWORK ADAPTER

Configure the NLB network adapter with a unique IP address and an appropriate subnet mask. The NLB network adapter does not need a gateway address because the traffic is not going to leave the network.

> **NOTE** If your RD Session Host Servers are virtualized and you choose to operate in Unicast mode, be sure to enable media access control (MAC) address spoofing on the NLB network adapter or hosts will not converge. For more on MAC address spoofing on virtual adapters, see "Configure MAC Address Spoofing for Virtual Network Adapters" at *http://technet.microsoft.com/en-us/magazine/ff458341.aspx.*

INSTALL NLB MANAGER

Next, you need to install the Network Load Balancing feature on each farm member. To do this, open Server Manager and select the Features section. Click Add Features, select the check box next to Network Load Balancing, and click Install.

You can also install the Network Load Balancing feature using Windows PowerShell using this command.

```
Import-Module Servermanager
add-Windows FeatureNLB
```

A successful install renders these results.

```
Success Restart Needed Exit Code Feature Result
------- -------------- --------- --------------
True    No             Success   {Network Load Balancing}
```

CONFIGURE THE NLB CLUSTER

Now that NLB is installed on each farm member, it's time to configure the cluster. To do so, follow these steps.

1. Open NLB Manager on one of the farm members from Start, All Programs, Administrative Tools, Network Load Balancing Manager or by typing **nlbmgr** in the Run text box on the Start menu. Right-click Network Load Balancing Clusters and choose New Cluster, as shown in Figure 9-7.

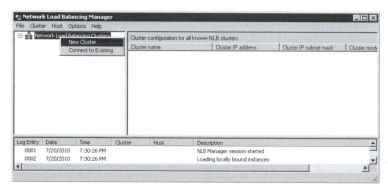

FIGURE 9-7 Open NLB Manager and create a new cluster.

2. In the Host input box, enter the name of one of the NLB hosts (one of the RD Session Host server farm members) and click Connect. All available network adapters on that server show up in the lower pane. Select the NLB dedicated network adapter that you have configured to use with load-balancing and click Next.

3. The IP address and subnet mask assigned to the network adapter will show up in the next window. The priority number is a unique number that differentiates the servers. Accept the default value. If you need to make any changes to the address, click Edit and make your changes. Leave the Initial Host State as Started, and click Next.

4. On the next screen, click Add and add a unique IP address and subnet mask that will be shared by all cluster members, and then click OK. When users request access to the farm, they will be sent to this address instead of a specific RD Session Host server ad-

dress. The address will appear in the Cluster IP address window, as shown in Figure 9-8. Click Next.

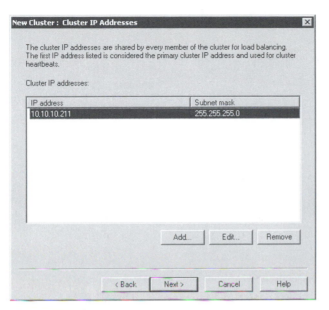

FIGURE 9-8 Add a unique cluster IP address and subnet mask.

5. On the Cluster Parameters page, accept the defaults, including Unicast for the Cluster Operation Mode setting, and click Next. All cluster host adapters must use the same operation mode or NLB will not function.

6. On the New Cluster: Port Rules page, you need to make a few changes to the default settings. Click Edit, and then change the starting and ending port range to 3389 (in both the To and From fields) because you will be using this cluster to load-balance RDP traffic only. In the Protocols section, select TCP. In the Filtering Mode section, choose Multiple Hosts to allow multiple hosts to handle traffic for this port rule. For Affinity, you have three choices.

- **None**   Multiple connections coming from the same IP address can be spread among the farm members.

- **Single**   Choosing this option gives affinity to connections coming from the same IP address; they will be terminated on the same farm member.

- **Network**   Choosing this option means that client connections within the same Class C address space are terminated on the same server.

Choose Affinity: None so that incoming connections can be sent to any member of the farm. (There's no reason to set affinity when the connections are being redirected, and doing so could make your load-balancing efforts useless by sending repeated connection requests to the same server.) Then click OK. Figure 9-9 shows these changes.

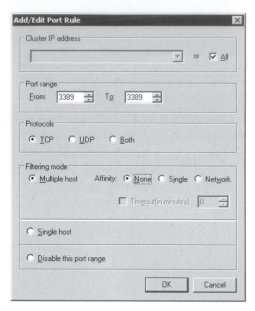

FIGURE 9-9 Change the port range, protocol, and filtering mode.

DIRECT FROM THE FIELD

NLB Cluster Operation Modes

Russ Kaufmann
Clustering MVP

When configuring an NLB cluster, you will have several options, one of which is to choose Unicast or Multicast mode.

Unicast uses a virtual MAC address, which is used instead of the physical MAC address (which is hard-coded on the network adapter) for all traffic that is covered by the port rules in the NLB configuration. Multicast adds the virtual MAC address and the physical MAC address on the network adapter. Multicast uses both the virtual MAC and the physical MAC addresses. Using both the virtual and the physical MAC addresses allows NLB members to communicate with each other as well as clients.

In both Unicast and Multicast, the virtual MAC is being used by multiple computers. If there are multiple servers using the same MAC address, a switch is not able to learn the port for the virtual MAC and is forced to send the packets destined for the virtual MAC to all ports of a switch. This is called *switch port flooding*. To limit the impact of network switch port flooding, you can use the following solutions.

- Create a virtual local area network (VLAN) for all your NLB servers.

- Use a hub or dumb switch for all your NLB servers and then connect the device to the rest of the network.

- Use Multicast mode and configure static mapping for the NLB cluster nodes in the switch so that it floods only the mapped ports instead of the entire switch.

- Use port mirroring so that all ports involved in the NLB cluster mirror each other.

In earlier versions of Windows, Unicast required two network adapters per NLB member so that one network adapter could be used for NLB traffic and the other network adapter could be used to manage the servers and used for any intra-cluster network needs, such as copying files between the nodes. Multicast mode was often used when only a single network adapter was available, because it would allow easier management of the servers and would also allow for intra-cluster communication by using the physical MAC. In Windows Server 2008 R2, there is no longer an issue with Unicast mode so that it needs a second network adapter in each node.

Multicast mode can have some support issues, such as the following.

- Multicast mode will multicast non-multicast (class D range) addresses, and many network devices don't support it.

- The CPU load on some network adapters can increase by 5 percent or more when handling Multicast traffic as opposed to Unicast traffic.

- Some routers might not support multicast addresses in their ARP implementation, so default NLB cluster access is limited to its own subnet. In these cases, you would need to create a static Address Resolution Protocol (ARP) entry in the router.

- Some routers don't support mapping the cluster (Unicast IP address) IP address to a multicast MAC address.

Because Unicast works well when using a single network adapter and does not have the supportability issues with Multicast, it is generally considered to be the best solution for NLB implementations.

ADD FARM DNS ENTRY

Now that you have NLB set up, you are ready to provide access to the farm via the cluster IP address. Set up a DNS host entry to map the IP address to the farm fully qualified domain name (FQDN). For example, you would map farm1.ash.local to 10.10.10.211 (the cluster IP address).

Configuring a Dedicated Redirector

If you have designated a dedicated redirector, you no longer need an initial load-balancing mechanism. The RDS farm connection brokering steps shown earlier in Figure 9-6 are slightly different in this scenario, as shown in Figure 9-10.

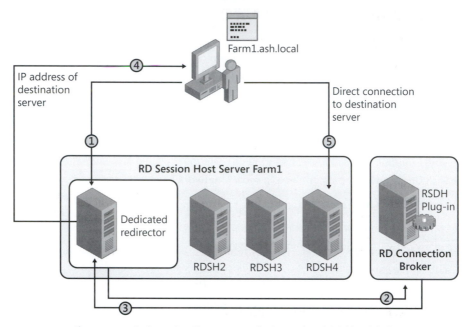

FIGURE 9-10 If you use a dedicated redirector, you don't need an initial load-balancing mechanism.

To configure a dedicated redirector for load-balancing initial RD Session Host server farm connections, you must do the following.

1. Give the RD Session Host server permission to join the RD Connection Broker.

2. Configure the RD Session Host server to become a dedicated redirector.

3. Add a DNS entry that maps the farm name to the IP address of the RD Session Host server that becomes a redirector.

First, add the RD Session Host server to the Session Broker Computers Group on the RD Connection Broker and then perform the following steps.

1. On the RD Session Broker computer, open RD Session Host Configuration. Open the RD Connection Broker Properties window by double-clicking the Member Of RD Connection Broker link located in the Edit Settings window.

2. Click Change Settings, and choose Dedicated Farm Redirection in the RD Connection Broker settings window.

3. Enter the FQDN of the RD Connection Broker Server, and the FQDN of the farm name in the corresponding input boxes at the bottom of the screen. Then click OK. You should get the pop-up message shown in Figure 9-11. (As the administrator, you can still connect to the server with a /admin connection.)

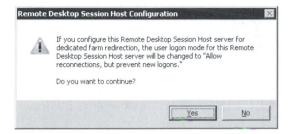

FIGURE 9-11 A dedicated redirector doesn't support user sessions, just incoming connection requests.

4. Add domain users to the Remote Desktop Users group on this server if they aren't already members. Even though people won't run sessions on this server, they must be able to connect to it.

5. On your DNS server, add a DNS host entry that maps the farm FQDN to the dedicated redirector's IP address.

Join RD Session Host Servers to a Farm

You can join RD Session Host servers to a farm via Remote Desktop Session Host Configuration, Group Policy, or Windows PowerShell.

Using Remote Desktop Session Host Configuration to Join a Farm

To join a farm using Remote Desktop Session Host Configuration, perform the following steps.

1. Open the tool on the RD Session Host server. Double-click the Member Of A Farm In RD Connection Broker setting listed in the Edit Settings window. The RD Connection Broker Properties tab will appear, as shown in Figure 9-12.

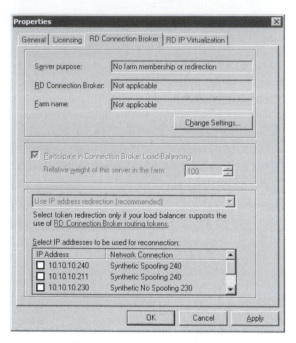

FIGURE 9-12 You can join a server to a farm from the RD Connection Broker properties tab in RD Session Host Configuration.

2. Click Change Settings. In the resulting RD Connection Broker Settings window, you specify how this RD Session Host server will interact with RD Connection Broker—that is, what the relationship is. Choose Farm Member and then enter the RD Connection Broker server FQDN and the farm name in the input boxes, as shown in Figure 9-13.

FQDN is a hierarchical naming format used with DNS to denote the location of a computer or resource in the DNS tree hierarchy. It's a good idea to use the DNS name for the farm, not its NetBIOS name, even though NetBIOS names will work for simple deployments. It's a form of planning ahead, because you must use the FQDN if any of the following conditions apply.

- You want to use DNS for name resolution (for example, if you're using IPv6, which WINS does not support).

- The farm certificate uses the FQDN in either the Subject or Subject Alternative Name fields.

- You want to use Kerberos authentication, not NTLM.

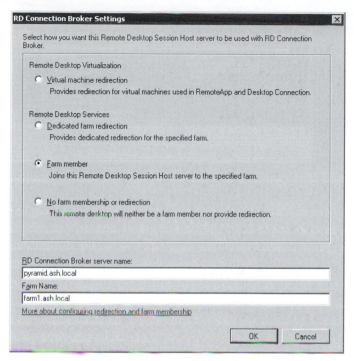

FIGURE 9-13 Add the RD Connection Broker server name and the farm name.

> **NOTE** For information on creating a Kerberos identity for an RD Session Host server farm, see *http://blogs.msdn.com/b/rds/archive/2009/05/20/creating-kerberos-identity-for-rd-session-host-farms-part-i-using-the-remote-desktop-services-provider-for-windows-powershell.aspx*.

3. Click OK and you will be back on the RD Connection Broker Properties tab. The check box next to Participate in Connection Broker Load Balancing is selected by default. Leave it selected.

4. Choose the relative weight of this farm server. The weight describes its capacity relative to the other RD Session Host servers in the farm. Although all RD Session Host servers should be configured identically, not all will necessarily have the same amount of memory or the same number of processor cores. For example, if a server is only 75 percent as powerful as other servers in the farm, then you can reduce its weight to allow it only 75 percent as many connections as the other servers. The default value is 100.

5. Also by default, the redirection method—how a client connects to the RD Session Host server once RD Connection Broker decides which server should accomodate the connection—is set to Use IP Address Redirection. If the initial load balancer allows clients to connect directly to RD Session Host servers in the farm, keep this default setting.

> **NOTE** Unless you know otherwise, always use IP address redirection. Some initial load-balancing configurations require all RD Session Host server traffic to be routed through the initial load balancer. Therefore, clients do not communicate directly with RD Session Host servers in the farm because they won't know their IP addresses. Instead, they talk to the load balancer, and the load balancer passes the communication to the appropriate RD Session Host server. In these situations, the load balancer must use routing token redirection instead of IP address redirection.

6. In the bottom section of this page, select the IP address that will be used for reconnections to this server.

> **NOTE** If you have more than one network adapter that you want to use, you can choose them all by checking the box next to each network adapter.

7. Click OK to apply the settings.

Perform this process for each member of the farm, taking care to use the same farm name and the same redirection method on all farm members.

Using Group Policy to Join a Farm

It's hard to keep the settings consistent if you're managing farm membership settings on each RD Session Host server. If you mistype the farm name on an RD Session Host server, for example, you'll create a new farm and that server will not be load-balanced with the other RD Session Host servers that you had intended to group it with. Assuming you have AD DS, the easiest way to configure an RD Session Host server farm and RD Connection Broker load balancing is to use Group Policy. The settings are located in Computer Configuration | Policies | Administrative Templates | Windows Components | Remote Desktop Services | Remote Desktop Session Host | RD Connection Broker.

Create a GPO and apply it to the organizational unit (OU) where the RD Session Host servers reside. Set the policies as described here.

- **Join RD Connection Broker** Enable this setting to join the RD Session Host servers to the farm specified in the RD Connection Broker Server Name policy setting.
- **Use RD Connection Broker Load Balancing** Enable this setting and the RD Session Host servers will participate in RD Connection Broker Load Balancing.

- **Configure RD Connection Broker Farm Name**   Enable this setting and specify a farm name. Because the GPO is applied to an OU holding the RD Session Host servers, all RD Session Host servers will know this farm name.

- **Configure RD Connection Broker Server Name**   Enable this setting and type the IP address or the FQDN of the server where RD Connection Broker is installed. RD Session Host servers in the farm will be serviced by this RD Connection Broker. Again, the FQDN is recommended.

- **Use IP Address Redirection**   Enable this setting unless your initial load balancer solution requires token-based redirection.

Any of these policy settings, if not configured or disabled, can be configured using RD Session Host Configuration on a per-service basis, although the settings in Group Policy take precedence if there is a conflict. One exception to this rule is the Join RD Connection Broker policy setting; if it is disabled in Group Policy, it cannot be configured via RD Session Host Configuration. If settings are configured via Group Policy, then the options to configure them in RD Session Host Configuration are dimmed, as shown in Figure 9-14.

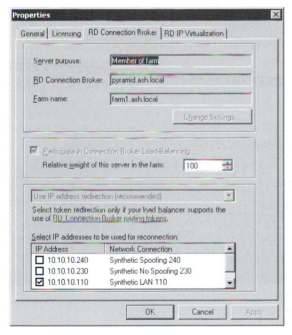

FIGURE 9-14 Configuring the RD Session Host server to join a farm via Group Policy blocks the ability to edit these settings in RD Session Host Configuration.

Using Windows PowerShell to Join a Farm

On an RD Session Host server farm member, open an elevated Windows PowerShell prompt and then do the following.

1. First, import the Remote Desktop Services Module with the following command.

   ```
   Import-module remotedesktopservices
   ```

2. Set the location to RDS with the following command.

   ```
   set-location rds:
   ```

3. Navigate to the RD Connection Broker settings directory with the following command.

   ```
   cd rdsconfiguration\ConnectionBrokerSettings
   ```

When you configure a server to join an RD Connection Broker server farm, all the settings to do so need to be run in one line of code. Therefore, you need to know what settings to specify beforehand. To know what items you will be setting and what the value options are for each setting, run this command.

```
get-childitem | format-list
```

These items in the resulting list correspond to the items that you would set in the RD Session Host Configuration had you done this via the graphical user interface (GUI).

Next, get the current redirectable address options that you have to choose from so that you can specify one or more IP addresses to use for IP address redirection later in the script.

```
PS RDS:\> cd RedirectableAddresses
PS RDS:\rdsconfiguration\ConnectionBrokerSettings\RedirectableAddresses>dir
```

Take a look at your redirectable address options; if you have more than one network adapter configured on the server, you will have multiple addresses to choose from. The results will look similar to this.

```
Directory: RDS:\rdsconfiguration\ConnectionBrokerSettings\RedirectableAddresses
```

Name	Type	CurrentValue	GP	PermissibleValues	PermissibleOperations
10.10.10.242	String		-		Get-Item
10.10.10.232	String		-		Get-Item
10.10.10.112	String		-		Get-Item
10.10.10.212	String		-		Get-Item
10.10.10.211	String		-		Get-Item

Now you have all the data that you need to configure the RD Session Host server to join an RD Connection Broker farm. Do this by running the following code, inputting the value options that work with your environment.

```
Set-Item ServerPurpose -value 3 -ConnectionBroker <FQDN-OF-RD-CONNECTION-
BROKER-GOES-HERE> -FarmName <FQDN-FARM-NAME-GOES-HERE> -IPAddressRedirection 1
-CurrentRedirectableAddresses <IP-ADDRESS-YOU-WANT-TO-USE-GOES-HERE>
```

NOTE To get help in setting the item ServerPurpose, run the following command.

```
get-help Set-Item -path .\Serverpurpose
```

To get help in understanding ServerPurpose parameters and their possible values, run this command.

```
get-help Set-Item -path .\Serverpurpose -param <The parameter you for which
you want possible values>
```

 ON THE COMPANION MEDIA A script to perform this process for all servers in an OU is included on the companion media in the JoinFarm.ps1 file. The script sets IP address redirection to use the first available network adapter option.

Naming RemoteApp And Desktop Connections

RemoteApp And Desktop Connections is a feature of Windows 7 or Windows Server 2008 R2 that allows the client to incorporate RemoteApp programs and VMs with the Start menu. Although RD Web Access supplies the content to the client, RD Connection Broker has one important role to play: You name the users' view of these RemoteApp And Desktop Connections from the Remote Connection Manager on the RD Connection Broker. To learn how to set up RemoteApp And Desktop Connections on the client, see the section entitled "Using RemoteApp And Desktop Connections" later in this chapter.

On the RD Connection Broker, open the Remote Connection Manager in the Remote Desktop Services administrative tools. Making sure you've selected the uppermost branch in the left pane (it should say Remote Desktop Connection Manager), click Display Name, located in the Properties group in the central pane, to open the dialog box shown in Figure 9-15.

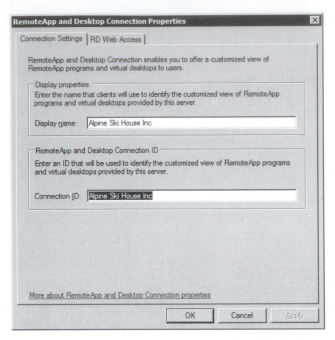

FIGURE 9-15 The name that you choose here will be the Display name for RemoteApp And Desktop Connections on the client.

You've got a lot of latitude in choosing a name: Names can be long, contain spaces, and will show mixed case. There's one caveat to this: You can't end the Display name with any character that Windows sees as either part of a file name (.) or a wildcard character (* or ?). That's why, in Figure 9-15, the "Inc" has no period. You can include any of these characters elsewhere in the Display name, but you cannot use any of them as the last character in the name.

Publishing and Assigning Applications Using RemoteApp Manager

Publishing RemoteApp programs requires having those applications already installed on the RD Session Host server. To make installed applications RemoteApp programs, you must perform the following steps.

1. Add those applications to the allow list of programs that can initiate a remote session, including the appropriate parameters.

2. Package those applications (as MSI files or RDP files) and apply the appropriate settings.

3. Distribute those applications.

The next sections will look at these steps in more detail.

Adding Applications to the Allow List

Before adding applications to the allow list, it's important to understand what adding applications to the allow list is and isn't. It *isn't* a form of software restriction policy or a way to enable AppLocker, as discussed in Chapter 6, "Customizing the User Experience." Adding an application to the allow list only enables a user to open a session with that application; after the remote session has begun, it's possible to start any other application on the RD Session Host server to which you have access. Do not consider the allow list as a step toward locking down the server.

So what *is* the allow list? Adding an application to the allow list makes it possible to start that application in a session (as a RemoteApp) and also to package it as a RemoteApp program for distribution. If you add an application to the allow list, package it, give that RDP file to someone, and *then* remove the application from the allow list, that RemoteApp file will not work any longer. In addition, if you previously configured the application to work with RD Web Access and then remove it from the allow list, it will no longer appear in the portal after you remove it from the allow list.

To add applications to the allow list, open the RemoteApp Manager (see Figure 9-16) from Start, Administrative Tools, Remote Desktop Services, RemoteApp Manager. This tool controls which applications are available as RemoteApp programs and how users reach those programs.

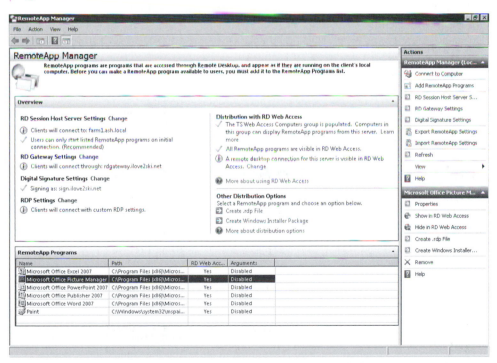

FIGURE 9-16 Configure RemoteApp programs using the RemoteApp Manager.

None of these settings apply, however, until you populate the allow list. To add an installed application to the allow list, you must add it to the RemoteApp Programs list located in the lower section of the middle pane (shown in Figure 9-16) by following the next set of steps.

NOTE You can add only applications on a terminal server running Windows Server 2008 or an RD Session Host server running Windows Server 2008 R2 to the allow list. Terminal servers running Windows Server 2003 cannot run RemoteApp programs or back an RD Web Access server, except to connect to a full desktop.

1. Click the Add RemoteApp Programs button in the Actions pane or right-click in the RemoteApp Programs section and choose Add RemoteApp Programs to start the RemoteApp Wizard. Click Next.

2. Choose the application(s) that you want to publish by selecting the corresponding check box in the RemoteApp Programs list (see Figure 9-17). If an installed application does not appear in the list, locate it by clicking Browse and navigating to the executable file.

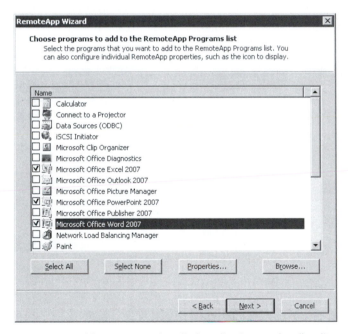

FIGURE 9-17 Add one or more installed applications to the allow list.

NOTE Applications are listed in alphabetical order, taken from the Start menu of the RD Session Host server on which you're running Remote App Manager. Use Browse to find applications that are not on the Start menu.

3. If adding a single application, you can edit the application settings by clicking Properties. The Properties section is discussed in the section entitled "Editing RemoteApp Properties" later in this chapter. If you've selected more than one application from the list, you can't edit the properties.

4. Click Next, review the settings that you have chosen, and click Finish. The application is now on the allow list.

Configuring Global RemoteApp Deployment Settings

Now look at the options in the middle pane; you'll use them to configure RemoteApp program deployment settings. The middle pane shows all the applications currently in the allow list and the options for configuring the RD Session Host server settings, RD Gateway settings, RDP common and custom settings, and digital signing options. If you click any of the Change hyperlinks here, you'll open the tabbed dialog box shown in Figure 9-18.

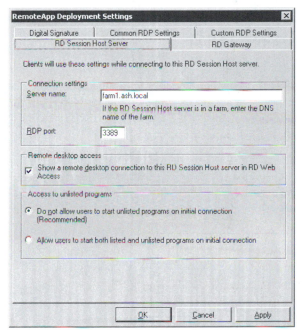

FIGURE 9-18 Click a Change link in the RemoteApp Manager Overview section to open the RemoteApp Deployment Settings dialog box.

NOTE You can also click the corresponding the RD Session Host Server Settings, RD Gateway Settings, or Digital Signature Settings options in the Actions pane to open the RemoteApp Deployment Settings tabbed dialog box.

Open the RemoteApp Deployment Settings dialog box to edit the global settings used to configure RemoteApp RDP and Windows Installer (MSI) distribution files. These settings also apply to RDP files created when a user clicks a RemoteApp icon in RD Web Access or Remote-App and Desktop Connections.

> **NOTE** If you change settings in the middle pane, RD Web Access and RemoteApp And Desktop Connections will use the updated settings. RDP files and .MSI files that you create from the RemoteApp Manager will not. You'll need to re-create them to make the new settings take effect.

RemoteApp deployment settings apply to all applications that you publish (unless you explicitly change the settings during creation) but will not affect applications you've already published. If you update these settings, any RDP or MSI files that you've already created will be out of date. You will need to recreate and redistribute them.

General RD Session Host Server Configuration

The RD Session Host Server tab contains three sections.

- **Connection Settings**   Specify the farm or server name (even though it says "Server," the farm name is a valid value) and port that clients will connect to when using RemoteApp programs. By default, the server name is the FQDN of the local server. Be sure to edit this setting to display the farm name if appropriate.

- **Remote Desktop Access**   RemoteApp programs aren't the only valid connection model. You can enable a full desktop connection to the RD Session Host server(s) available to users on the RD Web Access website by selecting the Show A Remote Desktop Connection To This RD Session Host Server In RD Web Access option.

- **Access To Unlisted Programs**   By default, Do Not Allow Users To Start Unlisted Programs On Initial Connection is selected. This setting does not prevent an application from starting after the remote connection has been made, but it prevents users from starting RemoteApp programs that are no longer on the allow list.

Configuring RD Gateway Settings

As described in Chapter 10, "Making Remote Desktop Services Available from the Internet," you can deploy RD Gateway to give users secure access to RemoteApp programs from outside the company network. If you do so, then the settings specified on the RD Gateway tab are applied when users start RemoteApp programs. You can also define the type of authentication that must be used when using RD Gateway. For example, for greater security, you could require smart card authentication. To use the same user credentials to access RD Gateway and the RD Session Host server, select the corresponding check box. Otherwise, users will be prompted for credentials twice.

NOTE Although Kerberos is the default authentication method for Windows Server 2008 R2, clients connecting via RD Gateway uses NTLM (which validates the domain only), not Kerberos (which validates the full name of the server). This is because you can't use Kerberos over the Internet. Kerberos requires that both client and server be domain-joined so that they can contact the authentication service. Therefore, for RD Gateway, you'll rely on either NTLM or smart card access.

You can also configure RD Gateway settings via Group Policy at User Configuration | Polices | Administrative Templates | Windows Components | Remote Desktop Services | RD Gateway. Read about using Group Policy to set RD Gateway settings in Chapter 10.

Signing RDP Files Automatically

Code-signing is probably familiar to you: You sign code to validate that you are authorizing its execution and are willing to state that it isn't malware.

Running an RDP file starts only code that's already present on the client, but you should still consider signing the code. An RDP file looks innocuous, but it has one major vulnerability: If you get an RDP file in an email message and are told to run it when you want to use an application, then you're not necessarily going to open this file to see where it's sending you. It's trivial to alter an RDP file to send it to a different server from the one originally specified. Then, if you connect to the malicious server, your credentials can be intercepted when you present them.

Signing an RDP file digitally provides users with the author's identity so they can make an informed decision when executing the RDP file. If users do not recognize the publisher of the code, they don't have to complete the connection. Digital signing also proves that the code is authentic; in other words, that it has not been tampered with or changed in any way after publishing. If a signed RDP file is altered in any way that changes how it's secured, the file is corrupted and won't start.

Background on Digital Certificates

The digital certificate used to sign an RDP file (or any other file) contains proof that the subject of the certificate (the web server, the user, the application, the entity) is indeed who or what it claims to be. Digital certificates are used for a variety of purposes, like authenticating servers, signing email, or authenticating users on a network.

When used to sign RDP files generated by the RemoteApp Manager, the digital certificate provides the software publisher identity to users of the RDP files. This gives users assurance that they will connect to a trusted RD Session Host server. It also assures that the RDP file code has not been altered in any way after it was published and signed using the certificate.

When purchasing a certificate, to prove that the subject of the certificate is real, the issuer of the certificate (the certificate authority, or CA) must verify the subject's identity. The CA does a background check to be sure that the person requesting the certificate is who he or she says. (The result is that you can't get signing certificates from a company that you don't belong to, or even to a company that you do belong to if you don't have authority to get them.) After the CA has verified the requestor's identity, the CA signs the certificate with its digital signature to show that the appropriate checking has taken place and to verify that the certificate subject is valid.

You can obtain a digital certificate from a public company such as VeriSign or Thawte. Alternatively, your company can maintain your own public key infrastructure (PKI), the system that maintains CAs and other systems related to digital certificates, and can issue and maintain your own digital certificates. In either case, a digital certificate is verified as legitimate by verifying the issuing CA signature used to sign the certificate. To verify the issuing CA signature, that CA certificate—which contains its digital signature—needs to be installed on the client in the Trusted Root certificate store. Users can add CA certificates to this store for every source they trust.

Microsoft operating systems come with some certificate authority CA certificates already installed in the Computer Certificates | Trusted Root CA store, as part of the Microsoft Root Certificate Program. Member certificates can be downloaded and installed using Windows Update. What this means is that users do not need to install anything to trust one of these CAs. This is important if users will be running RDP files on public or remote computers, where they might not have the permissions to install certificates (or don't know how to do so).

On Windows Vista and Windows 7, when an application needs to verify a certificate that has been signed by a CA, and that CA is not directly trusted (its certificate is not installed in the Trusted Root CA store on the computer), then the computer checks with Windows Update to see if the CA has been added to the Microsoft list of trusted authorities. If it has, then the certificate is automatically downloaded and installed in the Trusted Root CA store on the computer.

Computers running Windows XP and earlier can update their trusted root certificates by downloading the latest root update package from the Microsoft Updates Catalog.

> **NOTE** For more information on the Microsoft Root Certificate Program, go to *http://www.microsoft.com/technet/archive/security/news /rootcert.mspx?mfr=true.*

Companies that run their own PKI solution can choose to have their CA certificate signed by a public CA that is part of the Microsoft Root Certificate Program. This will save them from having to install their CA certificate on each of their clients, because the public CA that signed the company's CA root certificate would already have its certificate placed in the Computer Certificates/Trusted Root Certification Authorities folder.

To sign RDP files digitally, select the Sign With A Digital Certificate option. Then click Change and choose a digital certificate from the certificates installed on the RD Session Host server.

Adding the digital certificate also means that the RDP files created when a user clicks an application icon hosted by RD Web Access will also be signed. Just add the Secure Sockets Layer (SSL) or code signing certificate from the Digital Signature tab and RemoteApp Manager will sign all RDP files that it creates.

> **NOTE** If you need to distribute already created or manually created RDP files to users via email or network share, you can use the RDPsign.exe command-line tool to sign the files. See the section entitled "Signing Already-Created RDP Files" later in this chapter for more details.

You can tell an RDP file is signed if you open it in a text editor. The signature will be included in the file, as shown in Figure 9-19.

FIGURE 9-19 A signed RDP file includes the encrypted signature.

If you try to execute a signed file that has been tampered with, the remote desktop client will open, but the settings once contained in the signed RDP file will no longer be preselected. Also, the publisher of the RDP file will be unknown because you are no longer running a preconfigured RDP file (it was broken when the file was changed after it was signed).

When a user opens a signed RDP file, he or she will be presented with the screen shown in Figure 9-20.

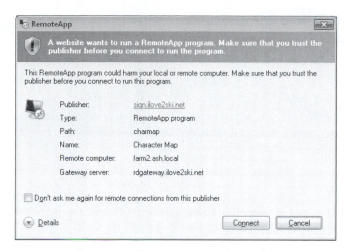

FIGURE 9-20 Signed RDP files show the user the publisher's identity before the code executes.

The user can then verify that he or she is executing the intended code from the correct source. The user can then execute the code by clicking Connect, or he or she can choose to click Cancel and not execute the file.

If you do not use digital signatures to sign RDP files, when users open a published RDP file, they will receive a warning (shown in Figure 9-21) stating that the publisher of the RDP file can't be identified.

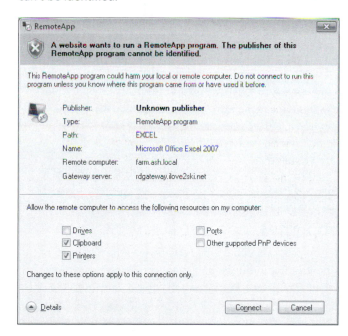

FIGURE 9-21 If a digital signature is not used to sign an RDP file, the user receives a warning that the publisher of the Remote Connection can't be identified.

The user either connects anyway by clicking Connect or clicks Cancel to cancel the connection.

Common RDP Settings Tab

Configure display settings and device redirection settings on the Common RDP Settings tab. These settings will be set in the RDP file and will be used as long as these settings are not specified through Group Policy. See Chapter 6 for more details on controlling device redirection.

Custom RDP Settings Tab

Add custom settings that are not specified in the common deployment settings of Remote-App Manager by typing the settings in this tab. (See the following sidebar, titled "Understanding RDP File Settings," for more details about available RDP settings.)

Understanding RDP File Settings

The RDP settings are passed to the endpoint when a user makes a connection. Not all options for an RDP file are exposed through the GUI of Mstsc.exe. To change the way a RemoteApp (or desktop) starts, you can edit the contents of the RDP file from a text editor such as Notepad. Most of these are reasonably self-explanatory, but it's good to examine what you can and can't control with an RDP file. (Not all settings here will be present in all RDP files, and desktops might have additional options.)

 ON THE COMPANION MEDIA A link to a website that provides all of the RDP file settings and their possible values is located on this book's companion media. The URL is *http://blog.kristinlgriffin.com/2010/10/rdp-settings-for-rdc-7.html*.

RDP file settings should not be changed if the RDP file is signed, because this will break the signature, corrupt the file, and render it unusable.

Editing RemoteApp Properties

You can edit a setting for a RemoteApp program either while adding it to the allow list, or after you've added it by right-clicking its entry in the list and choosing Properties. When you open the properties of a published application, you'll see a dialog box similar to the one shown in Figure 9-22.

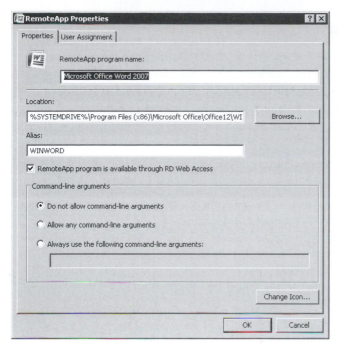

FIGURE 9-22 Edit RemoteApp settings in the RemoteApp Properties dialog box.

Choose an Appropriate Program Name

The RemoteApp program name is the user-friendly name for the RemoteApp. It's the same regardless of how you present the RemoteApp: via RD Web Access, RemoteApp And Desktop Connections, an .RDP file on a network share, or an .MSI file distributed via Group Policy.

If you're publishing the application only once, you're unlikely to edit its name. However, you can publish the application more than once, each time with individual settings, and you can name it according to its settings. For example, if you wanted to make it easy for members of the Accounting team to open their monthly reports, you could hard-code the RemoteApp to open the report file using the command-line arguments. (You'll find out how you would do this in the section entitled "Adding Command-Line Arguments" later in this chapter.) If you did so, it would make sense to edit the RemoteApp program name to show the name of the report instead of the name of the application.

Deliver via RD Web Access

Make the RemoteApp available via RD Web Access by selecting the option RemoteApp Program Is Available Through RD Web Access. Doing so makes it possible to display this application so it can be started through a website. You'll still need to do a little work to enable RemoteApp programs through a website. (See the section entitled "Delivering RemoteApp Programs and VMs Through RD Web Access" later in this chapter for more details about the process.)

Don't Change the Alias

The *Alias* property is a unique identifier for the application, defaulting to the application screen name. Although you can edit this property, it's best that you don't, because this is how the computer identifies each RemoteApp. The RemoteApp Manager uses Windows Management Instrumentation (WMI) interfaces that represent RemoteApp programs. The class *Win32_TSPublishedApplicationList* lists all RemoteApp programs in a list, identifying them by their aliases. If you change an alias, the class will not be able to find the RemoteApp in its list.

 CAUTION The RD Web Access website populates its list of applications by querying WMI, so editing the alias can cause a RemoteApp not to display in RD Web Access.

Adding Command-Line Arguments

People are so used to opening applications from the GUI that it's easy to forget that many applications support a number of command-line parameters. You can use them to automatically open files, to disable the splash screen, or even to open a document and highlight a particular section—it all depends on the application. For instance, to tell a RemoteApp instance of Microsoft PowerPoint 2010 to open Mydoc.pptx (stored on the file server COLFAX) as a slideshow when the PowerPoint application starts, add this command-line argument to the PowerPoint RemoteApp.

```
/S \\colfax\ash-company-files\Mydoc.pptx
```

By default, command-line arguments are not enabled for RemoteApp programs because no arguments are universally appropriate. By allowing users to specify their own arguments, you expose the RD Session Host server to attack, for example, through rogue websites. If you must enable arguments, select one of the following choices.

- **Allow Any Command-Line Arguments** Choose this option to allow users to assign parameters to a RemoteApp. Users can then open the RDP file in a text editor and add the arguments that they want to use for that connection, as shown in Figure 9-23. Users cannot add arguments to RemoteApps that they access via RD Web Access. But they can edit RemoteApps distributed by RemoteApp And Desktop Connections or by RDP or MSI file distribution by right-clicking the RemoteApp and opening it in a text editor.

NOTE If you digitally sign your RDP files, don't allow users to specify command-line arguments. If users edit the arguments, they'll corrupt the file.

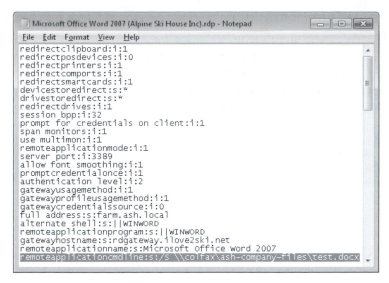

FIGURE 9-23 Add a command-line parameter to a RemoteApp RDP file.

- **Always Use The Following Command-Line Arguments**   If you choose this option and specify arguments, they'll be applied when that Remote App is started.

> **NOTE**   For best performance, it's always best to disable unnecessary images. For example, to remove the splash screen from the opening of any Microsoft Office application, add the */q* switch to the list of required command-line arguments. See the Additional Resources at the end of this chapter for pointers to command-line arguments for some sample applications.

The settings that you pick will always apply to that RemoteApp when it's started because they're defined on the server.

Editing the Application Icon

Applications come with a default icon, but you can change this. For example, if you edit the RemoteApp to open a document, you can change its icon to one that represents a document (Word has many alternate icons), not the application.

To change the icon that will represent the application, click the Change Icon button in the lower-right corner of the screen and choose a different icon. The path to the icon file must be a Universal Naming Convention (UNC) path so that the path will remain valid if you export the RemoteApp to another server.

Assigning Applications to Users

In Windows Server 2008, all users accessing the same RD Web Access site would see the same application set—you couldn't filter according to user identity. Although the default setting still allows all authenticated domain users (who are in the Remote Desktop Users group on the RD Session Host server) to run the applications, you can also allow only certain users to see applications. To configure this, turn to the User Assignment tab when configuring the RemoteApp properties, as shown in Figure 9-24.

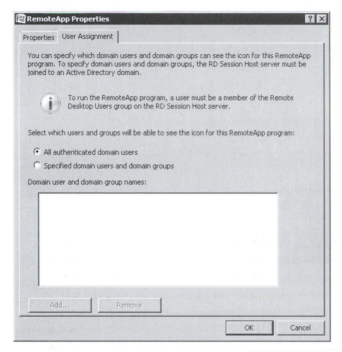

FIGURE 9-24 You can filter the contents of RD Web Access or RemoteApp And Desktop Connections by user identity.

To assign applications, just select the option for Specified Domain Users And Domain Groups and click Add. This will open the familiar search tool for finding users and groups in AD DS. Find the appropriate user or group and click OK, and then click OK again to confirm your selection when you see the user or group name in the list.

 CAUTION If you opt to assign the application to specified domain users and domain groups but don't add a user or group name to the input box, then the application will not be visible to anyone.

When assigning applications, keep the following in mind.

- The user or group accounts you assign them to must be domain accounts. You can't, for example, assign applications to a local user on the RD Web Access computer.

- The RD Web Access computer and RD Session Host server hosting the RemoteApp must be both domain-joined. They must be either in the domain for the user accounts or a trusted domain.

- You can only choose users or groups of users; there is no option to filter according to which computer the application set is viewed from.

- If someone can see an application and you don't think he or she should be able to, check the groups that have access to the application and the group memberships of the user who can unexpectedly see the application.

- The RD Web Access server must be a member of the Windows Authorization Access Group in the domain, so it has permission to check the group memberships for a user account. You can confirm this membership on a domain controller—to do this, open Active Directory Users And Computers and look in the Builtin folder to list all the built-in groups. Check the Members tab for the Windows Authorization Access Group. The RD Web Access server, or a group of which it is a member, must appear in this list.

Save the settings that you've adjusted. The application is now added to the allow list and can be displayed with the settings that you specified.

Maintaining Allow List Consistency Across the Farm

You can configure Remote App programs manually on each server in your farm. However, doing so is extra work and prone to error. Even if you manage to create exactly the same allow list on each RD Session Host server (which is required for RemoteApp to execute against that server), the chances are good that you won't edit all properties and icon settings correctly if you attempt to set up all the servers manually. If the properties are inconsistent across servers, then you might end up with odd behavior, such as an application starting a file when run on one server but not on another.

There are two ways you can deal with this: Publish the RemoteApp programs programmatically on all RD Session Host servers, and export the allow list from one server to import it on the other servers in the farm.

Editing Properties via Windows PowerShell

You can publish RemoteApp programs (add them to the allow list and configure display properties) from Windows PowerShell. This example publishes MSPaint.exe with an application name of MSPaint, and it is set to appear in the RD Web Access portal.

```
Import-module remotedesktopservices
set-location rds:
cd RemoteApp\RemoteAppPrograms
New-Item -applicationpath "c:\windows\system32\calc.exe" -applicationname "Calculator"
  -ShowInPortal 1
```

Exporting and Importing the Allow List

To export the allow list and associated settings, click the Export RemoteApp Settings link in the Actions pane of the RemoteApp Manager to open the dialog box shown in Figure 9-25.

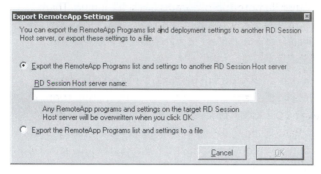

FIGURE 9-25 Export RemoteApp settings to a file or to other RD Session Host servers.

To export to single RD Session Host servers on the same network, choose the first option and provide the server's DNS name. Click OK and the settings will appear in the RemoteApp Manager of the specified server. Import the programs and settings to a server by clicking the Import RemoteApp Settings link in the Action pane of the RemoteApp Manager, and specifying the DNS name of the server from which to import the settings.

If you're configuring more than one server or the other server isn't yet online, choose Export The RemoteApp Programs List And Settings To A File and then choose the name and location to store the file. The created file will have an extension of .pub. On another RD Session Host server, open RemoteApp Manager and click the Import RemoteApp Settings link in the Actions pane. Locate the .pub file and click Open.

 ON THE COMPANION MEDIA See the companion media for a link to *http://blog.powershell.no/category/remote-desktop-services/*, where you can find a new Windows PowerShell module for RDS that includes cmdlets for importing and exporting allow lists.

One caution about importing and exporting the allow list: If you are signing the files digitally, you won't be able to create RDP or MSI files from a secondary server. Although it will appear that the signing settings have been exported for you to use when creating RDP files, this is incorrect. The required *certificate* will not be stored in the secondary server's certificate store. For this reason, it's best to designate one server as a management server. Create the RDP and MSI files from the designated management server and just import the allow list to the secondary servers. You can also install the signing certificate on each of the other RD Session Host servers and manually edit the RemoteApp digital certificate settings on each server to reflect the correct certificate.

Configuring Timeouts for RemoteApp Sessions

All RemoteApp programs for the same user that are run from the same server are run in the same session for greater efficiency. Therefore, when a user closes one RemoteApp, this doesn't close the entire session if other RemoteApp programs are still running. There is no option to log off or close a session from a RemoteApp. Doing so would terminate all RemoteApp programs the user started from that server simultaneously because all RemoteApp programs run in the same session.

Second, with RemoteApp programs, users are no longer starting and using applications from within another desktop. Instead, they open and close RemoteApp programs from their own desktop, and they no longer make a definitive decision about the state of their session by either disconnecting or logging off. Rather, they open and close RemoteApp programs as needed and do not have to think about the session. This is good from a user perspective, but it makes knowing when to disconnect a session a bit more complicated.

Because a RemoteApp session depends on the presence or absence of its RemoteApp programs, the logic for determining when the session should end is different from that of a desktop. The section entitled "RemoteApp Internals" earlier in this chapter explained the communication paths between the client-side application and the remote session. When the very last RemoteApp in a session is closed (signaled through a windowing event showing that the window is closed), and key processes are no longer running in the remote session, the connection determines that the session is complete and can be disconnected. The time that the session remains in a disconnected state depends on how you configure the Group Policy setting Set Time Limit For Logoff Of RemoteApp Sessions, located in Computer (or User) Configuration | Policies | Administrative Templates | Windows Components | Remote Desktop Services | Remote Desktop Session Host | Session Time Limits.

> **NOTE** RemoteApp programs and system tray icons that the user starts indirectly are included in this determination. As an example, let's assume a user opens a Microsoft Word document with a Word RemoteApp and the document contains a link to a Microsoft Excel spreadsheet. If the user also uses Excel as a RemoteApp, then clicking on the link indirectly opens the Excel RemoteApp. Both of these RemoteApp programs need to be closed for the session to be disconnected.

You don't necessarily *want* to terminate a session as soon as the last RemoteApp is closed. It's much faster to reconnect to an existing session than to re-create a new one (the process of loading all the processes to support the session is expensive). Therefore, you might want to edit the user or computer Group Policy to prolong the interval between disconnection and termination of RemoteApp sessions. This gives users a little time to realize that they have one more email to send and start Microsoft Outlook from the existing remote session, rather than waiting for a new session. To do so, when you enable the GPO setting Set Time Limit For Logoff Of RemoteApp Sessions, select the Enabled radio button and choose a time setting from the RemoteApp Session Logoff Delay drop-down menu, as shown in Figure 9-26.

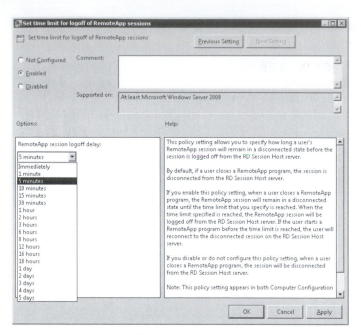

FIGURE 9-26 Use Group Policy to set a time limit for logoff of RemoteApp sessions.

> **NOTE** If you also enable the GPO setting Set Time Limit For Disconnected Session, then choose a time for that GPO that is longer than the time specified for RemoteApp Session Logoff Delay. Otherwise, sessions will always be terminated before the RemoteApp Session Logoff Delay Time limit is reached, thus rendering that GPO irrelevant.

There's a tradeoff between keeping responsive sessions and not overloading the RD Session Host server. If you choose to retain sessions for a long time, you might affect the RD Session Host server because the disconnected sessions remain active. Be sure that you have sufficient page file space to accommodate the disconnected sessions when they're not in use.

Signing Already-Created RDP Files

But what about RDP files that you have already created? To sign them, you can re-create them using the RemoteApp Manager or you can use the RDPsign.exe command-line tool to sign RDP files. To sign an RDP file using RDPSign, you need to retrieve the thumbprint from the signing certificate; this thumbprint is also known as the certificate *hash*. Certificates are located in the Certificate Store on the computer. To open the Certificate Store, start a Microsoft Management Console (MMC) and open the Certificates snap-in. Add the local computer store, not the user store. The SSL or code signing certificate will be located in the Personal Store folder. Find and double-click the certificate that you want to use to sign the

RDP file. Select the certificate's Details tab and scroll down to the Thumbprint value, as shown in Figure 9-27.

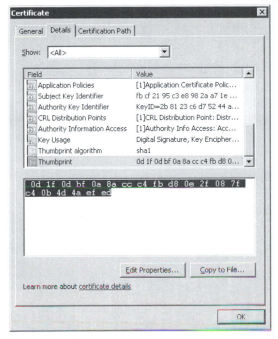

FIGURE 9-27 The certificate thumbprint is revealed in the Details tab of the certificate.

Highlight and copy the thumbprint to a text editor and remove the spaces so that you end up with 40 characters, such as 0d1f0dbf0a8accc4fbd80e2f087fc40b4d4aefed. You are now ready to sign an RDP file. RDPsign.exe is a command-line tool and contains a few parameters to note. Table 9-2 explains the parameters.

TABLE 9-2 RDPSign.exe Parameters

PARAMETER	DESCRIPTION
/sha1<hash>	Replace <hash> with the thumbprint of the certificate that you want to use to sign the RDP file.
/q	Quiet Mode—You will receive no output if the command is successful and very little if it fails.
/v	Verbose Mode—The opposite of Quiet Mode. It shows you all messages related to the execution.
/l	Tests signing the RDP file and tells you the results of the test, but does not actually sign the file.
/?	Typical command prompt for displaying help for the command. You can also type **rdpsign** and get the help information.

Open a command prompt, type **rdpsign**, add the hash, select a result display mode if you want, and then provide the location of the RDP file. The following example shows an Rdpsign command successfully executed.

```
C:\Users\admin>rdpsign /sha1 0d1f0dbf0a8accc4fbd80e2f087fc40b4d4aefed /v c:\Olympus.rdp
All rdp file(s) have been successfully signed.
```

You can also sign multiple files by adding them to the command line like this.

```
C:\Users\admin>rdpsign /sha1 0d1f0dbf0a8accc4fbd80e2f087fc40b4d4aefed
  /v c:\rdpfile1.rdp c:\rdpfile2.rdp c:\rdpfile3.rdp c:\rdpfile4.rdp
```

Users that start a signed RDP file will get an uneditable user interface, as shown in Figure 9-28.

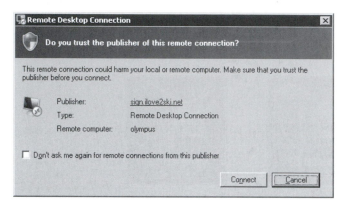

FIGURE 9-28 Signed RDP files are preconfigured and not editable.

Only if certain redirection was allowed at the time of creation will the user have the opportunity to disable it. If redirection is disabled, the user will not be given the opportunity to enable it.

Setting Signature Policies

Now you have a signed file, but what is to stop a user from tampering with the file, removing the signature in a text editor, making changes to the file, and then running it? By default, the answer is "Nothing." What you *can* do is allow users to run only RDP files that are signed. You control this in Group Policy with the Allow .RdpFiles From Unknown Publishers policy; by default, this setting allows users to run unsigned RDP files. Disable this policy to stop users from running RDP files from unknown publishers.

You can also specify a list of trusted certificate thumbprints so that when a user opens a signed RDP file that is signed by the trusted hash, users do not get the message asking them if they trust the file publisher. They will go straight to the login screen. This is true for RDP files signed via RemoteApp Manager or by RDPSign.exe. The setting to use is Specify SHA1 Thumbprints Of Certificates Representing Trusted .Rdp Publishers.

Both settings are available in the same location. To set the policies for computers, go to Computer Configuration | Policies | Administrative Templates | Windows Components | Remote Desktop Services | Remote Desktop Connection Client. For users, go to User Configuration | Policies | Administrative Templates | Windows Components | Remote Desktop Services | Remote Desktop Connection Client.

Distributing RemoteApp Programs

After adding publishing applications, you must get the RDP files to users so they can start those applications. You can do this in one of three ways.

- Create RDP files and make them available to users from a file share or by sending them in email.
- Create MSI files (which are installable versions of the same RDP files) and distribute them to users via Group Policy.
- Enable the applications in the allow list for display via RD Web Access or RemoteApp And Desktop Connections, and create the RDP files on demand when users click the icons.

This section will discuss the first two options; the third will be discussed in the section entitled "Delivering RemoteApp Programs and VMs Through RD Web Access" later in this chapter.

Distributing RDP Files

RemoteApp RDP distribution files are self-contained—the user does not install them. The user double-clicks the file, provides valid user credentials, an RDP session starts, and the application opens. Because the files are self-contained, you can distribute them to users via network share, website, email, and so on.

> **NOTE** To use RDP files from computers outside the corporate local area network (LAN), you need to deploy RD Gateway to provide secure access to RD Session Host servers in the network. For information about RD Gateway, see Chapter 10.

When users double-click a RemoteApp RDP file, they see a connection screen that either reveals the software publisher identity (so users know they are executing code from a trusted source), as previously shown in Figure 9-20, or indicates that the publisher is unknown, as shown in Figure 9-21.

To create an RDP file for distribution, click the Create .rdp File link in RemoteApp Manager. Click Next on the Welcome screen. The Specify Package Settings page appears, as shown in Figure 9-29.

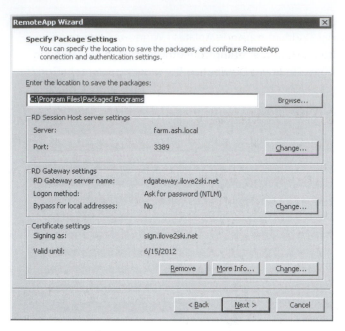

FIGURE 9-29 Specify RemoteApp MSI package settings, including a save location and any changes to server name, port, RD Gateway settings, or the default signing certificate.

Enter a location where you want to save the MSI package or browse to the location. RDP files (and MSI packages) are configured by default with the configuration settings that you set in RemoteApp Manager.

On this page, you can make any needed changes to the default RemoteApp settings for the MSI package by clicking the Change button next to the appropriate setting. Click Next, review your settings, and then click Finish. The created RDP file will be saved to the location you specified in the wizard.

Distributing MSI Files

You can also create MSI files and then distribute them via a file share, email, or Group Policy. An advantage of distributing MSI files is that you can configure the MSI install to place short-cuts on the user's desktop, the Start menu, or both. You can also associate file extensions with the RemoteApp program. The result is that the RemoteApp program will open when a user double-clicks a file with an associated extension. This is one of the main benefits for distributing RemoteApps this way because many users open applications and files by double-clicking the file.

To create an MSI file for distribution, perform the following steps.

1. Open RemoteApp Manager, click the Create Windows Installer Package link, and then click Next on the Welcome page of the RemoteApp Wizard. The Specify Package Settings page appears.

2. Enter a location where you want to save the MSI package, or browse to the location. Make any needed changes to the default RemoteApp settings for the MSI package by clicking the Change button next to the setting you want to change and entering the new setting. Click Next. The Configure Distribution Package appears, as shown in Figure 9-30.

FIGURE 9-30 Associate file extensions and create shortcut icons for RemoteApp programs.

3. In the top section, choose to put a shortcut on a client's desktop, the Start menu, or both by selecting the corresponding check box. If you choose to put a shortcut icon on the Start menu, then enter the name of the folder in which the icon will reside.

4. In the bottom section, you can choose to associate file extensions with the RemoteApp program by selecting the corresponding check box. Click Next, and then click Finish on the Review Settings page.

Creating RDP files and MSI packages might seem very similar, but another main purpose of creating MSI packages is to deploy RemoteApp programs via Group Policy. To use Group Policy to deploy RemoteApp MSI files, create a GPO and link it to an OU for the users or clients for which the Group Policy should apply. Navigate to either Computer Configuration | Policies | Software Settings or User Configuration | Policies | Software Settings, as appropriate. Right-click Software Installation and choose New Software Package. If you deploy RemoteApp MSI files using a computer policy, the application is assigned and installed automatically when the user boots the computer. Only administrators can uninstall the application.

> **NOTE** You can choose to either assign applications (installing them automatically) or publish applications (making them available for installation). It's a best practice to assign MSIs containing RDP files. Otherwise, the file associations linked with those RemoteApp programs won't work properly.

Delivering RemoteApp Programs and VMs Through RD Web Access

RD Web Access makes RemoteApp programs, remote desktops, and pooled and personal VMs available to users via the RD Web Access website or RemoteApp And Desktop Connections. When a user clicks an icon representing one of these resources, the RD Web Access role service creates a corresponding RDP file for that resource type, using the settings provided by the data source that offers the RemoteApp, remote desktop session, or the VM. The RDP file starts, and the user accesses the RemoteApp or remote desktop.

> **NOTE** RD Web Access also provides a way to connect remotely to other machines on the network via the Remote Desktop tab on the website interface. This is covered later in this chapter in the section entitled "Using the RD Web Access Website."

RD Web Access Sources

The source(s) that the RD Web Access role service queries for the resource data is configured on the RD Web Access website. It can be one or more RD Session Host servers, an RD Session Host server farm, or RD Connection Broker, as shown in Figure 9-31.

RD Web Access communicates with RD Session Host server sources using Windows Management Instrumentation (WMI), while it communicates with RD Connection Broker over remote procedure call (RPC). RD Web Access role service consumes the data that it receives from its source(s) and produces two data streams.

- Hypertext Markup Language (HTML) data that RD Web Access website displays as web pages
- An Extensible Markup Language (XML) feed that is consumed by the RemoteApp And Desktop Connections on clients running Windows 7 or Windows Server 2008 R2.

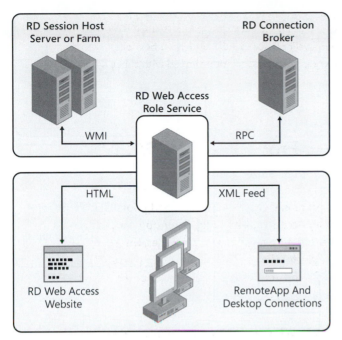

FIGURE 9-31 The RD Web Access role service gets RemoteApp, desktop session, and pooled and personal VM information from RD Session Host servers or RD Connection Broker.

NOTE It's important to understand that the RD Web Access role service is more than just a website. The role service is what polls the source(s) and gathers the data. The website is merely a way of telling the role service what source(s) to poll and then also displaying that data in a web browser.

The source dictates what *kind*s of resources are accessible via RD Web Access, as shown in Figure 9-32.

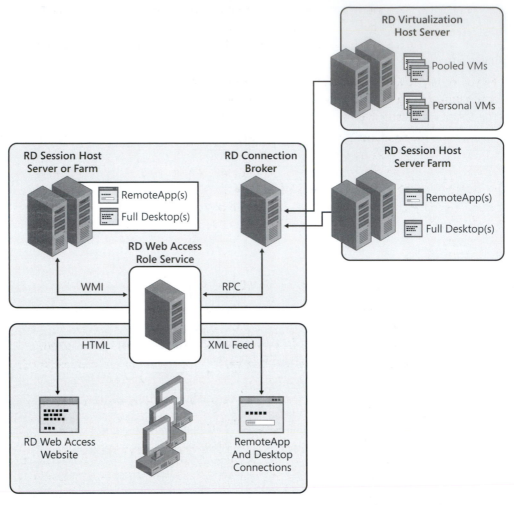

FIGURE 9-32 The RD Web Access source dictates the types of resources available via RD Web Access.

RD Session Host servers provide access to RemoteApp and full desktop sessions. If this is all you need to make available, then you have two ways to configure the RD Web Access source. You can configure the RD Session Host servers or farms as the RD Web Access sources, or RD Connection Broker can be configured to attain this data from the RD Session host servers and then pass it on to RD Web Access.

However, if you need to provide access to pooled and personal VMs, then you must use RD Connection Broker as the source, because only RD Connection Broker receives data from RD Virtualization Host servers regarding the VMs that they provide. Because RD Connection Broker can also be configured to consume resource data from RD Session Host servers and farms, it can act as an overall source for all available resources.

If you assign one or more RD Session Host servers or farm names as the source, the RD Web Access role service gets the resource data from this source by querying the WMI interfaces on the source to see what applications are on the allow list and are configured to be shown in the portal.

If you configure RD Connection Broker as the source, RD Web Access queries the RD Connection Broker using RPC. RD Connection Broker queries the RD Session host servers and farms that it knows about, gets the resource data, and passes it to RD Web Access.

Like RDP files created using the RemoteApp Manager, the dynamically created RDP files on the RD Web Access RemoteApp Programs tab adhere to the configuration settings specified in RemoteApp Manager. For example, if RemoteApp Manager global settings specify connecting to an RD Session Host server farm, then the RDP files created by RD Web Access RemoteApp Programs tab will also contain this setting. Likewise, if RemoteApp Manager contains RD Gateway settings, then RD Web Access RDP files are also set up to connect through RD Gateway.

Installing the RD Web Access Role Service

To install RD Web Access on a server running Windows Server 2008 R2, open Server Manager and follow these steps.

1. If the RD Session Host Services role is not installed, right-click Roles, click Add Roles, and then choose the Remote Desktop Services role. Then add the RD Web Access role service.

2. If the server already has the Remote Desktop Services role installed, right-click the Remote Desktop Services Role in Server Manager, click Add Role Service, and choose the RD Web Access role service.

3. Because this server acts as a web server, you must install Internet Information Services (IIS) 7.5 for it to work. If IIS 7.5 is not installed already, you will be prompted to add the role service. Click Add Required Role Services. You will see a screen with an introduction to IIS 7. Click Next, review the Web Server role services that will be installed for IIS, and click Next.

4. Confirm the installation instructions and then click Install.

5. When the installation completes, the installation results will show that the RD Web Access role service and the IIS role installed successfully. Click Close.

Alternatively, you can use Windows PowerShell to install RD Web Access like this.

```
Import-Module Servermanager
add-WindowsFeature RDS-Web-Access -restart
```

A successful install gives the following results.

```
WARNING: [Installation] Succeeded: [Remote Desktop Services] Remote Desktop Web Access.
RD Web Access requires additional configuration. On the Configuration page of the RD Web
Access website, you need to specify the source that will provide the RemoteApp programs
and desktops that will be displayed to users. For more information, see <a href="ts_
remoteprograms.chm::/html/e1e047ce-d080-4568-b987-378fef46bea2.htm">Configuring the RD
Web Access Server</a>.

Success Restart Needed Exit Code Feature Result
------- -------------- --------- --------------
True    No             Success   {Web Server (IIS) Tools, IIS Management Co...
```

> **NOTE** If you choose to install via the command line, then any needed components, such as IIS 7.5, that are not installed already will be installed automatically and will appear in the Feature Results section of the installation summary.

Implementing RD Web Access installs the RD Web Access website to the RD Web virtual path of the IIS default website. The install directory is located at %WinDir%\Web\RDWeb.

Configuring RD Web Access

After you install the RD Web Access role service, there are two things you must do to configure it.

- Give the RD Web Access a source or sources to query.
- Allow the RD Web Access source or sources to communicate with RD Web Access.

Access the RD Web Access website by opening Windows Internet Explorer and entering this URL: ***https://*servername/rdweb**, where *servername* is the name of the RD Web Access server. You can also access the RD Web Access website by clicking Start, Administrative Tools, Remote Desktop Services, Remote Desktop Web Access Configuration on the RD Web Access server. The site is made up of three tabbed pages, as shown in Figure 9-33.

- **The RemoteApp Programs tab**   Provides users with links to RemoteApp programs and their pooled and personal VMs. The contents of this page are filtered to show only those resources that the logged-in user is allowed to use.
- **The Remote Desktop tab**   Provides users with a way to connect remotely to other desktops located on the network that allow incoming RDP connections.
- **The Configuration tab**   Used to configure the sources that RD Web Access queries for RemoteApp programs, remote desktops, and pooled and personal VMs. You have to be a member of the TS Web Access Administrators local group or the Administrators local group on the RD Web Access server to see and edit the sources on this tab.

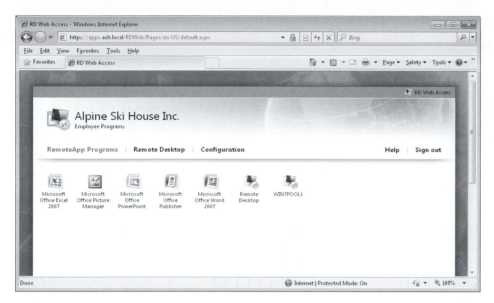

FIGURE 9-33 When you log in to the RD Web Access website, you have access to a tabbed interface.

Configuring the RD Web Access Source

To create the association between RD Web Access and its source or sources, perform the following steps.

1. Access RD Web Access by opening Internet Explorer and connecting to *https://server-name/rdweb,* or go to Start, Administrative Tools, Remote Desktop Services, RD Web Access Administration.

2. On the login page, enter a user name (in the form of *domain\username*) and password of an account that is a member of the TS Web Access Administrators group (domain administrators have this right).

3. Navigate to the configuration section of the website by clicking the Configuration tab, as shown in Figure 9-34. This tab is available only to members of the TSWeb Access Administrators group.

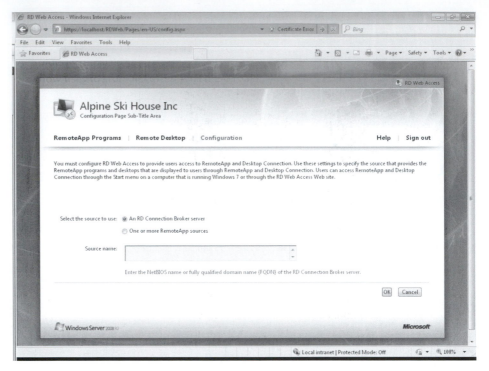

FIGURE 9-34 Click the Configuration tab to access the RD Web Access configuration area.

4. Select the radio button corresponding to the type of sources that will provide the RemoteApp and desktop information to RD Web Access.

5. Enter the name of the sources you want in the Source Name input box. If you chose the option One Or More RemoteApp Sources, separate each RD Session Host server or RD Session Host farm name source with a comma. When you are finished, click OK.

Each source that you choose for RD Web Access must be able to communicate with the role service. Grant this access by adding the RD Web Access computer account to the source's local TS Web Access security group.

RD Web Access Source Is One or More RD Session Host Servers and Farms

If you specify one or more RD Session Host servers or one or more RD Session Host server farms as the RD Web Access source, then each of those servers needs to have the RD Web Access server added to its TS Web Access Computers security group, as shown in Figure 9-35.

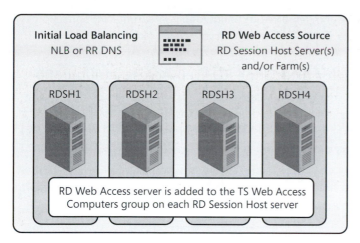

FIGURE 9-35 Give RD Web Access permission to query every RD Session Host server that is an RD Web Access source.

RD Web Access will query every individual RD Session Host server for its allow list and RemoteApp configuration. For farms, RD Web Access will choose one of the servers in each farm to query, but should that server become unavailable, it will query another farm member instead.

RD Web Access Source Is RD Connection Broker

For farm scenarios, if you specify an RD Connection Broker as the RD Web Access source, add the RD Connection Broker server to the TS Web Access Computers group on each farm member. Then add the RD Web Access computer account to the TS Web Access Computers group on the RD Connection Broker, as shown in Figure 9-36.

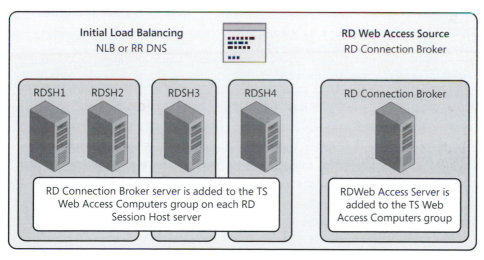

FIGURE 9-36 If RD Connection Broker is the RD Web Access source, RD Web Access gets allow list and RemoteApp configuration data from RD Connection Broker.

RD Web Access gets allow list and RemoteApp configuration data from RD Connection Broker, which gets the data from an RD Session Host server in each farm.

How a Dedicated Redirector Affects the RD Web Access Configuration

Using a dedicated redirector as your initial load balancer in a farm scenario also affects your RD Web Access configuration, because the redirector will act as the leader for the farm. Instead of querying a farm member for its allow list and configuration data, RD Web Access (or RD Connection Broker) will query the redirector.

In this scenario, if you use farm names as the RD Web Access source, you need to add the RD Web Access server computer account to the TS Web Access Computers group on the farm redirector or redirectors, as shown in Figure 9-37.

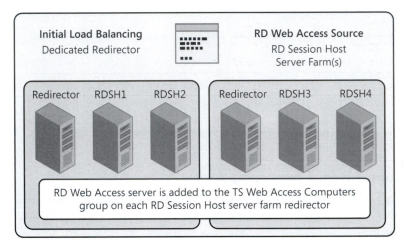

FIGURE 9-37 Add the RD Web Access server account to the RS Web Access Computers group on the redirector.

If you use RD Connection Broker as the RD Web Access source, you need to add the RD Connection Broker server computer account to the TS Web Access Computers group on the farm redirector or redirectors, and then add the RD Web Access server computer account to the TS Web Access Computers group on the RD Connection Broker, as shown in Figure 9-38.

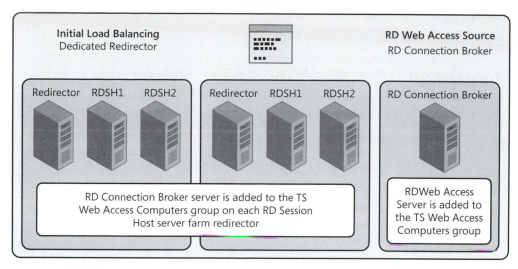

FIGURE 9-38 Add the RD Connection Broker server account to the RS Web Access Computers group on the redirector and add the RD Web Access server account to the TS Web Access Computers group on the RD Connection Broker.

Also, although the redirector is not accepting connections, it is a farm member in all other respects, and because RD Connection Broker or RD Web Access queries the redirector for allow list and RemoteApp configuration data, the redirector has to be configured identically to other farm members. This includes having the exact same RemoteApp settings. For example, if you do not add the farm certificate to a redirector, then when a RemoteApp is started from the website, it will be trying to reach the farm name, so it will show a certificate error when the name on the redirector certificate does not match the farm name, as shown in Figure 9-39.

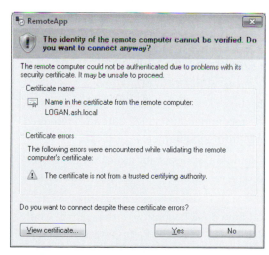

FIGURE 9-39 Avoid getting an error by adding the certificate containing the farm name to the RDP-Tcp Properties General tab of RD Session Host Configuration.

Configuring WebSSO

To minimize the number of times users must present credentials, enable Web SSO. Web SSO stores the credentials that a user uses to log on to the RD Web Access website and then uses them to authenticate the user when he or she opens a RemoteApp program via the website (or via RemoteApp And Desktop Connections on a client running Windows 7). The user does not receive any more login prompts when the user starts a RemoteApp.

> **NOTE** Web SSO works only for authentication to RemoteApp programs. There is no way to use Web SSO to pass credentials to a full desktop connection or VM connection.

To take advantage of Web SSO, the following must be in place.

- Clients must run Remote Desktop Connection (RDC) 7.0. Windows 7 comes with RDC 7.0. As discussed in Chapter 6, RDC 7.0 is available as an update for Windows XP SP3 and Windows Vista SP1 and SP2.

- RemoteApp programs must be signed with a SSL certificate or code signing certificate. If you are distributing applications from more than one farm or server, all RemoteApp programs must be signed with the same certificate. This is because Web SSO looks at the hash, or thumbprint, on the certificate. If you use different certificates for different farms, SSO will work only on a per-farm basis.

- Clients must trust the certificate used to sign the RemoteApp programs, meaning that the certificate that signed the SSL certificate must be located in the client's Computer Trusted Root Certification Authorities certificate store.

Customizing RD Web Access

RD Web Access lends itself to customization. Although a complete description of how to create a custom portal is outside the scope of this book, let's take a look at some of the options.

Configuring RD Web Access Remote Desktop Connection Options

Whereas with RemoteApps you'll configure settings from the RemoteApp Manager, the settings for Remote Desktops made available through RD Web Access are configured using settings on the IIS server hosting the website. We recommend using RD Gateway (described in Chapter 7) to provide secure access to desktops from the Internet.

To use RD Gateway with the RD Web Access Remote Desktops tab, you will need to provide the name of the RD Gateway server in IIS on the server that hosts the RD Web Access website.

On the RD Web Access server, open IIS. Expand the default website (or the website where you installed RD Web Access), expand the RDWeb folder, select the Pages folder, and in the pane on the right, double-click Application Settings. Double-click Default TSGateway, add the name of your RD Gateway server, and click OK. Then choose the TS Gateway authentication method by double-clicking GatewayCredentialsSource and specifying the corresponding number value as follows.

- **0** NTLM (password)
- **1** Smart Card
- **4** User Chooses Later (the default)

External users will access the Remote Desktops tab of the RD Web Access website and type in the name of the computer to which they want to connect. The connection will be made securely through RD Gateway.

If you do not want users to be able to use the Remote Desktop capabilities from the RD Web Access website, double-click Show Desktops and change the default entry (True) to False. This will hide the Remote Desktops tab. The changes take place immediately, so if the web page is open, refresh the page to see those changes. Allow or disallow the following resource redirection options by double-clicking each option and changing the value for the entry to True (enable) or False (disable).

- xClipboardxDriveRedirection
- xPnPRedirection
- xPortRedirection
- xPrinterRedirection

Alternatively, you can use a text editor such as Notepad to modify the Web.config file for the RD Web Access website located at %WinDir%/Web/RDWeb/Pages/Web.config. Locate these entries (under the heading<!-- Devices And Resources: Preset The Checkbox Values To Either True Or False -->) and change the value to "true" or "false" as needed as follows.

```
<add key="xPrinterRedirection" value="true" />
<add key="xClipboard" value="true" />
<add key="xDriveRedirection" value="true" />
<add key="xPnPRedirection" value="true" />
<add key="xPortRedirection" value="true" />
```

> **NOTE** If PnP, Port, and Drive redirection options are shaded and unavailable, add the website to the web browser's Trusted Sites list and they will become available.

When you allow other redirection capabilities (clipboard and printer redirection is enabled by default), they will not actually be enabled. However, by allowing other types of redirection you give users the option to enable that type of redirection when they initiate a connection via the Remote Desktops tab. When a user inputs a computer name and clicks Connect, the RDP file starts. The user can now click the Details button and enable the types of redirection that you have allowed by selecting the box next to the type of redirection that he or she wants to enable and then clicking Connect.

Why Do I See "Unknown Publisher" When Connecting to Remote Desktops?

Janani Venkateswaran
Program Manager

R DP file signing lets you put some user protection in place by allowing an RDP file's publisher to sign the file with a digital certificate. So, if you trust the publisher, you know you can trust the RDP connection. Unsigned files will show a warning label when they are started.

If you're using RD Web Access to make both RemoteApps and full remote desktops available, you might notice something odd if you're using RDP file signing. When you start RemoteApps, the dialog box will indicate that the files are signed (that is, they will identify the publisher of the file). When you start a connection from the Remote Desktops page, the dialog box will warn that the Publisher is not known, meaning that the file is unsigned.

Whether you click an icon on the RemoteApp Programs page or the Connect button on the Remote Desktops page, doing so creates an RDP file. There's one important difference between these approaches, however: When you click an icon on the RemoteApp Programs page, an RDP file that has been created from settings on the RD Session Host server is channeled to the client. When you click Connect on the Remote Desktops page, the client creates the RDP file. The following illustrations show this.

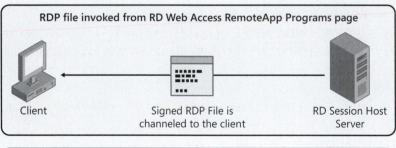

RDP file invoked from RD Web Access RemoteApp Programs page

Client — Signed RDP File is channeled to the client — RD Session Host Server

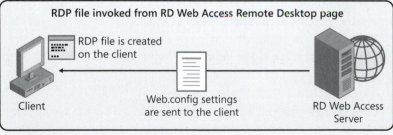

RDP file invoked from RD Web Access Remote Desktop page

Client — RDP file is created on the client — Web.config settings are sent to the client — RD Web Access Server

RDP signing is available for RemoteApps but not for connections to full desktops. Here's why: The RDP file created when you start a RemoteApp from RD Web Access is created on the RD Session Host server using the configuration settings set in RemoteApp Manager. You can specify a digital certificate in RemoteApp Manager with which to sign RemoteApps. If you have specified a digital certificate, the RDP file will be signed when it's created and then channeled to the client. Thus, the publisher of the RDP file will be identified to the client.

In contrast, an RDP file is created on the client when you click the Connect button on the Remote Desktops page, combining the settings specified in the Web.config file and Desktop.aspx on the RD Web Access server, along with any input from the user. There's no setting on the client to specify a digital certificate to use to sign RDP files that it creates. The client does not sign the file, and the publisher is shown as unidentifiable.

Customizing the RDC Client Update Settings

So far, the assumption is that the client already has RDC 6.1 or later installed, so it can start RemoteApps from RD Web Access. But what if the correct version *isn't* installed? To make it easier for users to get the correct version of the client, you can customize the link to point to an internal page hosting the required clients and service packs. This allows you to support users connecting to RD Web Access from an intranet with no Internet access or to standardize on a version of the client that you think appropriate.

To modify the target URL, log on to the RD Web Access server as an administrator and follow these steps.

1. Open IIS Manager by clicking Start, Administrative Tools, Internet Information Services (IIS) Manager.

2. In the navigation pane of IIS Manager, expand the server name, expand Sites, expand Default Web Site, and then click RDWeb. (By default, RD Web Access is installed to this location. If you installed RD Web Access to a different site, locate it and then click the site name.)

3. Under ASP.NET, double-click Application Settings. In the Actions pane, click Add, and then, in the Add Application Setting dialog box, do the following.

   a. In the Name text box, type **rdcInstallUrl**.

   b. In the Value text box, enter the target URL for the link.

NOTE To restore the link to point to the default URL, right-click the rdcInstallUrl application setting and then click Remove.

Alternatively, you can use a text editor such as Notepad to modify the Web.config file for the RD Web Access website directly. By default, the path of the configuration file is

%WinDir%\Web\RDweb\Web.config. To modify the file, under the <appSettings> section of the file, add an entry like this one, where *URL* is the target URL for the link.

```
<add key="rdcInstallUrl" value="http://URL" />.
```

This will update the page to the new location.

Changing RD Web Access RemoteApp Display

The default RD Web Access RemoteApp Programs web page is pretty basic—it shows the application icons, and that's about it. However, you can customize it to suit your needs. For instance, you might want to provide other links to web-based applications, documents, websites, or any other web-based content. RD Web Access doesn't have any easy way to add more data, but other frameworks, such as Microsoft SharePoint, do.

For example, you can integrate the Web Part that makes RemoteApp programs available on the RD Web Access website into a SharePoint website, as shown in Figure 9-40. The details of how to do this are outside the scope of this book, but there is a link to the step-by-step guide on the companion media.

 ON THE COMPANION MEDIA A link to "Customizing Remote Desktop Web Access by Using Windows SharePoint Services Step-by-Step Guide" is available on the companion media, or you can download it from *http://www.microsoft.com/downloads /details.aspx?displaylang=en&FamilyID=eb2b786f-2a70-4045-a899-6d7c9a794fbc.*

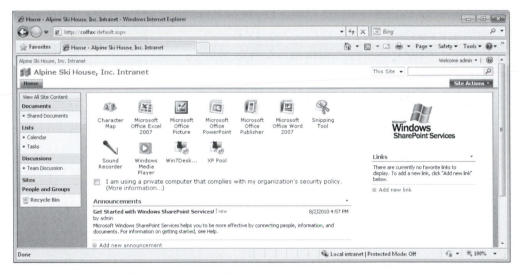

FIGURE 9-40 Add RD Web Access support to SharePoint.

Customizing Titles and Subtitles

There are three main pages of the RD Web Access website: RemoteApp Programs, Remote Desktop, and Configuration. Each page contains two lines in the upper-left portion of the page:

- The Page Title (the default is "Remote Desktop Services Default Connection")
- A page description or Subtitle area (the default is "Remote Desktop Services Default Connection")

Here is how to rename each page.

- All Page Titles are changed by editing the %WinDir%\Web\RDWeb\App_Data\ RDWebAccess.Config file line.

```
<WorkspaceSettings Name="YOUR TEXT HERE" ID="servername.domain.suffix"
    Description="" />
```

- However, if you set the Connection Settings on an RD Connection Broker server, these will show up as the Display name for all RD Web Access website pages.

- To change the Subtitle area of the Login page, open Login.aspx in a text editor and find and edit this string.

```
const string L_ApplicationName_Text = "YOUR TEXT HERE";
```

- To change the "Subtitle area" of the RemoteApp Programs page, edit the %WinDir%\Web\RDWeb\Pages\en-US\Default.aspx page line.

```
const string L_ApplicationName_Text = "YOUR TEXT HERE"
```

- To change the "Subtitle area" of the Remote Desktops page, edit the %WinDir%\Web\RDWeb\Pages\en-US\Desktops.aspx page line.

```
const string L_ApplicationName_Text = "YOUR TEXT HERE"
```

- To change the "Subtitle area" of the Configuration page, edit the %WinDir%\Web\RDWeb\Pages\en-US\Config.aspx page line.

```
const string L_ApplicationName_Text = "YOUR TEXT HERE"
```

Adding a Domain Name When Users Forget To

Users might forget to add the domain name as part of their login credentials. You can edit the website code to check this and, if the domain name is not present, add it to the login user name. To do this, open the Renderscript.js file located in the %WinDir%\Web\RDWeb\Pages folder, find the following code block, and change it from this

```
if ( objForm != null )
    {
strDomainUserName = objForm.elements("DomainUserName").value;
strPassword = objForm.elements("UserPass").value;
strWorkspaceId = objForm.elements("WorkSpaceID").value;
strRDPCertificates = objForm.elements("RDPCertificates").value;
```

to this

```
if ( objForm != null )
    {
strDomainUserName = objForm.elements("DomainUserName").value;

        // add default domain...
        if ( strDomainUserName.indexOf("\\") == -1 )
        {
strDomainUserName = "YOUR-DOMAIN-HERE"\\ + strDomainUserName;
objForm.elements("DomainUserName").value = strDomainUserName;
        }
strPassword = objForm.elements("UserPass").value;
strWorkspaceId = objForm.elements("WorkSpaceID").value;
strRDPCertificates = objForm.elements("RDPCertificates").value;
```

Substitute your domain NetBIOS name in the code where it says "YOUR-DOMAIN-HERE" (in bold in the code shown here).

Force RDC Connections Through RD Gateway via RD Web Access

By design, if you connect to a Remote Desktop through RD Web Access, the RDP file will bypass RD Gateway if the RD Session Host server and client are on the same network. RD Web Access uses Web.config to provide RDP settings to the client so the client can create its own RDP file for connecting to the RD Session Host server. None of those settings force the use of RD Gateway.

You can force the use of RD Gateway if appropriate by editing the web page presenting Remote Desktops. The *GatewayUsageMethod* property to the *IMsRdpClientTransportSettings* interface has five possible values. To force clients connecting to Remote Desktops via RD Web Access to use RD Gateway, change the value of this property from 2 (which selects the check box for the Bypass RD Gateway Server For Local Addresses option in the Remote Desktop Connection user interface) to 1 (which clears the check box for the Bypass RD Gateway Server For Local Addresses option in the Remote Desktop Connection user interface). See the following "Direct from the Source" sidebar for more details.

Forcing the Use of RD Gateway for Remote Desktops

Rob Leitman
Senior Software Development Engineer

Let's say that you're attempting to access a Remote Desktop via RD Web Access. Although the clients attempting to access the RD Web Access page are all on the same subnet as the RD Web Access server, you've configured the network so that they're actually connecting via the Internet, not the intranet. Therefore, you'd like to require that these clients use RD Gateway.

There's no check box on the Remote Desktops page to force the use of RD Gateway, but you can make it happen by editing Desktop.aspx from this

```
if ((DefaultTSGateway != null) && (DefaultTSGateway.length> 0)) {
RDPstr += "gatewayusagemethod:i:2\n";
```

to this

```
if ((DefaultTSGateway != null) &&(DefaultTSGateway.length> 0)) {
RDPstr += "gatewayusagemethod:i:1\n";
```

All Remote Desktop connections initiated from that RD Web Access site should now go through RD Gateway.

RDWA Customization: This Is A Private Computer Selected by Default

To preselect This Is A Private Computer on the RD Web Access login page, open the Logon.aspx page located at %WinDir%\Web\RDWeb\Pages\en-US\ using a text editor and make the following changes.

Remove the word "checked" from this code snippet.

```
<label><input id="rdoPblc" type="radio" name="MachineType" value="public"
    class="rdo" onclick"onClickSecurity()"  checked /></label>
```

Then add the word "checked" to the following code snippet.

```
<label><input id="rdoPrvt" type="radio" name="MachineType" value="private"
    class="rdo" onclick"onClickSecurity()" checked /></label>
```

Finally, save the file.

Troubleshooting RD Web Access Permissions

If you run into problems implementing RD Web Access, it's sometimes a permissions problem. Here are some general troubleshooting tips.

- Make sure that the correct computer accounts are added to the needed security groups on RD Session Host servers and RD Connection Broker.

- The Windows Authorization Access Group located in Active Directory Users And Computers needs to have the RD Connection Broker server in it if it is used in RD Web Access to check access control lists (ACLs) and do the filtering.

- If you have verified that the pertinent permissions have been given to the appropriate servers and you still receive Event id 1011 on the RD Connection Broker,

  - Look in the Event Viewer under Applications and Services Logs/Microsoft/ Windows/RemoteApp and Desktop Connection Management and and see if any errors exist there that will lead you to how to fix your issue.

  - Check to see that WMI Security and COM security are correct on each RD Session Host server. This is normally taken care of for you, but it is worth checking if you are having problems adding an RD Web Access source to the website. On each RD Session Host server, check the following.

WMI Security Settings:

1. Start the WMI Control MMC snap-in.

2. Right-click the WMI Control node and select Properties.

3. Go to the Security tab and navigate to Root, CIMV2, TerminalServices.

4. Highlight TerminalServices and click Security.

5. Confirm that local server\TSWeb Access Computers listed with Execute Methods, Enable Account, and Remote Enable is set to Allow.

DCOM Security Settings:

1. Start the Component Services MMC snap-in and navigate to Component Services, Computers, My Computer.

2. Right-click My Computer and select Properties.

3. Go to the COM Security tab, and under Access Permissions, click Edit Limits.

4. Make sure the TS Web Access Computers have all the permissions set to Allow.

5. Under Launch And Activation Permissions, click Edit Limits and confirm that the local server \TSWeb Access Computers is listed, with all the permissions set to Allow.

Using the RD Web Access Website

The RD Web Access role service supports two ways of presenting applications to users: the RD Web Access website and the RemoteApp And Desktop Connections tool in Windows 7. In this section, you'll learn how to use the RD Web Access website.

> **NOTE** To use RD Web Access, the clients must have RDC 6.1 or later installed. RDC 7.0 or later is recommended for the best user experience. See Chapter 6 for more information about RDC and where to get updated versions of the client.

Users access the RD Web Access website by browsing to *https://servername/rdweb* using Internet Explorer. The user will be presented with a login screen.

For these pages to work, the Microsoft Remote Desktop Services Web Access ActiveX control must be enabled. Clients logging onto the website for the first time should see a pop-up message that asks for permission to install the ActiveX control, as shown in Figure 9-41.

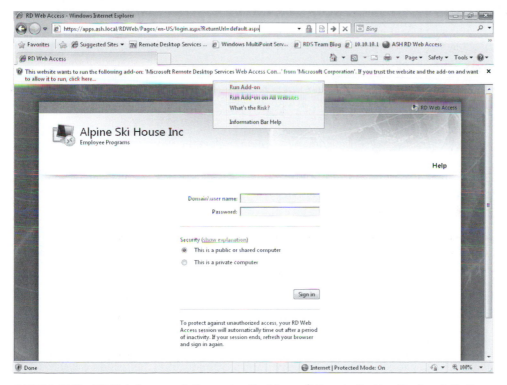

FIGURE 9-41 The RD Web Access website requires the Microsoft Remote Desktop Services ActiveX control to be enabled.

Right-click the Information Bar (a yellow bar) and choose Run Add-on to install the control. Users running Windows XP SP3 might not see this pop-up message. Instead, the user might log in and get the message shown in Figure 9-42.

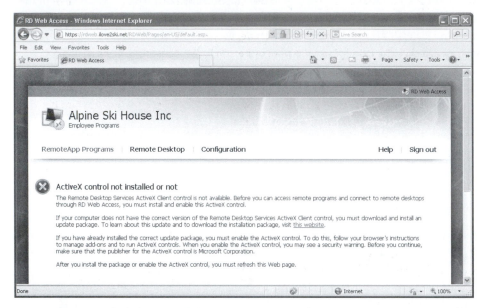

FIGURE 9-42 Users of Windows XP might receive a message telling them that the Remote Desktop Services ActiveX client is not available.

To install the control, click Tools/Internet Options, select the Programs tab, and click the Manage Add-ons button at the bottom of the dialog box. Select Show All Add-ons from the drop-down menu on the right side of the page. Then find the Microsoft RDP Client Control in the left pane, select it, and click the Enable button at the lower-right side of the page. Then click Close.

To log onto the website, enter a user name in the form of *domain\username,* such as ASH\ kristin.griffin. Enter the user's password. Choose a security mode that describes the computer that you are using, and then click Sign in.

Logging In

The RD Web Access login page has an option that specifies whether the computer used to access RD Web Access is a private computer, meaning you are the only one that uses the computer, or a public computer. If you pick the Private option, then the session will stay active longer if there is a period of inactivity.

When you have logged on to the website, you will be taken to the RemoteApps page shown in Figure 9-43.

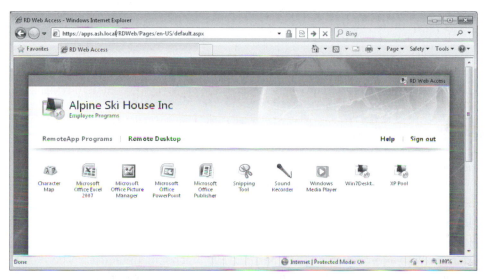

FIGURE 9-43 The RD Web Access RemoteApp Programs page offers a number of options.

When users open the RD Web Access website, they are provided with a web page with two tabs, the RemoteApp Programs tab and the Remote Desktops tab. The RemoteApp Programs tab contains links to available RemoteApps and VMs and also links to full desktop sessions for RD Session Host servers or farms as permitted in RemoteApp Manager. The Remote Desktops tab provides access to other remote desktops on the network.

When a user clicks a RemoteApp icon in RD Web Access (or chooses a desktop to connect to, as discussed in the next section, "Connecting to Resources), the ActiveX control in the browser creates a temporary RDP file in the user's Temp folder on the client. The RDP file will have a randomly generated name that begins with TSPORTAL and includes a five-digit number. Next, the ActiveX control calls Mstsc.exe and points it to the path of the new RDP file, as in this example for an RDP file named TSPORTAL#12345.

```
mstsc.exe /web/ webfilename:%userprofile%\AppData\Local\Temp\TSPORTAL#12345.rdp
```

This command starts Mstsc.exe exactly as if you had pointed it to any other RDP file, creating the connection.

Connecting to Resources

You can use the RD Web Access website to connect to RemoteApp programs, VMs, full desktops on a RD Session Host server, or even your personal computer.

The resources that a user sees are based on his or her access rights—that is, users see only resources that they in fact have permission to access. When a user clicks an application icon, this will start an RDP file and the RemoteApp executes. If you remove an application from the allow list on the RD Session Host server(s), the application is no longer displayed in the web part.

One of the biggest advantages of deploying RemoteApps using RD Web Access is that the RDP files created through the website use the settings specified in the RemoteApp Manager of the associated RD Session Host server. Therefore, they are always up to date. You don't need to redistribute RDP files to users whenever a change occurs in the RemoteApp Manager.

> **NOTE** You might notice that some settings do not change immediately in RD Web Access when you make a change to an RD Web Access source and you use RD Connection Broker as the source. This is because the RD Web Access service caches settings from RD Connection Broker for three minutes at a time for performance reasons.

A popular feature of RD Web Access (especially when combined with RD Gateway, as discussed in Chapter 10) has nothing to do with RemoteApp programs at all. Rather, it's the ability to connect to a computer desktop (such as your company computer desktop located in your office) from the Internet. This is useful for users who need access to their desktop computers from other locations (telecommuting), or for users who need access to more than one computer on the corporate network.

> **NOTE** The user needs to be a member of the Remote Desktop Users group of the specified computer to connect remotely to that computer.

From the Remote Desktops tab, a user provides the name of the computer to connect with, and an RDP file is created and opened. The user provides proper credentials, and the remote desktop session starts.

To get to your desktop, first make sure that the RD Web Access site is one of your Trusted
websites. Then click the Remote Desktop link to open the Remote Desktop page shown in
Figure 9-44.

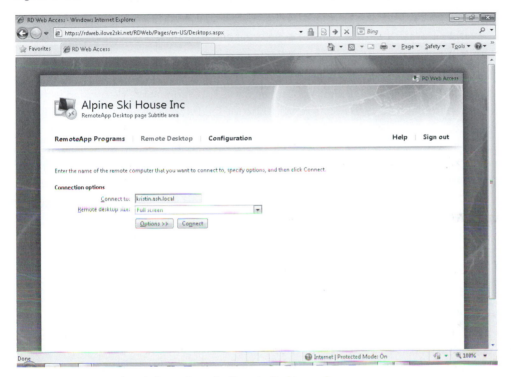

FIGURE 9-44 Access other desktops from the Remote Desktop webpage.

From here, users can connect to servers—and other computers that have Remote Desktop
enabled—by typing in the name of the computer, selecting the screen size, and clicking Connect. When a user clicks Connect, an RDP file pointing to the computer specified is created on
the user's computer, using the settings defined in Web.config on the RD Web Access server.

The Options button provides a set of RDP settings that the user can adjust, including device and resource redirection, whether to allow keyboard shortcuts in the remote desktop session, and the speed of the connection. However, if these options are specified using Group Policy or RD Configuration, then the settings specified by the user are ignored.

Using RemoteApp And Desktop Connections

RD Web Access is both a role service and a website. The role service supplies the website with the RemoteApp programs and VMs provided for the users, but it also supplies RemoteApp And Desktop Connections, a Control Panel setting on computers running Windows 7 and Windows Server 2008 R2. RemoteApp And Desktop Connections connects to a URL that you provide and populates the Start menu of the client with a new folder called RemoteApp And Desktop Connections.

The RD Web Access website is built with HTML generated from the RD Web Access server, but the RemoteApp And Desktop Connections application on the client is fed with an XML feed from the RD Web Access server. This XML feed works like an RSS feed, and like an RSS feed, it will be updated regularly as the contents of the data source are updated. If the administrator adds a RemoteApp or removes a VM pool, the change will appear in RemoteApp And Desktop Connections—there's no need for the user to log out and log back in again. Because the feed aggregator is built into the operating system, this feature is available only on Windows 7 and Windows Server 2008 R2. It's not part of the RDC 7 client; it just works with it. You can't add it to Windows XP or Windows Vista.

HOW IT WORKS

The Publishing Feed

The publishing feed populating RemoteApp And Desktop Connections on Windows 7 is essentially a Really Simple Syndication (RSS) feed from RD Web Access. Rather than being a list of new blog entries or news articles, like most common feeds, this one is a compilation of all the RemoteApp programs and VMs on the desktop, filtered according to the security credentials the user entered when logging on. The RSS feed aggregator is desktop-based, so the contents are visible—even though not accessible—even when the user is not logged on. If the user clicks a link, he or she will be prompted for credentials.

Configuring RemoteApp And Desktop Connections on Unmanaged Computers

One advantage to using RD Web Access to display RDS resources is that the computer the user connects from doesn't have to be a work computer. As long as users know which URL to connect to and the computer meets the minimum requirements for connecting (RDC 6.1 to use the RD Web Access website, or Windows 7 to connect to RemoteApp And Desktop Connections), then they can log on from anywhere they can connect. The computer they use does not have to be joined to the domain or have ever been connected to it.

To set up RemoteApp And Desktop Connections manually, follow these steps.

1. Open the Control Panel and click the icon for RemoteApp And Desktop Connections to open the initial screen. If no RemoteApp And Desktop Connections exist now, the right pane will be blank.

2. Click the link to add a new RemoteApp And Desktop Connection.

3. Type the URL the administrator provided in the text box. This URL will look something like this: *https://servername/rdweb/feed/webfeed.aspx*, where *servername* is the name of the RD Web Access server. Click Next.

4. You'll see a warning that you're connecting to the feed and this will download content to your computer. Click Next again to agree to this.

5. You'll see a process bar as the connection is made, and then you'll see a display screen showing that the connection was made successfully (see Figure 9-45). This page will show the name of the resource and the RemoteApp programs and VMs assigned to you.

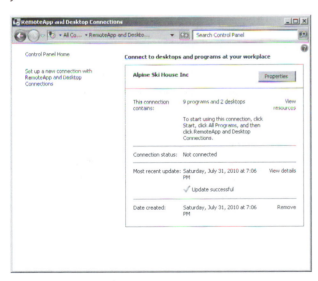

FIGURE 9-45 When you connect successfully to a RemoteApp and Desktop Connection feed, the number of resources at the time of connection will appear in the feed.

After you've connected to the feed, the contents will appear on the Start menu, as shown in Figure 9-46. It's possible to connect to more than one feed; the contents of each will appear as nested folders.

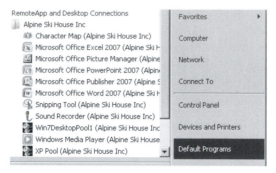

FIGURE 9-46 All RemoteApp And Desktop Connections appear on the Start menu.

Configuring to RemoteApp And Desktop Connections on Managed Computers

The simplest way to set up RemoteApp And Desktop Connections is using a script and Group Policy. The RDS team has created a Windows PowerShell script that you can run at user logon time to set up the connection on a computer—just configure the script to run at logon in Group Policy, as discussed in Chapter 5. The script is called Configure RemoteApp and Desktop Connection on Windows 7 Clients, and you will find a link to it on the companion media.

 ON THE COMPANION MEDIA You can download the Configure RemoteApp and Desktop Connection on Windows 7 Clients script located at *http://gallery.technet. microsoft.com/ScriptCenter/en-us/313a95b3-a698-4bb0-9ed6-d89a47eacc72* on the companion media.

Connecting to a RemoteApp from the Start Menu

Connecting to a RemoteApp in the feed is very simple: Click its icon on the Start menu to start the connection. At this point, one of two things will happen.

- If you've already logged into the RD Web Access website and Web SSO is enabled, you'll be able to start any RemoteApp in any farm without providing credentials again.
- If you have not already logged into RD Web Access or Web SSO is not enabled, you'll be prompted for your credentials to start the first RemoteApp in a farm.

If you click an icon for a VM pool or personal VM, you'll always need to provide your credentials because WebSSO does not work for VMs, just for RemoteApp programs.

Updating a RemoteApp and Desktop Connection

The feed will update regularly (refreshing itself every 24 hours; this doesn't mean you will necessarily wait 24 hours to see changes you made), but you can also force updates if required. To do so, open RemoteApp And Desktop Connections in the Control Panel and choose the connection, click Properties, and then click Update. Then click OK.

Removing a RemoteApp and Desktop Connection

Removing a connection is extremely simple. After you've connected the client to a feed, this connection will appear every time that you open RemoteApp And Desktop Connections. To remove it, click the Remove link. You'll be prompted to confirm that you want to remove the connection. Click Yes, and the connection is gone.

 CAUTION   The URL isn't cached anywhere, so don't break a connection that you might want to return to without having the URL available.

Summary

One of the best things about RDS is that it reduces the cost of adding one more user to the company or department. Rather than setting up a computer for each person, you just give access to the VM pool or to the RD Session Host server. To really take advantage of this flexibility, you'll need to deploy more than one server to build a farm.

At this point, you should know

- How to load-balance initial connections to a farm
- How you can display remote resources for users
- How to configure RD Web Access server to display RemoteApp programs and VMs and how to filter their display according to user identity
- How the roles supporting farm access work together
- Methods of customizing the resource display

So far, this book has focused on accessing VMs and RemoteApp programs from the LAN. In Chapter 10, you'll move on to information about supporting WAN scenarios with RD Gateway.

Additional Resources

These resources contain additional information and tools related to this chapter.

- For information on creating a Kerberos identity for an RD Session Host server farm, see the article on the team blog located at *http://blogs.msdn.com/b/rds /archive/2009/05/20/creating-kerberos-identity-for-rd-session-host-farms-part-i-using-the-remote-desktop-services-provider-for-windows-powershell.aspx*.

- See the companion media for a link to *http://blog.powershell.no/category/remote-desktop-services/*, where you can find a new Windows PowerShell module for RDS that includes cmdlets for importing and exporting allow lists.

- A link to "Customizing Remote Desktop Web Access by Using Windows SharePoint Services Step-by-Step Guide" is available on the companion media, or you can download it from *http://www.microsoft.com/downloads/details.aspx?displaylang= en&FamilyID=eb2b786f-2a70-4045-a899-6d7c9a794fbc*.

- Download the Configure RemoteApp and Desktop Connection on Windows 7 Clients script from *http://gallery.technet.microsoft.com/ScriptCenter/en-us/313a95b3-a698-4bb0-9ed6-d89a47eacc72*. (The link is also available on the companion media.)

- You can add command-line switches when starting Office applications. For example, see *http://office.microsoft.com/en-us/excel-help/command-line-switches-for-excel-HA010158030.aspx#BM4* to open Excel with custom options. Also, see *http://partners. adobe.com/public/developer/en/acrobat/PDFOpenParameters.pdf#page=5* to learn how to open Adobe Acrobat files with custom options.

Making Remote Desktop Services Available from the Internet

So far in this book, you have learned how to access RemoteApp programs, virtual machines (VMs), and Remote Desktop (RD) Session Host sessions when your users are located on your internal network. But what if they want to access these resources from home, from an Internet café, or another public place? The RD Gateway role service allows secure Remote Desktop Protocol (RDP) access from clients located outside the corporate network to resources located inside the corporate network, without needing any special software on the client, as long as it supports connecting via RD Gateway.

How RD Gateway Works

RD Gateway is an RDS role service that acts as a intermediary between the external client and the internal resource that the user wants to use. It governs who is allowed to connect via RD Gateway (Connection Access Policies, or CAPs) and what resources (VMs, sessions, even physical computers) the people who are allowed to connect can use (Resource Access Policies, or RAPs). This is how it works.

1. A user wanting access to an internal RDP resource runs the RDP file pointing to that resource, whether from a saved RDP file, from RemoteApp and Desktop Connections, from RD Web Access, or by starting a Remote Desktop Connection (RDC) and typing in the needed information to make the connection.

2. The RDP file is configured with the RD Gateway information defined locally, or when the resource was published, and the connection request goes to RD Gateway.

3. RD Gateway first authenticates the client and verifies that the client is authorized to make this connection by checking the user credentials against its RD Connection Access Policies (RD CAPs).

4. If the client is authenticated and authorized, RD Gateway then verifies that the client is allowed to connect to the requested resource by checking its RD Resource Access Policies (RD RAPs).

5. If the client is allowed access to the requested resource, RD Gateway establishes an RDP connection to the resource. Thereafter, all traffic for this connection is proxied through RD Gateway, as shown in Figure 10-1. RD Gateway forwards packets back and forth from the RD Session Host server and the remote client, sending RDP packets over port 3389 to the internal RDP resource, and Secure Sockets Layer (SSL)–encapsulated packets over port 443 to the remote client.

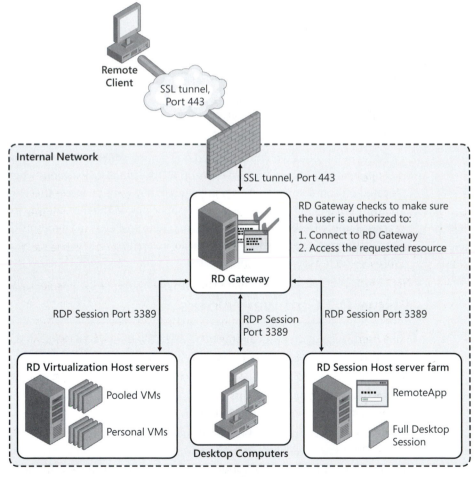

FIGURE 10-1 RD Gateway acts as the middleman for connections to RDP resources.

Understanding RD Gateway Authorization Policies

RD Gateway uses two distinct types of authorization policies, in consecutive order, to control connections to internal RDP resources. First, the connecting client's user, and optionally computer credentials, are checked against RD CAPs to see that the connecting client is allowed to access RD Gateway. Specifically, RD CAPs define

- Which users (specified by user group membership) can connect to RD Gateway
- From which computers (specified by computer group membership) users can connect (optional)
- Supported authentication methods (smart card or password)
- Which client devices will be redirected to the remote session
- Optional timeouts for active and idle sessions

RD CAPs are stored in a Network Policy Server (NPS), part of the Network Policy and Access Services role in Windows Server 2008 R2. The Network Policy and Access Services role is installed automatically when you install RD Gateway; if you like, you can elect to store the RD CAPs on a central NPS to allow multiple RD Gateway servers to draw their RD CAPs from the same server. (This also makes sense if you're using NPS for other reasons.)

> **NOTE** The section entitled "Using a Central NPS to Store RD CAPs" later in this chapter provides more information about how to set up centralized RD CAPs.

After the RD Gateway has established that its RD CAPs allow the user to connect, it checks the resource requested against its RD RAPs. RD RAPs specify which internal resources (specified by computer groups) a user is allowed to access via RD Gateway. This two-tiered system makes it possible to specify, for example, that a user can connect via the Internet but cannot connect to his or her desktop computer via RD Gateway, even though he or she can do so when connecting from the local area network (LAN).

Think of RD CAPs and RD RAPs as specifying *who* can get to *what*. RD CAPs define *who* can connect to RD Gateway, and RD RAPs define *what* internal resources user groups can connect to after they connect to RD Gateway. You can have multiple RD CAPs and RD RAPs in use at the same time. A user must meet the requirements specified on at least one RD CAP and one RD RAP to connect to RD Gateway and then to do anything after that.

To use RD Gateway, you must create at least one RD CAP and one RD RAP. But you might need more than one of each to control access to RD Gateway and to network resources more explicitly. Defining multiple RD CAPs and RD RAPs allows you to be very specific when granting network access instead of giving clients full access to every RDP-enabled device on the network that they could get to while on the LAN.

It's easiest if you group RD CAPs and RD RAPs conceptually. For instance, you can use two RD CAPs and two RD RAPs to specify the following connection requirements.

- Company Accounting Team Remote Access Authorization Policies

- RD CAP: Accounting user group members can establish a connection to RD Gateway, but only when they are using computers that belong to the Accounting computer group. These users can connect only using smart cards, and device redirection will be disabled.

- RD RAP: Accounting group users can then connect only to Accounting computers as well as the company RDS farm.

■ Company Sales Team Remote Access Authorization Policies

- RD CAP: Sales user group members can connect to RD Gateway from any computer. They can use password authentication, and clipboard and printer redirection are allowed.

- RD RAP: Sales user group members can connect to computers that are members of the Sales computer group.

> **NOTE** The next section will show you how to create an RD CAP and RD RAP as part of the RD Gateway installation procedures. For information on creating RD CAPs and RD RAPs post-installation, see the section entitled "Creating and Maintaining RD Gateway Authorization Policies" later in this chapter.

RD Gateway Requirements

RD Gateway is an RDS role service and therefore runs on Windows Server 2008 R2. Hardware requirements can vary, depending on the load the role service will accommodate. But in general, RD Gateway can accommodate a large number of concurrent connections on standard server hardware. For example, RD Gateway capacity planning information provided in the Windows Server 2008 R2 guide shows that a dual processor server with 4 GB of RAM can accommodate more than 1200 connections.

> **ON THE COMPANION MEDIA** Get the RD Gateway Capacity Planning in Windows Server 2008 R2 guide at *http://www.microsoft.com/downloads/en/details.aspx?displaylang=en&FamilyID=d31ac8fd-6ad8-4c5e-8dc3-a93fb55abc76*. This link is also available on the companion media.

It's also worth noting that RD Gateway can be virtualized. RD Gateway can also be limited as to the number of simultaneous connections it can accommodate, depending on the version of Windows Server 2008 R2 you are using. See the section entitled "Limiting Simultaneous Connections to RD Gateway" later in this chapter for more information on this limitation. Windows Server 2008 R2 Standard edition can accommodate a maximum of 256 connections. Foundation edition can accommodate a maximum of 50 simultaneous connections. Windows Server 2008 R2 Enterprise and Datacenter editions are unlimited.

To implement RD Gateway, you'll need certificates that allow the client and RD Gateway to set up a trusted communications channel, and the clients will need to use a supported operating system and RDP client.

First, you'll need a certificate for RD Gateway to use. For RD Gateway and remote clients to establish an encrypted connection to one another, you must install a server authentication certificate (an SSL certificate) in the RD Gateway server certificate store. You can get the certificate from a public certificate authority (CA), or if you maintain your own Public Key Infrastructure (PKI), you can generate your own server authentication certificate.

> **NOTE** For testing purposes, you can create a self-signed certificate using RD Gateway Manager, but it is not recommended to use self-signed certificates in a production environment.

Regardless of where you get the certificate, remote computers connecting to the RD Gateway server will attempt to verify the validity of the RD Gateway certificate. They do this by searching their own trusted root certificate store for the root CA certificate of the CA that signed the RD Gateway certificate. If the root CA certificate is there, the client trusts the root CA and therefore can trust the RD Gateway server (this is called the *chain of trust*). If not, then the connection will not be established.

It's often easiest if you use public certificates or have your own certificates signed by a public CA. You might not have control over the remote computers used to connect to RD Gateway if they're not company assets or computers belonging to the users connecting via the Internet. Therefore, either purchase an SSL certificate from a public CA that is part of the Microsoft Root Certificate Program or have your root CA certificate cosigned by a public CA that is part of this program. Members of this program have their root CA certificates already installed on Windows operating systems (and they can be updated by Windows Update), so you will decrease the chance of user connections failing due to certificate validation issues. If you use certificates that aren't already in the client's trusted store, users will need to install them before they can connect to RD Gateway.

> **NOTE** For more information on the Microsoft Root Certificate Program and certificates in general, see Chapter 9, "Multi-Server Deployments."

To work with RD Gateway, the SSL certificate must have the following attributes.

- The certificate must be a computer certificate because users will be authenticating with a server, not a person.
- The extended key usage for the certificate must be Server Authentication (OID 1.3.6.1.5.5.7.3.1).
- The certificate Subject name should match the Domain Name System (DNS) name that the client will use to connect. For instance, if remote users will connect to the RD Gateway name of rdgateway.ilove2ski.net, this needs to be the subject on the certificate. You can also use a wildcard certificate to work for all subdomains (for example, *.ilove2ski.net).

NOTE To specify multiple alternative names for a certificate, use a certificate that uses the Subject Alternative Name (SAN) attribute. For example, if you use both the .com and .net variations of your domain, you can specify both rdgateway.ilove2ski.net and rdgateway.ilove2ski.com. If the certificate uses the SAN attributes, then users can connect only using RDP 6.1 (available in Windows Vista SP1, Windows XP SP3, or Windows Server 2008) and later.

Second, you'll need to ensure that the clients can use RD Gateway. RD Gateway has the following client requirements.

- The clients must be running Windows XP (With Service Pack 2) or later. Windows CE and non-Windows clients don't work with RD Gateway natively.

- The clients must have RDC 6.0 or later installed, or RDC 7 to support all the features of RD Gateway in Windows Server 2008 R2.

NOTE Although you can technically connect to RD Gateway using RDC 6.0, we recommend using RDC 6.1 or later. RDC 6.0 lacks some important features such as the ability to access RD Web Access and the ability to use SAN certificates on RD Gateway. And remember, you need RDC 7.0 or later to get the latest feature set.

Installing RD Gateway

To install the RD Gateway Role Service, log on with an Administrator account and proceed through the wizard as described in the following steps.

1. Open Server Manager, add the Remote Desktop Services role, and choose the RD Gateway Role Service when prompted. If the Remote Desktop Services role is already installed, then select the Remote Desktop Services Role, click Add Role Service in the right pane, choose RD Gateway, and click Next.

2. You will be prompted to install any required role services required for RD Gateway, as shown in Figure 10-2. RD Gateway requires Internet Information Services (IIS) 7.5, which includes the required RPC over HTTP Proxy feature, RSAT Role Administration Tools, and Network Policy and Access Services, which is used to store RD CAPs. Click Add Required Role Services and then click Next.

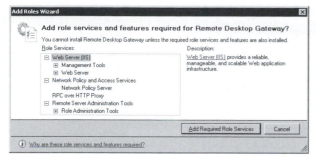

FIGURE 10-2 Install any required role services and features for RD Gateway.

3. You will be prompted to provide a server authentication certificate to use for establishing SSL connections. If you have already installed the required server authentication certificate in the server's Computer certificate store, it will appear in the list of certificates to choose from, as shown in Figure 10-3.

   Otherwise, you can create a self-signed certificate (you should use this type of certificate only for testing in a nonproduction environment). If you don't currently have a certificate installed, you can skip this step by selecting Choose A Certificate For SSL Encryption Later. Click Next.

CAUTION If the RD Gateway server has more than one server authentication certificate installed, the wizard will preselect the first one that it finds. This might not be the one that you intend to use, and if it does not meet the requirements and the user does not trust it, the connections won't work. If you have more than one server authentication certificate installed on the server, check to make sure that RD Gateway is configured with the right certificate.

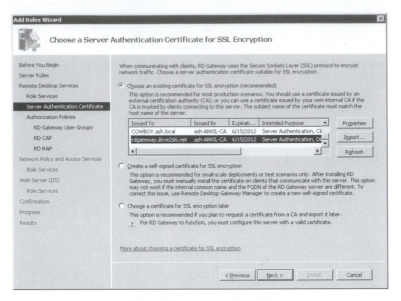

FIGURE 10-3 Choose an SSL certificate to use with RD Gateway.

4. On the next page, you'll be prompted to create the required RD CAP and authorization policies; do so by selecting the option Now and then clicking Next. (You can also opt to do this later using the RD Gateway Management Console, but remember that you must have at least one RD CAP specified before users can be authorized to connect to RD Gateway and at least one RD RAP to enable users to get to resources.)

5. Add the local or domain user groups that will be associated with both the RD CAP and the RD RAP. First, you will create an RD CAP. By default, the local Administrators group is already added to the input box. Members of the user groups added here are allowed to connect to RD Gateway. To add multiple user groups, type them and separate them with a semicolon, or click the Add button to pick a group from Active Directory Domain Services (AD DS). If the user groups that you want to add are located in different domains, you must use the Add button to add each one. Click Next.

6. Specify the name for the RD CAP (the default when you do this during installation is TS_CAP_01, but you can change it) and choose the Windows authentication method by which users specified in this RD CAP can connect to RD Gateway by selecting the check box next to Password or Smart Cards, or both boxes. Click Next.

7. Now you will create an RD RAP. Enter the name of the RD RAP (the default when you do this during installation is TS_RAP_01) and add a domain computer group that contains the resources to which user groups will connect. Alternatively, you can give users full access to internal RD Session Host servers and computers with Remote Desktop enabled by choosing Allow Users To Connect to Any Computer On The Network. Click Next.

8. If you are installing NPS, the Network Policy and Access Services introduction page appears. Click Next, and then click Next to install NPS.

9. If you previously chose to install IIS, then the Internet Information Services (IIS) introduction page appears. Click Next, and then click Next again to install the selected IIS role services.

10. Confirm the installation selections and click Install. When the installation is complete, you will see an Installation Results page showing that the installation is successful. Click Close.

Installing RD Gateway Using Windows PowerShell

You can install RD Gateway via Windows PowerShell by opening a command prompt and typing the following commands.

```
PS C:\Users\admin> import-module servermanager
PS C:\Users\admin> add-windowsfeature RDS-Gateway
```

A successful result will return the following information.

```
Success Restart Needed Exit Code Feature Result
------- -------------- --------- --------------
True    No              Success   {Network Policy Server, Web Server (IIS) T...
```

If you use Windows PowerShell to install RD Gateway, you are not prompted to install any dependent components; they are installed automatically as needed. Also, an RD CAP and RD RAP are not created, so you must configure the policies manually before users can use RD Gateway. Finally, RD Gateway will not be configured to use an SSL certificate. You will need to install an appropriate certificate if you have not done so already, and manually configure RD Gateway to use it.

Creating and Maintaining RD Gateway Authorization Policies

Post-installation, the first thing that you want to do to configure RD Gateway is to establish an RD CAP and RD RAP. You have the option of configuring an RD CAP and RD RAP when you install RD Gateway from the wizard, so you might have already configured one of each.

However, you can skip this step and configure them post-installation; you might not want to link the RD CAP and RD RAP as closely as the installation wizard does, and if you install via Windows PowerShell, you can't install an RD CAP or RD RAP while installing the role service. You'll need to know how to configure RD CAPs and RD RAPs post-installation and as your access strategy develops over time.

RD CAPs and RD RAPs work together to give remote users access to internal resources. Although the result relies on both of these items being configured, RD CAPs and RD RAPs are not necessarily tied to each other. That said, if you allow a user access to RD Gateway but do not give permission to connect to any resources, the connection will fail. Make sure that the RD CAPs and RD RAPs, although independent, complement each other.

> **NOTE** Using the installation wizard to create RD CAPs and RD RAPs makes it appear that the two are more linked than they are. The user groups that you specify in the RD CAP are merely supplied in the corresponding user group entry box for both RD CAPs and RD RAPs, but a user group can be associated with more than one RD RAP.

Creating an RD CAP

Creating an RD CAP after installation is similar to doing it using the installation routine described in the section entitled "Installing RD Gateway" earlier in this chapter. However, there are some differences that are pointed out in the following steps.

1. From RD Gateway Manager (located in the Remote Desktop Services tools), expand the Policies folder in RD Gateway Manager, right-click the Connection Authorization Policies folder, and choose Create New Policy, then choose Wizard to start the Create New Authorization Policies Wizard.

2. You still have the option to create both an RD CAP and an RD RAP, or to create only one or the other. If you choose to create both, the wizard will run through both the RD CAP and RD RAP wizards consecutively. This time, choose Create Only A RD CAP and click Next.

> **NOTE** If you configure RD Gateway to use a centralized NPS, then RD CAPs are not locally managed and stored. When RD CAPs are stored on a centralized NPS, you can create only an RD RAP instead of both an RD RAP and RD CAP. You will instead see a Central Network Policy Servers folder. If you right-click the folder and choose Configure Central RD CAP, this will actually take you to RD Gateway Properties, where you can adjust the settings for the centralized store. You have to create centralized RD CAPs on the centralized NPS server instead. For more information on centralized RD CAPs see the section entitled "Using a Central NPS to Store RD CAPs" later in this chapter.

3. Enter a name for the RD CAP (to help you distinguish RD CAPs, use a specific naming convention for your authorization policies, perhaps related to what user group it will apply) and click Next.

4. Specify the Windows authentication method (password, smart card, or both) that is required, and then add the user groups and the computer groups that are authorized to connect to RD Gateway, as shown in Figure 10-4. For example, you could choose to require smart-card authorization when using RD Gateway, even if users can log on with passwords while on the LAN.

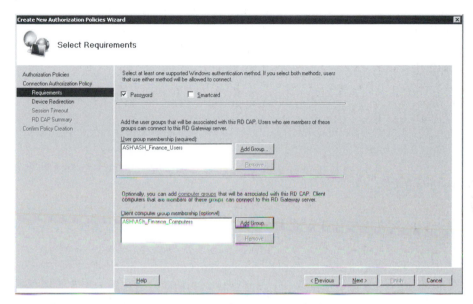

FIGURE 10-4 Select a supported Windows authentication method and add user and computer groups to which the RD CAP applies.

NOTE If you add both users and computer requirements to the RD CAP, then the two are cumulative; a user who is allowed to access RD Gateway must also be using a computer that is allowed to connect to RD Gateway.

Notice that this step differs from the RD Gateway installation wizard. The installation wizard asks you to supply local or domain user groups that will be associated with both the RD CAP and RD RAP. This wizard does not do this. Instead, it asks you to supply user groups for only the connection authorization policy. Click Next.

5. In Windows Server 2008 R2, RD Gateway can enforce device redirection; this is a change from Windows Server 2008, which did not enforce it. By default, the RD CAP allows all device redirection—the policies applying to the endpoint can limit further, but you can use RD Gateway to limit device redirection even more over the wide area

network (WAN) than is commonly done on the LAN. Disable device redirection for clients by selecting Disable Device Redirection For The Following Client Device Types and then selecting the boxes next to the devices that should not be redirected.

> **NOTE** RD Gateway cannot control audio redirection or smart card redirection.

This differs from the RD Gateway installation wizard, which does not give you the option to disable or limit device redirection at all. Instead, the initial RD CAPs created with the installation wizard will have device redirection enabled for all client devices.

You can also deny client connections to RD Session Host servers that do not enforce RD Gateway device redirection. If you choose this option, you will limit connections to Windows Server 2008 R2 and Windows 7 endpoints, because older operating systems do not enforce RD Gateway secure device redirection. Click Next.

> **IMPORTANT** Selecting the Only Allow Client Connections To Remote Desktop Session Host Servers That Enforce RD Gateway Device Redirection check box will prevent users from connecting to pooled or personal VMs that are running Windows Vista or Windows XP.

6. On the next page, you can set timeouts for active and idle sessions.

   To reclaim unused resources on RD Gateway, you can configure the gateway to disconnect idle sessions after a specified time period (defined in minutes). This will prevent users from walking away and leaving sessions open.

   You can also set a timeout for active sessions (in minutes). The session can be just disconnected; this forces the user to reinitiate the session and log on again. You can also choose to silently reauthenticate the user to the session. Choosing this option means that the user and session is reauthenticated and reauthorized, but without any impact on the user or session. However, if policies have changed, then the user would have to reauthenticate when the session timeout limit is reached, and the new polices would then take effect, thus keeping sessions consistently conforming to the most up-to-date policies.

7. Review the Summary page to make sure that you chose the right settings, and then click Finish.

> **NOTE** If you are familiar with the process of creating an RD CAP, you can skip the wizard and just fill in the requirements for the authorization by right-clicking the Connection Authorization Policies folder in RD Gateway and choosing Create New Policy, Custom. This will open a tabbed New RD CAP dialog box, which you can use to fill in the same settings for which you're prompted in the wizard.

Using RD Gateway to Restrict Device Redirection By User Group

In Windows Server 2008, disabling drive redirection from the RD CAP would have no effect if drive redirection was enabled on the client and the destination computers were protected via RD Gateway.

In Windows Server 2008 R2, this has changed. If drive redirection is disabled in RD Gateway, then it will be disabled no matter what the client and server have configured. If RD Gateway enables drive redirection, but the client or server disables it, then redirection is likewise disabled. This is great for restricting resources based on user group (remember that only printer redirection can be restricted in the user account in Active Directory Users And Computers). For instance, you could use precreated, signed RDP files to give users access to resources, and the RDP file would be configured to use RD Gateway for every connection. Then the policies on the RD Gateway would be configured to restrict certain device redirection based on user group membership. The file is read-only by the nature of it being signed, so tampering with it would break it.

This new RD CAP defines what combination of users (and optionally computers) are allowed to access RD Gateway, but it doesn't get users any farther than the RD Gateway because you haven't yet defined any resources that they are allowed to access. To define what resources users can access after they are allowed to connect to RD Gateway, you'll need to create an RD RAP, which is discussed next.

Creating an RD RAP

Creating an RD RAP using RD Gateway Manager is very similar to creating one using the installation wizard except that you are asked to associate user groups with the RD RAP. You can also create and use RD Gateway–specified computer groups in the RD RAP, which isn't an option when using the installation wizard. To do this, perform the following steps.

1. Expand the Policies folder in RD Gateway Manager, right-click the Resource Authorization Policies folder, choose Create New Policy, and then choose Wizard to start the Create Authorization Policies For RD Gateway Wizard.

> **NOTE** Even if you're using a centralized NPS to store RD CAPs, you still create RD RAPs on the local RD Gateway. RD RAPs are not stored by NPS.

2. Again, you can choose to create both an RD CAP and an RD RAP or to create only one or the other. If you choose to create both, then the wizard will run through both the RD CAP and RD RAP wizards consecutively. Choose Create Only A RDRAP and click Next.

3. Enter a name for the RD RAP (again, choose something descriptive) and click Next.

4. Add local or domain user groups associated with this RD RAP that can access the resources specified in it. To specify multiple user groups, separate them with a semicolon or click Add again to add another group. If the groups that you want to add are in different domains, you must use the Add Group button to add the user groups from each domain. Click Next.

5. Now, choose the resources that the specified user group(s) can connect to. You can allow users to connect to any network resource, specify one domain computer group, or specify one RD Gateway–managed computer group. If you are allowing access to an RD Session Host server farm, you must choose the Select An Existing RD Gateway–Managed Computer Group Or Create A New One option. The details of this option are discussed in the section entitled "Using RD Gateway Computer Groups to Enable Access to a Server Farm" later in this chapter. For now, choose Allow Users To Connect To Any Network Resources. Click Next.

> **NOTE** If you create an RD RAP during the initial installation, you won't have the option of choosing an RD Gateway–managed group.

6. Remember that RD Gateway acts as a proxy for the network resources to which users will remote. On the next page, specify the port that people are able to use via RD Gateway. By default, the gateway will allow connections only via port 3389, which is the default port for RDP. You can opt to configure another port (or ports separated with a semicolon), for example, if you've edited the port that RDP uses. You can also choose to allow connections through any port. Most of the time, you'll use 3389 for RDP traffic, so choose that option now. Click Next.

7. In the final page of the wizard, you'll see a summary of the settings that you've configured. Click Finish and the new RD RAP will be visible in the Resource Authorization Policies Folder.

> **NOTE** If you are familiar with the process of creating an RD RAP, you can skip the wizard and just fill in the requirements for the authorization by right-clicking the Resource Authorization Policies folder in RD Gateway and then choosing Create New Policy, Custom. This opens a tabbed New RD RAP dialog box, which you can use to fill in the same settings for which you're prompted in the wizard.

Modifying an Existing Authorization Policy

To modify an existing RD CAP or RD RAP in RD Gateway Manager, select the Connection Authorization Policies folder or the Resource Authorization Policies folder, respectively. You'll see the related authorization policies in the center pane. Double-click the policy that you want to edit. Edit the policy properties on each of the tabs as appropriate and then click OK to save and close the policy.

You also have the option to disable or enable a policy (for example, you might need to test the impact of a particular authorization policy). By default, all created policies are enabled. Disable a policy by clearing the Enable This Policy check box on the General tab of the policy.

Configuring RD Gateway Options

After you have installed RD Gateway and put the right RD CAPs and RD RAPs in place, you can tweak the configuration to suit your needs. The RD Gateway configuration options are contained in the Properties panel of the RD Gateway server. To manage RD Gateway, open the RD Gateway Management Console by going to Start/Administrative Tools/Remote Desktop Services/RD Gateway Manager. The RD Gateway Manager opens, as shown in Figure 10-5.

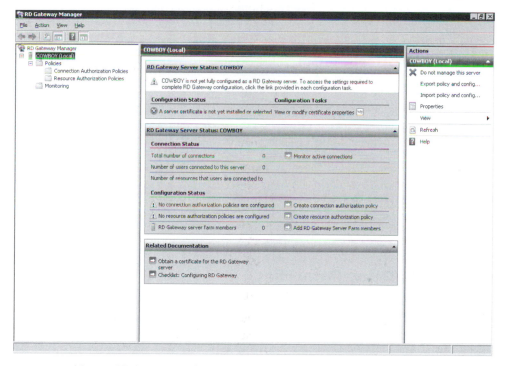

FIGURE 10-5 Manage RD Gateway via the RD Gateway Management console.

Click the server in the left pane to view the Connection Status and Configuration Status details in the middle pane. This pane contains three sections, each of which contains information and links to configuration pages in RD Gateway. The three sections are

- The Connection Status, which shows you how many connections are currently established with RD Gateway and how many resources users are connected to. When people are using RD Gateway, you can monitor and disconnect active connections here. Open the Monitor Active Connections page by clicking the corresponding link.

- The Configuration Status section, which tells you how many RD CAPs and RD RAPs are presently configured. If you have set up an RD Gateway farm, this section indicates how many servers are in that farm.

NOTE RD Gateway farms are discussed in the section entitled "Creating a Redundant RD Gateway Configuration" later in this chapter.

You can also create or modify RD CAPs and RD RAPs here by clicking the View Connection Authorization Policies link and View Resource Authorization Policies link, respectively.

Create or modify an RD Gateway farm by clicking the Add RD Gateway Server Farm Members link.

- The Related Documentation section, which provides links to RD Gateway configuration Help files.

RD Gateway lets you know if you skipped vital settings by displaying a red circle with an X or a yellow triangle with an exclamation point next to the settings that need further configuration. For example, recall that an installation using Windows PowerShell isn't complete. The RD Gateway Management Console will display the warnings shown in Figure 10-4 if you install RD Gateway using Windows PowerShell.

NOTE You can edit specific settings by clicking the link next to the green arrows in the middle pane of RD Gateway Manager.

Tuning RD Gateway Properties

After you have installed RD Gateway, it's time to configure it to suit your needs. Configure or edit RD Gateway settings by right-clicking the RD Gateway server in the left pane and choosing Properties. The server Properties dialog box appears, as shown in Figure 10-6.

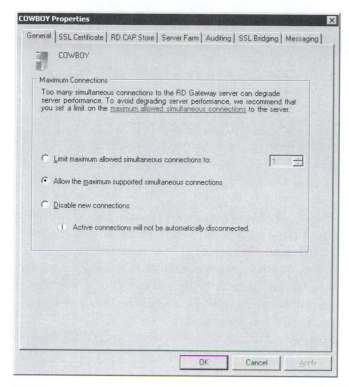

FIGURE 10-6 Configure or edit RD Gateway settings using the RD Gateway Properties dialog box.

From here, you can edit the settings as described in the following sections.

Limiting Simultaneous Connections to RD Gateway

The General tab of the RD Gateway Properties dialog box is where you specify the number of simultaneous connections that you will allow RD Gateway to handle. The maximum depends on the version of Windows that's installed. Windows Server 2008 R2 Standard Edition supports a maximum of 250 simultaneous connections through RD Gateway, and it is set by default to allow this maximum. (Windows Server 2008 R2 Enterprise and Datacenter editions have no limit and the Foundation edition supports a maximum of 50 simultaneous connections).

Instead of using the default setting, you can set a specific number of simultaneous connections (for performance reasons, for example). To do so, choose Limit Maximum Allowed Simultaneous Connections To. Then specify a number in the corresponding selection box. To drain connections from this server (for maintenance), select the Disable New Connections option button. Doing this does not allow any more new connections to RD Gateway, but it leaves the existing ones undisturbed until the user disconnects or ends the session.

Choosing an SSL Certificate to Use with RD Gateway

If you didn't define a certificate while installing RD Gateway, you'll need to do so afterwards, or when you're moving from a self-signed certificate to one signed by a trusted CA. Go to the SSL Certificate tab on the RD Gateway Properties dialog box to select an SSL certificate to use with RD Gateway.

> **NOTE** TLS is based on SSL, so the process to create an encrypted communication tunnel is the same for both. Refer to the section entitled "Transport Layer Security" in Chapter 8, "Securing Remote Desktop Protocol Connections," to see how SSL encryption works.

If you have already configured RD Gateway to use a certificate, the certificate information is displayed on this tab and the Select An Existing Certificate From The RD Gateway <*SERVER-NAME*> Certificates (Local Computer)/Personal Store option button is selected. You can choose another certificate that is already installed on the server by clicking the Import Certificate button and choosing from the certificates listed. Valid SSL certificates that are installed to the server's Computer Certificate Store Personal folder will be available in the Import Certificate pop-up dialog box. Choose a certificate and click Import.

If you do not have an SSL certificate installed on this server, you can create a self-signed certificate to use with RD Gateway. Use this certificate for testing purposes only; if it's used in a production environment, you could have issues with users who are not able to validate the certificate because it's not in their trusted root certificate store. A self-signed certificate also isn't verified by any authority.

To create a self-signed certificate, choose the Create A Self-Signed Certificate option and click the Create and Import Certificate button. The Create Self-Signed Certificate dialog box will appear, as shown in Figure 10-7.

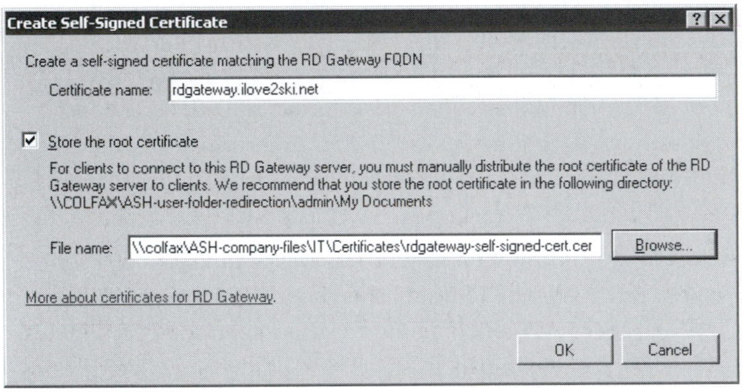

FIGURE 10-7 Create a self-signed certificate for RD Gateway.

Enter the fully qualified domain name (FQDN) of the RD Gateway into the Certificate name input box; this is the FQDN that is resolvable to external users. Because the certificate is self-signed, it will also act as its own root certificate. Clients must also have this certificate installed in their computers' certificate store in order to validate this same certificate used by RD Gateway. Therefore, the Store The Root Certificate check box is selected by default; this allows you to save the certificate to a file so that you can import it to the Trusted Root Certification Authorities certificate store on your test client. Click Browse, navigate to the chosen save location, and type a file name, or type the location and file name in the File Name box, and then click OK.

> **NOTE** To install the certificate on your test clients, open a Microsoft Management Console (MMC) on the client and add the Certificates snap-in. Expand the Certificates store tree and then right-click the Trusted Root Certification Authorities folder. Choose All Tasks, Import and follow the steps in the wizard to import the self-signed certificate file that you created from RD Gateway Manager.

You can also import a certificate to the server's certificate store and configure RD Gateway to use this certificate. To do so, select the Import A Certificate Into The RD Gateway <*SERVER-NAME*> Certificates (Local Computer)/Personal Store option button. Then click the Browse and Import Certificate . . . button. Browse to the certificate file that you want to import, select the file, and click Open.

Choosing an RD CAP Store

RD Gateway stores RD CAPs in an NPS store, which is why you had to install NPS when installing RD Gateway. The RD Gateway default installation uses a local NPS server to store RD CAPs, but you can use another NPS server for this purpose instead. This comes in handy when you have more than one RD Gateway server but both use the same RD CAPs (multiple RD Gateway servers act as a farm). Each RD Gateway server can be set to use a central NPS storage location and one set of RD CAPs instead of each maintaining its own RD CAPs. You might also opt for this setup if you already maintain an NPS server and want to use it to store RD CAPs instead of using NPS on the RD Gateway server. Use this tab to configure RD Gateway to use a central NPS store. To use a central server, select the Central Server Running NPS option, enter the central server's name or IP address into the input box, and click Add.

RD Gateway Server Farms

Select the Server Farm tab. This tab allows you to specify an RD Gateway server farm. If you load-balance RD Gateway servers but your inbound connections are seen as all coming from the firewall Internet Protocol (IP address), then you need to add each RD Gateway server that is part of the fault-tolerant solution to an RD Gateway farm on this tab. This makes sure that the two connections that occur per SSL connection (one inbound and one outbound connection) get sent to one RD Gateway server instead of being split between multiple RD Gateway servers.

> **NOTE** To load-balance RD Gateway servers, see the section entitled "Creating a Redundant RD Gateway Configuration" later in this chapter.

Auditing RD Gateway Events

For troubleshooting and planning purposes, auditing connection events is a good idea. The RD Gateway Auditing tab, shown in Figure 10-8, allows you to specify the RD Gateway events that you want to log.

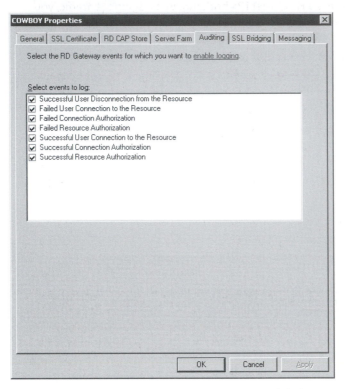

FIGURE 10-8 Logging RD Gateway events is enabled by default.

These events are logged in the Event Viewer under Application And Services Logs/Microsoft/Windows/TerminalServices-Gateway. By default, all available RD Gateway connection and authorization events are logged (the options are all checked on this tab). To modify which connection and authorization events are audited, select or clear the boxes corresponding to the available events in the Select Events To Log dialog box. Generally, failed events are more significant than successful ones because they can signal unauthorized attempts or annoyed users.

Using RD Gateway with SSL Bridging

Select the SSL Bridging tab. Positioning options for RD Gateway are covered in the section entitled "Placing RD Web Access and RD Gateway" later in this chapter. One option is to use Microsoft Forefront Threat Management Gateway (TMG) 2010 (the rebranded Microsoft Internet Security and Acceleration Server) or another SSL bridging device to bridge incoming SSL connections in the perimeter network to RD Gateway on the internal network.

If you do this, then you need to set up SSL bridging on this tab. SSL bridging means that SSL requests coming from the remote client are terminated at the bridging appliance and new requests are then initiated by the bridging appliance to RD Gateway. Enable SSL bridging by selecting the Use SSL Bridging check box. Next, you need to choose a bridging method.

The first bridging method is called HTTPS-HTTPS bridging. By bridging SSL traffic, you gain further control of the communication to and from RD Gateway. The bridging product acts as a policeman by decrypting SSL connections coming from outside the network, inspecting them for malicious code, and then re-establishing the SSL session with RD Gateway if the packets pass inspection. All traffic flowing to and from RD Gateway goes through the bridging appliance. To enable HTTPS-HTTPS bridging, select the HTTPS-HTTPS Bridging (Terminate SSL Requests And Initiate New HTTPS Requests) option button.

You can also bridge HTTPS-HTTP communications between the bridging device and RD Gateway, called *SSL offloading and termination*. HTTPS–HTTP bridging saves processor cycles: SSL packet processing generally takes more processor cycles than regular Hypertext Transfer Protocol (HTTP) traffic. By offloading the SSL communication to TMG or another bridging device, you save processing power.

Enable HTTPS-HTTP bridging by selecting the Use HTTPS-HTTP Bridging (Terminate SSL Requests And Initiate New HTTP Requests) option button. Click OK to save your selected settings.

HOW IT WORKS

Does SSL Bridging Offer Performance Benefits?

The short answer to this question is that it depends on what kind of bridging you're doing.

When deployed with a simple firewall, the RD Gateway server is still processing all the incoming SSL traffic. During SSL communication, there is a lot of back-and-forth to establish a secure communication between client and server. The client must initiate the connection, and the server's digital certificate must be validated by the client. Then a secret session key must be established to encrypt the communications. While all this communication is going on, the RD Gateway server must still act as a proxy for the incoming connection requests. On a busy server, this can consume a lot of processor cycles.

HTTPS-HTTPS SSL bridging adds an additional layer of security to the SSL communication by examining the contents of the SSL traffic and ensuring that it contains no malicious packets before sending it to the RD Gateway. However, HTTPS-HTTPS bridging does not offload the SSL processing; it only decrypts the Hypertext Transfer Protocol Secure (HTTPS) traffic to examine it before encrypting it again to send to the RD Gateway. The RD Gateway must still do all the SSL communication processing—but now it is just safer to do so. For any performance benefit, you must implement SSL offloading and termination with HTTPS-HTTP bridging. The catch is that you must balance the performance benefit of not processing the SSL traffic with the fact that, after it leaves the bridging device, the traffic is no longer encrypted. The traffic should be passing over the private network at this point, but for some implementations, this might still be a consideration.

RD Gateway Messaging

In RD Gateway for Windows Server 2008 R2, you now can send messages to users when they request access to resources via RD Gateway. (Use these messages to educate people on company policies, warn them of service outages, and the like.) To do so, you configure the settings on the RD Gateway Messaging tab, shown in Figure 10-9.

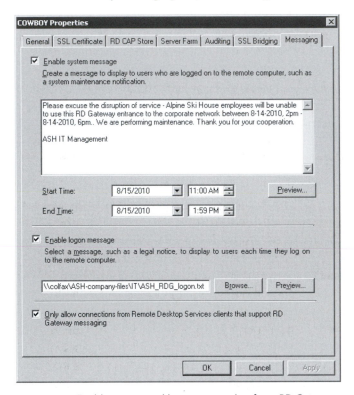

FIGURE 10-9 Enable system and logon messaging from RD Gateway.

You can configure two types of messages.

- **Logon Message** This message displays before a user is logged onto the requested session; for example, it could be a legal notice or company remote access policy.

- **System Message**   This message is displayed to users after they log on to a system, and only for a specified time period. System messages are good for notifying users of some future event, like a maintenance window, other planned downtime, or a pending change in access policies.

Logon messages are displayed each time that a user requests access to a resource via RD Gateway, but before they are logged onto the session. Configure a logon message by selecting the Enable Logon Message check box. Then click the Browse button and choose a text file that contains the logon message.

When a user requests a resource via RD Gateway before he or she is logged onto that resource, the user will see a logon message window like the one shown in Figure 10-10.

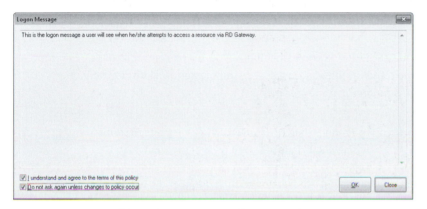

FIGURE 10-10 A user will see a logon message when attempting to access a resource via RD Gateway and RD Gateway logon messaging is enabled.

To log onto the remote desktop session, users must signify that they agree to the terms of the message by selecting the I Understand And Agree To The Terms Of This Policy check box. After users check the box and click OK, they are logged onto the remote session. If users do not agree to the terms of the message, then their only option is to click Close and cancel the request. If users agree to the message terms, then they can also select the Do Not Ask Again Unless Changes To The Policy Occur check box to suppress the logon message until the policy changes.

System messages are displayed right after a user logs onto a system, but only during the time period that you specify in the RD Gateway Messaging interface. To configure a system message, select the Enable System Message check box on the Messaging tab of the RD Gateway Properties dialog box. Type the message that you want to send into the system message input box. Finally, adjust the start and end time to reflect the time period during which users will see the message. Unlike logon messages, users cannot opt to suppress system messages. They will display every time that users invoke a new remote session during the specified time window, as shown in Figure 10-11.

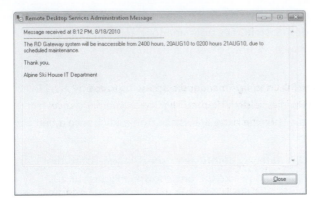

FIGURE 10-11 Users will receive a system message after they logon to the requested remote session.

Because system messages display only once per session, if a user opens multiple Remote-App programs on the same RD Session Host server, the message will display only once. All RemoteApp programs run in the same session.

 CAUTION If you use round robin DNS (RR DNS) or a dedicated redirector for RD Session Host farm initial load balancing RD Gateway, system messages will appear twice. This is because RD Gateway sees both the initial connection to the RD Session Host server and also the final connection to the determined destination server. Use network load balancing (NLB) to avoid double messaging.

Messages only display for connections made from RDC 7 or later. To prevent people from circumventing logon or system messages, you can deny RD Gateway connections from clients not running RDC 7.0 by selecting the Only Allow Connections From Remote Desktop Services Clients That Support RD Gateway Messaging check box.

Using RD Gateway Computer Groups to Enable Access to a Server Farm

As explained in the section entitled "Creating and Maintaining RD Gateway Authorization Policies" earlier in this chapter, RD RAPs define which resources a user can access via RD Gateway. However, AD DS does not have any way to represent a RD Session Host server server farm. To enable people to use a farm, you must either allow access to any network resource or create an RD Gateway–managed group that maps to the farm.

You can create an RD Gateway–managed computer group when creating an RD RAP using the Create Authorization Policies For RD Gateway wizard. When creating the RD RAP, you'll be prompted to determine whether the access should extend to the following.

- A specific domain computer group
- All computers with the specified port (normally 3389) open
- Members of an RD Gateway–managed computer group

If you opt to enable access to a computer group, you'll open a new page in the Authorization Policies Wizard, where you can create anew RD Gateway–managed computer group or select an existing one.

> **NOTE** You can also create or manage RD Gateway–managed computer groups by selecting the Resource Authorization Policies folder and then clicking the Manage Local Computer Groups link in the Actions panel on the right side of the RD Gateway Manager.

Associating RD RAPs with Computer Groups

To create a new RD Gateway–managed computer group, select Create A New RD Gateway-Managed Computer Group, enter a descriptive name for the group, and add the NetBIOS and FQDN names of each farm, as well as each farm member. If you want users to be able to connect to the farm by IP address, you can enter the IP address of the farm.

You must add all farm members to the group to enable access to the individual RD Session Host servers in the farm. The name of the farm must also be part of the managed computer group. For example, if your farm ("*FarmName*") includes two RD Session Host servers named RDSH1 and RDSH2 that belong to the domain called Mydomain.local, you must add the following names to the RD Gateway Computer Group mapping to *FarmName*.

- RDSH1 and RDSH1.mydomain.local
- RDSH2 and RDSH2.mydomain.local
- *FarmName* and *FarmName*.mydomain.local

If you change farm membership or add new servers, you will need to update the computer group to match. Each RD Gateway–managed computer group should include servers from only one farm. This will allow you to keep your resource permissions specifically defined.

> **NOTE** The names of RD Gateway–managed computer group members have to be resolvable in DNS or a host file, or you will see the error message shown in Figure 10-12 and you will not be allowed to add the entry.

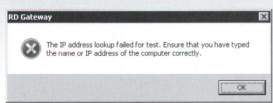

FIGURE 10-12 RD Gateway Managed Computer Group member names must be resolvable.

If you have already created an RD Gateway–managed computer group, then choose the Select An Existing RD Gateway–Managed Computer Group option and then highlight the group in the Existing Computer Groups box.

You can also edit an existing RD RAP to enable access to an RD Gateway–managed computer group. In RD Gateway, click the Resource Authorization Policies folder, then double-click the RD RAP that you want to edit. Select the Network Resource tab and then choose the Select An Existing RD Gateway-Managed Computer Group Or Create a New One option. From here, you can create a new group or select an existing one as described previously.

Managing Computer Group membership

To create, modify, or delete RD Gateway–managed computer groups, click the Resource Authorization Policies folder in RD Gateway. Choose Manage Local Computer Groups from the Actions menu in the right pane to open the dialog box shown in Figure 10-13.

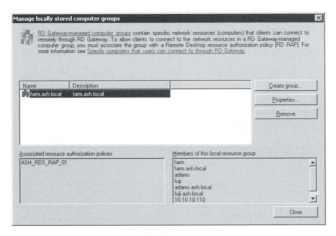

FIGURE 10-13 Edit or create RD Gateway–managed computer groups using the Manage Locally Stored Computer Groups dialog box.

Clicking existing computer groups reveals the RD RAPs that they are associated with in the lower section of the left pane and the computer group members in the lower section of the right pane (in Figure 10-13, for example, the group contains members of an RD Session Host server farm, so the farm FQDN and NetBIOS name are listed, along with all farm members and all NetBIOS names and IP addresses of the individual servers).

To create a new computer group, click Create Group. On the General tab, enter a name for the computer group. On the Network Resources tab, enter the names and optionally the IP addresses of the RD Session Host servers or computers that you want to add to the group. Click OK.

To edit an existing group, select the group and then click Properties and adjust the computer group name or the servers in the group as necessary. To delete an RD Gateway–managed computer group, click the group and click Remove.

Bypassing RD Gateway for Internal Connections

It's understandable that you want remote users to establish secure encrypted connections to desktops and servers located on the internal network. But for local users accessing resources on the same internal network, you can choose to bypass RD Gateway and allow them to connect directly to the resource. There are two places to do this: RDC on the client and RemoteApp Manager on the server, as follows.

- **Remote Desktop Client**   Open the RDC and click Options. Click the Advanced tab and then click the Settings button in the Connect From Anywhere section. Select Use These RD Gateway Server Settings, supply the server name, and then select the box next to Bypass RD Gateway Server For Local Addresses.

- **RemoteApp Manager**   Use this setting to bypass RD Gateway for RemoteApp programs and for RDP files created by RD Web Access. Open RemoteApp Manager, click the RD Gateway Settings link, select Use These RD Gateway Server Settings, supply the server name, and then select the box next to Bypass RD Gateway Server For Local Addresses.

> **NOTE**   To see how to force RDC connections initiated from RD Web Access to use RD Gateway, see the section entitled "Force RDC Connections Through RD Gateway via RD Web Access" in Chapter 9.

Using Group Policy to Control RD Gateway Authentication Settings

Three user Group Policy settings will help you control when clients use RD Gateway to connect to RDP resources, what authentication method(s) can be used to connect, and which RD Gateway server they use. The policies are located at User Configuration | Policies | Administrative Templates | Windows Components | Remote Desktop Services | RD Gateway and include the following options.

- **Set RD Gateway Authentication Method**   This policy specifies the authentication method that clients must use to connect to RD Gateway, as specified in the RemoteApp program settings on the RD Session Host server, in saved RDP files, or from the RDC. The choices are

- **Ask For Credentials, Use NTLM Protocol**   Secure credential passing using a hash.

> **NOTE**   For more information on NTLM, see *http://msdn.microsoft.com/en-us/library /aa378749(VS.85).aspx.*

- **Ask For Credentials, Use Basic Protocol** This option is only available using group policy—it is not available via RemoteApp Manager. Credentials are sent in cleartext and therefore are not secure.

- **Use Locally Logged-On Credentials** (enables single sign-on with RD Gateway)

- **Use Smart-Card**

You can allow users to change the authentication method by selecting the Allow Users To Change This Setting check box, or you can enforce the setting you choose by clearing this box. If users cannot change this setting, it will be in effect for all connections through RD Gateway. If this policy is not configured and no option is specifically selected by the user, then NTLM and smart cards can be used.

- **Enable Connection Through RD Gateway** Enabling this setting means that when users cannot create an RDP connection to a computer, they will attempt to connect via an RD Gateway that you specify in the Set RD Gateway Server Address policy described next.

You can enforce this setting by clearing the Allow Users To Change This Setting check box. If the policy is enforced, then users will attempt to connect through the RD Gateway address given in the Set RD Gateway Server Address policy described next. Clearing the check box means users will not use the address specified in the Set RD Gateway Server Address policy; instead, they are allowed to specify the RD Gateway that they wish to use.

- **Set RD Gateway Server Address** Specifies the RD Gateway address that users will attempt to connect to if they are unable to connect directly to an RDP resource. To enforce this setting, check the Allow Users To Change This Setting check box in the left pane.

 CAUTION If you enable the Enable Connection Through RD Gateway policy, you also must enable Set RD Gateway Server Address and provide the address. If you enable that policy but do not specify the address here, then user connections will fail.

Monitoring and Managing Active RD Gateway Connections

RD Gateway connections are monitored and managed from the Monitoring folder in RD Gateway Manager. The monitoring feature gathers data points about each active session and reports them in a table in the monitoring window. You can see all active RD Gateway connections by selecting the Monitoring folder of RD Gateway Manager, as shown in Figure 10-14.

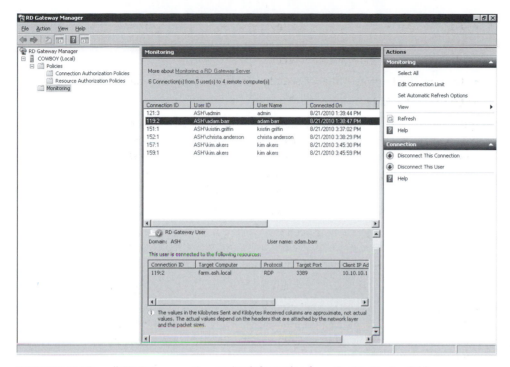

FIGURE 10-14 View all RD Gateway active session information from the Monitoring folder.

The specific data reported for each connection includes the following.

- **Connection ID** The Connection ID is formatted as *<A:B>*, where *A* is the Tunnel ID and *B* is the Channel ID. The Tunnel ID represents the client's connection to the RD Gateway, while the Channel ID represents the client's connection to the requested resource. The Tunnel ID is incremented each time a new connection is made to RD Gateway; if you restart the Remote Desktop Services Gateway service, the Tunnel ID count restarts at 1.

- **User ID** The User ID shows the domain and user name of the user who established the session, taking the form *domain\username*.

- **User Name** The session user's full name as specified in AD DS.

- **Connection On** States when a session was established.

- **Connection Duration** States how long a session has been active.

- **Idle Time** States how long a session has been idle.

- **Target Computer** The computer that the session is connected to.

> **NOTE** If there is no redirection, then RD Gateway monitoring displays the farm name (for example, Farm.ash.local). If there is redirection, RD Gateway monitoring displays the "host name" (for example, Fuji.ash.local).

- **Client IP Address**   The IP address of the client that is connecting. If you are connecting to RD Gateway from the other side of a firewall, the IP address listed will be the address of the firewall.
- **Target Port**   The port to which the user is connected.

Clicking any of the active sessions also shows the information about the selected session in the bottom pane, but will also reveal the total kilobytes sent and received in that session.

By default, RD Gateway updates the connection data every 30 minutes. To change this interval, right-click the Monitoring folder, choose Set Automatic Refresh Options from the context menu, and specify the new interval. Don't refresh too often; sampling takes processor cycles, so a high refresh rate can affect server performance. You can also disable automatic data refreshing by choosing the Do Not Refresh Automatically option. Click OK for the settings to take effect.

You can use this data to analyze the connections and tweak policy accordingly. For example, if your analysis indicates that a lot of connections go idle after 30 minutes, you could configure RD CAP timeouts to disconnect connections that are idle for more that 30 minutes and free resources for other users.

From the Monitoring folder, not only can you view connection data but you also can perform some tasks, such as disconnecting connections and changing the number of simultaneous connections allowed to RD Gateway. Disconnect connections from this folder according to the following rules.

- To disconnect a single session, right-click the session and choose Disconnect This Connection.
- A user can establish more than one RD Gateway session. To disconnect all a user's sessions, right-click a user's connection and choose Disconnect This User.
- To disconnect all RD Gateway sessions at once, right-click the Monitoring folder, choose Select All, and then right-click any of the highlighted sessions and choose Disconnect These Connections.
- To disconnect multiple connections at once, press Ctrl-click or Shift-click to select multiple connections, then right-click and choose Disconnect These Connections.

> **NOTE**   You don't have to disconnect connections manually if you plan to do maintenance on the RD Gateway. To drain RD Gateway sessions as users disconnect, configure the RD Gateway to stop accepting new connections, as described in the section entitled "Limiting Simultaneous Connections to RD Gateway" earlier in this chapter.

You can also edit the RD Gateway connection limit from the Monitoring folder. Right-click the Monitoring folder and choose Edit Connection Limit from the context menu. This brings up the General tab of the RD Gateway server Properties dialog box. Limit the sessions to a specific number, or put the RD Gateway into drain mode and click OK.

Creating a Redundant RD Gateway Configuration

For the most part, previous sections have tacitly assumed that you have one RD Gateway server. As with RD Session Host and RD Virtualization Host servers, however, one is not enough. The trouble isn't the number of simultaneous connections (the RD Gateway job isn't very taxing; one server can handle hundreds of simultaneous connections), but rather that a single RD Gateway server means a single point of failure. The job that RD Gateway performs is critical: Lose the gateway and you lose remote access to your corporate network, exclusive of other virtual private network (VPN) or Direct Access solutions.

Therefore, it's best to have two (or more) RD Gateway servers. This section discusses how to make this as easy as possible, including

- Configuring RD Gateway to work with NLB for load balancing and failover
- Centralizing the connection authorization policies
- Centralizing the resource authorization policies

Using NLB to Load-Balance RD Gateway Servers

RD Gateway doesn't have any load-balancing logic; a load balancer like NLB must provide this functionality and allows you to group multiple servers into a logical cluster. If one RD Gateway goes offline, any connections for which it was acting as a proxy will be disconnected. However, when the users automatically reconnect, they are sent to the working RD Gateway server and will be reconnected to their previous sessions. In the absence of the load-balanced farm, those connections would be severed completely.

NLB load-balances based on incoming network traffic to a virtual IP address, or *cluster IP address*, as shown in Figure 10-15.

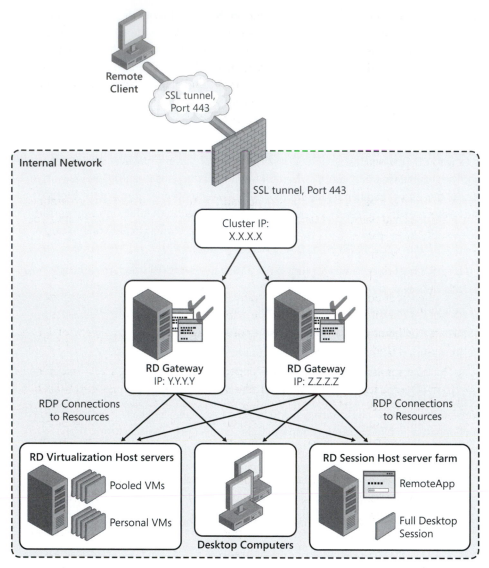

FIGURE 10-15 For redundancy, load-balance incoming connections to RD Gateway among multiple servers.

> **NOTE** Figure 10-15 does not include the RD Connection Broker because, although the broker plays a part in choosing which resource ultimately gets a connection, the final connection does not go through RD Connection Broker.

When you cluster RD Gateway servers, network traffic over port 443 isn't directed to a specific RD Gateway server. Instead, it goes to the cluster IP address representing the collection of RD Gateway servers. Then the load-balancing mechanism determines to which RD Gateway server the connection should be sent, generally based on the current load.

In this example, NLB is used as the load-balancing mechanism, and two network interface cards (NICs) are installed on each RD Gateway computer. One NIC will support incoming connections for management purposes, and NLB will use the other for load balancing. We recommend using static addressing for the management NIC; the NIC used for load balancing *must* be configured with a static IP address, subnet mask, and gateway address. When you have installed the NICs on the RD Gateway servers, install NLB on each RD Gateway server that will become part of the cluster. Either use Server Manager or install using Windows PowerShell using the following code.

```
Import-Module Servermanager
Add-WindowsFeature NLB
```

After installing NLB, create a server cluster and add the RD Gateway servers as members. Open the Network Load Balancing Manager by clicking Start, Programs, Administrative Tools, Network Load Balancing Manager, or by typing **nlbmgr** in the Start, Run box. Complete the following steps to create a server cluster.

1. Click Cluster and select New.

2. In the Host input box, enter the name of one of the RD Gateway servers and click Connect. NICs available to use with NLB will appear in the lower text box. Select the dedicated NIC that you have configured to use with load balancing (remember, it must have a static IP address) and click Next.

3. The IP addresses assigned to the NIC will appear. The priority number is a unique number that differentiates the servers. Accept the default value. The IP address in the lower text box will be dedicated to load balancing. It's possible that both NICs will show up in the text box (assuming that you have dual NICs); use the Edit and Remove buttons to adjust the dedicated IP address settings as needed. Leave the InitialHostState as Started and click Next.

4. Specify the cluster IP address by clicking Add and specifying the IPv4address and subnet mask or IPv6 address. When users request access to RD Gateway, they will be sent to this cluster address instead of a specific RD Gateway server address. Then the connection is sent by the load balancer to the appropriate RD Gateway server. Click Next.

5. Enter the public FQDN name that remote users use to access RD Gateway (for example, rdgateway.ilove2ski.net) and choose the cluster operation mode (Unicast or Multicast). All host adapters must use the same operation mode or NLB will not function. In this example, choose Unicast. Click Next.

6. For NLB to do its job, you need to indicate the ports that it should listen on for traffic. By default, it listens on ports 0 to 65535, and it load-balances the connections if the traffic appears on one of those ports. However, to accept incoming SSL connections, it needs to listen only on port 443. Edit the default rule to change the range From and To fields to 443.

7. Under Filtering Mode, choose Multiple Hosts to allow multiple hosts to handle traffic for this port rule. Now you have three Affinity choices.

- **None** Choosing this option means that multiple connections coming from the same IP address can be spread among the farm members.
- **Single** Choosing this option gives affinity to connections coming from the same IP address; they will be terminated on the same RD Gateway farm member.
- **Network** Choosing this option means that client connections within the same Class C address space are terminated on the same RD Gateway server.

Single is almost always the best choice. First, this will prevent RemoteApp connections in a single RDP session from being distributed across more than one RD Gateway server. Second, troubleshooting connection problems is easier when the connections for each session are coming through one RD Gateway server. Most important, each session connection requires two SSL connections: one from the client to the RD Gateway server, and one from RD Gateway to the client. Without server affinity, it's possible for a session's two needed SSL connections to get split between two servers. Because both the incoming and the outgoing connections are necessary to support the session, splitting the session between two servers doubles the chances that the session will be lost due to a downed RD Gateway server.

8. Choose the appropriate affinity setting and click OK. Then click Finish.

DIRECT FROM THE FIELD

Why You Should Use Single Affinity
Bohdan Velushchak
Operations Engineer

If SSL connections of a session get split between two servers, it actually reduces the resilience of the RD Gateway farm for failover. Here's how it happens. Imagine that you have many clients connecting to RD Gateway server A and also to RD Gateway server B. If either of the servers fails, clients connected through the failing server need to reconnect, but so do all those who have the split connections between servers A and B. The only circumstance under which you should not set affinity is if many clients are coming in from one IP address (for example, are working through a proxy server).

Not setting affinity adds complexity to the environment in several ways. You can have SSL connections split up and redirected to different servers, and as the administrator, you have no control over this. Second, in case of a failed server, more clients suffer (those who go through this server plus those who have a single SSL session served on the failed server). Third, in general, it reduces the predictability.

When you have any IP-based affinity on the NLB, the Server Farm feature is not used. There will be no situation when different SSL connections from the single client (so, from the same IP) will be sent to different RD Gateway servers, as IP affinity is set on NLB. So it doesn't matter if the Server Farm setting in RD Gateway is configured or not.

Don't use the affinity option included with some hardware load balancers. It does not provide any additional benefits to RD Gateway as opposed to using IP affinity, and it still requires the Server Farm setting to be configured.

 CAUTION Don't enable Single if all connections are proxied and appear to be coming from the same IP address (the address of the proxy server or firewall). In that situation, the Single option will direct all connections to the same RD Gateway server. When using a proxy server or firewall, choose None.

Next, you will need to add the other RD Gateway farm members by right-clicking the cluster and choosing Add Host To Cluster. Give the name of the server and then choose the dedicated IP address that you will use for this host, just as you did when setting up the first host. Because this server will be joining this cluster, you do not get to choose any other settings. Do this for each cluster member.

After you've created the cluster and added all RD Gateway cluster hosts, the Network Load Balancing Manager should look similar to Figure 10-16.

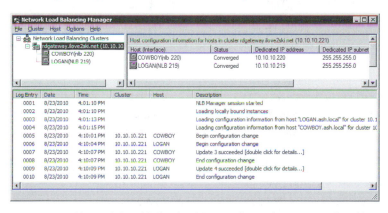

FIGURE 10-16 Network Load Balancing Manager has a cluster created and hosts converged.

All hosts should converge (note that hosts appear with a green square around the computer icons). If NLB can't hear a server heartbeat, the server state will display as "unreachable" with a red X on the computer icon. When the heartbeat resumes, the server reconverges. The details of changes in the environment show in the bottom pane.

To use RD Gateway, you will need to map the external DNS name (rdgateway.ilove2ski.net, the same name that you specified as the NLB) to the external IP address you designate that comes to your firewall, and then map that IP address to the internal cluster IP address. NLB will take care of passing the connection to the proper RD Gateway machine. This is shown earlier in Figure 10-15.

Preventing Split SSL Connections on RD Gateway

Setting affinity in a load balancer to a single server is the ideal, but it won't always work. For instance, if a large number of the RD Gateway connections will be coming from users behind a proxy, their IP addresses will all appear to be the same, and they will all get routed to one RD Gateway farm member. If you can't use IP affinity, then you must set up an RD Gateway farm on each RD Gateway farm member to avoid splitting up incoming and outgoing SSL connections for each session.

> **NOTE** Every SSL connection to RD Gateway actually consists of two SSL channels (RPC_IN_DATA and RPC_OUT_DATA).

By setting up the farm on each RD Gateway server, you're telling all the RD Gateway servers about each other. Doing so ensures that the SSL channels that are supporting the same connection will be routed through the same RD Gateway.

To set up an RD Gateway farm, follow these steps.

1. Open RD Gateway Manager, right-click the server, and choose Properties from the context menu to open the server Properties dialog box. Click the Server Farm tab, shown in Figure 10-17.

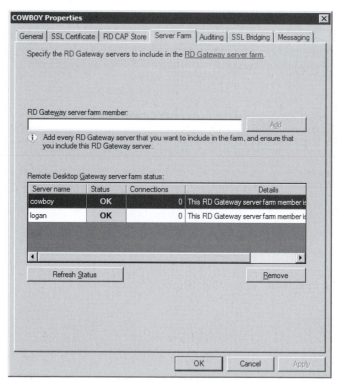

FIGURE 10-17 Add RD Gateway servers to the Server Farm tab if you don't use IP affinity in your load-balancing mechanism.

2. Add a server farm member to the RD Gateway Server Farm Member text box and click Add.

3. Do this for all server farm members and then Click OK.

4. Repeat this process for each RD Gateway server farm member. Connections supporting the same session should now be sent through the same RD Gateway server.

Maintaining Identical Settings Across an RD Gateway Farm

All RD Gateway servers in the server farm need to be configured identically or you'll get inconsistent experiences depending on which gateway server you connect to. You can make sure of this by exporting settings from a "master" server or by configuring all servers at the same time using Windows PowerShell.

Exporting and Importing Settings

One way to ensure that the server settings match is to export the settings from one RD Gateway server to a file and then import those settings to the other farm members. To export RD Gateway policy and configuration settings, open RD Gateway Manager, right-click the server, and choose Export Policy And Configuration Settings. Specify a name for the XML file in which the settings will be stored, point to a storage location, and then click OK.

To import RD Gateway server settings, right-click the RD Gateway server and choose Import Policy And Configuration Settings. Then specify the file that you want to import by typing the location or browsing to the file and then clicking OK.

Importing the settings is technically simple, but it does have a couple of potential "gotchas." To import settings from one RD Gateway server to another, the importing server must have an SSL certificate specified for the RD Gateway Properties, even if it is a self-signed certificate and not the ultimate certificate that you will use. If you do not specify a certificate and you try to import policy and configuration settings, you will see the following error.

```
The file cannot be imported because it might have been modified or corrupted.
```

If you cannot import policies from one RD Gateway server to another, it's possible that the exported settings refer to local security groups that don't exist on the server you're importing them to.

NOTE You will also get this error if RD RAPs are centrally stored. See the section entitled "Configuring a Central RD RAP Store" later in this chapter for more details.

Configuring the RD Gateway Farm Using Windows PowerShell

If you have more than one RD Gateway server, editing RD Gateway settings programmatically can help you to keep the RD Gateway configuration consistent across all RD Gateway farm members. You can use Windows PowerShell to make configuration changes on multiple RD

Gateway servers. In fact, you could create one script containing all RD Gateway configuration settings and run it against the organizational unit (OU) that contains the RD Gateway servers anytime you needed to make a change. For example, if you want to add the ASH-RDS-Users user group to an RD RAP called RD-RAP-01 on all RD Gateway machines in an OU called ASH_RDG_Farm, you would run the following script.

```
$objOU = "ASH_RDG_Farm"
$Domain = "ash"
$Suffix = "local"
$OU = [ADSI] "LDAP://OU=$objOU, DC=$Domain, DC=$suffix"
foreach ($child in $ou.psbase.children)
{
invoke-Command -computerName $child.name -scriptBlock {
$RDRAPName = "RDS-RAP-01"
$UserGroup = "ASH-RDS-Users@ASH"
Import-module remotedesktopservices
set-location rds:
cd gatewayserver\rap\$RDRAPName\
new-item usergroups -Name $UserGroup
}
}
```

To help you understand the RD Gateway folder structure in Windows PowerShell, run the following commands to navigate to the RD Gateway container, as shown in Figure 10-18.

```
PS C:\Users\admin> import-module remotedesktopservices
PS C:\Users\admin> set-location rds:
PS RDS:\> cd gatewayserver
PS RDS:\gatewayserver> dir
```

FIGURE 10-18 Manage RD Gateway settings programmatically using Windows PowerShell.

All RD Gateway configurable settings are located in the root or in containers in the gatewayserver directory. Use the dir and cd commands to enter subcontainers to get a full understanding of setting names and permissible operations.

 ON THE COMPANION MEDIA The script shown in this example is located on the companion media as the Add-RDRAP-UserGroup.ps1 file.

Using a Central NPS to Store RD CAPs

Maintaining identical settings gets you one-third of the way toward keeping the farm consistent. The second third is to provide a central storage location for the authorization policies.

To create a single store for RD CAPs, you can create a central NPS, either on one of the RD Gateway servers or on a different server altogether, and set all RD Gateway servers to use the central NPS. You might also do this if you already have an NPS running in your environment for other reasons and you decide to consolidate NPS functions onto one server.

The RD CAP Store tab in the RD Gateway Properties dialog box, shown in Figure 10-19, allows you to choose where to store RD CAPs.

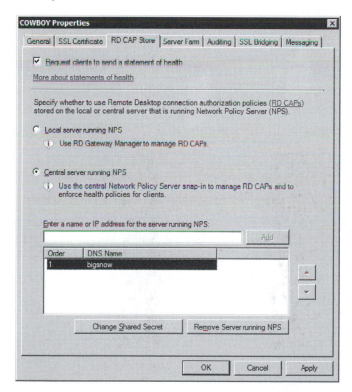

FIGURE 10-19 The RD Gateway Properties RD CAP Store tab shows you options for storing RD CAPs.

If you choose to use a central NPS, the new NPS will act as a Remote Authentication Dial-In User Service (RADIUS) server to the RD Gateway servers, and the RD Gateway servers will act as RADIUS clients to the NPS, as shown in Figure 10-20.

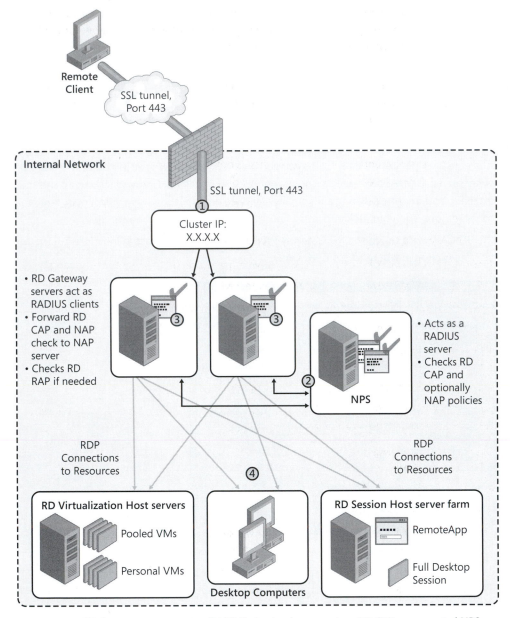

FIGURE 10-20 RD Gateway servers act as RADIUS clients when you store RD CAPs on a central NPS.

If you set up a central NPS for storing RD CAPs, the process to connect via RD Gateway will work like this.

1. A remote user requests connection to a resource via RD Gateway.

2. The RD Gateway server forwards the request to the centralized NPS, which checks the RD CAPs (and possibly other network access policies, too) and either allows or denies access based on whether the requester meets policy criteria.

> **NOTE** NPS can be used to check computer system health and uses network policies to accomplish this. You will learn more about this in the section entitled "Using NAP with RD Gateway" later in this chapter.

3. If the requestor meets policy requirements as defined in the connection and resource authorization policies, then the user is allowed to connect to RD Gateway.

4. RD Gateway does an RD RAP check and the connection is established or denied based on the results.

To configure RD Gateway to use a centralized NPS, you need to do the following.

1. Install the Network Policy and Access Services role on a server (or use an existing one).

2. Configure RD Gateway servers to use the new NPS location.

3. Configure the RD Gateway servers to forward network access requests to the new NPS.

4. Manually create new RD CAPs on the designated NPS.

These steps are described in the next sections.

INSTALL NETWORK POLICY AND ACCESS SERVICES (NPS)

First, install the Network Policy and Access Services role via Server Manager, or use Windows PowerShell to install NPS by running these commands.

```
Import-module servermanager
add-WindowsFeature NPAS
```

DIRECT THE RD GATEWAY SERVERS TO THE NPS

When the NPS server is ready, point the RD Gateway servers to the centralized RD CAP storage location. Perform the following steps on each RD Gateway Server.

1. Open RD Gateway Manager, right-click the server, and click Properties. Select the RD CAP Store tab and choose Central NPS Server. Type the name or IP address for the NPS and click Add.

2. The NPS must trust the RD Gateway to allow it to use its authorization policy store. Enter a shared secret password to use in validating the connection to the new NPS and click OK.

> **NOTE** After you point an RD Gateway server to another NPS, you can no longer create RD CAPs using RD Gateway Manager. The tools to create RD CAPs are disabled, and the RD CAP folder is replaced with a Central Network Policies folder that shows which NPS RD Gateway now uses to store RD CAPs, which are really Network Policies in NPS. In this case, you create and edit RD CAPs on the centralized NPS server instead.

CONFIGURE RD GATEWAY SERVERS AS RADIUS CLIENTS

Next, configure each RD Gateway server as a RADIUS client and point each server to the RADIUS server. By doing this, you are specifying where to forward NPS requests. On each RD Gateway server, do the following.

1. Open Network Policy Server (by clicking Start, Programs, Administrative Tools, and finally Network Policy Server).

2. Expand RADIUS Clients And Servers and select Remote RADIUS Server Groups.

3. In the right pane, double-click TS GATEWAY SERVER GROUP. The name of the central NPS server should be visible here. If it is not, add it by clicking Add and filling in the server name, then click OK. If there are any other servers listed, remove them by selecting them and clicking Remove, then click OK.

ENABLE ACCESS REQUEST FORWARDING

Next, make sure the NPS installed on each RD Gateway computer (the RADIUS client) forwards network access requests to the new centralized NPS (the RADIUS server). On each RD Gateway server, open NPS and complete these steps.

1. Expand the Policies folder. Click the Connection Request Policies folder, right-click TS GATEWAY AUTHORIZATION POLICY, and click Properties.

2. On the Overview tab, make sure that the policy is enabled and that the Type Of Network Access Server setting is Remote Desktop Gateway.

3. On the Conditions tab, make sure that NAS Port Type with a value of Virtual VPN is added. If it is not, click Add and then scroll down and select NAS Port Type. Click Add and then select the check box next to Virtual (VPN) in the Common Dial-Up And VPN Types box. Click OK.

4. On the Settings tab, click Authentication and confirm that the Forward Requests To The Following RADIUS Server Group For Authentication check box is selected, and that the TS GATEWAY SERVER GROUP is selected from the drop-down list.

5. Click Accounting. Confirm that the check box next to Forward Accounting Requests To This Remote RADIUS Server Group is selected and that TS GATEWAY SERVER GROUP is selected from the drop-down list.

ENABLE NPS TO TRUST THE RD GATEWAY SERVERS

To respond to requests from the RD Gateway servers, the central NPS server must trust them.

1. On the designated NPS, open the Network Policy Server management console, expand the RADIUS Clients and Servers folder, right-click RADIUS Clients, and choose New from the context menu.

2. Enter the name of an RD Gateway server in the Friendly Name input box, and its DNS name or IP address in the Address input box.

> **NOTE** If you are using NLB with multiple NICs installed on your RD Gateway servers, be sure to input the NLB IP address when creating RADIUS clients.

3. Next, accept the default Shared Secret Template (None), make sure the Manual option is selected, and enter the shared secret that you specified on the RD Gateway server RADIUS client. On the Advanced tab, accept the default configuration, and then click OK.

4. Repeat this for each RD Gateway server that will act as a RADIUS client.

The RADIUS clients will show up in the right pane, as shown in Figure 10-21.

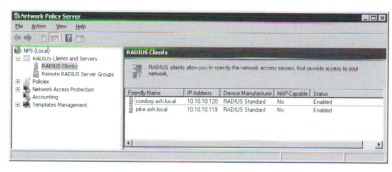

FIGURE 10-21 Add each RD Gateway server as a RADIUS client on the NPS.

Next, create a Connection Request Policy to allow RD Gateway servers to establish a connection to the NPS, as follows.

1. Expand the Policies folder, right-click Connection Request Policies, and choose New.

2. Give the policy a descriptive name, select Remote Desktop Gateway from the Type Of Network Access Server drop-down list, and click Next.

3. On the Conditions tab, click Add and select a condition for which the Connection Request Policy will be evaluated (and for which RD Gateway will pass). Click Add and enter the needed value for the condition. For example, add the Client IPv4 Address of the RD Gateway server. Leave the Settings tab settings as they are by default. Click OK.

   An RD Gateway Server must pass at least one Connection Request Policy, and it must also pass every condition within the policy. Therefore, you need to create a Connection

Request Policy for each RD Gateway server in your farm, each containing only conditions relevant to the individual RD Gateway server. For example, say that you have two RD Gateway servers with the following names and IP addresses.

- Cowboy.ash.local, 10.10.10.120
- Pike.ash.local, 10.10.10.119

4. Click Next through the rest of the Wizard screens and at the last screen click Finish.

To enable connections from both RD Gateway servers with these settings, set up two Connection Request Policies, one for each server, with the following conditions and values to allow connections from either of these two servers, as shown in Table 10-1.

TABLE 10-1 Create Connection Policies for Each RD Gateway Server Separately

CONNECTION POLICY NAME	CONDITION	VALUE
Cowboy	Client Friendly Name	Cowboy.ash.local
Cowboy	Client IPv4 Address	10.10.10.120
Pike	Client Friendly Name	Pike.ash.local
Pike	Client IPv4 Address	10.10.10.119

RECREATE RD CAPS ON THE NETWORK POLICY AND ACCESS SERVER

RD CAPs do not get transferred to the NPS when you choose to use a central NPS for storing them, so your next step is to re-create any existing RD CAP(s) on the new NPS.

An RD CAP is really a Network Access Policy; RD Gateway just makes it easier to create a policy with the settings that will work with RD Gateway. If you create an RD CAP on RD Gateway and then open the Network Policy Server console on the RD Gateway server, you will find that the RD CAP is created and stored under the Network Policies folder. Creating a network policy can accomplish the same thing as an RD CAP, and more. For example, a network policy can restrict access to RD Gateway based on the time of day or limit connecting clients to only those running a certain version of Windows or later. It's also important to know that a connection request must meet all settings and constraints configured in the network policy for the client to be allowed to access RD Gateway. Of course, just like local RD CAPs, you can create more than one network policy to accommodate different clients.

It's helpful to look at local NPS policies created by RD Gateway. Table 10-2 describes network policy settings and constraints, their values, and what RD CAP setting they correspond to when making a local RD CAP with the RD Gateway Wizard.

TABLE 10-2 Network Policy Conditions and Values That Correspond to Specific RD CAP Settings

NETWORK POLICY PROPERTIES TAB	NETWORK POLICY SETTING	NETWORK POLICY VALUE	CORRESPONDS TO RD CAP SETTING	RD CAP VALUE
Conditions tab	Machine Groups	A local or AD DS group	Client Computer Group Membership	A local or AD DS group
Conditions tab	Called Station ID	PW	Supported Windows Authentication Methods	Password
Conditions tab	Called Station ID	SC	Supported Windows Authentication Methods	Smart card
Constraints tab	Idle Timeout	Number of minutes	Enable Idle Timeout	Default = 120 minutes
Constraints tab	Session Timeout	Number of minutes	Enable Session Timeout	Default = 480 minutes
Settings tab	Vendor Specific	Vendor = Microsoft Attribute = TSG-Device-Redirection Attribute Value = 1073741824	Device Redirection	Enable all device redirection
Settings tab	Vendor Specific	Vendor = Microsoft Attribute = TSG-Device-Redirection Attribute Value = 1207959552	Device Redirection	Enable all device redirection plus setting: Only allow connections to RDSH that enforce RDG Device redirection
Settings tab	Vendor Specific	Vendor = Microsoft Attribute = TSG-Device-Redirection Attribute Value = 1	Device Redirection	Disable drive redirection
Settings tab	Vendor Specific	Vendor = Microsoft Attribute = TSG-Device-Redirection Attribute Value = 9	Device Redirection	Disable drive and clipboard redirection

Continued on the next page

NETWORK POLICY PROPERTIES TAB	NETWORK POLICY SETTING	NETWORK POLICY VALUE	CORRESPONDS TO RD CAP SETTING	RD CAP VALUE
Settings tab	Vendor Specific	Vendor = Microsoft Attribute = TSG-Device-Redirection Attribute Value = 11	Device Redirection	Disable drive and clipboard and printer redirection
Settings tab	Vendor Specific	Vendor = Microsoft Attribute = TSG-Device-Redirection Attribute Value = 15	Device Redirection	Disable drive, clipboard, printer and ports redirection
Settings tab	Vendor Specific	Vendor = Microsoft Attribute = TSG-Device-Redirection Attribute Value = 31	Device Redirection	Disable drive, clipboard, printer, ports and PnP redirection
Settings tab	Vendor Specific	Vendor = Microsoft Attribute = TSG-Device-Redirection Attribute Value = 134217759	Device Redirection	Disable redirection for all devices, plus setting: Only allow connections to RDSH that enforce RDG Device redirection

Although the intricacies of network policy creation on an NPS are outside the scope of this book, here is an example of how to create a simple policy that allows access to RD Gateway based on user group membership.

1. In the Network Policy Server Management Console, expand the Policies folder, right-click Network Policies, and choose New.

2. Give the policy a name, and for Type Of Network Access Server, choose Remote Desktop Gateway from the drop-down list. This specifies the type of network access server that will send connection requests to the NPS. Click Next.

3. At least one condition is required for this policy to be evaluated when a connection request is sent to NPS. Click Add and then choose a condition category. For example, choose Windows Groups. Click Add and then click Add Groups to add the group(s), one of which a user must be a member to access the RD Gateway server. Click OK a couple of times to return to the main dialog box and then click Next.

4   On the Specify Access Permission page, choose the Access Granted option and click Next.

5.   On the Configure Authentication Methods page, clear all the check boxes and then select the Allow Clients To Connect Without Negotiating An Authentication Method check box. Click No on the information pop-up window. Then click Next.

6.   Accept the defaults on the Configure Constraints page and click Next.

7.   On the Configure Settings page, select the RADIUS Attributes Standard option and then remove the default Framed-Protocol and Service-Type attributes. Click Next.

8.   On the Completing New Network Policy page, click Finish.

> **NOTE**   To save the NPS configuration to an XML file, run *netsh nps export*. For example, export the NPS configuration from a server named COWBOY to a network share with the following code.
>
> ```
> netsh nps export filename =
>     "\\colfax\ash-company-files\IT\Cowboy-NPS-Export.xml" exportPSK = YES
> ```
>
> Run the *netsh nps import* command to import an NPS configuration file.
>
> ```
> netsh nps import filename = \\colfax\ash-company-files\IT\Cowboy-NPS-Export.xml
> ```

Configuring a Central RD RAP Store

Unlike RD CAPs, RD RAPs can't be managed by NPS; they're actually implemented through the Authorization Manager. The Authorization Manager supports role-based access, so it's a good fit for RD RAPs. There is one failing from the point of creating a load-balanced farm: it does not support remote connections.

By default, RD RAP configurations are stored in an XML file located at %SystemRoot%\System32\Tsgateway\Rap.xml. However, you can tweak RD Gateway to get its RD RAPs from a central location so that all RD Gateway servers in the same load-balanced farm can have the same resource authorization policies without making you regularly export and import the RD RAPs. There's no user interface in the RD Gateway manager to do this, but you can change the location of the Rap.xml file by editing the registry.

First, copy the existing RD RAP to the network share. (If you don't, then when you update the storage location, RD Gateway will create a new copy of Rap.xml.) Next, open the Registry Editor and go to HKLM\SOFTWARE\Microsoft\Windows NT\CurrentVersion\TerminalServer-Gateway\Config\Core\RAPStore. Edit the value of this key to point to a network location. For example, change the registry key value from

```
msxml://%SystemRoot%\System32\tsgateway\rap.xml
```

to this.

```
msxml://\\colfax\ash-company-files\IT\rap.xml
```

Be sure to set the permissions on the network share that contains the Rap.xml file properly so that only RD Gateways are allowed write/read access. Otherwise, someone can circumvent the RD RAPs easily by editing the file.

Also, if you do not configure your RAP share with the correct permissions to allow RD Gateway servers to access the XML file, then NPS quarantines the user. The RDC that the client initiated will stop responding. You will have to use Task Manager to kill the attempted connection. The server will show an error in the event ID 6276 in the Security Event Log as follows.

```
Network Policy Server quarantined a user.
```

On the RD Gateway server, you will see

```
Event ID 642: The RD Gateway server cannot open the resource authorization policy store
on Authorization Manager (Azman).The following error occurred: "5".
```

There are a few issues with centrally stored RAPs that you should be aware of. First, making changes to centrally located RD RAPs takes some work, because you cannot edit the centrally located file from RD Gateway Manager. You have to repoint them to the local store location, modify the RD RAPs, and then re-copy the RAP.xml file to the central location and repoint the registry key to the central location. Also, to successfully export and import RD Gateway settings from one server to another, you also have to repoint RD RAPs to be stored locally, do the export and import, and then repoint the RD RAPs storage location registry entry to the central location. For these reasons, if you make changes to your RD Gateway configuration frequently, centrally stored RD RAPs might not work for you, due to the effort involved in keeping them centrally located.

Using NAP with RD Gateway

RD Gateway makes it easy to enable people to connect to internal network resources securely via the Internet. One trouble with allowing computers outside the network into the network to connect to RD Session Host servers is that you don't know where those computers have been. More to the point, you don't know what they bring with them.

It's easy to enforce certain policies on computers that are attached to the corporate network: you can update virus signatures, check for application updates, and so forth. But computers connecting to RD Session Host servers from outside the network, not updated according to the policies of that network, pose a different problem: How do you keep computers that you don't control from infecting the network?

One way is to check those computers *before* they connect to the network, make sure they conform to your organization's health policies, and permit access only if they do. The Microsoft technology that makes this possible is Network Access Protection (NAP). Using NAP, you can define a minimum set of policies to which a computer must conform before it can connect to a server via RD Gateway, and even help the computer become compliant if it isn't already. These health requirements can include policies such as the following.

- The computer must have an active firewall.
- The computer must have current antivirus signatures.
- Spyware protection must be enabled.

Basic NAP Concepts

NAP is a very big topic that covers a lot more than working with RD Gateway; it can also control access to other network resources like the wireless network and even getting an IP address from a Dynamic Host Configuration Protocol (DHCP) server.

Basically, when used with RD Gateway, NAP works like this: The client reports on its statement of health (SoH). NPS (on the RD Gateway server or on a centrally managed server) reads the reports and checks its network policies to determine whether the client complies with network and health policy requirements. If the client complies with policy, then RD Gateway checks its RD RAPs for a match. If the client matches an RD RAP, the client can connect to the requested resource.

As discussed in the section entitled "Using a Central NPS to Store RD CAPs" earlier in this chapter, the RD Gateway installation installs and uses a local NPS, but it can also access a central NPS. The configuration mainly depends on two factors: (1) whether you're clustering the RD Gateway servers and don't want to maintain CAPs on both servers; and (2) whether you're planning to use NAP for controlling access to any other network resources. For example, if you also use it to govern access to the wireless network, you'll most likely set up a central NPS to handle both cases.

To use NAP, a client must be running Windows XP SP3 or later.

How NAP Supports RD Gateway

To understand NAP, you must be familiar with the following NAP server and client components.

- **NPS**   The Network Policy Server role service of the Network Policy And Access role installed on a Windows Server 2008 R2 server. NPS is a RADIUS and proxy server. It also acts as an NAP network policy and health policy server, evaluating clients and determining their health compliance with company policies.
- **System Health Validators (SHVs)**   Specifies the settings that define what the organization considers a "health-compliant system." Each SHV interprets the health report sent from the client and creates a response report called the Statement of Health Response.
- **Statement of Health Response (SoHR)**   A report containing data about what network policy the client matched, and its resulting level of access.
- **System SoHR (SSoHR)**   A combination of all SoHRs from all SHVs. This is sent from NPS to the client.
- **NPS Administration Server (NPS AS)**   Passes SoHs to the SHV and passes SoH responses (SoHRs) to the NPS Service.

- **NPS Service**   Evaluates SoHRs and determines whether the NAP client is Compliant, Noncompliant, or Non-NAP-Capable, and packages SoHR responses into a System SoHR (SSoHR) report.
- **NAP Enforcement Server (NAP ES)**   Communicates with the client-side NAP Enforcement Client (NAP EC) component.

NAP client components include the following.

- **NAP Enforcement Client (NAP EC)**   The NAP client component that communicates with the NPS ES component.
- **System Health Agent (SHA)**   The client-side agent that monitors and creates a report of the client health as regards to various system health elements (for example, Antivirus, Antispyware, Windows Updates, and so on). The SHA gives this report to the NAP Agent. The SHA also performs system health updates as set forth by the remediation process. Every SHA has a corresponding SHV on the NPS.
- **Statement of Health (SoH)**   The report that the SHA creates. Each SHA creates its own SoH with data on the elements that the SHA reports on (for example, Windows Security elements, third-party antivirus, and so on).
- **System Statement of Health (SSoH)**   A report that contains all SHA reports.
- **NAP Agent**   This is a client-side agent that is built into Windows XP SP3 and later. It unpacks SSoHRs and distributes resulting SoHRs to the SHAs. It also packages SoHs into one SSoH that is sent to the server.

These components work together as shown in Figure 10-22.

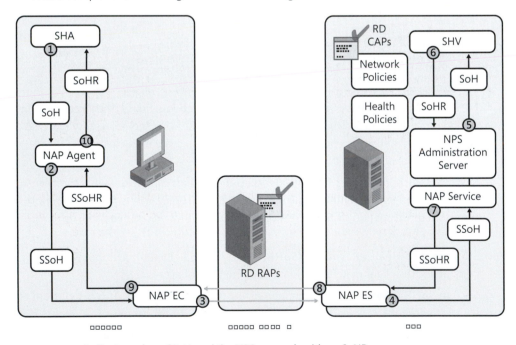

FIGURE 10-22 A client sends an SSoH, and the NPS responds with an SoHR.

1. When a client requests remote access to a resource (a remote desktop session, RemoteApp, or a VM), the client must send an SoH report to the NPS. The client SHAs create the SoH report(s), and each SHA passes the SoH to the NAP Agent.

> **NOTE** There can be more than one active SHA and corresponding SHV at a time. For example, you can implement third-party antivirus or antispyware SHAs and SHVs. For the purposes of this chapter, use the built-in client-side Windows SHA (WSHA) and server-side Windows SHV (WSHV), which monitor and report on the Windows Security Center settings (Windows Firewall, Windows Updates, and so on).

2. The NAP Agent combines the SHAs into the SSoH and passes this SoH to NAP EC.
3. The NAP EC passes the SSoH to the NPS ES on the NPS via RD Gateway.
4. The NPS ES passes the SSoH to the NPS Service, which unpacks the SSoH and passes each resulting SoH to the NPS Administration Server (NPS AS) component.
5. NPS AS passes each SoH made from the client-side SHA to its corresponding SHV.
6. The SHV checks the SoH against its requirements and sends the resulting SoHR to the NPS AS. The NPS AS passes the SoHR to the NPS Service.
7. The NPS Service compares the SoHR(s) against its network and health policies. It locates a network policy (which also references a health policy) that best matches the client health state. Health policies might look like the examples in Table 10-3.

TABLE 10-3 Example Health Policies That Describe the State of Connecting Clients

HEALTH POLICY NAME	HEALTH POLICY DEFINITION
Health-Policy-Pass	Client passes all SHV checks.
Health-Policy-Fail	Client fails one or more SHV checks.

> **NOTE** NPS needs access to AD DS to perform health validation for domain-joined clients.

Each network policy not only references a health policy, it contains access restrictions and remediation instructions as needed. Because of this, a computer client will always match a network policy (pass, fail, or not capable of using NAP). For example, Table 10-4 shows an example of Network Policies referencing Health Policies and dictating access and remediation accordingly.

TABLE 10-4 Example Network Policies That Reference Health Policies and Determine the Level of Client Access

NETWORK POLICY NAME	HEALTH POLICY NAME	NAP ENFORCEMENT
NAP-RD-Gateway-Pass	Health-Policy-Pass	Allow full access
NAP-RD-Gateway-Fail	Health-Policy-Fail	Limited access: Auto remediation and access with disabled device redirection
NAP-RD-Gateway-NonNAPClient	Health-Policy-NonNAPCapable	Deny access

The NPS Service creates an SSoHR that contains both its findings and the resultant level of access (and, if you want, remediation instructions) and sends it to the NAP ES.

8. The NAP ES passes the report to the NAP EC on the client via RD Gateway.

9. The NAP EC sends the SSoHR to the NAP Agent.

10. The NAP Agent unpacks it and sends each SoHR made from a specific SHV to the corresponding SHA.

If the policy and the client's health status are such that the client is allowed access to RD Gateway, then access to RD Gateway is granted. RD Gateway then checks its RD RAPs. If an RD RAP grants the client access to the requested resource, then the client is allowed to connect. The network policy that the client matched also determines the type of device redirection allowed.

NPS supports independent software vendors (ISVs) creating SHAs and corresponding SHVs. The native Windows SHVs (WSHVs) contain settings concerning the status of the categories shown in Table 10-5.

TABLE 10-5 Contents of the Windows Statement of Health

SYSTEM HEALTH AGENT	EXAMPLE OF WSHV SETTINGS WITH WHICH THE CLIENT MUST COMPLY
Firewall Status	The firewall must be enabled and currently running on all connections.
Antispyware	An antispyware application must be enabled and up to date.
Antivirus	An antivirus application must be enabled.
Automatic Updates	Auto-updating must be enabled.
Security Updates	The client must have checked for updates in the last 24 hours and must have Important and Critical updates installed.

The corresponding WSHA (remember, every SHV has a corresponding SHA), native to clients running Windows XP SP3 and later, monitors the Windows Security Center settings.

RD Gateway and NAP Remediation

In Windows Server 2008, if a client did not comply with enforced network policy, the client was locked out—the remediation that NAP supported was not available to RD Gateway clients. In Windows Server2008 R2, noncompliant clients can take advantage of NAP remediation. When a client does not pass a health check and Auto-Remediation is enabled in the matching network policy, the NAP agent on the client will be instructed to make necessary changes to the client to make it compliant. For example, if the network policy requires that a firewall be enabled, and the client uses Windows Firewall but it is turned off, the NAP Agent on the client will attempt to turn it on. With the firewall now enabled, the next time the client tries to connect, it will comply with the health policy and access will be granted to RD Gateway. Windows Updates can be instructed to get the latest updates from Windows Update servers or from Windows Server Update Services server. Windows Defender can be enabled if the health policy requires an antispyware program be enabled and the client uses Windows Defender. This is true for third-party software too, as long as it is registered with the Windows Security System on the client.

If the clients to be auto-remediated need access to other servers to update themselves, then those servers need to be accessible from outside the corporate network. For example, if you specify that Windows Updates need to be current and a client needs to get some updates to be compliant, and the way the client gets the updates is through Windows Software Update Services (WSUS), then the WSUS server must be accessible from the Internet so the remote client can get the updates. The same is true for third-party products. If your clients have a third-party firewall that they use, and it is registered with Windows Security Center, then the NAP Agent can report on its status.

CAUTION If you use a third-party tool with a Windows equivalent and auto-remediation cannot update the state of the third-party tool, then it will attempt to update the state of the Windows equivalent. For example, if you have a third-party firewall installed (but disabled) and auto-remediation cannot enable it, it will enable Windows Firewall instead. This could lead to unexpected results.

That is how NAP works. This next section explains configuring RD Gateway and NPS to use NAP to keep clients that don't meet system health policies away from RD Session Host servers, VMs, and other computers with remote desktop enabled. A full discussion of NAP is outside the scope of this book, so the information here concentrates on using NAP with RD Gateway only.

NOTE For a broader discussion of NAP, see *Windows Server 2008 Networking and Network Access Protection (NAP)* (Microsoft Press, 2008), by Joseph Davies and Tony Northrup with the Microsoft Networking Team.

Configuring NAP for Use with RD Gateway

In the following example, you will see how to make RD Gateway farm servers and a centralized NPS server work together to store and enforce RD CAPs and to perform client system health checks. To implement NAP with an RD Gateway farm and a centralized NPS, you need to do the following.

- Configure RD Gateway to work with NAP on the centralized NPS. This is the same setup you go through when configuring RD Gateway to use a centralized RD CAP storage location.

- Configure the NPS server to accept connections from RD Gateway and to evaluate incoming health reports.

- Configure clients as NAP clients.

This example assumes an RD Gateway farm and a centralized NPS server. If you have only one RD Gateway server and no separate NPS server, all setup will take place on the RD Gateway server.

CONFIGURING RD GATEWAY TO WORK WITH CENTRAL NAP

To configure RD Gateway to work with Central NAP, you need to do the following.

- Configure each RD Gateway server's local NPS with a Remote RADIUS Server Group to which the local NPS will forward requests.

- Configure each RD Gateway server's local NPS with a Connection Request Policy to forward connection requests to the Remote RADIUS Server Group.

- Enable health policy checking on each RD Gateway server.

- Note the RD Gateway SSL certificate Issued To name (shown on the SSL certificate) for future use in NAP client setup.

First, set up each RD Gateway server to forward connection requests to the centralized NPS. It will act as a RADIUS client, and the central NPS will act as the RADIUS server. Do this by creating a remote RADIUS server group on each RD Gateway server, as follows.

1. Open NPS, right-click Remote RADIUS Server Group, and choose New.

2. Enter a name for the group and add the central NPS server by clicking Add and entering the central NPS server's FQDN into the Server input box.

3. Select the Authentication/Accounting tab and enter the shared secret that the RD Gateway servers and the central NPS use to communicate. Then click OK.

Next, make sure you have a Connection Request Policy configured in each RD Gateway server's local NPS. This policy will forward connection requests to the remote RADIUS server group that you configured in the previous step, as follows.

1. In the NPS Management Console, right-click the Connection Request Policies folder and select New. Enter a policy name, and from the Type Of Network Access Server drop-down box, choose Remote Desktop Gateway. Click Next.

2. Add the NAS Port Type condition by clicking Add, choosing NAS Port Type from the bottom of the list. Click Add and then select the check box next to Virtual (VPN) and click OK. Then click Next.

3. On the Specify Connection Request Forwarding page, select Authentication and then select the Forward Requests To The Following Remote RADIUS Server Group For Authentication option.

4. In the drop-down box, make sure the remote RADIUS server group that you created earlier is selected. Click Next twice and click Finish.

Next, let's look at checking the health policy on RD Gateway. To do this, perform the following steps.

1. Open RD Gateway Manager, right-click the server, and choose Properties.

2. On the RD CAP Store tab, select the Request Clients check box to send an SoH. Click OK.

Note the Issued To name on the SSL certificate that you configured the RD Gateway server to use. You will use this name in the NAP client configuration. The name is located on the SSL certificate tab in the RD Gateway Properties.

CONFIGURING THE CENTRALIZED NPS TO WORK WITH RD GATEWAY

To configure the centralized NPS to work with the RD Gateway servers and to provide health checking, you need to do the following.

- Configure WSHV settings to reflect the organization definition of a healthy machine.
- Add the RADIUS clients to NPS.
- Add connection, network, and health policies to NPS.

First, configure the WSHV to reflect the health requirements you want computers to meet, as follows.

1. To edit the WSHV in the NPS console, expand Network Access Protection, expand System Health Validators, expand Windows Security Health Validator, and then highlight Settings.

2. You can create a New WSHV settings configuration by right-clicking Settings and choosing New. You can also edit the Default Configuration by double-clicking Default Configuration in the right pane. Doing so opens the WSHV shown in Figure 10-23.

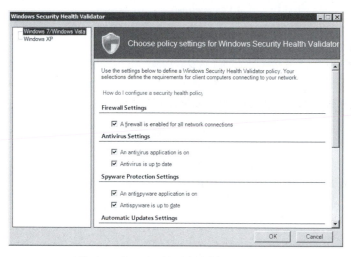

FIGURE 10-23 Windows Security Health Validator contains settings applying to Windows 7, Windows Vista, and Windows XP clients.

3. WSHV includes tabs that pertain to configurations for Windows XP, Windows 7, and Windows Vista clients. Select the boxes next to items you want to include as requirements for clients to gain access to RD Gateway. If your company uses Windows XP, Windows 7, and Windows Vista clients, then you need to set requirements on each of the appropriate tabs. When you're done, click OK.

Next, configure the central NPS with RADIUS client information so that connection requests can be received from the RD Gateway servers. You also need to configure the connection, network, and health policies required for RD Gateway to use NAP.

Fortunately, there is a wizard that will perform these duties. The NAP Wizard will do the following.

- Add specified RD Gateway servers as RADIUS clients.
- Create a Connection Request Policy that tells the NPS to process connection requests.
- Create three network policies (RD CAPs): one for compliant computers, one for non-compliant computers, and one for non-NAP-capable computers.
- Create two health policies that will be referenced by the compliant and noncompliant network policies.

Run the NAP Wizard and do the following.

1. On the central NPS, open the Network Policy Server console and select NPS (Local). From the Standard Configuration section in the middle pane, choose Network Access Protection (NAP) from the drop-down list and click the Configure NAP hyperlink to open the Configure NAP wizard shown in Figure 10-24.

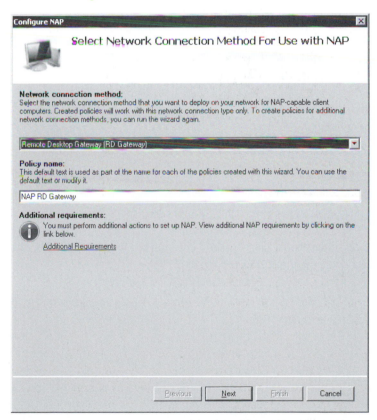

FIGURE 10-24 Choose the type of connection for which you're configuring NAP.

2. From the drop-down list, choose Remote Desktop Services Gateway (RD Gateway). Name your policy and click Next.

3. In the dialog box shown in Figure 10-25, add the RD Gateway servers that will act as NAP RADIUS clients. You should add all RD Gateway servers in the farm, as shown in Figure 10-25.

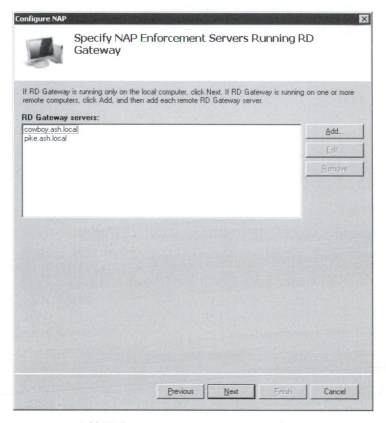

FIGURE 10-25 Add RD Gateway servers as NAP RADIUS clients.

Add RD Gateway servers by clicking Add and entering the information for an RD Gateway server, as shown in Figure 10-26.

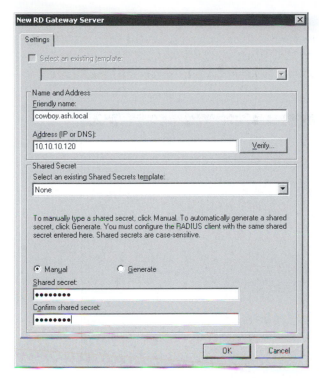

FIGURE 10-26 Add each RD Gateway as an NAP Enforcement server.

Input a friendly name (for example, the FQDN of the RD Gateway server), enter and verify each server's IP address, and type in the shared secret that will be used to join the RADIUS client with the RADIUS server. Click OK. Do this for each RD Gateway server in the RD Gateway farm. Click Next.

NOTE The shared secret that you input here must match the shared secret that you entered when you configured each RD Gateway server's remote RADIUS server.

From here, the process is much like creating an RD CAP, with the addition of selecting a WSHV.

4. Next, choose the device redirection settings to apply to the RD Gateway connecting clients and select the authorization methods that they're allowed to use. For example, the dialog box shown in Figure 10-27 is configured to allow password authentication and device redirection, and only allow clients supporting the redirection policies to use RD Gateway. Click Next.

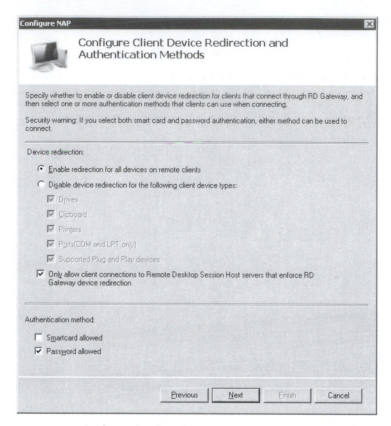

FIGURE 10-27 Configure the client device redirection and authentication methods.

5. On the next page, you can enable idle session timeouts and active session timeouts; this mimics the same settings that are set when creating an RD CAP. Configure these settings to your liking and then click Next.

6. On the next page, configure the user or computer group(s) that you want to allow to use RD Gateway. Click Add User or Add Machine to choose user or computer groups. Click Next.

7. Now, choose the System Health Validator to use with this configuration. In this example, we edited the default Windows Security Health Validator (WSHV) so this is the only one available. It is also selected by default.

> **NOTE** Although Windows Server 2008 R2 comes with only one SHV, the NAP model is extensible. ISVs can write their own sets of rules to cover conditions not accounted for in the default health validator.

Also on this page, choose what should happen when computers that are NAP-ineligible attempt to connect. By default, they're denied access, but you can also permit access and log the connection. Click Next to move to the review page.

8. Finally, the wizard will show your options for your review as shown in Figure 10-28. If the RADIUS clients and policies are what you intended, click Finish.

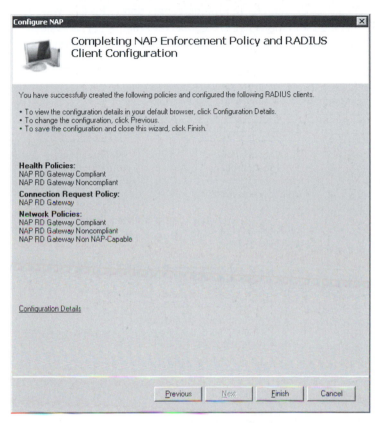

FIGURE 10-28 Review your NAP Enforcement policy settings and RADIUS client configuration settings.

After the NAP Creation Wizard finishes, you will find that it created one connection request policy, three network policies, and two health policies. These policies work together, first to accept connection information from RD Gateway, and then to evaluate whether clients requesting a connection to RD Gateway should be allowed or denied based on the health of the computer from which they are connecting, as well as the computer account and user account from which the client initiates the connection.

Figure 10-29 shows the relationships among these policies. This is what each type of policy does.

■ The Connection Request policy allows RD Gateway to send connection requests to NPS.

- Each of the three Network Policies contains information on the computer accounts and user accounts from which it accepts connections, as well as specifics on session timeout device redirection. In other words, a network policy should be very familiar to you—it is what an RD CAP really is.

- The two health policies—one a "passing" policy, the other a "failing" policy— determine the health of a computer requesting connection to RD Gateway. Using specifications that are set in the WSHV, the connecting client's SoH is evaluated. It will always meet the requirements of one of these policies (that is, it will either pass or fail).

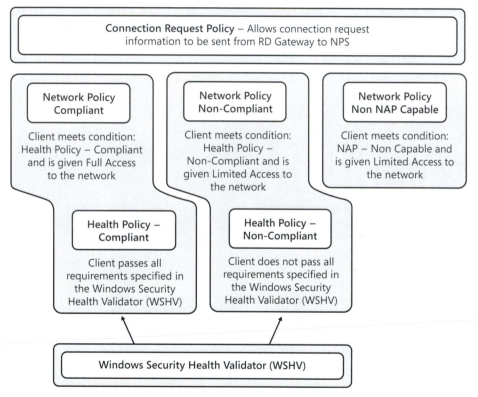

FIGURE 10-29 The relationships of policies created by the NAP Wizard make sure that a remote client will always meet the requirements of one network policy.

NAP clients will always fall into one of three scenarios shown in Figure 10-29. The client will meet the conditions specified in the Compliant or Non-Compliant network policy, or they will not be NAP-capable and therefore meet the condition of the Non-NAP-Capable network policy. The computers that meet the requirements for the Compliant network policy will be given full access to RD Gateway. Those computers that meet the requirements for either of the other two policies will be given the amount of access specified by the NAP Enforcement settings in each network policy respectively. NAP Enforcement settings were configured by the wizard, but you can tweak them as you see fit. They are located in each network policy on the Settings tab. Select NAP Enforcement.

CONFIGURING REMEDIATION SETTINGS

When you're trying to connect to the network through RD Gateway, it's helpful if a computer that doesn't meet the health policy can be fixed so that it does rather than the user just being told that it can't connect. NAP-enabled clients running RDC 7.0 and later can take advantage of auto-remediation. Clients running older versions of RDC cannot take advantage of auto-remediation, but they can still have their SoH evaluated.

NAP auto-remediation settings are configured automatically when you run the NAP Wizard and you create the three network policies. To see them, open the Network Policy Server Management tool on the NPS server, expand Policies, select Network Policies, and double-click the NAP RD Gateway Noncompliant policy. Select the Settings tab, and in the left pane, click NAP Enforcement. You will see that the Allow Limited Access option is selected, along with the Enable Auto-Remediation Of Client Computers check box. You can turn auto-remediation on for other policies as well by checking the Enable Auto-Remediation Of Client Computers check box.

Your clients need access to other services from other servers to become compliant—for example, they could be noncompliant because their virus signatures are out of date or they need Windows Updates. A server used for NAP remediation is called a *remediation server*. A remediation server must be available independently of RD Gateway for obvious reasons, and you'll need to tell clients about them. Create a remediation server group in NPS and then add the group to your NAP Non-Compliant policy so that clients that match this policy will know where to go for remediation.

To configure remediation groups from the NPS Management console, follow these steps.

1. Expand Network Access Protection, right-click Remediation Server Group, and choose New.

2. Enter a name for the group. Add the remediation servers by clicking Add and entering a descriptive name for the server and its publicly available FQDN or IP address (remember that you can't use RD Gateway to get to a remediation server). Then click OK.

> **NOTE**   You can also create Remediation Server Groups by clicking New Group on this same screen.

After you create a remediation server group, add it to the NAP RD Gateway Non-Compliant policy by following these steps.

1. Double-click the network policy, select the Settings tab, and select NAP Enforcement.

2. In the Remediation Server Group And Troubleshooting URL section, click Configure.

3. In the resulting dialog box, select the remediation server group from the drop-down list and click OK.

On the network policy Settings NAP Enforcement panel, notice that you can also enter a Troubleshooting URL when you click the Configure button in the Remediation Server Group And Troubleshooting URL section. Add a URL to a website that tells users how to update their machines to come into compliance with the corporate system health policies.

 CAUTION If you enable auto-remediation, do not add a troubleshooting URL to your noncompliant policy. This might look helpful, but if you do, auto-remediation is not performed on the client; instead, the client is just denied access.

CONFIGURING NAP ENFORCEMENT CLIENTS

For clients to be checked against NAP policies, you must perform the following steps.

- Enable the NAP client.
- Enable the RD Gateway Quarantine enforcement client (which tells the client to communicate the computer health status to the NPS).
- Add the RD Gateway to the Trusted Gateways list on the client.
- Add the RD Gateway certificate in Trusted Root Certification Authorities of the local computer certificate store.

NOTE Although online documentation on whether Windows Server 2008 can be a NAP client is conflicting, it cannot be a NAP client for RD Gateway using only components that come with the operating system. This is because the WSHA is not supported on Windows Server 2008. It is possible that you could integrate a third-party SHV and SHA and then use Windows Server 2008 as a NAP client for RD Gateway.

NOTE Windows Vista has the NAP client enabled by default. Windows XP SP3 and Windows 7 do not. Enable it by starting the Network Access Protection Agent service and then restarting the computer.

Enable the RD Gateway Quarantine enforcement client by adding the NAP Client Configuration snap-in to an MMC. Click Enforcement Agents, right-click the RD Gateway Quarantine enforcement client, and click Enable. An easier way to do this is to open an elevated command prompt and run this command.

```
netsh nap client set enforcement ID = "79621" Admin = "Enable"
```

Add the RD Gateway to the Trusted Gateways list by opening Regedit.exe and navigating to HKLM/SOFTWARE/Microsoft/Terminal Server Client/TrustedGateways. Add a new string value called GatewayFQDN. Then double-click GatewayFQDN and enter the FQDN name of the RD Gateway.

Easier yet, Microsoft provides a script that performs all these tasks. Download the text file Tsgqecclientconfig.txt (*http://www.microsoft.com/downloads/ details.aspx?familyid=cb986639-20e5-4f16-8e48-be68d23dc888&displaylang=en*) and rename it Tsgqecclientconfig.cmd. You will need to run the script with elevated privileges. Open an elevated command prompt, navigate to the directory where the script resides, and type **tsgqecclientconfig <RD Gateway FQDN>**. Successful results look like this.

```
tsgqecclientconfig.cmd rdgateway.ilove2ski.net
Setting the list of trusted TS Gateway servers to rdgateway.ilove2ski.net ...
The operation completed successfully.
Enabling the TS Gateway Quarantine Enforcement Client
The operation completed successfully.
Setting the Network Access Protection service startup type to Automatic...
[SC] ChangeServiceConfig SUCCESS
Starting the Network Access Protection service...
The Network Access Protection Agent service is starting.
The Network Access Protection Agent service was started successfully.
```

Restart the computer, and you're done.

ON THE COMPANION MEDIA The link to the Tsgqecclientconfig file is also located on the companion media.

Testing NAP with RD Gateway

To test NAP with RD Gateway, configure a client to match each of the three network policies (Compliant, Noncompliant, and Non-NAP-capable) and then try to connect to an RDS resource through RD Gateway. When testing each client configuration, check the system event logs on the NPS. Each connection should log successes or failures with details about what NAP network policy the client matched and why they denied access (if that is the case). Security Event IDs to look for are Event ID 6276 and Event ID 6272. Security Event IDs will show the status of Audit Success even if the client is denied access to RD Gateway because, technically, a noncompliant client matched a network policy. You will need to look at the details of these event logs to see which policy the client matched, what connection authentication they used, and other connection details.

AUTO-REMEDIATING NON-COMPLIANT CLIENTS

Clients that match the NAP RD Gateway Noncompliant policy will not be able to connect initially, even if configured as NAP Enforcement. They must first be brought into compliance. As shown in Figure 10-30, the client receives a message telling them that the computer did not meet the NAP health requirements.

FIGURE 10-30 If your computer does not comply with NAP health policies, you will see this error message when attempting to connect.

If you have kept the default configuration of this network policy and auto-remediation is enabled, then the NAP Agent will display a message telling you that it is trying to bring your computer into compliance. For example, if your WSHV requires that the firewall on the client be enabled and it is not, then the NAP Agent will attempt to turn it on, as shown in Figure 10-31.

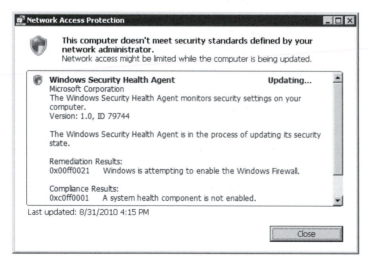

FIGURE 10-31 The WSHV will send instructions to the NAP Agent to get it to enable the Windows Firewall.

If the NAP Agent is successful, it will report that it has updated the computer and that the computer is now NAP-compliant, as shown in Figure 10-32.

FIGURE 10-32 After the client is updated and is NAP-compliant, the user can try the connection request again.

After the client has been updated and made compliant with the health policies, then the user can retry the connection. This time, the computer will match the NAP-Compliant network policy and the client will be able to connect to RD Gateway. Because the health policy is part of the connection policy, the RD Gateway will just have to check its RD RAPs before permitting the final connection.

Troubleshooting Declined Connections

You've set up the RD CAPs, RD RAPs, and network policies, but people still can't connect. Why not?

All too often, the error messages for a denied logon are cryptic. You know that a user was denied a connection to RD Gateway, but you don't know why. The Event Logs on both the RD Gateway server(s) and the NPS can help you find the source of the problem.

Identifying RADIUS Errors

For instance, if you have a fundamental problem between the RADIUS client (RD Gateway) and the NPS (if run on a separate computer), you will receive an error telling you that the connection was denied because the client did not meet the connection authorization requirements. Naturally, you will suspect that an RD CAP is blocking access. But in some cases, a problem between the RADIUS client and server might exist. To determine the real reason for a blocked connection, correlate the event logs in these three Event Viewer log places.

- In the RD Gateway server log located at Application Logs and Security/Microsoft/Windows/TerminalServices-Gateway/Operational. The denied connection will show up in this log as Event ID 201. You can see who tried to log on and generally why they were denied. Correlate this with the following Security log located at Windows Logs/Security: Look for Audit Failure log entries (event IDs 6273 and 6274) that correspond to the attempted logon time. Scroll to the bottom of these logs to find a reason code and a reason for the blocked connection.

- In the NPS Event Viewer. Check the System log for events with a source of NPS. For instance, if your RADIUS clients have dual NICs and they start communicating with the NPS from the wrong one (meaning that they are using an IP address not specified in the RADIUS Client field in the NPS Console), you will see Event ID 13 in your event logs.

Identifying RD RAP Errors

Connections that are blocked due to RD RAP policies are often simple. If a user is blocked by an RD RAP, he or she simply doesn't belong to a group that has access to the requested resource. The event is logged on the RD Gateway server at Application Logs and Security/Microsoft/Windows/Remote Desktop Services-Gateway/Operational.

RD RAPs can be tricky, though. You need to make sure that people connecting to resources can get to the resources along the way that the user might encounter before they reach their ultimate destination.

For example, if publishing pooled VMs, you must add not only the VMs to the RD RAP but also the redirector because the connection goes to the redirector first. If you don't add the redirector, the connection can't be redirected. The errors will be subtly different depending on the operating system on the client.

Connecting from a Windows 7 client will result in Event 301 being logged in the Operation log.

```
The user "ASH\kristin.griffin", on client computer "10.10.10.1", did not meet resource
authorization policy requirements and was therefore not authorized to resource
"humpback.ash.local". The following error occurred: "23002".
```

Connecting from a Windows XP client will also result in Event 301 being logged in the Operation log, but notice that the resource name is the downlevel DNS name of the redirector.

```
The user "ASH\hao.chen", on client computer "10.10.10.1", did not meet resource
authorization policy requirements and was therefore not authorized to resource
"humpback-vmredir". The following error occurred: "23002".
```

To do this in the easiest way, create an RD Gateway–managed group to accommodate both DNS names (the regular one and the one used for clients running Windows XP) for the purposes of redirection and then add the group to an RD RAP.

Identifying NAP Errors

Connections that are blocked due to NAP policies are fairly straightforward. The log files are found in two places.

- On the NPS, open Event Viewer, expand Custom Views/Server Roles, and click Network Policy And Access Services. This custom event log view contains all the event logs pertaining to NPS, including accounting events that occur on this server.

- By default, NPS logs accounting and authentication requests to a log file located at %SystemRoot%\System32\LogFiles. To adjust which events are logged or other settings such as the log location, open the Network Policy Server console, click Accounting, and then click the Configure Local File Logging link.

If you are having problems with your NAP health policy setup or remediation, the following troubleshooting tips can help.

- If your clients match only the NAP-Non-Capable network policy and they are really NAP-Capable clients, and your NAP client setup is correct, then you might have missed configuring each RD Gateway to request clients to send an SoH. Because no SoH is sent, the client is seen as Non-NAP-Capable. To fix this, on each RD Gateway server, in the RD Gateway Manager, right-click the server and select Properties. Navigate to the RD CAP Store tab and make sure that the Request Clients To Send A Statement of Health check box is selected.

- Running the Napstat.exe command at a command prompt shows the current NAP Agent status on the client. You can use this to see exactly what the NAP Agent is accomplishing when the client attempts to connect to a remote desktop resource.

- Use the following commands on each client to make sure that the NAP client configuration is correct.

  - **netsh NAP client show state**   Tells you if the NAP agent service is running. It should be. If it is not, then enable the service.

  - **netsh NAP client show group**   If you used Group Policy to set up the NAP client configuration, verify that the enforcement client is enabled via Group Policy by running this command. The enforcement client should return the following data.

    ```
    Name           = RD Gateway Quarantine Enforcement Client
    ID             = 79621
    Admin          = Enabled
    ```

  - **netsh nap client show config**   If you manually set up the NAP client configuration, verify that the enforcement client is enabled via the local policy by running this command. The enforcement client should return the following data.

    ```
    Name           = RD Gateway Quarantine Enforcement Client
    ID             = 79621
    Admin          = Enabled
    ```

- NAP client event logs could show you errors to help you correct client-side NAP issues. The NAP client event logs are located at Application and Services Logs/Microsoft/Windows/Network Access Protection/Operational.

- If the client NAP Agent is configured correctly and your network policies are working except for auto-remediation, check to see if you have both enabled auto-remediation and set a remediation server group and troubleshooting URL in the noncompliant policy. You cannot have a URL set and have auto-remediation work at the same time.

- Look in the System and Security Event Logs on the NPS for events pertaining to successful and declined connections.

- For auto-remediation to work, the client must be able to modify the firewall and other security settings. Make sure that Group Policy is not blocking the client from taking remediation action.

Placing RD Web Access and RD Gateway

RD Web Access is a good way to make RemoteApp programs available to users when it is impractical to distribute RDP files. To provide secure Internet access to RemoteApp programs through RD Web Access, you can publish RemoteApp programs to use RD Gateway. This section will focus on the placement of both RD Web Access and RD Gateway in your network.

> **NOTE**   Regardless of whether you place the RD Web Access server in a perimeter network or on the internal network, it's a good idea to replace the self-signed SSL certificate on the RD Web Access server with one signed by a public CA so that users can continue have an encrypted session with the website and also be able to trust the certificate without having to manually the website SSL cert to their trusted root store. As explained in Chapter 4, "Deploying a Single Remote Desktop Virtualization Host Server," a fresh install of the RD Web Access website will configure the site as a secured site, using a self-signed SSL certificate. Although this is fine for testing, using self-signed certificates is not recommended in production environments.

RD Gateway also uses SSL certificates to encrypt communication. We recommend SSL certificate options for both RD Gateway and RD Web Access, depending on their location in the network.

RD Web Access for External Access

One popular use of RD Web Access is to make RemoteApp programs easily available to users outside your network.

If you have a perimeter network, then it is wise to place the RD Web Access server in the perimeter to minimize your attack surface. That way, if your web server is compromised, your internal network will not be. You can also put RD Web Access in the internal network and publish the website through ISA/TMG or another firewall appliance. You can configure the RD Web Access website to have the same URL for both internal and external access, or create a separate URL for internal and external use.

If both internal and external users get RemoteApp programs from RD Web Access, you can provide the same external URL to people connecting from inside and outside the network. External users will resolve the URL through public DNS servers. For internal users to resolve this external URL, you will need to take one of the following approaches, split DNS or DNS doctoring, as follows.

- Split DNS creates a zone in your internal DNS servers for the external domain. You add an entry that maps the external DNS name to the internal IP address of the RD Web Access site.

At a high level, DNS doctoring maps internal and external addresses (you'll need to make sure your firewall supports this). An internal network client connects to an external DNS server for DNS resolution, and the external DNS server responds to the query. The firewall sees that the external DNS resolution IP address really translates to an IP address on the internal network. The firewall intercepts the DNS resolution response from the external DNS server and replaces it with the internal address. The common name of your SSL certificate should reflect the external name of the website as follows.

- Obtain a regular SSL certificate with the common name in the form *<external-DNS-hostname>.<external-domain-name>.<top-level-domain-name>*. For example, rdweb.ilove2ski.net.

- You could also use a wildcard SSL certificate with a common name reflecting the external domain space, such as *.ilove2ski.net.

> **NOTE** To save money, you can get a wildcard certificate that references the external domain name space and use it for both RD Gateway and RD Web Access, as well as to sign RemoteApps.

Alternatively, you could set up the RD Web Access server to use one URL for internal use and one for external use. To accomplish this, you can obtain a Subject Alternative Name (SAN) certificate. A SAN certificate (also known as a Unified Communications Certificate, or UCC certificate) contains multiple subjects. When you apply the SAN certificate to the website, the certificate will match both internal and external URLs, so a user won't get warning messages when trying to connect. For instance, in this example, the test environment internal domain name is Ash.local, but for users outside the internal network, the domain name Ilove2ski.net is used. So you would use a SAN SSL certificate on the RD Web Access website with the following two subjects: Apps.ash.local and Rdweb.ilove2ski.net.

SAN certificates are more expensive. If your budget will not accommodate a SAN certificate, you could use a standard SSL certificate (with one common name), allow HTTP and HTTPS access to the website, and then block port 80 at the firewall. This means that internal users could access an internal unencrypted HTTP address (no SSL certificate needed), and external users would still have to use an encrypted HTTPS address. Of course, this assumes that your company security policy allows unencrypted access to intranet sites from inside the corporate network.

> **NOTE** See the Additional Resources at the end of this chapter for links to information on DNS doctoring and SAN/UCC certificates.

RD Gateway Inside the Private Network

If you do not have a perimeter network, you can put RD Gateway in the internal network, as shown in Figure 10-33, with only port 443 opened in the firewall. The firewall permits incoming traffic to the RD Gateway on port 443 (SSL), and the gateway processes the incoming connections to make sure that they're permitted to access the network. When complete, the RD Gateway routes the connections to the resource via port 3389 (RDP).

Putting RD Gateway inside the network enables RD Gateway to communicate directly with AD DS so that it can pull its user and computer groups from a central location. (Without this ability, you'll need to set up local user groups and can't use domain computer groups to create RD CAPs and RD RAPs.) However, it also means that when an incoming connection is permitted, the network is wide open. You can restrict incoming connections to port 3389, and you can restrict the list of servers that the incoming connections can use. However, you can't easily define a set of permitted ports to use after the connection makes it inside the network. More important, if malicious code could reaches RD Gateway and RD Gateway is compromised, the private network is vulnerable.

> **NOTE** See the Direct from the Source sidebar entitled "TMG and RD Gateway Topology Scenarios" later in this chapter for information on protecting RD Gateway positioned in the internal network.

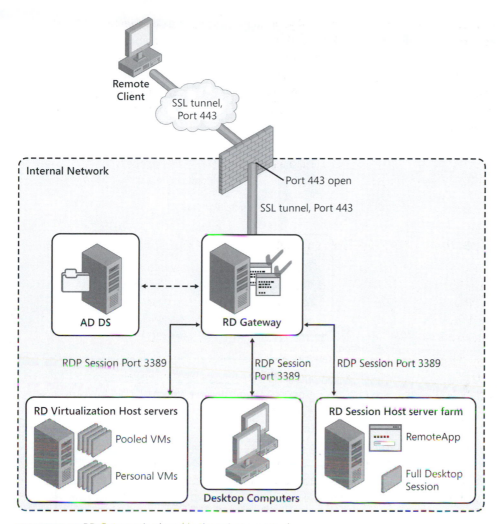

FIGURE 10-33 RD Gateway is placed in the private network.

RD Gateway in the Perimeter Network

To have a bit more control over which ports are open, you can use an additional firewall, as shown in Figure 10-34. This way, you can be sure that only port 3389 is open. Alternatively, you have the option of not limiting the ports that RD Gateway will permit and using the firewall to control the kinds of traffic that are available. The first firewall will have port 443 open. The second will have port 3389 open to permit RDP traffic to pass to the private network.

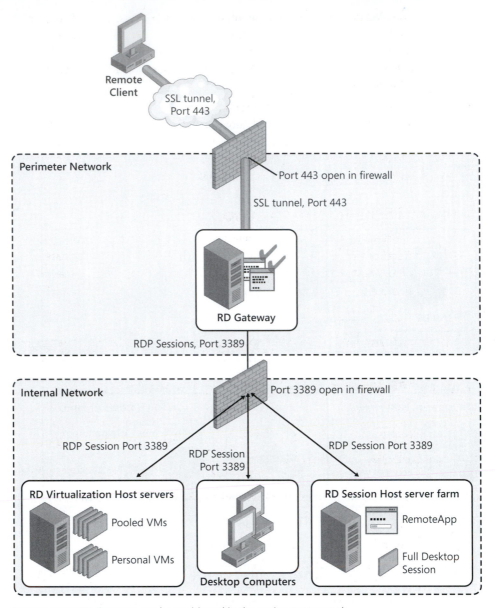

FIGURE 10-34 RD Gateway can be positioned in the perimeter network.

If you decide to position RD Gateway in the perimeter network, bear in mind that for RD Gateway to create RD CAPs that refer to domain accounts, it has to be able to communicate with AD DS. Otherwise, your users will have to present their credentials more often: They'll have to authenticate once to RD Gateway (placed in a workgroup with local accounts) and then again when RD Gateway allows the user to access an internal resource.

If you decide to provide RD Gateway in the perimeter network with access to AD DS, it's possible to do this without directly exposing AD DS to threats. For example, you can create a separate forest in the perimeter network, and create a one-way trust between the perimeter network AD DS and the internal corporate AD DS. You can also place a read-only domain controller in the perimeter network.

In these scenarios, you need to open specific ports to allow the needed traffic to pass between the perimeter network and the internal network. Refer to the following blog post (also included on the companion media) for information on firewall rules and port access needs with regards to RD Gateway in the perimeter network: *http://blogs.msdn.com/b/rds/archive/2009/07/31/rd-gateway-deployment-in-a-perimeter-network-firewall-rules.aspx.*

RD Gateway in the Internal Network and Bridged

To allow you to connect RD Gateway to AD DS while protecting the internal network, you can also use Microsoft Forefront Threat Management Gateway (TMG) 2010 (the new release of Microsoft ISA Server) or another SSL bridging device. Using SSL bridging is safer because TMG will first be decrypting the SSL traffic, inspecting packets, and denying packets with malicious code before traffic ever reaches RD Gateway.

DIRECT FROM THE SOURCE

TMG and RD Gateway Network Topology Scenarios

Tom Shinder
Microsoft DAIP

UAG Direct Access/Anywhere Access Team

There are several network topologies that work for using TMG or ISA as an HTTP/HTTPS bridge for RD Gateway.

Model 1: TMG in the Perimeter Network

In Model 1, TMG is located in the perimeter network between two other firewalls, and RD Gateway is located in the internal network. This scenario is popular with companies that already have a perimeter network in place. TMG, located in the perimeter network, receives the incoming packets destined for RD Gateway. TMG performs stateful and application-layer inspection of incoming packets for malware or exploits, denies any packets containing malicious code, and then repackages and forwards all good packets. One of the benefits of this model is that because TMG does not do any preauthentication of SSL traffic, there is no need for TMG to be part of the domain and there is no need to expose AD DS in the perimeter network. RD Gateway is located in the internal network and can therefore use domain user and computer groups in its RD CAPs and RD RAPs (see Figure 10-35).

Model 2: TMG as Back-end Firewall

In this model, TMG is the back-end firewall. This scenario is more popular in small to mid-sized companies. TMG performs the role of internal network edge firewall and also bridges incoming SSL traffic destined for RD Gateway on the internal network (see Figure 10-36). The benefit of this model is that companies don't have to invest in an extra firewall to create a perimeter network. It's also worth mentioning that ISA/TMG has had no documented exploits and has had fewer than 10 fixes in the history of the product's existence, so TMG is a good firewall solution.

Model 3: TMG in the Internal Network

In this model (shown in Figure 10-37), TMG is placed inside the internal network. Some might think that this poses security risks, but it really does not. First, consider that TMG is a firewall. So traffic coming in destined for RD Gateway must first pass through one or more edge firewalls and is then passed to another firewall, TMG. The benefit here is that no perimeter network is needed. Because of the way TMG publishes RD Gateway access, only the folder of the RPC directory is exposed. Further, TMG can be locked down further to provide access only to a particular file as well. TMG in this scenario can be a domain member or part of a workgroup—neither way poses an AD DS security risk because the TMG firewall protects itself from network attack—no traffic other than that enabled by System Policy is allowed to the firewall itself. And because of the design of the TMG firewall architecture, there is no practical mechanism that can be used to exploit the firewall itself for traffic that is exposed to the stateful packet and application layer inspection engines. In practice, the threat profile exposed by the workgroup TMG firewall is little different than that exposed by the domain member TMG firewall. And in fact, because of the increased number of security options available with a domain member TMG firewall, the over security posture of the domain member firewall is better than the workgroup firewall (assuming that you are using the TMG firewall for something other than publishing Remote Desktop Gateway).

For more information on TMG network topology, see *http://technet.microsoft.com /en-us/library/dd896975.aspx*.

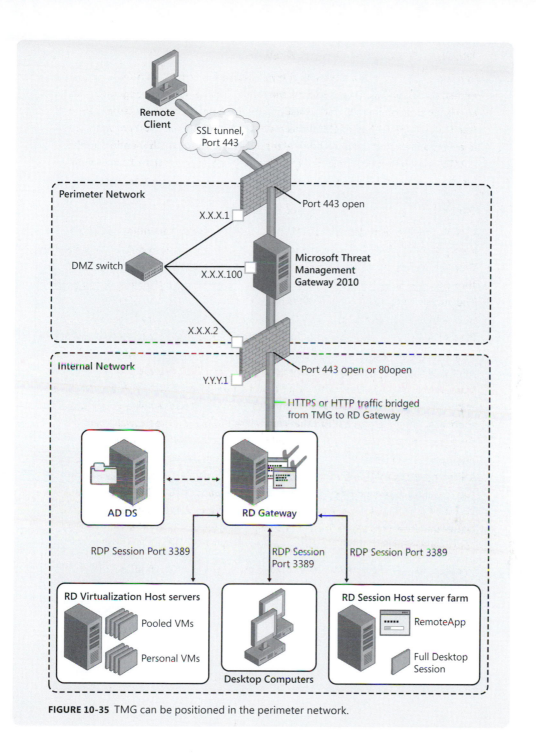

Remote
Client

SSL tunnel,
Port 443

Perimeter Network

X.X.X.1

Port 443 open

DMZ switch

X.X.X.100

**Microsoft Threat
Management
Gateway 2010**

X.X.X.2

Internal Network

Y.Y.Y.1

Port 443 open or 80open

HTTPS or HTTP traffic bridged
from TMG to RD Gateway

AD DS

RD Gateway

RDP Session Port 3389

RDP Session
Port 3389

RDP Session Port 3389

RD Virtualization Host servers

Pooled VMs

Personal VMs

Desktop Computers

RD Session Host server farm

RemoteApp

Full Desktop
Session

FIGURE 10-35 TMG can be positioned in the perimeter network.

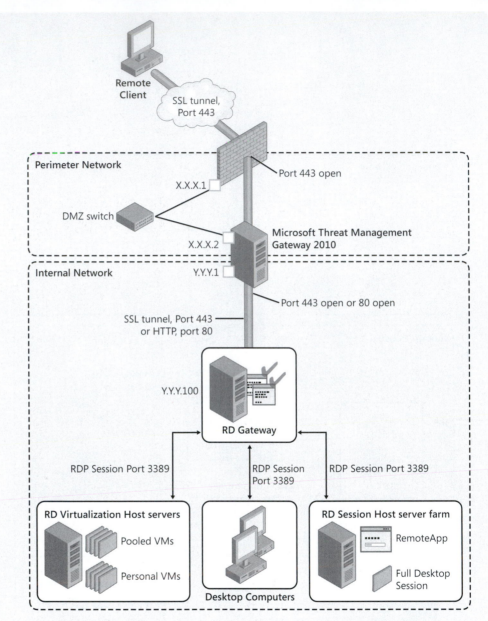

FIGURE 10-36 TMG can act as the internal network edge firewall and can also bridge RD Gateway traffic.

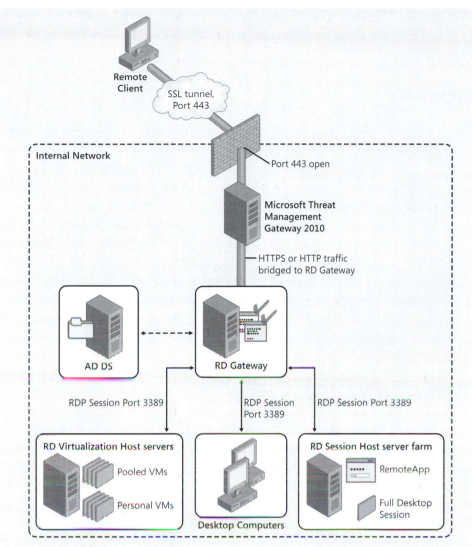

FIGURE 10-37 TMG can be positioned in the internal network and still inspect and bridge traffic to RD Gateway.

For more information on configuring RD Gateway with TMG/ISA Server, see *http://technet. microsoft.com/en-us/library/cc731353(WS.10).aspx*. Microsoft has also made a script available to help configure ISA Server for use with RD Gateway. Information about this script can be found at *http://blogs.msdn.com/b/rds/archive/2010/01/08/publish-rd-gateway-on-an-isa-server-using-a-script.aspx*.

ON THE COMPANION MEDIA These links are also available on the companion media.

Summary

One of the great values of RDS is that it enables people to work normally over the Internet. RD Gateway is an RDS role service that makes it possible to do this securely. This chapter has introduced you to a number of best practices for implementing RD Gateway.

- Load-balance RD Gateway servers to increase gateway uptime.
- When using an RD Gateway farm, centralize the RD CAP and RD RAP sources to simplify configuration. If centralizing isn't possible for some reason, use the export and import capabilities on the RD Gateway servers to maintain servers with identical settings.
- Enable server affinity to keep all SSL connections for a single session on the same RD Gateway server and to reduce the risk that a downed server will take down the session.
- Use NAP to conduct client system health checks and to determine if a client is compliant with company system health standards before it connects to the network using RD Gateway.

Additional Resources

The following resources are related to topics covered in this chapter. You can find the links and scripts on this book's companion media. A lot of the information in this chapter has focused on the various conditions under which connections are made, and you'll see resources here related to that as well.

- For more information on RD Gateway availability, configuration, and connection Event ID codes and possible resolutions, see *http://technet.microsoft.com/en-us/library /ee891285%28WS.10%29.aspx*.
- For more information on TMG network topology, see *http://technet.microsoft.com /en-us/library/dd896975.aspx*.
- For more information on configuring RD Gateway with TMG/ISA Server, see *http://technet.microsoft.com/en-us/library/cc731353(WS.10).aspx*.
- Microsoft has made a script available to help configure ISA Server for use with RD Gateway. Information about this script can be found at *http://blogs.msdn.com/b/rds /archive/2010/01/08/publish-rd-gateway-on-an-isa-server-using-a-script.aspx*.
- To learn more about NAP, see *Windows Server 2008 Networking and Network Access Protection (NAP)*, by Joseph Davies and Tony Northrup with the Microsoft Networking Team, available at *http://www.microsoft.com/mspress/books/11160.aspx*.

- For the NAP client configuration tool (Tsgqecclientconfig.cmd), go to *http://www.microsoft.com/downloads/details.aspx?familyid=cb986639-20e5-4f16-8e48-be68d23dc888&displaylang=en.*

- "Remote Desktop Services Gateway Server Protocol Routing Specification" is available for download from *http://msdn.microsoft.com/en-us/library/cc248485.aspx.*

- "Windows Security Health Agent (WSHA) and Windows Security Health Validator (WSHV) Protocol Specification" is available for download from *http://msdn.microsoft.com/en-us/library/cc215773.aspx.*

- "Statement of Health for Network Access Protection (NAP) Protocol Specification" is available for download from *http://msdn.microsoft.com/en-us/library/cc212976.aspx.*

- For more information on the Microsoft Root Certificate Program and certificates in general, see Chapter 9, "Multi-Server Deployments."

- Refer to the section entitled "Transport Layer Security" in Chapter 8, "Securing Remote Desktop Protocol Connections," to see how SSL encryption works.

- To see how to force RDCs initiated from RD Web Access to use RD Gateway, see the section entitled "Force RDC Connections Through RD Gateway via RD Web Access" in Chapter 9.

- Refer to the companion media for a script to add RD RAP user groups called Add-RDRAP-UserGroup.ps1.

- To understand RD Gateway deployment in a perimeter network and what firewall rules you will need to implement, see *http://blogs.msdn.com/b/rds/archive/2009/07/31/rd-gateway-deployment-in-a-perimeter-network-firewall-rules.aspx.*

- For an introduction to Network Access Protection, see *http://technet.microsoft.com/en-us/network/cc984252.aspx.*

- For information on NAP server side architecture, go to *http://msdn.microsoft.com/en-us/library/cc895519(v=VS.85).aspx.*

- For information on NAP client architecture, go to *http://msdn.microsoft.com/en-us/library/aa369702(VS.85).aspx.*

- For more information on deploying RD Gateway with NAP, see *http://blogs.msdn.com/b/rds/archive/2009/08/17/deploying-rd-gateway-r2-server-with-nap.aspx#_Steps_to_configure_2.*

- More information on configuring the RD Gateway NAP scenario is provided at *http://technet.microsoft.com/en-us/library/cc732172(WS.10).aspx.*

- Information on NAP Client Configuration can be found at *http://technet.microsoft.com/en-us/library/cc754803.aspx.*

- Quick fixes for NAP can be found at *http://technet.microsoft.com/ru-ru/library/dd348494%28WS.10%29.aspx.*

- For a description of the Remote Desktop Connection 7.0 client update for Remote Desktop Services (RDS) for Windows XP SP3, Windows Vista SP1, and Windows Vista SP2, as well as download links, see *http://support.microsoft.com/kb/969084*.

- Information on improving RD Gateway availability using NLB can be found at *http://blogs.msdn.com/b/rds/archive/2009/03/24/improving-ts-gateway-availability-using-nlb.aspx*.

- For information on customizing RD Gateway authentication and authorization schemes, see *http://blogs.msdn.com/b/rds/archive/2010/01/06/customizing-rd-gateway-authentication-and-authorization-schemes.aspx*.

Managing Remote Desktop Sessions

Previous chapters in this book explored how to set up and configure a Remote Desktop (RD) Session Host server and the supporting roles. Setting up the RD Session Host server puts users in a position to log on and use it . . . but administrators need a tool to keep track of what those users are doing and to help them, if necessary. That tool is the Remote Desktop Services Manager.

This chapter will explore how to use the session management tools—both command-line and graphical—to view and interact with running sessions. This chapter discusses

- The tools available in Windows Server 2008 R2 to help you manage sessions

- How to find and manage sessions on an RD Session Host server

- How to find and manage processes on an RD Session Host server

- How to get remote control of user sessions

- How to create custom server management groups in the Remote Desktop Services Manager

- How to use the command-line tools, scriptable interfaces, and Windows PowerShell to get information the graphical user interface (GUI) doesn't offer

Introducing RD Session Host Management Tools

Windows Server 2008 R2 has a set of tools for managing user sessions: The Remote Desktop Services Manager GUI and command-line tools to supplement it and enable scripting. Before delving into their usage, let's take a quick tour so that you can see what's possible.

HOW IT WORKS

Differences in Managing VMs and Sessions

The RDS session management tools work—with some limitations—for virtual machines (VMs), but fundamentally they're more designed for sessions than VMs. This means that you will work differently with sessions than with VMs.

Many people can use an RD Session Host server at the same time and can all be logged onto the same computer. Therefore, it's possible to aggregate information about processes and logons to individual sessions on a per-user basis. But while one RD Virtualization Host supports multiple VMs, the RD Virtualization Host does not see processes in each VM. You have to go to each VM for this information. If you know the server name and user name, you can control VMs remotely, disconnect or log off VM sessions, and even terminate processes in individual VMs, but you can't, say, terminate every instance of Sol.exe that's running on an RD Virtualization Host just by choosing to kill the process on that server.

Similarly, one VM has only one session so you might as well address users by name as by session ID. A user could have more than one session on an RD Session Host, but there's always a 1:1 mapping of users to sessions on a pooled or personal VM.

In short, most tools work for managing pooled and personal VMs as long as you're logged on to a session on an RD Session Host server to use the management tools. This chapter covers these tools in terms of managing RD Session Host sessions, but understand that these processes will work for pooled and personal VMs, too, and the chapter will note explicitly when they do not. However, be aware that the way you'll interact with a VM differs from how you'll interact with a session. For example, you might be checking an RD Session Host server to figure out if the amount of user sessions is causing a slowdown in user experience, but this would not be an issue for a pooled or personal VM.

The Remote Desktop Services Manager

Let's start by getting oriented. After you install the RDS role, the Remote Desktop Services Manager tool in Figure 11-1 is accessible by browsing to Start, All Programs, Administrative Tools, Remote Desktop Services, and finally Remote Desktop Services Manager. Using this tool, you can

- Display real-time data about current users, sessions, and processes
- Monitor, disconnect, and reset sessions
- View or interact with a user's session
- Send messages to users
- Terminate sessions and log off users

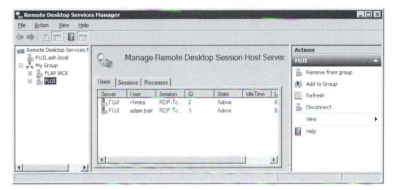

FIGURE 11-1 Use the Remote Desktop Services Manager to manage sessions on RD Session Host servers and pooled and personal VMs.

The left pane displays the available RD Session Host servers; by default, it will display only the server that you're currently logged on to, but you can add more. Although you can manage only one server at a time (you can't, for example, kill all instances of Sol.exe running in the farm from this tool), you can add more servers and even pooled and personal VMs. You'll learn about *how* to do this later in this chapter, in the section entitled "Organizing Servers and VMs in the Remote Desktop Services Manager."

The center pane displays the information for the currently selected server, including connected users, the sessions on the server, and the processes running on the server. Some of this data might be redundant, as it's just different ways of displaying data about the people logged on to the RD Session Host server, what they're doing there, and which sessions are open. It's different ways of looking at the same data.

The right pane displays the context-sensitive actions that you can take depending on the item you've selected in the left or center panes.

The Users tab contains current data pertaining to the users connected to the RD Session Host server and the associated sessions, as shown in Table 11-1.

TABLE 11-1 Data on the Users Tab of the Remote Desktop Services Manager

DATA	DESCRIPTION
Server	The server that the user is logged onto
User	The account name of the user who started the session
Session	The session associated with the user
ID	The Session ID that the RD Session Host server uses to identify sessions; each Session ID is unique on its server
State	The current state of the session (active, disconnected, reset, or idle)
Idle Time	The number of minutes since the last keyboard stroke or mouse movement in the session
LogOnTime	The date and time the user logged on

Much of the data located on the Sessions tab (see Table 11-2) mimics the data on the Users tab. However, the Sessions tab displays a few more session details, allowing you to view the protocol used to connect to the RD Session Host server (if applicable) and the names of the computers that users connect from (if the session is active).

TABLE 11-2 Data on the Sessions Tab of the Remote Desktop Services Manager

DATA	DESCRIPTION
Server	The RD Session Host server on which the session is running
Session	The session type
User	The user name associated with the session
ID	The number that identifies the session to the RD Session Host server
State	The current state of the session (active, disconnected, reset, or idle)
Type	The type of client used in the session (that is, RDP client or console connection)
Client Name	The name of the client that established the session
IdleTime	The number of minutes since the last keyboard stroke or mouse movement in the session
LogonTime	The date and time the user logged on
Comment	An optional field that isn't generally applicable because a user can't add a comment when connecting

The Processes tab (see Table 11-3) displays details about the processes currently running on each server, the associated sessions, and the users who invoked them.

TABLE 11-3 Data on the Processes Tab of the Remote Desktop Services Manager

DATA	DESCRIPTION
Server	The server on which the process is running
User	The user account that started the process
Session	The session number associated with the process
ID	The ID that identifies the session to the RD Session Host server
PID	The ID that identifies the process to the RD Session Host server
Image	The executable associated with the process

The Remote Desktop Services Manager displays similar information in many different ways to support various starting points that you might take to gather needed information. For example, if user Kim Akers has a problem with a program freezing or otherwise misbehaving in her session, you can use the Processes tab to stop the process and be sure that you picked the instance that belongs to her. If Kim needs help with her session, you can highlight the root of the Remote Desktop Services Manager to find out which server she is logged on to, shadow her session, and assist her. Fundamentally, though, the information that you can get about sessions is pretty straightforward: which users are logged on, whether they're using their session, which applications they're running, and which RD Session Host server they're connected to.

When you understand what information you can get from the Remote Desktop Services Manager, you can answer many questions even if the GUI doesn't anticipate them. For example, you can find out how many users are logging on during a particular interval in the morning or how many people are using a particular application. Knowing either of these pieces of information, you can take appropriate action: end processes, terminate sessions, or connect to a user's session to help him or her out. Going outside the Remote Desktop Services Manager, you could even use the information you get here to prompt you to purchase more licenses or add more servers, just to meet increasing demand.

This chapter will cover all the actions that you can perform using the Remote Desktop Services Manager. However, when you automate queries or changes, you'll want to know about the command-line tools and sometimes combine them with scripting such as Windows PowerShell or VBScript. Unfortunately, the GUI does not always refresh well, even in a small farm. To get the most reliable information about session status, the command-line tools might be more reliable.

 ON THE COMPANION MEDIA   You can run the Remote Desktop Services Manager tool from Windows 7 (Professional, Enterprise, or Ultimate editions only) with the Remote Server Administration Tools (RSAT), which includes both the Remote Desktop Services Manager and Remote Desktops. Download RSAT for Windows 7 from the Microsoft website at *http://www.microsoft.com/downloads /details.aspx?FamilyID=7D2F6AD7-656B-4313-A005-4E344E43997D&displaylang=en.*

Using the Status Dialog Box in the Remote Desktop Services Manager

James Baker
Program Manager II

I f you right-click an active remote connection in the Sessions or Users tab, you'll see a Status option in the context-sensitive menu. Click it, and you'll see a dialog box like the one shown in Figure 11-2.

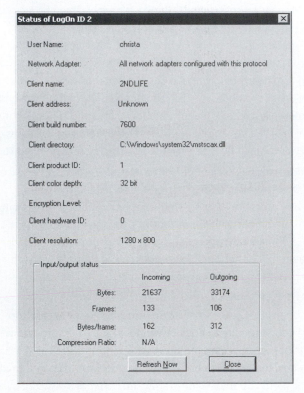

FIGURE 11-2 Examine a session's status to expose more details about a remote session, such as client color depth.

You can learn the following information from this dialog box.

- The User Name field, populated only when you open the Status dialog box from the Sessions tab, shows the name of the currently logged in user.

- Network Adapter tells you the name of the network adapter the user is connected to on the RD Session Host server. The information here will match what's in the Remote Desktop Session Host Configuration/RDP-Tcp/Network Adapter tab.

- Client Address tells you the client's Internet Protocol (IP) address for local connections. If the connection was started through RD Gateway, this address will not display.

- Client Build Number tells you the build number of the client operating system.

- Client Directory points you to the location on the client where the dynamic-link library (DLL) supporting the RDP client is stored.

- Client Color Depth indicates the color depth used in the RDP session.

- Encryption Level shows you the encryption setting managed through Group Policy or in RD Session Host Configuration, showing not the actual encryption setting but the option that the client sets as the encryption level.

- Client Resolution shows the resolution of the remote session.

- The Input/Output Status section shows the traffic passing between the remote session and the client.

Notice that a couple of the settings that you can see in the dialog box were left out of this list. Both the Client Hardware ID and the Client Product ID are hard-wired fields that will be the same for all clients. (They're here for legacy reasons.) Therefore, they don't give you any useful information.

Apart from those two fields, however, this dialog box shows you some information about the client experience that you can't get anywhere else. Want to understand why users are saying that their application looks grainy? Check the screen resolution here. Need to know the IP address that a client is using to connect to the RD Session Host server? Check it here. Beta-testing a new version of the client operating system? You can tell who's using the beta version by checking the build number. You can even use the Input/Output Status data to confirm that a session is not frozen; when the user moves the mouse, the number of incoming and outgoing bytes should update.

Command-Line Tools

In addition to the graphical tools, Windows Server 2008 R2, like previous versions of Windows Server, has command-line tools that you can use to view session information, manage a session's contents, control a user's session remotely, and so forth. These command-line tools are built on the same interfaces as the graphical tools, so any information you get from one (for example, Process ID) can be used in another.

Both Windows Server 2008 R2 and Windows 7 support the Remote Desktop Services command-line tools; these tools are part of the operating system. Table 11-4 lists the available command-line tools.

TABLE 11-4 Remote Desktop Services Command-Line Tools

COMMAND	DESCRIPTION
change logon or chglogon	Enable, disable, drain, or query information about logons from sessions on an RD Session Host server.
change port or chgport	List or change the COM port mappings to be compatible with MS-DOS applications.
logoff	Log off users and delete their session from the RD Session Host server.
msg	Send a message to a user or multiple users on an RD Session Host server.
query process or qprocess	Display information about all the processes currently running on an RD Session Host server.
query session or qwinsta	Display information about sessions on an RD Session Host server.
query termserver or qappsrv	List all the RD Session Host servers on a network.
query user or quser	Display information about the users connected to an RD Session Host server.
reset session or rwinsta	Terminate a session on an RD Session Host server.
shadow	Enable an administrator to view or interact with an active session of another user remotely on an RD Session Host server. You must run this command from within an RDP session on an RD Session Host for it to work.
tscon	Connect to another session on an RD Session Host server (you have to be in a remote session to connect to another remote session).
tsdiscon	Disconnect a session from a server.
tskill	Terminate a process running on an RD Session Host server. You can identify the process by image name or Process ID.
tsprof	Copies the Remote Desktop Services user profile from one user to another. This command-line tool is not available for Windows 7, and although it is available for Windows Server 2008 R2, it does not work. It was used in previous versions of Terminal Services.

The following command-line tools were removed in Windows Server 2008.

- **tsshutdn**   This command was used to shut down a terminal server. Use the shutdown command instead.

- **register**   This command was used to register a program.

- **cprofile**   This command was used to remove wasted space in a user profile and to delete file associations from the registry that were made to certain applications.

> **NOTE**   For those who like working in Windows PowerShell, Shay Levy, a Windows PowerShell MVP, built a Terminal Services PowerShell Module to help manage and monitor RDS sessions and processes. Download the module at *http://code.msdn.microsoft.com /PSTerminalServices*. The Uniform Resource Locator (URL) is located on the companion media. This tool is good for programmatically interacting with sessions or gathering information from multiple machines.

DIRECT FROM THE FIELD

A Custom PowerShell Module for RDS Session Management

Shay Levy
Windows PowerShell MVP

There are many command-line utilities to manage Remote Desktop Services from the command line. The major drawback of these utilities is that they output the result in text; you'll run a command, such as query.exe, against a server, get the result on screen, find a session ID or any other information you're looking for, and then execute a second command to manage that session. From an automation perspective, text output is *not ideal*, because you need to further parse the result and extract the information you need. In addition, text parsing is not always the safest method, because it is prone to errors and can lead to incorrect results.

To make the process of managing Remote Desktop Session Host servers more robust and accurate, I wrote the PSTerminalServices PowerShell module. Unlike command-line utilities, the functions of the module gives you back rich .NET objects that you can use to manage Remote Desktop users, sessions, and processes.

> **NOTE**   Rich .NET objects are not just a string of characters from a command-line tool. Each object implements a set of methods and properties. For example, a session object you get with the Get-TSSession function has an *IdleTime* property or a *Logoff* method.

Continued on the next page

One advantage of the functions is the ability to pipe the output of one command to another. For example, you can get all session objects from each RD Session Host server in a farm that have been idle for a certain length of time and pipe them to another command that disconnects them. Another advantage is the support of the risk mitigation common parameters: *WhatIf* and *Confirm*. The first parameter displays a message that describes the effect of the command instead of executing it, and the second one prompts you for confirmation before executing the command.

For example, this script finds sessions on domain-joined RD Session Host servers that have been idle for over an hour and disconnects the sessions.

```
"Server1","Server2" | Foreach-Object{
   Get-TSSession -ComputerName $_ -Filter {$_.IdleTime -gt (New-TimeSpan
-Hours 1) }
} | Disconnect-TSSession-WhatIf
```

The example script shown here and other examples are available at *http://blogs.microsoft.co.il/blogs/scriptfanatic/archive/2010/09/16/remote-desktop-services-r2-resource-kit.aspx*. The link is also available on the companion media. For information on installing the module, please refer to the module project Web page at *http://code.msdn.microsoft.com/PSTerminalServices*.

Connecting Remotely to Servers for Administrative Purposes

Chapter 4, "Deploying a Single Remote Desktop Virtualization Host Server," and Chapter 9, "Multi-Server Deployments," explained how connection brokering works. When you want to connect to a specific RD Session Host server to change its settings or manage a user session, you want to connect to a specific server. You don't want to go a random server in a farm and you don't want to pay an RDS client access license (CAL) when you aren't using the server, just managing it.

Prior to Windows Server 2008, to make an administrative connection, you'd use the */console* switch with the server name. Beginning in Windows Server 2008, this changed to the */admin* switch, which does not connect you to the console but does allow you to administer the server. Functionally, */admin* is equivalent to */console*.

Although the */admin* switch is functionally equivalent, it is not syntactically equivalent. If you use the */console* switch from Remote Desktop Connection (RDC) 6 or later, you might not notice that it doesn't work. The */console* switch is ignored—you still log on, but you will use up an RDS CAL. To start a remote session for administrative purposes, start RDC from the Run dialog box or command prompt and add the */admin* switch like this.

```
mstsc /admin
```

You can also specify the /admin switch when adding connections to the RSAT. The /console switch creates an admin connection when connecting from an older RDP client to a Windows Server 2008 R2 RD Session Host server. Plug in /admin when working from RDC 5.2 and Mstsc.exe will open a dialog box that explains the proper syntax for the command, because that version of the RDC client is not aware of the /admin switch. Unfortunately, this means that you'll need to change the connection syntax depending on whether you're connecting from a current or older version of Mstsc.exe.

Avoiding Administrative Lockouts

In Windows Server 2003, you could make two remote administrative connections and one console connection from the physical console, all without using a Terminal Services client access license (TS CAL). Windows Server 2008 and later permit two simultaneous administrative connections. This might look like a reduction in licensed connections, but the previous model was also a convenience. It was possible for two administrators to make connections, leave them connected, and effectively block anyone else from making an administrative connection to the terminal server because the remote logon count was at capacity. You had to have the console connection just to reset one of those remote connections.

Beginning in Windows Server 2008, you could choose to disconnect an administrative connection if you needed to make one and the number of admin connections was already at capacity. The other administrator will find his or her session as it was left, and you are not forced to log on from the console to disconnect the session.

Managing RD Session Host Servers from Windows 7

If you have only one RD Session Host server, you can probably do everything you need to do with the Remote Desktop Services Manager from the console. If you have multiple servers, you can even add them to one instance of the tool so that you can do everything from one place. But if you don't have physical access to an RD Session Host server, you can still get the same functionality to work from a Windows 7 laptop or workstation. The RSAT is a collection of tools used to manage Windows Server 2008 R2 (and Windows Server 2008) servers.

NOTE For those who have worked with Windows Server 2003, RSAT is equivalent to the Windows 2003 Server Administration Tools Pack (Adminpak.exe). There's also a version of RSAT for Windows Vista SP1 that allows management of Windows Server 2008 terminal servers.

RSAT is compatible with 32-bit and 64-bit Windows Server 2008 and 32-bit and 64-bit Windows Vista SP1 clients running Windows Vista Business, Enterprise, or Ultimate editions. RSAT for Windows 7 is not compatible with previous versions of Windows.

RSAT contains many more tools than that are discussed in this chapter, as it encompasses tools to manage other Windows Server 2008 R2 roles. The information in this chapter concentrates on the following RDS-specific RSAT tools.

- **Remote Desktop Services Manager** Used to manage RD Session Host servers
- **Remote Desktops** Used to connect to remote desktops from one window

Both of these tools get installed on Windows Server 2008 R2 when you install the Remote Desktop Services role. They work more or less the same way when installed on a computer running Windows 7.

To install RSAT on a Windows 7 client, download RSAT for Windows 7 from *http://www.microsoft.com/downloads/en/details.aspx?FamilyID=7d2f6ad7-656b-4313-a005-4e344e43997d.*

> **NOTE** RSAT for Windows Vista SP1 is located at *http://support.microsoft.com/kb/941314.*

Be sure to download the correct version (32-bit or 64-bit) of the RSAT MSU file. Install the tool by double-clicking the Microsoft Update Standalone Package (MSU) file and clicking OK to install the Update For Windows (KB958830).

After you've installed RSAT, you will need to enable it, because the installer does not enable all the tools by default. Open Control Panel and double-click Programs And Features. Then click Turn Windows Features On Or Off. Select the Remote Server Administration Tools check box, expand Role Administration Tools, and then expand this selection and select the check boxes next to Remote Desktop Services Tools. Then click OK.

When you have enabled the tools, you will find that a Remote Desktop Services folder is now visible in Administrative Tools. This folder contains links to the Remote Desktop Services Manager and Remote Desktops tools.

Organizing Servers and VMs in the Remote Desktop Services Manager

When you first start the Remote Desktop Services Manager, it will show you only the local server—not very useful if you're managing a server farm. You can add more servers to the console view in a couple of ways: by creating a custom group (or populating an existing group) or by importing all known farms and pools from an RD Connection Broker.

To create a new group, right-click the Remote Desktop Services Manager icon in the left pane and choose New Group from the context menu. In the dialog box that appears, type the name of the new group and click OK. This group will now appear in the left pane.

The Remote Desktop Services Manager starts with one default—and empty—group named My Group. To populate an existing group, right-click its icon in the left pane of the Remote Desktop Services Manager and choose Add Computer from the context menu. This will open the Select Computer dialog box, which you might have seen before when working with the Microsoft Management Console (MMC). From here, you can add computers to the group in one of three ways.

- If you know the name of the server or VM that you want to add to the console, select Another Computer, type the name into the text box, and then click OK. The server will appear in My Group.

- If you don't know the full name but know the letters that it begins with, click Browse. In the dialog box that opens, type the name or partial name of the server or VM and click Check Names. The name will appear in the Enter The Object Name To Select text box with an underline. If you typed the prefix and there's more than one match, then you can pick the right name from a list. (You can't add more than one name at a time.)

- If you have no idea of the name of the server, you'll need to search Active Directory Domain Services (AD DS) for it. From the second Select Computer dialog box, click Advanced to search AD DS. Click Locations to specify the organizational unit (OU) that the RD Session Host servers are in and then click Find Now to list all servers in that OU. From there, you can select servers one at a time to appear in the Select Computer dialog box.

Manually populating groups is time-consuming. Operating on the principle that you'd like to manage all the RD Session Host servers and VMs in one or more farms, regardless of their names, you can import server information from the RD Connection Broker. To do this, right-click the Remote Desktop Services Manager and choose Import From RD Connection Broker. Enter the name or IP address of the RD Connection Broker server from which you want to import and click OK. A new server management group will be created named RD Connection Broker(*servername*), and groups will be created beneath it named after your farm name(s) or VM pools, as shown in Figure 11-3.

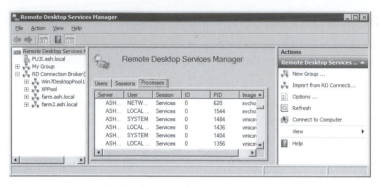

FIGURE 11-3 Import RD Session Host farms and VM pools from the RD Connection Broker into the Remote Desktop Services Manager.

NOTE When you import VM farms from the RD Connection Broker, it will import the VMs according to their VM names in Hyper-V Manager, not according to their computer names. Because the application programming interface (API) that the Remote Desktop Services Manager and the command-line tools are built on uses the computer name, you must make the VM name listed in Hyper-V Manager and the computer name match to manage VM sessions at all. If you don't, you won't see any activity inside the VMs from the Remote Desktop Services Manager (all tabs will be blank), and you won't be able to connect to the VMs using the Query command-line tools.

After importing the pools and farms into the Remote Desktop Services Manager, you must connect to each server to glean any useful data. This is a one-time process; after this, they will be connected when you open this tool on this particular server or workstation. Right-click each server and choose Connect. After all servers in each farm or all VMs in the pool are connected, you can highlight the group, user, session, and process data for all servers in the group appear together in the middle console pane. You can also click each server in the group and view just the data for that server.

Monitoring and Terminating Processes

One of the basic questions about remote sessions is what processes are executing inside those sessions. As discussed in previous chapters, some processes are common to all sessions, but other processes tell you what users are doing in their remote sessions. You can even use processes to determine whether a user is connected to a full desktop or to a RemoteApp program. In addition, you might need to terminate a stalled process in a session or terminate all instances of a specific application.

Monitoring Application Use

You can monitor processes on an RD Session Host server or VM from the Remote Desktop Services Manager or by using the query command-line tool with the *process* parameter, as shown here.

```
query process
```

From the Remote Desktop Services Manager, connect to the server or VM that you want to monitor and then select the Processes tab in the middle pane to display all processes running on that server. You can then sort the table by clicking the column heading you want to sort by (Server, User, Session, ID, PID, or Image).

You can accomplish the same thing at the command prompt by running the query process or qprocess command against an RD Session Host server or a VM. The syntax for both of these commands follows.

```
QUERY PROCESS [* | processid | username | sessionname | /ID:nn | programname]
   [/SERVER:servername]
```

```
*                   Display all visible processes.
processid           Display process specified by processid.
username            Display all processes belonging to username.
sessionname         Display all processes running at sessionname.
/ID:nn              Display all processes running at session nn.
programname         Display all processes associated with programname.
/SERVER:servername  The RD Session Host server or VM to be queried.
```

You can get a list of all processes running on an RD Session Host server. For example, the following command returns all processes running on the RD Session Host server FUJI.

```
query process * /server:fuji
```

You can also get more detailed information by specifying different parameters. For instance, to find all the processes running under sessions started by the user nancy.anderson on server FUJI, the command and data returned would look like this.

```
query process nancy.anderson /server:fuji
USERNAME            SESSIONNAME        ID    PID   IMAGE
nancy.anderson      rdp-tcp#2           4    3296  taskeng.exe
nancy.anderson      rdp-tcp#2           4    3736  rdpclip.exe
nancy.anderson      rdp-tcp#2           4    2680  dwm.exe
nancy.anderson      rdp-tcp#2           4    3700  explorer.exe
```

Another example of getting specific process-related information from the command line is to find all instances of a particular application running on an RD Session Host server. For instance, to find all sessions in which users are running Excel.exe on server FUJI, the command and results would look like this.

```
query process excel.exe /server:fuji
  USERNAME                 SESSIONNAME           ID     PID  IMAGE
  adam.barr                rdp-tcp#1              2     3156  excel.exe
  nancy.anderson           rdp-tcp#2              4     3044  excel.exe
  kristin.griffin          rdp-tcp#3              5     4088  excel.exe
  christa.anderson         rdp-tcp#4              6     3176  excel.exe
```

If you've used Windows PowerShell, you might be familiar with the Get-Process cmdlet. It's a useful tool that tells you a lot about the processes running on a computer, including working set, CPU time, and more information than qprocess can convey. Unfortunately, Get-Process is not multi-user-aware and reports only on the processes running in the current session. Similarly, you can't use the Stop-Process cmdlet very well on an RD Session Host server, because it is only aware of the processes running in the same session that it is.

Terminating Applications

When you know where an application is running, you can terminate it if you need to. A user's application might be unresponsive or a user might get past your lockdown schemes (for more information, see Chapter 7, "Molding and Securing the User Environment"). It's even possible to terminate a process for one user so that another user can use it without violating your application licensing. To terminate a process from the Remote Desktop Services Manager, connect to the server or VM where the process is running, select the Processes tab, right-click the process, and choose End Process.

You also can end a process from the command line by running the tskill command. The syntax is

```
TSKILL processid/processname [/SERVER:servername] [/ID:sessionid//A] [/V]
```

```
  processid           Process ID for the process to be terminated.
  processname         Process name to be terminated.
  /SERVER:servernameThe RD Session Host server or VM where the process is running (if
not specified, the local machine is the default).
      /ID or /A must be specified when using processname and /SERVER
  /ID:sessionid       End process running under the specified session.
  /A                  End process running under ALL sessions.
  /V                  Display information about actions being performed.
```

Notice that you can kill either a specific instance of an application on a server or all instances. To terminate an application running in a specific session, use the */ID:sessionid* parameter to specify that session. You need to know the session ID where the process is running, so you must first run the query session command to find out what the session ID is.

To illustrate, let's combine these two commands to effectively shut down one instance of an application. This example will terminate the Excel.exe process running in the session for user adam.barr on server FUJI. First, run the query session command to find the correct session ID.

```
C:\windows\system32>query session /server:FUJI
 SESSIONNAME        USERNAME                 ID  STATE   TYPE        DEVICE
 services                                     0  Disc
 console            Administrator             1  Active
 rdp-tcp#1          adam.barr                 2  Active  rdpwd
 rdp-tcp#0          administrator             3  Active  rdpwd
                    nancy.anderson            4  Disc
                    kristin.griffin           5  Disc
                    christa.anderson          6  Disc
 rdp-tcp                               65536  Listen
```

Then terminate Microsoft Excel by specifying the process name, the server, and the session ID.

```
C:\windows\system32>tskill excel /server:FUJI /ID:2
```

NOTE Notice that the process name is equivalent to the name of the executable minus the extension. Leaving off the extension is important; although executable names normally include the extension, the command won't work if you include it.

What if you forget to disable installations and discover a mahjong tournament taking place among the users on an RD Session Host server? You can also terminate a process (in this example, mahjong) running in all sessions on an RD Session Host server by using the /A switch in this way.

```
tskill mahjong /server:FUJI /A
```

Monitoring and Ending User Sessions

Before you start monitoring and ending sessions in the Remote Desktop Services Manager, you should recognize the different session types that you will see and what they are for. Four types of sessions appear in the Remote Desktop Services Manager.

- **Console** Session supports someone logged on locally (at the physical console). This session is not accessible via RDP.
- **RDP-Tcp** Remote RDP session.
- **Services** Session used by server services.
- **Listener** Session listens for incoming connection requests.

For our purposes, you're going to work most often with the RDP-Tcp sessions.

Switching Between Sessions

Let's say that you have logged on to your Windows 7 desktop via RDP with your domain credentials so that you can work on that computer from a remote location. When you do so, the console session switches to the RDP session and the console goes back to the logon screen. The same functionality is behind the ability to move between sessions on an RD Session Host server, using the Remote Desktop Services Manager or the tscon command. You can switch between your own sessions if you have more than one, or (if you know the password) you can connect to another user's session and disconnect your own. Connecting to a session using this functionality automatically disconnects the session you started from.

There are a few caveats to using the Connect functionality.

- It works only to connect to an RDP-Tcp session from another RDP-Tcp connection on the same server. You can connect to an active or a disconnected session.

- You cannot connect to a RemoteApp session, only a full desktop.

- Although you can connect to another session from an administrative (/admin) connection, you can't connect to an administrative connection from another RDP-Tcp connection.

- When you are prompted for a password while connecting to a session from the Remote Desktop Services Manager, the password is obscured on the screen. When you supply the password to the command-line tool, the password might be displayed on the screen, in cleartext, if you want. Therefore, be careful how you use tscon when anyone is standing behind you!

> **NOTE** If you attempt to connect to a local logon session from tscon, you'll see error code 31, telling you, "A device attached to the system is not functioning." If you attempt to connect to an /admin remote connection, you'll get an error message that access is denied.

DIRECT FROM THE SOURCE

What Happens to the Password I Type into tscon?

Al Henriquez
Software Development Engineer II

Meher Malakapalli
Senior Development Lead

The Connect tool (whether implemented from the command line or the GUI) implements this functionality through the WTSConnectSession function described on MSDN at *http://msdn.microsoft.com/en-us/library/bb394782(VS.85).aspx*. For the purposes of the IT pro, this function takes three important parameters: *logonID*, *targetlogonID*, and *password*.

Basically, this function accepts the domain name and user name of the person initiating the request. If these do not match, then the person initiating the request must type in the password of the account that owns the target session. One key fact to note is that Connect works only on the same RD Session Host server—you can't connect to a session on another server. Therefore, the credentials don't go over the network except when you type them into the RDP window, and then they're protected by RDP encryption.

The bottom line is that when you connect to another session, the credentials that you provide are protected. They never leave the RD Session Host server and they are removed from memory as soon as the function is finished with them.

To use the Connect functionality from the Remote Desktop Services Manager or the tscon command, follow these steps.

1. Start an RDP session to the RD Session Host server hosting the session to which you want to connect.

2. Find the correct session. From the Remote Desktop Services Manager, find the correct session from the Users or Sessions tab in the center pane. If using the command prompt, find the session ID by typing **query session**.

3. Connect to the session. From the Remote Desktop Services Manager, right-click the session and choose Connect from the context menu. From the command prompt, type **tscon***sessionID* **/password:***password* to enter the password with the command, or **/password*** to be prompted for the password. You'll need to include all of this information in the command.

> **NOTE** You must supply the password when connecting from the command prompt or the command will fail. When connecting from the Remote Desktop Services Manager, you are prompted for the password if connecting to a session that is not your own.

4. Assuming that you provide the correct password and it's possible to connect to the session, you will connect immediately to the new session and see any applications or files open in the other session. The person whose session that was will be disconnected. If the password isn't valid, you'll see an error message.

So why do this? The functionality is most useful if RemoteApp functionality isn't in the picture. In Windows Server 2003 and earlier, the only way to publish individual applications was by limiting a session to a single application. By using Connect, it was possible (if awkward) for a user to move between individual applications on the same terminal server.

Today, this command isn't applicable to most situations because the only sessions that you should be able to connect to (assuming reasonably secure domain password protection) are your own. One possible scenario for using Connect in this present version of RDS is if you were logged on to an RD Session Host server as both a user and an administrator, using two different accounts. You could switch to your administrator persona by connecting to the session, but you'd disconnect your user persona.

Closing Orphaned Sessions

An *orphaned session* is one that is no longer being used. An orphaned session can occur for a number of reasons. For example, if you do not limit users to one session and don't set a time limit for resetting idle and disconnected sessions, you might encounter sessions that were left open by users. You might also find orphaned sessions if users get disconnected from their sessions and you are not using the RD Connection Broker (which will reconnect users to disconnected sessions). In this instance, when the users reconnect to the farm, they might open a new session and unknowingly abandon the other session.

There are several ways to decrease orphaned sessions. You can configure Group Policy objects (GPOs) to end idle and disconnected sessions automatically after a certain period of inactivity, or you can use the RD Connection Broker to reconnect users to their disconnected sessions. However, if these avenues are blocked for you, you should know how to terminate orphaned sessions.

First, you must determine which sessions are really abandoned. A good way to tell if a session is not being used is to look for active and disconnected sessions that have been idle for a certain period of time, such as if you have shift workers and a session is idle for longer than the normal daily shift hours. Check the Users or Sessions tab of the Remote Desktop Services Manager or use the query user command to figure out which sessions to terminate by finding out how long sessions have been idle. For example, to check the Idle Time setting for all sessions on server FUJI, you can run the following command.

```
C:\windows\system32>query user /server:FUJI
```

USERNAME	SESSIONNAME	ID	STATE	IDLE TIME	LOGON TIME
administrator	console	1	Active	none	7/26/2010 6:51 PM
adam.barr	rdp-tcp#1	2	Active	57	7/30/2010 4:55 PM
administrator	rdp-tcp#0	3	Active	.	7/27/2010 6:37 PM
nancy.anderson	rdp-tcp#2	4	Active	48	7/30/2010 4:55 PM
kristin.griffin	rdp-tcp#3	5	Active	7	7/30/2010 4:56 PM

NOTE See the section entitled "Auditing User Logons" later in this chapter for more examples of how to use the query user command.

The results will show the state, idle time (if applicable), and logon time of each session.

At this point, you have a couple of options: you can disconnect the session or terminate it. Disconnecting the session causes it to use fewer resources on the server while leaving open the applications and data in use in the session. Terminating the session (also called *resetting the session*) will end the session completely. Disconnecting is not invasive; users can get back to where they were by logging on again, but it does continue to use resources on the server. Terminating sessions frees resources, but it can lead to file locking issues because it's an ungraceful exit and files might not close properly.

> **NOTE** RDS does not support concurrent user licensing, just per-user or per-device. Therefore, if you're using a native RDS environment (and aren't running add-ons that are licensed on a concurrent-user basis), it's immaterial from a licensing perspective whether you disconnect or terminate a session. Adding third-party software that does support concurrent user licensing can affect the best practices that apply to you.

Disconnecting Sessions

Disconnecting a session using the Remote Desktop Services Manager is easy. Find the session to disconnect, right-click it, and choose Disconnect from the context menu. You must be connected to the same server as the session you're disconnecting.

To disconnect a session from the command prompt, use tsdiscon. The syntax is simple.

```
TSDISCON              [sessionid/sessionname] [/SERVER:servername] [/V]
  Sessionid           The ID of the session.
  Sessionname         The name of the session.
  /SERVER:servername  Specifies the RD Session Host server (default is current).
  /V                  Displays information about the actions performed.
```

As you can see, when using the command-line tool, you can specify the server on which you want to disconnect a session.

 CAUTION If you run tsdiscon without arguments, you'll disconnect your own session even if you're sitting at the console. You won't lose any data because the session will continue running and you can just reconnect, but disconnecting yourself is disconcerting and should be avoided.

Terminating Sessions

You can terminate a session easily from the Remote Desktop Services Manager or the command prompt.

To terminate a session from the Remote Desktop Services Manager, highlight the session on the Users or Sessions tab, right-click, and choose Reset. You'll see a dialog box telling you that you're resetting this user's session. Click OK, and then the session will reset. All processes belonging to that user will be terminated immediately.

You can also terminate active and disconnected sessions from the command line using one of these three utilities (their syntax is shown here).

```
RESET SESSION {sessionname | sessionid} [/SERVER:servername] [/V]
RWINSTA {sessionname | sessionid} [/SERVER:servername] [/V]
LOGOFF [sessionname | sessionid] [/SERVER:servername] [/V]
```

Reset session and rwinsta are functionally the same in that they terminate the connection ungracefully—the session never has a chance to close open files or save the profile changes. Logoff is a little different in that, although it won't save open files, it will at least write back changes to the profile.

The syntax for all three commands requires that you use the session name or session ID to identify the session you want to close, so you will need to get this information from the Remote Desktop Services Manager or from the command line by using the query user command. The syntax is

```
QUERY USER [username | sessionname | sessionid] [/SERVER:servername]
```

For instance, to reset a disconnected session for user paul.koch on server FUJI, run these commands. The following example checks for Paul's session after resetting it just to make the point that this session no longer exists.

```
C:\Users\Administrator>query session paul.koch /server:FUJI
 SESSIONNAME        USERNAME                ID  STATE   TYPE        DEVICE
                    paul.koch                5  Disc
C:\Users\Administrator>reset session 5 /server:FUJI
C:\Users\Administrator>query session paul.koch /server:FUJI
No session exists for paul.koch
```

Providing Help with Remote Control

In addition to the methods just described, another way to interact with user sessions is to shadow them. Inevitably, every user, at one time or another, calls the Help desk to get assistance from the IT staff. And as helpful as staff can be, and as willing to describe their unfortunate circumstances as users can be, it is sometimes best to experience the problem to solve it efficiently. Windows Server 2008 R2 (like its predecessors) gives you the ability to observe the user session or even take control of the session so that you can act as the user and experience the difficulties a user has. Hopefully, this experience provides a clearer picture of the situation and leads to a speedy resolution of the Help desk ticket.

You can control Remote Control settings from three locations.

- **Group Policy** Used to specify Remote Control settings for all RD Session Host servers in a farm

- **Remote Desktop Session Host Configuration** Used to specify Remote Control settings on a per-server basis
- **Active Directory Users And Computers** Used to specify Remote Control settings on a per-user basis

The ability to control or *shadow* a user's session remotely is enabled by default on the Remote Control tab of each user's account Properties dialog box, as shown in Figure 11-4.

> **NOTE** Even though Remote Control is enabled by default in domain user account properties, these settings are used only when you use Remote Desktop Session Host Configuration (instead of Group Policy) to stipulate Remote Control settings, and only when Remote Desktop Session Host Configuration is set to Use Remote Control With Default User Settings. You will look at Remote Desktop Session Host Configuration Remote Control settings later in this section.

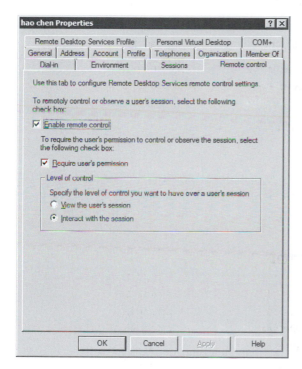

FIGURE 11-4 Remote Control is enabled by default on AD DS user accounts.

If you do not want to be able to view or interact with sessions opened by the user, clear the Enable Remote Control check box.

By default, the user's permission is required for an administrator to interact with the user's session. When you invoke remote control of a user session, the user receives a prompt similar to Figure 11-5 requesting that he or she grant you permission to control the session. If the user clicks No or doesn't respond, the person requesting remote control will see a message that access is denied.

FIGURE 11-5 If the user's permission is required for shadowing the session, the user will see this notice.

Not everyone wants users to be aware that their sessions are being shadowed; some companies use this feature for auditing the work habits of their employees. If Require User's Permission is not enabled, then you can gain remote control (for viewing or interacting, depending on the level of control option selected) of the user session without her knowledge or permission.

When you attach to the session in these circumstances, the user sees nothing and is not aware of your presence unless you interact with the session in some way.

 CAUTION If you decide to interact with user sessions without user knowledge or permission, check with your company's legal and human resources (HR) departments first, to make sure that the company is legally protected and that HR policies reflect this need.

By default, administrators have full control of the user session. This means you can manipulate the session (use the keyboard and mouse, and so on) as if you are the user. This level of control can be changed to allow only observation by selecting the option View The User's Session. At this level, you can observe the user's session, but you cannot control it in any way.

Remote Control settings can also be set using RD Session Host Configuration on each server or by using Group Policy. Group Policy settings take precedence over RD Session Host Configuration settings.

Enabling Remote Control via Group Policy

You can configure Remote Control settings with either a user Group Policy (to affect certain groups of users) or a computer Group Policy (to affect all users who log on to a server or server farm). These settings are located at

- Computer Configuration | Policies | Administrative Templates | Windows Components | Remote Desktop Services | RD Session Host | Connections | Set Rules For Remote Control Of Remote Desktop Services User Sessions

- User Configuration | Policies | Administrative Templates | Windows Components | Remote Desktop Services | RD Session Host | Connections | Set Rules For Remote Control Of Remote Desktop Services User Sessions

> **NOTE** If both of these Group Policy settings are enabled and there is a conflict, the computer policy settings will take precedence.

Opening either of these GPO settings reveals the screen shown in Figure 11-6.

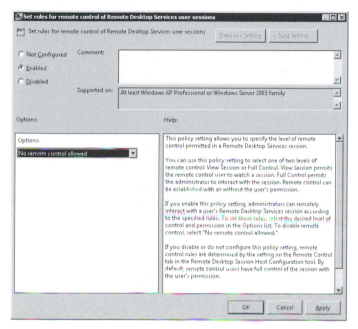

FIGURE 11-6 The Set Rules For Remote Control Of Remote Desktop Services User Sessions GPO setting dialog box allows you to choose the settings you want for remote sessions.

Enable the GPO setting and then specify whether user permission is required for interaction with the user session and what level of control will be allowed. Do this by choosing the appropriate option from the Options drop-down menu. The options available are the following.

- **Full Control With User's Permission** With the user's permission, you can take action in the session just as if you were the user.

- **Full Control Without User's Permission** Without the user's permission and without the user receiving any notification beforehand, you can take action in the session just as if you were the user.

- **View Session With User's Permission** With the user's permission, you can view the session but cannot interact with it in any way.

■ **View Session Without User's Permission** Without the user's permission and without the user receiving any notification, you can view the session but cannot interact with it in any way.

If these Group Policy settings are set to Not Configured, then Remote Control settings are controlled by RD Session Host Configuration. Enabling either of these Group Policy settings overrides Remote Control from the RD Session Host Configuration, and the setting options there will be disabled.

To disable remote control of user sessions, choose the No Remote Control Allowed option from the Options drop-down menu.

> **NOTE** Disabling the Set Rules For Remote Control Of Remote Desktop Services policy has the same effect as not configuring it.

Enabling Remote Control via RD Session Host Configuration

RD Session Host Configuration is used to set Remote Control settings on a per-server basis. On a server, open RD Session Host Configuration, double-click the RDP-Tcp connection, and then click the Remote Control tab shown in Figure 11-7.

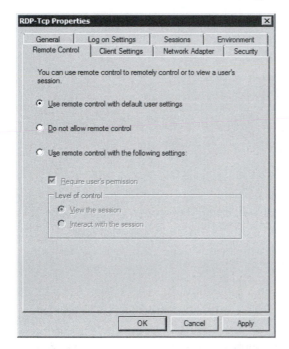

FIGURE 11-7 Configure Remote Control via the RD Session Host Configuration RDP-Tcp Properties dialog box.

There are two ways to enable remote control.

- Enable remote control and specify whether user permissions are required to shadow the user session and the level of control (view only or interact) permitted when shadowing the session.

- Enable remote control and use the Remote Control settings set in each user's account properties to specify whether shadowing that user's session is allowed, whether the user's permission is required, and the level of control (view only or interact) permitted when shadowing the session.

You can disable remote control of user sessions created on the server by choosing Do Not Allow Remote Control.

By default, only administrators have the right to shadow sessions. To give another user or user group permissions to shadow sessions, follow these steps.

1. Open RD Session Host Configuration and double-click RDP-Tcp.

2. Navigate to the Security tab and click OK to the warning that pops up telling you to modify the Remote Desktop Sessions group. Then click Advanced.

3. Add the user account or the user group whose sessions you would like to be able to shadow by clicking Add and entering the name of the user or group. Then click OK.

4. In the Permissions Entry For RDP-Tcp dialog box, select the Remote Control check box.

5. Then click OK in each of the three dialog boxes that are open to save the changes.

The settings are applied at logon, so the users to whom you granted this right must log off and log back on before they can remote control others' sessions.

Shadowing a User Session

Before you try to shadow a session, there are two things to keep in mind. First, you can shadow a session only from another RDP session because you're basically intercepting the graphics output of the shadowed session and sending it to your own session. You can't send RDP updates to a local logon, just as you can't connect to an RDP session from a local logon. (You'll see this when you start the Remote Desktop Services Manager from the console session; there's a warning that these tools will be disabled.)

Somewhat more insidiously, you can't shadow all remote sessions. To be precise, you can only shadow sessions connecting to a full desktop using a single monitor. It will *appear* that you can shadow other sessions, because nothing in the user interface prevents you from connecting to a session hosting RemoteApp programs, and you won't see any warnings. However, shadowing RemoteApp programs isn't supported and really doesn't work well. The problem is that enabling RemoteApp programs requires detailed communication between server and client to position the window correctly. This communication doesn't extend to both the computer from which the administrator is shadowing the session and the original client. If the administrator shadowing the session moves the application window, it might disappear from the session when the administrator restores control, or it might just render the application unresponsive. Therefore, although it is technically possible to shadow a RemoteApp session, it's pretty useless. Before shadowing, be sure that you're connecting to a full desktop session.

> **NOTE** Neither the Remote Desktop Services Manager nor the command-line tools make it easy to distinguish between full desktops and RemoteApp sessions. To learn how to distinguish between sessions running RemoteApp programs and those running a full desktop, see the section entitled "Differentiating RemoteApp Sessions from Full Desktop Sessions" later in this chapter.

Shadowing a session is simple, and you can do it from the Remote Desktop Services Manager or from a command prompt.

To shadow from the GUI, create an RDP connection to a server or desktop and run the Remote Desktop Services Manager. On the Users tab in the middle pane, right-click the user whose session you want to shadow and select Remote Control. If the user's permission is required, the user will receive a remote control request and can accept or deny it.

On the server, you will see a dialog box asking you to specify a key sequence to end the shadow session (shown in Figure 11-8). Ctrl+Tab is the default choice, but you can choose other options if the default doesn't work for you.

FIGURE 11-8 Choose a hot key sequence to end a shadow session.

Your screen might freeze briefly while the user is alerted to your shadow request if shadowing is configured to notify the user (and the user's screen might blink once when you connect).

After the user grants you permission to shadow the session, your session will be replaced with the user's session desktop. If settings only permit you to view the session, then you will be able to see the user's actions, but you won't be able to interact with the session. Otherwise, you can take part in the session as if you were the user. To stop shadowing, simply press the hot key sequence that you selected when establishing the session; the shadow session will disappear and you will be back to your desktop. The user's session will continue as normal.

You can also start a shadow session from the command line. Again, you'll need to establish an RDP session first and run the command from it. To get remote control of a session from the command line, use the *shadow* command and provide the name of the session ID to which you want to connect. To shadow a session on a remote computer, add the name of the server, as in this example of shadowing session 2 on server FLAPJACK.

```
shadow /SERVER:flapjack 2
```

When you start a shadow session from the command line, there is no prompt for you to choose a hot key sequence to end the shadow session. To end the shadow session, use the hot key sequence Ctrl+*.

> **NOTE** The asterisk above the number 8 does not work to stop shadowing. Use the asterisk on your numeric keypad.

Troubleshooting Session Shadowing

If you try to shadow a user session and can't, there are a couple of steps you can take to troubleshoot the problem.

First, make sure that the user's session is allowed to be shadowed. This setting can be configured through Group Policy (for users or computers), the user account properties, or in RD Session Host Configuration. If you find that the settings in these areas are set correctly and you are still being denied, check with the user. It might be that the user is mistakenly answering "No" to the request to let you remote-control the session.

Second, use the error messages to help you diagnose the problem. Any error messages that you might receive when trying to shadow a session are most helpful when you're trying to shadow a session from the same server as the session you're trying to shadow is connected to. For instance, if you are trying to shadow a user session from the same server that the user is logged on to, and RD Session Host Configuration is set not to allow remote control, you will receive a message like this.

```
shadow 3
Your session may appear frozen while the remote control approval is being negotiated.
Please wait...
Remote control failed. Error code 7051
Error [7051]:The requested session is not configured to allow remote control.
```

However, if you are initiating the shadowing operation from a computer other than the one that hosts the session that you want to shadow, you will not get such a straightforward message. Instead, if there's a problem, you will receive a cryptic message like this.

```
shadow 3 /SERVER:FUJI
Your session may appear frozen while the remote control approval is being negotiated.
Please wait...
Remote control failed. Error code 2
Error [2]:The system cannot find the file specified.
```

Typically, if you see error code 2, it means either that the user denied your request to shadow the session or shadowing the session is not allowed.

If you'd like to save yourself the trouble of trying three different tools to find the current Remote Control settings and where they're set, query the *Win32_TSRemoteControlSetting* Windows Management Instrumentation (WMI) class from Windows PowerShell.

> **NOTE**   The methods and properties for this class can be found at *http://msdn.microsoft.com /en-us/library/aa383817(VS.85).aspx.*

To view the Remote Control settings for a computer, open Windows PowerShell and enter the following command.

```
get-wmiobject -namespace "root\cimv2\terminalservices" -class
    Win32_TSRemoteControlSetting
```

The important part of the output is at the bottom, where you'll see values such as this.

```
Caption                  :
Description              :
InstallDate              :
LevelOfControl           : 0
Name                     :
PolicySourceLevelOfControl : 0
RemoteControlPolicy      : 1
Status                   :
TerminalName             : RDP-Tcp
```

The key properties *LevelOfControl*, *PolicySourceLevelOfControl*, and *RemoteControlPolicy* provide answers to the following questions: Do you have permission to shadow this session? Where is this policy set?

 ON THE COMPANION MEDIA   The Windows PowerShell script, Shadowcheck.ps1, helps automate the commands detailed here.

LevelOfControl can have values from 0 to 4, with the following meanings.

- 0 = Remote control is disabled.
- 1 = Administrator has full control; user must grant permission to be shadowed.
- 2 = Administrator has full control; user permission is not required.
- 3 = Administrator can view the shadowed session; user must grant permission to be shadowed.
- 4 = Administrator can view the shadowed session; user permission is not required.

The *PolicySourceLevelOfControl* shows where the value of *LevelOfControl* comes from. A value of 0 means that this value is set on a per-server basis, a value of 1 indicates that it's set by Group Policy, and a value of 2 means that it's the user account policies.

The value of the *RemoteControlPolicy* property indicates whether Remote Control settings are configured on a per-user basis (1) or a per-server basis (0).

You can observe the changes to these settings by editing the Remote Control settings from RD Session Host Configuration. Try editing the settings to see how the value of the *LevelOfControl* property changes when you disable remote control, and you'll see the value change when you run the script.

Another reason you might see errors when trying to shadow sessions has to do with screen size. If you try to shadow a session that is using one monitor from another session that is spanning multiple monitors, you will not be able to shadow the session. Trying to shadow from a Windows 7 client using multiple monitors to a session using fewer monitors results in the session being disconnected and you will get the following error.

```
Remote control failed. Error code 120
Error [120]:This function is not supported on this system.
```

> **NOTE** Shadowing from a Windows XP client to an RD Session Host server remote session does not work. It results in the session being disconnected, and you will get this error.
>
> ```
> Remote control failed. Error code 31
> Error [31]:A device attached to the system is not functioning.
> ```

Preparing for Server Maintenance

When you need to update an application, you certainly don't want users to be connected to it at the time. Therefore, you'll need some method of keeping users off the server when necessary. This is generally known as putting the server into *drain mode*, where existing connections are allowed to continue but no new ones are allowed in (and the RD Connection Broker won't route any connections there).

When preparing for maintenance, there are three steps you should perform, in order.

1. Disable new logons.
2. Inform users of the planned downtime.
3. Shut down the RD Session Host server programmatically.

Disabling New Logons

You can put a server into drain mode via RD Session Host Configuration or the command line.

From RD Session Host Configuration, move to the Edit Settings area in the middle pane and double-click User Logon Mode. This will open a dialog box presenting three options.

- **Allow All Connections**   This is the default user mode. All connections are allowed.

- **Allow Reconnections, But Prevent New Logons**   This is drain mode. Users with existing sessions are allowed to reconnect or to stay connected to the server, but new connections are blocked.

- **Allow Reconnections, But Prevent New Logons Until The Server Is Restarted**   This is temporary drain mode. The server will not accept new connections (and the RD Connection Broker will not route connections to it) until the server is rebooted. After the server has rebooted, this setting will revert to Allow All Connections.

Choose the option that suits your needs and click OK.

To change user logon mode from the command prompt, you'll use the change logon command. You must execute this command from the server whose user logon mode you're changing; the tool does not offer a remote option. The change logon syntax is pretty simple.

- **/query**   Returns the state of the server

- **/enable**   Enables logons that had been disabled

- **/disable**   Disables all incoming connections, including reconnections

- **/drain**   Puts the server into drain mode

- **/drainuntilrestart**   Puts the server into temporary drain mode (until the system is restarted)

If you're familiar with this tool from previous versions of Windows Server, you might notice the options for enabling drain mode and temporary drain mode. Otherwise, the syntax hasn't changed since Windows Server 2003.

Notice that change logon offers an option that RD Session Host Configuration does not: */disable*. Drain mode prohibits new connections but does allow users to reconnect to existing sessions. If you're serious about removing users from the server, use change logon */disable* to prevent any incoming connections, even reconnections. However, use this option with care. Disabling logons when users have existing sessions open can result in lost data or profile changes in the orphaned sessions. Drain mode, combined with reminders to users that you will be shutting down the server and requests to users to log off their sessions, is a safer option.

Each of these options allows you to configure only one server, though. To set the logon mode on more than one server at a time, use either Group Policy or script the logon mode via WMI. To edit the User Logon Mode via Group Policy, go to Computer Configuration | Policies | Administrative Templates | Windows Components | Remote Desktop Services | Remote Desktop Session Host | Connections | Allow Users To Connect Remotely Using Remote Desktop Services.

Group Policy is most useful for longer-term changes affecting many servers (you wouldn't edit Group Policy for a temporary change to two servers), whereas WMI is better for faster or more directed changes. Group Policy isn't practical for, say, changing the logon mode for two RD Session Host servers in the farm while the other two keep accepting logons, but WMI works well for this.

One way to check for the current logon mode via WMI on the local computer is to run the following Windows PowerShell script. (To run this script on a remote computer, replace the value of *$strComputer* with the name of the other computer.)

```
$strComputer = "."
$RDSH = get-wmiobject -class "Win32_TerminalServiceSetting" -namespace
    "root\CIMV2\terminalservices" `
-computername $strComputer
switch ($RDSH.AllowTSConnections)
{
   0 {"User logons are disabled."}
   1 {"User logons are enabled."}
   default {"The user logon state cannot be determined."}
}
switch ($RDSH.SessionBrokerDrainMode)
{
   0 {"Allow all connections."}
   1 {"Allow incoming reconnections but prohibit new connections."}
   2 {"Allow incoming reconnections but until reboot prohibit new connections."}
   default {"The user logon state cannot be determined."}
}
```

For example, this script will return the following message if the server is in temporary drain mode.

```
User logons are enabled.
Allow incoming reconnections but until reboot prohibit new connections.
```

 ON THE COMPANION MEDIA This script is also available on the companion media as CheckLogon.ps1.

Notice that this script has to query two properties to return all the information. The *AllowTSConnections* property corresponds to the */enable* and */disable* switches, and *SessionBrokerDrainMode* corresponds to the */drain* and */drainuntilrestart* switches. As before, you are using the switch statement to evaluate the actual values and make interpreting the output easier. The efficiency of running a script to get the information you need is somewhat reduced if you have to look up the return values on MSDN to know what they mean.

Sending Messages to Users

Shutting down an RD Session Host server or VM without telling users is apt to annoy them. Even if you plan to start maintenance after work hours, it's still a good idea to let users know that they should shut down their sessions completely, not just disconnect them. You can also send messages for less drastic reasons, such as telling a user to resend a print job or warning users to shut down an application.

One way to communicate with your user base is by sending messages from the Remote Desktop Services Manager or by using the msg command-line tool. Using these tools, you can communicate with individuals, selected groups, or everyone logged on to the server. You can even wait for acknowledgement of your message.

> **NOTE** Using the techniques described in the rest of this chapter, you can send messages to users logged on to VMs as well as users logged on to sessions. Only one person will be logged on to each VM, however, so the broadcast functionality won't work on VMs as it does for sessions. That is, you can't use it to send a message to all VMs on an RD Virtualization Host.

From the Remote Desktop Services Manager, right-click a session on an RD Session Host or VM and select Send Message. You will see a dialog box like the one in Figure 11-9.

FIGURE 11-9 Send a message to a user logged on to an RD Session Host server or a VM with the Send Message tool.

The message contains the sender's user name and the time that the message is sent. Type your message in the Send Message dialog box and click OK. The user will see a message box like the one in Figure 11-10.

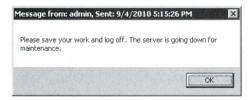

FIGURE 11-10 Users get your messages in a pop-up window.

Unlike the shadowing feature, sending messages is supported for RemoteApp programs. Users running RemoteApp programs or full desktop sessions receive the same message box; the only difference is that RemoteApp programs users get a message box on their local desktop, whereas users running a full desktop session receive the message in that session window.

You can also use the msg command-line utility to send a message to a session like this.

```
msg nancy.anderson /SERVER:FUJI Nancy, Tech Support has reviewed your case, and will be
with you in 5 minutes.
```

If you are not running the msg command from the same RD Session Host server as the one where the session is hosted, then you must specify the server (or VM) as shown in the example. You can specify sessions based on user name, session ID, or session name. Use the query command or the Remote Desktop Services Manager to get any of these data points.

If you have not limited users to one session per server, then you might need to send a message to every session that user has open. If you provide the user name as an argument, the message will appear in all sessions belonging to that user. To send a message to all sessions on a server, use the * argument. For example, to send a message to every session on server FUJI, run this command.

```
msg * /SERVER:FUJI This server will be rebooted at 3pm.  Please close your RemoteApp
programs.
```

You can also send a message to all users on an RD Session Host server, session IDs, or session names contained in a file. Using a file to specify who should receive a message can be helpful if you need to communicate with a group of users, but not every single person using the server. For instance, maybe you need to tell all users from the accounting department on server FUJI to shut down the accounting application. To do this, first create a file containing the user names of the accounting department users. This is most easily done from Windows PowerShell with the following script, which gets the names of the users in the ASH_Accounting_Users OU and adds them to a file named c:\scripts\ash-acct-users.txt. Obviously, you'll need to modify the Lightweight Directory Access Protocol (LDAP) paths and file name for your purposes.

```
$OU = [ADSI] "LDAP://OU=ASH_Accounting_Users, DC=ASH, DC=local"
$UserList = "c:\scripts\ash-acct-users.txt"
foreach ($child in $ou.psbase.children)
{
out-file -filepath $UserList -append -inputobject $child.name
}
```

 ON THE COMPANION MEDIA   The script to get the names of members of an OU and dump them to a file is on the companion media as GetUsers.ps1. Use this script any time you want to get the names in a collection. It can be modified easily to return computers as well as users, and to point to different locations. Because it queries AD DS directly, the list that it produces will always be up to date.

When you have the names in the file, then you can run the msg command as shown here.

```
msg @ c:\scripts\ash-acct-users.txt /SERVER:FUJI Please close the accounting
application.
```

Shutting Down and Restarting RD Session Host Servers

When you've drained the server of users and notified anyone who is still connected to the server, you can shut it down. You've probably shut down a server from the GUI; shutting down an RD Session Host server is no different. However, because you might not have shut it down from the command prompt, the focus is on that option here.

> **NOTE** The tsshutdown command used in Windows Server 2003 was discontinued in Windows Server 2008 and Windows Vista. Use the shutdown command instead. You must be an administrator to shut down or reboot an RD Session Host server. Users do not get access to the Shut Down, Restart, Hibernate, or Sleep option on the Start menu when working in a session. Nor can they execute the shutdown command.

Shutting down and rebooting an RD Session Host server from the Start menu is no different from shutting down or rebooting a Windows Server 2008 R2 server (without RDS installed) or a Windows 7 client. Go to Start and then click the arrow to the right of the lock button on the lower right of the menu. A menu pops up; choose either Restart or Shut Down.

When you choose to shut down or restart a server, you will see a pop-up window in which you need to choose a reason for the shutdown/reboot from the Option drop-down menu. Also, indicate whether the action was planned or unplanned, type any comments that you want to add in the Comments window, and click OK. This information is recorded in the server System Event Log (Event ID 1074). This logging is helpful for keeping track of who rebooted or shut down a server, and why they did so. Giving detailed information in the Comments area can make it easier for another administrator to figure out the exact reason for a reboot. For instance, if you install an application update, you can add a comment in the Shut Down Windows dialog box indicating exactly which one it was, which saves time if someone else needs the details later.

You can also use the shutdown command to shut down or restart a server from the command line. This command can be run from a Windows Server 2008 R2 server or even a Windows 7 client. The command syntax is

```
shutdown [/i | /l | /s | /r | /g | /a | /p | /h | /e] [/f] [/m \\computer][/t xxx]
    [/d [p|u:]xx:yy [/c"comment"]]
```

> **NOTE** Typing *shutdown* at a command prompt gives you the same command syntax and arguments as typing *shutdown /?*.

Table 11-5 shows a list of the command-line arguments available for the shutdown command.

TABLE 11-5 Arguments for the shutdown Command

ARGUMENT	INPUT	DETAILS
No arguments		Displays the command syntax and arguments. This is the same as typing /?.
/?		Displays the command syntax and arguments.
/i		Displays the GUI Shutdown. This must be the first option if used with other options. Use this option to shut down or reboot more than one computer at a time.
/l		Log off the computer. This cannot be used with the /m or /d option.
/s		Shuts down the computer.
/r		Restarts the computer.
/g		Restarts the computer and then starts registered applications.
/a		Aborts a system shutdown, but can be used only against the shutdown command given with a timeout period (/t *xxx*).
/p		Turns off the local computer with no timeout or warning. Can be used with the /d and /f options.
/h		Hibernates the local computer. Can be used with the /f option.
/e		Supposed to be used to document the reason for an unexpected shutdown of a computer, but it does nothing. Use the /c argument instead.
/m	*computername*	Specifies the target computer to shutdown or reboot.
/t	*xxx*	Set the timeout period before shutdown or reboot to *xxx* seconds. The valid range is 0–600, with a default of 30. Using /t *xxx* implies the /f option.
/c	"comment"	Add a comment about the reason for the restart or shutdown. Maximum of 512 characters allowed.
/f		Forces running applications to close without forewarning users; /f is automatically set when used in conjunction with /t *xxx*.

Continued on the next page

ARGUMENT	INPUT	DETAILS
/d	[p|u:]xx:yy	Indicates the reason for the restart or shutdown; *p* indicates that the restart or shutdown is planned; *u* indicates that the reason is user-defined. If neither *p* nor *u* is specified, the restart or shutdown is unplanned; *xx* is the major reason number (positive integer less than 256); *yy* is the minor reason number (positive integer less than 65536). (See Table 11-6 for a reason code reference.)

Instead of running through every option the shutdown command offers, the following information highlights some options applicable to an RDS environment.

Using the command-line utility means that you can shut down or reboot a server remotely. For instance, to shut down the server FUJI from a remote Windows 7 client, the command looks like this.

```
shutdown /m \\FUJI
```

Use the */r* command to reboot a server like this.

```
shutdown /r /m \\FUJI
```

As with shutting down or rebooting from the GUI, it's good to document why the event is occurring. Use the */c* argument to add a comment to the event to get recorded in the event log. For example, this command shuts down FUJI and adds a comment to explain the reason for the shutdown.

```
shutdown /r /m \\FUJI /c Installed accounting application update.
```

To document the planned reason for a shutdown or to restart via the command-line interface (CLI), use codes that correspond to the Option drop-down menu in the Windows Shut Down dialog box. The syntax for choosing a reboot code is *shutdown /d [p|u:]xx:yy*. The letters *p* and *u* indicate a planned action or user-defined action, respectively. The letter combination *xx* indicates the major reason number code; *yy* indicates the minor reason error code. Table 11-6 shows the reasons and corresponding code numbers.

TABLE 11-6 Major and Minor Number Codes Corresponding to Reasons for a Server Shutdown or Reboot

TYPE E = EXPECTED U = UNEXPECTED P = PLANNED	MAJOR	MINOR	TITLE/EXPLANATION
U	0	0	Other (Unplanned)
E	0	0	Other (Unplanned)
E P	0	0	Other (Planned)

TYPE E = EXPECTED U = UNEXPECTED P = PLANNED	MAJOR	MINOR	TITLE/EXPLANATION
U	0	5	Other Failure: System Unresponsive
E	1	1	Hardware: Maintenance (Unplanned)
E P	1	1	Hardware: Maintenance (Planned)
E	1	2	Hardware: Installation (Unplanned)
E P	1	2	Hardware: Installation (Planned)
P	2	3	Operating System: Upgrade (Planned)
E	2	4	Operating System: Reconfiguration (Unplanned)
E P	2	4	Operating System: Reconfiguration (Planned)
P	2	16	Operating System: Service pack (Planned)
	2	17	Operating System: Hot fix (Unplanned)
P	2	17	Operating System: Hot fix (Planned)
	2	18	Operating System: Security fix (Unplanned)
P	2	18	Operating System: Security fix (Planned)
E	4	1	Application: Maintenance (Unplanned)
E P	4	1	Application: Maintenance (Planned)
E P	4	2	Application: Installation (Planned)
E	4	5	Application: Unresponsive
E	4	6	Application: Unstable
U	5	15	System Failure: Stop error
E	5	19	Security issue
U	5	19	Security issue
E P	5	19	Security issue
E	5	20	Loss of network connectivity (Unplanned)
U	6	11	Power Failure: Cord Unplugged
U	6	12	Power Failure: Environment
P	7	0	Legacy API shutdown

For instance, to reboot the server FUJI and document the reboot as being due to application maintenance, the command is

```
shutdown /r /m \\FUJI /d p:4:1
```

Running the preceding command remotely produces Event ID 1074 in the System Event Log on the server that is rebooted, with a description of the action that occurs. The data includes the user name that initiated the request, the IP address of the computer the request comes from, and the reason for the request.

```
The process wininit.exe (10.10.10.23) has initiated the restart of computer FUJI on
behalf of user ASH\Administrator for the following reason: Application: Maintenance
(Planned)
```

Shutdown.exe is also helpful if you need to reboot many servers. To do so, run the following command.

```
shutdown /i
```

This command brings up the dialog box named Remote Shutdown Dialog, shown in Figure 11-11, which gives you the ability to specify more than one computer to shut down or restart.

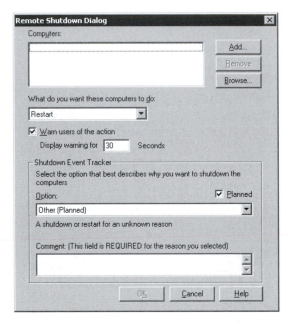

FIGURE 11-11 The Remote Shutdown dialog box allows you to shut down specific computers.

Click Add and type the name of the computer that you want to shut down or restart. Do this for all computers you want to shut down or restart and then choose the action you want to perform from the What Do You Want These Computers To Do drop-down menu.

- Restart
- Shutdown
- Annotate Unexpected Shutdown

Choose the reason for this action by selecting the appropriate choice from the Option drop-down menu and add any comments in the Comment text box. Then click OK.

As an example, if you perform scheduled server maintenance, such as running some updates every Sunday, and include a reboot, you can automate the reboot process by creating a scheduled task with the Windows Server 2008 Task Scheduler or by using the command-line tool schtasks. For example, to reboot the server FUJI every Sunday night at midnight, use the schtasks command as shown here.

```
schtasks.exe /create /SC WEEKLY /D SUN /RU admin@ash.local /RP "xxxxxxxx" /TN RebootFUJI
/TR "C:\windows\system32\shutdown.exe /m \\FUJI /r /c FUJI-WindowsUpdates-Reboot" /ST
12:00
```

 ON THE COMPANION MEDIA This scheduled task is located on the companion media as Schedreboot.bat.

If a shutdown or reboot attempt fails, Event ID 1073 is logged in the System Event Log of the server that fails to reboot. The log won't tell you why the action failed, but it will at least let you know that it did fail and which user account issued the command. If you like, you can use Schtasks.exe to create a task that performs an action such as running a script that emails you every time the event ID appears. The details of Server-reboot-failed.vbs are in the next sidebar, "Direct from the Field: Email Yourself When a Reboot Fails."

```
schtasks.exe /Create /TN EventLog-1073 /TR "cscript\\colfax\ash-company-files\IT\
Scripts\server-reboot-failed.vbs" /SC ONEVENT /EC System /MO *[System/EventID=1073]
```

 ON THE COMPANION MEDIA This scheduled task is located on the companion media as Emailonfail.bat. The scheduled task executes Server-reboot-failed.vbs, which you can access from *http://theessentialexchange.com/blogs/michael /default.aspx*. This link is also on the companion media.

Email Yourself When a Reboot Fails

Michael Smith

Exchange MVP, Smith Consulting

When performing remote reboots, you're not present to see whether the reboot works . . . and it can waste a lot of time if you think a server reboots when it doesn't. One solution is to email yourself when a shutdown or reboot fails. You'll need a Simple Mail Transfer Protocol (SMTP) server running in your domain (you can install the SMTP server feature built into Windows Server 2008 or you can use another SMTP server), the Microsoft Collaboration Data Objects (CDOs) installed on the computer creating the email, and a script to do the emailing. You can edit this sample script to conform to your needs.

```
Option Explicit
'''----- script configuration area
Const strSMTPServer = "arvon.ash.local"
Const strFrom       = "alerts@ash.local"
Const strTo         = "adam.barr@ash.local "
'''----- end configuration area


Dim objMail                 ' the CDO object
Dim objWSHNetwork           ' windows-script-host network object
Dim strNetBIOSComputer      ' the netbios name of our computer


''' get the NetBIOS computer name
Set objWSHNetwork   = CreateObject ("WScript.Network")
strNetBIOSComputer = objWSHNetwork.ComputerName
Set objWSHNetwork   = Nothing


''' do the real work to send the message
Set objMail = CreateObject ("CDO.Message")
objMail.Configuration.Fields.Item ("http://schemas.microsoft.com/cdo/
    configuration/sendusing")                           = 2
objMail.Configuration.Fields.Item ("http://schemas.microsoft.com/cdo/
    configuration/smtpserver")                          = strSMTPServer
objMail.Configuration.Fields.Item ("http://schemas.microsoft.com/cdo/
    configuration/smtpserverport")                      = 25
objMail.Configuration.Fields.Update
objMail.From    = strFrom
objMail.To      = strTo
objMail.Subject = "Critical error!! " &strNetBIOSComputer& " failed to
    reboot " & Now
```

```
objMail.Textbody = "Critical error!! " &strNetBIOSComputer& " failed to
    reboot " & Now &vbCRLF
objMail.Send
Set objMail = Nothing
```

 ON THE COMPANION MEDIA   A link to the preceding code is provided on this book's companion media. You can access it from the blog at *http://theessentialexchange.com/blogs/michael/archive/2008/10/06/script-for-from-the-field.aspx*. The CDO installer can be downloaded from *http://www.microsoft.com/downloads/en/details.aspx?FamilyID=e17e7f31-079a-43a9-bff2-0a110307611e*.

Applying RDS Management Tools

Thus far, the examples in this chapter have focused on the tools themselves. This section will show you how to combine these tools to get the information that you need when it's not supplied directly by the tools themselves.

Differentiating RemoteApp Sessions from Full Desktop Sessions

One good example of applying the RDS management tools is when you have to determine whether you can shadow a session. As explained earlier in this chapter, shadowing Remote-App sessions isn't supported and can lead to some very odd behavior. Therefore, it's good to avoid shadowing a RemoteApp session. Unfortunately, this is easier said than done, because the Remote Desktop Services Manager doesn't spell out the difference. You can find the RemoteApp sessions if you know that RemoteApp sessions use Rdpshell.exe and full desktops use Explorer.exe as the shell. You also have to know where to find this information.

Here's how to find it: From the Remote Desktop Services Manager, the User tab and Session tab reveal no differences between desktop and RemoteApp sessions. Go to the Processes tab, however, and you can see one difference: The shell processes for the two types of sessions are different, as discussed in Chapter 2, "Key Architectural Concepts for Remote Desktop Services," and Chapter 6, "Customizing the User Experience." As you might remember, desktop sessions use Explorer.exe as a shell and Userinit.exe to start Windows Explorer; RemoteApp sessions use Rpdshell.exe and Rdpinit.exe, respectively. Therefore, if user Hao Chen calls you to ask for help with his application, you can check the Processes tab to determine if Hao is running a desktop session that you can shadow.

Identifying Full Desktop Sessions

You can find RemoteApp sessions from the command line using the query commands. The query session command will help you find the sessions hosting Rdpinit.exe and Rdpshell.exe, and query process will help you find out whether a user's session contains those processes.

To find out which sessions on server FUJI are running Rdpshell.exe, run this command.

```
query process RDPshell.exe /SERVER:FUJI
```

The results show that Paul Koch is running a RemoteApp and therefore should not be shadowed.

USERNAME	SESSIONNAME	ID	PID	IMAGE
paul.koch	rdp-tcp#1	3	3132	rdpshell.exe

Let's say that you know the user whose session you want to shadow. You can ask the user to describe the session's appearance and figure out if he is running a RemoteApp, but that's slow and unreliable. The better alternative is to query the Remote Desktop Services Manager for the processes that the user is running. To query the processes running for user Kim Akers on server FUJI, run this command.

```
query process kim.akers /SERVER:FUJI
```

In this example, Kim Akers is not running Rdpinit.exe or Rdpshell.exe, so shadowing the session is supported.

USERNAME	SESSIONNAME	ID	PID	IMAGE
kim.akers	rdp-tcp#1	3	2276	taskeng.exe
kim.akers	rdp-tcp#1	3	3480	rdpclip.exe
kim.akers	rdp-tcp#1	3	3884	dwm.exe
kim.akers	rdp-tcp#1	3	3560	explorer.exe
kim.akers	rdp-tcp#1	3	2660	winword.exe
kim.akers	rdp-tcp#1	3	3676	splwow64.exe
kim.akers	rdp-tcp#1	3	3880	powerpnt.exe
kim.akers	rdp-tcp#1	3	3436	excel.exe

The preceding command also reveals the session ID, which you need to shadow Kim's session, like this.

```
shadow /SERVER:FUJI 3
```

Auditing Application Usage

Many administrators want to know if their company is compliant with their application licensing requirements. Unfortunately, this isn't easy to determine at the best of times, and it gets harder when an RD Session Host deployment is involved. First, application licensing for an RD Session Host server can be tricky. You need to read the application's fine print (the application vendor determines the licensing requirements, not Microsoft), and if you must be able to demonstrate compliance for legal reasons, you might need to clarify the details with the application's vendor. (Not all license agreements are written with virtualization in mind.) Second, Windows Performance Monitor doesn't offer a way to keep track of how many instances of a process are open on a server, other than adding a process counter and manually counting how many processes have the same name.

You *could* count application instances from the Remote Desktop Services Manager by counting processes on each RD Session Host server and adding up the results of each count, but why would you? The query process or qprocess command provides a way to do the same thing programmatically. With a little help from some other scripting objects, the query process command can be the basis of a rudimentary application metering tool.

> **NOTE** The Get-Process Windows PowerShell cmdlet isn't session-aware, so it will return only processes in the current session.

This series of scripts will do the following.

- Find all RD Session Host servers in an OU.
- Query all servers to get a list of the processes running on each one.
- Ignore all processes that aren't the application that the script is designed to count.
- Email you if more people are using the application than you have licenses.
- Keep a log file of this data for trending.

 ON THE COMPANION MEDIA Some of these tasks also apply to other inventory tasks. To make it easier for you to reuse the code, they are included on the companion media as RDSHServerFarmNames.vbs, RDSHNames.bat, QueryRDSH.vbs, ProcCleanup.vbs, CheckFile.vbs, and Count-Email.vbs. Appaudit.vbsis the combination of these scripts into one application metering script, and it is also available on the companion media.

Use this tool not only to keep track of your licensing, but also to let you know if an application's usage is decreasing. If you're considering retiring an application, recording how many instances are running over time can give you the data you need to know about how many people are still using it.

Get the Server Names

First, you'll need the names of all the RD Session Host servers. How you do this depends on whether the servers are in a domain or a workgroup. (The workgroup model will support both domains and workgroups, but the domain model doesn't work for workgroups because it depends on reading OU memberships.) In both cases, you'll collect the names of the RD Session Host servers and put them into a file.

Assuming that all identically configured RD Session Host servers are in the same OU, one way to do this is to query that OU and return its members, writing the names to a file. The companion media contains a Windows PowerShell script that does this (called Getservers.ps1), but you can also do this with VBScript (RDSHServerFarmNames.vbs on the companion media), as shown in the following code snippet.

```
' =====Configuration Area================
strRDSTextFile = "FarmServers.txt"
strRDSLDAPPath = "LDAP://OU=ASH_RD_Farm1, DC=ash, DC=local"
sScriptDirPath = "\\colfax\ash-company-files\IT\AUDIT\"
' =====End Configuration Area============
Set objRDSOU = GetObject(strRDSLDAPPath)
objRDSOU.Filter = Array("Computer")
' ==================================
' If file exists add data, if not, then create file and add data
Set objFSO = CreateObject("Scripting.FileSystemObject")
If objFSO.FileExists(sScriptDirPath&strRDSTextFile) Then
'do nothing
Else
Set objRDSTextFile = objFSO.CreateTextFile(sScriptDirPath&strRDSTextFile)
objRDSTextFile.Close
End If
Set objRDSTextFile = objFSO.OpenTextFile(sScriptDirPath&strRDSTextFile, ForWriting)
For Each objRDSItem in objRDSOU
    strRDSComputer = objRDSItem.CN
    objRDSTextFile.WriteLinestrRDSComputer
Next
objRDSTextFile.Close
WScript.Quit
```

This won't work in the workgroup scenario, because workgroups don't have OUs. In that case, you'll need to rely on the query termserver command, as in the following example. This is a bit more complicated, because the command-line tool returns some extra data and you'll need to remove it from the file. This section relies on both RDSHNames.bat and QueryRDSH.vbs on the companion media.

```
' =====Configuration Area================
objRDSBATFile = "\\colfax\ash-company-files\IT\scripts\RDSHNames.bat"
' =====End Configuration Area============
' Run batch file query termserv
' requires batch file
' batch file code is: query termserv>\\colfax\ash-company-files\IT\scripts\RDSHNames.txt
Set WSHShell = CreateObject("Wscript.Shell")
WSHShell.Run (objRDSBATFile),0, True
' Query termserv command adds two lines of header info to file
' This removes this extraneous information
' =====Configuration Area================
strRDSFile = "\\colfax\ash-company-files\IT\scripts\RDSHNames.txt"
' =====Configuration Area================
Set objFSO = CreateObject("Scripting.FileSystemObject")
Set objRDSFile = objFSO.OpenTextFile(strRDSFile, ForReading)
Do until objRDSFile.AtEndOfStream
objRDSFile.SkipLine
objRDSFile.SkipLine
strRDSLines = objRDSFile.ReadAll
Loop
objRDSFile.close
' Remove carriage return at end of file
Set objNewRDSFile = objFSO.OpenTextFile(strRDSFile, ForWriting)
objNewRDSFile.WritestrRDSLines
Set objNewRDSFile = objFSO.OpenTextFile(strRDSFile, ForReading)
strRDSLines = objNewRDSFile.ReadAll
objNewRDSFile.close
strFileContents = strRDSLines
intLength = Len(strFileContents)
strEndofString = Right(strFileContents, 2)
If strEndofString = vbCrLf Then
                strFileContents = Left(strFileContents, intLength - 2)
                Set objNewRDSFile = objFSO.OpenTextFile(strRDSFile, ForWriting)
                objNewRDSFile.WritestrFileContents
                objNewRDSFile.Close
End if
Set objRDSFile = Nothing
Set objNewRDSFile = Nothing
wscript.quit
```

List Processes on the RD Session Host Servers

When you know the names of the RD Session Host servers in an OU, query each server by typing **query process *<executable>* /server:*<server name>***. To make it easy, automate this process by running a batch file that runs the query process command against the saved server list and pipes that data to a file, as shown here.

```
FOR /F %%G IN (\\colfax\ash-company-files\IT\AUDIT\FarmServers.txt) DO query process *
    /server:%%G >>\\colfax\ash-company-files\IT\AUDIT\Processes\processes.txt
```

Why use a batch file? Mostly because it's easy. There's no reason to reinvent the wheel and try to pull all the process data from all the servers when query process does the same thing so succinctly. This batch file is on the companion media as Processes.bat.

Extract the Application Name

When you saved to a file the list of all processes running on all servers in an OU, you will need to focus on the particular process for which you need a usage count. Run this script to keep only lines in the text file that contain the application name. In this script, you are looking for Excel.exe, but you can edit the script to adjust the application name as required. The script is on the companion media as ProcCleanup.vbs.

```
' =====Configuration Area=================
sScriptDirPath = "\\colfax\ash-company-files\IT\AUDIT\"
sFldrProcesses = "Processes"
sProcDirectoryPath = sScriptDirPath& "\" &sFldrProcesses
sProcessesTxt = "processes.txt"
objProcessesFile = sProcDirectoryPath& "\" &sProcessesTxt
objFindApp.Pattern = "excel.exe"
' =====End Configuration Area============
Set objFindApp = CreateObject("VBScript.RegExp")
Set objFSO = CreateObject("Scripting.FileSystemObject")
Set objTextFile = objFSO.OpenTextFile(objProcessesFile, ForReading)
Do Until objTextFile.AtEndOfStream
        strSearchString = objTextFile.ReadLine
        Set colMatches = objFindApp.Execute(strSearchString)
        If colMatches.Count> 0 Then
                For Each strMatch in colMatches
                strNewContents = strNewContents&strSearchString&vbCrLf
                Next
        End If
Loop
objTextFile.Close
Set objTextFile = objFSO.OpenTextFile(objProcessesFile, ForWriting)
objTextFile.WritestrNewContents
objTextFile.Close
WScript.Quit
```

ON THE COMPANION MEDIA The text file contents produced by the preceding script contains a carriage return at the end of the file, which for line-counting purposes will increase the count by 1. This carriage return has been deleted in CheckFile.vbs, which is located on the companion media.

Record Application Instances and Email Alerts

Now run Count-Email.vbs (on the companion media) to count the lines left in Processes.txt (the file produced by the preceding scripts) and send an email to a specified address if the count is higher than the number of licenses that you own. This section will also record the count to a text file each time that you run the script so that you can tell how application usage changes over time.

```
' =====Configuration Area================
sScriptDirPath = "\\colfax\ash-company-files\IT\AUDIT\"
sFldrProcesses = "Processes"
sProcDirectoryPath = sScriptDirPath& "\" &sFldrProcesses
sProcessesTxt = "processes.txt"
objProcessesFile = sProcDirectoryPath& "\" &sProcessesTxt
' =====End Configuration Area============
Set objFSO = CreateObject("Scripting.FileSystemObject")
If objFSO.FileExists(objProcessesFile) Then
'do nothing
Else
    Wscript.Echo "Error - Processes file missing."
    WScript.Quit
End If
'Count the lines in the file processes.txt
Set objProcessesFile = objFSO.OpenTextFile(objProcessesFile, ForReading)
objProcessesFile.ReadAll
' If the count > licenses owned then email alert
Dim objLicensesOwned 'The number of application licenses owned
' =====Configuration Area================
objLicensesOwned = 0
' =====End Configuration Area============
' WScript.EchoobjProcessesFile.line& " " & "objects still counted"
If objProcessesFile.line>objLicensesOwned then
' =====Configuration Area================
Const strSMTPServer = "cathedral.ash.local"
Const strFrom       = "admin@ash.local"
Const strTo         = "kristin@ash.local"
' =====End Configuration Area============
' get the NetBIOS computer name
Set objWSHNetwork   = CreateObject ("WScript.Network")
strNetBIOSComputer = objWSHNetwork.ComputerName
```

Continued on the next page

```
Set objWSHNetwork  = Nothing
Set objMail = CreateObject ("CDO.Message")
objMail.Configuration.Fields.Item
   ("http://schemas.microsoft.com/cdo/configuration/sendusing")      = 2
objMail.Configuration.Fields.Item
   ("http://schemas.microsoft.com/cdo/configuration/smtpserver")     = strSMTPServer
objMail.Configuration.Fields.Item
   ("http://schemas.microsoft.com/cdo/configuration/smtpserverport") = 25
objMail.Configuration.Fields.Update
objMail.From     = strFrom
objMail.To       = strTo
objMail.Subject = "Licensing Check!! " & Now
objMail.Textbody = "Licensing Check!! "  & " The application count in use is "
   &objprocessesFile.line& " which is higher than number of licenses purchased " & Now
objMail.Send
Set objMail = Nothing
               End if
' Create or append data to log file
' =====Configuration Area================
objApp = "excel.exe"
strProcLogDir = "\\colfax\ash-company-files\IT\Reports"
strProcLogFile = "processcountlog.txt"
' =====End Configuration Area============
   Sub subAppend
   ' Append count to the log file processcountlog.txt
   Set objProcLogFile = objFSO.OpenTextFile(strProcLogDir& "\" &strProcLogFile,
   ForAppending, true)
   strProcLogText = NOW & "/The # of instances of " &objApp& " running is "
   &objProcessesFile.Line
   ' Writes strText to processcountlog.txt
       objProcLogFile.WriteLine(strProcLogText)
   objProcLogFile.close
   End Sub
' Check that the directory folder exists, if not create file
If objFSO.FolderExists(strProcLogDir) Then
'do nothing
Else
   Set objProcLogFolder = objFSO.CreateFolder(strProcLogDir)
objProcLogFolder.close
End If
' If log file exists append data, if not, then create file and append data
If objFSO.FileExists(strProcLogDir& "\" &strProcLogFile) Then
   call subAppend
Else
   Set objProcLogFile = objFSO.CreateTextFile(strProcLogDir& "\" &strProcLogFile)
objProcLogFile.Close
```

```
    call subAppend
End If
WScript.Quit
```

 ON THE COMPANION MEDIA   The AppAudit.vbs script found on the companion media combines all the scripts in this section into one script. This sample is designed for our environment, so you'll need to edit it to work for your specific situation. Areas to change are highlighted in the script as Configuration Areas. Any batch files referenced will need to be edited to suit your environment and put in appropriate path locations as specified in the script. Batch files are also located on this resource kit's companion media.

Auditing User Logons

Like application usage auditing, you can use the built-in tools to get you some information to help with capacity planning. One part of capacity planning, after all, is knowing how many people are using an RD Session Host server and how these numbers are increasing over time. That way, you can scale the hardware before users start wondering why the server is slow. It's also helpful to review logon patterns. As discussed in Chapter 2, there is a great deal of process creation associated with establishing a user session. If many users log on to the server at the same time, you might need to adjust the amount of memory available to support this pattern. Starting a process requires two to three times the memory that it takes to keep it running.

It's hard to plan for intense logon periods or increasing numbers of users if you don't know about them. Using the query user command, you can create a rudimentary user auditing tool.

To find out how many users have a session open on an RD Session Host server, open the Remote Desktop Services Manager and select the Users tab. All users with sessions will be listed there. You can also get this information by running the following command from a Windows 7 client or a Windows Server 2008 R2 server.

```
query user /server:SERVERNAME
```

That approach is fine for getting real-time data to help you solve a real-time issue, such as determining if your server is overloaded with user connections and performing poorly. But to get a sense of the average number of users logging onto a server, you will need to compile a user count over time. To get this count over time, you can run query user and pipe the data to a file like this.

```
query user /server:SERVERNAME>> c:\userlogons.txt
```

Closing Unresponsive Applications

If a user's application stalls, one way to handle the problem is to stop the process for that application. How you do this depends on whether you want to stop all instances of that process on the RD Session Host server or just the one that's causing trouble.

In this scenario, the user's application is not responding. You must terminate the process associated with the application. If you have a farm, first you will need to find out which server hosts the user session.

Do this by opening the Remote Desktop Services Manager and adding the servers for an RD Connection Broker farm. Then, for each server, click the Users tab and find the user. If you have not limited users to one session, then you will need to check all servers and find all sessions the user might have established. After you know all the places the user is connected, you must locate the stalled application.

How simple this is depends on your policies on having multiple sessions. If you support only one session per user, then all you need to do is click the Processes tab on the server that hosts the user session containing the stalled application, sort by Image, find the process associated with the user and the stalled application, right-click anywhere in the line entry, and choose End Process. If your user has multiple sessions, then you need to check the processes on each server, locate the specific server and user session in which the process is running, and terminate the process.

You can also accomplish all this from the command line. In this example, hao.chen, a user in the ash.localdomain, has been running the Excel RemoteApp. It has become unresponsive and needs to be terminated. This domain has a server farm and limits users to one session at a time.

First, you need to locate the server that hosts hao.chen's session. Run the qprocess command against every server in the farm until you find hao.chen.

```
C:\windows\system32>qprocess excel.exe /server:bigfrog
 USERNAME              SESSIONNAME        ID    PID  IMAGE
 paul.koch             rdp-tcp#1           4   2720  excel.exe
 adam.barr             rdp-tcp#2           5   3228  excel.exe

C:\windows\system32>qprocess excel.exe /server:FUJI
 USERNAME              SESSIONNAME        ID    PID  IMAGE
 hao.chen              rdp-tcp#1           4   2776  excel.exe
 nancy.anderson        rdp-tcp#3           5   3392  excel.exe
 alex.robinson         rdp-tcp#4           6   3532  excel.exe
```

Now stop the Excel.exe process associated with hao.chen. Do this by specifying the PID associated with the process shown in the preceding query.

```
C:\windows\system32>tskill 2776 /server:FUJI
```

> **NOTE** You can also specify the process by using the *session ID* and *process name* switches. Refer to the section entitled "Monitoring and Terminating Processes" earlier in this chapter for other examples of terminating processes.

If other users also complain, and it is apparent that all instances of Excel are stalled, you can terminate them all by running tskill, but use the *processname* parameter (the image name minus the executable extension) and the switch */A* (which tells tskill to kill all instances of the *processname*).

```
C:\windows\system32>tskill excel /server:FUJI /A
```

Then run **qprocess** again and see that there are no longer any instances of Excel.exe running.

```
C:\windows\system32>qprocess excel.exe /server:FUJI
No Process exists for excel.exe
```

Summary

This chapter has explained how to manage current RDP sessions using the graphical and command-line tools. Some of the best practices covered include the following.

- If you plan to import VM pools from RD Connection Broker to work in the Remote Desktop Services Manager, make sure the computer names match the VM names in Hyper-V. The importing function will report the VM names, not the computer names, and the management API uses the computer names.

- For the most accurate information across multiple servers, use the command-line tools.

- For best password security, do not use tscon from the command line, because it displays the password on the screen in cleartext.

- If you must remove a session from an RD Session Host server forcibly, use the logoff command rather than resetting the session. Although logoff won't save user data, it will write profile changes back to the profile server, whereas resetting the session does not.

- Don't try to shadow RemoteApp sessions. Use the Remote Desktop Services Manager or the query session or query process command to determine whether a session is displaying a full desktop or a RemoteApp.

- When preparing for user maintenance, use the */drain* switch with the change logon command to drain users slowly from the RD Session Host server rather than using the */disable* switch.

- You can use the command-line tools to help you learn patterns of application usage and user logons and save those inventories to a log file.

Additional Resources

This chapter includes a number of tools for checking settings and running inventory, all of which are on the companion media.

- For more details about how there can be multiple instances of the same process on an RD Session Host server, see Chapter 2, "Key Architectural Concepts for Remote Desktop Services."

- For more details about the session startup process, see Chapter 3, "Deploying a Single Remote Desktop Session Host Server."

- To learn how to configure Remote Control settings via Group Policy review the section entitled "Enabling Remote Control via Group Policy" in this chapter.

- To download RSAT for Windows 7, go to *http://www.microsoft.com/downloads /details.aspx?FamilyID=7D2F6AD7-656B-4313-A005-4E344E43997D&displaylang=en*.

- Microsoft MVP Shay Levy has created the Terminal Services PowerShell Module, which allows you to perform many Remote Desktop Services Manager tasks from Windows PowerShell. Get it here: *http://code.msdn.microsoft.com/PSTerminalServices*.

- Information on the Win32_TSRemoteControlSetting Class can be found at *http://msdn.microsoft.com/en-us/library/aa383817(VS.85).aspx*.

- A Windows PowerShell module for monitoring VDI and RD Session Host server sessions is available at the Microsoft Script Center at *http://gallery.technet.microsoft.com /ScriptCenter/en-us/e8c3af96-db10-45b0-88e3-328f087a8700*.

- Other scripts to accomplish other management tasks such as enabling or listing the remote control settings for a user account, farm and VDI usage reports, reporting session idle information, and more can be found at the Microsoft Script Center in the Remote Desktop Services section at *http://gallery.technet.microsoft.com/ScriptCenter /en-us/*.

- Microsoft MVP Michael Smith created a script that sends an email when an event ID occurs. Get this script at *http://theessentialexchange.com/blogs/michael /archive/2008/10/06/script-for-from-the-field.aspx*.

- The CDO installer can be downloaded from *http://www.microsoft.com/downloads/en /details.aspx?FamilyID=e17e7f31-079a-43a9-bff2-0a110307611e*.

Licensing Remote Desktop Services

Remote Desktop Services (RDS) works only for a limited time without licensing, so to complete this book, you'll learn more about that issue, including

- The licensing models for RDS
- How to install the RDS Licensing role service
- How to activate license servers
- How to install and manage license packs
- How to point an RD Session Host server to a license server
- How RD Session Host assigns licenses
- How to run usage reports

The RDS Licensing Model

As RDS gains more functionality, the licensing model has to adjust to include this new functionality. In Windows 2000 Server, the licensing model was entirely per-device (meaning that every device connecting to a terminal server needed a license). Windows Server 2003 introduced per-user licensing for terminal servers, giving companies a choice of how they wanted to license access. Windows Server 2008 introduced new roles like Terminal Services Gateway, which didn't perform a license check but still required a license to use them.

The addition of native virtual machine (VM) support in Windows Server 2008 R2 introduced added complexity. First, remote access to client operating systems is governed by rules separate from those for remote access to a server operating system. Second, VM deployments are helped by some partner technologies (for example, System Center Virtual Machine Manager and App-V) that were not part of the former TS client access license (CAL). Third, some people want VMs only, and some people want all the functionality of RDS: VMs, RD Session Host sessions, remote access to RDS resources, and so forth.

The final version has worked out to a two-tier model.

> **NOTE** For answers to frequently asked questions about RDS licensing, see *http://www.microsoft.com/windowsserver2008/en/us/rds-product-licensing.aspx*.

- **RDS Licensing**   Licensing to access RD Session Host sessions (including VMs) and to use other RDS role services (such as RD Gateway, RD Connection Broker, and RD Web Access).
- **VDI Licensing**   Licensing to access pooled or personal VMs hosted on the RD Virtualization Host server and to use RD Connection Broker provide access to pooled and personal VMs. This licensing model is intended for people who need only Virtual Desktop Infrastructure (VDI) and don't need other RDS role services (for example, RD Gateway for WAN access).

RDS Licensing

RDS CALs give users or devices the right to access and use any of the RDS role services. This is why RDS CALs are part of the requirements for VDI access, as shown in the section entitled "VDI Licensing" later in this chapter. RDS CALs also include the rights to use App-V to deploy applications to RD Session Host servers. There are four RDS licensing options to choose from, and which option you choose depends on how your company operates. The four RDS licensing options are

- **Per-User Licensing**   Each user that will use RDS role service(s) needs to have an RDS User CAL. Purchase RDS User CALs when your users will access RDS role service(s) from multiple machines. This model allows users to access RDS resources from any computer because the license is tied to the user, not the device. RDS Device CALs, conversely, are tied to the accessing device.

- **Per-Device Licensing** Each device that will use RDS role service(s) needs to have an RDS Device CAL. Purchase RDS Device CALs when multiple users will access RDS role service(s) from a set number of client devices. A good example of when RDS Device CALs are the better choice is shift work—when multiple users at different times of the day will use one machine to access RDS resources. RDS Device CALs are also required to access pooled or personal VMs.

- **RDS External Connector** This license option allows multiple external users (users who are not part of your company and for whom you do not provide licensing) to access one specific server. Each server accessed would need a license. For example, if you were going to license access to an RD Session Host server on one server, via RD Gateway on another server, you would need a license for both servers.

- **Services Provider License Agreement (SPLA)** This licensing is specifically for hosting providers and independent service vendors (ISVs) that host RDS and provide RDS access rights as part of their offering.

> **NOTE** For more information on SPLA, see *http://www.microsoft.com/hosting/en/us/licensing/splabenefits.aspx*.

Of the four options, RDS (Per-User or Per-Device) CALs are most commonly used with RDS. RD Session Host servers can be configured only in Per-User or Per-Device mode, but not both. Most people purchase one type of RDS CAL. You might use both if providing both VMs and sessions: Per-User CALs to access RD Session Host servers and RDS Per-Device CALs to use pooled and personal VMs.

HOW IT WORKS

2008 TS CALs vs. 2008 R2 RDS CALs

Windows Server 2008 R2 is a minor release, not a major one. So Windows Server 2008 TS CALs can be used for licensing connections to both Windows Server 2008 terminal servers and Windows Server 2008 R2 RD Session Host servers. Older licenses would need to be replaced with Windows Server 2008 R2 RDS CALs. Windows Server 2008 TS CALs and Windows Server 2008 RDS CALs both include the right to use App-V to install applications on RD Session Host servers. Windows Server 2008 TS CALs are no longer offered for sale and have been replaced with RDS CALs.

VDI Licensing

The VDI licensing model is device-based, meaning that you buy a license for each device that will access pooled or personal VMs hosted on RD Virtualization Host servers. It has three components.

- Licensing for the client devices that will access virtual desktops
- RDS CALs for each device that will access RD Virtualization Host server and use RD Connection Broker to gain access to the VMs
- Licensing for management components

Connection Licensing with and Without Software Assurance

Software Assurance (SA) simplifies VDI licensing. VDI licensing has changed a bit. Prior to July 2010, you needed to purchase a VECD license for each device that would access pooled or personal VMs. VECD rights are now included as part of SA.

> **NOTE** Non-SA customers will need to purchase Virtual Desktop Access (VDA) licensing, which is discussed in the next section.

Devices covered by SA can run up to four VMs locally on the desktop and access up to four VMs on servers in the datacenter. Devices covered by SA also include "roaming rights"—the single primary user of an SA-licensed device can access pooled or personal VMs from any PC without having to purchase any additional licenses.

Companies will need to purchase Virtual Desktop Access (VDA) licensing for devices not covered by SA that will be used to access pooled and personal VMs., You'll need VDA for devices like thin clients, non-Windows-based devices, and devices that are not part of your organization (such as contractors' computers). It also covers Windows devices for companies that don't subscribe to SA. Each VDA license does the following.

- Includes SA benefits for Windows such as 24x7 call and web support (how much depends on your investment in SA) and access to deployment planning services.
- Allows concurrent connections to up to four VMs.
- Includes primary user roaming rights

The primary user of a device that is covered by a VDA license can access his or her VDI desktop from non-corporate machines, such as personal laptops or hotel computers.

Licensing for Management Components

To manage a VDI implementation using more than just the tools in Remote Desktop Services, you need licensing for each management product that you want to use with your VDI and RDS implementation. These products include

- **System Center Virtual Machine Manager (SCVMM)** To provision and manage VMs

- **Microsoft Desktop Optimization Pack (MDOP)** Includes use of App-V to deliver applications to virtual desktops

- **System Center Configuration Manager (SCCM)** To configure RD Virtualization Host servers

- **System Center Operations Manager (SCOM)** To manage RD Virtualization Host health and performance monitoring

The right to use these products to manage your VDI implementation is included in the VDI Suite licenses, discussed next.

VDI Suites

Instead of requiring the purchase of separate RDS licensing and management licensing, Microsoft provides two subscription-based VDI licensing bundles: VDI Standard Suite and VDI Premium Suite.

VDI Standard Suite includes

- Per-Device CAL for accessing VDI desktops only, not sessions

- Use of management products to manage VMs and hosts (SCVMM, MDOP, SCCM, and SCOM)

- Use of RD Connection Broker to provide access to pooled and personal VMs

VDI Premium Suite includes all the benefits of the VDI Standard Suite, as well as the following.

- RDS CAL for accessing both virtual desktops and sessions

- Use of App-V to deliver applications to RD Session Host servers

In certain circumstances, you will not need to purchase anything extra to have the right to access pooled or personal VMs. For example, if you don't need to use extra management tools to manage VDI, your client devices are covered by SA, and you already own RDS Per-Device CALs, then you don't need any further licensing to access pooled or personal VMs. However, if you want to use the management tools (SVCMM, SCCM, SCOM, and MDOP), then you have to either purchase VDI Suite CALs (which includes the rights to these tools) or purchase individual licensing for the tools you want to use.

> **NOTE** A brochure with licensing examples to help you understand what VDI licenses you will need given different scenarios is available at *http://download.microsoft.com /download/7/8/4/78480C7D-DC7E-492E-8567-F5DD5644774D/VDA_Brochure.pdf*. The link is available on the companion media.

License Tracking and Enforcement

Some RDS license options are enforced while others are not. The same is true for tracking license allocation. Table 12-1 shows which licenses are tracked, enforced, both, or neither.

TABLE 12-1 Tracking and Enforcement of RDS Licenses

RDS LICENSE TYPE	TRACKED	ENFORCED
RDS User CAL	Yes	No
RDS Device CAL	Yes	Yes
External Connector Licenses	No	No
VDI Standard Suite	No	No
VDI Premium Suite	No	No

> **NOTE** VDI Licensing will be tracked and enforced in Windows Server 2008 R2 SP1.

Per-User licensing is tracked but not enforced, whereas Per-Device licensing is tracked and enforced. This does not mean that you are not bound by your license agreement, however—you are required to purchase the proper amount of licenses for your environment whether or not the licensing model is enforced. You can have up to two concurrent administrative connections to an RD Session Host server for administrative purposes. Administrative connections do not require an RDS CAL.

> **NOTE** Putting the RD Session Host servers into Per-User mode can help you avoid outages because Per-User licensing isn't enforced. It's okay to run in Per-User mode, even if you have purchased Per-Device RDS CALs. For that reason, in an emergency, flip the switch. You won't be able to use the License Server application to keep track of how many RDS Per-Device CALs are used, but as long as you have enough licenses to accommodate your connecting devices, this is in compliance with the End User License Agreement (EULA). Then you can fix your downed license server. To be clear, this does not remove your responsibility to be licensed according to EULA.

How RD License Servers Assign RDS CALs

When a client connects to an RD Session Host server, the server requests the type of license from the client that the server is configured to understand. If the RD Session Host server is in Per-Device mode, it requests a Per-Device license. The client presents the license from its store in the registry. If the RD Session Host server is in Per-User mode, it requests a Per-User license. Per-User licenses are stored as a property on a user account object in Active Directory Domain Services (AD DS), so the RD Session Host server can check this when user credentials are presented. (If you use Per-User licensing in a workgroup, then Per-User licenses aren't tracked.)

All licenses are assigned for a random period of 52 to 89 days so that unused licenses can return to the license pool automatically. Beginning seven days before the license expires, when that license is presented at logon, the RD Session Host server will try to renew it for another period of 52 to 89 days.

> **NOTE** It's possible to revoke a Per-Device CAL manually if you don't want to wait for the automatic revocation to kick in. The section entitled "Revoking RDS CALs" later in this chapter talks more about this.

If the client does not have a valid license or if the license it has is within seven days of expiring, then the RD Session Host server must attempt to obtain a license for the client at each login. If the server cannot find a license server to renew the license before it expires or no license is available, the license will expire. What happens then depends on the circumstances described in Table 12-2. Notice that there are circumstances in which an RD Session Host server in Per-User mode will permit the connection when an RD Session Host server in Per-Device mode will not.

TABLE 12-2 Processes When a Client Requests a License

CIRCUMSTANCE	PER-USER	PER-DEVICE
The RD Session Host server has never found a license server but is in its grace period.	The RD Session Host server will issue a temporary license that lasts up to 90 days.	The RD Session Host server will issue a temporary license that lasts up to 90 days.
The RD Session Host server has never found a license server and is out of the grace period.	The RD Session Host server will not permit the connection.	The RD Session Host server will not permit the connection.
The RD Session Host server has found a license server but the license server has no RDS CALs installed and is not activated. The license server is in the grace period.	The client will be allowed access for up to 120 days.	The client will be allowed access for up to 120 days.

Continued on the next page

CIRCUMSTANCE	PER-USER	PER-DEVICE
The RD Session Host server has found a license server but the license server has no RDS CALs installed. The license server is out of its grace period.	The RD Session Host server will permit the connection.	The RD Session Host server will not permit the connection.
The RD Session Host server has found a license server with RDS CALs available.	The RD Session Host server will give the license server the name of the user attempting to connect to the RD Session Host server. The license server will then contact AD DS to set a property on that user's account object to show that the person has used a license.	The RD Session Host server will contact the license server with the hardware ID (HWID) of the computer attempting to connect to the RD Session Host server. The license server will then assign an RDS CAL to that HWID and create a record of the assignment.

If you watch a license server when a user is logging onto an RD Session Host server in Per-Device mode, you might notice that before issuing a permanent license to the device, the license server will first issue a temporary license. This temporary license is given to the client device prior to the user logon. The reason is that you need a license to connect, but until the user who initiated the connection has presented credentials, the RD Session Host server can't tell whether that user has permission to log on to the RD Session Host server and therefore will not allocate a license unnecessarily.

> **NOTE** Prior to Windows Server 2000 SP2, a terminal server issued a permanent RDS CAL when the connection was initiated. Unfortunately, this meant that it was very easy for a malicious person to drain TS CALs from a license server because the person didn't even need a valid account to attempt the connection and have TS CAL assigned to the connecting computer.

When the user logs on from a client device a second time, then the RD Session Host server will attempt to get a valid RDS Device CAL for the device. If the RD License server does not have any, then the client can continue to access the server for up to 90 days, or until the client is issued a real RDS Device CAL, whichever comes first.

What if a license server the RD Session Host server connects to doesn't have any licenses of the right kind available? Prior to Windows Server 2008 R2, the license server would forward the request to another license server that it had discovered (the license servers would search for and discover other license servers), a feature called CAL Forwarding. Windows Server 2008 R2 no longer uses license server discovery (discovery could be interrupted by so many situations it wasn't reliable), so CAL Forwarding has been removed. Instead, you must point a RD Session Host server to the license server(s) it should use. If one license server cannot fulfill the request, the RD Session Host server will proceed to the next one in the list until it finds one that *can* fulfill the request or until it runs out of license servers.

DIRECT FROM THE SOURCE

CAL Forwarding Deprecated in Windows Server 2008 R2

Silvia Doomra
Software Design Engineer, Test

Because CAL Forwarding is deprecated in Windows Server 2008 R2, how can you make sure that your RD Session Host server contacts the second license server in case the first one doesn't have the requested type of CALs?

In Windows Server 2008 R2, the concept of auto-discovery of license servers doesn't exist. Hence, you need to configure each RD Session Host server with the license server name to make sure that the RD Session Host server can contact the RD License server. If you have multiple license servers in your environment, to make sure that if all the CALs of one license server are consumed, your RD Session Host server will contact the next one in the list automatically, then specify all the license servers on the RD Session Host server. It will always contact the first license server specified in the list. If the first license server is out of CALs, the RD Session Host server will then contact the second license server in the list and so on.

In summary, to ensure that all the license servers can be contacted by RD Session Host servers, specify their names on each RD Session Host server.

You will learn how to specify RD License servers in the Specified License Server List in the section entitled "Configuring RD Session Host Servers to Use License Servers" later in this chapter.

Setting Up the RDS Licensing Infrastructure

To set up the license server so that there is a source for RDS CALs, you'll need to do the following.

1. Install the RD Licensing role service.
2. Activate the license server(s) to register it with the Microsoft Clearinghouse.
3. Add the RD License server(s) to AD DS.
4. Install RDS CALs on RD License server(s).
5. Configure RD Session Host server(s) to use the RD License server(s).
6. Allow RD Session Host server(s) to communicate with RD License server(s).

The next sections explain how to accomplish each of these steps.

Installing RD License Server

RDS Licensing can be installed on any Windows Server 2008 R2 server that supports RDS. You can install this role service on a domain controller or member server. To install the Remote Desktop Licensing role service, follow these steps.

1. If you haven't previously installed any RDS roles on the computer, start Server Manager, right-click Roles in the tree view on the left, and choose Add Roles.

> **NOTE** If you are installing RDS Licensing on a computer that already has RDS installed, then you'll start from the Role Services section of Server Manager. In the Remote Desktop Services section, the screen will show the installed role services. Click Add Role Services to jump to the page in the wizard where you choose to add the licensing service.

2. Click through the introduction to RDS and on the next page, select the check box next to the Remote Desktop Licensing role service. Click Next.

3. Do not set a discovery scope, as it does not apply to Windows 2008 R2 license servers. Click Next.

> **NOTE** Discovery settings apply only to terminal servers running Windows Server 2008 and earlier. RD Session Host servers cannot use discovery to find license servers; you must explicitly specify the licensing server that an RD Session Host server will use.

   If needed, you can change the default location of the licensing database by clicking the Browse button and choosing a different location. Click Next.

4. Click the Install button on Confirm Installation Selections page.

5. After the installation is complete, you'll see a confirmation message and a reminder to configure the RD Session Host servers to point to the license server. Click Close.

You can also install the Remote Desktop Licensing role service using Windows PowerShell like this.

```
PS C:\Users\admin> import-module servermanager
PS C:\Users\admin> add-WindowsFeature RDS-Licensing
```

Installing using Windows PowerShell doesn't give you the option of doing any configuration. When you install this way, the license server will be set up with all the default settings, will not be activated, and will have no RDS CAL packs installed. The licensing database will be installed to the default location.

To remove the RD Licensing role services using Windows PowerShell, run this command. You might need to restart the server to complete the removal.

```
Remove-WindowsFeature RDS-Licensing
```

RD License Server Connection Methods

RD License servers must communicate with the Clearinghouse when you add or migrate licenses, and activate or deactivate a license server.

> **NOTE** For details on how the communication with the Clearinghouse works, see the section entitled "Background: How RDS CALs Are Tied to an RD License Server" later in this chapter.

There are three methods that the RD License server can use to communicate with the Clearinghouse when performing these tasks.

- **Automatic Connection** With this method, you enter the needed information into the appropriate RD License server wizard interface and the RD License server contacts the Clearinghouse automatically to perform the chosen activity. When possible, this is the easiest method.

- **Web Browser** Use this method when the RD License server does not have Internet access but you can access the Internet from another computer. The RD License server directs you to a website (*https://activate.microsoft.com/*) to perform the chosen activity. The RD License server also gives you the information you will need.

- **Telephone** Use this method when you do not have Internet access. The RD License server will ask you for your country or region and then provide you with the appropriate phone number to call the Clearinghouse.

The method by which you will communicate with the Clearinghouse is specified in the RD License server's Properties dialog box. When you install the RD License server, this is set to Automatic Connection, but you can change it when you activate RDS CALs. You can also change this method in the RD License Server Manager at any time. Change the connection method in the RD License Server Manager by right-clicking the server and choosing Properties. On the Connection Method tab, use the Connection Method drop-down box to choose a connection method and click OK. Again, however, the Automatic Connection method of communicating with the Clearinghouse is simplest.

Activating the License Server

You're not quite ready to install license packs on the license server. The license server has not yet been activated and therefore cannot issue permanent RDS CALs. This is indicated in the RD Licensing Manager pane by a red X (see Figure 12-1).

FIGURE 12-1 Activate the RD License server to issue permanent RDS CALs.

Activating a license server registers it with the Clearinghouse so that any licenses that you install on it will be associated with that server.

> **NOTE** Beginning in Windows Server 2008 R2, RD Licensing allows you to move licenses from one license server to another without having to call the Clearinghouse. For details on this process, see the section entitled "Migrating RDS CALs from One License Server to Another" later in this chapter.

To activate the license server, open the RD Licensing Manager. The interface here is pretty straightforward. Any license servers (locally installed, or to which you connected) will appear under All Servers. License servers that are marked with a red X are not yet activated and can only issue temporary RDS CALs. You can't make RDS Per-User CAL reports yet because you have no RDS Per-User CALs installed for which to create reports.

> **NOTE** To manage more than one license server from RD Licensing, right-click All Servers and choose Connect. When prompted, type the name of the license server to connect to.

Why Are There Windows 2000 TS CALs on My Windows 2008 R2 License Server?

Because you haven't yet installed any RDS CALs on the license server, you may wonder why the license server contains a reference to Windows 2000. That's the result of a decision made in the Windows 2000 era. At that time, any Windows 2000 Professional computer had a license to access a Windows 2000 Server terminal server. Many people referred to this as a "built-in" license, but this is misleading. There was no license built into Windows Server 2000 Professional, just the ability to pull from the Unlimited pool on the license server.

Beginning with Windows XP and Windows Server 2003, no client operating system has been able to draw from this Unlimited pool, but it's still available if you have (a) Windows 2000 Server terminal servers using the license server and (b) Windows Server 2000 Professional clients that will be using those license servers. If you don't have both, this Unlimited license pool is totally irrelevant. Even if you have Windows 2000 Professional clients, they cannot draw from the Unlimited pool to access a Windows Server 2008 RD Session Host server or a Windows Server 2008 or Windows Server 2003 terminal server.

To activate the license server, select it, choose Action, Activate Server, or right-click the license server and then choose Activate Server from the context list. This will start the Activate Server Wizard.

Click Next and then choose a method to contact the Clearinghouse to activate the server. If at all possible, use the Automatic Connection option, as it's less prone to error than either the website or the telephone options. The Clearinghouse manages licensing for Microsoft, including activating license servers, issuing RDS CALs and associating them with a license server, and recovering licenses. When you contact the Clearinghouse to activate a server, you'll receive an X.509 certificate to identify the server. Installing RDS CALs on the activated server associates them with that certificate and validates their authenticity.

Next, you'll need to provide some basic company information to the Clearinghouse to associate you with the activated server. This information is required. Type in your first name, last name, and company name, and then select your country or region from the corresponding drop-down menu.

 CAUTION If you're tempted to put in a false name, as some people do when asked to provide contact information, be aware that this information is designed to allow the Clearinghouse to find you in its system if you need to have licenses reissued or need other support. We recommend using your real name. If you put in a false name, remember it!

Next, the wizard will prompt you for some additional optional information that the Clearinghouse can use to contact you and further identify you: email address, organizational unit (OU), company address, city, state or province, and postal code.

Click Next, watch the status bar for a few seconds until you see the activation is complete, and you're finished. The license server is now activated and ready for you to install RDS CALs. When you go back to the RD Licensing Server console, the server will now have a green icon with a check mark indicating that it is activated.

NOTE Although the Activate Server Wizard will prompt you to install RDS CALs right away, you can skip this step for now and the license server will allow access for up to 120 days (until the grace period expires). The grace period ends at 120 days or when you install at least one license pack.

Activating an RD License Server Using Windows PowerShell

You can also activate an RD License server using Windows PowerShell. Activate the RD License server using the Automatic Connection method with the following command (Table 12-3 shows the Activation reason codes), but most reason codes apply only to reactivation. If activating the server for the first time, always use code 5.

```
PS RDS:> Set-Item -path LicenseServer\ActivationStatus -Value 1 -ConnectionMethod AUTO
   -Reason <REASON FOR ACTIVATION GOES HERE>
```

TABLE 12-3 RD License Server Activation Reason Codes

CODE	REASON
0	The server was redeployed.
1	The certificate was corrupt.
2	The private key was compromised.
3	The activation key expired.
4	The server was upgraded.
5	The server is being activated for the first time.

NOTE To understand what parameters you might need to supply in Windows PowerShell, use the Get-help cmdlet. For example, to get the needed parameters for setting the RD License server activation status in Windows PowerShell, run this command.

```
PS RDS:\LicenseServer> get-help Set-Item -path .\ActivationStatus
```

Then you can check to see what the possible values are for those parameters. For example, to get an explanation for the possible values of the parameter reason in the previous command, run the following.

```
PS RDS:\LicenseServer> get-help Set-Item -path .\ActivationStatus
    -param Reason
```

After the License server is activated, you should note the License Server ID and the required and optional information that you used to activate the license server. If you ever need to contact the Clearinghouse (for example, to get your RDS CALs reissued), this is the information that they will use to verify who you are and to help you further. If your license server dies in the future and you cannot get to this information, then working with the Clearinghouse becomes much harder.

In the RD Licensing Manager, right-click the license server and choose Properties from the context menu. Write down the License Server ID located on the Connection Method tab and also all information on the Required Information and Optional Information tabs. We recommend that you keep all your original purchase information and receipts.

NOTE You can get this information using Windows PowerShell like this.

```
Import-module RemoteDesktopServices
Set-Location RDS:
PS RDS:\>  get-item .\licenseserver\LSID | format-list
PS RDS:\>  get-item .\licenseserver\configuration | format-list
```

Background: How RDS CALs Are Tied to an RD License Server

When you activate an RD License server with the Clearinghouse, the Clearinghouse issues an X.509 digital certificate to the RD License server. This certificate is used to encrypt communications with the Clearinghouse. Figure 12-2 depicts the process of activating an RD License server and installing RDS CALs.

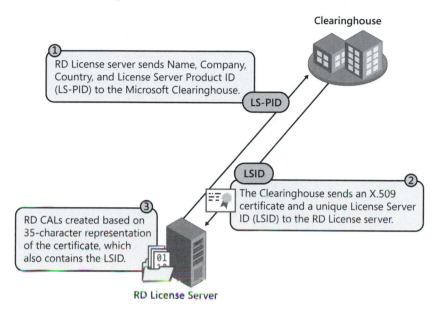

FIGURE 12-2 The Clearinghouse issues an LSID to the RD License server, which is matched to the LSID contained in the RDS CALs.

1. You activate the RD License server. The RD License server sends information to the Clearinghouse identifying the RD License server. This information includes

   - First Name and Last Name
   - Company
   - Country
   - License Server Product ID (LS-PID)

   The LS-PID is server-specific because it is created from the Windows Product ID (PID), a unique identifier created when you install the operating system. It contains the Microsoft Product Code (MPC) that identifies the operating system and the Channel ID that specifies the channel through which you purchased your operating system (Retail, Original Equipment Manufacturer [OEM], Volume Licensing Programs, Evaluation, or Checked Build).

2. The Clearinghouse issues an X.509 certificate to the RD License server. The certificate is used to establish secure communications between the RD License server and the Clearinghouse. The Clearinghouse also sends a unique License Server ID (LSID) to the server.

   This certificate is not stored in the regular computer certificate store on the server. Instead, it is stored in the registry at HKLM\SYSTEM\CurrentControlSet\Services\TermServLicensing\Parameters. The following four keys exist here.

   - **L$TermServLiceningSignKey-12d4b7c8-77d5-11d1-8c24-00c04fa3080d**
     This key is created from the license server's certificate.

   - **L$TermServLicensingExchKey-12d4b7c8-77d5-11d1-8c24-00c04fa3080d**
     This key is created from the license server's certificate.

   - **L$TermServLicensingServerId-12d4b7c8-77d5-11d1-8c24-00c04fa3080d**
     The unique LSID sent from the Clearinghouse.

   - **L$TermServLicensingStatus-12d4b7c8-77d5-11d1-8c24-00c04fa3080d**
     The last run state of the license server database.

3. You install RDS CAL packs. RDS CALs are created based on a 35-character alphanumeric representation of the digital certificate that was issued to the RD License Server. This 35-character sequence contains the LSID. When RDS CALs are installed, the RD License server matches the LSID in the 35-character sequence with its own LSID, which was issued by the Clearinghouse. If they match, then the RDS CALs are installed. If they do not match, the server rejects the installation.

> **NOTE** If you see Event ID 17 logged and you find the license server is only issuing temporary licenses, see *http://support.microsoft.com/kb/2021885*. You might have a corrupted certificate. Reactivate the license server as described in the Knowledge Base article to resolve the problem.

The key point is that *the LSID issued to the RD License server is created from the LS-PID*. The LS-PID is created from the unique operating system PID. This process ties the RDS CALs to the RD License server operating system installation.

Communication from the RD Session Host servers and the clients is encrypted based on the RD License server certificate, as shown in Figure 12-3.

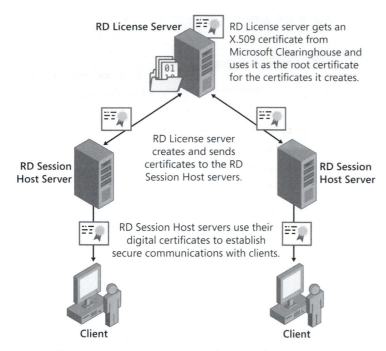

RD License server gets an X.509 certificate from Microsoft Clearinghouse and uses it as the root certificate for the certificates it creates.

RD License Server

RD License server creates and sends certificates to the RD Session Host servers.

RD Session Host Server

RD Session Host Server

RD Session Host servers use their digital certificates to establish secure communications with clients.

Client

Client

FIGURE 12-3 The RD License server issues certificates to the RD Session Host servers.

1. The license server gets an X.509 certificate from the Clearinghouse based on its PID.

2. The license server creates digital certificates signed with its own certificate and issues them to the RD Session Host servers (RD Session Host servers request RDS CALs on behalf of the users or computers connecting to them).

3. The RD Session Host servers use their digital certificates to establish secure communications with clients to check for and to issue RDS CALs.

The result is that to establish secure communication, the client verifies the RD Session Host server certificate by checking the signature on the certificate.

The RD Session Host server certificate is signed by the RD License server certificate. After it gets a certificate from a license server, it will never try to get another certificate, even if the license server is changed. This is because the certificate issued by one RD License server is valid for all other RD License servers. Communication happens using the original certificate only.

> **NOTE** For Per-User licensing, the RD Session Host server doesn't have to send anything to or get anything from the client because all the RDS CAL usage information is stored in AD DS.

Adding License Servers to AD DS

After the initial installation and activation, the RD Licensing Manager will show a yellow warning sign next to the license server, as shown in Figure 12-4. This is because the license server has not yet been added to the Terminal Server License Servers group in AD DS. You must add the license server to this group for every domain for which the license server will allocate licenses.

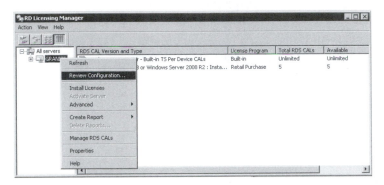

FIGURE 12-4 Add the RD License server to the Terminal Server License Servers group in AD DS by selecting Review Configuration in the RD Licensing Manager.

To do so, select the server in RD Licensing Manager, right-click it, and select Review Configuration. Click Add To Group and then click Continue in the resulting pop-up box that tells you that you must have Domain Admins privileges to do this. Then click OK in the second pop-up box that tells you the account was added to the Terminal Services License Group in AD DS.

Installing RDS CALs

To install the RDS CAL license packs using the automatic connection method, perform the following steps.

1. Open RD Licensing Manager and choose Actions, Install Licenses or right-click the server and select Install Licenses. Click through the opening dialog box of the Install Licenses Wizard to get to the page shown in Figure 12-5.

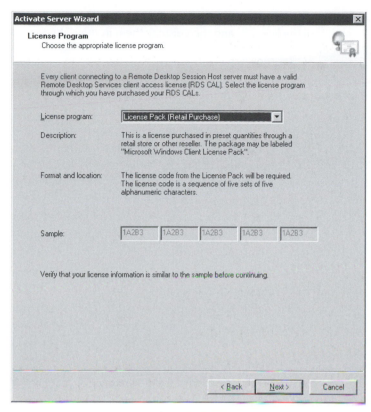

FIGURE 12-5 Choose the type of license packs you'll install.

2. From the License Program drop-down menu, choose the license program that you used to purchase your RDS CALs (for this example, you will choose to install a retail license pack). The corresponding Format and Location information area will tell you what further information you will need to provide on the next page(s). Click Next.

3. The next page(s) can vary slightly, depending on which License Program you chose, because the information that you need to enter next is unique to the license program. However, the general step is the same: enter the license information that the interface prompts for. For example, for CALs purchased from the Retail Purchase program, type in the license code or key for your CAL purchase and click Add. The code will show up in the list of entered license codes. You can enter as many here as you have available. When you're finished, click Next.

> **NOTE** The Microsoft RDS team has provided an example of how to use Windows PowerShell to add a License Key Pack to an RD Licensing server (and how to perform other license server management) online at *http://blogs.msdn.com/b/rds/archive /2010/04/07/manage-remote-desktop-licensing-by-using-windows-powershell.aspx*.

4. After you have entered all the required information, the RD License server will contact the Clearinghouse, install the licenses, and then display them in the right pane of the RD Licensing Manager.

Configuring RD Session Host Servers to Use RD License Servers

Since Windows Server 2003 R2, it's been recommended that you point a terminal server to a particular license server to avoid the uncertainty that automatic discovery introduces. In Windows Server 2008 R2, this is the only option: License Server Discovery has been removed. CAL Forwarding (the ability of one license server to forward a request to another license server because a terminal server would find one license server and then stop looking, even if the license server had no licenses available) has also been removed. Now you must configure the RD Session Host server(s) to use specified RD License server(s), and an RD Session Host server can request licenses from more than one license server if it must.

An RD Session Host server can get licenses from any of the RD License servers it is configured to use. If the first license server that it queries does not have the requested RDS CAL, the RD Session Host server will continue querying RD License servers that it knows about until it either gets a CAL to issue to a client, or determines that no CALs are available from any of its known RD License servers.

> **NOTE** For more information on how this change replaces CAL Request Forwarding in Windows 2008, see the sidebar entitled "Direct from the Source: CAL Forwarding Deprecated In Windows Server 2008 R2" earlier in this chapter.

Make RD License servers known to RD Session Host servers by doing either of the following.

- Add RD License servers to RD Session Host Configuration on a per-server basis.
- Add RD License servers to RD Session Host Configuration via Group Policy.

To specify an RD Session Host server's known license server(s), do the following.

1. Open RD Session Host Configuration, and, in the middle pane, double-click Remote Desktop License Servers.

2. Select the licensing mode by selecting the Per Device or Per User option.

3. Click the Add button at the bottom of the page, highlight a license server located in the Known License Servers pane, and click the Add> button to add it to the Specified License Servers pane. Do this for every license server that you want to add to the RD Session Host server configuration.

    Only local license servers and those registered as SCP entities in AD DS will appear in the Known License Servers pane. To add RD License servers that do not appear in the pane, type the server name or IP address in the lower-left input box and click the corresponding Add> button to add it to the Specified License Servers list. Then click OK.

To use Group Policy to configure RD Session Host servers with known RD License servers, do the following.

1. Create a Group Policy Object (GPO) and enable this policy: Computer Configuration | Policies | Administrative Templates | Windows Components | Remote Desktop Services | Remote Desktop Session Host | Licensing | Use The Specified Remote Desktop License Servers.

2. Specify the RD License server or servers that you want the RD Session Host servers to use. Do this by name (NetBIOS or FQDN) or by server IP address, separated with a comma as shown here.

   ```
   colfax.ash.local,blueridge.ash.local.
   ```

3. Apply the GPO to the OU where the RD Session Host servers reside.

> **NOTE** You can point an RD Session Host server to a license server in another domain, but if the RD Session Host server is configured for Per-User licensing, a trust relationship must exist between the domain where the license server is located and the AD DS for the user accounts. This is because RDS Per-User CAL usage is stored in AD DS. When a user gets a CAL, the RD License server updates their user account property to show that that user has a CAL, so it must be able to write to the user account. It must also be able to query it to run a report on Per-User CAL usage.

Configuring RD License Servers to Allow Communication From RD Session Host Servers

If you restrict RD License servers to only answering requests from specified RD Session Host servers, then you must add those servers to the Terminal Server Computers group on each RD License server.

> **NOTE** For more information on restricting RD License server responses to specific RD Session Host servers, see the section entitled "Restricting Access to RDS CALs" later in this chapter.

Migrating RDS CALs from One License Server to Another

In older versions of Terminal Services, if you lost your TS License server, or if you wanted to move your TS CALs to another TS License server, you had to call the Clearinghouse to get your TS CALs reissued. This process has been automated in Windows Server 2008 R2 so that migrating CALs from one RD License server to another is now easily done via the RD Licensing

Manager. You can also migrate RDS CALs from offline RD License servers to online RD License servers. So if you only have one RD License Server and it dies, creating another RD License server and migrating the RDS CALs to the new location is simple: You just need to reenter your CAL License information to complete the process. To migrate RDS CALs from one license server to another, do the following.

1. Open the RD Licensing Manager on the RD License server to which you want to migrate licenses, expand All Servers, right-click the RD License Server, and choose Manage RDS CALs. This starts the Manage RDS CALs Wizard.

2. Click Next on the Welcome page and, on the next page, choose the Migrate RDS CALs From Another License Server To This License Server option. In the corresponding drop-down box, choose the reason for the migration. Then click Next.

3. Depending on the migration reason you chose in the previous step, the next screens will vary.

   - If you are replacing the source license server with this license server, then the following will happen.

     a. You will be prompted for the source license server name or IP address.

     b. Then you will reenter your license CAL program and code information as you did when you originally installed it.

   - If the source server is not online, then

     a. Select the check box for the option The Specified Source License Server Is Not Available On The Network. Doing so will then require you to choose the operating system of the source license server from the available drop-down box. You will also need to enter the source server License Server ID.

     b. Reenter your license CAL program and code information as you did when you originally installed it.

   - If your source server is no longer functioning, select the check box for the option The Source Server Is No Longer Functioning. Then click Next.

4. If you indicated that your source license server was not available or not functioning, on the next page, you are required to agree not to use the licenses installed on the source server. Select the check box next to the agreement and click Next.

5. On the next pages, reenter your License Program information and corresponding license information as you did when you first installed the licenses on the source license server. Click Next and the licenses will be migrated to the destination server.

Rebuilding the RD License Server Database

You can also completely rebuild the licensing database using the Manage RDS CALs Wizard. You might do this if your license server database or license server certificate becomes corrupt or compromised, or if the license server is being redeployed. To do this, perform the following steps.

1. Open the RD Licensing Manager on the RD License server to which you want to migrate licenses, expand All Servers, right-click the RD License Server, and choose Manage RDS CALs. This starts the Manage RDS CALs Wizard.

2. Click Next on the Welcome page and, on the next page, choose the Rebuild The License Server Database option. In the corresponding drop-down box, choose the reason for the rebuild. Then click Next.

3. Rebuilding an RD License server database deletes any RDS CALs installed on it, so have your purchase agreement information on hand. The next page tells you this. Select the Confirm Deletion Of RDS CALs Currently Installed On This License Server check box. Then click Next.

4. The next page confirms that the RD Licensing database has been deleted. Click Next and then follow the prompts to reenter your RDS CAL purchase information as you did when you originally installed the RDS CALs.

Backing Up an RD License Server and Creating Redundancy

Before Windows Server 2008 R2, creating redundancy for your TS Licensing implementation meant creating multiple license servers, splitting TS CALs between them, and relying on the license servers to forward CAL requests to other license servers (CAL Forwarding). With Windows Server 2008 R2, this redundancy is done a little differently. Now the RD Session Host servers are responsible for checking with each license server that it knows about to satisfy a CAL request.

We recommend having more than one license server implemented in your environment. This way, you can split your RDS CALs among two (or more) license servers and configure the RD Session Host servers to use all the license servers. If one license server goes down, then there is another that continues to issue RDS CALs while you bring the downed server back online. And if one license server runs out of RDS CALs, the requests are re-sent to the next license server listed in the RD Session Host server's Known RD License Servers list. If you're completely out of licenses, then server redundancy won't help you (although Per-User licenses are not enforced).

This takes care of redundancy. But what about losing data if an RD License server dies? As explained in the following sidebar, what you lose depends on the circumstances.

Does Backing Up a Windows Server 2008 R2 License Server Help You?

In previous versions of Terminal Services, you had to contact the Clearinghouse if you wanted to rebuild a license server. Beginning in Windows Server 2008 R2, this became unnecessary, because you can now migrate RDS CALs to a new server. This is true even if the original server is out of commission.

If you don't back up a license server and the server fails, what have you lost?

You haven't lost the licenses. Using the RD Licensing tool, you can migrate them to a new server. If the original license server has failed, you can still reinstall the licenses on a new server by saying that the server is out of commission and agreeing not to use the licenses twice.

You haven't lost the ability for people or devices that already had licenses to connect. An RD Session Host server does not check with the license server every time someone connects. It checks only when a user or a device without a license or one with a license that needs to be renewed connects. Anyone who still has a currently working license will continue to be able to connect.

You don't lose the ability for new devices to connect, because they would get a temporary RDS CAL and would be able to use it until it expired or the device could be issued a real RDS CAL.

Devices with expired licenses would not be able to get a license and so would not be able to connect. But this is dealt with easily by running more than one RD License server.

You might have lost your usage reports, depending on whether you were issuing Per-Device or Per-User licenses. Per-User licensing records are stored in AD DS, since the license usage is reported as a property set on a user's account. Per-Device license reports are stored on each license server. Therefore, losing a license server would prevent you from reporting accurately on Per-Device RDS CALs already issued. However over time, as client RDS Per-Device licenses expire and they get new ones, your reporting will become accurate again.

Because installation of an RD License server and RDS CAL migration is an easy and quick process to accomplish, if you have redundancy built into your licensing implementation (meaning that you have implemented more than one license server and split the RDS CALs among them), you might not need to back up the individual license servers.

If your reporting is crucial to you, and you cannot wait for clients to be reissued licenses and for your count to become accurate over time once again, then you can maintain backups of your RD License servers so you can restore them if necessary and regain full functionality and reporting. An RD License server licensing database is stored as part of the system state data (it's in %SystemRoot%\Windows\System32\Lserver). As long as the system state is backed up, you can restore it to the same machine and get a full recovery of the RD License server.

Each operating system installation uses server-specific encryption that is unique to that installation. Every new installation of the operating system changes the crypto keys used in the server-specific encryption.

To be fully functional without having to migrate licenses, the RD License Server restore needs three things.

- RD License Server database directory.
- Licensing registry keys.
- Crypto keys from the operating system (those that crypto application programming interfaces [APIs] use; these are machine-specific). This is required to prevent piracy.

If you back up the RD License server system state, then you can restore to the same hardware and you will have a fully functioning RD License server. Unissued RDS CALs will be restored and available.

Microsoft also supports restoring a system state backup to a different physical computer if the new computer has the same hardware and if you take bare metal restore (BMR) backups. Windows Server 2008 R2 Windows Backup can make BMR backups.

Situations in which you would need to do a new installation and then migrate the RDS CALs to the new installation are those in which you are unable to restore the system state and the LServer folder successfully. For instance, Microsoft does not support restoring the system state to dissimilar hardware. In this case, it's possible that you will need to start over with a new license server and then migrate the licenses.

 ON THE COMPANION MEDIA See *http://support.microsoft.com/kb/249694* for more information on requirements for restoring a system state to different hardware. The link is also located on the companion media.

Managing and Reporting License Usage

When users log onto an RD Session Host server that is set to Per-User mode, the RD Session Host server checks to see if each user has the licensing property set in the user account properties in AD DS. If the licensing property is set, then a user can log on; if not, the licensing server will ask the domain controller to update the user account to show that it's using an RDS CAL. To track per-user licensing, you must have a domain.

You can't find evidence of this user CAL in the user account properties in AD DS; this is not exposed in the user interface. However, you can run a report on the license server to see how many user CALs have been allocated. To do so, open RD Licensing, right-click a server, and choose Create Report, Per User CAL Usage.

 CAUTION Only choose an activated server to create the report. The Create Report command will function if the server has no CALs or hasn't been activated, but it will return an empty set.

Choosing this option will open the dialog box shown in Figure 12-6.

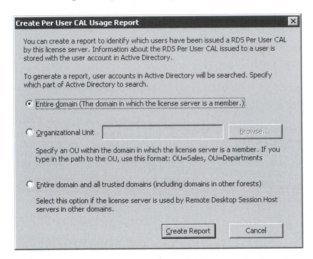

FIGURE 12-6 Choose a location for which to run the Per-User RDS CAL Usage Report.

To generate the report, specify the part of AD DS to search for the data, as follows.

- **Entire Domain** The domain that the license server belongs to.

- **Organizational Unit** A particular OU where user accounts are stored that is also part of the domain where the license server resides. Choose this option to restrict a search to a particular OU, if you want to get usage for only a subset of users.

- **Entire Domain And All Trusted Domains** Includes domains in other forests in the search, but choosing this option will increase the time needed to generate the report.

For this example, choose Entire Domain (the default) and click Create Report. After RD Licensing Manager creates the report, it appears in the RD Licensing Manager, as shown in Figure 12-7.

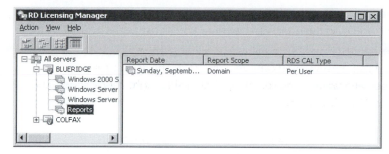

FIGURE 12-7 Use an RDS CAL usage report to determine how many per-user CALs you've consumed.

To view the report, save the data to a file. Right-click the report, select Save As from the context menu, and provide a location to save the report to create a comma-delimited file at that location. Open the file in Notepad (or any program that can open .csv files) to view a report like the one shown in Figure 12-8.

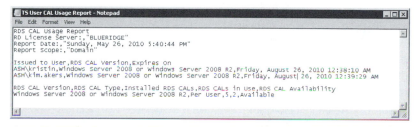

FIGURE 12-8 RDS UCAL usage report results can be seen.

Although Per-User RDS CAL usage is not enforced, the data gained from this reporting feature will help you to demonstrate compliance with the RDS EULA. The report contains the following data.

- The license server the report was run on
- The RDS CAL type (which will be always per-user; at this time, Windows Server does not create reports on Per-Device RDS CAL usage)
- The Report date
- The Report scope (domain, OU, and so on)
- The number of CALs installed on the server, how many are currently in use, and how many are currently available
- Which users have been issued a CAL, and when that CAL will expire and be returned to the pool

> **NOTE** A script to generate RDS Per-User CAL usage across domains is available at
> http://blogs.msdn.com/b/rds/archive/2009/11/09/per-user-cal-reporting-script.aspx.

RD Licensing Manager also shows you explicitly which machines have been allocated an RDS Per-Device CAL. In the RD Licensing Manager, expand the license server and select the Per Device License CALs group. Allocated licenses appear in the right pane.

 ON THE COMPANION MEDIA A script that counts allocated RDS Per-Device CALs for servers in a named OU is available on the companion media. The script also sends an email if the count is higher than the specified threshold value. The script is called PerDeviceCAL-Count-Alert.vbs.

NOTE A script for tracking Per-Device licensing on a per server basis is available at *http://blogs.msdn.com/b/rds/archive/2007/08/10/generating-per-device-license-usage-reports-for-ts-license-servers-running-windows-server-2008.aspx.*

Revoking RDS CALs

Unlike Per-User licensing, Per-Device licensing is enforced. When a user logs on to an RD Session Host server that is set to Per-Device licensing mode, the computer from which the user logged on is issued an RDS Per-Device CAL on its second logon (remember that the computer gets a temporary CAL on its first logon). The CAL is associated with a computer for an interval of 52 to 89 days. Either it must be renewed before it expires, or the CAL goes back into the pool so that the license server can allocate it to another client.

If you are replacing a few computers with new ones and have few enough CALs that you can't wait for the old allocations to expire, you might choose to revoke some RDS CALs to fill in the gap.

You can't revoke all RDS CALs at once. Microsoft has limited the ability to revoke RDS CALs to 20 percent of the Per-Device RDS CALs installed. For example, if your license server manages 100 RDS Per-Device CALs and 200 Windows Server 2003 Device CALs, you can revoke 20 and 40 CALs, respectively. Manual revocation is not intended to be used as concurrent-connection licensing by allowing you to revoke RDS CALs on devices not currently being used.

To revoke an RDS Per-Device CAL, in the RD Licensing Manager, right-click the CAL entry corresponding to the computer and select Revoke CAL from the context menu. The RD Licensing Manager will display a message confirming that the RDS CAL has been revoked, and the RDS CAL status in the Licensing Manager will be displayed with a status of Revoked.

This CAL is then available immediately in the device CAL pool and can be assigned to another computer. When you reach your limit for revoking licenses, you cannot revoke a license again for two months.

You might notice that you can still log on to the RD Session Host server from a computer whose device CAL you have revoked, but its license will still be revoked in the Licensing Manager and the client device won't get a new one. The revocation worked; what you're seeing is the way the bookkeeping associated with revocation functions. If you revoke a client's RDS CAL, that computer can still connect until the RDS CAL that it was originally given expires. If you're following licensing guidelines, this should be a moot point, because the whole point of revoking licenses is to remove them from a computer that will no longer be used as an RD Session Host server client. Just don't be surprised if that client PC can still connect to the RD Session Host server for a while longer.

> **NOTE** You can't revoke Per-User licensing. You don't need to, because Per-User licensing is not enforced, and if you delete a user account because the user has left, the CAL assigned to the account will no longer appear in the count.

Restricting Access to RDS CALs

RDS CALs cost money. You probably want some control over who's able to use them. You might want to ensure that users don't set up RD Session Host servers to experiment and use the production RDS CALs, or that the department paying for the RDS CALs is the one using them. If other departments want to use RDS CALs, they can purchase their own.

If your license server is part of a workgroup, you probably don't have much to worry about, because only RD Session Host servers in the workgroup can use it. If the license server is in a domain, the license server is registered as a service connection point (SCP) in AD DS when the role service is installed. The license server will then show up as a "known license server" in RD Session Host Configuration when you begin adding license server(s). Because the license server is known, it's more easily accessible by RD Session Host servers in the same forest.

> **NOTE** If SCP registration failed or did not occur (for example, if AD DS was not available when you installed your license server), you can register the license server manually as an SCP in AD DS by right-clicking the license server in the RD Licensing Manager and clicking **Review Configuration**.

But there's also a way to ensure that only certain RD Session Host servers can allocate licenses from a particular RD License server. If your license server is part of a domain, then you can enable a group policy to limit RDS CAL disbursement to those RD Session Host servers that are part of the license server's Terminal Server Computers local computer group.

> **NOTE** This procedure has no effect on RD License servers that are part of a workgroup.

The Terminal Server Computers local computer group is created on the RD License server the first time the Remote Desktop Services Licensing Service starts. By default, this group is empty. To block rogue RD Session Host servers from stealing RDS CALs (or users in other departments from "borrowing" them), follow these steps.

1. Add RD Session Host servers to the Terminal Server Computers group on the RD License server.

2. Create a GPO and enable the Security Group setting of the RD License server.

3. Apply the GPO to the OU where the RD License server resides.

In Server Manager, expand Configuration/Local Users and Groups/Groups.

NOTE If you install your license server on a domain controller, then the Terminal Server Computers group is located in the AD DS/Users folder.

In the Terminal Server Computers group add the authorized RD Session Host server(s) to the group, and click OK. You must add the RD Session Host servers individually to this group—you can't group all the RD Session Host servers together and then add that group to the RD Session Host servers group.

You can also use Windows PowerShell to add RD Session Host server(s) to the Terminal Server Computers group with this command.

```
PS RDS:\> new-item -path licenseserver\terminalservercomputers -name <servername@domain>
```

Remove computers with this command.

```
PS RDS:\>remove-item -path licenseserver\terminalservercomputers\<servername@domain>
```

NOTE Replace *<servername@domain>* with your server name and domain, such as olympus@ash, for example.

On the domain controller, open the Group Policy Management console and create a new GPO named something descriptive, such as RD License Restrictions. Right-click the new GPO and choose Edit. Navigate to Computer Configuration | Administrative Templates | Windows Components | Remote Desktop Services | RDS Licensing. Locate the License Server Security group setting, double-click it, select Enable, and then click OK.

Apply this policy to the OU containing the RD License server and then reboot the license server.

If the License Server Security Group GPO is enabled and applied to the license server, the RD License server will show a message to that effect in the RD Licensing Configuration dialog box. To see the message, right-click the server and choose Review Configuration.

Preventing License Upgrades

An RD License server will always attempt to issue the most appropriate version of RDS CAL to an RD Session Host server that requests it on behalf of a connecting client. For example, if you have a license server with both Windows Server 2003 CALs and Windows Server 2008 R2 RDS CALs installed, and a client connects to a Windows Server 2003 terminal server, the RD Licensing server will attempt to issue a Windows Server 2003 CAL. But if the license server runs out of Windows Server 2003 CALs, it will issue an available RDS CAL instead. This is because RDS CALs can be used with the version of Windows for which they were made, as well as for any previous version back to Windows 2000.

It could be that you don't want your older systems to use RDS CALs when they run out of their own. You can choose to allow an RD License server to distribute only CALs that are made for the version of RD Session Host server or terminal server that the client accesses. Do this by enabling the following policy, either locally or via the Group Policy Management console.

Computer Configuration Policies | Administrative Templates/Windows Components | Remote Desktop Services | RD Licensing | Prevent License Upgrade

If you enable this policy, then instead of distributing RDS CALs when lower version CALs would be more appropriate but are not available, the RD License server will issue temporary CALs, which will last 90 days. After 90 days, the client will be denied access if you are using Per-Device licensing.

Using the Licensing Diagnosis Tool

After setting up licensing so that your RD Session Host servers and RD License servers can find each other, you can double-check your work using the Licensing Diagnosis tool on the RD Session Host servers.

On the RD Session Host server, open the Remote Desktop Session Host Configuration console, and then click Licensing Diagnosis. The tool runs and produces a report like the one shown in Figure 12-9.

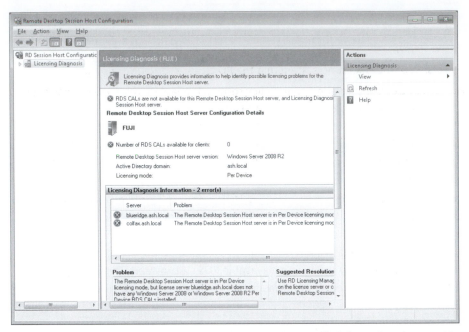

FIGURE 12-9 The Licensing Diagnosis tool gives RD Licensing specific information about problems.

The report shown in Figure 12-9 states that Licensing Diagnosis discovered that although this RD Session Host server is configured to use RDS Per-Device CALs, none are available. To get more details, click the entry for the license server located in the Summary window to show more details, like those shown in Figure 12-10.

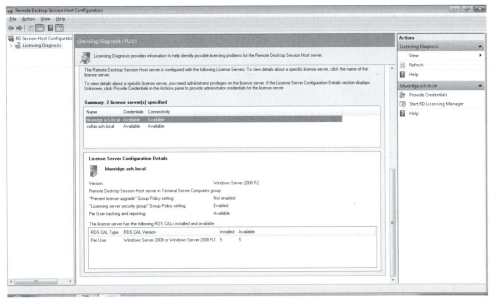

FIGURE 12-10 Click on the discovered license server in the Licensing Diagnosis report summary section to get more RD Licensing information.

As you can see, Licensing Diagnosis reports on a few other items you might find useful for troubleshooting licensing issues or for getting quick RD Licensing information. The report also shows the following.

- The version of the operating system that the RD License server is running.

- The Prevent License Upgrade Group Policy setting. If enabled, this GPO defines how RDS CALs are given to clients if no appropriate version of CAL is available for the client's operating system version. If no earlier version of RDS CAL is available for a pre-Windows Server 2008 R2 RD Session Host server connecting to your license server, by default the license server will issue an RDS CAL. If you don't want this to happen, then enable this GPO.

- The License Server Security Group Policy setting. If this policy is enabled, then the RD Session Host server must be listed in the RD License server's Terminal Server Computers group to use the RD License server.

- Which RDS CALs are installed and available. If you just want a quick glance at your RDS CAL availability, you can view it here instead of using the RDS Licensing Manager on the RD License server.

Summary

RDS licensing has changed in Windows Server 2008 R2, both to accommodate the addition of VMs (and the management tools many people want to support them) and to make the licensing more robust. This chapter has explained those changes and described best practices to keep licensing available, including the following.

- Per-Device licensing for sessions is enforced, but Per-User licensing is tracked. VDI licensing is not enforced.
- If you require VDI only, you might be able to use the VDI licensing CAL.
- Discovery of other license servers is no longer an option. You must configure an RD Session Host server to use a license server or multiple license servers.
- For maximum availability, we recommend having more than one license server, with the licenses split between them.
- Use Group Policy to prevent unauthorized RD Session Host servers from consuming licenses.

Additional Resources

- For more on SPLA, see *http://www.microsoft.com/hosting/en/us/licensing /splabenefits.aspx.*
- For examples to help you understand VDA, see *http://download.microsoft.com /download/7/8/4/78480C7D-DC7E-492E-8567-F5DD5644774D/VDA_Brochure.pdf.*

- For an explanation of the licensing grace period, see *http://technet.microsoft.com /en-us/library/cc738962(WS.10).aspx*.

- For more on RDS CALs, see *http://technet.microsoft.com/en-us/library/cc753650.aspx*.

- Locate a number for the Microsoft Clearinghouse at *http://support.microsoft.com /kb/291795*.

- For more information on backup and recovery in Windows Server 2008 R2, see *http://technet.microsoft.com/en-us/library/dd979562(WS.10).aspx*.

- For information on how to move the system state to new hardware, see *http://support.microsoft.com/kb/249694*.

Index

About the Authors

KRISTIN GRIFFIN was born in California and grew up a military brat, part of a loving and happy family. She has worked with Terminal Services/Remote Desktop Services since Windows 2000 and has implemented RDS for a diverse set of customers, including distributors, law offices, and commercial contracting firms. Formerly a senior IT consultant for a Virginia-based Internet and application service provider, she is now a Seattle-based independent consultant and author. Kristin was honored to receive the Microsoft MVP award for Remote Desktop Services beginning in 2009. You can find her answering questions on the Microsoft RDS Technet Forum (*http://social.technet.microsoft.com/Forums/en /winserverTS/threads*). She also keeps a blog concentrated on RDS tips, setup, and troubleshooting advice at blog.kristinlgriffin.com. In her spare time Kristin enjoys photography, computer graphics, camping, traveling, stained glass, woodworking, and buying more tools from the hardware store. Most of all she enjoys being with her family. She takes her German shepherd dog with her wherever she goes.

A former military brat, CHRISTA ANDERSON lived in various places in the western United States until a visit to Virginia ended in a 20-year stay on the East Coast. She returned to Seattle in 2007, where she enjoys the arts and outdoors in a city with a lot of both. Christa's interest in travel and environmental issues contributed to her enthusiasm for presentation remoting, beginning with Citrix WinFrame in the middle 1990s. A former Terminal Services MVP and freelance technical author and speaker for over a decade, she is now a program manager on the Remote Desktop Virtualization team at Microsoft. She promises to talk about something other than the book now.

System Requirements

To use this book's companion CD-ROM, you need a computer equipped with the following minimum configuration:

- Microsoft Windows Server 2008 R2, Windows Server 2008, Windows 7, Windows Vista, Windows Server 2003, or Windows XP
- An appropriate processor depending on the minimum requirements of the operating system)
- At least 2 GB of system memory (depending on the minimum requirements of the operating system)
- A hard disk partition with at least 1 GB of available space
- Appropriate video output device
- Keyboard
- Mouse or other pointing device
- Optical drive capable of reading CD-ROMs

Some items on the companion media have specific requirements. The companion CD-ROM contains numerous links to scripts, tools, Knowledge Base articles, and other information. To view these links, you will need a Web browser and Internet access.

The companion CD-ROM also includes scripts that are written in VBScript (with a .vbs file extension), Windows PowerShell (with a .ps1 file extension) and a few batch files. The Windows PowerShell scripts require that you have Windows PowerShell 2.0 installed. To run these scripts, your system must meet the following additional requirements;. Windows Server 2008 R2 and Windows 7 include Windows PowerShell 2.0. For Windows XP SP3, Windows Vista SP1, and Windows Server 2003 you must download and install Windows PowerShell 2.0. The Windows PowerShell 2.0 download is located at *http://support.microsoft.com /kb/968929*.

- Scripts intended for execution on the local server that depend on specific counters and interfaces will not execute correctly unless the appropriate Remote Desktop Services role service is installed. (For example, a script that queries RD Gateway interfaces will not return results unless the RD Gateway role service is installed.)

The scripts on the CD are not signed. To run them on your computer, we recommend setting the Windows PowerShell Execution Policy to "RemoteSigned." To do this, start Windows PowerShell and type **Set-ExecutionPolicy RemoteSigned**.

This setting will allow you to run the scripts on the CD, and it is more secure than setting this policy to"Unrestricted.

> **NOTE** For more information on using the Set-ExecutionPolicy cmdlet see: *http://www.microsoft.com/technet/scriptcenter/topics/msh/cmdlets/set-execution-policy.mspx.*

When you run a Windows PowerShell script, you need to provide the full path to the script. To use the VBScript scripts and batch files, double-click them, or execute them directly from a command prompt.

Finally, the CD contains a few files created in Visio 2010, so you will need to have the Visio 2010 viewer to view these files. It also contains a few PDF files so you will need a PDF reader to view these files.

Get Certified—Windows Server 2008

Ace your preparation for the skills measured by the Microsoft® certification exams—and on the job. With 2-in-1 *Self-Paced Training Kits*, you get an official exam-prep guide + practice tests. Work at your own pace through lessons and real-world case scenarios that cover the exam objectives. Then, assess your skills using practice tests with multiple testing modes—and get a customized learning plan based on your results.

EXAMS 70-640, 70-642, 70-646

MCITP Self-Paced Training Kit: Windows Server® 2008 Server Administrator Core Requirements

ISBN 9780735625082

EXAMS 70-640, 70-642, 70-643, 70-647

MCITP Self-Paced Training Kit: Windows Server 2008 Enterprise Administrator Core Requirements

ISBN 9780735625723

EXAM 70-640

MCTS Self-Paced Training Kit: Configuring Windows Server® 2008 Active Directory®

Dan Holme, Nelson Ruest, and Danielle Ruest

ISBN 9780735625136

EXAM 70-647

MCITP Self-Paced Training Kit: Windows® Enterprise Administration

Orin Thomas, et al.

ISBN 9780735625099

EXAM 70-642

MCTS Self-Paced Training Kit: Configuring Windows Server 2008 Network Infrastructure

Tony Northrup, J.C. Mackin

ISBN 9780735625129

ALSO SEE

Windows Server 2008, Administrator's Pocket Consultant, Second Edition

William R. Stanek

ISBN 9780735627116

EXAM 70-643

MCTS Self-Paced Training Kit: Configuring Windows Server 2008 Applications Infrastructure

J.C. Mackin, Anil Desai

ISBN 9780735625112

Windows Server 2008 Administrator's Companion

Charlie Russel, Sharon Crawford

ISBN 9780735625051

Windows Server 2008 Resource Kit

Microsoft MVPs with Windows Server Team

ISBN 9780735623613

EXAM 70-646

MCITP Self-Paced Training Kit: Windows Server Administration

Ian McLean, Orin Thomas

ISBN 9780735625105

microsoft.com/mspress

What do you think of this book?

We want to hear from you!

To participate in a brief online survey, please visit:

microsoft.com/learning/booksurvey

Tell us how well this book meets your needs—what works effectively, and what we can do better. Your feedback will help us continually improve our books and learning resources for you.

Thank you in advance for your input!

Stay in touch!

To subscribe to the *Microsoft Press® Book Connection Newsletter*—for news on upcoming books, events, and special offers—please visit:

microsoft.com/learning/books/newsletter